Studies in International Law of the Sea and Maritime Law
Internationales Seerecht und Seehandelsrecht

Herausgegeben von
Prof. Dr. Doris König
Prof. Dr. Nele Matz-Lück
Prof. Dr. Alexander Proelß
Prof. Trine-Lise Wilhelmsen

Band 6

Aleke Stöfen-O'Brien

The International and European Legal Regime Regulating Marine Litter in the EU

Nomos

The Deutsche Nationalbibliothek lists this publication in the Deutsche Nationalbibliografie; detailed bibliographic data are available on the Internet at http://dnb.d-nb.de

a.t.: Trier, Univ., Diss., 2015

ISBN 978-3-8487-2680-6 (Print)
978-3-8452-7017-3 (ePDF)

British Library Cataloguing-in-Publication Data
A catalogue record for this book is available from the British Library.

ISBN 978-3-8487-2680-6 (Print)
978-3-8452-7017-3 (ePDF)

Library of Congress Cataloging-in-Publication Data
Stöfen-O'Brien, Aleke
The International and European Legal Regime Regulating Marine Litter in the EU
Aleke Stöfen-O'Brien
453 p.
Includes bibliographic references.

ISBN 978-3-8487-2680-6 (Print)
978-3-8452-7017-3 (ePDF)

1. Edition 2015

Preface

The dissertation was accepted by the Faculty of Law of the University of Trier during the winter semester of 2014. This monography reflects the state of the law as of August 2015.

I owe a considerable debt of gratitude to my supervisor, Professor Dr. Alexander Proelß, for sparking my interest in all aspects of law of the sea and international public law and for his constant encouragement and advice during the time spent writing this monography. I should also like to thank Professor Dr. Brunhilde Bloemeke for her valuable recommendations as second examiner.

I am grateful to the German Research Foundation (Deutsche Forschungsgemeinschaft) for making available the necessary funding to allow me to pursue my doctoral studies, which were conducted under the auspices of the 'Graduate School on Cooperation of Science and Jurisprudence in Improving Development and Use of Standards for Environmental Protection – Strategies for Risk Assessment and Management'. This provided an ideal environment within which it was possible to conduct research and to expand one's knowledge related to interdisciplinary questions relevant to my chosen subject. In particular, exchanging and engaging with colleagues from other disciplines as well as implementing joint projects both within and outside the university was particularly enriching. My thanks go to my Graduate School colleagues and lecturers for their support, collaboration, and surely at times, patience in addressing diverse questions. I am especially grateful to Joscha Beninde, Daniela Matenaar, Dr. Katja Rohde and Charlotte Wesch.

I would also like to acknowledge the role of my colleagues at the Institute of Technology and Environmental Law at the University of Trier. The Institute's comprehensive and specialised library as well as the collaborative working environment provided excellent working conditions. Thanks go, in particular, to Amber Rose Maggio, Jessica Schröter, as well as Helga Hartmann and Veronika Weber for their company and support.

Beyond the university setting, I would also like to express my heartfelt thanks to Stefanie Werner from the German Federal Environment Agency (Umweltbundesamt). Her advice and guidance on this topic were invaluable and I am fortunate that I was in a position to learn from her vast expertise in different settings. Furthermore, I would like to thank the staff of the Black Sea Commission, the International Commission for the Protection of the Rhine, the International Commission for the Protection of the Elbe River and the International Commission for the Protection of the Danube for their kind support in providing information on the topic.

I would like to thank my family for their constant support over many years throughout all of my studies. My very deepest gratitude goes to my husband Killian, whose unwavering support has accompanied me over the years. He has celebrated the highs and patiently supported me during the lows, all throughout the writing process. His intellectual advice has been invaluable, as have the timely reminders that there are other things in life than writing a monography. Finally, I would not be in the position to write a foreword such as this without the support and guidance of my family. My deepest gratitude goes to Ulrike Stöfen, Dr. Peter Stöfen and Dr. Axel Staudte as well as my triplet siblings, Frederike and Eggert for their constant support and it is with heartfelt thanks that I dedicate this monography to them.

Table of Contents

List of Abbreviations

Art.	Article
Barcelona Convention	Convention for the Protection of the Marine Environment and the Coastal Region of the Mediterranean
Barcelona Convention 1976	Convention for the Protection of the Mediterranean Sea Against Pollution from 1976
BAT	Best Available Technique
BC	Barcelona Convention
BEP	Best Environmental Practice
BlS LBP	Land-Based Pollution Protocol in the context of the Bucharest Convention
2009 BlS-LBP	Revised Land-Based Pollution Protocol in the context of the Bucharest Convention (2009)
BlS ML SAP	Strategic Action Plan for the Management and Abatement of Marine Litter in the Black Sea region
BlS SAP	Strategic Action Plans for the Environmental Protection and Rehabilitation of the Black Sea
BlSC	Bucharest Convention
CJEU	Court of Justice of the European Union
COP	Conference of the Parties
CP(s)	Contracting Party (Parties)
DDT	dichlorodiphenyltrichloroethane
DG	Directorate General of the European Commission
DG ENV	Directorate General for the Environment of the European Commission
EC	European Community
EcoQO	Ecological Quality Objective
Ed(s).	Editor (Editors)
EEA	European Environment Agency
EEC	European Economic Community
EEZ	Exclusive Economic Zone
EIA	Environmental Impact Assessment
EIHA	OSPAR's Environmental Impacts of Human Activities Committee
EPIL	Max Planck Encyclopedia of Public International Law
EQS	Environmental Quality Standard
EQSD	Environmental Quality Standard Directive
EU	European Union
FAO	Food and Agricultural Organisation of the United Nations
GEcS	Good Ecological Status

GES	Good Environmental Status
GESAMP	Joint Group of Experts on the Scientific Aspects of Marine Environmental Protection
GPA	Global Programme of Action for the Protection of the Marine Environment from Land-Based Activities
HC	Helsinki Convention
HELCOM	Helsinki Commission
HELCOM HOD	HELCOM Heads of Delegation
HELCOM LAND	HELCOM Land-based Pollution Group
HELCOM RAP ML	HELCOM Regional Action Plan on Marine Litter
ICGML	Intersessional Group on Marine Litter (OSPAR)
ICJ	International Court of Justice
ICZM	Integrated Coastal Zone Management
ICZMP	Protocol on Integrated Coastal Zone Management in the Mediterranean
IGR	Inter Governmental Review (GPA)
ILM	International Legal Materials
IMCO	International Maritime Consultative Organisation
IMO	International Maritime Organisation
IOC	Intergovernmental Oceanographic Commission
IRBD	International River Basin District
ITLOS	International Tribunal for the Law of the Sea
London Convention, LC	Convention on the Prevention of Marine Pollution by Dumping of Wastes and Other Matter from 1972
London Protocol, LP	Protocol to the 1972 Convention on the Prevention of Marine Pollution by Dumping of Wastes and Other Matter
MAP	Mediterranean Action Plan
MARPOL	The International Convention for Prevention of Pollution from Ships (1973/1978)
MED POL	Programme for the Assessment and Control of Marine Pollution in the Mediterranean
MEDU	Coordinating Unit for the Mediterranean Action Plan
MEPC	Marine Environment Protection Committee (IMO)
MoU	Memorandum of Understanding
MPEPIL	Max Planck Encyclopedia of Public International Law
MSFD	Marine Strategy Framework Directive
NEAS	Strategy of the OSPAR Commission for the Protection of the Marine Environment of North-East Atlantic 2010-2020
NGO	Non-Governmental Organisation
NOAA	National Oceanic and Atmospheric Administration
OECD	Organization for Economic Co-operation and Development
OJ	Official Journal of the European Union
OSPAR	The Convention for the Protection of the Marine Environment of the North-East Atlantic (1992)

OSPARCOM	OSPAR Commission
OSPAR RAG ML	OSPAR Regional Action Plan on Marine Litter
PAHs	polycyclic aromatic hydrocarbons
Para.	Paragraph
PBT	persistent, bioaccumulating and toxic compounds
PCB	polychlorinated biphenyls
PCDD/PCDF	polychlorinated dibenzo-p-dioxins and polychlorinated dibenzo-furans
PCIJ	Permanent Court of International Justice
POPs	Persistent Organic Pollutants
PRF	Port Reception Facilities
PRF Directive	Port Reception Facilities Directive
QSR	Quality Status Report
RAP ML Med	Regional Action Plan on Marine Litter Management in the Mediterranean
RBD	River Basin District
Res.	Resolution
Rio Declaration	Rio Declaration on Environment and Development
Stockholm Conference	1972 United Nations Conference on the Human Environment in Stockholm
Stockholm Declaration	1972 Declaration of the United Nations Conference on the Human Environment
TEU	Treaty on the European Union
TFEU	Treaty on the Functioning of the European Union
TSG ML	Technical Subgroup on Marine Litter
UN	United Nations
UNCED	United Nations Conference on Environment and Development
UNCED	United Nations Conference on Environment and Development
UNCLOS	UN Convention on the Law of the Sea
UNEA	United Nations Environment Assembly of the United Nations Environment Programme
UNEP	United Nations Environment Programme
UNGA	UN General Assembly
UNTS	United Nations Treaty Series
UNTS	United Nations Treaty Series
UWWTD	Urban Waste Water Treatment Directive
WFD	Water Framework Directive
WG PRESSURE (HELCOM)	Working Group on Reduction of Pressures from the Baltic Sea Catchment Area (within HELCOM)
ZaöRV	Zeitschrift für ausländisches öffentliches Recht und Völkerrecht
ZUR	Zeitschrift für Umweltrecht

Introduction

Each year 6.4 million tons of waste enter our seas. The resultant litter, or in the American discourse marine debris, is a complex environmental issue with scientific, aesthetic, economic and societal impacts. The most well-known story about marine litter relates to the so-called garbage patches in the ocean in which the discarded waste accumulates and rotates within ocean currents. By way of a preliminary statement marine litter is defined as "any persistent, manufactured or processed solid material discarded, disposed of or abandoned in the marine and coastal environment."[1]

Marine litter includes several types of solid substances ranging from 5 nm microplastics to discarded vessels. The disposal of radioactive waste stored in barrels in the sea or sunken armadas on places of maritime battles account, strictly speaking, for marine litter. However, since plastic constitutes approximately 80% of the material, it can be assumed to be an environmental problem of the 20th century, the major starting point of which is demarcated by the production and commercialisation of plastic as an industrial resource in the 1950s. Admittedly, the seas have been used for centuries as a disposal place for human litter; but the production of plastic has changed the discourse and consequences of the discarded waste.

Marine litter is not an acute environmental catastrophe, but rather a long-term and latent problem. It is not only an aesthetic issue when washed ashore on a pristine beach; it is also known to harm marine organisms, the environment and potentially also human beings. The sources of marine litter are manifold and not entirely known. They range from waste disposal from land-based garbage, disposal of waste from vessels, accidents and unintentional introduction due to lack of knowledge. The complexity of the consequences of marine litter and the marine ecosystems, marine organisms and potentially also human beings are diverse and scientifically demanding. The interdependence of the environment is so mul-

1 *Coe/Rogers*, Marine debris, 1997, xxxi.

tifaceted and complex that humans cannot exhaustively understand and recognise all potential consequences of their littering actions.

With a view to the starting point of "modern marine litter" it is quite surprising that the extent of the problem has only very recently found substantial attention and interest by decision-makers, the media, civil society and individuals. Consequently, there is a time delay between the occurrence of the issue and the global perception of its risks and adverse consequences outside of interested circles.

John Steinbeck wrote in his book "The Log from the Sea of Cortez" about boat expeditions he made in 1940 in the Gulf of California "The debris from ships from hundreds of miles around is piled on this beach-mountains of sea-washed piles of it, mixed in with bottles and cans and pieces of clothing. It is the termination of some great sweeping in the Pacific."[2]

Steinbeck perceived the issue as an aesthetic problem. The adoption of the Convention on the Prevention of Marine Pollution by Dumping of Wastes and other matter from 1972 (London Dumping Convention) under which plastic may, in principle, not be dumped as well as Annex V of the International Convention for the Prevention of Pollution from Ships from 1973/1978 on prevention of pollution by garbage from ships are illustrative of the prevalence of a certain level of awareness of the consequences of plastic in the environment prevailing at that time.

Also, certain authors indicated the potential threat and damage arising from marine litter in the 1980s and 1990s.[3] It is therefore striking that awareness of the broader public for this pollutant has been (more or less) dormant in the policy and legislative context for approximately 30 years, until it was categorised as a high priority on the agenda of decision-makers. Marine litter is a rather 'abstract' problem that generally does not affect people's lives until they are directly exposed to it themselves such as during holidays at the ocean.

---

2 *Steinbeck/Ricketts,* The log from the Sea of Cortez, 1995, 206.

3 *Baur/Iudicello,* Ecology Law Quarterly 17 (1990) 71; *Joyner/Frew,* Ocean Development & International Law 22 (1991) 33; *Timagenis,* International control of marine pollution, 1980, 18 *et seq.*

Definition of marine litter

The definition of marine litter has been subject to many amendments over time. In 1997, *Coe* and *Rogers* outlined that scientists use the following definition of marine litter: "Marine litter is defined as any persistent, manufactured or processed solid material discarded, disposed of or abandoned in the marine and coastal environment."[4] Consequently, the definition contained four criteria that identify marine litter:

- A substance (a processed physical material)
- Fate in the environment (persistence)
- Activity leading to the introduction of marine litter
- Location of introduction

With a view to the factual background[5], this definition lacks certain elements. Primarily, it ignores the land-based dimension of marine litter. Also, it does not include additional activities such as unintentional or accidental introduction. In 2005, the United Nations Environment Programme (UNEP) proposed a refinement of the definition of marine litter that is, for the most part, identical with the definition mentioned above. It reads as follows

> "Marine litter is defined as any persistent, manufactured or processed solid material discarded, disposed of or abandoned in the marine and coastal environment.
> Marine litter consists of items that have been made or used by people and deliberately discarded into the sea or rivers or on beaches; brought indirectly to the sea with rivers, sewage, storm water or winds; accidentally lost, including material lost at sea in bad weather (fishing gear, cargo); or deliberately left by people on beaches and shores."[6]

Despite the vague and rather descriptive terms of the refined definition, it is preferable to the older version. This is mainly due to the inclusion of the catchment areas of rivers and other activities. This definition serves, unless otherwise provided, as the reference definition in the context of the

---

4 *Coe/Rogers*, Marine debris, 1997, xxxi. This appears to be based on the definition that is used in the Global Programme of Action for the Protection of the Marine Environment from Land-Based Activities (GPA).

5 See the discussion on the sources of marine litter in chapter 1 of this study.

6 *UNEP*, Marine litter, an analytical overview 2005, 3.

study.[7] The definition is, however, not a legal definition *per se*, since it is not used in a legally binding document.[8]

Legal approaches to addressing marine litter

Marine litter is part of the greater regulatory context of marine pollution and environmental law. Both regimes are interlinked and regulate a diverse range of substances, sources of pollution and consequences that pose a challenge with regard to marine litter aspects. Marine litter is only one of many types of polluting substances, thus the provisions of the regulatory agreements are sometimes not suitable or adequate for the specific problems and challenges posed. Therefore a legal analysis of marine litter makes understanding and interpreting the broadly formulated provisions and obligations through a marine litter perspective indispensable. Whereas sectoral aspects such as shipping or dumping as a source of marine litter have been intensively researched in legal studies, literature exclusively focusing on legal aspects addressing every source of marine litter is not abundant.[9]

Marine litter as a tragedy of the commons

Marine litter considerations must also be seen in the context of "sustainable development." The Brundtland report of the World Commission on Environment and Development from 1987 defines this notion as "development that meets the needs of the present without compromising the ability of future generations to meet their own needs."[10] The two underlying and linked dimensions of sustainable development are "intragenerational equi-

7 This definition is also used in the context of the EU: *Galgani/Fleet/van Franeker et al.,* Marine Strategy Framework Directive, Task Group 10 Report Marine Litter, 2010, 4.

8 As will be demonstrated in the course of the study, the incorporation of a definition of marine litter into legally binding instruments has only been pursued in recent years: see chapter 4.

9 See for early accounts of studies that relate to legal questions regarding marine litter: *Lentz,* Marine Pollution Bulletin 18 (1987) 361; *Bean,* Marine Pollution Bulletin 18 (1987) 357; *Joyner/Frew,* Ocean Development & International Law 22 (1991) 33. See also *Trouwborst,* Utrecht Journal of International and European Law 27 (2012) 4.

10 *World Commission on Environment Development,* Our Common Future, 1987, 43.

ty" and "intergenerational equity" [11] that relate broadly to the right to development and the use of resources. Intergenerational equity implies that "[t]he right to development must be fulfilled so as to equitably meet developmental and environmental needs of present and future generations."[12] On the other hand, intergenerational equity "requires equity in the distribution of the outcomes of development within one generation as much as internally (within one national society) as internationally (between developed and developing States)."[13] Even though the legal status of sustainable development in international law is debated, the essence of the concept contains important considerations in respect of marine litter regulations. The "plastic footprint" in the seas links our generation with that of many others that are limited in using this resource.[14]

The sustainable use of (non-renewable) resources is also linked to the tragedy of the commons.[15] Already in 1968 Hardin outlined his visionary view on the tragedy of the commons as a social problem in which the unlimited availability of a resource leads to a depletion of it, for example fish. With regard to pollution he states that:

> In a reverse way, the tragedy of the commons reappears in problems of pollution. Here it is not a question of taking something out of the commons, but of putting something in--sewage, or chemical, radioactive, and heat wastes into water; noxious and dangerous fumes into the air, and distracting and unpleasant advertising signs into the line of sight. The calculations of utility are much the same as before. The rational man finds that his share of the cost of the wastes he discharges into the commons is less than the cost of purifying his wastes before releasing them. Since this is true for everyone, we are locked

---

11 *Barral,* European Journal of International Law 23 (2012) 377, 380. *Birnie, Boyle* and *Redgewell* also include the integration of environmental protection and economic development, the right to development, the sustainable utilization and conservation of natural resources as elements of sustainable development: *Birnie/Boyle/Redgwell,* International law and the environment, 2009, 116 *et seq*. The core of the concept of sustainable development is in need of substantiation *Proelß,* Völkerrecht, in *Bothe/Dolzer/Kau et al.,* Völkerrecht (2013) 352–438, 417.

12 Principle 3 of the Rio Declaration on Environment and Development, *UN*, UN Doc. A/CONF.151/26 (vol. I); 31 ILM 874 (1992) (Rio Declaration) (emphasis added).

13 *Barral,* European Journal of International Law 23 (2012) 377, 380.

14 See only the reference of ecological footprint concept of *Wackernagel* in *Meadows/Randers/Meadows,* Grenzen des Wachstums: das 30-Jahre-Update, 2006, 301.

15 *Brown Weiss,* Sustainable development and international law, in *Lang,* Sustainable development and international law (1995) 17–33, 18.

> into a system of "fouling our own nest," so long as we behave only as independent, rational, free-enterprisers.[16]

Challenges of marine litter regulatory efforts

The conceptual problems of legal efforts regulating marine litter issue are quite complex. Marine litter is a transboundary issue that emanates from the territory of a State or is disposed of in the High Seas, but potentially has consequences and impacts in other places than their location of introduction. The transboundary issue of marine litter therefore necessitates particular questions.

The functions of a regulatory framework to address marine litter are on the one hand to establish obligations on States to prevent transboundary harm, to protect the marine environment and to take measures; they however also establish rights for States. The regulatory framework of marine litter should also have the function to translate socially acceptable levels of marine litter pollution and to integrate scientific knowledge on its risks into a legal context. Regulatory efforts are, however, aggravated by certain problems. With a view to the manifold sources and impacts as well as the variety of potentially applicable instruments, it is argued that the different possible solutions and regulatory approaches run the risk of creating a fragmented regulatory regime. The scientific uncertainties and knowledge gaps that prevail regarding the sources and consequences also pose a challenge when undertaking a legal evaluation of the issue.

Determining the aim of a regulatory framework of marine litter

The potential aims that marine litter regulation can achieve are important considerations before embarking on a legal analysis of the subject. Whereas in other areas of environmental regulation it is possible to eliminate emissions (such as major point sources), the success of establishing objectives of marine litter regulations is limited. The legacy of polluting activities and the persistence of the material aggravate the determination of a time scale of the finalization of the problem. In this regard, aiming to eliminate the overall pollution of the sea by litter is not feasible at the moment due to the pre-existing pollution load. Clean-up efforts are at this stage developed in pilot studies. These should, however, serve to complement measures that are aimed at preventing the introduction of marine lit-

---

16 *Hardin,* Science 162 (1968) 1243, 1244.

ter. It is suggested that starting from the current *status quo*, a conceivable aim is the reduction or elimination of the introduction of litter overall. The impact of efforts following this objective might potentially only be visible several decades later.

All existing legal responses serve as mechanisms to prevent the introduction of marine pollution. Therefore, the aim of this legal analysis is to understand what *agreements establish the current regulatory regime* that serves to eliminate or reduce the introduction of marine litter. In this regard, their scope, function and underlying logic are important assessment parameters. An additional element is to illustrate what *legal measures are currently in place* to specifically address the issue. The identification of regulatory gaps and particularities will be a central purpose of the study. Central questions in this context are: *which jurisdictional level and actors or institutions* (global, regional or in the EU) and *which level of specificity of legal measures* are the most suitable to address the reduction of the introduction of marine litter.

Scope of the study

Due to the many potentially applicable instruments, the geographical scope of the study is limited to those instruments that are applicable in the four seas surrounding Europe: the North-East Atlantic, the Baltic Sea, Mediterranean Sea, and Black Sea. Even though such an approach potentially runs the risk of ignoring the transboundary impact of polluting activities from outside these territories, a geographical delimitation allows for greater focus throughout the study so as to enable an in-depth discussion. The four seas surrounding Europe represent a particular interesting study area since several regulatory layers are applicable to their conservation. Not only are they covered by public international law, but they are also subject to the effects of provisions of European Union law. European Union law is to be differentiated from public international law and constitutes a legal order *sui generis* whereby the distinguishable element of this regulatory order is based on its supranational character as well as a comprehensive body of instruments that is applicable also to the sources and impacts of marine litter.

The study is divided into four chapters. The first chapter presents the *factual aspects of marine litter* used as a basis and reference framework for the subsequent legal assessment. It intends to present the sources and consequences of marine litter so as to guide and reflect upon existing or future regulatory responses. It is argued that the factual background and its associated uncertainties and knowledge gaps are important considerations when assessing existing legal responses. Ultimately, developing and/or implementing legal responses without taking adequate consideration of the factual circumstances would, in most cases, significantly diminish the effectiveness of such instruments, rendering them ineffective and failing to address the issue at the core. Additionally, understanding the adverse consequences and risks associated with marine litters an important yardstick in measuring the urgency and level of action taken as well as determining the acceptability of polluting effects. Due to the debate on microplastics as an "emerging pollutant", the consequences of this type of marine litter will be a particular focal point. The factual background is then taken as a starting point to establish requirements for an effective regulatory regime of marine litter.

In the second chapter, the *global regulatory framework* of marine litter in general will be examined by way of analysing pertinent principles, treaties and other programmes. Following an overview on how the issue of marine litter has been dealt with over the last decades in different instruments and declarations of public international law, the role of principles in guiding and interpreting legal norms is elucidated. Thereafter, pertinent treaties and action programmes with a global scope will be analysed with regard to their role in a marine litter context. Due to the broad substantive and geographical scope of these instruments, the fundamental obligations pertinent to marine litter of these frameworks will be analysed. An aspect to which particular attention is paid is whether marine litter considerations are directly or indirectly addressed and whether and to what extent the defined requirements for an effective regulatory regime are fulfilled.

In the third chapter, the regulatory regime governing the *four Regional Seas Conventions surrounding Europe* will be analysed. Depending on the Regional Seas Convention in question, its scope, protocols and subsequent implementing actions are measured against the requirements of an effective regulatory regime. The analysis is not limited to legally binding instruments *per se*, but also extends to include soft law i.e. non-binding recommendations or monitoring instruments as the case may be. A particular question will be whether regional approaches to the issue of marine litter could result in increased protection standards and tailor-made solutions that effectively address the introduction of marine litter.

In the fourth chapter, the complex body of regulation in the *European Union* will be analysed. In this regard, the competence of the EU and its institutions to act on the different aspects of marine litter such as waste management or marine environmental protection will be analysed. In a second step, the application of principles as embodied in EU primary law will be discussed with regard to their specific implementation and application to the various questions associated with marine litter. Before embarking on a systematic analysis of the secondary law instruments that directly or indirectly relate to marine litter, the issue will be classified in the overall strategic work of the EU and its institutions. This chapter aims to understand whether the assumption that EU law plays a major role in reducing the introduction of marine litter into the seas surrounding the EU, can be confirmed.

Chapter 1: Sources and consequences of marine litter

Marine litter is not only an acute environmental problem, but due to plastic and other persistent synthetic materials, it is also a chronic, cumulative and complex issue. The following discussion on the consequences, sources and possible monitoring strategies serves as a fundamental background for the ensuing questions relating to regulatory answers. In particular the impacts of marine litter are a starting point to assess the gravity of the problem.

A. Sources of marine litter

In the regulatory legal framework relating to marine litter, sources are generally differentiated according to their geographic origin.[17] Knowledge about the pathways and influx vectors of marine litter are prerequisites for the adoption of effective measures. This classification is necessitated by the multicausal origins and the inadequate knowledge about the sources of marine litter in general. The underlying logic behind this, also from a legal point of view, is that marine litter pollution can only be prevented by taking measures at the source. A regulatory response at the source is, however, aggravated by the diffuse nature of sources and the multiplicity of entry points and activities that cause marine litter. Consequently, one cannot only reduce the sources to mere geographic factors, rather such an assessment needs to integrate the influence of other factors leading to the emission of solid waste such as weather conditions, physical structures of waste management and the behavioural patterns of individuals.[18] With a

17 See only the International Convention for the Prevention of Pollution from Ships (MARPOL) (London) of 2 November 1973, in force 2 October 1983 as amended by the 1978 Protocol (London), of 01 June 1978; 1340 UNTS 61 and the Convention on the Prevention of Marine Pollution by Dumping of Wastes and Other Matter (London Dumping Convention) (London, Mexico-City, Moscow, Washington) of 29 December 1972, in force 30 August 1975; 1046 UNTS 120; 11 ILM 1294 (1972).

18 *Ryan/Moore/van Franeker et al.,* Philosophical Transactions of the Royal Society B: Biological Sciences 364 (2009) 1999, 2000.

view to structuring this analysis, the different sources and activities known to add to the problem are divided into two main categories: land-based pollution and ocean-based pollution. Since a sectorial perspective, dealing with each source or activity individually, without observing the overall context, does not reflect the complex causal relations and the variety of activities, the distinction between land-based and ocean–based sources and activities is also made as both sources are currently addressed by a different regime of instruments and mechanisms.

I. Landward factors and activities leading to the introduction of waste into the marine environment

The matter of land-based pollution of marine litter is highly controversial in the academic debate. An overview of possible sources estimated that 50-90% of marine litter stems from land-based activities.[19] This percentage is explained by the large geographical scope including the catchment areas of rivers, bays and estuaries that take up and transport solid waste to the oceans. Rivers play an important role in introducing inland pollution into the marine environment. Their catchment areas or drainage basins include small streams and rivers that collect surface water.[20] Consequently, waste from leakages of landfills and overflown sewage systems, notwithstanding their distance to large rivers or the coast, could end up ultimately in the sea. Rivers and estuaries are thus the major transport vectors in this

19 The percentages are taken from the different regionals overviews of Marine Litter: A Global Challenge, 2009, chapter 2. Depending on the region in question, the percentage of land-based pollution differs. However, the exact amount of the ratio between land-based and ocean-based pollution is disputed. *Hammer et al.* suggested in a study in 2012, that land-based pollution amount to approximately 12% and ocean-based pollution to approximately 88% of marine litter sources. Nevertheless, given the vast drainage basin of rivers and the amount of coastal urbanization, these figures should be carefully handled: *Hammer/Kraak/Parsons,* Reviews of Environmental Contamination and Toxicology, in *Whitacre,* Reviews of Environmental Contamination and Toxicology (2012) 1–44, 9. *Andrady* on the other hand outlines that 80% are land-based pollution and 18% of marine litter sources are from the fishing industry: *Andrady,* Marine Pollution Bulletin 62 (2011) 1596, 1597.

20 In this way, a variety of pollutants is introduced into the freshwater including fertilisers introduced by agricultural run - offs, thermal pollution and chemicals: *Wither/Bamber/Colclough et al.,* Marine Pollution Bulletin 64 (2012) 1564, 1564.

regard and most often the mouths of rivers and deltas have high accumulation rates of marine litter.[21] The transport of small solid particles after incineration of waste or tyre and road wear particles via the atmosphere is also an aspect in the management of land-based marine litter.[22] In regard to land-based sources, the differentiation between diffuse and point sources is at times difficult to draw. Whereas pipelines from sewage structures ending in rivers or industrial are clearly point sources, surface runoffs with no identifiable point of discharge are diffuse sources.

Hot spots, major sources of pollution, are entry points of marine litter from "a specific area, land use or point source, defined by latitude and longitude or eastings and northings."[23] The use of hot spots in marine litter monitoring is an important tool to evaluate the sources and activities that lead to the introduction of waste in the environment.[24] As it is estimated that 40% of the world's population lives in distance of 100km to the coast, hot spots can be urban agglomeration or tourist and cargo ports.[25] This explains the assumption that almost 58% of marine litter has its origin in shoreline and recreational activities.[26] Land-based sources come from a broad range of activities and sources. In the following the dominant types and sources of marine litter are categorised.

---

21 *Denuncio/Bastida/Dassis et al.,* Marine Pollution Bulletin 62 (2011) 1836, 1940; *Galgani/Leaute/Moguedet et al.,* Marine Pollution Bulletin 40 (2000) 516, 525. However, in 1973 researcher observed that waste in the estuary of the Thames was washed upstream: *Board,* Marine Pollution Bulletin 4 (1973) 165, 165 *et seq.*

22 Atmospheric transport plays an important factor in the introduction of other types of pollution such as metals and organic substances to the marine environment: *Zoller,* Völker - und europarechtliche Aspekte des Mittelmeerumweltschutzes, 1996, 42 and *Clark,* Marine pollution, 2007, 131.

23 *UNEP,* UNEP/EAS/GPA/HS. 1/4 2002, Regional Workshop on Identification of Pollution Hot Spots in the East Asian Seas Region, 2002, 4.

24 The Adriatic Sea for example is considered as one of the marine litter hot spots in the world, due to the heavily populated coastline: *Lazar/Gračan,* Marine Pollution Bulletin 62 (2011) 43, 43.

25 *Agardy/Alder,* Coastal Systems, in *Hassan/Scholes/Ash,* Ecosystems and human well-being (2005) 513–548, 515.

26 *UNEP*, Marine litter, an analytical overview 2005, 4. Nevertheless, in different statistics, differing elements and variables are taken that potentially lead to varied results. This relates thus one the one hand to studies that use "number of items" found or the volume in kg or m^3: *Interviewes/Görlitz/Stöfen et al.,* Issue Paper to the "International Conference on Prevention and Management of Marine Litter in European Seas", 16.05.2013, 12.

1. Urban agglomerations

Litter from urban agglomerations is usually indicated by everyday objects such as plastic bags, plastic containers for food and beverages, food packages for chips and sweets. However, a particular often occurring type of litter associated with an urban environment are cigarettes butts/cigarettes that account for 37.4% and 29.1% of marine litter found in the Baltic Sea and the Mediterranean respectively, placing them first on the list of objects found.[27] These objects enter the sea either by strong winds that transport the objects directly to the sea or in close waters or are flushed through the storm drains that carry the runoffs of rain.[28]

2. Sanitary and sewage-related waste

Sewage is a water-carried waste and transport amongst others household waste water, precipitable water and waste water from industrial production sites.[29] The sanitary system of household waste water holds amongst others personal care products such as disposed cotton buds and sanitary towels. It is also in this context, that microparticles contained in tooth paste and peeling scrubs for face and body can enter the aquatic environment.[30] Waste water from industrial production sites potentially includes, besides chemicals and metals, solid objects such as plastic resins used in plastic product production. Usually, industrial and sanitary wastewaters are carried in separate system to the treatment or disposal site, however particularly in older cities, the so-called combined sewer carries both types of wastewaters. During wet weather overflow in which the sewage system does not have the capacity to contain the access of water during natural

---

27 *UNEP*, Marine Litter: A Global Challenge, 2009, 197.

28 *UNEP*, Marine litter, an analytical overview 2005, 20; *Morritt/Stefanoudis/Pearce et al.*, Marine Pollution Bulletin 78 (2013) 196, 196 *et seq.*

29 Currently only limited data is available for this source in a marine litter setting: *Öko-Institute.V.*, Study on the land-sourced litter (LSL) in the marine environment, 2012, 33; *Habib/Locke/Cannone,* Water, Air and Soil Pollution 103 (1998) 1, 1 *et seq*.

30 *Fendall/Sewell,* Marine Pollution Bulletin 58 (2009) 1225, 128. See for an early account of the role of sewage systems in carrying synthetic fibers: Habib/Locke/Cannone, Water, Air and Soil Pollution 103 (1998) 1, 2.

catastrophes (storm or floods), untreated waste water is accidentally discharged into the environment.[31]

3. Pollution from waste disposal

Another important source, particular in the Black Sea Region and the Mediterranean, are illegal and legal waste disposal sites.[32] In some parts of the world, communities use the marine environment as dump sites for their municipal waste. Solid wastes can enter the marine environment by washouts from strong floods, missing or inefficient drainage or overfilled landfills.[33] In cases the storm water drainage or the bottom liner systems of landfills are defective, the collection of runoffs cannot be guaranteed and solid waste is in that way released. The leakage of medical waste and syringes disposed in landfills is known to have been the cause for the so-called syringe tide during the 1980s at the east coast of the United States of America.[34]

Solid waste management practices include a broad range of aspects such as the waste handling of individuals but also from insufficient waste management infrastructures.[35] Besides accidental pollution after strong rains, fly tipping poses a particular problem as missing cover systems facilitates the transport of waste via the air or the water to rivers that are in

---

31 *Sheavly/Register,* J Polym Environ 15 (2007) 301, 302.

32 *UNEP*, Marine Litter: A Global Challenge, 2009, 41 and 99.

33 Overfilled landfills that have reached their capacity since the 1990s have caused a waste management problem in the city of Naples that necessitated disposing of the waste at alternative sites, including the coast: *Alessio Vinci,* Why Naples is drowning in garbage, 08.01.2008, http://edition.cnn.com/2008/WORLD/europe/01/07/naples.rubbish.background/, last accessed 27.08.2015. Also, the infamous Saida landfill in Lebanon receives 300 tons of solid waste per day. Since it is located only 200 meters from the coast and has no leachate collection system, it the cause of sever environmental hazards in the area: *United Nations Development Programme - Lebanon,* The Rehabilitation of Saida Dumpsite, http://www.lb.undp.org/content/lebanon/en/home/operations/projects/environment_and_energy/project-id---00083622---the-rehabilitation-of-saida-dumpsite.html, last updated 23.04.2013, last accessed 27.08.2015.

34 *Editor of Marine Pollution Bulletin*, *American News,* Marine Pollution Bulletin 19 (1988) 554.

35 *UNEP*, Marine Litter: A Global Challenge, 2009, 99.

proximity.[36] Illegal landfills, those in which a systematic disposal of waste in non-authorised landfills is pursued, increase the risk of run offs due to the unsupervised discharge of diverse types of litter.[37]

4. Tourism and recreational activities

Notwithstanding the legal assessment whether beaches are to be categorised as land-based or ocean-based sources of pollution, the inclusion of beaches in a marine litter context is of particular importance due to the pressures exerted by tourism and recreational activities along the coast. Beach goers are often guilty of littering or leaving behind their food and beverage containers which are easily transported into the water. It is estimated that for example in the Mediterranean Sea, recreational activities along the shoreline contribute to more than 50% of the marine litter problem.[38] Particular hot-spots for marine litter are recreational areas (including resorts and beaches) and ports. However, in the assessment of this problem, one must be aware that not all litter found at beaches has its origin from beach goers, it could be washed ashore after the transport by ocean circulation.[39]

II. Uses of the ocean that lead to marine litter

The various activities that are taking place on the ocean could potentially lead to the intentional or unintentional introduction of marine litter. These include shipping, the offshore industry including oil and gas platforms, fishing and recreational activities. Depending on the specific activity pattern in the region, the percentage of sea-based pollution differs immensely. Besides shipping and fishing, other potential sources of marine litter such

---

36 See only: *Zylstra,* Journal of Arid Environments 89 (2013) 13, 13 *et seq.*

37 See only the "history" of cases concerning illegal landfills in Greece: *European Commission*, Environment: Commission takes Greece back to Court over illegal landfills and asks for fines, Press Release, Brussels, IP/13/143, 21.02.2013.

38 *UNEP*, Marine Litter: A Global Challenge, 2009, 98.

39 *Widmer/Hennemann,* Journal of Coastal Research 26 (2010) 993, 997.

as dumping or disposal from oil platforms are only marginally studied, but can on a local scale be the dominant sources.[40]

Historically, the disposal of unwanted waste at sea was viewed as belonging to the freedom of the High Seas.[41] Corresponding to the motto "out of sight, out of mind," States were able to avoid costly terrestrial waste disposal programs. The dumping of sewage sludge or destroyed appliances, vessels or car batteries as well as tyres in the marine environment equally pollute the marine environment.[42] Contrary to other aspects of marine pollution, any concrete statement and facts about these offshore sources are difficult to make as "there are no recent and certain figures on the amounts of marine litter worldwide. Nor are there any such global figures on the annual input of marine litter to the marine and coastal environment."[43] Overall, the identification of the sources of marine litter poses several challenges that include different monitoring strategies and the subjective element of classifying the particular pieces of litter.[44] Consequently, it is very challenging to provide concrete and final answers in order to completely fill the knowledge gap in regard to the amount and sources of marine litter overall.

---

40 Shipping as a source of marine litter has been a key research area that is also depicted in the amount of articles published on this topic: *Barnet,* Shipping and Marine Debris in the Wide Caribbean: Answering a Difficult Challenge, in *Coe/Rogers,* Marine debris (1997) 219–228; *Wade,* The Challenges of Ship-Generated Garbage in the Caribbean in *Coe/Rogers,* Marine debris (1997) 229–238.; *Koss,* Dealing with Ship-Generated Plastics Waste on U.S. Navy Surface Ships, in *Coe/Rogers,* Marine debris (1997) 263–270; *Wallace,* A Strategy to reduce, control and minimise vessel-source marine debris, in *Coe/Rogers,* Marine debris (1997) 277–288; *Horsman,* Marine Pollution Bulletin 13 (1982) 167.

41 *Hafner,* Meeresumwelt, Meresforschung und Technologietransfer, in *Graf Vitzthum,* Handbuch des Seerechts (2006) 347–460, 389.

42 *Davies,* Marine Pollution Bulletin 19 (1988) 2; *Parmentier,* International Negotiation 4 (1999) 433, 434. See for a legal definition of dumping in the marine environment chapter 2 section C.V.1. Even in 1994, it was suggested to use deep ocean disposal for land-based waste in order to face the global waste problem that was expected to rise due to population and economic growth. The selection of suitable seabed burial site was to take, *inter alia,* into consideration location where "particle-by-particle sedimentation has continued for millions of years": *Laughthon,* Marine Policy 18 (1994) 453, 453 *et seq.*

43 *UNEP*, Marine litter, an analytical overview 2005, 4.

44 *Koutsodendris/Papatheodorou/Kougiourouki et al.,* Estuarine, Coastal and Shelf Science 77 (2008) 501, 507; *Avery-Gomm/O'Hara/Kleine et al.,* Marine Pollution Bulletin 64 (2012) 1776, 1781.

1. Shipping

Shipping as a source of marine pollution covers a wide range of industries and activities with different goals. As with land-based pollution, ocean-based pollution can occur accidentally, during normal operation or through intentional discharge. The distinction between operational and accidental pollution is necessary in order to adequately address and outline "existing responses and prevention mechanisms in the legal sphere."[45] Depending on the type of shipping, different quantity and kinds of waste occur. This becomes apparent when considering the different functions of shipping including primarily: transporting goods (merchant shipping) and people (cruise shipping and ferries). Furthermore, fishing is pursued from a vessel and could theoretically be considered as falling under the broad category of shipping, however it is treated in a separate part as its associated type of marine litter has outstanding ecological as well as socio-economic implications. While the operational pollution from shipping is the primary cause of marine litter, accidental pollution can equally contribute on a local as well as regional level for increased marine litter appearances.

a) Operational pollution

In 2011 the world fleet of propelled-sea going merchant ships comprised 104,304 vessels with an average age of 22 years.[46] The information about the age is important in determining the construction and design standard of the ships in regard to their operational waste management but also in regard to their safety profile. It is estimated that annually 1.4 billion tons of litter enter the marine environment from vessels;[47] yet any assessment of

45 *Kachel,* Particularly Sensitive Sea Areas, 2008, 31.

46 *IMO*, Maritime Knowledge Center, International Shipping Facts and Figures-Information Resources on Trade, Safety and Security, 06.03.2013, http://www.imo.org/KnowledgeCentre/ShipsAndShippingFactsAndFigures/TheRoleandImportanceofInternationalShipping/Documents/International%20Shipping%20-%20Facts%20and%20Figures.pdf, 3.2., last accessed 27.08.2015. The statistics includes vessel of 100 gross tonnes or above.

47 *Watters/Yoklavich/Love et al.,* Marine Pollution Bulletin 60 (2010) 131, 131. However the specific amount remains to this date highly debated.

this data is exacerbated by "considerable statistical weaknesses."[48] Operational litter stems from activities on board and includes sewage, tank residues bunker oil, ballast water and also solid waste. Solid waste such as disused packaging accumulates during operational activities related for example, to the catering for the crew or guests.[49] Cruise shipping is a rapidly growing tourism sector that has drawn 18.8 million passengers in 2010.[50] It is estimated that a cruise ship with a capacity of 2000-3000 passengers generates 7.000-10.5000 kilogram of solid waste per day.[51] Usually this incidental waste is disposed of in reception facilities in ports; however illegal discharge of the waste also occurs, mainly due to economic considerations.[52]

b) Accidental pollution

Accidental pollution is usually associated with oil-tankers that release, in case of collision with external objects or grounding, oil. As seen in famous cases such as the Exxon Valdez oil spill in Alaska and the Deepwater Horizon incident in the Gulf of Mexico, an oil plague can substantially affect the ecological balance of the entire ecosystems of the region which is even more so aggravated by the chemical substances and detergents used

48 *IMO*, MEPC 59/6/3, Interpretations of and amendments to MARPOL and related Instruments, Report of the Correspondence Group for the Review of MARPOL Annex V, 02.04.2009, 6.

49 *Vauk/Schrey,* Marine Pollution Bulletin 18 (1987) 316, 318.

50 *IMO*, Maritime Knowledge Center, International Shipping Facts and Figures-Information Resources on Trade, Safety and Security, 06.03.2013, http://www.imo.org/KnowledgeCentre/ShipsAndShippingFactsAndFigures/TheRole-andImportanceofInternationalShipping/Documents/International%20Shipping%20-%20Facts%20and%20Figures.pdf, 3.8.5., last accessed 27.08.2015.

51 *Oceana*, Contamination by cruise ships, http://na.oceana.org/sites/default/files/o/fileadmin/oceana/uploads/europe/reports/cruise_ships_eng.pdf, last accessed 27.08.2015. The same study estimated that each passenger generates 3,5kg of solid waste per day. Due to the nature of long distances journeys, it is assumed that litter made of tin and glass comes primarily from vessels *Koutsodendris/Papatheodorou/Kougiourouki et al.,* Estuarine, Coastal and Shelf Science 77 (2008) 501, 508.

52 See section B.II.2.a. of chapter 3 and section B.VI.6. of chapter 4. Also, some ports may not be adapted to receive certain types of vessel-based garbage or do not have adequate port reception facilities: *Ninaber,* MARPOL Annex V, Commercial Ships, and Port Reception Facilities: Making it Work, in *Coe/Rogers,* Marine debris (1997) 239–251, 239 *et seq*.

in the clean-up to disintegrate the oil.[53] Accidental pollution leading to solid waste being emitted into the marine environment occurs as a consequence of collisions, groundings or sinking of vessels, explosions, or loss of cargo.[54] These events can be inflicted by severe weather conditions, incorrect stowage or navigational errors. With an increase in transported tonnage, higher transport speeds and larger ships that necessitate specific maritime safety measures, the risk of collisions and accidents could potentially increase. Another, admittedly, seldom occurring phenomena was the debris that was washed into the ocean after the tsunami along the Japanese coast in 2011. The strong floods took with their withdrawal, several objects from inland and the coastal waters that subsequently formed a risk for the safety of navigation in the marine environment.[55] A so-called ghost ship floating towards the coast of Canada or a dock from the fishing port of Misawa, Japan landed at a beach on the West Coast of the United States of America, attest the transboundary impacts of these events. [56]

2. Fisheries

Fisheries can be the source of a particular type of marine litter, so-called ghost-nets that have a particular impact on the environment and also in socio-economic terms.[57] Ghost nets are drifting fishing nets that are accidentally lost during fishing or are intentionally discarded by fishermen.[58] Rea-

---

53 See for example *Allan/Smith/Anderson,* Environmental Science & Technology 46 (2012) 2033, 2038 *et seq.*; *Kujawinski/Kido Soule/Valentine et al.,* Environmental Science & Technology 45 (2011) 1298, 1298. Accidents with chemical tankers might have even more serious consequences, as the chemicals react with the marine environment (water and air) or between incompatible chemicals.

54 It is estimated that over 10.000 containers are lost at sea each year. *KIMO*, Maritime Safety and Pollution, www.kimointernational.org/MaritimeSafetyandPollution.aspx,b last accessed 27.08.2015.

55 *BBC News,* Japan tsunami ′ghost ship' drifting to Canada, 24.03.2012, http://www.bbc.co.uk/news/world-us-canada-17500008, last accessed 27.08.2015.

56 *NOAA,* Japan Confirms Dock on Washington Coast Is Tsunami Marine Debris, 18.01.2013, http://usresponserestoration.wordpress.com/2013/01/18/japan-confirms-dock-on-washington-coast-is-tsunami-marine-debris/%C3%A4.

57 See for studies on this topic: *Butler/Gunn/Berry et al.*, Journal of Environmental Management 123 (2013) 14.

58 Illegal, unregulated and unreported fishing is also known to cause ghost fishing: *Wilcox/Hardesty/Sharples et al.,* Conservation Letters 6 (2013) 247, 248.

sons for the loss or abandonment of fishing gear could be overcapacity, gear conflicts or economic reasons such as avoiding paying disposal fees.[59] Illegal, Unreported and Unregulated Fisheries could also lead to lost or abandoned nets. These discarded fishing nets continue to float in the water column and accidentally catch marine animals that entangle in the nets and face starvation, injuries or drowning as they are not able to free themselves from the nets. This process is called "ghost-fishing." Certain types of nets and fishing methods are particularly prone to be accidentally lost and perform ghost fishing due to strain on the material.[60] Passive gears such as gillnets, trammel and wreck nets are particularly prone to be lost and deploy in the water and continue to fish.[61] Furthermore, the geomorphic circumstances such as during seamount fisheries with trawling gear for example, test the material as netting can be caught at the steeply irregular sea floor and can be lost in this activity.[62] Additionally, aquaculture and the practice of wet storage of nets could be potential sources of marine litter.

B. Classification and types of marine litter

On the basis of this descriptive introduction to the diverse sources of marine litter, it is apparent that different types of marine litter are existent. In order to provide a coherent classification of marine litter, the litter sizes are broadly divided into macro-litter (litter sizes with a diameter larger than 20mm), meso-litter (diameter between 5- and 20mm)[63] and micro-lit-

---

59 *Wilcox/Hardesty/Sharples et al.,* Conservation Letters 6 (2013) 247, 254; *Brown/Magnus*, Policy framework for improving management of the deep-water net fishery of the West and North of Great Britain and Ireland, 2006, 4.

60 *Barco/D'Eri/Woodward et al.,* Marine Pollution Bulletin 60 (2010) 1477, 1477.

61 Before the 1950s, the material used in ropes for fishing gear were made of natural fibers such as hemp, therefore they were quicker to disintegrate than nylon ropes: *Gregory,* Philosophical Transactions of the Royal Society B: Biological Sciences 364 (2009) 2013, 2014.

62 *Pham/Gomes-Pereira/Isidro et al.,* Deep Sea Research Part II: Topical Studies in Oceanography 98 (2013) 204, 205.

63 Barnes/Galgani/Thompson *et al.*, Philosophical Transactions of the Royal Society B: Biological Sciences 364 (2009) 1985, 1986.

ter or microplastics.[64] However, these sizes differ subtly between various scholars and authorities.[65]

Some authors suggest an additional type of classification: mega-litter which is used to describe pieces of litter bigger than 100mm diameter.[66] As these types of classification of marine litter relate only to the waste already present in the sea, the differentiation in size might *prima facie* not be an important tool in the prevention of marine litter. Notwithstanding this, such a general classification serves as a first indication of the composition of marine litter that allows for adequate and comprehensive solutions for the several types of marine litter. The term marine litter for legal matter is too diverse and is composed of such a broad range of materials and characteristics, that a first indication according to the size can provide a starting point for the assessment of associated risk and environmental consequences.[67] Marine litter can therefore stem from diverse materials such as glass, plastic, metal, leather and styrofoam. Macro-litter includes, for example, ghost fishing nets and cargo lost from vessels. Smaller debris can occur as consequences of polluting activities but also as a product of fragmentation due to abrasion. The final product of this fragmentation processes are microparticles that can be found in exponential amounts in every part of the marine environment.[68] The amount of litter in the marine

---

64 *Barnes/Galgani/Thompson et al.,* Philosophical Transactions of the Royal Society B: Biological Sciences 364 (2009) 1985, 1986; *Chesire/Adler/Barbière,* UNEP/IOC Guidelines on Survey and Monitoring of Marine Litter, 2009; *GESAMP*, Proceedings of the International Research Workshop on the occurrence, effects, and fate of microplastic marine debris, 2010, 19; *Arthur/Baker/Bamford* (eds.), Proceedings of the International Research Workshop on the occurrence, effects, and fate of microplastic marine debris, September 2008, NOAA Technical Memorandum NOS-OR&R-30, 10.

65 *Ryan/Moore/van Franeker et al.,* Philosophical Transactions of the Royal Society B: Biological Sciences 364 (2009) 1999, 2000. See only: *Van Cauwenberghe/ Vanreusel/Mees et al.,* Environmental Pollution 182 (2013) 495, 495 who define it as being less than 1 mm.

66 *Barnes/Galgani/Thompson et al.,* Philosophical Transactions of the Royal Society B: Biological Sciences 364 (2009) 1985, 1986; *McCoy,* Marine Pollution Bulletin 19 (1988) 25.

67 The size of the litter fragments allows to make statements in regard to their likelihood of carrying invasive alien species and the organisms that settle on their surfaces: *Morét-Ferguson/Law/Proskurowski et al.,* Marine Pollution Bulletin 60 (2010) 1873, 1877.

68 See for an in-depth discussion of the sources and impacts of micro-litter (or microplastic), section A.IV.a and b of this chapter.

environment leads to the assumption that the quantities of microparticles will even increase in the following years and decades.[69] This fact is very alarming in that these small particles have a high potential influence on marine organisms as the small size allows them to be ingested. Despite the fragmentation processes, the durability especially of plastic is still uncertain, but seems to last from 3 to 10 years which can be potentially extended to 30-50 years due to the additives used.[70]

I. Spatial appearance of marine litter

Marine litter can be found virtually in all places of the ocean, on the deep sea floor, in the water column, on the surface, as microparticles in the sand and sediments,[71] even in the unpopulated Polar Regions.[72] The distribution of marine litter is dependent, albeit not exclusively, on three key factors: the behaviour of litter in water,[73] hydrodynamic and weather conditions. The fate of plastic in the marine environment is referred to as the "lifecycle model" of marine litter[74] as it undergoes different processes in the marine environment.

Strong residual cycles in the ocean lead to convergence zones within which litter accumulates.[75] The frequently mentioned "Great Pacific Garbage Patch" in the central North Pacific subtropical gyre is the most prominent example of such a convergence zone and is estimated to cover

---

69 *Barnes/Galgani/Thompson et al.,* Philosophical Transactions of the Royal Society B: Biological Sciences 364 (2009) 1985, 1994.

70 *Derraik,* Marine Pollution Bulletin 44 (2002) 842, 844.

71 *Van Cauwenberghe et al.* were able to proof microplastics on the deep-seafloor: *Van Cauwenberghe/Vanreusel/Mees et al.,* Environmental Pollution 182 (2013) 495.

72 *Walker/Reid/Arnould et al.,* Marine Pollution Bulletin 34 (1997) 61; *Bergmann/ Klages,* Marine Pollution Bulletin 64 (2012) 2734; *Zarfl/Matthies,* Marine Pollution Bulletin 60 (2010) 1810.

73 *Yoon/Kawano/Igawa,* Marine Pollution Bulletin 60 (2010) 448, 450 *et seq.*

74 *Chesire/Adler/Barbière*, UNEP/IOC Guidelines on Survey and Monitoring of Marine Litter, 2009, 6.

75 In contrary to how the gyres are sometimes depicted (for example: *Zürich Museum,* The Seventh Continent — Musings on The Plastic Garbage Project, http://www.domusweb.it/en/design/2012/08/27/the-seventh-continent--musings-on-the-plastic-garbage-project.html, last accessed 27.08.2015, these are not „islands" of floating litter.

an area of France and Spain combined.[76] Other convergence zones such as the South Pacific subtropical gyre also accumulate marine litter.[77] While the presence of litter in the sea is somewhat easier to prove in this case, temporal and long-term factors such as the North Atlantic oscillation and ocean circulation influence the drift speed and residual times of marine litter. The role of ocean currents in the distribution of (buoyant) marine litter was demonstrated by the "friendly floaters" incident in the Pacific Ocean, when, in 1992, 29.000 rubber ducks fell off a vessel during a storm and are still being washed ashore today.[78] This case study provided valuable evidence that hydrodynamic factors such as velocity, turbidity and the density of water play an important role in the distribution of marine litter.

Moreover, geographic factors such as islands or ridges that serve as barriers are also major factors which need to be considered when assessing the average drift time or estimated residence time in determining the source and destination of marine litter.[79] Even though litter usually floats on the water surface, some types of litter lose over time their positive buoyancy and become denser than water through a fouling process brought about by algae, or bacteria and consequently sink to the seafloor where they become sedimented. The biofouling process during which bacterial cells are adsorbed to the litter fragment leading to the attachment of larvae and spores, initiates the adherence of specific invertebrates and algae.[80] Other man-made material such as ghost-nets float in the water col-

---

76 The size of the garbage patch is disputed. In this context, the "definition" of the patch according to the density and occurrence of plastic in the environment are variable: *Hammer/Kraak/Parsons,* Reviews of Environmental Contamination and Toxicology, in *Whitacre,* Reviews of Environmental Contamination and Toxicology (2012) 1–44, 2; *Moore,* Marine Pollution Bulletin 42 (2001) 1297; *Martinez/Maamaatuaiahutapu/Taillandier,* Marine Pollution Bulletin 58 (2009) 1347.

77 *Eriksen/Maximenko/Thiel et al.,* Marine Pollution Bulletin 68 (2013) 71; *Martinez/Maamaatuaiahutapu/Taillandier,* Marine Pollution Bulletin 58 (2009) 1347.

78 Similarly, marine litter has also been found in areas that are remote from human activities: *Kühn/van Franeker,* Marine Pollution Bulletin 64 (2012) 1252. As plastic marine litter is constantly exposed to currents and ocean dynamics, it serves as a potential pathway for chemicals with a strong sorption behavior to be transported into remote areas: *Zarfl/Matthies,* Marine Pollution Bulletin 60 (2010) 1810, 1814.

79 *Widmer/Hennemann,* Journal of Coastal Research 26 (2010) 993, 997; *Galgani/Leaute/Moguedet et al.,* Marine Pollution Bulletin 40 (2000) 516, 526; *Acha/Mianzan/Iribarne et al.,* Marine Pollution Bulletin 46 (2003) 197.

80 *Lobelle/Cunliffe,* Marine Pollution Bulletin 62 (2011) 197, 197; *Ye/Andrady,* Marine Pollution Bulletin 22 (1991) 608, 608.

umn until they become further disintegrated by abrasion or foul and sink to the seafloor.[81] Recent findings have suggested that the deep sea is a major sink for microplastics.[82]

Benthic and seafloor debris pose a monitoring challenge. In several studies it has been demonstrated that marine litter on the seafloor is not exposed to external factors such as solar radiation and oxidation which are believed to slow down the degradation and fragmentation process.[83] It is estimated that most of the litter on the seafloor is accumulated in proximity to the coast with the amount decreasing in inverse relation to the distance to the coast.[84] Additionally, the influence of strong underwater currents and inputs from large rivers cause a degree of seasonal and temporal variation of the distribution of marine litter on the seafloor.[85] The estimation of the amount of marine litter both entering the marine environment and already present therein proves a challenge due to its temporal spatial appearances.[86]

II. Monitoring of litter in the marine environment

Monitoring marine litter is a key instrument to estimate the amount of litter in the oceans and is used to identify its sources. It is considered as the most important parameter to evaluate the effectiveness of management in-

---

81 *Gregory/Andrady,* Plastics in the marine environment, in *Andrady,* Plastics and the environment (2003) 379–403, 384; *Williams/Simmons/Fricker,* Marine Pollution Bulletin 26 (1993) 404, 404; *Holmström,* Nature 255 (1975) 622, 622; *Thompson,* Science 304 (2004) 838, 838.

82 *Woodall/ Sanchez-Vidal/ Canals et al.*, Royal Society Open Science 1 (2014), 140317, 140317.

83 *Watters/Yoklavich/Love et al.,* Marine Pollution Bulletin 60 (2010) 131, 137.

84 In the North-West Mediterranean, the density of marine litter is with approximately 1935 fragments/km^2 very high: *Koutsodendris/Papatheodorou/Kougiourouki et al.,* Estuarine, Coastal and Shelf Science 77 (2008) 501, 507. In other studies, it was calculated that the weight of one km^2 amounts to 13.4kg: *Koutsodendris/ Papatheodorou/Kougiourouki et al.,* Estuarine, Coastal and Shelf Science 77 (2008) 501, 504.

85 *Galgani/Leaute/Moguedet et al.,* Marine Pollution Bulletin 40 (2000) 516, 526.

86 *Madzena/Lasiak,* Marine Pollution Bulletin 34 (1997) 900, 906; *Law/Moret-Ferguson/Maximenko et al.,* Science 329 (2010) 1185, 1188.

struments and decisions.[87] The assessment of the presence of marine litter is difficult due to the temporal variability of marine litter in the different zones of the marine environment and the difference in its size and material.[88] The monitoring methodologies for marine litter vary among scientists and depend on the specific spatial location (beach, water surface, water column and seafloor) and the type of litter concerned.[89] The differing approaches and disaccords in the scientific community towards monitoring methodologies potentially circumvent significant and generally accepted evidence that can be made available when deciding on adequate legal responses to the problem at hand. The need for harmonised methodological standards has in recent years been acknowledged by the OSPAR Commission and the Member States of the European Union which have initiated concepts to harmonise data collection.[90] In the following, a brief overview of the monitoring challenges related to specific spatial locations will be provided in order to outline the scientific challenges in the assessment of the *status quo*.

Litter washed ashore is the first sign of the presence of marine litter. Counting the amount and different types of marine litter establishes an assessment of the sources, composition and trends of the litter. Beach monitoring methodologies can be the counting of the items of marine litter at beaches as well as aerial pictures of the beaches.[91] The interpretation of the data can lead to diverse outcomes as the studies focus not on the entire range of marine litter but often have priority research areas (for example on PET bottles or specific polymers).[92] Moreover, microparticles, as small as sand, have been monitored by sand filtration. The amount and presence

---

87 *De Jonge/Elliott/Brauer,* Marine Pollution Bulletin 53 (2006) 5, 5; *Henderson,* Marine Pollution Bulletin 42 (2001) 584, 586.

88 *Coe*, Marine debris, 1997, 8; *Ryan/Moore/van Franeker et al.,* Philosophical Transactions of the Royal Society B: Biological Sciences 364 (2009) 1999, 2000.

89 *Coe*, Marine debris, 1997, 8.

90 D*e Jonge/Elliott/Brauer,* Marine Pollution Bulletin 53 (2006) 5, 14 *et seq*. See for further information on the policy and legal aspects section C.III. of chapter 3 and section B.VII.2.ee. of chapter 4. See equally the efforts of UNEP in harmonising approaches to the monitoring of marine litter in the framework of the lifecycle of marine litter: *Chesire/Adler/Barbière*, UNEP/IOC Guidelines on Survey and Monitoring of Marine Litter, 2009; *GESAMP*, Proceedings of the International Research Workshop on the occurrence, effects, and fate of microplastic marine debris, 2010.

91 *Nakashima/Isobe/Magome et al.,* Marine Pollution Bulletin 62 (2011) 762.

92 *Nakashima/Isobe/Magome et al.,* Marine Pollution Bulletin 62 (2011) 762, 767.

of marine litter at beaches varies depending on the weather conditions, the season and the exposure of the specific beach to ocean currents and coastal population concentration. For this reason, a well-considered site selection and a regular monitoring scheme are necessary in order to produce significant data. Furthermore, researching and counting the abundance of beach litter has also been pursued in the framework of citizen science projects or coastal clean-ups, during which volunteers remove and also count the objects found along the beach.[93]

Large floating litter[94] items are surveyed by aerial and boat surveys as well as net trawls. Even though aerial surveys can cover large areas, this method allows only the larger debris items that can be seen from the airplane to be surveyed which necessitates skilled observers in order to make available an exact account of pieces of litter. The information provided by aerial surveys can generate predictions and modelling information of the drift route and future interferences with species habitats or traffic routes. However, aerial surveys are limited by weather and seasonal conditions and are cost-intensive.

C. Consequences and impacts of marine litter

Marine litter causes long-range damage, since the impact or damage is usually not in close proximity to the source. The distribution and drift of marine litter into every zone of the ocean, necessitates that the consequences of marine litter must be addressed both on a temporal as well as spatial scale. In the following, the risks posed by marine litter will be assessed with a view to understanding which kind of material and size of marine litter are particularly harmful. It is submitted that the extent of harm of marine litter depends on the specific marine species, the type and size of material, its biodegradation potential as well as the chemical adsorbed or contained in plastic. The complexity of depicting the impacts of marine litter stems on the one hand from the many uncertainties that are yet unclear and on the other hand from the many possible forms of impacts. The impacts of marine litter on marine and coastal biodiversity and

93 See only: *Hidalgo-Ruz/Thiel,* Marine Environmental Research 87-88 (2013) 12.

94 It is estimated that more than 5 trillion plastics pieces that weigh over 250, 000 tons are afloat in the world's ocean: *Eriksen/Lebreton/Carson et al.*, Plos One (2014), 10 December 2014.

habitat are as of yet not entirely known. There are knowledge gaps on its impacts on population of affected species and ecosystems.[95] In order to structure the discussion, two central categories of impacts are analysed: ecological impacts (entanglement and transport vector for invasive species) as well as toxicological influences by ingestion. Here, the accumulation of chemicals via contaminated litter as a result of environmental exposure is particularly interesting. Whereas marine litter can consist of many other materials such as cloths or treated wood, it is estimated that approximately 60-80% of marine litter consists of this endurable material.[96] Therefore, the following section will specifically address the impacts associated therewith.

I. Ecological impacts

Even though ingestion by marine litter is also an ecological impact, it will be dealt with in a separate section due to the potential toxicological dimension of ingested plastic both for marine organisms as well as humans. The following section sketches out the ecological impacts of marine litter such as entanglement and as a vector for invasive species. Whereas adverse ecological impacts prevail, some species can potentially benefit from marine litter. Barnacles, polychaete worms and hydroids use litter as "mobile homes."[97]

1. Entanglement

Primarily marine mammals (e.g. seals) and birds have been reported to become entangled in marine litter leading to death through drowning, suffo-

---

95 UNEP/CBD, Report of the Expert Workshop Report of the Expert Workshop to Prepare Practical Guidance on Preventing and Mitigating the Significant Adverse Impacts of Marine Debris on Marine and Coastal Biodiversity and Habitats (UNEP/CBD/MCB/EM/2014/3/2), 2-4.12.2014, Annex IV, https://www.cbd.int/doc/?meeting=MCBEM-2014-03 (last accessed 27.08.2015).

96 *Derraik*, Marine Pollution Bulletin 44 (2002) 842, 843; *Moore,* Environmental Research 108 (2008) 131, 131.

97 *Barnes,* Nature 416 (2002) 808, 808.

cation or strangulation.[98] Migratory species are in particular prone to become entangled.[99] Moreover, birds use plastic filaments as nesting material which can equally cause entanglement of both adults and juveniles. In those cases in which the entanglement does not have a mortal ending, the filament can severely injure the animals leading to restricted movement and thus reduced predation activity and potential amputation of the entangled body part.[100] Ghost nets and monofilament lines are suggested to be the main sources of entanglement.[101] Even though the detection of entangled taxa at sea is difficult due to their sinking or predation,[102] already in 1997 *Laist* estimated that 136 species are affected by entanglement.[103] The smothering of the seafloor, by sunken litter fragments, poses a risk to benthic species as well as their habitat in general. The potential impacts of marine litter on the benthic fauna and flora stem from a poor water quality or physical damages caused by marine litter. In particular sea grass beds and coral reefs are especially fragile ecosystems that are vulnerable to the impact of marine litter.

98 *Derraik,* Marine Pollution Bulletin 44 (2002) 842, 846 ; *Good/June/Etnier et al.,* Marine Pollution Bulletin 60 (2010) 39, 39; *Henderson,* Marine Pollution Bulletin 42 (2001) 584, 588.

99 *Laist,* Impacts of Marine Debris: Entanglement of Marine Life in Marine Debris Including a Comprehensive List of Species with Entanglement and Ingestion Records, in *Coe/Rogers,* Marine debris (1997) 99-140, 100.

100 *Barco/D'Eri/Woodward et al.,* Marine Pollution Bulletin 60 (2010) 1477, 1477; *Raum-Suryan/Jemison/Pitcher,* Marine Pollution Bulletin 58 (2009) 1487, 1487; *Votier/Archibald/Morgan et al.,* Marine Pollution Bulletin 62 (2011) 168, 168; *Hartwig/Clemens/Heckroth,* Marine Pollution Bulletin 54 (2007) 595. Other non-lethal impacts are scarification patterns: *Simmonds,* Journal of Marine Biology 2012 (2012) 1, 6.

101 *Laist,* Impacts of Marine Debris: Entanglement of Marine Life in Marine Debris Inclduing a Comprehensive List of Species with Entanglement and Ingestion Records, in *Coe/Rogers,* Marine debris (1997) 99-140, 104.

102 *Ibid.*, 100.

103 *Laist,* Impacts of Marine Debris: Entanglement of Marine Life in Marine Debris Inclduing a Comprehensive List of Species with Entanglement and Ingestion Records, in *Coe/Rogers,* Marine debris (1997) 99-140, 102. In the early stages of the research on the impacts of plastic in the water column, it was estimated that floating and sunken fragments of plastic pose a lesser degree of damage *Ye/Andrady,* Marine Pollution Bulletin 22 (1991) 608, 608.

2. Transport vectors for hitch-hiking of non-native species and smothering of marine habitat

Marine litter potentially serves as a primary or a secondary vector for the introduction of non-native species. This potentially concerns also pathogens. Litter particles provide for the means of transport of alien species into a new ecosystem. Marine species use pelagic plastic and bottles as rafting materials on which they are carried to other sea regions.[104] Alien species may invade new ranges and possibly cause the extinction of other species.[105] Sessile organisms, such as tube worms and coralline algae, colonise floating plastic pieces and therefore expand the habitat range of certain species.[106] Moreover, the fouling process on the pieces of plastic assembles epibiota that is consequently introduced to new regions where it has not been present beforehand during the drifting process. The size of individual plastic fragments plays an important role in facilitating the introduction of invasive species.[107]

II. Toxicological influences of marine litter by ingestion

It is estimated that over 312 species of seabirds are affected by the ingestion of marine litter.[108] Here, in particular the so-called surface feeders such as albatrosses and shearwaters as well as plankton-feeding divers are particular vulnerable to ingest marine litter.[109] There are at least 26 species of cetaceans known to ingest plastic.[110] In the western Mediterranean 35%

---

104 Jones/Ingolfsson/Olafsson *et al.*, Migrations and dispersal of marine organisms, in Proceedings of the 37th European Marine Biology Symposium held in Reykjavik, Iceland, 5-9 August 2002, 2003, 60; *Barnes,* Nature 416 (2002) 808, 808.

105 *Aliani/Molcard,* Hydriobiologia 503 (2003) 59, 65 *et seq.*

106 *Barnes,* Nature 416 (2002) 808, 808.

107 *Morét-Ferguson/Law/Proskurowski et al.,* Marine Pollution Bulletin 60 (2010) 1873, 1877; *Barnes,* Nature 416 (2002) 808, 808.

108 *Laist,* Marine debris, in *Coe/Rogers,* Marine debris (1997) 99–140, 102. During a study of sampled fulmars in the North Sea, 95% of the fulmars had plastic in their stomach *van Franeker/Blaize/Danielsen et al.,* Environmental Pollution 159 (2011) 2609, 2609.

109 *Institute for European Environmental Policy/Poseidon Aquatic Resource Management Ltd joint report,* Ghost Fishing by Lost Fishing Gear, 2005, 45.

110 *Baird/Hooker,* Marine Pollution Bulletin 40 (2000) 719, 720.

of loggerheads turtles analysed had litter in their gastrointestinal tract.[111] Animals are affected by marine litter due to normal behaviour patterns such as feeding themselves or their offspring.[112] Ingestion of litter by animals occurs because of misidentification of litter as a source of food,[113] as a secondary ingestion of prey[114] or through regurgitation from parent to chick.[115] Marine litter causes blockages of the digestive tract resulting in the obstruction of gastric enzyme production, malnutrition, limited growth or starvation.[116] Additionally, further consequences are limited reproductive fitness or a reduced capacity to avoid predators.[117] Moreover, sharp objects can inflict internal injuries and ulceration.[118] In fish, buoyant pieces of plastic can disturb the function of the air bladder so that the fish is prevented from diving into deeper water layers.[119] Whereas some marine species are able to pass pieces of litter through the digestive tract, seabirds are not known to be able to egest waste and are therefore used as a target species to monitor the presence and accumulation of marine litter in animals.[120] In 2012, the case of a sperm whale that was found dead on the coast in Spain drew the attention of scientist and media alike. Whereas the whale appeared to be emaciated, the inspection of the abdomen demonstrated a gastric rupture that was caused by impaction with plastic litter.[121] A further analysis demonstrated that the sperm whale had ingest-

111 *Lazar/Gračan,* Marine Pollution Bulletin 62 (2011) 43, 45.

112 *Lazar/Gračan,* Marine Pollution Bulletin 62 (2011) 43, 43; *Fry/Fefer/Sileo,* Marine Pollution Bulletin 18 (1987) 339, 339.

113 The plastic in planktivorous fish was dominantly white, clear or blue, thus leading to the conclusion that the fish had mistaken the plastic as plankton: *Boerger/Lattin/Moore et al.,* Marine Pollution Bulletin 60 (2010) 2275, 2277; *Campani/Baini/Giannettiet al.,* Marine Pollution Bulletin 74 (2013) 225, 226.

114 *Eriksson/Burton,* AMBIO: A Journal of the Human Environment 32 (2003) 380, 382.

115 *Fry/Fefer/Sileo,* Marine Pollution Bulletin 18 (1987) 339, 339.

116 *Possatto/Barletta/Costa et al.,* Marine Pollution Bulletin 62 (2011) 1098, 1101; *Boerger/Lattin/Moore et al.,* Marine Pollution Bulletin 60 (2010) 2275, 2277.

117 *Gregory,* Philosophical Transactions of the Royal Society B: Biological Sciences 364 (2009) 2013, 2016.

118 *Ryan/Jackson,* Marine Pollution Bulletin 18 (1987) 217, 219.

119 *Boerger/Lattin/Moore et al.,* Marine Pollution Bulletin 60 (2010) 2275, 2277.

120 *Derraik,* Marine Pollution Bulletin 44 (2002) 842, 845.

121 *De Stephanis/Giménez/Carpinelli et al.,* Marine Pollution Bulletin 69 (2013) 206, 207.

ed over 59 plastic items, weighing almost 18kg and covering $37m^2$.[122] A striking fact in this regard is that the most commonly ingested plastic item consisted of cover material of greenhouses that can be found along the Spanish coast as well as flower pots. Even though this represents one limited example, albeit spectacular, on how ingestion can impact marine organisms, it also shows that the bioavailability of plastic depends on the size of the materials itself or the species which has ingested the material in question.

1. Chemicals contained in plastic

The many different characteristics and functions of plastic are mainly due to the additives. Phthalates such as *Di-2-ethylhexyl phthalate* and *dibutyl phthalate* and bisphenol A are such additives that were or are used in plastic manufacturing. As phthalates are not chemically bound to the polymer they may leach into the surrounding environment. Bisphenol A is primarily taken up by ingestion of contaminated food.[123] In this regard plastic bottles and containers made out of polycarbonates are possible pathways.[124] Bisphenol A is a suspected endocrine disruptor, as it impacts the reproductive system by binding to oestrogen receptors. Several bioassays using micro-invertebrates and fish, for example, *Debenest et al.* assessed the ecotoxicity of tetrabromobisphenol A and its derivates that are used in plastic and electronical equipment.[125] In particular the rainbow trout assay, a standardised test system for aquatic toxicity, rendered a significant toxicity.[126]

---

122 *de Stephanis/Giménez/Carpinelli et al.,* Marine Pollution Bulletin 69 (2013) 206, 208.

123 *Vandenberg/Hauser/Olea et al.*, Reproductive Toxicology 24 (2007) 139, 140. The toxicity of these plasticisers is subject to controversial discussions among scientists.

124 There are however bottles that are produced free of Bisphenol A.

125 *Debenest/Gagné/Petit et al.*, Comparative Biochemistry and Physiology Part C: Toxicology & Pharmacology 151 (2010) 407, 408. See only, *OECD*, OECD Guideline for testing acute fish toxicity testing.

126 *Ibid.,* 411.

2. Material science of plastic

Plastic is derived from the Greek word "plastikos" which signifies "fit for moulding".[127] This exemplifies the many possibilities of plastic in its use, shape and function. Any combination of properties can be chemically engineered to accommodate almost any use and application under differing thermal, chemical and biological conditions.

Plastic is a light-weight and versatile product that is used in all sectors but particularly in the building and construction, agricultural, food and medical sectors. World plastic production has grown rapidly since its commercialisation in the 1950s and amounted in 2012 to 241 million tons of produced plastic.[128] The plastic production in the year 2012 in the European Union, Switzerland and Norway amounted to 20.4% of the total world´s production.[129] The biggest market share in the range of application constitutes packaging at 39.4%[130], most of which tends to be quickly disposed of after usage.[131] It is estimated that in Europe 25 million tons of post-consumer plastic waste are generated each year.[132] Plastic is seen to be an important factor in reducing fuel usage during transportation due to lightweight construction units which readily leads to the prediction that a further demand and therefore supply can be expected.[133] It is assumed that there is a correlation between the growth of plastic pollution and the abundance of plastic in the seas.[134]

Biopolymers have been used in the production of leather and birch-tar for several hundred years. The production of chemically modified natural material such as collagen and nitrocellulose is believed to have started in the 19th century.[135] A further development came with Alexander Parkes

---

127 *Hammer/Kraak/Parsons,* Reviews of Environmental Contamination and Toxicology, in *Whitacre,* Reviews of Environmental Contamination and Toxicology (2012) 1–44, 2.

128 *Plasticseurope*, Plastics the fact 2013, 2013, 11.

129 *Ibid.*

130 *Plasticseurope*, Plastics the fact 2013, 2013, 13.

131 Most packages have a lifetime of less than a year: *Selke,* Plastics and the environment, in *Andrady,* Plastics and the environment (2003) 139–183, 139.

132 *Plasticseurope*, Plastics the fact 2013, 24.

133 *Thompson/Moore/Vom Saal et al.,* Philosophical Transactions of the Royal Society B: Biological Sciences 364 (2009) 2153, 2164.

134 *Wright/Thompson/Galloway,* Environmental Pollution 178 (2013) 483, 484.

135 Plasticseurope, Plastics the fact 2013, 2013, 1.

who invented celluloid, the first thermoplastic, in 1862[136] and Leo Baekeland who produced the first real synthetic mass-produced plastic.[137] Depending on the materials used in the production, one can distinguish between fossil based plastic and synthetic plastic. The fossil based plastics are derived from natural products such as cellulose, natural gas and most importantly crude oil. Crude oil is the basic building block of plastic and almost 8% of the world´s oil production is used for the purpose of plastic fabrication.[138] It is distillated so that the different components are fragmented into hydrocarbon chains. These hydrocarbon chains differ in the composition, size and structure of their molecules.

One of these fractions is naphtha, the crucial element for the production of plastic. In a further step, naphtha is broken down by means of cracking, a thermal splitting process, to smaller structural units, monomers that form molecular chains, so-called polymers.[139] In the polymerisation process, the compounds are formed into a polymer chain. These polymer chains can be made up of carbon chain or individual polymers linked together. Depending on the structure of polymers, the structure and indeed function of the plastic changes. Plastic can be broadly classified into two categories that are determined by their engineering behaviour: thermoplastics and thermosets.[140] The first category, thermoplastics, are carbon-chain polymers that allow them to be repeatedly remoulded and reformed. Plastics from this family include Polyvinyl chloride (PVC) used in transparent food packaging[141] and polycarbonate (PC) processed for sunglasses and DVDs, for example. Thermosets on the other hand undergo a chemical reaction during fabrication and thus cannot be reprocessed or remolded. Polyester used in automobile and boat hulls belongs to this type of plastic. Virgin

---

136 *Fenichell,* Plastic: The making of a synthetic century, 1996, 17.

137 The man-made polymer was Bakelit that was made by Baekeland in 1907: *Andrady,* Common Plastics Material, in *Andrady,* Plastics and the environment (2003) 77, 77.

138 *Thompson/Moore/Vom Saal et al.,* Philosophical Transactions of the Royal Society B: Biological Sciences 364 (2009) 2153, 2153.

139 *Andrady,* Common Plastics Material, in *Andrady,* Plastics and the environment (2003) 77, 79.

140 *Ibid.*, 78.

141 *Andrady,* Common Plastics Material, in *Andrady,* Plastics and the environment (2003) 77, 78.

plastic polymers are usually not used by themselves but are mixed with additives in order to provide them with particular properties.[142]

Additives such as plasticisers, flame retardants, colorants and stabilisers are combined with the polymers during processing.[143] Plasticisers, for example, are used to guarantee the elasticity and flexibility of plastic at extreme temperatures and to soften the plastic for daily usage (soles). Common plasticisers are bisphenol A, and phthalates that are used as can liners and artificial fragrances.[144] They are commonly used in PVC and PC. Plasticisers space the polymers apart by bedding themselves between the chains of plastic polymers. Nonylphenol was used in PVC as an anti-fog and anti-static compound. Stabilisers are added as compounds in order to reduce the effects of aging and weathering through sunlight and ozone and include lead, tin, barium and cadmium.[145] Further potential properties include the resistance to various chemical products, the electrical conductivity and the glass transition temperature that are achieved by introducing additives. In order to decrease the risk of fire, bromated flame retardants such as polybromated biphenyl are added to the plastic.

3. Microplastics

A particular aspect of the marine litter debate relates to the aspect of microplastics. These have increasingly gained attention given the correlation between the size of microplastics, which increases the bioavailability for marine organisms.[146] Even though they are considered as an emerging pollutant, they have already been studied as early as the beginning of the 1990s.[147] Microplastics are fragments of plastics that are smaller than 5mm, their size ranges between 7 and 30 µm and 5 mm. However, there is an ongoing scientific discussion about the limits of the size range and the

---

142 *Ibid.*, 105.

143 See only table 2.7: *Andrady,* Common Plastics Material, in *Andrady,* Plastics and the environment (2003) 77, 106.

144 *Talsness/Andrade/Kuriyama et al.,* Philosophical Transactions of the Royal Society B: Biological Sciences 364 (2009) 2079, 2080.

145 *Andrady,* Common Plastics Material, in *Andrady,* Plastics and the environment (2003) 77, 100.

146 *Browne/Galloway/Thompson,* Integrated Environmental Assessment and Management 3 (2007) 559, 559.

147 *Derraik,* Marine Pollution Bulletin 44 (2002) 842, 842.

monitoring methodologies.[148] Microplastics is a collective term since one can differentiate between so-called primary microplastics and secondary microplastics. Microplastics pose a (toxicological) risk for marine organisms and potentially also humans through ingestion. In this regard, studies are currently underway on whether the ingestion of microplastic poses an additional pathway for chemicals associated with or adsorbed to plastic to enter the food chain of marine organisms or humans.[149]

a) Primary microplastic

Primary microplastics stem from the direct release of primary products such as small plastic pellets or abrasives.[150] Even though the topic has been already acknowledged in the 1990s, the dimension of the use of microplastics in personal care products has only recently begun to receive enormous attention.[151] Primary microplastics are, for example, plastic exfoliator beads in skin cleansers, face scrubs or hand wash.[152] Whereas formerly exfoliating materials in personal care products were made of oatmeal, apricot or walnut husks, the cosmetic industry has replaced these by micro-beads usually made of polyethylene, largely speaking for reasons of cost.[153] The microplastics are later released into the environment through effluents of waste water treatment plants, since it is assumed that these substances pass through the preliminary treatment filters.[154] Moreover, *Browne et al.* have demonstrated that the washing of a single garment pro-

148 *Gray/Lattin/Moore,* Marine Pollution Bulletin (2012) 2190, 2191.

149 The potential ecological and human health risks of microplastics are relatively new research fields and are currently associated with a large degree of uncertainty: *GESAMP, Kershaw, P.J. (ed.),* GESAMP Report No.90, (2015), 30.

150 These "primary" products also include macerated waste, shot-blasting and industrial cleaning products respectively that enter the marine environment either directly or via urban waste water systems: *GESAMP*, Proceedings of the International Research Workshop on the occurrence, effects, and fate of microplastic marine debris, 2010, 11.

151 See only Gregory who described the use of plastic beads in hand wash in the 1990s *Gregory,* Marine Pollution Bulletin 32 (1996) 867. *GESAMP, Kershaw, P.J.(ed.),* GESAMP Report No.90 (2015), 18.

152 *Fendall/Sewell,* Marine Pollution Bulletin 58 (2009) 1225. See also for an overview:.

153 *Ibid.*, 1225.

154 *Fendall/Sewell,* Marine Pollution Bulletin 58 (2009) 1225, 1225.

duces more than 1900 fibres per wash, which ultimately pass through the filter system of waste water plants and are contained in sewage.[155] In this way, particles are also released into the marine environment. Additionally, possible other sources of microplastics are airborne and runoff particles from tyres and road wear particles.[156] Primary microplastics that have been found in the marine environment were made of polypropylene and polyethylene.[157]

b) Secondary microplastic

Despite the long-term durability of plastic items in the marine environment, plastic undergoes transformation processes. As has been depicted above, microplastics can be the result of a fragmentation process in the marine environment. In the Great Pacific Garbage Patch in the central North Pacific, the ratio between plankton and microplastics is 1 to 6.[158] Plastic fragments primarily due to UV radiation; furthermore fragmentation can result due to mechanical forces such as waves and grinding as well as biological activity.[159] Carbon-based plastic floating at the water surface for example is subject to photo-oxidation.[160] Photolytic reactions modify the surface properties of plastic. Even though it has been found that microbial biofilms developing on the surface of plastic do not provide for organisms that are able to degrade polyethylene, it plays an important role in the weathering and aging process of plastic.[161] The cold water temperature in the marine environment in relation to the high thermal resistance of plastic makes it a long-lasting and slowly degrading substance in

155 *Browne/Crump/Niven et al.,* Environmental Science & Technology 45 (2011) 9175, 9177.

156 *Panko/Chu/Kreider et al.,* Atmospheric Environment 72 (2013) 192.

157 *Mato/Isobe/Takada et al.,* Environmental Science & Technology 35 (2001) 318, 318; *Ashton/Holmes/Turner,* Marine Pollution Bulletin 60 (2010) 2050; *Teuten/Rowland/Galloway et al.,* Environmental Science & Technology 41 (2007) 7759.

158 *Moore/Moore/Leecaster et al.,* Marine Pollution Bulletin 42 (2001) 1297, 1297.

159 *GESAMP,* Proceedings of the International Research Workshop on the occurrence, effects, and fate of microplastic marine debris, 2010, 119. Boring isopods have damaged polystyrene floats under docks and caused in this way microplastics *Davidson,* Marine Pollution Bulletin 64 (2012) 1821.

160 *Teuten/Saquing/Knappe et al.,* Philosophical Transactions of the Royal Society B: Biological Sciences 364 (2009) 2027, 2039.

161 *Ibid.*; *Cooper/Corcoran,* Marine Pollution Bulletin 60 (2010) 650.

the marine environment. For these reasons, the quantity of plastic fragments is therefore expected to increase in the seas and oceans.[162] However, knowledge gaps still prevail as to the amount, sources and trends of microplastics in general.[163]

4. The uptake of microplastics

Different factors influence the uptake of microplastics into marine organisms.[164] The stranded sperm whale demonstrated that the size of the plastic is a key factor for the bioavailability of plastic.[165] In this regard, the size of microplastics allows for greater ingestion by lower trophic organisms. Whereas some of these organisms have a lower selectivity when taking in food,[166] the passive feeding behavior of higher trophic planktivores such as baleen whales potentially leads to the greater likelihood of an uptake of microplastics.[167] The specific spatial distribution of plastic also increases the bioavailability for organisms in the water column and on the sediment.[168] An explanation why plastic microspheres are ingested by plantivores is that their specific gravity that is similar to algae.[169] Benthic deposit feeders and benthic scavengers could ingest suitable sizes of microplastics.[170] The blue mussel *Mytilus edulis*, is a suspension feeder known to capture and ingest microplastics.[171] Even though bivalves such as the *Mytilus edulis* can sort the captured particles before ingestion, it appears that microplastics cannot be entirely rejected as pseudofaeces and

162 *Liebezeit/Dubaish,* Bulletin of Environmental Contamination and Toxicology 89 (2012) 213.

163 *Zarfl/Fleet/Fries et al.,* Marine Pollution Bulletin 62 (2011) 1589, 1589.

164 *Wright/Thompson/Galloway,* Environmental Pollution Pollution 178 (2013) 483, 484.

165 *Ibid.*

166 *Wright/Thompson/Galloway,* Environmental Pollution 178 (2013) 483, 484.

167 *Fossi/Panti/Guerranti et al.,* Marine Pollution Bulletin 64 (2012) 2374.

168 *Wright/Thompson/Galloway,* Environmental Pollution 178 (2013) 483, 486.

169 *Ibid.*

170 *Wright/Thompson/Galloway,* Environmental Pollution 178 (2013) 483.

171 *v. Moos/Burkhardt-Holm/Köhler,* Environmental Science & Technology 46 (2012) 11327.

are therefore ingested.[172] Whereas field surveys of vertebrates that have ingested microplastic include fish, seabirds and marine mammals, laboratory experiments have demonstrated that amphipods, lugworms, barnacles as well as marine zooplankton are also able to ingest microplastics.[173] Even though it has been confirmed that several species have taken up plastic, there are currently also several prognostic modelling activities in place, that need to be further substantiated by experimental and field data.[174]

In humans, it is known that microplastics can also be inhaled.[175] *Liebezeit* and *Liebezeit* found small particulate material in honey, suggesting that ingestion of these particles could also be a route of transfer into the human body.[176]

5. Adsorption of chemicals and metals onto microplastics

Microplastics are believed to play an important role in the adsorption of chemicals due to their low polarity and as their volume ratio provide a greater surface than macroplastics.[177] Consequently, the plastic fragments act like “hydrophobic adsorbents”.[178] The high degree of marine plastic that has adsorbed contaminants is derived from the low density of plastic which causes it to float at the sea-surface microlayer where the hydrophobic contaminants’ concentrations are up to 500 times higher than in the

---

172 *Wright/Thompson/Galloway,* Environmental Pollution 178 (2013) 483, 487; *v. Moos/Burkhardt-Holm/Köhler,* Environmental Science & Technology 46 (2012) 11327, 11335.

173 *Koelmans/Besseling/Foekema*, Environmental Pollution 187 (2014) 49, 54 ; *Chua/Shimeta/Nugegoda et al.*, Environmental Science & Technology (2014), just accepted script 02.06.2014; *GESAMP, Kershaw, P.J. (ed.),* GESAMP Report No.90 (2015), 30.

174 *Koelmans/Besseling/ Foekema*, Environmental Pollution 187 (2014) 49, 54.

175 *Browne/Crump/Niven et al.,* Environmental Science & Technology 45 (2011) 9175, 9177.

176 In *Liebezeit/Liebezeit,* Food Additives & Contaminants: Part A (2013) 1, 2, also *Wagner/Oehlmann,* Environmental Science and Pollution Research 16 (2009) 278, 279.

177 *Mato/Isobe/Takada et al.,* Environmental Science & Technology 35 (2001) 318, 318; *Frias/Sobral/Ferreira,* Marine Pollution Bulletin 60 (2010) 1988.

178 *Mato/Isobe/Takada et al.,* Environmental Science & Technology 35 (2001) 318, 318.

water column.[179] In addition, production pellets that were released within the marine environment are also known to accumulate metals.[180] The weathering effects of plastic in the marine environment are key factors for the adsorption of metals and hydrophobic persistent pollutants onto plastic particles and facilitate their fragmentation to edible sizes.[181] Through weathering, the plastic surfaces become porous and, consequently, provide for excellent adsorption conditions.[182]

Polychlorinated biphenyls (PCBs) are a group of 209 manufactured organic chlorides that share a similar biphenyl–structure which only differs in regard to the quantity of chloratome. The chlorination degree determines the physical as well as chemical characteristics and has therefore an impact on toxicological profiles. Due to the PCB's versatile characteristics such as inertness and temperature-stability, it has been widely used in the production process of hydraulic systems and cold storage systems. Moreover they have been applied as flame retardants as well as plasticisers in plastics and paintwork. Due to their broad field of application as well as their persistence, PCB is ubiquitous in the atmosphere, water and soil. PCB cannot be broken down by photolysis or microorganisms and thus potentially remains in the environment for years. Despite the ban of the original "dirty dozen" of POP by the Stockholm Convention on Persistent Organic Pollutants since 2001,[183] their persistence and semi-volatility fa-

---

179 *Teuten/Rowland/Galloway et al.,* Environmental Science & Technology 41 (2007) 7759, 7759.

180 *Ashton/Holmes/Turner,* Marine Pollution Bulletin 60 (2010) 2050, 2054.

181 *Ashton/Holmes/Turner,* Marine Pollution Bulletin 60 (2010) 2050; *Browne/Galloway/Thompson,* Environmental Science & Technology 44 (2010) 3404, 3408.

182 *Thompson/Moore/Vom Saal et al.,* Philosophical Transactions of the Royal Society B: Biological Sciences 364 (2009) 2153, 2156.

183 40 ILM 532 (2001). The Stockholm Convention was adopted 22 May 2001 and entered in force 17 May 2004. It establishes a listing-approach in which substances listed in Annex A are to be eliminated, substances in Annex B to the Convention must be restricted and Annex C substances must be reduced with a view to their unintentional production. The original "dirty dozen" POPs are: Pesticides: *aldrin, chlordane, Dichlordiphenyltrichlorethan (DDT), dieldrin, endrin, heptachlor, hexachlorobenzene, mirex, toxaphene; Industrial chemicals: hexachlorobenzene, polychlorinated biphenyls (PCBs*); and by-products: *hexachlorobenzene; polychlorinated dibenzo-p-dioxins and polychlorinated dibenzofurans (PCDD/PCDF),* and *PCB*s. The Fourth Conference of the Parties (COP) to the Stockholm Convention amended in 2009 Annexes A, B and C to the Convention and added nine new POPs (decision SC-4/10-SC-4/18). During the Fifth

cilitates their transport over long-distances to remote areas where they resettle in sediments for example. In 1972, PCB was detected on polystyrene spherules and it was suggested that these were adsorbed from surrounding seawater.[184] *Mato et al.* showed in 2001 that many hydrophobic contaminants were accumulated on marine plastic, reaching concentrations of PCB that were 10^6 higher than in the adjoining water.[185] Chlorinated hydrocarbons are lipophilic, having a strong affinity to lipids and are therefore known to accumulate in the surface layer of the sea that contains fatty acids.[186] As plastic usually floats on the surface, it adsorbs the hydrocarbons and is thus to be regarded as a growing concern with a view to the increasing amount of plastic in the marine environment. Even though the toxicological characteristics of most of these are well known, the degree of the bioavailability of adsorbed POPs in microplastics remains unclear.[187]

A variation in the contaminants concentration levels among plastic fragments has been observed.[188] Possible factors explaining these variations are difference in the material, weathering, the partition coefficient, thermal and chemical processes or the residence time in the sea. It is contentious whether the colour or the age of the plastic fragment, indicated by a fouling process at the plastic´s surface, are determining factors for a higher adsorption rate of chemicals.[189]

Meeting of the COP in May 2011, Annex A to the Stockholm Convention was amended to include *endosulfan* and its related isomers (decision SC-5/3). See also: *Sohn/Noyes,* Cases and materials on the law of the sea, 2004, 727.

184 *Carpenter/Anderson/Harvey et al.,* Science 178 (1972) 749, 749. For an early account on research that suggested the correlation between the intake of plastics and PCB concentrations in marine organisms *Ryan/Connell/Gardner,* Marine Pollution Bulletin 19 (1988) 174.

185 *Mato/Isobe/Takada et al.,* Environmental Science & Technology 35 (2001) 318, 324;*Lobelle/Cunliffe,* Marine Pollution Bulletin 62 (2011) 197; *Rochman/Manzano/Hentschel et al.,* Environmental Science & Technology (2013) 13976, 1376.

186 *Clark,* Marine pollution, 2007, 134.

187 *GESAMP*, Proceedings of the International Research Workshop on the occurrence, effects, and fate of microplastic marine debris, 2010, 26; *Andrady,* Marine Pollution Bulletin 62 (2011) 1596.

188 *Frias/Sobral/Ferreira,* Marine Pollution Bulletin 60 (2010) 1988, 1991.

189 See for a summary of this discussion in: *GESAMP,* Proceedings of the International Research Workshop on the occurrence, effects, and fate of micro-plastic marine debris, 2010, 23.

6. Trophical transfer of persistent microplastics

The trophical transfer of persistent microplastics within food chains is of relevance not only to top-level predators but also to humans as potential consumers due to trophic biomagnification of microplastics.[190] The bioaccumulation of plastic and associated substances could occur after the predation of organisms which ingest and accumulate microplastics. Whereas this assumption could, for example, apply to the predation of microplastics-contaminated marine invertebrates, few studies have effectively researched the potential transfer across marine trophic levels.[191] *Eriksson* and *Burton* suggested that the accumulation of plastic pieces in fur seals feeding was associated with the fact that they had ingested prey that had itself previously ingested marine litter.[192]

Farrell and *Nelson* assessed the trophic transfer of microplastics into crabs (*carcinus maenas)* via *mytulis edulis*. It was observed that microplastics had accumulated in the hemolymph and tissue of *carcinus maenas* which indicates that microplastics have the potential to reach higher trophic levels.[193] For human consumers this therefore potentially constitutes a health risk,[194] since the consumption of mussels containing microplastics could possibly serve as a vector to introduce microplastics into humans.

7. Toxicological considerations

As the ingestion of plastic is known to occur in more than 200 species, plastics "serve as carriers of organic contaminants to wildlife."[195] With regard to microplastics, the physical and chemical consequences of inges-

---

190 *Talsness/Andrade/Kuriyama et al.,* Philosophical Transactions of the Royal Society B: Biological Sciences 364 (2009) 2079, 2079.

191 *Wright/Thompson/Galloway*, Environmental Pollution 178 (2013) 483, 489; *Farrell/Nelson,* Environmental Pollution 177 (2013) 1.

192 *Eriksson/Burton,* AMBIO: A Journal of the Human Environment 32 (2003) 380, 384.

193 *Farrell/Nelson,* Environmental Pollution 177 (2013) 1, 3. Almost all of the ingested microplastics was cleared from the crabs after 21 days.

194 *Ibid.*

195 *Teuten/Saquing/Knappe et al.,* Philosophical Transactions of the Royal Society B: Biological Sciences 364 (2009) 2027, 2028.

tion depend on certain factors.[196] The smallest particles are known to be mobile within bodily tissues and cause harm to the fitness of organisms through particle toxicity. Potential toxic effects of microplastics can be cell damage,[197] cell death, inflammation, lysosomal instability, infections and tumor formation.

It is argued that the possibility of microplastics accumulation within an organism is a factor for causing physical impacts.[198] *Browne et al.* (2008) demonstrated in laboratory studies that microplastics can accumulate in the digestive cavity and tubules of bivalve molluscs.[199] Additionally, the translocation of microplastics in the organism has been demonstrated in *Mytilus edulis.*[200] Even though the precise mechanism for translocation across the epithelial lining remains yet unknown, *Browne et al.* were able to prove that microspheres had translocated from the gut to the circulatory system.[201] The occurrence of microplastic in the haemolymph in *Mytilus edulis* did not coincide with toxic effects.[202] It is suggested that the smaller the sizes of microparticles, the accumulation of it in the circulatory fluid is likely to increase which in return also increases the likelihood of translocation.[203] Another factor is the shape of microplastics, which have a specific shape-related toxicity, which relates to the potential greater contact area.[204] The larger volume ratio could facilitate the exchange of contaminants. An additional factor in an ecotoxicological context is the possibility of the organism to excrete microplastics.[205] Species with a particular small body mass may be particularly vulnerable to the toxicological effects. Here, two factors appear to be important, these are the residence time and volume of ingested plastic.[206]

---

196 *Wright/Thompson/Galloway,* Environmental Pollution 178 (2013) 483, 488.

197 *v. Moos/Burkhardt-Holm/Köhler,* Environmental Science & Technology 46 (2012) 11327.

198 *Wright/Thompson/Galloway,* Environmental Pollution 178 (2013) 483, 488.

199 *Browne/Dissanayake/Galloway et al.,* Environmental Science & Technology 42 (2008) 5026, 5028.

200 *Ibid.*, 5026.

201 *Browne/Dissanayake/Galloway et al.,* Environmental Science & Technology 42 (2008) 5206, 5026.

202 *Ibid.*, 5030.

203 *Wright/Thompson/Galloway,* Environmental Pollution 178 (2013) 483, 488.

204 *Ibid.*, 489.

205 *Wright/Thompson/Galloway,* Environmental Pollution 178 (2013) 483, 489.

206 *Andrady,* Marine Pollution Bulletin 62 (2011) 1596, 1596.

In regard to the marine environment, the toxicity of chemicals contained in plastic have two central sources: synthetic man-made chemicals added during plastic fabrication and persistent, bioaccumulating and toxic compounds (PBT) that are ubiquitously present in the marine environment.[207] Studies have shown that there is a positive correlation between the amount of ingested plastics and the concentration of lower-chlorinated congeners.[208] PCB as a hydrophobic and poorly metabolised contaminant is amplified along the food chain.[209] However, the bioavailability of the additives or adsorbed POPs contained in the plastic is not entirely known and is in need of further research.[210] *Chu/Shimeta/Nugegoda et al.* have found that PBDE derived from microplastic can be assimilated into the tissue of amphipods. Even though chemical uptake from microplastics is lower than the uptake of free available chemicals in the marine environment, microplastics are therefore able to transfer PBDE into marine organisms.[211] Nonetheless, few studies have demonstrated the adverse consequences of the uptake of contaminated microplastics.[212] *Koelmans/Gouin/Thompson et al.* indicate that uptake of microplastics may not significantly alter the contaminant level in the marine organism.[213]

However, potential effects of ingested particles could be inflammatory responses (immune system), cellular damage and other possible physiological, ecological or behavioural responses.[214] Thus, whereas manual impacts such as entanglements are clearly visible, "the potential impacts of

---

207 The term PBT is borrowed from *GESAMP*, Proceedings of the International Research Workshop on the occurrence, effects, and fate of micro-plastic marine debris, 2010.

208 *Yamashita/Takada/Fukuwaka et al.,* Marine Pollution Bulletin 62 (2011) 2845, 2845; *Colabuono/Taniguchi/Montone,* Marine Pollution Bulletin 60 (2010) 630, 630.

209 *Teuten/Saquing/Knappe et al.,* Philosophical Transactions of the Royal Society B: Biological Sciences 364 (2009) 2027, 2040.

210 *Andrady,* Marine Pollution Bulletin 62 (2011) 1596.

211 *Chua/Shimeta/Nugegoda et al.*, Environmental Science & Technology (2014), just accepted script 02.06.2014.

212 *Wallace* in *Koelmans/Gouin/Thompson*, Environmental Toxicology and Chemistry 33 (2014) 5, 9.

213 *Koelmans/Besseling/Wegner et al.*, Environmental Science & Technology 47 (2013) 7812, 7812.

214 *Wright/Thompson/Galloway,* Environmental Pollution 178 (2013) 483, Table 2. .

micro-plastics may be quite subtle […] and it may be difficult to extrapolate experimental results to population and ecosystem scales."[215]

A second aspect is the transfer coefficient across trophic levels that are introduced via microplastics. Many POPs are known to be subject to trophic transfer among the trophic chain. PCB as a hydrophobic and poorly metabolisable contaminant is amplified along the food chain.[216] The octanol-water partition coefficient and the metabolic transformation rate are important considerations when assessing the possibility of trophic transfer. Thus even though the association of microplastics and POPs is known, further research is currently needed to understand potential bioaccumulation of chemicals contained or adsorbed on microplastics.[217] A further aspect of this problem is whether the consumption of marine organisms that have been contaminated by microplastics has an impact on human health.[218] It is suggested that humans could potentially be affected by these chemicals after ingesting affected organisms.[219] *Van Cauwenberghe and Janssen* detected a high concentration of microplastic in comercially grown mussels. From this, one could conclude that the annual dietary exposure for European shellfish consumers could amount to 11,000 microplastics per year.[220] However, there still remain substantial knowledge gaps regarding the fate and toxicity of microplastics in humans.[221] Studies have demonstrated plastic particle toxicity in humans. *Wick/Malek/Maner et al.* used an *ex vivo* human placental perfusion model to understand whether nanoparticles can cross the placenta as model particles and the study demonstrated that beads of a diameter of up to 240 nm were capable of being taken up by the placenta.[222] However, since most people will be exposed "to complex mixtures of organic compounds at low concentra-

---

215 *GESAMP,* Proceedings of the International Research Workshop on the occurrence, effects, and fate of micro-plastic marine debris, 2010, 18.

216 *Teuten/Saquing/Knappe et al.,* Philosophical Transactions of the Royal Society B: Biological Sciences 364 (2009) 2027, 2040.

217 *Wright/Thompson/Galloway,* Environmental Pollution 178 (2013) 483, 490; *Andrady,* Marine Pollution Bulletin 62 (2011) 1596.

218 *GESAMP*, Proceedings of the International Research Workshop on the occurrence, effects, and fate of micro-plastic marine debris, 2010, 8.

219 *Frias/Sobral/Ferreira,* Marine Pollution Bulletin 60 (2010) 1988, 1992.

220 *Van Cauwenberghe/Janssen,* Environmental Pollution 193 (2014) 65, 65.

221 *GESAMP, Kershaw, P.J. (ed.),* GESAMP Report No.90 (2015), 53.

222 *Wick/Malek/Manser et al.,* Environmental Health Perspectives 118 (2009) 432.

tions", this problem most probably has a limited long-term public health dimension.[223]

III. Socio-economic impacts

Marine litter has an impact on a variety of marine sectors such as fishing, shipping, tourism and aquaculture. However, a knowledge gap exists regarding pertinent socio-economic impacts.[224] Polluted beaches impose a twofold economic problem: first, aesthetic as well as hygienic concerns may deter visitors or tourist. It has been demonstrated that polluted beaches could cause 50% of the tourist revenue.[225] Secondly, the clean-up costs that are to be sustained by local communities are substantial.[226] Aside from the aesthetic problems related to marine litter, sanitary and medical waste washed ashore has been a problem in the past that poses a serious threat to human health.[227]

Additionally, marine litter has an economic impact for the operator of vessels which cannot operate due to entanglement or propeller fouling.[228] Entangled plastic in nets and cages around aquaculture farms reduces the water circulation that potentially leads to poor sanitary conditions. The impact of ghost nets stems from their continuing catching of target species and the capture of non-target fish and shellfish as well as the disturbance of the marine ecosystem that could impact incidentally on target species. The fibres used for ropes, cordage and fishing are made out of nylon and other synthetic materials, therefore making them endurable, buoyant and resilient.[229] The economic impact heavily depends on the capacity to con-

---

223 *Ibid.*; *Liebezeit/Liebezeit,* Food Additives & Contaminants: Part A (2013) 1, 2; *Wagner/Oehlmann,* Environmental Science and Pollution Research 16 (2009) 278, 279.

224 Interviewes/Görlitz/Stöfen *et al.*, Issue Paper to the "International Conference on Prevention and Management of Marine Litter in European Seas", 16.05.2013, 11.

225 *Ballance,* South African Journal of Science 96 (2000) 210, 212.

226 The beach-clean ups in the The Hague municipality costs annually € 626,709: *UNEP,* Marine Litter: A Global Challenge, 2009, 115.

227 *Ivar do Sul/Costa,* Marine Pollution Bulletin 54 (2007) 1087, 1099.

228 *UNEP*, Marine Litter: A Global Challenge, 2009, 115.

229 Spectra (registered trade mark) used in fishing twine is supposed to be 15 times stronger than steel and more durable than polyester: *Barco/D'Eri/Woodward et al.,* Marine Pollution Bulletin 60 (2010) 1477, 1478.

tinue ghost fishing which is related to the type of fishing gear, its decomposition status and its suspension in the water.[230] The fishing capacity of ghost nets is highly variable and depends on the destruction of nets by vessels and the process of fouling that makes the nets visible.[231] A study in selected Swedish fishing areas found that during a period of 28 months, the catch capacity of the ghost nets accumulate between 3 and 906 tonnes. Taking into consideration that the commercially exploited landing of cod in this area amounted to 28,345 tonnes of cod, the continued catch rate of the ghost fisheries in this instance could lie between 0.01 and 3.2%.[232] This great span in the quantification of the overall estimated ghost catches and therefore lost resources, stems from the difficult assessment methods. Thus the outlook and estimation vary immensely, reaching from 1% of the overall landed catches, and consequently not impacting the yield[233] to "non-trivial portion of target fishery population."[234]

IV. Preliminary conclusion

Hidden within the broader issue of marine litter lies a complex set of potential and as yet not fully understood ecological and ecotoxicological impacts. Even though sub-lethal effects are known that alter the biological and ecological behaviour of individuals of marine species, there remain substantial knowledge gaps on its impacts on populations, habitats and ecosystems. This limited knowledge is an obstacle to effectively address and manage the problem. Drawing from the scientific findings, it could be concluded that plastic, in particular, poses one of the central challenges due to its low biodegradation potential in the marine environment. It has an impact on the different "life stages", whether as a macroplastic or as microplastic. Besides the more mechanical impacts such as entanglement or as a vector for invasive species, the ecotoxicological influences it might have,are not yet entirely tangible. However, the toxicity of contaminated

230 *Institute for European Environmental Policy / Poseidon Aquatic Resource Management Ltd joint report,* Ghost Fishing by Lost Fishing Gear 2005, 6–8; *Good/June/Etnier et al.,* Marine Pollution Bulletin 60 (2010) 39, 39.

231 *Institute for European Environmental Policy / Poseidon Aquatic Resource Management Ltd joint report,* Ghost Fishing by Lost Fishing Gear 2005, 6.

232 *Ibid.*

233 *Brown/Macfayden,* Marine Policy 31 (2007) 488, 490.

234 *Good/June/Etnier et al.,* Marine Pollution Bulletin 60 (2010) 39, 40.

microplastic and the subsequent exposure to these in animals as well as humans is probably one of the key leverage points when addressing the issue from a regulatory point of view. Even though marine organisms and humans are exposed to similar chemicals via other exposure pathways, microplastics pose a particular problem due to the potential dimension of their ecotoxicological impacts and the longevity and persistence of plastic itself. As has been demonstrated by *Chua*, microplastics play a role in transferring PBDE into marine organisms.[235] Drawing from the experiences in relation to the long-term effect of chemicals that have been prohibited such as PCB, the persistence and toxicity of plastic in general indicates that actions should not be postponed with a view to direct and imminent impacts it might have.

D. Preliminary conclusion – Uncertainties and knowledge gaps

The above discussion has demonstrated that marine litter is a complex and cumulative problem. Even though the different pathways and possible sources were broadly depicted, uncertainties remain regarding the specific importance of each source and the percentage of unknown, underestimated or diffuse sources. The manifold sources of marine litter thus pose a challenge with regard to addressing them. This is also reinforced by the diverse types and materials that can be associated with marine litter. The specific spatial distribution of marine litter, being essentially omnipresent in the world oceans, also contributes to its potential to cause harm to the marine environment and its organisms. Consequently, marine litter is not only restricted to the water surface but it can also be found in the water column and sediments. Most strikingly, the distribution mechanisms of the oceans such as currents and oscillation disperse marine litter into far remote areas such as Polar Regions and uninhabited islands in the Pacific that are far away from civilisation. Therefore, the long-range spatial distribution of marine litter thus constitutes a transboundary problem in which usually the polluter does not feel the consequences of its impacts.

The environmental impacts of marine litter are diverse and can range from entanglements in ghost nets to ingestion of marine litter as well as

---

235 *Chua/Shimeta/Nugegoda et al.,* Environmental Science & Technology (2014), just accepted script 02.06.2014.

litter as a vector for alien species. Microplastics stemming both from primary or secondary plastics sources pose a particular risk due to their size that facilitates their bioavailability. The particle toxicity of these microparticles can be explained by the adsorbed POPs or already contained additives. Whereas the bioavailability of these contaminants is suspected to be influenced by factors such as the accumulation and translocation of microplastics in the marine organism, further research is necessary.

Although the transfer of POPS across trophic levels has been already proven, only very little or scarce data relating to the trophic transfer of contaminants introduced by ingested microplastics is available. Furthermore, the large dilution of contaminants and the complex trophic webs pose a challenge in further determining adverse impacts.[236]

The correlation between increased plastic production and consumption leads to the conclusion that the marine litter problem is potentially increasing over time. A particular worrisome aspect is the summation of the legacy of polluting activities with a view to the continuous input of tons of new litter. Due to its persistence, the plastic introduced is expected to stay for more than generations in the marine environment, potentially creating a perpetual problem if it is not addressed soon. The associated dimension of cumulative effects of litter adds to the complexity of potential impacts and consequences. With increasing knowledge, different aspects of the issue are emerging. This relates for example to the assumption that engineered plastic nanoparticles could be ingested by filter feeders.[237]

The knowledge of sources, fragmentation rates, abundance and trends of marine litter and microplastics in the oceans are important for the development of monitoring tools and strategies as well as targeted legal responses. It is clearly discernible that definitions and agreement on the risks of marine litter both for the marine environment, marine organisms and also humans will be only with difficulties achieved. This also relates to thresholds of (acceptable) risks or quality standards on the status of the marine environment. This is not only due to the many sources and fate of marine litter, but also with regard to its complex adverse consequences on different scales.

236 *Law/Hanke/Angelidis et. al.*, Marine Strategy Framework Directive, Task Group 8 Report on contaminants and polluting effect, 2010, 9.

237 *Andrady,* Marine Pollution Bulletin 62 (2011) 1596.

E. Requirements for an effective and integrated protection instrument

The analysis and synopsis of the origins, distribution and consequences of marine litter demonstrate that regulating the sources and activities leading to the introduction of marine litter into the marine environment is a complex and multifaceted task. It necessitates the integration of a broad range of sources and activities that vary immensely in their degree of pollutive effect. The introduction of marine litter is, *inter alia*, related to behavior of individuals, spatial planning activities, accidental, deliberate and operational introduction both on and offshore. One striking aspect is the prevailing lack of knowledge that is expressed in only fragmented and partial information on particular sources and activities. This leads to an uncertainty in regard to the actual (long)-term impacts of marine litter. Thus drawing from the empirical evidence, the following aspects should be elements in an effective and integrated protection instrument.[238]

Prevention at the source

An effective protection instrument should be based on the premise of the prevention of the introduction of marine litter at the source. A source-based approach that tackles the introduction of marine litter at its origins is therefore the most fundamental aspect of a regulatory regime. The underlying logic is that the removal of litter from the sea or the beach is very costly and could potentially incentivise continuous polluting activities.[239] A direct regulation at the source should be generally preferred to an approach that also takes into consideration indirect - thus primary and secondary - impacts and consequences caused by marine litter. This regulatory approach would be reactionary in that it addresses for example the smothering of habitats by sedimented plastic, entanglements or ingestion of marine organisms only after the litter has been introduced. Such an approach could dilute the protection standard at the source.

Even though the focus of an effective regulatory regime should be primarily a substance and source-oriented approach, measures related to the

238 The development of creating a protection instrument is based on the corresponding part of: *Fritz,* Integrierter Umweltschutz im Völkerrecht, 2009, 85 *et seq.*: *Fritz* elaborates on criteria relating to the integrated environmental protection in international law.

239 See for such a clean-up activity: *Martin,* Marine Pollution Bulletin 74 (2013) 165.

protection of biodiversity also play a role in advancing the protection regime. A regulation that prevents pollution in general, naturally also contributes to the protection of biodiversity. Depending on the protection standard of the biodiversity regulations, a source and pollution-based approach always profits from existing obligations to protect the environment as a whole.

Integrated approach to address all sources including diffuse sources

The regulatory instruments shall integrate, as far as possible, all land - as well as offshore - based pollution in order to avoid an unnatural fragmentation or separation between both compartments. Pollution by marine litter is not geographically confined to its place of introduction, but may due to hydrographic circumstances, be easily transported to even remote areas thereby becoming a transboundary impact. This aspect is particularly important in that diffuse or non-attributable sources of pollution necessitate a carefully selected yet dynamic standard setting approach. The standard setting approach needs to be coined by a precautionary approach that integrates risks and uncertainties. Additionally, the regulatory instrument must allow for the integration of new scientific knowledge on sources and consequences so as to prioritise actions. However, it is admitted that the multitude of sources is a complex and non-linear system, which cannot be addressed by one single instrument.

Integrating scientific knowledge

Knowledge is a prerequisite for adequate and effective measures that address the sources and entry points of marine litter. Due to the prevailing knowledge gap, the risk prevails that sources yet not known or underestimated are not integrated into the regulatory response. The scientific uncertainty in regard to exact data on entry points and sources of marine litter as well as to the complex impacts and consequences are focal points in this regard. Due to the missing knowledge about the potential complex interactions, such an approach should follow a flexible and precautionary approach in order to allow for new evidence on damages or impacts that are yet not describable or predictable. A cyclical assessment that ensures a continuously monitoring activity is an important tool to understand the *status quo* and to describe trends and changes in the distribution or density of marine litter. In order to understand the scale of the problem, it is indispensable to aim at harmonised monitoring methodologies and comparable data collection efforts. Fundamentally, monitoring efforts should always be linked to the introduction to source-based measures in order to evaluate their effectiveness.

Coordination vs. fragmentation

The factual situation as depicted above clearly demonstrates that a multitude of different actors and potential polluters need to be addressed when establishing a comprehensive protection regime. Developing a suitable regime therefore requires involving stakeholders on the international, regional, national, local and individual level. From a functional point of view, the different potential responses to any of the sources of marine litter, automatically run the risk of merely being one of many. Some of the potential measures are highly technical in nature such as waste management, whereas others deal for example with awareness rising of the individual. The entire range of possible measures and actors necessitates different focal points and priority setting. A weakness of this approach is that small ad-hoc or singular activities address a smaller aspect of the problem, but would not necessarily introduce a structural change. A structural change could be for example a coherent regulatory approach to the handling of vessel-based pollution in a region or common solid waste management standards. Whereas it is of course admitted that small and individual measures are clearly necessary in the overall set of measures, an overall coordination and streamlining of measures is indispensable.

Chapter 2: Global regulatory framework relating to marine litter

This chapter discusses the global framework regulating marine litter. This entails a discussion of globally applicable agreements made under public international law. The aim of this chapter is to present the range of global agreements applicable to the regulation of marine litter. First, the analysis intends to clarify and illustrate the role of principles of public international law in interpreting vague legal norms and to guide implementation measures. Thereafter, an assessment of the chronology of the measures developed on the introduction of marine litter either directly or indirectly will be made, in order to gain a comprehensive understanding of the key elements at the core of the current framework as well as of the general tendencies and trends evident within it. Here, the discussion is not only delimited by legal agreements *sensu stricto*, but also the relevance of soft-law instruments will be highlighted in a second step. Third, the pertinent globally applicable agreements and conventions are analysed with regard to their role in contributing to eliminate the introduction of marine litter. A particular aspect in this regard is whether the sectoral approach of each of these agreements or programmes leads to a fragmentation that ignores diffuse sources.

A. Principles and their approaches to address marine litter

Before a detailed discussion of pertinent treaties, the following section sets out to sketch and analyse relevant principles in the context of marine litter mitigation. The principles discussed in the following are not those "metalegal principles" that are taken from a philosophical context.[240] The principles discussed are what *De Sadeleer* refers to as "directing principles", which are, however, not congruent with those principles as stipulated in Art. 38 (1) (c) International Court of Justice (ICJ) Statute.[241] Additionally,

240 *Wolfrum,* General International Law (Principles, Rules, and Standards), in Max Planck Encyclopedia of Public International Law (MPEPIL), B.6.

241 *De Sadeleer,* Environmental Principles, 2002, 6 and 249; *Sands/Peel,* Principles of international environmental law, 2012, 188; *Wolfrum,* General International

it has been considered to transfer the theory of principles of national law into public international law.[242] A central aspect is the delimitation between principles and rules which are both accepted as legal norms.[243] *Dworkin* states that legal principles and legal rules:

> point to particular decisions about legal obligation in particular circumstances, but they differ in the character of the direction they give. Rules are applicable in an all-or-nothing fashion…[A principle] states a reason that argues in one direction, but does not necessitate a particular decision… All that is meant, when we say that a particular principle is a principle of our law, is that the principle is one which officials must take into account, if it is relevant, as a consideration inclining in one way or another.[244]

Consequently, principles do not evoke specific legal consequences.[245] They rather serve as an obligation to optimise in which "express normative values are to be realised through an optimised balancing of conflicting principles in line with the principle of proportionality."[246] In international law principles serve the purpose of framing proposals and arguments in in-

---

Law (Principles, Rules, and Standards), in Max Planck Encyclopedia of Public International Law (MPEPIL), B.7. *Maurmann* also deals with a differentiation between these principles: *Maurmann,* Rechtsgrundsätze im Völkerrecht am Beispiel des Vorsorgeprinzips, 2008, 30.

242 The possibility of this transfer has recently been confirmed, see only: *Winter,* The Legal Nature of Environmental Principles in International, EC and German Law, in *Macrory/Havercroft/Purdy,* Principles of european environmental law (2004) 11–27, 15; *Epiney/Scheyli,* Strukturprinzipien des Umweltvölkerrechts, 1998, 81 *et seq*; *Maurmann,* Rechtsgrundsätze im Völkerrecht am Beispiel des Vorsorgeprinzips, 2008, 30; *Proelss,* German Yearbook of International Law 53 (2010) 65, 80.

243 *Alexy,* Theorie der Grundrechte, 1986, 40 *et seq.*

244 *Dworkin,* Taking rights seriously, 1977, 26.

245 *Proelss,* German Yearbook of International Law 53 (2010) 65, 77.

246 *Ibid.*

ternational negotiations,[247] dynamisation of public international law,[248] a reference to ethics and moral[249] as well as a structural element.[250]

The inherent nature of any marine pollution regime necessitates rather precise technical standards and regulation that can only marginally be covered by those principles.[251] In this regard, the application of the principle and the inherent legal consequences:

> must be considered on the facts and circumstances of each case, having regard to several factors, including: the source of the principle; its textual content and language; the particular activity at issue; the environmental and other consequences of the activity; and the circumstances in which it occurs (including the actors and the geographic region).[252]

This section is therefore dedicated to an analysis of the principles regarding their role in the systematisation of "positive legal norms" that are stipulated in a given legal agreement.[253] The significance of a preluding discussion on the application and interpretation of the principles is twofold. On the one hand it serves the purpose of understanding how principles can generally guide decisions and regulatory options in a marine litter context. Additionally, these principles also serve as "tools of interpretation"[254] and are thus important parameters when assessing diverse legal problems. For the purpose of this study, it has been chosen to concentrate on three central

---

247 *Bodansky,* The art and craft of international environmental law, 2011, 201.

248 *Winter,* The Legal Nature of Environmental Principles in International, EC and German Law, in *Macrory/Havercroft/Purdy,* Principles of european environmental law (2004) 11–27, 22; *Epiney/Scheyli,* Strukturprinzipien des Umweltvölkerrechts, 1998, 15. Principles serve as guidance for further developments that can also integrate scientific knowledge.

249 *Verschuuren* argues that environmental principles serve as linking elements between the "morality of aspiration" and "morality of duty": *Verschuuren,* Principles of environmental law, 2003, 25 *et seq.*

250 *Epiney* and *Scheyli* coined the phrase "Strukturprinzipien": *Epiney/Scheyli,* Strukturprinzipien des Umweltvölkerrechts, 1998, 15. *Sands* outlines that "the principles and rules of general application [...] provide a framework that shapes the structure and development of international environmental law": *Sands/Peel,* Principles of international environmental law, 2012, 237.

251 *Molenaar,* Coastal State Jurisdiction over Vessel-Source Pollution, 1998, 42.

252 *Sands/Peel,* Principles of international environmental law, 2012, 188.

253 See for more information on the different roles of principles: *Wolfrum,* General International Law (Principles, Rules, and Standards), in Max Planck Encyclopedia of Public International Law (MPEPIL), B.54.

254 *Ibid.*, B.57.

principles and their application will be subject of further scrutiny due to their importance to the topic at hand: the polluter-pays-principle, the preventive principle and the precautionary principle.

In particular, any discussion on the properties and effects of a substance is inherently associated with the risks and uncertainties that the introduction of that particular substance entails. A proper understanding of the relevance of the 'preventive principle' and the 'precautionary principle' are seen as a prerequisite to systematise and understand the selected instruments in a marine litter context. As a consequence thereof, a common understanding also helps to clarify vague or inadequately defined legal terminology that are important in the legal discourse of marine litter regulation. Due to the scope and objective of the study, it is not primarily aimed at elaborating in detail on the legal status and the ensuing consequences of the principles *per se*.[255] Rather; the objective is to identify "how" these principles impact marine litter regulation by guiding interpretation and decision-making in international law. Because of their prominent role, those principles that are explicitly endorsed in the EU framework will be specifically addressed in the pertinent chapter.[256]

I. Polluter-pays-principle

The polluter-pays-principle is in its essence an economic instrument in which externalities from polluting activities should be borne by the polluter causing it.[257] What appears *prima facie* to be a rather simple and clear concept is, however, not homogenously applied among different le-

255 See for further references on these aspects: *Sands/Peel,* Principles of international environmental law, 2012, 187 *et seq*.

256 Besides the three central principles that will be further analysed below, the principle of co-operation also plays an important role in preventing marine pollution. It has been stipulated in the majority of international and regional marine protection agreements and has also been confirmed and applied in several court decisions and awards. See only the MOX Plant Case in which the International Tribunal for the Law of the Sea (ITLOS) has confirmed the duty to co-operate as a fundamental principle in the prevention of marine pollution: ITLOS v. Order 3 December 2001 – 41 ILM 405 - The MOX Plant Case (Ireland v United Kingdom). See further on this aspect section C.VI. of this chapter.

257 *Molenaar,* Coastal State Jurisdiction over Vessel-Source Pollution, 1998, 44. The origin of this notion stems from *Arthur Pigou* who established that external costs such as pollution should be internalised by the polluter in form of taxes, see:

gal instruments. Whereas the origin of the principle can be found in recommendations of the Organization for Economic Co-operation and Development (OECD) from the 1970s,[258] the principle was first listed as Principle 16 in the Rio Declaration:

> National authorities should endeavour to promote the internalization of environmental costs and the use of economic instruments, taking into account the approach that the polluter should, in principle, bear the cost of pollution, with due regard to the public interest and without distorting international trade and investment.

From a material and normative application of the principle as envisaged by the Rio Declaration, it becomes clear that the simple premise of the polluter paying the damage for its polluting activity is limited by the addendum "in principle". This means that discretion prevails to what degree the polluter has to bear the costs of pollution.

1. The application of the polluter-pays-principle in agreements

The polluter-pays-principle has been incorporated within a number of international agreements. The OSPAR Convention[259] on the protection of the marine environment of the North-East Atlantic for example makes its application legally binding and confirms that "the polluter pays principle, by virtue of which the costs of pollution prevention, control and reduction measures are to be borne by the polluter."[260] This definition does not, contrary to Principle 16 of the Rio Declaration, establish discretion on the proportion of the costs to be attributed to the polluter. It expands the application of the principle by referring also to those measures that relate to the prevention and control of pollution. However, since these measures are also in need of further concretisation, the polluter-pays-principle fails to

---

Weimann, Umweltökonomik, 1991, 26; *Costanza/Bartmann,* Einführung in die ökologische Ökonomik, 2001, 45 *et seq.*

258 *Boyle,* Polluter Pays, in Max Planck Encyclopedia of Public International Law (MPEPIL), A.1.

259 Convention for the Protection of the Marine Environment of the North-East Atlantic (OSPAR Convention) (Paris) of 22 September 1992, in force 25 March 1998; 2354 UNTS 67; 32 ILM 1069 (1993).

260 Art. 2 (2) (b) OSPAR Convention.

effectively create specific legal obligations in the framework of the OSPAR Convention.[261]

Whereas the OSPAR Convention as a minimum defines broad theoretical elements of the polluter-pays-principle, the Helsinki Convention[262] applicable to the marine environmental protection of the Baltic Sea establishes an obligation to apply the principle but does not define its content and application.[263] In the absence of a further definition, no concrete normative obligations regarding the exact application of the polluter-pays-principle as stipulated in Art. 3 (4) HC can be distinguished, due to lack of legal substance. Even though the application of the principle is mandatory under the Helsinki Convention, it depends on the States how they apply the polluter-pays-principle in their territory. A potential caveat in this regard could be the heterogeneous application and implementation of the polluter-pays-principle in each country that could lead to different legal standards regarding the acceptance of polluting activities.[264]

2. Function of the polluter-pays-principle in marine litter context

The polluter-pays-principle has a preventive function due to its deterrent effects. In this regard, its application should dissuade potential polluters from polluting in order to reduce the financial consequences of their actions. Admittedly, an understanding of the preventative function of the principle requiring its application before any environmental damage has occurred is a broad interpretation of the role of the principle. However, with regard to marine litter, the preventative function of the principle should be emphasised due to its limitations. Even though the polluter-pays-principle is highly relevant in the context of any marine pollution regulation, it faces certain limitations. Its application to diffuse sources with no clearly distinguishable polluter poses a challenge as potential

261 *Proelß,* Meeresschutz im Völker- und Europarecht, 2004, 205.

262 Convention on the Protection of the Marine Environment of the Baltic Sea Area (Helsinki Convention, HC) (Helsinki) of 09 April 1992, in force 17 January 2000; 33 ILM 1540 (1992). The two Conventions will be further analysed in chapter 4.

263 Art. 3 (4) HC. Consequently, "[t]he Contracting Parties shall apply the polluter-pays-principle.".

264 See also the application of the principle in the Helsinki Convention system of port reception facilities, chapter 4.

sanctions cannot be imposed. With a view to marine litter considerations, the application of the principle is also limited to determine the extent of damage that was caused by singular sub-threshold activities for example. The identification of the polluter overall is difficult in light of the diverse and sub-threshold activities that result in marine litter.

Also, the legacy of polluting activities and the persistency of marine litter aggravates the application of the polluter-pays-principle since the identification of newly introduced material is difficult. Therefore, a link between the preventative principle and the polluter-pays-principle is indispensable.[265] The polluter-pays-principle potentially plays an important role in implementing instruments that aim to prevent pollution in the first place. However, a potential caveat is its concrete and effective application that forms the basis of its deterrent effect.

II. The role of the preventive principle in a marine litter context

The 'prevention' of the introduction of polluting substances into the environment is one of the central objectives of the subsequently analysed instruments. Whereas the goal to be obtained is clear, the principle of prevention has been subject to diverse academic debate and discussion on its application and role. A "preventative logic"[266] is that "prevention is better than cure."[267] It can be differentiated from the precautionary principle by "the understanding of risk."[268] Consequently, "preventive measures are thus intended to avert risks for which the *cause-and effect relationship is already known* (for example, chronic pollution, repetitive risks)."[269] Given the effects of marine pollution by plastic are documented, the application of this principle is evident. Furthermore, the principle of prevention has to be differentiated from the "duty to avoid transboundary environmental harm."[270] Such a differentiation derives from their differing goals. Even

---

265 *De La Fayette,* The International Journal of Marine and Coastal Law 14 (1999) 247, 256. *De La Fayette* highlights the relation between the polluter-pays-principle and BET and BAP.

266 The term is borrowed from *Trouwborst,* Erasmus Law Review 2 (2009) 106.

267 *Trouwborst,* Erasmus Law Review 2 (2009) 106, 110.

268 *De Sadeleer,* Environmental Principles, 2002, 74.

269 *De Sadeleer,* Environmental Principles, 2002, 75 (emphasis added).

270 *Trouwborst,* Erasmus Law Review 2 (2009) 106, 111. However, the following authors do not make such a distinction: *Beyerlin/Marauhn,* International environ-

though both approaches aim to prevent transboundary pollution, the no harm rule is "a compromise between the territorial sovereignty of the state of origin of the environmental harm, on the one side, and the territorial integrity of the state likely to be affected by this harm, on the other."[271] The preventive principle "seeks to protect the environment as an end in itself."[272] In that regard, the primary purpose of the preventive principle is to prevent pollution, ergo harm in the first place, the transboundary relation is incidental or secondary. The unclear "normative structure" of the principle of prevention has as a consequence that one cannot extract general, predefined obligations from it. In the absence of clear provisions, the preventive principle can be understood as an "obligation of conduct" in which the State has to act accordingly so as to prevent harm.[273]

The Pulp Mills Case of the International Court of Justice (ICJ) has contributed in some ways to further refine the elements of principle of prevention.[274] In this case, the ICJ decided on the long-standing dispute between Argentina and Uruguay about the construction of two pulp mills directly at the boundary river between those two countries.[275] The ICJ differentiated between substantive and procedural elements of the principle of prevention.[276] Even though the ICJ claimed that there was a "functional link" be-

---

mental law, 2011, 41 *et seq.*; *Birnie/Boyle/Redgwell,* International law and the environment, 2009, 143. *Birnie/Boyle/Redgewell* outline that they are referring to an obligation that "is more than a principle", *ibid. Beyerlin and Marauhn* differentiate between a "prohibitive" and "preventive" dimension of the no-harm-principle, *Beyerlin/Marauhn*, International environmental law, 2011, 40.

271 *Beyerlin/Marauhn,* International environmental law, 2011, 40.

272 *Trouwborst,* Erasmus Law Review 2 (2009) 106, 112.

273 *Birnie/Boyle/Redgwell,* International law and the environment, 2009, 147; *Kiss/ Shelton,* International environmental law, 2004, 205.

274 *ICJ,* Pulp Mills on the River Uruguay (Argentina v. Uruguay), Judgement of 20 April 2010, ICJ Rep.2010, 14; *Proelß,* Dynamik und Nachhaltigkeit des Öffentlichen Rechts, in *Ruffert,* Dynamik und Nachhaltigkeit des Öffentlichen Rechts (2012) 611–625, 623.

275 See for a detailed case note: *De Mulder,* Review of European Community & International Environmental Law 19 (2010) 263.

276 *Proelß,* Dynamik und Nachhaltigkeit des Öffentlichen Rechts, in *Ruffert,* Dynamik und Nachhaltigkeit des Öffentlichen Rechts (2012) 611–625, 616 *et seq.* Here, the ICJ characterised both elements in the following: "[…] whereas the substantive obligations are frequently worded in broad terms, the procedural obligations are narrower and more specific […]"; *ICJ*, Judgement Pulp Mills, ICJ Rep. 2010, 14, 49 (§ 77).

tween those two elements regarding prevention,[277] it did not seize the opportunity to further analyse their interrelationship.[278] It established, however, the relevance of co-operation and the principle of prevention.[279] Regarding the substantive obligations, the ICJ further addressed the question when and how a State has to act in order to prevent harm.[280] The ICJ deduced from Art. 41 of the River Statute that a State has thus complied with the exigency contained therein when it has acted with "due diligence."[281] The interface between the prevention of harm and due diligence[282] was also confirmed by the ICJ when it expanded on the duty of due diligence as "an obligation which entails not only the adoption of appropriate rules and measures, but also a certain level of vigilance in their enforcement and the exercise of administrative control applicable to public and private operators, such as the monitoring of activities undertaken by such operators."[283]

Judging from this, due diligence potentially implies in a marine litter context that measures are not only developed but also enforced. However, the content and application of due diligence duties "may not easily be described in precise terms"[284], since "the measures considered sufficiently diligent at a certain moment may become not diligent enough in light, for instance, of new scientific or technological knowledge."[285] Consequently, due diligence also relates to a developing standard of technology and regulation.[286]

---

277 *Vernet,* Pulp Mills on the River Uruguay (Argentina v Uruguay), in Max Planck Encyclopedia of Public International Law (MPEPIL), F.34.

278 *ICJ*, Judgement Pulp Mills, Joint Dissenting Opinion of Judges Al-Khasawneh/ Simma, ICJ Rep.2010, 14, 108, 120 (§ 26 *et seq.).*

279 *ICJ,* Judgement Pulp Mills, 14, 56 (§ 102).

280 *De Sadeleer,* Environmental Principles, 2002, 63.

281 *ICJ,* Judgement Pulp Mills, 14, 69 *et seq*. (§ 197). See also: *Kiss/Shelton,* International environmental law, 2004, 205. It is questionable whether a State can be accounted for a transboundary environmental damage if it has acted with due diligence: *Proelß,* Raum und Umwelt im Völkerrecht, in *Bothe/Dolzer/Kau et al., Völkerrecht (*2013) 352–438, 412 *et seq*.

282 *Sands/Peel,* Principles of international environmental law, 2012, 200.

283 *ICJ*, Judgement Pulp Mills, 14, 69 (§ 197).

284 *ITLOS*, Responsibilities and Obligations of States Sponsoring Persons and Entities with Respect to Activities in the Area, Advisory Opinion, Seabed Dispute Chamber of 01 February 2011 (No 17), ILM 50 (2011), 455, 36 (§ 117).

285 *Ibid.*

286 *Birnie/Boyle/Redgwell,* International law and the environment, 2009, 148.

In the following, a comparative overview of a few key agreements addressing marine pollution will be made in order to illustrate the elements of the preventive principle as standardised in certain treaties. Since the principle of prevention is differently implemented and applied among treaties, the OSPAR Convention and the Helsinki Convention will be exemplarily analysed.[287] The Helsinki Convention substantiates in Art. 3 (1) HC the preventive principle. It states: "[t]he Contracting Parties shall individually or jointly take all appropriate legislative, administrative or other relevant measures to prevent and eliminate pollution in order to promote the ecological restoration of the Baltic Sea Area and the preservation of its ecological balance."

The duty to apply the preventive principle is substantiated by Art. 3 (3) HC which prescribes that "in order to *prevent* and eliminate pollution of the Baltic Sea Area the Contracting Parties shall promote the use of Best Environmental Practice and Best Available Technology" (emphasis added). Consequently, the Helsinki Convention contains an evolving standard of pollution prevention and elimination.

Even though the OSPAR Convention does not explicitly endorse the preventive principle, it contains a provision implementing the essence of the principle.[288] Accordingly, Art. 2 (3) (a and b) OSPAR Convention states that:

> [i]n implementing the Convention, Contracting Parties shall adopt programmes and measures which contain, where appropriate, timelimits for their completion and which take full account of the use of the latest technological developments and practices designed to *prevent* and eliminate pollution fully (emphasis added).

When implementing this obligation, the Contracting Parties are under the obligation to consider best available techniques, best environmental practice and also clean technology.[289] The inclusion in the OSPAR Convention can be evaluated as a positive element that incorporates a dynamic reaction to evolving techniques and standard.[290] *De la Fayette* states that the clause "where appropriate" might imply that opting for clean technology

287 See further on the role of these two conventions in the marine litter context: chapter 4.

288 *Proelß,* Meeresschutz im Völker- und Europarecht, 2004, 206.

289 Art. 2 (3) (a and b) OSPAR Convention.

290 See also *Proelß,* Meeresschutz im Völker- und Europarecht, 2004, 206.

might not be adequate at times.[291] Generally, the implementation of the preventive principle as set forth in both the Helsinki and the OSPAR Convention is highly relevant for the problem of marine litter. The duty to apply the BAP and BET potentially integrates a broad range of potential sources of marine litter such as waste management practices.[292] In the subsequent chapters, the understanding of the principle of prevention and its role in the discourse in marine litter regulation will be analysed in detail by means of pertinent implementation measures.

III. The precautionary principle

In the following, the content and application of the precautionary principle in an environmental law setting will be discussed with particular focus being put on how the precautionary principle could affect the regulation of marine litter. In an international context, Principle 15 of the Rio Declaration provides a (non-binding) definition of the principle

> In order to protect the environment, the precautionary principle shall be widely applied by States according to their capabilities. Where there are threats of serious or irreversible damage, lack of full scientific certainty shall not be used as a reason for postponing cost effective measures to prevent environmental degradation.

Even though its exact meaning and content is subject to diverse interpretations,[293] the essence of the precautionary principle is to take anticipatory

---

291 *De La Fayette,* The International Journal of Marine and Coastal Law 14 (1999) 247, 248.

292 In the OSPAR Convention framework this has been already pursued. See only: OSPAR Recommendation 2000/1 on Best Environmental Practice (BEP) for the Reduction of Inputs of Agricultural Pesticides to the Environment through the Use of Integrated Crop Management Techniques, Annex 8, Ref. § 5.25a adopted in Copenhagen, 2000 and OSPAR Recommendation 2012/5 for a risk-based approach to the Management of Produced Water Discharges from Offshore Installations (OSPAR 12/22/1, Annex 18), adopted in Bonn, 2012. See for a comprehensive discussion on the role of BAT and BEP: *Proelß,* Meeresschutz im Völker- und Europarecht, 2004, 207.

293 *Proelss,* German Yearbook of International Law 53 (2010) 65, 73; *Marr,* The precautionary principle in the law of the sea, 2003, 7; *Hewison,* The International Journal of Marine and Coastal Law 11 (1996) 301, 312 *et seq.; Trouwborst,* Precautionary Rights and Duties of States, 2006, 23; *De Sadeleer,* The effect of uncertainty on the thresholds levels to which the precautionary principle appears to

decisions in order to avoid uncertain future risks. A distinction between prevention and the precautionary principle is that whereas prevention always implies the control of concrete and determinable danger, precaution relates to a "high degree of uncertainty surrounding the probability of risk."[294] In a marine litter setting, the boundaries between uncertainty and risks are constantly changing, therefore potentially shifting the relevance of the precautionary principle. This is due to the increasing scientific knowledge and research efforts providing new insights. However, this developing knowledge also potentially leads to an understanding or awareness of additional (secondary) risks such as those relating to ecotoxicological effects and potentially bioaccumulation.[295] Consequently a demarcation between preventative or precautionary actions appears to be difficult. Here, *Trouwborst* argues correctly that

> It seems to do more justice to the pertinent practice of States, however, to view the precautionary principle as an expanded version of the preventative principle, as effectively comprising the latter, or – probably most accurately – as the 'most developed form' of prevention.[296]

As mentioned above, the precautionary principle is differently defined in various international agreements, a factor explained by the diverging perceptions of what constitutes risk.[297] An additional explanation for the diversity of application is also that the formulation of the precautionary principle is fitted to a specific problem standardised in a treaty.[298] This in particular applies to the regulation of marine pollution in which the precautionary principle has been defined in some key agreements.

---

be subject (1), in *Applegate,* Environmental risk (2004) 454-479, chapter 4. The diversity of the content and exact meaning of the principle is also derived from the diverse definitions and interpretations in international agreements.

294 *De Sadeleer,* Environmental Principles, 2002, 75.

295 See results of chapter 1 of this study.

296 *Trouwborst,* Erasmus Law Review 2 (2009) 106, 124.

297 See for a discussion on this aspect section A.III.2. of this chapter.

298 *Trouwborst,* Precautionary Rights and Duties of States, 2006, 21.

1. The implementation of the precautionary principle in the context of the introduction of polluting substances in the marine environment

The second North Sea Conference[299] in 1987 introduced the concept of the precautionary principle also in relation to the introduction of substances in its so-called London Declaration: "in order to protect the North Sea from possibly damaging effects of the most dangerous substances, a precautionary approach is necessary which may require action to control inputs of such substances even before a causal link has been established by absolutely clear scientific evidence."[300]

Also, the Declaration calls for the "principle of precautionary action" in the context of riverine and estuaries as a source of toxic substances:

> by reducing polluting emissions of substances that are persistent, toxic and liable to bioaccumulate at source by the use of the best available technology and other appropriate measures. This applies especially when there is reason to assume that certain damage or harmful effects on the living resources of the sea are likely to be caused by such substances, even where there is no scientific evidence to prove a causal link between emissions and effects.[301]

Only three years later during the third North Sea Conference in 1990, the Hague Declaration broadened the scope of the application of the precautionary principle and adopted it as a premise for "their future work."[302] Consequently, the Contracting Parties "will continue to apply the precautionary principle, that is to take action to avoid potentially damaging impacts of substances that are persistent toxic and liable to bioaccumulate even where there is no scientific evidence to prove a causal link between emissions and effects."[303]

OSPAR Convention

Despite the broad application, the application of the principle is limited to those substances that are assumed to be toxic or liable to bioaccumulate[304]

299 See further on the North Sea Conferences section C.I. of chapter 3.

300 Ministerial Declaration of the Second International Conference on the Protection of the North Sea, 25 November 1987 (London), para.VII.

301 London Declaration 1987, para.XVI (1).

302 Ministerial Declaration of the Third International Conference on the Protection of the North Sea, 8 March 1990 (The Hague), 2.

303 The Hague Declaration 1990, 2.

304 *Marr,* The precautionary principle in the law of the sea, 2003, 61.

which is somewhat counterproductive, since this characteristic might not yet be established. These overall considerations were also reflected in the subsequent OSPAR Convention which introduced the precautionary principle in Art. 2 (2) (a) OSPAR Convention. The Contracting Parties shall accordingly apply:

> the precautionary principle, by virtue of which preventive measures are to be taken when there are reasonable grounds for concern that substances or energy introduced, directly or indirectly, into the marine environment may bring about hazards to human health, harm living resources and marine ecosystems, damage amenities or interfere with other legitimate uses of the sea, even when there is no conclusive evidence of a causal relationship between the inputs and the effects.

The OSPAR Convention therefore explicitly encompasses the precautionary principle and establishes the obligation to apply the principle.[305] Contrary to the Hague Declaration, the duty to apply the precautionary principle is not directly linked to any persistent or toxic characteristic. The application in the OSPAR Convention is broader and does not distinguish between specific characteristics. The addendum that no conclusive evidence is necessary ("reasonable grounds") implies that there is a shifting of the burden of proof towards the Contracting Party that seeks to rely on the environmental safety of its activities.[306] The principle is nevertheless limited to those circumstances in which a substance or energy has been introduced into the marine environment.[307] Even though the material scope integrates direct and indirect sources, this potentially limits the principle to specific activities. Moreover, the application requires that a threshold of a "reasonable grounds for concern" be reached prior to action being taken.[308] Therefore one could rather speak of a limited shifting of the burden of proof.[309]

---

305 See for a discussion on the value of the inclusion of the precautionary principle in the OSPAR Convention: *Marr,* The precautionary principle in the law of the sea, 2003, 61; D*e La Fayette,* The International Journal of Marine and Coastal Law 14 (1999) 247, 254.

306 *Proelß,* Meeresschutz im Völker- und Europarecht, 2004, 204.

307 *De La Fayette,* The International Journal of Marine and Coastal Law 14 (1999) 247, 255.

308 *Marr,* The precautionary principle in the law of the sea, 2003, 61.

309 *Proelß,* Meeresschutz im Völker- und Europarecht, 2004, 204.

Helsinki Convention

In the Helsinki Convention, the introduction of the precautionary principle as a legal norm was seen as a major innovation.[310] The Helsinki Convention explicitly lists the precautionary principle and defines it by stating:

> [The Contracting Parties] shall take preventive measures when there is reason to assume that substances or energy introduced, directly or indirectly, into the marine environment may create hazards to human health, living resources and marine ecosystems, damage amenities or interfere with other legitimate uses of the sea, even when there is no conclusive evidence of a causal relationship between inputs and their alleged effects.[311]

The precautionary principle of the Helsinki Convention therefore encompasses a wider scope than established in the OSPAR Convention.[312] The Helsinki Convention does not require a specific threshold of likelihood of harm in order to apply ("reason to assume").[313] The application of the principle is "affranchised from subjective elements, therefore the provision as set out in the Helsinki Convention entail less discretion for the parties."[314] One can thus conclude that there is a *prima facie* obligation under the Helsinki Convention to apply the precautionary principle in every situation. This establishes a broad protection standard in which the precautionary principle is not limited to specific characteristics of a substance.

Similar to the OSPAR Convention, a shortcoming of the precautionary principle in the Helsinki Convention is that it only refers to circumstances in which substances or energy are introduced. The limited application to energy and substances potentially excludes other activities regulated under the Convention such as the protection of the biodiversity.[315] However, the broad scope in regard to pollution including its direct and indirect sources is laudable in regard to regulating marine litter.

---

310 *Jenisch,* The International Journal of Marine and Coastal Law 11 (1996) 47, 63.
311 Art. 3 (2) HC (emphasis added).
312 *Marr,* The precautionary principle in the law of the sea, 2003, 63; *Ebbesson,* The Stockholm declaration and law of the marine environment, in *Nordquist/Moore/Mahmoudi,* The Stockholm declaration and law of the marine environment (2003) 155–164, 159.
313 *Marr,* The precautionary principle in the law of the sea, 2003, 63.
314 *Hjorth,* Baltic environmental cooperation, 1996, 13 *et seq.*
315 Ebbesson, German Yearbook of International law 43(2000) 38.

Furthermore, the Helsinki Convention also implements the precautionary principle by distinguishing between "hazardous substances"[316] and "harmful substances." Art. 5 HC in conjunction with Annex I HC introduces a provision specifically for the regulation of "harmful substances." In this regard the States are obliged to prioritise and assess potential risks that are associated with certain substances. In light of the absence of a definition of what constitutes "harmful", Annex I HC establishes priority groups of harmful substances and also identifies criteria that shall be consulted in the evaluation of the harmfulness of a substance. One of the criteria is the "risk of undesirable changes in the marine ecosystem and irreversibility or durability of effects"[317] that clearly demonstrates precaution and is highly relevant for any marine litter discussion.

2. The precautionary principle in the marine litter context - how to interpret risks and uncertainty?

The precautionary principle is distinguished from the principle of prevention by its degree of uncertainty and risks. In order to frame the discussion on these two concepts from a legal point of view, their relationship needs to be considered. The concept of risk is intertwined with the precautionary principle.[318] Risk is defined as being the probability of an event occurring multiplied by a quantification of the seriousness of the harm caused (Risk=Probability x Gravity (of harm)).[319] Risk therefore implies that there are "known impacts" and "known probabilities."[320] A measure to respond to this risk is to take preventive actions that target the known danger. Uncertainty, on the other hand, relates to "likely impacts" but "unknown probabilities."[321] In the context of uncertainty, it is not clear what measures should be taken to address the negative impacts, ultimately resulting in the application of the precautionary principle. Following this logic, uncertainty can become risk through the results of research.

---

316 Art. 2 (8) HC.

317 Regulation 1 (1) indent 7 Annex I HC.

318 *D Sadeleer,* Environmental Principles, 2002, 150.

319 *Trouwborst,* Precautionary Rights and Duties of States, 2006, 27.

320 *Grandjean,* Science for precautionary decision-making, in *European Environment Agency*, Late lessons from early warnings: science, precaution, innovation (2013) 623-642, 623.

321 *Ibid.*

The uncertainty element as contained in the implementation of the precautionary principle poses a challenge to any scientific undertaking.[322] *Gray* argues that "[t]he precautionary principle should not be part of science, since by definition it does not have to rely on scientific evidence."[323] With regard to marine litter, uncertainty prevails on the exact sources, the amount of litter, its interactions and consequences on the marine environment, organisms and, potentially, also human beings. From this, one can conclude that the precautionary principle is applicable in the context of marine litter as it is impossible to speak about a quantified or even quantifiable risk. A direct interpretation of the precautionary principle in this regard is not to wait until all scientists have found a consensus on every aspect of the scientific questions, but with a view to uncertainty, to take action.

This applies in particular to the issue of microplastics, with their diverse risks and uncertainties. The precautionary principle can thus be also used when establishing thresholds of harm.[324] When assessing risks and adverse consequences of an activity or a polluting substance, an important parameter is the boundary of the risk. This is important since, "[t]he notion of risk thus only becomes fully effective when it affects values or interests."[325] The boundary of risks thus relates, *inter alia*, to threshold values that seem to suggest that there exists an acceptable amount of pollution and an inacceptable amount. However, the complexity of the marine litter problem and its multiple impacts indicate that there are potentially also many thresholds. From an anthropocentric point of view, the impacts and consequences of marine litter seem *prima facie* inextricably linked with the degree to which it disturbs humans or human activities. Whereas the disturbance or annoyance of marine litter is not felt far away from the beach, it becomes an immediate nuisance as soon as people are prevented from swimming due to the presence of marine litter. It remains to be seen whether and to what degree the current legal framework defines the boundaries of (un)acceptable marine litter pollution in light of an application of the precautionary principle and the associated notions of risk and uncertainty.

---

322 *Gray,* Marine Pollution Bulletin 21 (1990) 174.
323 *Gray,* Marine Pollution Bulletin 21 (1990) 174, 175.
324 *De Sadeleer,* Environmental Principles, 2002, 155.
325 *Ibid.,* 150.

B. Marine litter considerations in the development of environmental law

The following section sets out the historical background of the issue of marine litter as it has been developed over the last decades. The purpose of this section is to understand how marine litter considerations have found way into the framework regulating marine pollution. Marine litter has in the past only been a subcategory in the marine pollution framework and has increasingly been identified as a specific issue necessitating focused regulatory solutions. With regard to the convoluted international development regarding marine pollution, the analysis is limited to those events and documents that are of particular relevance for the regulation of marine litter.[326] A good starting point for this analysis is the 1972 United Nations Conference on the Human Environment in Stockholm (Stockholm Conference)[327] as it is widely accepted to mark the beginning of "the modern era" of international environment law.[328] Admittedly, individual events such as the establishment of the International Maritime Consultative Organisation (IMCO) in 1958[329] under the 1954 International Convention for the Prevention of Pollution of the Sea by oil are also important developments that have had a consequence on the regulation of marine litter in the

326 Since many activities and documents exist that are limited either in their geographic scope or exclusively address a singular source or activity, the exact starting point cannot be readily estimated. The first workshop on marine litter dates back to 27-29. November 1984 in Hawaii that was organised by the American National Oceanographic and Atmospheric Administration (NOAA) and addressed the fate and impact of marine debris, see http://www.globalgarbage.org/blog/index.php/conferences-and-workshops/, last accessed 27.08.2015.

327 See for a concise description of the events leading to the Stockholm Conference: *Shelton,* Stockholm Declaration (1972) and Rio Declaration (1992), in Max Planck Encyclopedia of Public International Law (MPEPIL), B.

328 *Sand,* The Evolution of International Environmental Law, in *Bodansky/Brunnée/Hey,* The Oxford handbook of international environmental law (2007) 31–43, 33. According to *Sand*, the development of international environmental law has developed in three major periods. These are the "traditional era" pre-1972 United Nations Stockholm Conference on the Human Environment, the "modern era" from the 1972 Stockholm Conference to the 1992 United Nations Conference on Environment and Development (UNCED) in Rio de Janeiro, and the "post-modern" after the UNCED.

329 Convention on the International Maritime Consultative Organization (Geneva) of 06 March 1948, in force 17 March 1958; 289 UNTS 175.1982. The Intergovernmental Maritime Consultative Organisation officially changed its name to International Maritime Organisation.

long-term.[330] Nonetheless this is an isolated event that is also limited by the substantive scope of the IMCO at that time. Moreover, in consideration of the plethora of relevant documents that address the different categories of sources, a preliminary systematisation of documents is necessary so as to demonstrate how the issue of marine litter has been approached in the past. All of these documents must be put into context within the regime regarding marine pollution and some will be subject to a more thorough analysis in the course of the study.

The Stockholm Conference was convened because of the increasing concern about environmental degradation that was primarily triggered through major catastrophes such as oil spills.[331] The outcome of the Stockholm Conference, the Declaration of the United Nations Conference on the Human Environment (Stockholm Declaration) did not directly address marine litter as a substance of concern. However its provision on pollution of the sea indirectly addressed the issue.[332] Principle 6 of the Stockholm Declaration states that:

> [t]he discharge of toxic substances or of other substances and the release of heat, in such quantities or concentrations as to exceed the capacity of the environment to render them harmless, must be halted in order to ensure that serious or irreversible damage is not inflicted upon ecosystems.[333]

Moreover, principle 7 stipulates that: "States shall take all possible steps to prevent pollution of the seas by substances that are liable to create hazards to human health, to harm living resources and marine life, to damage amenities or to interfere with other legitimate uses of the sea."

---

330 *Sand,* The Evolution of International Environmental Law, in *Bodansky/Brunnée/Hey,* The Oxford handbook of international environmental law (2007) 31–43, 33. See for a summary on the development of treaties addressing different forms of marine pollution: *Timagenis,* International control of marine pollution, 1980, part two and three.

331 *Shelton*, Stockholm Declaration (1972) and Rio Declaration (1992), in Max Planck Encyclopedia of Public International Law (MPEPIL), A.1.

332 *UN*, U.N. Doc. A/Conf.48/14/Rev. 1(1973), Declaration of the United Nations Conference on the Human Environment of 16 June 1972 (Stockholm Declaration); 11 ILM 1416 (1972). For a further discussion on the declaration, see *Birnie/Boyle/Redgwell,* International law and the environment, 2009, 48 *et seq.*; The Stockholm declaration and law of the marine environment, 2003. See for further information on the Action Plan that was developed to implement the provisions of the Declaration: *Timagenis,* International control of marine pollution, 1980, 102 *et seq*.

333 Emphasis added.

Thus, principles 6 and 7 of the Stockholm Declaration establish that the oceans have a limited assimilative capacity regarding certain substances.[334] Principle 7 puts a positive duty on States ("shall") that is nevertheless limited by the non-binding status of the Stockholm Declaration. Their wording implies that there is a permissible pollution load and a certain threshold above which the notion of serious damage is established. Exceeding this limit constitutes an unaccepted amount of pollution.[335] This important notion of the causal relationship between the introduction of substances and their consequences has found its way into several relevant legal documents such as the UN Convention of the Law of the Sea (UNCLOS) subsequently and attests the continuous importance of the Stockholm Declaration.[336]

The International Maritime Organisation (IMO),[337] responsible for the safety of shipping and the protection of the marine environment, has addressed the introduction of ocean-based litter at an early stage. The adoption of Annex V on garbage from ships in the context of the International Convention for the Prevention of Pollution from Ships (MARPOL)[338] from 1973 and 1978 respectively as well as the Convention on the Prevention of Marine Pollution by Dumping of Wastes and other matter from 1972 (London Dumping Convention)[339] provide a sectoral approach to regulating marine litter long before its impacts has been perceived gener-

334 See for a detailed overview on marine pollution aspects in the Stockholm Declaration: *Timagenis,* International control of marine pollution, 1980, 87 *et seq*.

335 See for a further discussion on the conference and declaration *Birnie/Boyle/Redgwell,* International law and the environment, 2009, 49.

336 United Nations Convention on the Law of the Sea (Montego Bay) of 10 December 1982, in force 14 November 1994; 1833 UNTS; 21 ILM 1261 (1982); *Molenaar,* Coastal State Jurisdiction over Vessel-Source Pollution, 1998, 49; *Birnie,* Impact on the Development of international law on Cooperation, in *Nordquist/Moore/Mahmoudi,* The Stockholm declaration and law of the marine environment (2003) 85–100, 92, see section C. of this chapter.

337 See for IMO's treaty-making activities: *Blanco-Bazán,* International marine environmental law, in *Kirchner,* International marine environmental law (2003) 31–47, 32 *et seq*.

338 International Convention for the Prevention of Pollution from Ships (MARPOL) (London) of 2 November 1973, in force 2 October 1983 as amended by the 1978 Protocol (London), of 01 June 1978; 1340 UNTS 61.

339 Convention on the Prevention of Marine Pollution by Dumping of Wastes and Other Matter (London Dumping Convention) (London, Mexico-City, Moscow, Washington) of 29 December 1972, in force 30 August 1975, 1046 UNTS 120; 11 ILM 1294 (1972).

ally as a serious problem.[340] These agreements will be thoroughly analysed in subsequent sections of this chapter.

The United Nations Conference on Environment and Development (UNCED) that took place in Rio de Janeiro from 3 to 14 June 1992 was an important step for the development of environmental policy. [341] Among the soft-law instruments adopted during the UNCED, the Rio Declaration on Environment and Development (Rio Declaration)[342] and its implementing action plan Agenda 21: Programme of Action for Sustainable Development (Agenda 21)[343] can be seen as the most pertinent instruments regarding the issue of marine litter of UNCED.

The Rio Declaration established, following a similar concept to the Stockholm Declaration, 27 (non-binding) principles. Even though no reference is made to marine litter or marine pollution, it is nevertheless relevant in relation to marine litter. The preamble recognises the "integral and interdependent nature"[344] of the earth´s ecosystem and integrates a holistic and interdependent understanding of that concept.[345] Furthermore, the Rio Declaration introduces a precautionary and anticipatory approach while also encouraging the polluter-pays-principle on a global level.[346] Agenda 21 serves as an implementation tool to implement the Rio Declaration and contains, to this end, quite detailed recommendations and measures.

Even though other dedicated chapters such as chapter 18 of the Agenda 21 on the protection of freshwater are also highly relevant for the topic at hand, chapter 17 of Agenda 21 on the protection of the oceans is the most pertinent. Chapter 17 does not focus primarily on the control of sources,

---

340 *Molenaar* estimated in 1998 that "although often regarded as relatively harmless, ship-generated sewage and garbage can cause significant local pollution, particularly in harbours and estuaries" *Molenaar,* Coastal State Jurisdiction over Vessel-Source Pollution, 1998, 17.

341 *Gold,* Gard Handbook on Protection of the Marine Environment, 2006, 69. In the framework of UNCED, the UN Framework Convention on Climate Change United Nations Framework Convention on Climate Change, in force 21 March 1994, 1771 UNTS 107 and the UN Convention on Biological Diversity, in force on 29 December.1993, 1760 UNTS 79; 31 ILM 818 (1992) were adopted.

342 *UN*, Rio Declaration on Environment and Development, UN Doc. A/CONF. 151/26 (vol. I); 31 ILM 874 (1992).

343 *UN*, A/CONF.151/26, Agenda 21: Programme of Action and Sustainable Development, 13.06.1992.

344 Recital 4, Rio Declaration.

345 *Fritz,* Integrierter Umweltschutz im Völkerrecht, 2009, 132.

346 Principle 15 and 16 Rio Declaration.

but "more broadly on the prevention of environmental 'degradation' and the protection of ecosystems."[347] In particular, it links sustainable development with the management of coastal zones and provides detailed measures regarding land-based pollution. Marine litter is identified amongst others as one of "the contaminants that pose the greatest threat to the marine environment."[348] In addressing environmental degradation, Agenda 21 establishes that "a precautionary and anticipatory rather than a reactive approach is necessary."[349] It also stipulates the objective to reduce the risk of long-term or irreversible adverse effects on the marine environment, which is directly relevant to marine litter. Also, in 1995, the Global Programme of Action for the Protection of the Marine Environment from Land-Based Activities (GPA) was adopted that addresses marine litter as one of the major sources substances.[350]

The impact of marine litter as an issue of global importance has been recognised by the UN General Assembly that has drawn attention to the consequences of marine litter and the fragmented knowledge base.[351] Recently, the UNGA has stressed the need to integrate waste management in the coastal zone, ports and maritime industries. To this end, it has stressed that waste management options such as recycling, reuse, reduction and disposal as well as economic incentives such as cost recovery systems are suitable measures to reduce marine litter.[352]

Twenty years after UNCED, the follow-up conference "Rio+20" in 2012 has initiated an important impetus in a marine litter context. In the outcome document of the conference, States "commit to take action to, by 2025, based on collected scientific data, achieve significant reductions in marine debris to prevent harm to the coastal and marine environment."[353]

---

347 *Birnie/Boyle/Redgwell,* International law and the environment, 2009, 384.

348 Para. 17.18, Agenda 21.

349 Para. 17.21, Agenda 21.

350 *UN*, UNEP(OCA)/LBA/IG.2/7, GPA, Intergovernmental Conference to adopt a Global Programme of Action for the Protection of the Marine Environment from Land-Based Activities, 05.12.1995, 7. A further discussion on the relevance of the GPA regarding marine litter is pursued in section D.III. of this chapter.

351 *UNGA*, A/RES/60/30, United Nations General Assembly, Resolution 60/30 on Oceans and the law of the sea, 08.03.2006, paras.65-70.

352 *UNGA*, A/RES/65/37, United Nations General Assembly, Resolution 65/37 on Oceans and the law of the sea, 17.03.2011, para.137.

353 *UNGA*, A/RES/66/288, United Nations General Assembly, Resolution 66/288 on "the Future we want", An-nex, Conference Report Rio+20 United Nations Con-

Consequently, marine litter is explicitly identified as an important environmental concern for the first time in an outcome document of these international universal summits.[354] Despite the laudable identification, the wording appears to be weak and at the early stages of regulatory responses. It can be by no means compared to the strong wording of the Stockholm Declaration ("shall") that is a child of a different environmental protection generation. It remains to be seen how and to what degree the States are using the subsequently analysed instruments to take actions to achieve this aim. Most recently, the first session of the United Nations Environment Assembly of the United Nations Environment Programme that was held in Nairobi in 2014 adopted a resolution on marine plastic debris and microplastics.[355] The resolution addresses amongst others the need for further examination and research on the key sources of marine debris, potential management techniques as well as its impact. It also emphasised the application of the precautionary approach with regard to the lack of full scientific certainty and encourages the cooperation with other international organisations also with a view to microplastics.

With a view to the different documents, it is easily conceivable that marine litter has been increasingly gaining attention in international organisations. It has been indirectly addressed in the framework of marine pollution instruments and therefore many diverse and usually distinctly separated fora play a role in developing and potentially providing solutions to this issue.

ference on Sustainable Development, 11.09.2012, para.163. See for a further discussion on Rio+20 and ocean considerations: *Liebermann/Yang,* Ocean Yearbook 27 (2013) 67.

354 The Stockholm or Rio Declarations are such outcome documents.

355 *UNEA*, UNEP/EA.1/10, United Nations Environment Assembly of the United Nations Environment Programme, Resolution 1/6. Marine plastic debris and microplastics, 02.09.2014.

C. UNCLOS

I. The UN Convention of the Law of the Sea (UNCLOS) – framing marine environmental protection activities

The modern law of the sea has been shaped by the UN Convention of the Law of the Sea (UNCLOS) which came in force on 16 November 1994 after lengthy negotiations.[356] The aim of UNCLOS is to establish "a legal order for the seas and oceans which will facilitate international communication and that will promote […] the equitable and efficient utilization and […] the study, protection and preservation of the marine environment."[357] This claim has resulted in UNCLOS being often referred to as the "constitution of the seas."[358] The umbrella function of UNCLOS includes the regulation of a broad range of activities and issues that facilitate "the realisation of a just and equitable international economic order which takes into account the interests and needs of mankind as a whole and, in particular, the special interests and needs of developing countries, whether coastal or land-locked."[359]

The following section examines how marine pollution is addressed in the framework of UNCLOS.[360] UNCLOS follows a zonal approach in which each zone is subject to different rights and obligations for the

356 United Nations Convention on the Law of the Sea (UNCLOS) (Montego Bay) of 10 December 1982, in force 14 November 1994; 1833 UNTS 3; ILM 1261 (1982). UNCLOS is the result of a codification process of the law of the sea that has its origins in the Hague Codification Conference in 1930 on territorial waters and further processed with the 1958 and 1960 Geneva Conferences on the law of the Sea: *Nelson*, Reflections on the 1982 Convention on the law of the Sea, in *Freestone/Barnes/Ong,* The law of the sea (2006) 28-39, 28 *et seq*. See also *Boyle,* The American Journal of International Law 79 (1985) 347, 348 *et seq*. and *Timagenis,* International control of marine pollution, 1980, chapter 16, for an account of the developments immediately before the Third Conference on the Law of the Sea in 1973. For a historical overview on the development of the law of the sea, see *Graf Vitzthum,* Begriff, Geschichte und Rechtsquellen des Seerechts, in *Graf Vitzthum,* Handbuch des Seerechts (2006) 1–134, 9 *et seq.*

357 Preamble, para.4 UNCLOS.

358 *UN*, Ocean: the sources of life, UNCLOS 20th anniversary (1982-2002), http://www.un.org/Depts/los/convention_agreements/convention_20years/oceanssourceoflife.pd, last accessed 27.08.2015.

359 Preamble, para.5 UNCLOS.

360 See for a further overview on UNCLOS: *Beyerlin/Marauhn,* International environmental law, 2011, 119 *et seq.*

States,[361] consisting of the territorial sea, international straits, the contiguous zone, archipelagic waters, the exclusive economic zone (EEZ), the continental shelf, the high seas and the 'Area'.[362]

II. The definition of marine pollution in the context of regulatory measures

A first starting point in the discussion is whether and how the problem of marine litter can be categorised within the regulatory context of UNCLOS. UNCLOS defines pollution as

> the introduction by man, directly or indirectly, of substances or energy into the marine environment, including estuaries which results or is likely to result in such deleterious effects as harm to living resources and marine life, hazards to human health, hindrance to marine activities, including fishing and other legitimate uses of the sea, impairment of quality for use of sea water and reduction of amenities.[363]

The definition of pollution embodies a broad understanding of the concept. Pollution according to UNCLOS already occurs in case in which it is *likely* that a substance results in a deleterious harm. Therefore, the starting point is not the substance itself, but its effects on the environment.[364] The wording of the definition also "implies a mandate of protective measures before any harm can actually occur."[365] Consequently, UNCLOS reflects a "precautionary spirit."[366] This can also be seen in the "elasticity" of the concept of marine pollution towards potential new polluting substances that does not only consider material, but also energetic substances were in

361 *Treves,* Law of the Sea, in Max Planck Encyclopedia of Public International Law (MPEPIL), E.23.

362 *Ibid.* Other zones that are also referred to include, *inter alia,* internal waters, historic bays and the contiguous zone.

363 Art. 1 (4) UNCLOS.

364 *Freestone/Rayfuse,* Marine Ecology Progress Series 364 (2008) 227, 229.

365 *Marr,* The precautionary principle in the law of the sea, 2003, 52.

366 *Fritz,* Integrierter Umweltschutz im Völkerrecht, 2009, 209. As the precautionary principle was not widely recognised at the time at which UNCLOS was drafted, the Convention does not expressly embody the precautionary principle. However, it does indeed do so implicitly: *Proelß,* Meeresschutz im Völker- und Europarecht, 2004, 82 *et seq.* See also the Southern Bluefin Tuna Cases (Australia v. Japan; New Zealand v. Japan), Request for Provisional Measures, Order of 27 August 1999, ITLOS Reports 1999, 280.

the definition.[367] Another progressive element constitutes the inclusion of indirect or diffuse sources of pollution from tributaries and the atmosphere.

In the absence of a definition of what constitutes "deleterious effects", the listing of examples that could account for these effects already provides a first indication. Since these adverse consequences include harm to living resources and marine life, hazards to human health, hindrance to marine activities such as fishing and other legitimate uses of the sea and impairment of quality of use of sea water, it is clear that UNCLOS accounts for damages of anthropogenic use but also refers to the marine environment generally.[368] However, the wording seems to indicate that there is a threshold which "excludes an introduction of substances or energy which has to be only a minor impact in this respect."[369]

The element of the "legitimate uses of the sea" implies an anthropocentric approach in which the degree of damage is determined by users of the sea. The complexity of ecologic systems such as the marine environment and the strong interaction between its constituent elements, though, represent a challenge to determining the impairments and deleterious effects. The elements and concept included in the definition of pollution in UNCLOS clearly include aspects of marine litter. The definition outlines three parameters that help to place marine litter in the system of pollution management: the anthropogenic origin of the substance, the source (indirect or direct) and (deleterious) environmental, economic and health impacts. Marine litter can be therefore subsumed under the broad definition of pollution that integrates several of the adverse consequences of marine litter in its scope.

---

367 *Fritz,* Integrierter Umweltschutz im Völkerrecht, 2009, 209.

368 *Dotinga/Oude Elferink,* Ocean Development & International Law 31 (2000) 151, 159.

369 *Ibid.*

III. The obligation to preserve and protect the marine environment as stipulated by UNCLOS in the context of marine litter regulation

Marine environmental protection is a horizontal issue referred to in several provisions throughout UNCLOS.[370] The integrative protection approach as exemplified in the preamble third indent to UNCLOS, recognises the interdependency and presence of complex interactions within the marine environment and beyond and consequently proposes that "the problems of the ocean space are closely interrelated and need to be considered as a whole." In integrating both the marine environment as well as the estuaries UNCLOS avoids a separation between the aquatic ecosystems that is comprised of the marine environment and its connected freshwater systems.[371] This approach must absolutely be borne in mind throughout any consideration of the regulation of marine litter within UNCLOS.

The ambitious approach of some Contracting Parties to achieve with the conclusion of UNCLOS "a unified and comprehensive approach" to the protection of the marine environment[372] is reflected in Part XII UNCLOS which is dedicated to marine environmental protection measures. The dedication of a specific part signifies that a particular value was attached to this aspect during negotiations. It establishes a fundamental marine environmental protection framework and constitutes on a global level an agreement that provides obligations, responsibilities and powers of States in all aspects of marine environmental protection.[373]

Part XII UNCLOS provides for introductory and general provisions, followed by more specific sections that refer, amongst others, to technical assistance, prescriptive and enforcement jurisdiction.[374] Accordingly,

370 See only in Art. 19 (2) (h) UNCLOS (innocent passage in the territorial sea); Art. 39 (2) (b) UNCLOS and Art. 42 (1) (b) UNCLOS (transit passage through straits used for international navigation); Art. 56 (1) (b) (iii) UNCLOS and Art. 61 to 65 UNCLOS (EEZ); Art. 79 (2) UNCLOS (Continental Shelf); Art. 94 (4) (c) UNCLOS (duties of the flag State); Art. 116 to 120 UNCLOS (conservation and management of the living resources of the High Seas); Art. 123 UNCLOS (enclosed or semi-enclosed seas) and Art. 142 (3), Art. 145 and Art. 165 UNCLOS (the 'Area').

371 *Fritz,* Integrierter Umweltschutz im Völkerrecht, 2009, 209.

372 *Sohn/Noyes,* Cases and materials on the law of the sea, 2004, 689.

373 *Boyle,* The American Journal of International Law 79 (1985) 347, 350.

374 *Hafner,* Meeresumwelt, Meresforschung und Technologietransfer, in *Graf Vitzthum,* Handbuch des Seerechts (2006) 347–460, 367. For example section 1 refers to general provisions, section 2 to global and regional co-operation, section

Art. 192 UNCLOS sets out the general obligation that States must "protect and preserve the marine environment." The obligation to do so is unqualified and extends to all zones as well as to all activities that are conducted in the maritime area.[375] This would seem to be unequivocal and essentially universally accepted.

The measures foreseen by Art. 194 (1) UNCLOS not only stipulate in a reactionary way that measures be taken to reduce or control pollution that has already occurred in the marine environment, but rather follow a preventive approach aiming to prevent pollution at the source. The measures to prevent pollution should amongst others aim to "minimise to the fullest possible extent"[376]

> the release of toxic, harmful or noxious substances especially those which are persistent, from land-based sources from or through the atmosphere or by dumping" and pollution from vessels, in particular measures for preventing accidents and dealing with emergencies, ensuring their safety of operations at sea, preventing intentional and unintentional discharges, and regulating the design, construction, equipment, operation and manning of vessels.[377]

Despite the rather vague standard of "possible extent", this provision exhibits the broad scope of UNCLOS's protection regime that integrates different interactions and consequences of introduced pollutants. These provisions demonstrate the integrated approach taken by UNCLOS providing leeway for the later inclusion of matters that were, at the time of the negotiation of UNCLOS, not necessarily considered to be a significant pollutant, such as marine litter. In taking these measures, particular attention should be made to preserving "rare or fragile ecosystems as well as habitat of depleted, threatened or endangered species and other forms of marine

---

3 to technical assistance and section 4 to monitoring and environmental assessment.

375 *Dotinga/Oude Elferink,* Ocean Development & International Law 31 (2000) 151, 159. *Proelß* argues that Art. 192 UNCLOS reflects customary law: *Proelß,* Meeresschutz im Völker- und Europarecht, 2004, 78. *Hafner*, however, raises doubts in regard to the specificity of the provision *Hafner,* Meeresumwelt, Meresforschung und Technologietransfer, in *Graf Vitzthum,* Handbuch des Seerechts (2006) 347–460, 367.

376 Art. 194 (3) UNCLOS.

377 Art. 194 (3) (a-b) UNCLOS. Additionally, these measures further extent to pollution from installations that are used in the exploration of natural resources of the sea-bed and subsoil (Art. 194 (3) (c) UNCLOS) and pollution stemming from other installations.

life."[378] UNCLOS` regulatory approach does not follow a substance-based approach but a source-based or origin-based approach. This means that it does not enumerate specific substances but rather regulates the sources of these substances. UNCLOS stipulates five types of pollution sources: land-based pollution, pollution from seabed activities subject to national jurisdiction, pollution from activities in the Area, pollution by dumping, pollution from vessels and pollution from or through the atmosphere.[379] Whereas this aspect could *prima facie* lead to the conclusion that UNCLOS outlines a fragmented approach to address sources of marine pollution, the broad and integrative definition of pollution can be clearly used to argue to the contrary. Bearing in mind the overarching aims stated in the preamble as well as in Art. 1 (4) UNCLOS would seem to further strengthen this supposition. The underlying ties that are knotted by this definition, avoid a biased and one-sided consideration of pollution control as established by UNCLOS. Additionally, since UNCLOS provisions on marine pollution were seen in the negotiation as "basic principles and rules,"[380] it thereby deliberately "avoided enumerating new standards for particular forms of pollution."[381] Hence, the source-based approach serves to lay the foundation for the broadest possible level of protection, particularly when considered teleologically and holistically.

The obligation in Art. 194 (1) UNCLOS to take "all measures [...] that are necessary to prevent, reduce and control pollution of the marine environment from any source", implies that a broad range of measures are available to do so.[382] However, these specifications are limited in that the measures need to be "consistent with this Convention."[383] In developing and taking measures to prevent and pollution of the marine environment, "States may not transfer damage or hazards or transform one type of pollution into another."[384] In this context, section 5 of Part XII UNCLOS de-

378 Art. 194 (5) UNCLOS.

379 In the negotiation towards UNCLOS, several delegations emphasised the importance to differentiate between the different kinds of pollution. See for example: *Sohn/Noyes,* Cases and materials on the law of the sea, 2004, 696.

380 *UN*, UNCLOS Third Committee, 5th Meeting July 15-16 1974, UNCLOS III 312-13, Delegate of Sweden: Mr. Delin, para.8.

381 *Tan,* Vessel-source marine pollution, 2006, 195.

382 *Dotinga/Oude Elferink,* Ocean Development & International Law 31 (2000) 151, 160.

383 Art. 194 (2) UNCLOS.

384 Art. 195 UNCLOS.

termines the competences to establish material norms to address the five source categories of UNCLOS. Section 6 of Part XII UNCLOS is dedicated to enforcement competences of the Contracting Parties regarding pollution, prevention and control measures established in section 5 Part XII UNCLOS. Given its substantive relevance, this analysis is limited to examining three sources of pollution that account for the primary pathways of marine litter into the marine environment: land-based pollution, vessel-based pollution and dumping. It will address UNCLOS' regulatory regime using a problem-based approach. This implies that it is not intended to generally discuss the different rights and obligations of States to prevent marine pollution in an abstract way.

Instead, the following analysis is based on three scenarios or activities that could account for instances of typical introduction of marine litter into the marine environment. Such illustrative scenarios are depicted in order to highlight the role of UNCLOS as a general framework, since, unlike certain other issues, a sum of activities leads to the introduction of marine litter. In this context, one must not necessarily balance certain risks of newly emerging activities or technology against the underlying provisions of UNCLOS such as in the case of climate engineering or sub-seabed carbon capture and storage for example. Marine litter is (usually) the outcome of activities that are part of "routine" operations[385] or individual behaviour. The problem-based approach thus aims to underline the role of UNCLOS in framing and broadly regulating human activities, while specifically addressing marine litter considerations.

(1) The first scenario relates to land-based activities in a State during which non-toxic and non-radioactive synthetic solid material is released in the drainage system and is subsequently washed into the ocean.
(2) The second scenario relates to a vessel that sets out on a journey to deliberately dispose of solid man-made material from land in the ocean in order to avoid its disposal in an overfilled landfill site. The captain of the vessel intends to pursue this activity in the EEZ and the territorial sea of a third State.
(3) In a third scenario, a large vessel disposes of the food packaging material accumulated during a voyage within the EEZ and partially in the

385 As mentioned in chapter 2, only in very rare cases, major accidents or incidents such as wreckage or tsunamis lead to the introduction of marine litter.

territorial sea of a third State in order to avoid paying disposal fees in the harbour.

These three scenarios of course only schematically represent possible marine litter sources.[386] Admittedly, a moderation of the scenarios by changing the nationality of the vessel operators or the location of disposal has differing legal consequences. Also, the scenarios are only considered in a vacuum relating to UNCLOS´s provisions in order to demonstrate its underlying regulatory approach that is ultimately reflected in implementing agreements that further substantiate its obligations. In the following, the first scenario on land-based pollution will be treated individually, whereas scenarios two and three will be largely dealt together in pertinent sections on ocean-based pollution due to the (mainly) similar regulatory techniques and jurisdictions. Since the scenarios relate to the categories of pollution as regulated under UNCLOS, a discussion on these categories will be effected in a specific section after the jurisdictions of the different actors of the law of the sea are analysed.

IV. Pollution from land-based sources

Considering the first scenario, it is necessary to understand whether the State of origin of the land-based pollution is under an obligation to eliminate the pollution originating from its territory under UNCLOS. Additionally, the question will be addressed whether other riparian States have the right under UNCLOS to intervene in this context.

1. Prescriptive jurisdiction

According to Art. 207 (1) UNCLOS, States are under the obligation to "prevent, reduce and control pollution of the marine environment from land-based sources, including rivers, estuaries, pipelines and outfall structures." The geographic scope of land-based sources thus includes inland point and diffuse sources, the catchment area of rivers and the coast. Consequently, the case depicted above is applicable under UNCLOS. Even

386 See chapter 2. For the purpose of this study, it is assumed that the vessels are not warships or other government ships operated for non-commercial purposes as referred to in Art. 29 to Art. 32 UNCLOS that enjoy immunities.

though, UNCLOS prescribes that measures taken should "*take into account* internationally agreed rules, standards and recommended practices and procedures,"[387] this is to be done under consideration of regional characteristics and the economic capacity of developing States.[388] At the time of negotiations of UNCLOS, the "social and economic cost"[389] of higher standards of land-based pollution "was seen as unacceptably high."[390] Consequently, a "balance between national legislation and international rules is evidently in favour of national laws and regulations"[391], this also reflects sovereignty.[392]

UNCLOS additionally obliges States to "endeavour to harmonise their policies in this connection at the appropriate regional level."[393] Consequently, Art. 207 UNCLOS does not impose any obligation to adhere to "minimum international standards" as it does with other sources of pollution.[394] Besides the weak legal obligations to address land-based pollution on a global level, UNCLOS further makes reference to material obligations that should be particularly considered when establishing relevant measures. A particular focus is thereby put on those measures that are designed to "minimise, to the fullest extent possible, the release of toxic, harmful or noxious substances, especially those which are persistent, into the marine environment."[395]

---

387 Art. 207 (1) UNCLOS (emphasis added).

388 Art. 207 (4) UNCLOS.

389 *Birnie/Boyle/Redgwell,* International law and the environment, 2009, 454.

390 *Ibid.*

391 *Yankov,* The Law of the Sea Convention and Agenda 21: Marine Environment Implications, in *Boyle/Freestone,* International law and sustainable development (1999) 271–295, 280 as cited by *Tanaka,* Zeitschrift für ausländisches öffentliches Recht und Völkerrecht 66 (2006) 533, 543. See also for a critical evaluation of UNCLOS' provisions addressing land-based pollution: *Hassan,* Protecting the marine environment from land-based sources of pollution, 2006, 83 *et seq*.

392 *Hassan,* Protecting the marine environment from land-based sources of pollution, 2006, 44.

393 Art. 207 (3) UNCLOS. *Birnie/Boyle/Redgwell,* International law and the environment, 2009, 454 speak of a "hortatory character" of Art. 207 UNCLOS. The establishment of agreements and measures on a regional addressing land-based pollution, will be discussed in chapter 4 of this study.

394 *Boyle,* Marine Policy 16 (1992) 20, 25. Reasons for the rather weak elaboration of standards regarding land-based pollution is, *inter alia,* the pressure by developing States that ask for the recognition of their needs *Boyle,* The American Journal of International Law 79 (1985) 347, 354.

395 Art. 207 (5) UNCLOS.

Even though no further specifications with regard to the potential substances are given, this clause can be understood to emphasise and strengthen the application of UNCLOS regarding any marine litter consideration. Particularly the reference to the persistency of the introduced substance is relevant in the context. Yet again, no threshold criteria is given as to when a substances is "toxic", "harmful" or "persistent", consequently, providing the Contracting Parties a broad degree of discretion in implementing this provision. In summary, the broad specifications regarding land-based pollution are based on the still prevailing understanding of the territorial sovereignty of States which has also been reflected in the implementation process.[396] Notwithstanding this, States are, in essence, obliged to act against possible polluting activities stemming from their territory. However, this obligation is not absolute due to the weak wording of Art. 207 UNCLOS.[397] The approach taken by UNCLOS to address land-based pollution is distinguished by flexible provisions.[398] It remains to be seen whether the regulation of land-based pollution is strengthened by other, not necessarily explicit, references in the framework of UNCLOS.

2. Enforcement of land-based pollution

Art. 213 UNCLOS regulating the enforcement of land-based pollution merely states that "states shall enforce their laws and regulations adopted in accordance with article 207." A State is under the obligation to:

> adopt laws and regulations and take other measures necessary to implement applicable international rules and standards established through competent international organizations or diplomatic to prevent, reduce and control pollution of the marine environment from land-based sources.

The enforcement structure emanating from Art. 213 UNCLOS "lacks any means for its direct enforcement."[399] States have rather opted to develop

396 See for a detailed discussion on this aspect: chapter 4.

397 *Hassan,* Protecting the marine environment from land-based sources of pollution, 2006, 82.

398 *Rothwell/Stephens,* The international law of the sea, 2010, 379.

399 *Boyle,* Marine Policy 16 (1992) 20, 25. *Tanaka* argues that the rules are "so general that further specifications are required" *Tanaka,* Zeitschrift für ausländisches öffentliches Recht und Völkerrecht 66 (2006) 533, 543.

regional or subregional approaches to address the issue of land-based pollution.[400]

However, in case of disputes between States, UNCLOS establishes the obligation to settle disputes by peaceful means.[401] The Mox Plant Case constitutes an example in which land-based pollution was at the core of the dispute.[402] In the case, the Republic of Ireland opposed the plans of the United Kingdom to build a mixed oxide fuel (`Mox') plant in Sellafield, located at the Irish Sea.[403] It is the largest civil nuclear complex in the UK in which fuel rods from nuclear power stations are reprocessed. Ireland was concerned about the environmental impacts of the discharge of radioactive materials from this plant into the Irish Sea and the transport of reactor fuel elements via the sea.[404] Ireland claimed that the discharges of the plant were "incompatible with the United Kingdom´s obligation to protect and preserve the marine environment" (Article 192 LOSC)"[405] and that these violated the obligations contained in Article 207 and 2013 UNCLOS.[406]

Leaving aside procedural aspects of this case that do not play a further role in this context, the International Tribunal for the Law of the Sea (ITLOS) held that "the duty to cooperate is a fundamental principle in the prevention of pollution of the marine environment under Part XII of the

---

400 *Birnie/Boyle/Redgwell,* International law and the environment, 2009, 455.

401 Art. 279 UNCLOS.

402 *ITLOS*, Mox Plant Case (Ireland v. United Kingdom) Request for Provisional Measures and Statement of Cases in Ireland of 9 November 2001, ITLOS Reports 5 (2001), 95. See for an overview on *Stephens,* International courts and environmental protection, 2009, 232 *et seq.* The Mox Plant Cases and arbitrations related to the proceedings of Ireland against the United Kingdom under UNCLOS, the OSPAR Convention and also the European Court of Justice. Amongst others the case has been subject to substantial academic debate about the relationship and jurisdiction between courts, see only: *Shany,* Leiden Journal of International Law 17 (2004) 815; *Lavranos,* Leiden Journal of International Law 19 (2006) 223; *Lavranos,* The Law & Practice of International Courts and Tribunals 5 (2006) 479; *Brown,* The International Journal of Marine and Coastal Law 17 (2002) 267; *Kwiatkowska,* The International Journal of Marine and Coastal Law 18 (2003) 1; *Hassan,* Protecting the marine environment from land-based sources of pollution, 2006, 190 *et seq.*; *Fitzmaurice,* The International Journal of Marine and Coastal Law 18 (2003) 541.

403 *ITLOS*, Mox Plant Case, § 1.

404 *Ibid.*, § 8 and 9.

405 *Ibid.,* § 113.

406 *Ibid.*, § 114.

Convention and general international law."[407] It also stated that "prudence and caution require that Ireland and the United Kingdom cooperate in exchanging information concerning risks or effects of the operation of the MOX plant and in devising ways to deal with them, as appropriate."[408] Additionally,

> Ireland and the United Kingdom shall cooperate and shall, for this purpose, enter into consultations forthwith in order to:
> (a) exchange further information with regard to possible consequences for the Irish Sea arising out of the commissioning of the MOX plant;
> (b) monitor risks or the effects of the operation of the MOX plant for the Irish Sea;
> (c) devise, as appropriate, measures to prevent pollution of the marine environment which might result from the operation of the MOX plant.[409]

The Mox Plant Case has demonstrated that under certain circumstances, dispute settlement can serve the role of further refining the obligations arising under UNCLOS. Admittedly, the Mox Plant Case deals with radioactive substances that are in principle not comparable to marine litter considerations. It is not suggested to use dispute settlements as a mean of enforcement only; nevertheless the duty to co-operate could be a first starting point in this regard.

The prescriptive and enforcement jurisdiction provisions in respect of land-based marine litter are particularly limited in UNCLOS. This is primarily due to the principle of territorial sovereignty. In this regard, the country of origin is under the obligation to control any pollution from its territory. However, no precise measures are provided under UNCLOS. Other States have therefore very limited capacity to interfere with inland polluting activities of other States as illustrated by the Mox Plant Case.[410] A possible additional approach to address pollution from land-based sources could be seen in the obligation to co-operate as prescribed in UNCLOS. Admittedly, it is not possible to derive specific actions from this. The issue of land-based pollution therefore appears to be in need of further

407 *Ibid.*, § 82.
408 *Ibid.*, § 84.
409 *Ibid.*, § 89.
410 This assumption holds true for "minor" or "diffuse" pollution such as in the case of marine litter. It is argued that in case of major or hazardous pollution from one territory of a State to another, the legal situation has to be differently evaluated.

concretisation in different fora and it is not possible to provide a satisfactory solution to the problem posed using UNCLOS.

V. The regulation of ocean-based pollution

Whereas the material scope regarding land-based pollution is rather limited, the provisions regarding dumping as outlined in Art. 210 UNCLOS and vessel-based pollution in Art. 211 UNCLOS are more differentiated.

1. Dumping as a source of marine litter

The second scenario will be considered in the context of UNCLOS. According to Art. 56 (1) (b) (iii) UNCLOS the coastal State has the jurisdiction to protect and preserve the marine environment within its EEZ. The provisions relates to Part XII UNCLOS in which dumping is, *inter alia*, also regulated. Dumping is, in the framework of UNCLOS, defined as "any deliberate disposal of wastes or other matter from vessels, aircraft, platforms or other man-made structures at sea" and "any deliberate disposal of vessels, aircraft, platforms or other man-made structures at sea."[411] States are thus under the obligation to "adopt laws and regulations to prevent, reduce and control pollution of the marine environment by dumping."[412] Art. 210 UNCLOS does not contain specific technical obligations, but rather provides the legal basis for regulating dumping activities. It primarily establishes a situation in which the coastal State has "the right to permit, regulate and control such dumping after due consideration of the matter with other States which by reason of their geographical situation may be adversely affected thereby."[413] The geographical scope of those measures extends both to the territorial sea, the EEZ and the continental shelf of a coastal State.[414] Consequently, the vessel that sets out on a journey to dump its waste is under an obligation to ask for the permission of

411 Art. 1 (5) (a) (i and ii) UNCLOS.
412 Art. 210 (1) UNCLOS.
413 Art. 210 (5) UNCLOS. Tacit acceptance of dumping therefore is not accepted: *Frank,* The European Community and marine environmental protection in the international law of the sea, 2007, 290.
414 Art. 210 (5) UNCLOS.

the coastal State. The coastal State may opt not to grant such permission for dumping. It is, nonetheless, entitled to grant such permission under the terms of UNCLOS, which also includes the due consideration of the matter with States that may be adversely affected by the actions.

In the development of national measures, the States "acting especially through competent international organisations or diplomatic conference, shall endeavour to establish global and regional rules, standards and recommended practices and procedures to prevent, reduce and control such pollution."[415] However, this obligation is limited by the weak clause to "endeavour to establish global and regional rules, standards and recommended practices and procedures to prevent, reduce and control such pollution."[416] This reference norm to endeavour refers not only to the International Maritime Organisation but also to the International Energy Agency and Regional Seas Conventions.[417] On an international level, the London Convention and the London Protocol are the primary mechanisms to further substantiate the broad provisions of UNCLOS. In addition, regional standards on dumping have been developed.[418]

2. Operational pollution from seagoing vessels

The substantive law relating to vessel-based pollution as established in Art. 211 UNCLOS is significantly more detailed than the provisions of Art. 207 and 210 UNCLOS. This is, *inter alia*, due to the specific nature of shipping as a key factor to the global economy and the balance between the freedom of navigation on the one hand and the protection of the marine environment on the other hand.[419] Consequently, "States, acting through the competent international organization or general diplomatic conference, shall establish international rules and standards to prevent, reduce and control pollution of the marine environment from vessels

415 Art. 210 (4) UNCLOS.

416 Art. 210 (4) UNCLOS.

417 *Frank,* The European Community and marine environmental protection in the international law of the sea, 2007, 291.

418 *Ibid.* See only the plural of "competent international organizations" (Art. 210 (4) UNCLOS in comparison to the singular reference in Art. 211 (1) UNCLOS.

419 *Ibid.,* 191.

[…]."[420] These should be re-examined from time to time.[421] Also, contrary to other provisions, the States shall not only endeavour to act, but are explicitly obliged to develop measures.

Art. 211 UNCLOS differentiates between substantive laws regarding coastal State measures in the territorial sea, the EEZ and vessels flying the flag of a State. As a general rule, the coastal State has to respect the right to innocent passage of third State vessels as is stipulated in Art. 17 UNCLOS through the territorial sea.[422] The passing of a vessel may become "non-innocent" under certain circumstances. According to Art. 19 UNCLOS, a passage of a vessel may become non-innocent after it has conducted, *inter alia,* "any act of wilful and serious pollution contrary to this Convention."[423] Consequently, the test whether an activity constitutes a breach of innocent passage is a two-step test and relates to two cumulative criteria. On the one hand, it has to be determined whether the act of pollution was wilful, i.e. whether it was intentionally and deliberately carried out. Secondly, the seriousness of the pollution of the pollution must be stated to reach a certain minimum level of gravity. The cumulative nature of both the intention and the degree of damage "represent a significant threshold."[424] With a view to the fact that marine litter can be subsumed under the pollution definition of UNCLOS, it remains to be determined whether the addendum "serious" pollution implies a somewhat different meaning than that arising out of the definition in Art. 1 (1) (4) UNCLOS. Since no

420 Art. 211 (1) UNCLOS.

421 Art. 211 (1) UNCLOS.

422 It is however not uncontended whether the innocence passage through the territorial sea constitutes customary law. Whereas *Proelß,* Meeresschutz im Völker- und Europarecht, 2004, 87 argues in favour of the status, *Rothwell/Stephens,* The international law of the sea, 2010, 76 rejects the thought. *Rothwell* refers in this context to State practice regarding prior notification schemes in several countries: *ibid.* The same author admits that UNCLOS has further contributed in refining the specific elements. See only Arts.17-19 UNCLOS. See for an early account of the different contentious elements of the innocent passage: *Emanuelli,* The Canadian yearbook of international 11 (1973)13, 13.

423 Art. 19 (2) (f) UNCLOS. In the Corfu Channel case, the ICJ held that a mere breach of national laws according to Art. 21 UNCLOS does not *ipso facto* constitutes a breach of innocent passage: *ICJ,* Corfu Channel Case (United Kingdom of Great Britain and Northern Ireland v. Albania), Merits, Judgement of 9 April 1949, ICJ Rep.1949, 4.

424 *Molenaar,* Coastal State Jurisdiction over Vessel-Source Pollution, 1998, 197.

definition of "serious" is provided in UNCLOS,[425] the determination of what constitutes "serious" has to be also considered. It is argued that in this regard, two central elements need to be considered: the quantity of pollution and its characteristics.

Regarding the quantity of pollution, the discarding of some few packaging materials cannot be said to result in non-innocent passage.[426] A somewhat different conclusion could be reached if a ship were to discard a substantial amount of plastics and packaging material. However, were this to occur during an emergency accident, this would not comply with the wilful element and therefore cannot render the passage non-innocent.[427]

The other aspect of the determination of "serious" relates to the characteristics of the discarded substance, i.e. the causal link between the polluting activity and the negative effects of the polluting substance. This approach can be derived from the definition of pollution from UNCLOS that is also based on the adverse consequences of the introduced substances on the environment.[428] Here, first indications what kind of elements could be used in the determination of the seriousness of the pollution are given. Nevertheless, the causal link between the introduction of a small amount of packaging materials and adverse consequences is significantly limited by an utter inability to establish a sufficient degree of harm. The vagueness of the term 'serious' thus provides the coastal State with a broad discretion for its interpretation.[429] A further limitation of the discretion is evident in the cumulative nature of this provision. *Molenaar* rightly points out that "intentional operational discharges will in general not also be 'serious'."[430]

Where coastal States develop national measures with the objective of preventing, reducing and controlling marine environmental pollution from vessels that are registered within their jurisdiction, these measures "shall at least have the same effect as that of generally accepted international rules and standards established through the competent international orga-

---

425 *Ibid.*

426 Different: *Joyner/Frew* who do not differentiate between the seriousness of pollution and sees the disposal of plastic as an act of "serious pollution" under Art. 19 UNCLOS: *Joyner/Frew,* Ocean Development & International Law 22 (1991) 33, 39 footnote 58.

427 *Molenaar,* Coastal State Jurisdiction over Vessel-Source Pollution, 1998, 197.

428 See section C.II. of this chapter.

429 *Molenaar,* Coastal State Jurisdiction over Vessel-Source Pollution, 1998, 197.

430 *Ibid.*

nisation or general diplomatic conferences."[431] A similar minimum standard must also be adhered to when establishing measures in the EEZ.[432] Since UNCLOS does not further define what "generally accepted international rules and standards" constitute, this has been subject to substantive legal writing.[433] It is undisputed that within the meaning of Art. 211 UNCLOS, the IMO is the only body that may take measures on shipping.[434] In that regard MARPOL is the most important implementing treaty.[435] The mandate and allocation of powers can thus be interpreted as an attempt "to avoid a fragmentation of maritime law" [...] that places "considerable constraints on the efforts of individual States, or regions, to introduce rules which diverge from those agreed at a global level."[436] Under these strict provisions, Art. 211 (3) UNCLOS establishes nevertheless the competence of the coastal States to demand requirements regarding pollution control and prevention as a condition for the entry of foreign vessels into their port or internal waters. In practice this relates, for example, to discharge

---

431 Art. 211 (2) UNCLOS. See also Art. 21 (f) UNCLOS in regard to laws and regulations of a coastal State to protect its marine environment regarding innocent passage.

432 Art. 56 (1) (b) (iii) UNCLOS provides that the coastal States has jurisdiction with regard to the protection and preservation of the marine environment.

433 *Walker*, Definitions for the law of the sea, 2012, 92 *et seq.*; *Proelß,* Meeresschutz im Völker- und Europarecht, 2004, 87 *et seq.*; *Ringbom*, Competing norms in the law of marine environmental protection, 1997, 5.

434 In this context, Art. 211 (6) UNCLOS stipulates that the coastal State may after consultation through ('the organization') IMO with any other State concerned and where it has "reasonable grounds for believing that a particular, clearly defined area of their respective exclusive economic zones is an area where the adoption of special mandatory measures for the prevention of pollution from vessels is required [...] in relation to its oceanographical and ecological conditions [...]" may adopt "laws and regulations for the prevention, reduction and control of pollution from vessels implementing such international rules and standards or navigational practice as are made applicable, through the organization, for special areas." The reference norm assigns the IMO as the pertinent UN specialised agency the mandate to act and substantiate UNCLOS' legal framework on vessel-based pollution: *Proelß*, Meeresschutz im Völker- und Europarecht, 2004, 86; *Secretariat of IMO,* LEG/MISC.7 Implications of the United Nations Convention on the Law of the Sea for the International Maritime Organization, 19.01.2012, 7.

435 *Hafner,* Meeresumwelt, Meresforschung und Technologietransfer, in *Graf Vitzthum,* Handbuch des Seerechts (2006) 347–460, 387.

436 *Ringbom*, Competing norms in the law of marine environmental protection, 1997, 5.

requirements requiring rubbish to be disposed of at port reception facilities.[437]

3. Enforcement measures of ocean-based pollution prevention measures

In regulating ocean-based pollution such as vessel-based pollution and dumping, UNCLOS has "developed specific rules seeking to allocate jurisdiction over vessels traversing the sea."[438] Thus, "the pollution control standards [...] may be prescribed and enforced by any one or more of three state actors- the flag state, coastal state and port state."[439] The enforcement structure of Art. 216 UNCLOS dealing with dumping envisages three actors that can enforce national measures and "applicable international rules and standards." Consequently, the coastal State can enforce dumping measures within its territorial sea, its Exclusive Economic Zone and on its continental shelf.[440] Second of all, the flag State has the possibility to enforce measures regarding vessels flying its flag or listed in its registry.[441] Third, any State has the possibility to enforce measures during the "act of loading of wastes or other matter occurring within its territory or at its off-shore terminals."[442] In this context, "applicable" rules refer to those standards arising out of treaties and customary law.[443]

The enforcement regime of vessel-based pollution in the law of the sea evolved over time. The enforcement structure of UNCLOS is primarily based on the premise that the flag States under which the vessels fly have the primary responsibility in ensuring that their vessels comply with those standards and rules.[444] According to Art. 92 UNCLOS, it is the primary

437 See for an extensive discussion on this aspect chapter 4.

438 *Tan,* Vessel-source marine pollution, 2006, 23.

439 *Ibid.*

440 Art. 216 (1) (a) UNCLOS.

441 Art. 216 (1) (b) UNCLOS.

442 Art. 216 (1) (c) UNCLOS. The use and application of generally accepted international rules and standards is an expression for the need to ensure consistency and uniformity of UNCLOS: *Frank,* The European Community and marine environmental protection in the international law of the sea, 2007, 26.

443 *Ibid.*, 291.

444 *Mansell,* Flag state responsibility, 2009, 53 *et seq*. The "[f]lag State jurisdiction is the oldest expression of maritime jurisdiction": *Gavouneli,* Functional jurisdiction in the law of the sea, 2007, 34.

right of the flag State to exercise jurisdiction over the ships sailing under its flag, irrespective of the ship's geographical location.[445] Art. 217 UNCLOS applies to the enforcement rules by flag State. Accordingly,

> States shall ensure compliance by vessels flying their flag or of their registry with applicable international rules and standards, established through the competent international organization [...] and with their laws and regulations adopted in accordance with this Convention for the prevention, reduction and control of pollution of the marine environment from vessels.[446]

This obligation also entails the duty to ensure that the vessels carry on board those certificates that are obligatory according to international rules and standards.[447] Furthermore, it extends also to requirements regarding the design, construction, equipment and manning of vessels.[448] In case of violation of these conditions, the flag State can institute investigations and, where appropriate, "proceedings in respect of the alleged violation."[449] If a third State requests the flag State in writing to investigate any violation by a vessel flying its flag, the flag State is under the duty to comply with this demand and commence proceedings in case sufficient evidence are available.[450] The outcome of the proceedings and consequent actions must be communicated to the requesting State and the IMO and

---

445 See Art. 94 UNCLOS for a catalog of duties of the flag State. According to Art. 94 (4) (c) UNCLOS, States are under the obligation to ensure that the master and to the extent possible also the crew "observe pertinent international regulations relating to the prevention, reduction and control of marine pollution." In the Lotus case, the Permanent Court of International Justice (PCIJ) outlined that: "[v]essels on the high seas are subject to no authority except that of the state whose flag they fly. In virtue of the principle of the freedom of the seas, that is to say the absence of any territorial sovereignty upon the high seas, no state may exercise any kind of jurisdiction over foreign vessels upon them" (emphasis added): The Lotus case (France v. Turkey), Judgement of 07 September 1927, PCIJ, Ser.A, No 10, para.25. On the high seas, the "exclusivity of flag State jurisdiction is not absolute": *Rayfuse,* Non-flag state enforcement in high seas fisheries, 2004, 22. See only Art. 92 UNCLOS in which "[s]hips sail under the flag of one State only and, save in exceptional cases expressly provided for in international treaties or in this Convention, shall be subject to its exclusive jurisdiction on the high seas.".

446 Art. 217 (1) UNCLOS.

447 Art. 217 (3) UNCLOS.

448 Art. 217 (2) UNCLOS.

449 Art. 217 (4) UNCLOS.

450 Art. 217 (6) UNCLOS.

has to be made available to all States.[451] In order to establish a deterrent effect, the national law should envisage penalties that are "adequate in severity to discourage violations wherever they occur."[452]

The flag State enforcement regime is, however, significantly weakened in that the flag State is at the same time "user" and therefore potentially also "polluter" of the marine environment but is also committed to establish protective measures.[453] These conflicting and opposing functions therefore necessarily have as a consequence that the flag State has to balance economic interests against environmental measures which in turn, has ultimately led to weak flag State enforcement standards.[454] Unfortunately, the past has shown that, contrary to the expectations, numerous flag States do not always exercise their jurisdiction effectively.[455] Flag State jurisdiction would be in regard to vessel-based pollution, such as operational waste, an important factor in ensuring compliance, however, its limited effectiveness has therefore also repercussions on marine litter prevention from that source.

4. Enforcement by coastal States

The mandate of the coastal State to enforce laws is limited by both geographic (internal waters, territorial sea and EEZ) and by material preconditions. This refers to the competences of a coastal State to inspect and institute proceedings against a vessel that has violated national laws and regulations or applicable international marine environmental rules and stan-

---

451 Art. 217 (7) UNCLOS.

452 Art. 217 (8) UNCLOS.

453 Proelß speaks of this as a "*Personalunion*" between those two functions: *Proelß,* Meeresschutz im Völker- und Europarecht, 2004, 99.

454 Additionally, so-called "flags of convenience" pose a limitation to the effectiveness of flag State jurisdiction: *Rayfuse,* Non-flag state enforcement in high seas fisheries, 2004, 25. This is the "practice of flagging out or reflagging to avoid control", *ibid.*

455 *Mansell,* Flag state responsibility, 2009, 95 *et seq.*; *Rayfuse,* Non-flag state enforcement in high seas fisheries, 2004, 24. Reasons for this being, *inter alia,* "lack of political to regulate capacity" or "lack of financial and technical expertise": *Rayfuse,* Non-flag state enforcement in high seas fisheries, 2004, 24. Modes of non-flag State enforcement are for example the right of approach, the right of visit and search and arrest, see for further information, *ibid.*, 61 *et seq.*

dards.[456] A coastal State may commence proceedings against a vessel in its port or at an off-shore terminal regarding any violations:

> of its laws and regulations adopted in accordance with this Convention or applicable international rules and standards for the prevention, reduction and control of pollution from vessels when the violation has occurred within the territorial sea or the exclusive economic zone of that State.[457]

A somewhat different ground applies in case the vessel has during the navigation in the territorial sea of a State violated national laws or applicable international laws. In this context, the coastal State may "undertake physical inspection of the vessel relating to the violation and may, where the evidence so warrants, institutes proceedings, including detention of the vessel."[458] If a vessel navigating in the EEZ or the territorial sea of a State has violated national or international applicable laws, the "State may require the vessel to give information regarding its identity and port of registry, its last and its next port of call and other relevant information required to establish whether a violation has occurred."[459] If this information were evidently false or if the violation justifies this, the coastal State may undertake physical inspection of the vessel. This right is however limited by the precondition that there are "clear grounds" that a violation as stipulated in Art. 220 (3) UNCLOS has resulted in a substantial discharge causing, or threatening significant pollution of the marine environment.

In case there is evidence that such a violation has resulted "in a discharge causing major damage or threat of major damage to the coastline or related interests of the coastal State, or to any resources of its territorial sea or exclusive economic zone"[460] the State may institute proceedings.[461] The definition of "(threat) of major damage" and "interests" of the coastal State include a wide-scope of material damage. However despite this, the provision establishes a threshold of significance. After all, in case minor violations would be pursued, this would potentially hollow out the coastal State enforcement regime and it would from a practical point of view be extremely difficult to handle such an amount. However, this approach con-

456 Art. 220 (1) UNCLOS.
457 Art. 220 (1) UNCLOS.
458 Art. 220 (2) UNCLOS.
459 Art. 2210 (3) UNCLOS.
460 Art. 220 (6) UNCLOS.
461 The coastal State may allow the vessel to proceed despite proceeding against it, in case bonding or "other appropriate financial security" are assured.

stitutes from a perspective of marine litter a weakness since it is indeed those minor polluting activities that lead to the overall effect.

5. Enforcement through port States

The weakness and inadequate implementation of the flag State´s duty has led to the strengthening of the port State regime.[462] The origin of also supporting non-flag port States to supplement the enforcement of treaty obligations is derived from, *inter alia*, increased environmental awareness.[463] The intention behind the strengthening of the port State jurisdiction is that the port State functions as an organ of the international community.[464]

Port State jurisdiction:

> derives from the territorial sovereignty states enjoy in their internal waters under customary international law such that a state may, under its municipal law, prosecute a vessel for the breach of an international standard committed in

---

462 See for a comprehensive historical overview on the development of port State jurisdiction: *Anderson,* Port States and Environmental Protection, in *Boyle/Freestone,* International law and sustainable development (1999) 325–344.; *McDorman,* Journal of Maritime Law & Commerce 28 (1997) 305, 305 *et seq*. UNCLOS does not provide a definition of port State: *Molenaar,* Ocean Development & International Law 38 (2007) 225, 227. It has been chosen to follow *Molenaar´*s understanding of port State as "encompassing jurisdiction over the port´s own maritime zones (in its capacity as coastal State) as well as over the high seas and the maritime zones of other coastal States": *Molenaar,* Port State Jurisdiction: Towards Mandatory and Comprehensive Use, in *Freestone/Barnes/Ong,* The law of the sea (2006) 192–209, 194. Also port State jurisdiction "concerns the port state's powers to prosecute ships and impose fines on them for violation of international rules and standards": *Bang,* The International Journal of Marine and Coastal Law 23 (2008) 715, 717.

463 *Rayfuse,* Non-flag state enforcement in high seas fisheries, 2004, 65.

464 *Hafner,* Meeresumwelt, Meresforschung und *Technologietransfer*, in *Graf Vitzthum,* Handbuch des Seerechts (2006) 347–460, 408. "Port State jurisdiction clearly does not just serve the national interests, but can also further the interests of the international community, by among others things, ensuring [...] marine environmental protection [...]" (emphasis added): *Molenaar,* Ocean Development & International Law 38 (2007) 225, 225. Port State jurisdiction has only been explicitly articulated in 1973 in the context of the IMCO Conference on Marine Pollution, before that "no significant port State powers of jurisdiction were exercised in respect of pollution offences committed outside the normal limits of the State's coastal jurisdiction [...]": *Bang,* Journal of Maritime Law & Commerce 40 (2009) 291, 293.

> port or committed before the ship entered the port where the offense is continuing in port.[465]

According to Art. 218 (1) UNCLOS a State

> may undertake investigation and where the evidence so warrants, institute proceedings in respect of any discharge from that vessel outside the internal waters, territorial sea or exclusive economic zone of that State in violation of applicable international rules and standards established through the competent international organization or general diplomatic conference.[466]

Port State jurisdiction can therefore be territorial, quasi-territorial or extraterritorial.[467] Quasi-territorial jurisdiction covers the jurisdiction of a port State in its EEZ or continental shelf.[468] Under certain preconditions, the port State can also act in the name of flag States, the State in which waters' the violation has taken place or any State "damaged or threatened by the discharge violation."[469] However, "even though the provisions of Article 218 are very clear, it will be difficult to put them into practice."[470] In a survey on the practical application of Art. 218 UNCLOS in different

---

465 *Bang/Jang,* Ocean Development & International Law 43 (2012) 170, 171.

466 See for an analysis of the port State enforcement provision in UNCLOS: *Di Schiano Pepe,* Port Sate Control as an Instrument to Ensure Compliance with International Marine Environmental Obligations, in *Kirchner,* International marine environmental law (2003) 137–156, 142 *et seq*. The enforcement jurisdiction under Art. 218 UNCLOS deals only with discharges and not with violation of construction, design, equipment or manning: *Bang,* Journal of Maritime Law & Commerce 40 (2009) 291, 299. The term "applicable international rules and standards" does not relate "to resolutions, guidelines and codes that are not yet considered 'generally accepted international rules and standards (GAIRS)": *Bang,* Journal of Maritime Law & Commerce 40 (2009) 291, 293.

467 *Molenaar,* Port State Jurisdiction: Towards Mandatory and Comprehensive Use, in *Freestone/Barnes/Ong,* The law of the sea (2006) 192–209, 196.

468 *Ibid.* Extraterritorial jurisdiction relates to behavior beyond the territorial of a State. Here, a sufficient jurisdictional link is necessary. See for an analysis *Di Schiano Pepe,* Port Sate Control as an Instrument to Ensure Compliance with International Marine Environmental Obligations, in *Kirchner,* International marine environmental law (2003)137–156.

469 Art. 218 (3) UNCLOS. The port State may thus not act *motu proprio*, but a third State must prompt him to do so. Furthermore, in case the demanding flag or coastal State request so, the port State is under the obligation to submit the records of the investigation (Art. 218 (4) UNCLOS).

470 *Keselj,* Ocean Development & International Law 30 (1999) 127, 138. See for a critique of Art. 218 UNCLOS: *Bang,* Journal of Maritime Law & Commerce 40 (2009) 291, 299 *et seq*.

countries, *Bang* found out that no port State analysed had indeed "prosecuted foreign vessels for unlawful discharges committed outside their national waters or EEZ under Article 218 of the LOS Convention."[471] Reasons for this included the lack of interests of port States or concerns about "pre-empted flag States"[472] and remote damage from illegal discharges that usually do not directly cause harm to the environment of port States. Also, the proof of evidence of any discharge, particularly those in the high seas, is very difficult to produce.[473]

It is argued that particular with a view to the source of vessel-based litter, port State jurisdiction and Port State Control could be a central factor in increasing the protection standard.[474] This is due to the fact that port State jurisdiction can serve as a legal tool to control requirements relating to onboard generated waste. UNCLOS's port State regime "formed the basis for the development of Port State Control (PSC) regimes, which, […] have become the main tool to ensure flag State compliance with international safety and anti-pollution standards."[475] The necessity to develop such a regime is the consequence of the weak implementation and enforcement practice of flag States, sub-standard vessels[476] and "to eliminate so-called port shopping, to enhance the efficiency of port states' inspections by means of harmonization between port states and sharing of information."[477] As *Frank* rightly puts it "in an ideal world PSC should not

---

471 Ibid, 299 *et seq.* The analysed countries were, *inter alia*, the United States of America, Latvia, Lithuania and the Netherlands.

472 *Ibid.*, 313.

473 *Keselj,* Ocean Development & International Law 30 (1999) 127, 138; *Bang,* Journal of Maritime Law & Commerce 40 (2009) 291, 313.

474 See for a further analysis of the approach taken in the EU regarding port reception facilities, chapter 4 of this study. There is a distinction between port State control and port State jurisdiction: *Rayfuse,* Non-flag state enforcement in high seas fisheries, 2004, 69. Port State control does not coincide with the enforcement jurisdiction of Art. 218 UNCLOS: *Di Schiano,* Port Sate Control as an Instrument to Ensure Compliance with International Marine Environmental Obligations, in *Kirchner,* International marine environmental law (2003) 137–156, 147.

475 *Frank,* The European Community and marine environmental protection in the international law of the sea, 2007, 205. In the case of Port State Control, "unlike PSJ, the port state does not prosecute the vessel for an alleged breach of its legislation": *Bang,* The International Journal of Marine and Coastal Law 23 (2008) 715, 717.

476 *Rayfuse,* Non-flag state enforcement in high seas fisheries, 2004, 67.

477 *Bang/Jang,* Ocean Development & International Law 43 (2012) 170, 171.

even be necessary."[478] Even though the premise of the flag State as the primary enforcement actor prevails, "action by port States is required to prevent the operation of substandard ships."[479] To this end, so-called Memoranda of Understandings (MoU) on Port State Control were signed in different geographical regions.[480] A particular relevant MoU on Port State Control in the context of this study is the Paris MoU on PSC in which for participating authorities port State procedures and obligations are further established.[481]

6. Discussion on scenarios

The scenarios as outlined above are discussed separately since these do not exclusively relate to the jurisdiction of the different actors, but are rather based on two of the pollution catgeories as regulated under UNCLOS. In the following, a broad overview of the specific pollution control jurisdictions is given for the scenario on dumping of litter and vessel-based pollution.

Scenario 2

UNCLOS establishes a regime in which the coastal State has jurisdiction according to the provisions of UNCLOS and is entitled to permit activities within areas under its jurisdiction including dumping of litter. With regard to the case at hand, this implies that the vessel can be granted permission before commencing with dumping activities. The coastal State may alternatively decide not grant the permission to dump the material. Additionally, in this regard, however, also the flag State of the vessel is under the

---

478 *Frank,* The European Community and marine environmental protection in the international law of the sea, 2007, 205.

479 See in this regard the preamble to the Paris Memorandum of Understanding on Port State Control (Paris MoU on PSC) that was signed in 1982 by then 14 European States. Nowadays 27 States participate in this framework. See also: *Molenaar,* Ocean Development & International Law 38 (2007) 225, 244; *Rayfuse,* Non-flag state enforcement in high seas fisheries, 2004, 67 *et seq.*

480 See for an overview on the development of port State control: *Keselj,* Ocean Development & International Law 30 (1999) 127; *Bang/Jang,* Ocean Development & International Law 43 (2012) 170, 171.

481 See for further information: *Bang,* The International Journal of Marine and Coastal Law 23 (2008) 715, 730 *et seq.*

obligation to enforce rules and standards so as to ensure that any dumping activities are carried out in accordance with UNCLOS. In this regard the flag State is at the same time user and has the function to enforce marine environmental protection standards. This demonstrates the ambiguity of this category of jurisdiction.

Scenario 3

In the case at hand, the flag State of the vessel is under the obligation to prevent pollution by the disposal of packaging waste as it is required to enforce marine environmental protection measures. However, in doing so, it is under the constant demand to strike a balance between its environmental protection obligations on the one hand and to further its economic interests on the other hand.

The concerned coastal State within whose area of jurisdiction, the vessel aims to dispose its waste, may legislate for national laws on this matter. A coastal State must not accept the innocent passage of a vessel through its territorial sea in cases of serious pollution. It has been demonstrated that the disposal of small amounts of packaging material does not render the passage non-innocent. This is, in particular, due to the fact that in the applicable test two cumulative elements need to be proven. Whereas the intentional discharge of operational pollution such as packaging material fulfils the criteria of "wilful", the seriousness of the act must however be denied in these circumstances. In case of polluting activities in the EEZ, the State may equally prescribe laws that need to be in accordance with UNCLOS.

In this case, the coastal State and the port State could invoke measures to enforce its protection standards. A major challenge in this regard is posed by the evidence to prove the polluting activity, since the identification of the source is extremely difficult. Consequently, regarding the disposal of vessel-based pollution, the port State potentially has a crucial role to play. This relates amongst others the control of delivery of waste after a vessel has entered the port.

7. Preliminary Conclusion

The distribution of competences to establish and enforce legal standards to prevent and control marine pollution naturally lies in the heart of any discussion on polluting activities. Whereas other types of marine pollution such as oil spills or emergency situations have a clearly definable source, the diffuse nature of marine litter pollution aggravates an effective enforcement. Also, due to the rather minimal amounts and singular activities, the persecution of any offenders is extremely difficult. With regard to the three scenarios as depicted at the outset of this section, it can be concluded that the regulation of marine litter stemming from different sources is subject to a complex regulatory framework. Without claiming that the described incidences can be entirely answered and evaluated, they nevertheless help to demonstrate the requirements and challenges of law of the sea that surface in a marine litter context. The scenario on land-based pollution demonstrated that in regard to this source, UNCLOS provides only in an extremely limited way prescriptive and enforcement jurisdiction. Therefore, UNCLOS can only with limited effect serve as a regulatory source in regard to marine litter stemming from land-based activities. With regard to both scenarios related to ocean-based pollution, UNCLOS creates a more detailed prescriptive and enforcement jurisdiction. However, one of the central finding in this regard is that the flag State has the primary duty to enforce environmental protection standards. However, as has been discussed above, the flag State is both user and potential polluter of the marine environment. Therefore the flag State is under pressure to balance environmental protection obligations and economic interests. This has ultimately a consequence on the introduction of marine litter either through dumping or operational waste, as flag State jurisdiction is not always exercised effectively.

VI. The duty to co-operate as endorsed by UNCLOS and its implication for marine litter regulation

UNCLOS contains different aspects of the duty to co-operate.[482] Whereas UNCLOS remains silent on a definition of co-operation generally, it is also difficult to derive substantive obligations of the duty to co-operate *per se*.[483] Whereas States have to merely "endeavour" to co-operate in developing measures addressing land-based pollution, the obligation to co-operate regarding vessel-based pollution is absolute, as this is to be done

482 See only Art. 64 (1), 65, 118 and 197 UNCLOS respectively.

483 *Dzidzornu,* Ocean Development & International Law 33 (2002) 263, 268.

through competent international organisations or diplomatic conferences. Besides the sectoral, source-based obligation to co-operate, UNCLOS provides a broader backdrop that entails the protection of the marine environment in its entirety.

In the context of marine pollution prevention, UNCLOS opens the possibility and indeed puts an emphasis on regional co-operation. Art. 197 UNCLOS further formalises the co-operation by obliging that

> States shall co-operate on a global basis and, as appropriate, on a regional basis, directly or through competent international organizations, in formulating and elaborating international rules, standards and recommended practices and procedures.

In doing so, the co-operation should also be based on "characteristic regional features."[484] The duty to co-operate as outlined by UNCLOS is not only a significant framework regarding pollution prevention measures. It also extends to the exchange of information and data and the role of scientific research in pollution of the marine environment.[485] States are thus under an obligation to promote studies and support scientific research "directly or through competent international organisations."[486]

A particularly important reference regarding marine litter is the specification that States "shall endeavour to participate actively in regional and global programmes to acquire knowledge for the assessment of the nature and extent of pollution, exposure to it, and its pathways, risks and remedies."[487] Despite the rather weak obligation "to endeavour" to pursue those programmes, the provision demonstrates the need to gain comprehensive knowledge not only on the polluting substance itself but also with its interactions and causation with the marine environment. Furthermore, the data gained through scientific research and programmes as envisaged by Art. 200 UNCLOS should then be used to establish "appropriate scientific criteria for the formulation and elaboration of rules, standards and recommended practices and procedures for the prevention, reduction and control of pollution of the marine environment."[488] The importance of Art. 200 and 201 UNCLOS vis-à-vis marine litter is not only the reference

484 Art. 197 UNCLOS.

485 Art. 200 and 201 UNCLOS.

486 Art. 200 sent.1 UNCLOS.

487 Art. 200 sent.2 UNCLOS.

488 Art. 201 UNCLOS. See also Part XIII UNCLOS on marine scientific research, in particular section 2.

to the prevailing knowledge gap, but its role as a legal basis to introduce scientific research and joint research programmes in global and regional contexts.

VII. Marine litter considerations in semi-enclosed seas under UNCLOS

In its environmental protection regulatory scope, UNCLOS identifies an additional concept that is based on the notion of regionalisation. The underlying motivation to include this norm is to address the inherent vulnerabilities towards anthropogenic impacts in so-called enclosed or semi-enclosed seas.[489] This is even more interesting in that all four Regional Seas that are particularly considered in this study are either entirely or partially considered as an enclosed or semi-enclosed sea.[490] Enclosed or semi-enclosed seas are defined in Art. 122 UNCLOS as "a gulf, basin or sea surrounded by two or more States and connected to another sea or the ocean by a narrow outlet or consisting entirely or primarily of the territorial seas and exclusive economic zones of two or more coastal States." Despite legal uncertainties relating both to the relation between the two types of enclosed seas and the exact addressees of the norm,[491] the introduction of

489 *Posselt,* Umweltschutz in umschlossenen und halbumschlossenen Meeren, 1995, 29.

490 Whereas the Mediterranean, the Black and Baltic Sea are in their entirety considered as semi-enclosed seas: *Treves,* Regional Approaches to the Protection of the Marine Environment, in *Nordquist/Moore/Mahmoudi,* The Stockholm declaration and law of the marine environment (2003) 137–154, 139, the North–East Atlantic is included by virtue of reference to the North Sea: *UN*, UN/ECLAC, LC/CAR/L. 24, Major issues in the management of enclosed or semi-enclosed seas, with a particular reference to the Caribbean Sea, 18.11.2004, 1.

491 During the negotiations towards adopting UNCLOS, the issue of semi-enclosed seas remained controversial. This was also due to the determination of the concepts or region since the political *status quo* at that time was also coined by ideological regionalism. See for an account of possible outcomes: *Alexander,* Ocean Development & International Law 2 (1974) 151. *Treves* argues that region refers to "maritime" regions rather than "land" regions *Treves,* Regional Approaches to the Protection of the Marine Environment, in *Nordquist/Moore/Mahmoudi,* The Stockholm declaration and law of the marine environment (2003) 137–154, 139. Also, the differentiation between semi - and enclosed seas has been subject to legal discussion: *Posselt,* Umweltschutz in umschlossenen und halbumschlossenen Meeren, 1995, 25. A particular aspect in this regard is the freedom of navigation in these seas which has been subject of discussion dur-

specific norms dedicated to this topic emphasises the importance of adopting specific rules under UNCLOS.[492]

Those riparian States around an enclosed or semi-enclosed sea according to Art. 122 UNCLOS "should co-operate" directly with each other or by means of regional organisations. This in particular refers to four areas of co-operation that are listed in Art. 123 UNCLOS. Amongst others the co-operation extends to "the rights and duties with respect to the protection and preservation of the marine environment" and the "scientific research policies."[493] Also highly relevant in this context is the reference to the co-operation with other "interested States or international organisations" as outlined in Art. 123 (d) UNCLOS. The reference to the protection of the marine environment consequently also includes the sources of pollution as entailed in Part XII UNCLOS. However, *Treves* highlights that judging from the provisions, UNCLOS emphasises a regional approach particularly regarding land-based sources.[494]

VIII. Preliminary conclusion

UNCLOS is based on a zonation approach which does not necessarily reflect the complexity and interactions of the marine ecosystem. However, the particular environmental protection approach clearly indicates that UNCLOS in principle encompasses and considers the challenge arising out of the regulation of the marine environment. UNCLOS is the legal framework which structures any marine litter regulatory measures that refer in a broad sense to the law of the sea. Generally, "the subject of ocean governance is extremely broad, potentially involving an analysis of the in-

---

ing the negotiations of UNCLOS: *Posselt,* Umweltschutz in umschlossenen und halbumschlossenen Meeren, 1995, 26.

492 *Milan,* Archiv des Völkerrechts 25 (1987) 92, 94.

493 Art. 123 (b and c) UNCLOS respectively. Art. 123 (a) UNCLOS refers to the management, conservation, exploration and exploitation of the living resources of the sea.

494 *Treves,* Regional Approaches to the Protection of the Marine Environment, in *Nordquist/Moore/Mahmoudi,* The Stockholm declaration and law of the marine environment (2003) 137–154, 138. However, UNCLOS does not rule out regional co-operation with regard to vessel-based pollution, see only the pertinent provisions in the Helsinki Convention and Port State Control, *ibid.*, 140 *et seq.*

teraction among a large number of legal and policy instruments, as well as global and regional organizations and other bodies."[495]

The understanding of what constitutes pollution under UNCLOS has repercussions on the discussion of marine litter. A categorization of the different regulatory aspects leads to the conclusion that UNCLOS does not necessarily follow a substance-based approach, but rather that of a source-based approach. This approach automatically allows for a progressive and wide material scope that integrates newly emerging pollutants. Three aspects of marine litter regulation are of central importance in UNCLOS. First, it encompasses all sources of pollutants as well as substances. However, the regulatory framework on land-based pollution is substantially less rigid than ocean-based pollution sources. Even though States are under the obligation to control pollution emanating from their territory, neighbouring States enjoy very limited capacity to intervene with regard to transboundary pollution. Second, it redistributes and redefines the balance of prescriptive and enforcement powers between coastal, port and flag States. This aspect is in particular important with regard to the enforcement of standards relating to ocean-based activities such as dumping and shipping that are also sources of marine litter. With a view to ensure compliance with environmental protection standards, it has been argued that strengthening port State jurisdiction and Port State Control is an important parameter. This is necessary since flag State jurisdiction has not been effectively applied in the past. Third, it contains co-operation clauses that relate to the transboundary impact of marine litter. As will be demonstrated later in this study, UNCLOS forms the legal basis for a set of measures at the international implementation level, but also in the setting of regional measures.[496]

495 *De La Fayette,* The Role of the United Nations in International Ocean Governance, in *Freestone/Barnes/Ong,* The law of the sea (2006) 63–74, 63.

496 See for example on the role of port reception facilities of vessel-based pollution in the Baltic Sea and the European Union, section B.II.2.a. of chapter 3 and section B.VII.6.of chapter 4 respectively.

D. The implementation and substantiation of environmental standards in public international law

Due to the broad range of pertinent treaties that regulate aspects of the prevention of the introduction of marine litter, a selection of treaties must be made which address the outlined research questions in a problem based manner. The following agreements were selected with a view to their scope in regulating the prevention of the introduction of marine litter. Consequently, three agreements will be analysed: these are MARPOL, as an instrument addressing vessel-based pollution; the London Convention and the London Protocol, as instruments covering dumping and finally, the Global Programme of Action for the Protection of the Marine Environment from Land-Based Activities (GPA).[497]

I. International Convention for the Prevention of Pollution from Ships, as modified by the Protocol of 1978 relating thereto (MARPOL)

In the following it will be analysed whether MARPOL as the "pre-eminent international convention" [498] covering the prevention of vessel-based accidental and operational pollution meets the requirements for an adequate protection standard that contributes to prevent the introduction of marine litter.[499] MARPOL superseded the Convention on the Prevention of Pollution of the Sea by Oil and is distinguished by a broad regulatory scope that not only aims to protect the marine environment from oil pollution but covers several aspects of vessel-based pollution.[500]

---

497 *UN*, UNEP(OCA)/LBA/IG.2/7, Global Programme of Action for the Protection of the Marine Environment from land-based Activities (GPA), Intergovernmental Conference to adopt a Global Programme of Action for the Protection of the Marine Environment from Land-Based Activities, 05.12.1995.

498 *Gold,* Gard Handbook on Protection of the Marine Environment, 2006, 201.

499 *Gold,* Gard Handbook on Protection of the Marine Environment, 2006, 201.

500 *Tan,* Vessel-source marine pollution, 2006, 129; *Birnie/Boyle/Redgwell,* International law and the environment, 2009, 402; *Gold,* Gard Handbook on Protection of the Marine Environment, 2006, 201, see also section D.I. of this chapter. MARPOL addresses pollution by oil (Annex I), pollution by noxious liquid substances in bulk (Annex II), pollution by harmful substances carried by sea in packaged form (Annex III), pollution by sewage from ships (Annex IV), pollution by garbage (Annex V) and air pollution from ships (Annex VI).

The general obligation arising under MARPOL is "[...] to prevent the pollution of the marine environment by the discharge of harmful substances or effluents containing such substances in contravention of the Convention."[501] The scope of the convention is broad which is exemplified by the definition of what constitutes discharge, as "any release howsoever caused from a ship and includes any escape, disposal, spilling, leaking, pumping, emitting and emptying."[502] In order to distinguish between other forms of marine pollution it is furthermore defined that discharge in the context of MARPOL does not include:

(i) dumping within the meaning of the Convention on the Prevention of Marine Pollution by Dumping of Wastes and other Matter, done at London on 13 November 1972; or
(ii) release of harmful substances directly arising from the exploration, exploitation and associated offshore processing of sea-bed mineral resources; or
(iii) release of harmful substances for purposes of legitimate scientific research into pollution abatement or control. [503]

Accidental pollution is equally covered under MARPOL and is "an event involving actual or probable discharge into the sea of a harmful substance or effluents containing such a substance" (Art. 2 (6) MARPOL 73). Most interestingly, MARPOL has introduced the threshold of "harmful substance" which establishes a limit as to when a substance is harmful to the marine environment. This approach is indicative of a preventive/precautionary spirit. The provided definition of harmful substance entails three elements that demonstrate the causation between the discharged substance and the adverse effect, these are: hazard for human health, harm to living resources and marine life and damage to amenities or to interfere with other legitimate uses of the sea.[504]

---

501 Art. 1 MARPOL.

502 Art. 2 (3) (a) MARPOL.

503 Art. 2 (3) (b) MARPOL.

504 Art. 2 (2) MARPOL 73. The definition reads as follows: "any substance which, if introduced into the sea, is liable to create hazards to human health, to harm living resources and marine life, to damage amenities or to interfere with other legitimate uses of the sea, and includes any substance subject to control by the present Convention.".

A ship in the context of the Convention is “a vessel of any type whatsoever operating in the marine environment and includes hydrofoil boats, air-cushion vehicles, submersible, floating craft and fixed or floating platforms.”[505] The inclusion of this broad scope of types of vessels potentially strengthens the protection regime as each category of vessels could also contribute to the introduction of marine litter even though this might not yet have been proven or known.

The material obligations regarding the prevention of pollution from ships are substantiated in the Annexes that form, in conjunction with Art.I MARPOL, an integral part of the Protocol. MARPOL Annex V on pollution by garbage from ships is consequently an integral part of MARPOL, however its status as an “optional annex” signifies that States may opt not to be bound by its provisions.[506] Currently, 144 States are bound by MARPOL Annex V representing 98.47% of the world tonnage.[507] In the following, the material scope of MARPOL Annex V will be analysed with a view to its regulatory technique in preventing pollution by accidental and operational ship waste. It is important to outline that MARPOL Annex V was amended in 2011, which entered in force on 1 January 2013.[508] The amendments made in regard to the issue of marine litter are significant and will be highlighted in the following.[509] In so doing, a comparison (where

505 Art. 21 MARPOL.

506 Art. 14 (1) MARPOL. MARPOL Annexes III and IV are equally optional annexes. *Bang* argues that only MARPOL Annex I and II can be considered as GAIRS under UNCLOS: *Bang,* Journal of Maritime Law & Commerce 40 (2009) 291, 299.

507 *IMO*, Summary of Status of Conventions as at 09.01.2013, http://www.imo.org/About/Conventions/StatusOfConventions/Pages/Default.aspx, last accessed 27.08.2015.

508 MARPOL Annex V entered in force on 31.12.1988 and has been amended in 1989 (MEPC 28/4, Annex 2); 1994 (MP/CONF.2/8; 1995 (MEPC Resolution 37/22/Add.1, Annex 13); 2000 (MEPC 45/20, Annex 3); 2004 (MEPC 51/22, Annex 6) and 2011 (Resolution MEPC.201(62), Amendments to the Annex of the Protocol of 1978 relating to the International Convention for the Prevention of Pollution from ships, 1973, Revised MARPOL Annex V, 15.07.2011).

509 In the amendment towards Annex V, the non-governmental organization Clean-Shipping Coalition argued that “to illustrate this enforcement and compliance problem one needs only to look at the existing situation in respect of plastics. The discharge of plastic has been prohibited by MARPOL Annex V for many years, yet on most beaches, and certainly on any that are close to a shipping route, it is easy to find plastic items which are strongly related to shipping; e.g., synthetic ropes, nets, cans, etc. A prohibition on the discharge of plastics exists but the reg-

possible) will be made between MARPOL Annex V 2004 version and the amended version of 2011.

1. MARPOL Annex V Regulations for the prevention of pollution by garbage from ships

MARPOL ANNEX V is the only worldwide applicable instrument explicitly addressing a known (point) source of marine litter.[510] It contains four fundamental elements that determine the protection standard in relation to the disposal of garbage by ships. These are the discharge standards of garbage from ships, the reception facilities of ship waste in ports, operational obligations such as the keeping of garbage record book and Port State Control. The pollution protection regime afforded by MARPOL Annex V is not only limited, as perhaps one might well reasonably have been inclined to do, to the disposed waste itself. Rather a further factor determining the specific protection regime is the area of the sea in which the activity occurred. MARPOL Annex V promulgates a general discharge prohibition that varies depending on the discharge location and type of waste. The discharge location of the ship waste is a determining factor as Regulation 6 MARPOL Annex V in conjunction with regulation 1 (14) MARPOL Annex V prescribes special discharge requirements for so-called "Special Areas" and areas outside of these Special Areas.

---

ulations in the existing Annex V are such that illegal discharging has continued, and in our view the proposed revised Annex V has not adequately addressed the issues that have allowed this to happen": *IMO*, MEPC 62/6/2, Issues arising from the Committee's work on the revision of MARPOL Annex V, sub-mitted by the Clean Shipping Coalition (CSC), 23.05.2011, 5. See for an overview on the role of non-governmental organisations in international organisations relating to maritime aspects: *Suarez,* Towards sustainable Ocean Development: The Particpation and Contribution of Non-governmental Organisations to the Work of International Organizations in the Ocean Sector, in *Ehlers/Lagoni,* International maritime organisations and their contribution towards a sustainable marine development (2006) 53–75.

510 It is submitted that shipping is in essence a diffuse point source. A single polluting vessel is a point source; however the cumulative and non-attributable effects of several polluting vessels that are not sanctioned render it "diffuse", see chapter 2. Nevertheless, the labeling in this regard has no legal implications.

a) Role of the distinction between special areas and outside Special Areas under MARPOL Annex V for the regulation of marine litter

The area–based management approach followed by MARPOL Annex V makes a distinction between areas outside of and within Special Areas.[511] Simply put, if an area is not considered a Special Area as stipulated in regulation 14 MARPOL Annex V, the specific discharge requirements for areas outside of Special Areas apply.[512] A Special Area is defined as "a sea area where for recognised technical reasons in relation to its oceanographic and ecological condition and to particular character of its traffic the adoption of special mandatory methods for the prevention of sea pollution by garbage is required."[513] In regard to the study at hand, these Spe-

511 Another area-based instrument that is available under the IMO scope is the concept of Particularly Sensitive Sea Areas (PSSA). It is defined as "an area that needs special protection through action by IMO because of its significance for recognised ecological, socio-economic, or scientific attributes where such attributes may be vulnerable to damage by international shipping activities": *IMO*, Assembly resolution A 24/Res.982, Assembly Resolution on Revised Guidelines for the Identification and Designation of Particularly Sensitive Sea Areas, adopted on 01. December 2005, 06.02.2006, para.1.2 (PSSA Guidelines). Whether an area can be designated is a case-by-case decision in which the MEPC is the primary platform. An area can be designated as a PSSA after it has been demonstrated that is fulfills one of the eligibility criteria (PSSA Guidelines, para.4) and demonstrate vulnerability of impacts from shipping (PSSA Guidelines, para.5). If a PSSA is established, so-called associated protective measures can be adopted, that could include ship routeing measures, discharge restrictions (such as arising under MARPOL) and prohibited activities such as mandatory no anchoring areas. Marine litter considerations potentially fall under the PSSA regime, in the context of measures relating to discharge standards or the prevention of accidents. See for a comprehensive discussion on this topic: *Kachel,* Particularly sensitive sea areas, 2008.

512 A similar area-based management approach is also pursued in other MARPOL Annexes. As an example, MARPOL Annex VI regulates air pollution from ships in emission control areas "[…] where the adoption of special mandatory measures for emissions from ships is required to prevent, reduce and control air pollution from NO_{X} or SO_{X} […]" (Regulation 2 (8) MARPOL Annex VI). The "clearly defined areas" as stipulated in Art. 211 (6) UNCLOS are not necessarily limited to MARPOL Special Areas provisions. Whereas "[o]riginally Article 211 (6) UNCLOS may have been primarily related to the MARPOL […] special areas provisions", its broad wording also allows for "discharge and CDEM standards, and navigational measures […]": *Molenaar,* Coastal State Jurisdiction over Vessel-Source Pollution, 1998, 405.

cial Areas are of particular importance as several the European Seas are considered as Special Areas: the Mediterranean Sea,[514] the Baltic Sea,[515] the Black Sea[516] and the North Sea.[517] Consequently, the North-East Atlantic as one of the areas to which further attention is devoted within this study, is only partially designated as a Special Area under MARPOL Annex V.

The coming into effect of the specific obligations of a Special Area under MARPOL Annex V is linked to two requirements that must be fulfilled: more restrictive discharge standards and adequate port reception facilities along the coast of the sea area that are adequately designed to receive the specific garbage.[518] The existence of port reception facilities in

513 Regulation 14 MARPOL Annex V. The procedural steps for the designation of a special area under MARPOL were originally outlined in a guidelines that addressed both special areas under MARPOL as well as the Particularly Sensitive Sea Area in Assembly resolution A. 720 (1) (1991) that was subsequently amended by Assembly resolution A. 927(22): *IMO*, MEPC 63/9, Identification and Protection of Special Areas and Particularly Sensitive Sea Areas, Consequential amendments to the Guidelines for the Designation of Special Areas under MARPOL, 25.11.2011.

514 The Mediterranean is included with regard to its "proper sea and the gulfs and seas therein that are limited in the East in regard to the Black Sea by the 41∘N parallel and in the West by the Strait of Gibraltar at meridian 5∘36 ′W", Regulation 1 (14.1) MARPOL Annex V.

515 The Baltic Sea Special Area extends to the proper sea, the Gulf of Bothnia as well as the Gulf of Finland and its open access to the North-Sea is defined by the parallel of the Skaw in the Skagerrak at 57∘44.8′N", Regulation 1 (14.2) MARPOL Annex V. This definition differs slightly to the definition of the Baltic Sea as used in the Helsinki Convention which states that the Skaw in the Skagerrak is defined at 57°44.43′N (Art. 1, sent. 1 Helsinki Convention).

516 The Black Sea is the "proper Black Sea and its boundary to the Mediterranean is determined by the parallel 41∘N", Regulation 1 (14.3) MARPOL Annex V. The special status is not in force.

517 The North Sea is also a Special Area under MARPOL Annex V and includes the "proper North Sea which is defined by the following boundaries: southwards of latitude 62∘N and eastwards of longitude 4∘W; the Skagerrak forms the eastward boundary east of the Skaw by latitude 57∘44.8′N and the English Channel and its approaches eastwards of longitude 5∘W and northwards of latitude 48∘30′N.F", Regulation 1 (14.6.1-3) MARPOL Annex V. Also, the Gulfs area, the Red Sea, the Wider Caribbean Region and the Antarctic Area are covered under the Special Area regime of MARPOL Annex V.

518 Regulation 5 (4) (a and b) MARPOL Annex V in conjunction with Regulation 7 (1) MARPOL Annex V. The adoption of the Mediterranean, the Baltic Sea and the Black Seas as a Special Area under MARPOL Annex V was on 2 November

all ports must be notified by MARPOL Contracting Parties along the bordering coast in order that the increased protection for the Special Area will take effect.[519] In the European context this lack of notification signifies that the MARPOL Annex V Special Areas requirements have not come into effect for the Black Sea.[520] This necessitates a further comparative analysis between the protection standards of areas within and outside the Special Areas under MARPOL Annex V.

b) Discharge standards

Notwithstanding this specific regional protection approach, the overall protection standard of MARPOL Annex V in regard to the introduction of waste can be considered as comprehensive and adequate as the disposal at sea of "all garbage" is generally prohibited.[521] In order to ensure legal certainty, garbage is defined as

> all kinds of food wastes, domestic wastes and operational wastes, all plastics, cargo residues, cooking oil, fishing gear, and animal carcasses generated during the normal operation of the ship and liable to be disposed of continuously or periodically except those substances which are defined or listed in other Annexes to the present Convention.[522]

This newly introduced definition of garbage and the listing of the constituent elements of garbage provides for an increases legal certainty and

---

1973. The adoption of the North-Sea was on 17 October 1989. The entry in force of the Special Areas under MARPOL Annex V of Mediterranean, the Baltic Sea and the Black Sea was 31 December 1988. The entry in force of the North Sea Special Area under MARPOL Annex V was on 18 February 1991: *IMO*, Special Areas under MARPOL, http://www.imo.org/OurWork/Environment/Pollution-Prevention/SpecialAreasUnderMARPOL/Pages/Default.aspx, last accessed 27.08.2015.

519 Regulation 5 (4) (b) MARPOL Annex V.

520 *IMO*, Special Areas under MARPOL, last accessed 27.08.2015.

521 Regulation 3 (1) (a) MARPOL Annex V.

522 Regulation 1 (9) MARPOL Annex V.

facilitated interpretation.[523] Furthermore, the inclusion of food waste,[524] domestic waste[525] and cargo residues[526] is aimed at harmonising the definition used in all MARPOL Annexes and to contribute to clear and transparent concepts.[527] A particular important aspect is that plastic has also been defined:

> Plastic means a solid material which contains as an essential ingredient one or more synthetic organic high polymers and which is formed (shaped) during either manufacture of the polymer or the fabrication into a finished product by heat and/or pressure. Plastics have material properties ranging from hard and brittle to soft and elastic.[528]

The inclusion of a definition of plastic into MARPOL Annex V, indicates that the Contracting Parties have recognised the importance of this source material for the marine environment.[529] Also, this indicates that the ad-

---

523 The former version of garbage of MARPOL Annex V was defined as: "all kinds of victual, domestic and operational waste excluding from fish and parts thereof, generated during normal operation of the ship and liable to be disposed of continuously or periodically except those substances which are defined or listed in other Annexes to the present Convention." See for example: IMO, MEPC 58/6/5, Interpretations of and amendments of MARPOL and related instruments, status Report on the Review of MARPOL Annex V, 01.08.2008, para. 22.

524 Regulation 1 (8) MARPOL Annex V: "Food waste means any spoiled or unspoiled food substance and includes fruits, vegetables, dairy products, poultry, meat products and food scraps generated aboard ship.".

525 Regulation 1 (4) MARPOL Annex V: "Domestic wastes means all types of wastes not covered by other Annexes that are generated in the accommodation spaces on board the ship. Domestic wastes do not include grey water.".

526 Regulation 1 (2) MARPOL Annex V: "cargo Residues means the remnants of any cargo which are not covered by other Annexes to the present Convention and which remain on the deck or in holds following loading or unloading, including loading and unloading excessed or spillage, whether in wet or dry condition or entrained in wash water but does not include cargo dust remaining on the deck after sweeping or dust on the external surfaces of the ship.".

527 *IMO*, MEPC 58/6/5, Interpretations of and amendments of MARPOL and related instruments, status Report on the Review of MARPOL Annex V, 01.08.2008, para.22; *IMO*, MEPC 61/7/2, Interpretations of, and amendments to, MARPOL and other related instruments, Report of the Correspondence Group for the Review of MARPOL Annex V, submitted by New Zealand, 28.06.2010, 3.

528 Regulation 1 (11) MARPOL Annex V.

529 See only the Report of the Correspondence Group for the Review of MARPOL Annex V in which estimations of the extent of the marine litter problem has been depicted, also with a view to plastics: *IMO*, MEPC 59/6/3, Interpretations of and

verse consequences of plastic as a major percentage of marine litter are acknowledged.

Moreover, the newly introduced definition of fishing gear[530] is highly pertinent as it is often referred to in the context of the discussion on marine litter.[531] With a view to the particular challenge of ghost nets, IMO therefore skilfully exercises its competences as the regulation of on board ship waste is covered by its statues, whereas fisheries management such as the use of certain types of nets does not fall under its mandate.

In respect of these categories and definitions, the basic premise enumerated in MARPOL Annex V is that the disposal of all garbage at sea is prohibited with the exception of certain discharges that are due to accidental loss or aimed to ensure the safety of the ship or the crew.[532] While the MARPOL Annex V 2004 version provided for a general prohibition of "all plastics", the material scope of permitted disposal outside of the Special Areas was significantly wider as it included amongst others the disposal of dunnage, linen, metal, bottles and crockery.[533] The protection regime after the 2011 amendment of MARPOL Annex V was significantly strengthened. Accordingly, regulation 1 (9) MARPOL Annex V, in conjunction with regulation 3 MARPOL Annex V, applies an approach for ar-

---

amendments to MARPOL and related Instruments, Report of the Correspondence Group for the Review of MARPOL Annex V, 02.04.2009, 6 *et seq*.

530 Regulation 1 (6) MARPOL Annex V : "Fishing gear means any physical device or part thereof or combination of items that may be placed on or in the water or on the sea-bed with the intended purpose of capturing, or controlling for subsequent capture or harvesting, marine or fresh water organisms.".

531 *IMO*, MEPC 54/21, Report of the Marine Environment Protection Committee on its Fifty-Fourth Session, 27.02.3006, 54; *IMO*, MEPC 59/6/14, Interpretations of, and Amendments to, MARPOL and related Instruments, comments on the Report of the Correspondence Group for the Review of MARPOL Annex V, 22.05.2009, 1.

532 Regulation 7 MARPOL Annex V.

533 Under MARPOL Annex V 2004 version, a further distinction of permitted material for disposal is made between on the one hand dunnage, lining and packing materials that float and on the other hand food waste and all other garbage including paper products, rags, glass, metal bottles, crockery and similar refuse. Whereas both categories shall be disposed of "as far as practicable from the nearest land," a certain minimum distance from land had to be maintained. With a view to the category of dunnage and packing material this amounts to 25 nautical miles from the nearest land, while food wastes and all other garbage such as glass, metal and crockery can be disposed of 12 nautical miles from land after it has been passed through a comminuter or grinder.

eas outside Special Areas under MARPOL Annex V that is broadly comparable to the scope of protection of the Special Areas in MARPOL Annex V 2004 version.[534]

Consequently, ships outside Special Areas may only discharge "where practicable" cargo residues, food waste, cleaning agents and carcasses of animals[535] while the ship is en route and abides to a minimum distance to the nearest land.[536] With a view to the discharge permitted within Special Areas under MARPOL Annex V the substances allowed are reduced to ground or comminuted food waste that is not contaminated, cargo residues contained in wash water and cleaning agents.[537] The latter two substances may only be introduced in case both are not harmful to the environment and if the ports of departure and destination are within a Special Area and have no adequate port reception facilities. Generally, when garbage is

---

534 Accordingly, regulation 5 (2) MARPOL Annex V 2004 version prohibited the discharge of all plastic as well as of other garbage except of food wastes that has been entered through a grinder into the special areas under MARPOL Annex V.

535 The issue of animal carcasses has been during the negotiations to the amended MARPOL Annex V a very controversial topic and was in its original form considered as falling under the scope of the London Convention or London Protocol. Due to question of practicability such as the time aspect in applying for a dumping permission under the London Convention or London Protocol and the consequential hygienic aspect, the Correspondence Group decided to include the discharge of animal carcasses in MARPOL Annex V: *IMO*, MEPC 59/6/3, Interpretations of and amendments to MARPOL and related Instruments, Report of the Correspondence Group for the Review of MARPOL Annex V, 02.04.2009, 15; *IMO*, MEPC 61/7/2, Interpretations of, and amendments to, MARPOL and other related instruments, Report of the Correspondence Group for the Review of MARPOL Annex V, submitted by New Zealand, 28.06.2010, 3.

536 Regulation 4 MARPOL Annex V. In this regard, a distinction is made between ground or comminuted food waste whereby ground food waste that passes through a screen with openings no greater than 25 mm may be discharge with a distance of at least 3 sea miles from land and not ground food waste 12 sea miles from land. Cargo residues contained in wash water may be discharged from a distance of at least 12 sea miles from land and "as far as practicable". Carcasses of animals that are carried on board as cargo and which have died during the journey may be discharge as far as possible from the nearest land.

537 Regulation 6 MARPOL Annex V. During the negotiations of the revised MARPOL Annex V, the issue of cleaning agents or additives contained in deck washing was discussed among Contracting Parties to be considered as garbage: *IMO*, MEPC 61/7/2, Interpretations of, and amendments to, MARPOL and other related instruments, Report of the Correspondence Group for the Review of MARPOL Annex V, submitted by New Zealand, 28.06.2010, 5.

mixed or contaminated by other substances that are subject to a different discharge requirement as defined by the Annex, the more stringent requirement prevails.[538]

c) Operational requirements under MARPOL

In order to be able to control and manage the onboard generated waste, MARPOL Annex V requires that provision be made for a system of waste management on board.[539] The specific operative duties under which a vessel operates is based on the size of the vessels, measured both by length as well as gross tonnage regarding the operative duties. First, ships of a minimum length of 12 m or fixed and floated platforms must display placards that advise of the pertinent discharge obligations and that are written in the working language of the ship´s crew or when necessary in English, French or Spanish in order to inform staff as well as passengers on the discharge requirements.[540] Every ship of a minimum of 100 gross tonnages and every ship that is certified to carry more than 15 persons and fixed or floating platforms are obliged to carry a Garbage Management Plan.[541]

The plan shall "provide written procedures for minimizing, collecting, storing, processing and disposing of garbage including the use of the equipment on board."[542] In order to further substantiate the provisions made in regulation 10 MARPOL Annex V, Guidelines for the development of Garbage Management Plans are established that contain information on procedures on collecting and processing garbage.[543] The approach

538 Regulation 4 (3) and 6 (4) MARPOL Annex V.

539 Regulation 10 MARPOL ANNEX V.

540 The requirement to write the placards in English, French or Spanish is necessary when the ships lay to ports that are under the jurisdiction of other Parties of the Convention.

541 In the MARPOL Annex V 2004 version, the trigger point for developing a garbage management plan was for vessels of 400 gross tonnage and above (Regulation 9 (2)). The reduction in the gross tonnage is to be welcomed as according to the motto "every little helps", the quantity of ships required to develop waste management on boards is increased. Whether and what kind of effect the waste management plans have in regard to preventing the introduction will be analysed in the following.

542 Regulation 10 (2) MARPOL Annex V.

543 The amendment of MARPOL Annex V is accompanied by the amendment of the Guidelines for the Implementation of MARPOL Annex V (adopted by Resolu-

used by the Guidelines on Garbage Management Plans is distinguished by complementary techniques to manage garbage that include the reduction at the source, onboard processing, the discharge into the sea in case permitted and the landing of garbage in port reception facilities.[544] Furthermore in relation to regulation 10 (2) MARPOL Annex V, the guidelines provide further information regarding the person in charge of carrying out the plan.

Additionally, every ship of 400 gross tonnages or more, every ship that is certified to carry more than 15 persons that travels to ports or offshores terminals that are under the jurisdiction of another Party to the Convention as well as every fixed or floating platform shall have a Garbage Record Book.[545] Every incineration or discharge either in the sea or in reception facilities must be recorded in this book. MARPOL Annex V outlines clear requirements in regard to the form of the Garbage Record Book that is specified in an appendix to MARPOL Annex V as well as regarding the language and concrete information contained in it.[546] Regarding the exceptions to the discharge prohibitions made under regulation 7 MARPOL Annex V, these shall also be entered into the Garbage Record Book. Similar requirements are also on ships of less than 400 gross tonnages which shall in the case of discharges or accidental losses note these in the ship´s official log-book with a reference to the measures taken to prevent or minimise the risk of discharge or accidental loss.[547] A stricter requirement is imposed on the accidental loss or discharge of fishing gear subject to regulation 7 (1) (3 and 4) MARPOL Annex V. This shall be reported to the

tion MEPC .219(63), 02.03.2012) and the Guidelines for the development of Garbage Management Plans (adopted by Resolution MEPC .220(63), 02.03.2012). For this purpose an Intersessional Correspondence Group was established during MEPC 62 in 2010: *IMO*, MEPC 63/7, Report of the Intersessional Correspondence Group on Reviewing the Guidelines for the Implementation of MARPOL Annex V and the Guidelines for the Development of Garbage Management Plans, 25.11.2011.

544 Paragraph 3.1. Guidelines for the development of Garbage Management Plans.

545 Regulation 3 MARPOL Annex V.

546 Regulation 10 (3) (1 and 2) MARPOL Annex V.

547 Regulation 19 (4) MARPOL Annex V. The issue of obliging vessels of 100 gross tonnages or more to keep Garbage Record Books was discussed in the Correspondence Group in the context of lost fishing gears. However the proposal was not supported: *IMO*, MEPC 59/6/3, Interpretations of and amendments to MARPOL and related Instruments, Report of the Correspondence Group for the Review of MARPOL Annex V, 02.04.2009, Annex 2, 2.

flag ship State and, in case it is located in waters under jurisdiction of a coastal State, also to this State.[548] This newly included provision reflects the growing concern about the impacts of lost fisheries on the marine environment and navigation. The Garbage Record Book can be used during inspection while the ship is in ports or offshore terminals to control whether the MARPOL Annex V provisions have been adhered to. As an example, the port authority can retrace the last discharge of garbage in ports or sea and can estimate whether the indicated quantity of remaining waste on board is realistic with a view to the time passed on sea.

d) Port reception facilities

The third element in the regulatory regime of MARPOL Annex V are port reception facilities of ship waste that receive the onboard generated waste. The role of port reception facilities plays an important part in the compliance with discharge requirements. Consequently, the making available of port reception facilities contributes to the prevention of the discharge of waste into the marine environment. In the regime of MARPOL ANNEX V, the presence of adequate port reception facilities is an integral precondition for higher protection standards in the form of the designation of Special Areas under MARPOL Annex V.[549] However, neither port reception facilities nor the "adequacy" of port reception facilities are directly defined or regulated in the MARPOL provisions itself, which amounts to an expression of "a serious and deliberate deficiency in the regime formation process […]."[550] The lack of concepts and understanding of the role of ports States in port reception facilities has been the subject of controversial discussions within IMO.[551] Generally, the fundamental understanding of port reception facilities is based on an interplay between ships ad-

---

548 Regulation 10 (6) MARPOL Annex V.

549 Port Reception facilities are not defined in MARPOL Annex V, but a definition is provided in: *IMO*, MEPC.1/Circ.67, Guide to Good Practice for Port Reception Facility Providers and Users and "refers to any fixed, floating or mobile facility capable of receiving MARPOL residues/wastes from ships and fit for that purpose" (para. 12).

550 *Tan,* Vessel-source marine pollution, 2006, 265.

551 *IMO*, Comprehensive manual on port reception facilities, 1999, 15 ; *Tan,* Vessel-source marine pollution, 2006, 256.

hering to discharge standards and coastal States providing reception facilities for the ship waste.[552]

The disposition of adequate port reception facilities has not comprehensively been pursued due to concerns of ports and States that the incidental costs on the ship operators using those facilities may impact the ports' or States' competitiveness.[553] In the context of MARPOL Annex V, the facilities must be adapted to receive the garbage "without causing undue delay to ships and according to the ships using them."[554] The criteria used to assess the adequacy of a port reception facility are outlined in MEPC resolution.83 (44) on Guidelines for ensuring the adequacy of port waste reception facilities according to which a reception facility is adequate "when mariners use it; it entirely meets the needs of the ships regularly using it; do not provide mariners with a disincentive to use them; and contribute to the improvement of the marine environment."[555]

On the basis of these rather broad and vague criteria of the definition of adequacy, one can conclude that MARPOL does not stipulate any concrete prescriptive requirements for port reception facilities. It is interesting to note that MARPOL Annex V does not directly oblige ships to dispose of their generated waste in port reception facilities. Whereas MARPOL Annex V provisions require under certain conditions an obligation to carry a

---

552 *Tan,* Vessel-source marine pollution, 2006, 253.

553 *Ibid.*, 255 *et seq*. According to *Tan*, "unfortunately states have consistently ignored their obligation to provide adequate reception facilities in ports. Instead, their response to growing environmental pressure has been to tighten further the regulations on onboard discharges [...]." In order to receive information about inadequate port reception facilities, IMO has issued a standard format for communicating any inadequacies. The consolidated format for reporting alleged inadequacies of port reception facilities was approved by means of MEPC/Circ.215 in September 1988 and revised in 1998 and 2007 respectively: *IMO,* MEPC.1/Circ. 469/Rev. 1, Revised Consolidated Format For Reporting alleged Inadequacies of Port Reception Facilities, 13.07.2007, 1. During the preparation of the amendment procedure, the Correspondence Group on the amendment of MARPOL Annex V stated that the overall consensus was that the provision of adequate port reception facilities is "a function of the broader issue of waste management capacity [...] and for which other UN bodies offer experience and programmes": *IMO*, MEPC 59/6/3, Interpretations of and amendments to MARPOL and related Instruments, Report of the Correspondence Group for the Review of MARPOL Annex V, 02.04.2009, 10.

554 Regulation 8 MARPOL Annex V.

555 *IMO*, Guidelines for ensuring the adequacy of port waste reception facilities, 2000, 5 (Guidelines for ensuring the adequacy of port waste reception facilities).

garbage management plan on board, no reference is made in regard to waste management strategies in the receiving ports. This potential regulatory gap is filled by reference to pertinent non-binding guidance documents.[556] Regarding the waste management in ports, the role of a waste management strategy is stressed, as this is seen "as a powerful tool to establish a coherent system of waste handling practices and facilities [...]."[557] A "waste management strategy is a systematic approach, which outlines how, and by whom, waste is managed."[558] Despite the detailed guidance on waste handling in ports that can be used for interpretation by the Contracting Parties, its mention in non-binding guidance documents could potentially undermine the environmental protection standard that is established by the general discharge prohibition of MARPOL Annex V. The imprecise provisions on port management as outlined by Annex V could, with a view to its implementation on a national level, be problematic as they offer great flexibility and leeway for the implementing Contracting Parties regarding the form of the reception facilities.[559]

e) Port State Control

MARPOL Annex V also relates to Port State Control and operational requirements.[560] This implies that a ship that is in a port or an offshore terminal of another Contracting State can be inspected by authorised officers "concerning operational requirements under this Annex, where there are clear grounds for believing that the master or crew are not familiar with essential shipboard procedures relating to the prevention of pollution by garbage."[561] The specific procedure relating to Port State Control in the

556 See *IMO*, Resolution MEPC.83(44), Guidelines for ensuring the adequacy of port waste reception facilities, 13.04.2000 as contained in Annex 2 of the Report of the Marine Environment Protection Committee on its Forty-Fourth Session, MEPC 44/20, 12.04.2000; *IMO*, Manual on port reception facilities; *IMO*, MEPC.1/Circ.67, Guide to Good Practice for Port Reception Facility Providers and Users, 20.07.2009.

557 *IMO*, Manual on port reception facilities, 34.

558 *Ibid.*

559 See for a detailed study on the development and issues related to port reception facilities in: *Tan,* Vessel-source marine pollution, 2006, 251 *et seq.*

560 Regulation 9 MARPOL Annex V.

561 Regulation 9 MARPOL Annex V.

MARPOL setting is regulated at large in MARPOL and is prefixed in Art. 5 MARPOL Convention.[562] With a view to clarifying aspects of Port State Control in the context of IMO and to guide national authorities, the Contracting Parties of IMO have adopted procedures for Port State Control.[563]

Amongst others the provision "clear grounds" is defined as "evidence that the ship, its equipment or its crew does not correspond substantially with the requirements of the relevant conventions or that the master or crew members are not familiar with essential shipboard procedures relating to the safety of ships or the prevention of pollution."[564] With regard to MARPOL Annex V relevant inspection elements are whether the ship personnel is aware of the elements of the Guidelines for the implementation of MARPOL Annex V such as the reduction of potential garbage or the garbage handling and storage procedures.[565] In case a vessel has been identified as a sub-standard ship that due to its "[…] equipment or operational safety is substantially below the standards required by the relevant convention or whose crew is not in conformance with the safe manning document,"[566] the port State may take action in response.[567]

On a regional level, the Paris MoU on PSC stipulates that each port State establishes an effective control system regarding several internation-

---

562 Regulation 9 (3) MARPOL Annex V.

563 *IMO*, Assembly resolution Res.A.882(21), Procedures for Port State Control, amending Resolution A.787(19), 2001, London, 1. The first resolution relating to Procedures for Port State Control has been adopted in 1981 (IMO, Assembly resolution A.466 (XII) on Procedures for the Control of Ships). Since then, several amendments and resolution were adopted that addressed the issue. The IMO Sub-Committee on Flag State Implementation recommended the development of a single document, a development that resulted in the adoption of Assembly resolution A.787(19) on Procedures for Port State Control, 23.11.1995, this has been amended by Assembly resolution A.882(219 on Amendments to the Procedures for Port State Control, 25.11.1999 and Assembly resolution A.1052(27), Procedures for Port State Control, 20.12.2011 (Procedures for Port State Control).

564 Procedures for Port State Control, 1.7.2. Examples are given that include, *inter alia*, "the absence of principal equipment or arrangements required by the conventions or general impressions or observations that serious deficiencies exist in the safety, pollution prevention or navigational equipment": Procedures for Port State Control, 2.4.2.1.

565 Procedures for Port State Control, Appendix 7, 18.3.1.

566 Procedures for Port State Control, 1.7.10.

567 Procedures for Port State Control, 3.3. Measures could be the detention of ships and procedures for rectification of deficiencies and release.

al agreements.[568] As a basic rule, the national inspective authorities have to achieve 25% of inspections measured against the average number of individual foreign merchant ships entering their ports during the three last calendar years. MARPOL aspects are also covered under the Paris MoU.[569] Consequently, all relevant procedural and material provisions contained in MARPOL have to be examined. This extends also to operational violations of the discharge standards of MARPOL Annex V that integrates vessel-based sources of marine litter. The inspections in the context of the Paris MoU on PSC regarding MARPOL Annex V deficiencies have resulted in 402 finding of deficiencies in 2010, 347 deficiencies in 2011 and 303 deficiencies in 2012.[570] Since these deficiencies relate to procedural obligations arising of MARPOL Annex V, the Paris MoU therefore serves as an enforcement mechanism to reduce the sources of marine litter from vessels.

2. Preliminary Conclusion

The adoption of MARPOL and particularly Annex V both prior and since the amendments thereto constitutes one of the major singular events in addressing marine litter at an early stage. Whereas the discharge standards and the provisions of port reception facilities are important elements in regard to vessel-based pollution, the regime established by MARPOL Annex V has been criticised for not effectively reducing the input of vessel-based pollution. Admittedly, the complex interaction between diverse interests and jurisdiction of coastal, flag and port States along with other

---

568 See for an overview on the elements of the Paris MoU on PSC: *Güner-Özbek,* Paris Memorandum of Understanding- an Example of International Co-operation and its Perspectives, in *Ehlers/Lagoni,* International maritime organisations and their contribution towards a sustainable marine development (2006) 105–134. The Paris MoU on PSC establishes a white, grey and black list of flag State performance; see only Annex 7 Paris MoU in PSC on ship risk profile. The Paris MoU on PSC is not legally binding: *ibid.,* 122. During the negotiations the States preferred a MoU since this ensure a certain degree of practicability when negotiating the instrument itself but also subsequent amendments.

569 *Secretariat Paris MoU on PSC*, The Paris MoU on Port State Control, 01.07.2014, 2.1.6, https://www.parismou.org/system/files/Paris%20MoU%2C%20incl%2037th%20amendment%20%28final%29.pdf, last accessed 27.08.2015.

570 *Secretariat Paris MoU on PSC*, Annual Report 2012, The Hague, 46.

stakeholders such as port authorities, ship owners and registration companies makes for an extremely ambitious undertaking. With this in mind, the revised MARPOL Annex V can be seen as an important step in increasing legal certainty. This is in particular due to the definitions contained therein. However, it is argued that discharge obligations in every port would potentially increase the protection standard. It remains to be seen how and to what degree, the newly revised MARPOL Annex V serves to reduce the introduction of marine litter from vessel-based sources. In this regard, the compliance and control of its material standards are important aspects. Also, the regional implementation of these standards further clarifies the potential role of MARPOL Annex V in preventing the introduction of marine litter from vessel-based pollution. This is possible, since

> MARPOL prescriptive standards are indeed maximum standards in respect of Article 218 jurisdiction and of coastal State jurisdiction exercised beyond territorial waters (and in respect of CDEM matters in the territorial sea), they are minimum standards vis-à-vis port States and coastal State jurisdiction in the territorial sea on non-CDEM matters.[571]

II. The regulation of dumping as a source of marine litter

Dumping is not an isolated activity as it stands in close relationship with "efficient waste management policies and the effective regulation of land-based pollution-based alternatives."[572] The disposal of (primarily) land-based chemical, industrial and radioactive waste into the ocean has previously been pursued in the understanding that the ocean has an endless assimilative capacity for human produced waste.[573] Substances that were considered as being too toxic for direct dumping were either incinerated before being dumped or filled into containers so as to reduce their toxic

571 *BMT Group*, Study on the Economic, Legal, Environmental and Practical Implications of a European Union System to Reduce Ship Emissions of SO2 and NOx, 2000, A4.159.

572 *Frank,* The European Community and marine environmental protection in the international law of the sea, 2007, 308.

573 *Davis,* Marine Policy 14 (1990) 191, 193.

characteristics.[574] Even though some materials were indeed inert to their surroundings, some dumped pollutants such as PCB are still persistent in the oceans[575] and have a direct link to the potential toxicity of marine litter.[576]

The global regulatory regime that addresses dumping[577] as a source of marine pollution is established by the London Convention and the London Protocol.[578] The Contracting Parties to the London Convention adopted the London Protocol in 1996 with a view to bringing the Convention in "line with the modern approach to waste management and emerging principles of international environmental law."[579] Irrespective of the two agreements, the institutional setting is shared, implementing a vision of "two instruments-one family."[580]

The London Convention was elaborated in the understanding "that the capacity of the sea to assimilate wastes and render them harmless, and its ability to regenerate natural resources, is not unlimited."[581] The strategy to

---

574 *Saila,* Marine Pollution Bulletin 2 (1971) 125, 125. In the Baltic Sea, mustard gas was discarded in this fashion. The containers occasionally posed a problem to fishers as some were captured by trawlers.

575 *Davis,* Marine Policy 14 (1990) 191, 193.

576 See for a discussion on this aspect chapter 1.

577 For a review on the development of the dumping regime, see *Frank,* The European Community and marine environmental protection in the international law of the sea, 2007, 288 *et seq.*; *De La Fayette,* The International Journal of Marine and Coastal Law 13 (1998) 515; *Davies,* Marine Pollution Bulletin 19 (1988) 2.

578 See for an overview on the development of these agreements: *VanderZwaag/ Daniel,* International Law and Ocean Dumping: Steering a Precautionary Course Aboard the 1996 London Protocol, but Still an Unfinished Voyage, in *Johnston/ Chircop/McDorman et al.,* The future of ocean regime-building (2009) 515–571, *517 et seq*.

579 *Frank,* The European Community and marine environmental protection in the international law of the sea, 2007, 295.

580 *IMO*, LC 28/15, Report of the Twenty-Eight Consultative Meeting of Contracting Parties to the Convention on the Prevention of Marine Pollution by Dumping of Wastes and Other Matter 1972 and First Meeting of Contracting Parties to the 1996 Protocol to the Convention on the Prevention of Marine Pollution by Dumping of Wastes and Other Matter 1972, 06.12.2006, 12. Even though the documents of the London Convention and the London Protocol refer to the time frame of the meeting, in the following the date of publication of the reports will be used when citing those documents.

581 Preamble, para.2 London Convention (LC). *Brubaker,* Marine pollution and international law, 1993, 74 *et seq.* In 1994, Laughton outlined that with a view to the global waste problem, deep ocean disposal could be a suitable alternative in

regulate dumping has been pursued in a twofold manner. The London Convention pursues a "listing approach" which establishes a dumping prohibition for all substances listed in Annex I ('black list') and in principle allows for the dumping of Annex II and other substances after a prior special or respectively a prior general permit has been issued.[582]

Both the London Convention and London Protocol define dumping as "any deliberate disposal of wastes or other matter from vessels, aircraft, platforms or other man-made structures at sea and any deliberate disposal at sea of vessels, aircraft, platforms or other man-made structures at sea."[583] The London Protocol extends this definition by classifying the storage of waste or other matter in the sea-bed and subsoil and the abandonment of man-made structures to the aim of disposal as dumping.[584] Waste or other matter in the context of both the London Convention and London Protocol is defined as "material and substance of any kind, form or description."[585] Judging from the vague and broad definition of waste, marine litter considerations can be certainly subsumed under this definition.

The London Protocol which was adopted to implement aspects of the Agenda 21,[586] applies a so-called 'reverse listing approach'[587] which es-

---

places that were remote from earthquakes or turbidity currents. He states that "[…] I believe that the instrument of the LC is too blunt. The oceans have a capacity both for storage and for irretrievable disposal that must ultimately be put to use for the benefit of mankind": *Laughthon,* Marine Policy 18 (1994) 453, 455.

582 All other wastes or matters that are not listed in Annex I and II to the Convention require a prior general permit, Art.IV (1) LC. See for a comprehensive analysis of the London Convention: *Brubaker,* Marine pollution and international law, 1993, chapter 6.

583 Art.III (1) (a) (i and ii) LC and Art. 1 (4 (a) (i and ii) London Protocol (LP).

584 Art. 1 (4) (a) (iii and iv) LP. Dumping does not, *inter alia*, include the "placement of matter for a purpose other than the mere disposal thereof, provided that such placement is not contrary to the aims of this Protocol (Art. 1 (4) (b) (ii) LP). See only: *IMO*, LC 28/15, Report of the Twenty-Eight Consultative Meeting of Contracting Parties, 6 *et seq*. for a discussion on the definition and issue of placement in the context of the placement of artificial reefs.

585 Art.III (4) LC and Art. 1 (8) LP.

586 *De La Fayette,* The International Journal of Marine and Coastal Law 13 (1998) 515, 516.

587 The 'reverse listing' approach reflects the precautionary principle. "This argument rests on the consideration that even in the absence of scientific evidence, the 1996 Protocol categorically excludes all dumping of industrial waste and

tablishes a general dumping prohibition that is merely repealed for certain matters listed in Annex 1 thereto.[588] The stated objective is described in Article 2:

> Contracting Parties shall individually and collectively protect and preserve the marine environment from all sources of pollution and take effective measures, according to their scientific, technical and economic capabilities, to prevent, reduce and where practicable eliminate pollution caused by dumping or incineration at sea of wastes or other matter. Where appropriate, they shall harmonize their policies in this regard.[589]

The implementation of the LP is to be guided by the precautionary approach and the polluter-pays-principle.[590]

---

heavy metals on the basis of the mere assumption that such wastes could be detrimental to the marine environment": *Marr,* The precautionary principle in the law of the sea, 2003, 123.

588 According to Art. 20 LP, Annexes form an "integral part to the Protocol." *VanderZwaag* and *Daniel* see the reverse listing approach as a form of the precautionary "thrusts" of the LP: *VanderZwaag/Daniel,* International Law and Ocean Dumping: Steering a Precautionary Course Aboard the 1996 London Protocol, but Still an Unfinished Voyage, in *Johnston/Chircop/McDorman et al.,* The future of ocean regime-building (2009) 515–571, 520. Originally, the seven categories of Annex I LP included dredged material, sewage sludge, fish waste or material resulting from industrial fish processing operations, vessels and platforms or other man-made structures at sea, inert, organic geological material and bulky items (Art. 1 (1-7) Annex 1 LP). On 2 November 2006, pertinent amendments to Annex 1 LP were made in order to regulate carbon capture and storage-activities under the LP: *IMO*, LC 28/15, Report of the Twenty-Eight Consultative Meeting of Contracting Parties, 6. These amendments came in force on 10 February 2007. For each of the categories, guidance documents are developed: *VanderZwaag/Daniel,* International Law and Ocean Dumping: Steering a Precautionary Course Aboard the 1996 London Protocol, but Still an Unfinished Voyage, in *Johnston/Chircop/McDorman et al.,* The future of ocean regime-building (2009) 515–571, 527 *et seq.*

589 Art. 2 LP.

590 See for a discussion on the "precautionary thrusts of the Protocol" in the context of different aspects regulated by it: *VanderZwaag/Daniel,* International Law and Ocean Dumping: Steering a Precautionary Course Aboard the 1996 London Protocol, but Still an Unfinished Voyage, in *Johnston/Chircop/McDorman et al.,* The future of ocean regime-building (2009) 515–571, 519 *et seq.*

1. Marine litter aspects in the LC

Among the substances listed in Annex I LC are persistent plastics and other persistent synthetic materials. Therefore the dumping is prohibited under the 'black list'.[591] Persistent plastic are further defined as "other persistent synthetic materials, for example netting and ropes, which may float or may remain in suspension in the sea in such a manner as to interfere materially with fishing, navigation or other legitimate uses of the sea."[592] The wording "in such a manner" implies that the criteria of 'floating' and 'interfere' are cumulative.[593] This potentially reduces the protection standard that is intended by the London Convention. Despite a few indications such as fishing and navigations, it remains unclear what the definition and concept of "material interferences" is.[594] It merely establishes a threshold. If no material interferences occur, then the substance is not covered under the black list, therefore it may be dumped. That would somehow contradict the approach of the London Convention that relies on the fact that the environment has a limited assimilative capacity. On the other hand, the list appears to be illustrative ("for example") and is therefore not exhaustive.

However the 'black list' is subject to exceptions that are also relevant for marine litter. Certain Annex I LC substances such as persistent plastics may be dumped if they "are rapidly rendered harmless by physical, chemical or biological processes in the sea provided they do not [...] make edible marine organisms unpalatable, or [...] endanger human health or that of domestic animals."[595] Even though an option is provided for revision in case the harmlessness of a substance is doubted, these considerations appear to be highly anthropocentric in nature. Also, the term "rapidly" has been criticised due to diverse possible interpretations.[596] Certainly, during the time of adoption of the LC, the awareness and knowledge on the persistency of plastics in the ocean was most likely less developed.[597] Addi-

591 Art.IV (a) LC in conjunction with Annex I LC.

592 Annex I (4) LC.

593 *Timagenis,* International control of marine pollution, 1980, 205.

594 *Ibid.*, 206.

595 Regulation 8 (i) and (ii) Annex I LC.

596 *Timagenis,* International control of marine pollution, 1980, 226.

597 During the Third Consultative Meeting of the Parties to the Convention in 1978 Interim Guidelines for the Implementation of paragraphs 8 and 9 Annex I LC were adopted (1978 Interim Guidelines): *Timagenis,* International control of marine pollution, 1980, 226.

tionally, paragraph 9 Annex I LC outlines that Contracting Parties may allow the dumping of certain Annex I LC substances if these occur as "trace contaminants" in sewage sludge or dredged material. This exception clause also relates to persistent plastic. Whereas it potentially did not relate to the knowledge during the drafting of the LC, the so-called trace contaminants of plastic have clear relevance in today´s use of microplastics or fibres.[598]

Due to continuous amendments of the London Convention, the permissible substances that may be dumped under the London Convention and the London Protocol have increasingly been limited.[599] Even though the placement of persistent plastic in the 'black list' indicates a far reaching outlook, the exceptions as outlined above indicates that the London Convention contains weakness regarding an effective marine litter protection regime.

2. Aspects of marine litter considerations in the LP

Whereas the London Protocol in itself does not specifically relate to any particular marine litter considerations, it has to be analysed whether and to what degree the eight categories of waste outlined in Annex 1 LP potentially (directly or indirectly) relate to marine litter considerations. According to Art. 4 (1) (b) LP, "[t]he dumping of wastes or other matter listed in Annex 1 shall require a permit. Contracting Parties shall adopt administrative or legislative measures to ensure that issuance of permits and permit conditions comply with provisions of Annex 2."

The obligations under Annex 2 LP relate, *inter alia*, to a waste prevention audit, dump-site selection and the assessment of potential effects and permit and permit conditions. The provision of the permit should ensure "as far as practicable, that environmental disturbance and detriment are minimised and the benefits maximised."[600] In order to assist in the inter-

598 The 1978 Interim Guidelines provide that under certain circumstances the trace contaminants shall not be accepted for dumping, for example when "they are present in otherwise acceptable wastes or other materials to which they have been added for the purpose of being dumped": *Timagenis,* International control of marine pollution, 1980, 226.

599 *De La Fayette,* The International Journal of Marine and Coastal Law 13 (1998) 515, 521.

600 Annex 2, para.17 LP.

pretation of the LC and LP; so-called Generic as well as Specific Guidelines were adopted that "embody a mechanism to guide national authorities in evaluating applications for dumping of wastes in a manner consistent with the provisions of the London Convention 1972 or the 1996 Protocol thereto."[601] The Guidelines for the assessment of wastes or other matter that may be considered for dumping[602] were complemented by specific guidelines for each category listed under Annex 1 LP.[603] The approach of establishing guidelines is also an application of the precautionary approach under the LP whereby "when applying these Guidelines, uncertainties in relation to assessments of impacts on the marine environment will need to be considered and a precautionary approach applied in addressing these uncertainties."[604]

With a view to the definition of marine litter as outlined above, it is submitted that essentially almost every waste category could be classified as marine litter. Consequently, applying the very broad definition that is not limited to the size of marine litter, the disposal of vessels could *prima facie* account for the introduction of marine litter. It is also in this regard that marine litter aspects are to be included in the assessment. In the Specific Guidelines for assessment of vessels[605] a pollution prevention plan

601 *IMO*, LC 33/15, Report of the Thirty-Third Consultative Meeting and the Sixth Meeting of the Contracting Parties, 08.11.2011, 19. See also: *IMO*, LC 28/15, Report of the Twenty-Eight Consultative Meeting of Contracting Parties, 38. The Guidelines integrate aspects of uncertainty and therefore recommend a precautionary approach: *Marr,* The precautionary principle in the law of the sea, 2003, 124.

602 *IMO*, LC 19/10, Report of the Nineteenths Consultative Meeting of Contracting Parties to the Convention on the Prevention of Marine Pollution by Dumping of Wastes and Other Matter, 14.11.1997, Annex 2. These are referred to as Generic Guidelines.

603 The Guidelines may be found in: *IMO*, LC/SG 21/11, Report of the Twenty-Fourth Meeting of the of the London Convention and London Protocol Scientific Group, Twenty-Fourth Meeting of the Scientific Group, 24.07.2001. Additionally, Specific Guidelines for Assessment of Carbon Dioxide Streams for Disposal into sub-seabed geological formations (CO_2 Specific Guidelines) were adopted in 2007: *IMO*, LC 29/17, Report of the Twenty-Ninth Consultative Meeting and the Second Meeting of Contracting Parties, 14.12.2007.

604 CO_2 Specific Guidelines.

605 *IMO*, LC/SG 24/2/Add.4, Waste Assessment Guidance: Completion of the Reformatting of the Waste-Specific Guidelines adopted in 2000, Twenty-Fourth Meeting of the London Convention and London Protocol Scientific Group, 23.02.2001.

must be established with "the purpose of [...] to assure that wastes (or other matter and materials capable of creating floating debris) potentially contributing to pollution of the marine environment have been removed to the *maximum extent*."[606] The wording of removal to the "maximum extent" could potentially constitute a loophole for marine litter considerations. According to regulation 2 Annex I LP, vessels, platforms or other man-made structures at sea

> may be considered for dumping, provided that material capable of creating floating debris or otherwise contributing to the pollution of the marine environment has been removed to the maximum extent and provided that the material dumped poses no serious obstacle to fishing or navigation.

Even though the 'reverse listing' approach of the London Protocol clearly indicates that only the listed substances may be dumped, the collective term "vessels" implies that also many smaller pieces and also that of plastic might still be acceptable in this context.

Additionally, the dumping of sewage could potentially be a source of microplastics or microfibres. This is even more so relevant in that the Specific Guidelines for Assessment of Sewage Sludge (Specific Guidelines for Sewage Sludge) relate to human sludge, thus residues from municipal sewage treatment plants.[607] The elements contained therein such as the assessment of possible alternatives to sea-based dumping, the characterisation of the chemical properties and dump site selection and the assessment of potential effects are important parameters in assessing the risks of the substances contained in the sewage sludge. However, the possible long-term adverse consequences of microplastics could potentially be ignored under the current form. Since these guidelines are understood as "living documents" that are continuously updated,[608] it should be emphasised that with increasing knowledge an amendment in this regard could be advisable.

---

606 *Ibid.*, 6 (emphasis added).

607 Specific Guidelines for Sewage Sludge, 4.

608 *VanderZwaag/Daniel*, International Law and Ocean Dumping: Steering a Precautionary Course Aboard the 1996 London Protocol, but Still an Unfinished Voyage, in *Johnston/Chircop/McDorman et al.*, The future of ocean regime-building (2009) 515–571, 527.

3. Boundary issues between the LC/LP and MARPOL Annex V

The very generically formulated definition of what constitutes waste could potentially offer a broad scope of application for both the LC and LP. At the same time, it is delimited by an additional clause which outlines activities that are not to be considered as dumping. Consequently, dumping does not include

> the disposal into the sea of wastes or other matter incidental to, or derived from the normal operations of vessels, aircraft, platforms or other man-made structures at sea and their equipment, other than wastes or other matter transported by or to vessels, aircraft, platforms or other man-made structures at sea, operating for the purpose of disposal of such matter or derived from the treatment of such wastes or other matter on such vessels, aircraft, platforms or other man-made structures.[609]

This implies that dumping must be the sole purpose of the ship's voyage. This reference clause links the dumping regime with that of MARPOL in that it clearly delimits that the discharge of on board generated waste during normal operations is not to be considered as dumping.[610] However, in the past the definition of waste under 'normal operations' has been subject to diverse interpretations. Thus, vessels have relied on this concept and anecdotal evidence persists of ship´s crew having thrown old furniture's overboard before the ship continued the journey to port for overhauling.[611] Even though the boundary issue between normal operations and dumping is not necessarily of great practical relevance,[612] the question of how to deal with spoilt cargo is of importance also regarding the newly amended MARPOL Annex V.[613] Spoilt cargos is for example, frozen beef in dam-

---

609 Art.III (b) (i) LC and Art. 1 (4) (b) (i) LP.

610 *VanderZwaag/Daniel*, International Law and Ocean Dumping: Steering a Precautionary Course Aboard the 1996 London Protocol, but Still an Unfinished Voyage, in *Johnston/Chircop/McDorman et al.*, The future of ocean regime-building (2009) 515–571, 524.

611 *Ibid.*

612 *IMO*, MEPC 65/7, Interpretations of, and Amendments to MARPOL and related instruments, Draft revised guidance to manage spoilt cargoes, 03.01.2013, Annex, 9. The Draft revised guidance to manage spoilt cargo lists 28 incidents in the time frame from 1984-2009 in which a permit had been issued to dispose of spoilt cargo.

613 See section D.II.3. of this chapter on a further discussion.

aged containers, cement packed in bags or alumina spoilt by water ingress.[614]

Since the definition of garbage under MARPOL Annex V does not include spoilt cargo, it is not regulated under MARPOL Annex V.[615] Consequently, a non-regulation of the issue could lead to an increased fragmentation in marine environmental protection as it is permissible to dump spoilt cargo under the conditions of the London Convention or London Protocol respectively, only if the ship possesses a permit. To clarify these issues, a Joint London Convention/MEPC Correspondence Group was established in 2005 with the mandate to develop guidelines and interpretations regarding boundary issues between both conventions, in particular with a view to spoilt cargos.[616] Whereas the Correspondence Group had initially adopted a Guidance document on managing spoilt cargo during MEPC 59 in 2009, the newly amended MARPOL Annex V necessitated a revision of this Guidance in order to ensure coherence between the instruments.[617] In 2012, a Revised Guidance on the management of spoilt cargos was adopted by the governing bodies of the London Convention and the London Protocol which was then forwarded to the MEPC which adopted these in May 2013.[618] The Guidance document outlines that the documentation of spoilt cargo onboard could be done in the Garbage Record Book.[619] Also, it suggested developing contingency plans for the management of spoilt cargo which serves to "facilitate timely decision-making by State regulatory authorities and minimise delays to ship."[620] Even though this side issue of spoilt cargos appears to be of marginal im-

---

614 *IMO*, MEPC 65/7, Interpretations of, and Amendments to MARPOL and related instruments, Draft revised guidance to manage spoilt cargoes, Annex, 8.

615 *Ibid.*, Annex, 2.

616 The Joint Correspondence Group is led by Canada: *VanderZwaag/Daniel*, International Law and Ocean Dumping: Steering a Precautionary Course Aboard the 1996 London Protocol, but Still an Unfinished Voyage, in *Johnston/Chircop/ McDorman et al.*, The future of ocean regime-building (2009) 515–571, 524.

617 *IMO*, MEPC 65/7, Interpretations of, and Amendments to MARPOL and related instruments, Draft revised guidance to manage spoilt cargoes, 1.

618 *IMO*, LC-LP.1/Circ.58, Revised Guidance on the management of spoilt cargos, 03.07.2013, 1. See also an information flyer that was developed on the issue: *IMO*, LC 35/15, Report of the Thirty-Fifth Consultative Meeting and the Eight Meeting of Contracting Parties, Annex 9 Information flyer on spoilt cargos–managing spoilt cargo, 21.10.2013.

619 Revised Guidance on the management of spoilt cargos, 3.

620 *Ibid.*

portance, it constitutes a case study on the many small and at times seemingly innocuous activities that lead to the introduction of marine litter.

4. The dumping regime in the context of land-based waste management

The increased regulation of ocean dumping has a direct link to waste management strategies on land. The very limited opportunities available to discharge waste in the marine environment signify an increased need to find land-based alternatives. With a view to the complementary issues of land-based pollution, the London Protocol establishes the obligation on Contracting Parties not to transfer one type of pollution into another.[621] Both the London Convention and London Protocol adopted in 2006 a partnership agreement between the UNEP Global Plan of Action for the Protection of the Marine Environment from Land-based Activities.[622] The initially proposed areas of co-operation were sub-sea disposal through outfalls of tailings and associated wastes from mining operations and habitat destructions.[623] In June 2009, Canada proposed an extension to the co-operation to the field of marine litter as an overarching issue.[624] Since its inception, the work on marine litter has however been constantly postponed. Most recently, action on it has been deferred to 2014.[625]

---

621 Art. 3 (3) LP. This corresponds also with the obligations under Art. 195 UNCLOS.

622 *IMO*, LC/SG 32/8, Coastal Management issues associated with activities- Initial proposals for co-operation between the London Convention and Protocol and the UNEP Global Programme of Action for Protection of the Marine Environment from Land-based Activities (GPA) discussed during the Thirty-Second Meeting of the Scientific Group of the London Convention and the Third Meeting of the Scientific Group of the London Protocol Scientific Group, 24.04.2009.

623 *Ibid.*

624 *IMO,* LC/SG 32/15, Report of the Thirty-Second Meeting of the Scientific Group of the London Convention and the Third Meeting of the Scientific Group of the London Protocol, 29.06.2009, 42. A first initiative on a collaboration between IMO and the GPA has been established 1999: *De La Fayette,* Environmental Policy and Law 30 (2000) 51, 60. The issue appears however to have been dormant until the new initiative in 2009.

625 *IMO*, LC 33/15, Report of the Thirty-Third Consultative Meeting and the Sixth Meeting of the Contracting Parties, 08.11.2011, 39. During the Thirty-Fifth Consultative Meeting of Contracting Parties to the London Convention, the Joint Work Programme of the Scientific Group (2014-2016) also contained a reference to marine litter. In regard to the co-operation with other UN agencies and indus-

What can be seen however is that instead of comprehensively addressing the issue of marine litter as a whole, a selection of sectoral 'projects' relating to minor concerns in the marine litter issue debate has been made. This refers, *inter alia,* to (more or less) successful attempts to collect information on the presence of storage facilities of industrial wastes near the coasts[626] and sewage treatment facilities and sewage sludge management.[627] The postponement of measures aimed at reducing marine litter comprehensively is to be lamented. A consequent follow-up of measures addressing marine litter would have been very suitable vis-à-vis the timeliness of the issue in 2009.[628]

5. Preliminary conclusion

The dumping regime established by the LC marks one of the early key events of marine litter regulation. The characteristics and potential adverse consequences of plastics were at the time already, in principle, acknowledged. However, the exceptions to the black list that also touch upon plastic can be seen as weakness of the LC regarding the marine litter debate. The 'reverse listing' approach of the LP consequently applies to marine litter considerations and excludes a vast amount of different marine litter types. However, there are certain loopholes that potentially do not regulate aspects of marine litter in the dumping regime established by the LP. This relates on the one hand to aspects of floating debris when disposing of vessels and microplastics or fibres aspect in sewage sludge. Admittedly,

---

try organizations, marine litter is listed as a "high priority" for the years 2014 and 2015 with a target completion date in 2015: *IMO*, LC 35/15, Report of the Thirty-Third Consultative Meeting and the Sixth Meeting of the Contracting Parties, Annex 11, 3.

626 *IMO*, LC/SG 34/15, Report of the Thirty-Fourth Meeting of the Scientific Group of the London Convention and the Fifth Meeting of the Scientific Group of the London Protocol, 24.05.2011, 43.

627 *Ibid.* Both attempts demonstrate that the approach of the Contracting Parties is not necessarily distinguished by a great political will. Regarding the collection of information on storage facilities, "the Secretariat indicated to hesitate with collection of information on this issue through questionnaires to national LC/LP Administrations, fearing a poor return rate, and that an invitation of case studies might be more productive", *ibid.*

628 See only the impetus in the Regional Seas Conventions (as discussed in chapter 4).

the scientific uncertainties and knowledge gaps that still remain in regard to sewage sludge as a source of these materials, makes this only a marginal concern, only given the level of knowledge currently available on this issue. Also, the risk assessment and dumping guidelines as instruments reflecting a precautionary approach further serve as guidelines in considering these potential pathways of marine litter.

The issue of spoilt cargo, though marginal, is an interesting example on how two different ocean pollution treaties address, in essence, similar aspects. This is also true for the interface between land-based pollution and ocean dumping. Whereas the co-operation between the London Convention and London Protocol Contracting Parties with the GPA is an important element in overcoming the 'fragmentation' of land- and ocean-based pollution, the missing concrete actions should be critically evaluated.

III. The regulatory framework of land-based marine litter in the absence of a legally-binding global agreement

Since land-based pollution potentially accounts for the majority of marine litter sources, its regulation will be particularly considered in this section. However, in practice the introduction of marine litter by land-based pollution is a multifaceted problem that has its origins in many different actors and activities. Any effective regulation has to address a broad range of small and large activities from individuals and companies. The activities are in their nature separate but have a common consequence. The cumulative effects of land-based pollution are in particular a challenge in a regulatory framework. Whereas each activity on its own does not necessarily result in a significant impact, the sum of activities and pollutants create the problem. This is also aggravated by the variability in their causation. Marine litter can be chronically released, causing a continuous, below threshold impact, whereas in other cases accidental and singular events can lead to heavy pollution loads. Consequently, the difficulty to give an exact account of the causes and origins of marine litter from land-based pollution also aggravates determining the amount of solid waste entering the ocean.

Even though pollution occurs on the sovereign territory of a State, the impact of marine litter is potentially transboundary. With the increased consolidation of regulations addressing offshore sources of marine litter in the 1970s, the land-based regulations on how to deal with the disposal of household and industrial solid waste gained importance.[629] However, even though the question of solid waste management still remains at the core of the issue, land-based marine litter is also associated with behavioural, educational and cultural aspects that is apparent in tip-dumping and (unintentional) littering.[630] Since land-based pollutants also include nutrients, heavy metals, chemicals, radioactive material and sewage, the complexity of regulation is far more than compared to other regimes.[631] Notwithstanding that, land-based pollution has been an issue of concern, but this understanding "was not accompanied by general agreement on the most effective means of combating the threat."[632] This relates primarily to the opposing views of establishing a globally legally binding agreements or regulating the issue through national measures given that the pollutants originate from sovereign territory.[633] In this context, some preliminary remarks are in order. Contrary to other areas in international public law, regional strategies in the form of Regional Seas Conventions that, amongst others, addressed land-based pollution were established before a global instrument was envisaged.[634] Only after the realization that some of the regional treaties were not entirely successful due to the lack of political will of States to implement and develop regional obligations, a global approach has been developed.[635]

---

629 *Timagenis,* International control of marine pollution, 1980, 17.

630 *Jeftic/Matte-Baker/Schomaker,* The state of the marine environment, 2006, 28.

631 See for example the Mox Plant Case as discussed in section C.IV.2. of this chapter. Also, an option to ban land-based chemicals that could have potentially an impact on the marine environment is to ban those substances such as envisaged by the 2002 Stockholm Convention on Persistent Organic Pollutant: *Sohn/Noyes,* Cases and materials on the law of the sea, 2004, 727.

632 *Mensah,* The International Legal Regime for the Protection and Preservation of the Marine Environment from Land-based Sources of Pollution in *Boyle/Freestone,* International law and sustainable development (1999) 298–324, 298.

633 *Ibid.*

634 This relates for example to the 1974 Nordic Environmental Protection Convention, the 1974 Convention for the Prevention of Marine Pollution from land-based sources. See for a concise listing of relevant Regional Conventions: *Tanaka,* Zeitschrift für ausländisches öffentliches Recht und Völkerrecht 66 (2006) 533, 550.

635 *Nollkaemper,* Legal Regulation of Upland Discharges of marine debris: From Local to Global Controls and Back, in *Coe/Rogers,* Marine debris (1997) 293–305, 294 *et seq*. However, *Nollkaemper* admits that some instruments (for the Baltic, Black Sea, the Northeastern Atlantic and the Mediterranean) "are covered by more-or-less operational programs for land-based pollution.".

1. Marine litter issues in the development of global land-based pollution measures

Whereas the Stockholm Conference in 1972 provided rather broad principles relating to marine pollution and in particular to land-based pollution, the subsequent increased environmental awareness had an important role in shaping the agenda for establishing more concrete standards for land-based pollution.[636] In 1985, UNEP adopted the Montreal Guidelines for the Protection of the Marine Environment Against Pollution from Land-based Sources.[637] The Guidelines were developed in the understanding that, at that time, a legally binding instrument addressing land-based pollution globally was not achievable.[638] The Montreal Guidelines provided detailed information that were based on existing agreements such as the pertinent obligations of UNCLOS and the 1974 Helsinki Convention[639] and served to promote the implementation of UNCLOS as well as establishing the background for further adoptions of pertinent instruments.[640] Chapter 17 of Agenda 21 called, with a view to land-based pollution, for the convening of an inter-governmental conference with the aim of adopting a global programme of action to address land-based pollution.[641] The propagated conference took place in 1995 in Washington DC, USA. The conference adopted the Washington Declaration on the Protection of the Marine Environment from Land-based Activities (Washington Declara-

---

636 *Hassan,* Protecting the marine environment from land-based sources of pollution, 2006, 89.

637 *UNEP*, Protection of the Marine Environment Against Pollution from Land-Based Sources (Montreal Guidelines), Environmental Policy and Law 14 (1985) 77. See further *Hassan,* Protecting the marine environment from land-based sources of pollution, 2006, 89 *et seq.*

638 *Mensah,* The International Legal Regime for the Protection and Preservation of the Marine Environment from Land-based Sources, in *Boyle/Freestone,* International law and sustainable development (1999) 298–324, 302.

639 Convention on the Protection of the Marine Environment of the Baltic Sea Area (1974 Helsinki Convention) (Helsinki) of 22 March 1974, in force 03 May 1980; 13 ILM 546 (1974), see also section B. of chapter 3.

640 *Yankov,* The Law of the Sea Convention and Agenda 21: Marine Environment Implications and *Mensah*, The International Legal Regime for the Protection and Preservation of the Marine Environment from Land-based Sources, in *Boyle/Freestone*, International law and sustainable development (1999) 298–324, 302 and 271–295, 283 respectively.

641 Para. 17.26, Agenda 21.

tion) and also the non-binding Global Programme of Action for the Protection of the Marine Environment from Land-Based Activities (GPA).[642] This event marks thus a renunciation from the fragmented and regional protection approaches of land-based pollution to a supplementary global regulatory level.

The Washington Declaration sets a more strategic framework that underlines the purpose of establishing the GPA.[643] Accordingly, the GPA aims to "preventing the degradation of the marine environment from land-based activities by facilitating the realization of the duty of States to preserve and protect the marine environment."[644] It furthermore intends to "assist States in taking actions individually or jointly within their respective policies, priorities and resources."[645] From their inception, the GPA and also the Washington Declaration highlight the main contaminants that emanate from land-based sources, amongst others also litter.[646]

2. Implications of marine litter as a priority contaminant in the framework of the GPA

In the constituent document establishing the GPA, specific sections for each priority contaminant are listed in which targets and objectives for ad-

642 *UN*, UNEP(OCA)/LBA/IG.2/7, Global Programme of Action for the Protection of the Marine Environment from land-based Activities (GPA), Intergovernmental Conference to adopt a Global Programme of Action for the Protection of the Marine Environment from Land-Based Activities, 05.12.1995; *Mensah,* The International Legal Regime for the Protection and Preservation of the Marine Environment from Land-based Sources, in *Boyle/Freestone,* International law and sustainable development (1999) 298–324, 307; *Hassan,* Protecting the marine environment from land-based sources of pollution, 2006, 95 *et seq.*

643 *Sohn/Noyes,* Cases and materials on the law of the sea, 2004, 725.

644 *UN*, UNEP(OCA)/LBA/IG.2/7, GPA, Intergovernmental Conference to adopt a Global Programme of Action for the Protection of the Marine Environment from Land-Based Activities, 05.12.1995, 7.

645 *Ibid.*

646 *UN*, UNEP(OCA)/LBA/IG.2/7, GPA, Intergovernmental Conference to adopt a Global Programme of Action for the Protection of the Marine Environment from Land-Based Activities, 05.12.1995, 11.; *Tanaka,* Zeitschrift für ausländisches öffentliches Recht und Völkerrecht 66 (2006) 533, 546; *Hassan,* Protecting the marine environment from land-based sources of pollution, 2006, 96. Besides litter, these are sewage, persistent organic pollutants, radioactive substances, heavy metals, oils, nutrients, sediment mobilisation.

dressing the input of the substances are proposed. Corresponding to the overall legal value of this document, the necessity and specific actions and regulatory approaches of marine litter are vaguely elaborated. Before proposing specific marine-litter related targets and objectives, the multiple sources of marine litter are identified and also the particular impact of resin pellets and the combustion of plastic are mentioned.[647] The two central objectives of the GPA regarding marine litter primarily address waste management strategies and stipulate the establishment of environmentally sound waste collection services for coastal communities and the reduction of generation of solid waste and improved management.[648] The proposed actions for national governments range from simply providing garbage bins in public areas, to education and awareness campaigns and the use of spatial planning when planning dump sites in coastal areas.[649]

On the regional scale "actions should include the promotion of regional cooperation for the exchange of information on practices and experiences regarding waste management, recycling and reuse, and cleaner production, as well as regional arrangements for solid-waste management."[650] The international actions were to include the development of a "clearing-house mechanism on waste management, recycling and reuse and waste mini-

---

647 *UN,* UNEP(OCA)/LBA/IG.2/7, GPA, Intergovernmental Conference to adopt a Global Programme of Action for the Protection of the Marine Environment from Land-Based Activities, 05.12.1995, 55.

648 *Ibid.* With regard to the reduction of solid waste, the GPA draws on the pertinent paragraphs of Agenda 21 that calls for efficient waste collection services by the year 2000 and adequate waste services for all urban populations by 2025 (Para. 21.39, Agenda 21).

649 *UN*, UNEP(OCA)/LBA/IG.2/7, GPA, Intergovernmental Conference to adopt a Global Programme of Action for the Protection of the Marine Environment from Land-Based Activities, 05.12.1995, 55.

650 *Ibid.*, 19.

mization technology"[651] and capacity building.[652] Even though these measures appear to be beneficial, they merely provide general strategic targets rather than setting specific legally binding targets and timetables.[653] In a broader context, the GPA proposes procedures on how to identify and develop management strategies and also establishes a review and evaluation mechanism.[654]

Since its inception, there have been three Inter-governmental reviews (IGR) on the implementation progress of the GPA.[655] These on the one hand reflect on the progress of implementation and also propose new strategies for the general orientation of the GPA. Generally, marine litter

---

651 Even though the concept of clearing-house mechanism is not defined in the marine litter section itself, a definition of its function is given: "a referral system through which decision makers at the national and regional level are provided with access to current sources of information, practical experience and scientific and technical expertise relevant to developing and implementing strategies to deal with the impacts of land-based activities" *ibid.*, 22. In *UNGA*, Assembly Resolution A/RES/51/189 on Institutional arrangements for the implementation of the Global Programme of Action for the Protection of the Marine Environment from Land-based Activities, 21.02.1997, the General Assembly called IMO to develop a clearing-house mechanism for oil and litter (para.9 *et seq.*). This was at the time however not followed-up due to financial constraints: *De La Fayette,* Environmental Policy and Law 30 (2000) 51, 60. In 1999, Canada led a pilot project in co-operation with IMO to prepare a clearing-house mechanism for oil and litter, which was scheduled to end in 2000: *ibid.*

652 *UN*, UNEP(OCA)/LBA/IG.2/7, GPA, Intergovernmental Conference to adopt a Global Programme of Action for the Protection of the Marine Environment from Land-Based Activities, 05.12.1995, 56.

653 *Nollkaemper,* Legal Regulation of Upland Discharges of marine debris: From Local to Global Controls and Back, in *Coe/Rogers,* Marine debris (1997) 293–305, 304.

654 *International Institute for Sustainable Development,* Earth Negotiations Bulletin 25 (2012) 1, 2.

655 *UN,* UNEP/GPA/IGR.3/INF/3/Rev. 1, Progress in implementing the GPA at the National Level, IGR Third session Manila, 04.01.2012, 2. The first IGR of the GPA was held in Montreal, Canada in 2001, the second IGR in 2006 in Bejing, China, the third IGR was held in Manila in January 2012. During IGR 1, the Montreal Declaration was adopted that focused on strengthening the collaboration between ocean and freshwater management and financing the GPA, see: *Sohn/Noyes,* Cases and materials on the law of the sea, 2004, 725. The 2006 Bejing Declaration marked a change in the strategic orientation from international and regional management to national and local initiatives on land-based pollution: *UN*, UNEP/GPA/IGR.3/INF/3/Rev. 1, Progress in implementing the GPA at the National Level, IGR Third session Manila, 04.01.2012, 4.

has also in the context of these reform processes remained a priority substance.[656] This has also been confirmed during the IGR 3 in 2012 which placed marine litter again on the agenda as a priority issue in the GPA.[657] Even though increased attention was thus paid to the problem of marine litter, the report "The state of the marine environment" that was produced as a preparation for IGR 2 in 2006 stated that "the problem of marine litter has steadily grown worse, despite both national and international efforts to control it."[658] As a consequence of this realisation, the GPA has played a significant role addressing the prevailing lack of coordination with other institutions and programmes that are relevant in the field of marine litter. This is even more so interesting since the GPA in itself has no legal personality and therefore is not able to adopt any legally binding measures.

3. The role of the GPA to overcome the fragmented approach in addressing marine litter

In 2005, the GPA and UNEP´s Regional Seas Programme established the "Global Initiative on Marine Litter".[659] The Marine Litter Initiative envisaged the establishment of regional strategies on marine litter that are pri-

---

656 *International Institute for Sustainable Development,* Earth Negotiations Bulletin 25 (2012) 1, 4; *UN*, UNEP/GPA/IGR.3/3, Policy guidance for implementing the GPA over the period 2012–2016, IGR Third session, 01.11.2011, 6. In the context of the second IGR, four out of the original source categories were identified that were in particular need of increased attention: sewage and management of municipal waste water, nutrient over-enrichment, marine litter and physical alteration and habitat destruction: *Jeftic/Matte-Baker/Schomaker,* The state of the marine environment, 2006, 33 and 37. In the preparation towards the third review of the GPA for the period 2012-2016, three priority source categories were identified: nutrients, sewage and marine litter. The reduction of source categories was made with a view to guide, in a target-oriented manner, the financial resources and expenditures. Even though the GPA still is not legally binding, the prioritization has as a consequence that these three sources will be primarily addressed in programmes and initiatives.

657 Marine litter is accordingly next to nutrients and wastewater one of the three priority issues: *UN*, UNEP/GPA/IGR.3/CRP.1/Rev. 1., Manila Declaration on Furthering the Implementation of the GPA Activities, IGR Third session, Manila, 26.01.2012, 3.

658 *Jeftic/Matte-Baker/Schomaker,* The state of the marine environment, 2006, 28.

659 *UNEP Regional Seas Programme*, Global Initiative on Marine Litter, http://www.unep.org/regionalseas/marinelitter/initiatives/unepglobal/default.asp, last

marily developed and implemented through the Regional Seas Conventions.[660] The coordinative technique that is pursued primarily relies on reinforcing existing programmes and structures that are already in place. Amongst others, this refers to using Regional Seas Conventions as an implementation platform which are much more suitable to develop and carry out tailored programmes.[661] Furthermore, in June 2012 the Global Partnership on Marine Litter was launched. It is a voluntary multistakeholder coordination mechanism in which all partners such as States, inter-governmental organisation, academia, private sector or non-governmental organisations can participate. Even though the GPA has remained, due to its non-binding character, a rather weak instrument in the context of land-based pollution, its role in coordinating different aspects of marine litter is remarkable. The GPA has increasingly played a significant role in harmonising and streamlining actions on marine litter, despites its functional limited competences and non-binding provisions. The repercussions of its role as a coordinative platform have for example also impacted the marine litter regulation in the European Seas.

E. Conclusion

The precautionary principle and the polluter-pays-principle provide guidance in implementing any marine litter regulatory measures. Despite their heterogeneous application with respect to different treaties, they play an important role in helping to guide and implement any marine litter related measures. In particular the precautionary principle facilitates the decision-making vis-à-vis the uncertainty and knowledge gaps that are inherent in any marine litter discourse.

---

accessed 27.08.2015. See for a comprehensive discussion on the role and function of this Initiative in chapter 4.

660 A thorough assessment of the role of UNEPs and GPA´s Initiative on marine litter will be effected in chapter 4 of this study. Also, the establishment of the "Global Partnership on Marine Litter" that serves "as a catalyst for change" is another aspect of marine litter considerations under GPA, see: *UN*, UNEP/GPA/IGR.3/INF/6, Progress in the implementation of UNEP's marine litter activities 2007-2011 and the way forward from 2012 to 2016, IGR Meeting on the implementation of the GPA Third session, Manila, 12.01.2012, 10.

661 *Ibid.*, 12. See chapter 4.

However, the inherent nature of public international law regarding the regulation of marine pollution has certain limits. The task to create a suitable regulatory framework that effectively corresponds to the complex interactions of substances in the marine environment, that is at least acceptable to the majority of States, is a challenge to say the least! The development of international law has demonstrated that the expansion and specialisation of the different subjects and actors is increasing and becomes more tailor-made to a specific problem. The results are functional agreements that serve the purpose of addressing, for example, a specific source of pollution in an –at times- highly detailed and technical manner. Even though this approach in principle corresponds to the regulatory needs of marine litter, the regulation at the source, it follows a sectoral manner. This means that each source is addressed distinctly on its own, while considering interactions between the regimes in a very limited way.

From this, it follows that the measures and provisions might be highly specialised but fail to adress in a systematic way any boundary issues between the different agreements. A clear distinction has to be made regarding offshore and onshore sources of pollution. Admittedly, UNCLOS follows in essence an integrated approach which integrates all kind of sources and also acknowledges the interrelation of the ocean. The legal framework established by UNCLOS establishes several points of contacts for the marine litter discussion. The main focus in this regard is the wide definition of pollution and the primarily pollution prevention approach of Part XII UNCLOS. Whereas the different enforcement and prescriptive jurisdiction are important starting points in ensuring compliance, the analysis has demonstrated that strengthening port State jurisdiction and Port State Control are important parameters in increasing compliance with international discharge standards.

An analysis of the sectoral agreements relating to pollution from shipping and dumping has shown that the MARPOL regime in particular could potentially play an important role in addressing this issue. In the end, it is a legally binding instrument that is specifically designed to address the introduction of marine litter at a known source. In the context of MARPOL, the assessment of the recent amendments of MARPOL Annex V, relating to vessel-based garbage, has demonstrated that these potentially increase the protection standard of discharges. This relates to the newly introduced broad and comprehensive definition of waste and the overall prohibition to discharge waste. The extension of this concept has also significantly increased the material protection standard. This is due to the reduction in exceptions and clearly worded provisions. Concurrently, the protection standard between Special Areas and outside Special Areas under Annex V are increasingly aligned. From this, it follows that the overall influx of vessel-based garbage could be reduced.

Albeit the discharge standards have been raised, the port reception facilities provisions under MARPOL Annex V remain somewhat vague and offer great flexibility for Contracting Parties. Despite their importance in the context of the discharge standards, the concept of port reception facilities in the instrument remains fairly subordinated. The disposition of adequate port reception facilities, one of the elements of Special Areas, has not been comprehensively pursued. A further potential caveat in this regard, is the missing link to establish waste management strategies in the receiving harbours. It remains, however, to be seen how and to what degree these framing concepts are implemented and applied on a regional level.

Even though the GPA is by its normative nature a weak and non-committal action-program, it has had a significant impact in regard to marine litter aspects. This however does not derive from standard setting or the development of material law. A preliminary analysis has demonstrated that the additional value of the GPA is its coordinative role. The continuous classification of marine litter as a priority source category has on the one hand ensured a certain degree of consistency and attention for this issue. On the other hand, its liaison with other international conventions and also actors such as UNEP has triggered important, albeit non-binding actions.

An assessment of the global applicable treaties and the GPA demonstrates the potential benefits that follow from globally applicable international law, whereby a certain common denominator is created, laying the ground for specific sectoral environmental protection. However, the very nature of these agreements is, for the most part, confined to a sectoral, one source-specific category of pollution, which is its weakness. The different economic and environmental protection interests that are to be considered in their development or furtherance naturally impact their overall scope. Classifying marine litter in their context therefore appears at times somewhat copious. Admittedly, MARPOL Annex V is specifically dedicated to address the issue of marine litter by vessel-based pollution.

Nonetheless, it is submitted that the international regulatory regime that is established by these treaties is an indispensable mechanism in the overall marine litter regulation. Whereas some of the agreements lack legally binding provisions or only contain broad and vague elements, it allows for a worldwide minimum environmental protection standard. The requirement to take into consideration transboundary environmental pollution, is an important consideration. The sectoral and somewhat fragmented approach on an international scale does not entirely render satisfactory results from a marine litter perspective. This relates primarily to the issue of diffuse sources and the need to address the knowledge gap.

Chapter 3: The role of the European Regional Seas Conventions to prevent the introduction of marine litter

The protection of specific seas or ecosystems through regional regulatory agreements plays an important role in the concretisation of the global regulatory framework.[662] The significance of Regional Seas Conventions can also be attributed to their scope and approach, which is tailored to the vulnerabilities and anthropogenic activities occurring in the particular marine region where they apply.[663] The thematic priorities in the Regional Seas Conventions are necessitated on the one hand by the prevailing ecosystems but also developed through the work of the States that share a common water body.

Regional marine environmental measures were primarily established by UNEP´s Regional Seas Programme, launched in 1974 as an outcome of the Stockholm Conference.[664] It serves as an umbrella programme under which 13 Regional Seas Programmes aim to address the protection of the shared marine environment.[665] Not every Regional Sea is administered under the UNEP´s Regional Seas Programme, as is the case with regard to some of the waters surrounding the EU. The Mediterranean Sea is covered under UNEP´s Programme whereas the Baltic Sea, Black Sea and the North-East Atlantic are associated with UNEP´s Regional Seas Programme as partner agreements but are governed through independent programmes.[666]

---

662 *König,* Marine Environment, International Protection, in Max Planck Encyclopedia of Public International Law (MPEPIL), D.37; *Birnie/Boyle/Redgwell,* International law and the environment, 2009, 393.

663 *Franckx,* The International Journal of Marine and Coastal Law 13 (1998) 307. 320.

664 *UNEP*, Marine Litter: A Global Challenge, 2009, 15; *Ehlers,* The International Journal of Marine and Coastal Law 8 (1993) 191, 191.

665 See for further information on the Regional Seas Programmes: http://www.unep.org/regionalseas/about/default.asp.

666 *UNEP Regional Seas Programme*, Non-UNEP Administered and Independent Programmes, http://www.unep.org/regionalseas/programmes/nonunep/default.asp, last accessed 27.08.2015. The programmes for the Baltic Sea and the North-East Atlantic are nevertheless considered as associated partner pro-

The issue of marine litter has increasingly obtained a more prominent position within the work of UNEP following a decision of UNEP´s Governing Council in 2004 that categorised marine litter as a priority issue.[667] The decision further strengthened UNEP´s Marine Litter Initiative. The initiative is established so as to contribute "to the scientific and substantive understanding of marine litter and subsequently to the management of a global problem with devastating effects on ecosystems, economies and human well-being."[668]

A. UNEP´s Marine Litter Initiative and the Regional Seas Conventions

UNEP´s Marine Litter Initiative has provided a significant stimulus for several initiatives and projects in different Regional Seas. As a first step, a "feasibility study on sustainable management of marine litter" was conducted which can be considered as a milestone in addressing marine litter, since it comprehensively considered the issue without exclusively focusing on individual sectoral sources or solutions.[669] Whereas the need to act was a central conclusion of the study, the most preferred course for follow-up actions was not finally determined. The considered options were to either follow an *ad hoc* approach or rather a streamlined and coordinated way of addressing the issue.[670] However, it was quickly decided to entrust UNEP´s Regional Seas Programme with the competence to serve as a coordination platform. The challenge at the time was to establish pertinent measures that would be at the same time broad and generic enough to be applicable to several Regional Seas, but that would also define concrete

grammes to UNEP´s Regional Seas Programme as they pursue a similar objective and follow comparable approaches in achieving this aim: *Gold,* Gard Handbook on Protection of the Marine Environment, 2006, 256. The Black Sea Programme was originally initiated under the auspices of UNEP, but subsequently became an independent programme.

667 *UNEP*, Marine litter, an analytical overview, 2005, ii. See for further information *Kiss/Shelton,* International environmental law, 2004, 86 *et seq*.

668 *UNEP Regional Seas Programme*, Global Initiative on Marine Litter, http://www.unep.org/regionalseas/marinelitter/initiatives/unepglobal/default.asp, last accessed 27.08.2015.

669 See for a summary of the study: *UNEP*, Marine Litter, an analytical overview, 2005.

670 *Ibid.*, 37.

measures so as to guide States in developing adequate (legislative) measures.

The work in this context was framed by MoUs on the development of marine litter management activities that were established between the Regional Seas Coordinating Office and Secretariats of the Regional Seas Conventions, even when these were not directly administered under UNEP.[671] From a legal point of view, the Marine Litter MoUs have no legal effect as would be the case, for example, were they established by a treaty within the meaning given to that term, for example, under the Vienna Convention on the Law of Treaties.[672] Therefore no legal rights and duties are established for the signatories. Their role is rather that of a co-operation agreements between UNEP and the individual Regional Seas Secretariats.

The MoUs, despite their diverse addressees, establish four elements: the review of the status of marine litter in the region through monitoring, the preparation of a Regional Action Plan or Regional Strategy on sustainable management of marine litter, the organisation of a regional meeting of national authorities and experts on marine litter and, a practical measure, the organisation of a Clean Up Day.[673] The Regional Strategy was to include amongst others, a programme of enhancement of national or regional legal and administrative instruments and the development of regional and na-

671 *UNEP*, Marine Litter: A Global Challenge, 2009, 7. Even though the former document speaks of "agreement" in this regard, other sources indicate that the nature of the agreements were MoU: *UNEP Regional Seas Programme,* Regional Seas Activities – ongoing MoU 2007 activities, marine litter regional action plan, http://www.unep.org/regionalseas/news/default.asp, last accessed 27.08.2015 and *UNEP*, Marine Litter: A Global Challenge, 2009, 107. Also, in the language of UNEP, the Secretariats were called: Regional Seas Coordinating Units, *ibid.* 17. Besides the two MoUs that were adopted in the Black Sea Region, no other MoUs were available. Thus, no further information can be given regarding the adoption of each agreement. Therefore, the information that "agreements" were signed with five regional organizations in 2005, another five in 2006 and with two more during 2007 and 2008, *ibid.*, 17, only provisionally outlines the timeframe of these activities. In the Baltic Sea, no MoU has been signed for the purpose. UNEP rather co-financed a project on marine litter.

672 Convention on the Law of Treaties (VCLT, Vienna) of 25 May 1969, in force 27 January 1980; 1980 UKTS 58. It is of course the case that the Convention on the Law of Treaties only addresses States Parties. As the MoUs were concluded between International Organisations, the terms of the VCLT cannot apply. It is submitted, however, that many of the provisions might nonetheless find an analogous application.

673 *UNEP*, Marine Litter: A Global Challenge, 2009, 7.

tional strategies for an integrated management of marine litter.[674] Furthermore, the Regional Strategy should include programmes on the co-operation with the private sector, NGOs and the scientific community, information and outreach activities, sectoral activities and fundraising activities.[675] These elements are thus measurable and include specifications that serve on the one hand as guiding principles for their implementation and on the other hand establish a yardstick to evaluate whether pertinent measures were taken. A particularly positive aspect of this approach is that these elements primarily address the prevailing knowledge gap regarding marine litter and aim to increase awareness of the diverse problems associated with it.

The development of a Regional Strategy on marine litter was to be implemented in three phases.[676] Phase one refers to the assessment of the regional situation which should be used to prepare the second phase, the Regional Strategy itself. Subsequently, in phase three the Regional Strategies were to be implemented and integrated into the "Programme of Work of the respective Regional Seas Programmes and the implementation of the Regional Strategy at the national and regional level."[677]

In 2009, UNEP published a comprehensive review of the results and findings and provided an overview of pertinent data and measures on marine litter that were available in the specific regions.[678] The purpose of the present study is not to double the comprehensive work pursued by UNEP, but it is rather aimed at using its knowledge base as a starting point to further assess the legal options and peculiarities contained within the specific regimes. The four Regional Seas Conventions that apply to the waters surrounding the EU will be analysed with a view to their specific role in substantiating pertinent international obligations and their interpretation and scope of legal measures to address marine litter.

The assessment does not intend to afford a comparison of the differences between UNEP's Regional Seas Programmes and its partner pro-

---

674 *Ibid.*, 17.

675 *UNEP*, Marine Litter: A Global Challenge, 2009, 17.

676 To ensure a coherent and harmonised application, the Regional Seas Programme prepared in November 2006 the Guidelines for the Development and Implementation of Regional Strategies for Addressing Marine Litter, *ibid.*, 17.

677 *UN*, UNEP (DEPI)/ MED WG.334/Inf.5, Results of the assessment of the status of marine litter in the Mediterranean, Meeting of the MED POL Focal Points, 19.05.2009, 3.

678 *UNEP*, Marine Litter: A Global Challenge, 2009, 7.

grammes, as UNEP serves as an instrument to coordinate and consequently ensure harmonious and coherent environment protection approaches.[679] Its objective is rather to contextualise and understand the approaches that are taken generally to address issues of pollution in the differing Conventions and to put these in the setting of marine litter regulation. The specific primary obligations in the form of the provisions contained in the treaties as well as the related annexes and, where applicable, the subsequent recommendations and initiatives will be analysed so as to delineate and characterise the protection approach to the problem of marine litter pursued by each Convention. Since the diverse impacts and consequences of marine litter and its multiplicity of sources require a systematic approach, each Regional Sea Convention will be analysed with a view to specific focal topics. The choice of the main focus is derived both from the factual situation prevailing in the region and the measures available in the framework of each Regional Sea Convention.

B. Marine litter in the regulatory framework of the Baltic Sea

The Baltic Sea is one of the largest semi-enclosed brackish water areas in the world.[680] The narrow opening to the North Sea results in a reduced influx of oxygen-rich waters from the North Sea. Consequently, the saline concentration and volume of oxygen-rich water are proportionately low. Moreover, the residence time of the transferred water in the Baltic Sea amounts to 35 years, which consequently makes the sea vulnerable in respect of negative anthropogenic influences such as pollution.[681] The high

679 *Fritz,* Integrierter Umweltschutz im Völkerrecht, 2009, 215.

680 *Täufer,* Introduction to the Baltic Sea, in *Czybulka,* Marine nature conservation and management at the borders of the European Union (2012) 25–28, 25.

681 *HELCOM,* Ecosystem Health of the Baltic Sea 2003–2007: HELCOM Initial Holistic Assessment, Baltic Sea Environmental Proceedings (No 122), 2010, 7. Since the Baltic Sea is a relatively shallow sea that has only very limited access to the open seas, eutrophication and hazardous substances are one of the main human pressures: *Täufer,* Introduction to the Baltic Sea, in *Czybulka,* Marine nature conservation and management at the borders of the European Union (2012) 25–28, 26.
See for a discussion on the legal implications of the specific Baltic Sea hydrographical and geomorphic characteristics: *Jenisch,* The International Journal of Marine and Coastal Law 11 (1996) 47.

population density of over 85 million citizens around the Baltic Sea exerts further pressures on the fragile environment. This problem was recognised in the early 1970s and addressed by the establishment of an international convention aiming to ensure the protection of the marine environment from all sources, the 1974 Convention on the Protection of the Marine Environment of the Baltic Sea Area.[682] The geopolitical changes surrounding the Baltic Sea Area in the 1990s and the impetus of progressive environmental developments prior to the Rio Conference made the adoption of an amended Helsinki Convention in 1992 possible.[683] The treaty was established in the spirit of the Rio Declaration and intends at working "to embody developments in international environmental policy and law"[684] under the auspices of the advancement of specific environmental goals. As a so-called "second generation regional treaty"[685], the Helsinki Convention

---

682 The 1974 Convention on the Protection of the Marine Environment of the Baltic Sea Area "had an important influence on the formulation of the marine pollution provisions of the 1982 UNCLOS and of UNEP′s regional seas treaties": *Birnie/Boyle/Redgwell,* International law and the environment, 2009, 395. See for a general discussion on the 1974 Convention on the Protection of the Marine Environment of the Baltic Sea Area in the context of other Regional Seas obligations: *Fitzmaurice,* The 1974 Convention on the Protection of the Marine Environment of the Baltic Sea Area, in *Platzöder/Verlaan,* The Baltic Sea (1996) 312 *et seq.*; *Brubaker,* Marine pollution and international law, 1993; *Jenisch,* The International Journal of Marine and Coastal Law 11 (1996) 47.

683 *Frank,* The European Community and marine environmental protection in the international law of the sea, 2007, 35. The Contracting Parties are: Denmark, Estonia, Finland, Germany, Latvia, Lithuania, Poland, Russia, Sweden and the European Union. The 1992 Helsinki Convention is the first Regional Seas agreement that has implemented the obligations arising out of Agenda 21: *Birnie/Boyle/Redgwell,* International law and the environment, 2009, 395. See also: *Ehlers,* The International Journal of Marine and Coastal Law 8 (1993) 191; *Jenisch,* The Development of Environmental Standards in the Baltic Sea, in *Ehlers/Wolfrum/Borgese,* Marine issues (2002) 63–72; *Plasman,* The International Journal of Marine and Coastal Law 13 (1998) 325.

684 Preamble, para.12 HC.

685 *Doris König,* Marine Environment, International Protection, in Max Planck Encyclopedia of Public International Law (MPEPIL), D.38; *Treves,* Regional Approaches to the Protection of the Marine Environment, in *Nordquist/Moore/Mahmoudi,* The Stockholm declaration and law of the marine environment (2003) 137–154, 144 (who names them "two generations instruments"). Second-generation regional treaties are those regional agreements that have been revised in the follow-up process of the Rio-Conference in 1992 in order to integrate new developments.

sets out to apply the precautionary principle, the polluter-pays-principle and to ensure the participation of the civil society, all of which has moved the scope of the Convention beyond the prevention of pollution.

The Convention applies to the protection of the marine environment of the Baltic Sea Area, which comprises the entire Baltic Sea and is delimited by its entrance. The only access to open sea is defined as the parallel of the Skaw in the Skagerrak at 57 44.43´N.[686] The Baltic Sea Area is defined by Art. 4 HC as comprising the water-column and the seabed, although the subsoil is not directly mentioned in this provision. The subsoil is however integrated amongst others in the norm controlling land-based pollution including any pollution caused by the disposal under the sea-bed, *i.e.*, the subsoil, with access from land by tunnel, pipeline or other means.[687] Air as a medium which is usually excluded from the scope of such conventions, is functionally included in that emissions, which are inducted from a point or diffuse input on land and reach the sea airborne, are considered as falling under its scope.[688] The internal waters are included in the scope of the Convention.[689]

The concept of the protection of a coastal zone extending both seawards and landwards was introduced in the form of a recommendation which requires Parties to take measures to ensure the environmental integrity of land as well as marine areas. Nevertheless, the Contracting Parties are free to delimit the boundaries of the landward limits of their internal waters, which they must then communicate to the depositary at the time of the deposit of the instrument of ratification, approval or accession.[690] The subjective nature of the individual designation of the internal waters could be potentially problematic. It may theoretically have as a consequence that landward borders of the internal waters are differently designated among the Contracting Party. Additionally, the designation made in regard to estuaries seems to be obsolete, as Art. 2 HC in conjunction with Art. 6 (1) HC provides for the integration of the riverine system, consequently applying a functional limited drainage basin approach as all land-sources

686 Art. 1 sent.1 HC. This geographical delimitation differs slightly from the geographic provisions stipulated in the Special Area under MARPOL Annex V.

687 Art. 2 (2) sent. 2 HC.

688 Art. 2 sent. 1 HC.

689 *Ehlers,* The International Journal of Marine and Coastal Law 8 (1993) 191, 1996 *et seq.*

690 Art. 1 sent.3 HC.

"reaching the sea waterborne" are included in the scope. This implies that there must be a link between the inland source and its influx into the Baltic Sea, otherwise these provisions fall under the regime of inland water protection. The geographic scope extending both to inland and air pollution opens the regulatory approach to address diffuse pollution that is carried by rivers or is airborne. The integration of the riverine system also has an effect on the potential geographic scope of the Convention.

The Helsinki Convention contains an accession clause stating that all States being "*interested* in fulfilling the aims and purposes of the convention"[691] can accede upon invitation of all Contracting Parties to the Convention. It is simply a matter of logic and common sense that Belarus and Ukraine, as countries whose sovereign territories are included in the catchment area of the Baltic Sea, are at least granted observer status. The relevance of the broad interpretation of the geographical scope of the Convention can particularly be seen with respect to the regulation of land-based pollution in the framework of the catchment area of the Baltic Sea. The Baltic is comprised of the territorial waters and Exclusive Economic Zones of the riparian States only.[692]

I. The institutional framework established by the Helsinki Convention

The Baltic Marine Environment Protection Commission (HELCOM) serves as an intergovernmental supervisory institution. HELCOM is the executive body of the Helsinki Convention and is comprised of a chairperson who serves for a period of two years and is supported by administrative staff. The Commission appoints the Executive Secretary, who shall perform administrative functions and other tasks entrusted by HELCOM.[693] An international secretariat is established in Helsinki, in order to support the work of the Commission.[694] Art. 20 HC sets out the functional provisions and duties of HELCOM. Apart from secretarial work,[695] HEL-

691 Art. 35 (2) HC.

692 *Röckmann,* International Co-operation for Sustainable Fisheries in the Baltic, in *Ehlers/Lagoni,* International maritime organisations and their contribution towards a sustainable marine development (2006) 239–258, 239.

693 Art. 21 (5) HC.

694 Art. 21 (3) HC.

695 *Röckmann,* International Co-operation for Sustainable Fisheries in the Baltic, in *Ehlers/Lagoni,* International maritime organisations and their contribution to-

COM has the duty to keep the implementation of the Convention under continuous observation[696] and to make recommendations relating to the purpose of the Convention.[697] HELCOM has no prescriptive power in terms of being able to create binding legal norms and, therefore, its recommendations are not legally binding and are thus best described as "soft law".

The terminology "soft law" is used to indicate that the instrument is not itself law *sensu stricto,* yet its importance within the general framework of international legal development is quite substantial.[698] The elaboration of recommendations, for example, indicates that they were preceded by intense intergovernmental co-operation, discussions and meetings. Thus, the contents of these recommendations reflect State practice and manifests general consent towards certain concepts and basic principles that are acceptable and practicable for all States.[699] Moreover, especially as a result of its non-binding character, a potentially positive aspect of a recommendation may be found in the possible progressive content which can be integrated. Since their elaboration is based on the principle of co-operation, the HELCOM Recommendations establish a certain degree of flexibility to address arising environmental problems as they arise.[700] To assist with the planning of recommendations and the specifications of the substantive articles as set out in the treaty, the organisational structure of the HELCOM envisages the creation of permanent working groups charged with

---

wards a sustainable marine development (2006) 239–258, 239; *Jenisch,* The Development of Environmental Standards in the Baltic Sea, in *Ehlers/Wolfrum/Borgese,* Marine issues (2002) 63–72, 67.

696 Art. 20 (1) (a) HC.

697 Art. 20 (1) (b) HC. See for example: HELCOM Recommendation 29/2 on marine litter within the Baltic Sea Region, 05.03.2008. Moreover, its task is to review the contents of the Convention including its Annexes and recommend changes in regard to substantive norms, as well as the adoption of new annexes or the amendment of existing annexes Art. 20 (1) (c) and (d) HC.

698 *Birnie/Boyle/Redgwell,* International law and the environment, 2009, 36.

699 *Ibid.*, 35. *Toope,* Formality and Informality, in *Bodansky/Brunnée/Hey,* The Oxford handbook of international environmental law (2007) 107–124, 119.

700 *Fitzmaurice,* International legal problems of the environmental protection of the Baltic Sea, 1992, 81. During the negotiations leading up to the 1992 Helsinki Convention, it was considered to provide HELCOM with competence to adopt binding recommendations *Jenisch,* The Development of Environmental Standards in the Baltic Se, in *Ehlers/Wolfrum/Borgese,* Marine issues (2002) 63–72, 69.

preparing background material on more technical aspects and to propose issues for discussion at the meeting of the Heads of the Delegations to HELCOM.[701]

II. Primary and secondary Helsinki Convention provisions regarding pollution

The Helsinki Convention is not only restricted to a sectoral approach,[702] *i.e.*, the protection of area-specific environmental issues, but it encompasses the environment as a whole. This comprehensive or holistic approach is reflected in the preamble, indicating the fragile state of the marine environment which is composed of "exceptional and ecological characteristics living resources."[703] The comprehensive approach that encompassed all sources was already embedded in the 1974 Helsinki Convention, a document that served as a guideline in the establishment of the 1982 UNCLOS and also other UNEP`s Regional Seas Conventions.[704]

The regulatory approach of the Convention is made up of substantive articles and legally binding annexes[705] which refer to specific pollution types and substantiate the provisions as set out in the Convention: The introduction of harmful substances (Annex I), land-based pollution sources (Annex II), exemptions from the general prohibition of dumping of waste and other matter (Annex V), pollution from ships (Annex IV), prevention

701 *Täufer,* Introduction to the Baltic Sea, in *Czybulka,* Marine nature conservation and management at the borders of the European Union (2012) 25–28, 34. There are five permanent working groups (WG) which were established after the revision of HELCOM main groups in September 2014: WG GEAR (Group on the Implementation of the Ecosystem Approach), WG MARITIME (Maritime Group), WG PRESSURE (Working Group on Reduction of Pressures from the Baltic Sea Catchment Area), formerly WG LAND (Land-based Pollution Group), WG RESPONSE (Response Group) and WG STATE AND CONSERVATION (Working Group on the State of the Environment and Nature Conservation).

702 *Graf Vitzthum,* Raum und Umwelt im Völkerrecht, in *Graf Vitzthum,* Völkerrecht (2007) 387–490, 457 (issues such as the combat against pollution from land, the protection of the air, animals or plants).

703 Preamble, para. 1 HC.

704 *Birnie/Boyle/Redgwell,* International law and the environment, 2009, 388.

705 According to Art. 28 HC, the Annexes attached to the convention form an integral part of it.

of pollution from offshore activities (Annex VI) and response to pollution incidents (Annex VII).

The obligation to prevent pollution stipulated in Art. 3 (1) HC reads:

> [t]he Contracting Parties shall individually or jointly take all appropriate legislative, administrative or other relevant measures to prevent and eliminate pollution in order to promote the ecological restoration of the Baltic Sea Area and the preservation of its ecological balance.

The Helsinki Convention stipulates thus a positive duty to eliminate and prevent pollution that is to be achieved by a comprehensive framework integrating different sources of pollution. Additionally, the aim to restore the Baltic Sea is extremely ambitious, even though the reference status of the "restoration" is open for interpretation. This comprehensive protection approach is additionally strengthened by an obligation to prevent and eliminate pollution by harmful substances from all sources (Art. 5 HC in conjunction with Annex I HC). Consequently, a distinction is made between hazardous and harmful substances that imply a differentiated approach towards the pollutants entering the Baltic marine environment. [706] It provides the possibility to prioritise substances according to their potential harm to the environment. A harmful substance in the context of the HC is defined as "any substance, which, if introduced into the sea, is liable to cause pollution."[707] Read together with Art. 3 (2) HC, that definition thus constitutes, with a view to the potentially toxic interactions of pollutants and plastics, a precautionary approach that is highly suitable for the issue of marine litter.[708]

In preventing and eliminating pollution, the Contracting Parties are obliged to promote the use of BEP and BAT.[709] It is further outlined that

706 Hazardous substances "means any harmful substance which due to its intrinsic properties is persistent, toxic or liable to accumulate" (Art. 2 (4) (8) HC). This provision is consequently relevant for the toxicological potential of marine litter.

707 Art. 2 (4) (7) HC. Regulation 1 (2) (i) HC lists *inter alia* "persistent materials which may float, remain in suspension or sink" as a priority substance. From this one can conclude that plastics which usually have these characteristics are also considered as a harmful substance in the Helsinki Convention.

708 Similar: *Marr,* The precautionary principle in the law of the sea, 2003, 63. See also a discussion on this aspect in chapter 3.

709 Art. 3 (3) HC. Despite the wording that provides merely a weak obligation ("to promote") to endorse the use of those practices and thus does not constitute an absolute obligation regarding their application, the introduction is seen as ensuring a modern technological standard. Criteria and general provisions in relation

BEP shall be used for all sources and BAT for point sources.[710] While the definition of BEP as "the application of the most appropriate combination of measures" does not contribute to a clarification of the concept, the proposed measures such as public information, the availability of collection and disposal systems and recycling, recovery and re-use[711] help to shed light on the content. BAT on the other hand signifies "the latest stage of development (state of the art) of processes, of facilities or of methods of operation which indicate the practical suitability of a particular measure for limiting discharges."[712]

The various substantive provisions on pollution control in the Baltic Sea can be seen as an overarching framework in which each polluting substances is integrated. Irrespective of the inclusion of several substances, the Contracting Parties can prioritise those substances that are seen to need most urgently regulation. Against this backdrop, it is important to understand that marine litter in the framework of HELCOM was until only very recently "not prioritised in the Baltic Sea Region as a major problem."[713] This understanding could potentially lead to the situation in which lesser attention is paid to the issue of marine litter. Having in mind the obligation of Art. 3 (1) HC, that obliges the Contracting Parties to "[…] promote the ecological restoration of the Baltic Sea Area and the preservation of its

---

to Best Environmental Practice and Best Available technology are furthermore substantiated in Annex II HC.

710 Regulation 1 (2) Annex II HC as well as in relation to land-based pollution, Art. 6 (1) HC.

711 Regulation 2 (1) Annex II HC. In the choice of BEP, consideration is to be made amongst others of the precautionary principle, the associated risks and social and economic implications of the planned measures (Regulation 2 (2) Annex II HC).

712 Regulation 3 (1 and 2) Annex II HC.

713 *HELCOM News*, 1/2008 Newsletter, Marine litter a concern, but not a major problem, 31 *et seq.*; *HELCO*M, HELCOM 29th Meeting (29/2008), Agenda Item 3 Matters arising from the subsidiary bodies, Document Code 3/11, 2. A focus is for example laid on the input of nutrients. The excess of nutrients leads to algal blooms and increased growth of macroalgae which leads to increased oxygen consumption and oxygen depletion in the bottom water. This potentially has a strong impact in semi-enclosed seas such as the Baltic Sea that has only a limited exchange with oxygen rich waters. This assumption has changed recently most prominently with the pertinent passage in the HELCOM Copenhagen Ministerial Declaration "Taking Further Action to Implement the Baltic Sea Action Plan-Reaching Good Environmental Status for a healthy Baltic", 03.10.2013 (Copenhagen, Denmark) (HELCOM Copenhagen Ministerial Declaration). See for a discussion on the relevance of this document, section F of this chapter.

ecological balance" such a statement can be described as careless or, at best, premature.

As established elsewhere, the persistence and toxicology of marine litter may amount, in the long-term, to a significant problem for the marine environment. Consequently, a case study on how marine litter is addressed and regulated in the Helsinki Convention also serves as a yardstick on how comprehensive the established regime addresses initially less prioritised substances. It needs also to be seen how this is reflected in the work and projects of the HELCOM.

1. The land-based pollution approach of the Helsinki Convention

The comprehensive geographic scope of the Helsinki Convention is strengthened by the definition of land-based pollution as:

> pollution of the sea by point or diffuse inputs from all sources on land reaching the sea waterborne, airborne or directly from the coast. It includes pollution from any deliberate disposal under the seabed with access from land by tunnel, pipeline or other means.[714]

---

714 Art. 2 (2) HC. See for a review of the approach to land-based pollution as followed by the Helsinki Convention 1974: *Hassan,* Protecting the marine environment from land-based sources of pollution, 2006, 118 *et seq.*; *Brubaker,* Marine pollution and international law, 1993, 100; *Täufer,* Introduction to the Baltic Sea, in *Czybulka,* Marine nature conservation and management at the borders of the European Union (2012) 25–28. In 1992 the Baltic Sea Joint Comprehensive Environmental Action Programme (JCP) was established with a time framework of 20 years. It aimed to reduce pollution through international co-operation and the so-called hot-spot approach. 192 hot-spots of both industrial and agricultural pollution were chosen that were believed to contribute with high emissions to the pollution level of the Baltic Sea. The inclusion as well as withdrawal of hot spots was at time controversial, as the criteria used for these procedures were not clear and contained complex requirements. Consequently, the removal of a hot spot has been subject to controversial discussions: *Kremser,* The Baltic Sea Joint Comprehensive Environmental Action Programme, in *Ehlers/Wolfrum/Borgese,* Marine issues (2002) 105–118, 108; *HELCOM,* HELCOM Land 17th Meeting (17/2012), Agenda Item 6: Joint Comprehensive Environmental Action Programme-Request for additional information for the decision to delete hot spots No.54 in Lithuania, Document code 6/16. This "naming and shaming approach" was sought to be reversed by a "Baltic Green Spot" concept that would demonstrate good practice, see *HELCOM,* HELCOM HOD 35th Meeting (35/2011), Agenda Item 3: Matters

In recognition of the Contracting Parties' sovereignty,[715] the Helsinki Convention´s approach to land-based pollution is couched in terms of "close regional co-operation."[716] An obligation to co-operate regarding the input of shared watercourses is established through Art. 6 (4) HC that stipulates the co-operation between two or more riparian Contracting Parties or, if interested or concerned, third States.

The threshold to act is quite low, as Art. 6 (4) HC specifies that if the input of substances is "liable to cause pollution of the marine environment" the concerned parties are obliged to take measures.[717] The procedures and measures related to land-based pollution are substantiated in Annex III HC.[718] Annex III has a twofold approach to land-based pollution as it addresses both pollution from industry and municipalities[719] as well as pollution from agriculture.[720] While both parts are primarily concerned with regulating the introduction of nutrients,[721] part I contains some relevant approaches on standard setting regarding marine litter. It establishes treatments standards for municipal and waste waters and water management in industrial plants. In doing so, it follows a permitting approach that substantiates Art. 6 (3) HC as this provisions allows for the introduction of harmful substances from point sources "in negligible quantities" upon the granting of a prior permit.[722] Whereas no yardstick for a further specification of "negligible" is provided, Annex III HC establishes

arising from the HELCOM Groups - Draft Criteria for Green Baltic Spots, Document Code 3/12.

715 Art. 6 (1) sent. 2 HC.

716 Preamble, para.5 HC.

717 (emphasis added). The obligation to co-operate is not absolute and does not "amount to a procedural obligation to cooperate" *Ehlers,* The International Journal of Marine and Coastal Law 8 (1993) 191, 203. The threshold of "liable" is a reflection on the preventative and precautionary principle.

718 See for a general discussion on the role of Annex II HC in the context of the overall Baltic Sea protection regime: *Ehlers,* The International Journal of Marine and Coastal Law 8 (1993) 191, 201 *et seq.*

719 Part I Annex III HC.

720 Part II Annex III HC.

721 HELCOM, HELCOM Initial Holistic Assessment, Baltic Sea Environmental Proceedings (No 122), 2010, 9; *Ehlers,* Marine Environment Protection - The Baltic Sea Example, in *Ehlers/Wolfrum/Borgese,* Marine issues (2002) 92–104, 94.

722 The permit may be regularly reviewed and the Contracting Parties are obliged to monitor and control permitted emissions (Art. 6 (3) HC).

principles and procedures that give guidance in the permitting process.[723] In the application process, information should be contained regarding the site of discharge, the treatment of solid waste and the possible impacts on the environment.[724]

Furthermore, the operator of the industrial plant that intends to make use of the right to emit should, in the permitting process, include and describe the planned activities. The option to emit "negligible" quantities into the environment constitutes a loophole in the general prohibition of pollution as laid down in the Helsinki Convention. There is a tangible risk that it may be a significant source of harmful substances if no coordination process takes place that monitors the cumulative charge of each individual permits in the entire catchment area of the Baltic Sea.

2. The prevention of pollution from ships

The substantive article of the Helsinki Convention regarding ship pollution strives "to protect the Baltic Sea Area from pollution by ships."[725] In achieving this, the provision refers to measures as outlined in Annex VI of the Helsinki Convention.[726] The Contracting Parties are to achieve this by cooperating within the IMO and to promote and ensure an effective and harmonised implementation of IMO rules.[727] This is also as relevant as the

723 However, the wording "undertake to apply the following principles and procedures" indicates that these procedural aspects are not legally binding in their form (Part 1, Regulation 3, Annex III HC).

724 Part I, Regulation 3 (1) Annex III HC.

725 Art. 8 (1) HC. See for an introduction on the issue of shipping in the framework of HELCOM: *Brusendorff/Ehlers,* The International Journal of Marine and Coastal Law 17 (2002) 351.

726 See for a discussion: *Ehlers,* The International Journal of Marine and Coastal Law 8 (1993) 191, 204.

727 Regulation 1 Annex IV HC. *Treves* outlines in this regard that regional rules to vessel-based pollution are also permissible under UNCLOS in that the term "international" of Art. 211 (1) UNCLOS and the reference to "cooperative agreements" of Art. 211 (3) UNCLOS "are very likely to be of regional character" *Treves,* Regional Approaches to the Protection of the Marine Environment, in *Nordquist/Moore/Mahmoudi,* The Stockholm declaration and law of the marine environment (2003) 137–154, 139. Also, *Treves* argues that vessel-based pollution "[…] approach of the Helsinki Convention remains one of subsidiarity to the global rules …]", *ibid.,* 141.

Baltic Sea is designated as a Special Area under MARPOL Annex V which provides for a higher protection standard of permissible discharges into the marine environment. The explicit obligation to endorse IMO rules and instruments strengthens their application as, within the regime created by the Helsinki Convention, the Contracting Parties are thus under a duty to implement those obligations, percolating down from two legally binding sources.[728]

a) Port Reception Facilities

Regarding marine litter from vessel-source pollution, the Helsinki Convention enjoys a pioneering role in establishing a unique system of ships' waste reception and handling in ports. This is already embodied in Art. 8 (2) HC that stipulates the obligation to "develop and apply uniform requirements for the provisions of reception facilities for ship-generated wastes, taking into account, *inter alia* the special needs of passengers ships operating in the Baltic Sea Area." The focal point adopted by HELCOM on port reception facilities relates to a detailed regulatory and technical framework that helps to ensure a coordinated application of norms. This, in turn, guarantees equal standards for port operators avoiding competitive distortions[729] and an increased protection regime that potentially reduces illegal discharges into the Baltic Sea. The port reception regime in the Baltic Sea Area is further substantiated in detail by Regulation 6 An-

728 According to Regulation 4 (1) Annex IV HC, the Contracting Parties are obliged to apply MARPOL Annex I–V thus ensuring a broad protection scope. With a view to embody developments of international law, the developments and future provisions such as the denial of entry into ports of vessels that continue to operate beyond the "anniversary of the date of delivery in 2015" are spelt out (Regulation 4 (2) (c) Annex IV HC). This regulation is based on the revised Regulation 13G MARPOL Annex I.

729 *Tan,* Vessel-source marine pollution, 2006, 255 *et seq.* Accordingly, "apart from direct construction and maintenance cost [of the port reception facilities], states fear that the imposition of charges for the use of reception facilitates may affect their *port's commercial competitiveness*. This concern would be especially pertinent if neighboring ports do not require the use of such facilities. Consequently, the uneven provision of reception facilities has raised concern throughout the world-particularly in Europe- over the distortion in competition arising among different ports and shipping companies" (emphasis added).

nex IV HC that establishes a mandatory discharge of all wastes as outlined in MARPOL Annex V to a port reception facility.[730]

Since MARPOL does not establish such a mandatory system of discharge of all waste, the argumentation that regional rules potentially undermine globally accepted standards such as MARPOL needs to be considered. As MARPOL establishes minimum standards, it is permissible to implement increased environmental protection standards.[731] In implementing Art. 211 (3) UNCLOS that allows for the establishment of particular entry requirements for the prevention and reduction of vessel-based based pollution, the mandatory discharge is permissible when a port State chooses to make use of its territorial sovereignty of a port State.

The mandatory discharge is, however, exempted for "special arrangements" that relate, for example, to passenger ferries engaged in short voyages as well as "minor amounts of wastes."[732] Furthermore, a vessel may retain "minor amounts of wastes on board" when their discharge constitutes an unreasonable burden.[733] This provision could theoretically lead to a circumvention of the mandatory discharge; nevertheless, it has been established in a (non-binding) recommendation that, in relation to ships garbage covers, "all collected garbage ready for delivery at the time of departure must be delivered."[734]

Since the design and provisions of port reception facilities have not been coherently addressed on the global scale,[735] HELCOM has further substantiated certain elements by providing for additional soft law instruments. The Strategy on Port Reception Facilities and a plethora on perti-

730 Regulation 6 (B) Annex IV HC. Regulation 6 concerning mandatory discharge of all wastes to a port reception facility of Annex IV HC was made legally binding through its inclusion in the Annex, see before HELCOM Recommendation 21/2 on Amendments to Annex IV "Prevention of Pollution from Ships" of the Helsinki Convention, 20.03.2000. See for information on the categories of waste included in the mandatory discharge regime: HELCOM Recommendation 22/3 on Unified interpretations to ensure a harmonised and effective implementation of the strategy for port reception facilities for ship-generated wastes and associated issues, 21.03.2001.

731 See chapter 2 in this context.

732 Regulation 6 (C) (1 and 3) Annex IV HC. No definition is provided to clarify the exact content and understanding of minor amount of waste. Any granted exemption must be communicated to HELCOM.

733 Regulation 6 (C) (2) Annex IV HC.

734 Part. C, para.3 HELCOM Recommendation 22/3. This excludes food waste.

735 See chapter 2.

nent recommendations have been adopted that address the handling of wastes in ports, the economic framework of port reception facilities and notification obligations.[736] Despite their character as soft law, thus their non-binding status, their impact is substantial as they create an exemplary best practice that had an impact on actions taken in other fora.[737]

b) The no-special-fee-system as a means to reduce vessel-based pollution

In order to provide a further incentive regarding the disposal of waste in ports, a particular cost recovery system for the discharge of waste is established in the framework of the Helsinki Convention regime. The so-called "no-special-fee-system" was established by HELCOM Recommendation 28E/10 with a view to preventing operational and illegal discharges into the sea by promoting the discharge of ship's waste in ports and to avoid undesirable waste streams between ports.[738] The no-special-fee-system in the Baltic Sea Area establishes an (indirect)

> charging system where the cost of reception, handling and disposal of ship-generated wastes, originating from the normal operation of the ship, as well as of marine litter caught in fishing nets, is included in the harbour fee or otherwise charged to the ship irrespective of whether wastes are delivered or not.[739]

The fundamental element of the no-special-fee-system is that no additional costs are imposed on ships using the port reception facilities, therefore removing expenses for discharge that could otherwise be avoided by circumventing the discharge. HELCOM Recommendation 28E/10 was

736 Pertinent recommendations include: HELCOM Recommendation 31E/4 on Proper handling of wastes/landfilling, 20.05.2010 outlines harmonised requirements on proper handling of inert, non-hazardous and hazardous waste, and requires introduction of modern landfill techniques and the phasing out of improper dumping sites and HELCOM Recommendation 23/1 on Notification on ship′s waste, 06.03.2002 requires notification by ships of the intended use of a reception facility as a prerequisite to ensure the use and efficient operation of port reception facilities.

737 See chapter 4.

738 Preamble, para.3 HELCOM Recommendation 28E/10 on the Application of the no-special-fee system to ship-generated wastes and marine litter caught in fishing nets in the Baltic Sea Area, 15.11.2007.

739 Part 1 (1) HELCOM Recommendation 28E/10.

amended by enlarging its scope to also include besides, ship-generated waste, litter caught in fishing nets.[740] Consequently, in line with the mandatory discharge of waste, the recommendation proposes to establish a no-special-fee-system for MARPOL Annexes I, IV and V substances and recommends extending the charging system to "marine litter caught in fishing nets."[741]

With a view to stifling from an environmental perspective undesirable competition among ports, a harmonised application of the no-special-fee-system is foreseen in both the Baltic Sea Areas as well as in the North Sea Regions.[742] In calculating the waste management fee, the recommendation stipulates fair, transparent and non-discriminatory criteria. Even though Recommendation 28E/10 states that fees should be independent of the size of the ship,[743] it offers for an option to scale the fee according to:

> a high quality standard of the applied waste management procedures and waste processing equipment on board [that] can also be taken into account in scaling the waste management fee, having in mind the general aim of minimisation of waste production, and the benefit of waste separation.[744]

This provision provides the ports with a degree of flexibility in determining the proportionate fraction for garbage discharge in the harbour fee and can be seen to encourage operators to apply BEP and BAT with a view to economise their expenditures. Furthermore, ships that are engaged in "regular services" can be exempted from the no-special-fee-system where they satisfy the precondition that evidence is adduced for regular traffic and waste management practices on board.[745] In line with the co-operation requirement, those exemptions should be communicated to other Port States

740 *UNEP*, Marine Litter: A Global Challenge, 2009, 36; HELCOM Recommendation 28E/10.

741 Preamble, paras.8 and 9 HELCOM Recommendation 28E/10.

742 Para.5 HELCOM Recommendation 28E/10.

743 Para.4 (1) HELCOM Recommendation 28E/10.

744 Para.4 (2) HELCOM Recommendation 28E/10.

745 3 HELCOM Recommendation 28E/10. "Regular services" means "a series of ship crossings operated so as to serve traffic between the same two or more ports, or a series of voyages from and to the same port without intermediate calls, either: (i) according to a published timetable, or (ii) with crossings so regular or frequent that they constitute a recognisable schedule. A crossing should be considered as frequent if the ship visits the port once a fortnight.".

along the route and also to HELCOM in order to prevent abuse that could lead to illegal discharges.[746]

c) The role of the polluter-pays-principle and cost recovery

In the choice of establishing fees for the disposal of on board generated garbage, several options are available. Due to the role of incentives for disposal at ports, an assessment of options for disposal fees of vessel garbage is an economic instrument that is categorised at the interface between economic considerations and environmental protection. An evaluation of the options should look at incentives of both waste minimisation and (economic) incentives to discharge the waste in ports, but also on the system of cost recovery. Cost recovery refers to "a mechanism to generate revenue, which is used to cover the capital, operational and administrative costs of operating port reception facilities."[747] The costs of equipment, staff costs and also the fees for the disposal or recycling of the waste are also expenses that are to be covered.[748] IMO has identified six systems for recovering the costs of port reception facilities. These are, besides the no-special-fee-system, the direct-fee-system, the contract-system, the fixed-fee-system, the combined-system and the free-of-charge system.[749] These systems are opposed to one another in the way they recover costs. The direct-fee-system envisages the payment of a direct fee for every lot of garbage that is discharged by the vessel operator, whereas the free-of-charge-system does not charge the vessels for their waste disposal in ports.

The notion underlying the direct-fee-system is the implementation of the polluter-pays-principle in that the waste producer covers all expenses

746 For the purpose of promoting a dialogue forum and exchange of good practices on implementing and operating port reception facilities for sewage, the HELCOM Cooperation platform on port reception facilities in the Baltic Sea was established in 2011, see http://helcom.fi/helcom-at-work/groups/maritime/prf-cooperation-platform, last accessed 27.08.2015. Even though this cooperation platform is currently limited to sewage issues, such a cooperation forum could be also imaginable for waste produced onboard of vessels.

747 *Carl Bro a/s*, A Study on the Availability and Use of Port Reception Facilities for Ship-Generated Waste December 2005, 4.

748 *Carpenter/Macgill,* Marine Pollution Bulletin 42 (2001) 257, 258.

749 *IMO*, Comprehensive manual on port reception facilities, 1999.

associated with the disposal of the waste.[750] However, additional costs associated with the disposal of garbage could be a disincentive to discharge in ports. With these economic considerations in mind the free-of-charge-system provides an incentive to discharge but of course depends on subsidies or revenues of certain taxes to cover the incurred costs.[751] Along the range of choices, the contract system entails that a vessel that regularly calls at a port, can conclude an agreement between the operator of the port reception facility on the volume and rate of a monthly or annual volume of delivered waste.[752] The fixed-fee and the combined-fee-system rely on a garbage disposal fee which is separately paid from the port fees.[753] Whereas in the fixed-fee-system, the amount paid for waste disposal is already determined, the combined-system charges a fixed sum plus an additional charge that depends on the volume and type of waste.[754]

The no-special-fee-system proposed provides an economic incentive to dispose of the garbage as the payment of the general port fee is not avoidable. This could in turn lead to a situation in which a ship might pay less than the actual waste discharge would cost in case a direct garbage fee would apply.[755] This additional sum must then be compensated by ports where there is, in some cases, a need to recover the additional costs. Such a system could also lead to "waste tourism" in which vessels would retain their generated waste on board and discharge it in a port which applies this cost recovery model, consequently providing an additional and disproportionate burden on that port.

Since the vessel owner pays a proportion of the actual costs of disposal, the no-special-fee-system implements the polluter-pays-principle. However, in order to keep the port fee at a reasonable, competitive price, the vessel´s payment may ultimately not cover the entire external costs incurred portside, such as additional costs that are not covered by the fee imposed e.g extra disposal requirements in relation to sectoral specific waste

750 As established in chapter 2 of this study, the application of the polluter-pays-principle is legally binding in the Helsinki Convention. However, due to a lack of definition in the convention text, no specific elements are prescribed that could guide the Contracting Parties in implementing or applying it.

751 *IMO*, Comprehensive manual on port reception facilities, 1999, 245.

752 *Ibid.*, 240.

753 *Ibid.*, 243 *et seq.*

754 *Ibid.*, 244 *et seq.*

755 See for an overview in this regard *Carl Bro a/s*, A Study on the Availability and Use of Port Reception Facilities for Ship-Generated Waste December 2005, 9.

(fishing gear etc.). The Helsinki Convention merely obliges the Contracting Parties to apply the principle without further defining its application or content. As has been previously shown, the polluter-pays-principle stipulated in Art. 3 (4) HC does not make reference to the principle of proportionality regarding to what degree costs should be covered.[756] In essence, all vessels will be required to pay the same amount, notwithstanding the fact that the overall amount of waste produced may vary greatly, ranging from no waste whatsoever to considerable amounts that are more expensive to dispose of than the flat-fee demanded by port authorities. Nevertheless, in particular with a view to the consequences of illegally discharged waste, a balance must be drawn between the economic incentive of an "adequate" price and the provision of port reception facilities.

Consequently, the no-special-fee-system could play an essential role in providing economic incentives to encourage vessel operators to dispose of their waste in ports. The proposed scaling of prices according to environmental criteria such as an effective waste minimisation and existence of a recycling scheme on board, serves as an incentive to make use of the port reception facilities. However, a coherent and harmonised cost recovery scheme implemented in all Baltic Sea ports is necessary to avoid any competitive distortions. To this end, the provisions on waste management and vessels engaged in regular service between ports should be further defined and outlined so as to achieve a common pricing and cost recovery standard.

In the context of the port reception facilities discourse, it is argued that the application of the wide sense of the polluter-pays-principle, thus the entire internalisation of cost, does not lead to the desired outcome of reducing illegal discharge. With a view to the aim of reducing and controlling pollution, a partial internalisation of cost should be the preferred course. This option does not contravene relevant provisions of Helsinki Convention, bearing in mind a teleological interpretation of its overall aim to reduce or eliminate pollution.

756 See for a reference chapter 3.

3. The role of monitoring of marine litter

In the Baltic Sea area, the understanding that a sound scientific knowledge is a prerequisite for an adequate legal instrument has resulted in a history of comprehensive monitoring programmes.[757] This is also substantiated in a norm on the development of assessment methodologies. Consequently, Art. 24 (2) HC aims to develop methods to assess "the nature and extent of pollution, pathways, exposures, risks and remedies in the Baltic Sea Area." In this context, HELCOM Recommendation 29/2 on marine litter within the Baltic Sea Region has been adopted and does not, as the title might indicate, relate to the prevention of marine litter but rather focuses on its monitoring and data collection.[758] The reason for this approach is the "[…] need to [for] such data for evaluation of implementation of the existing regulatory framework concerning marine litter in the Baltic and for identification of needs for additional measures."[759]

HELCOM thus implements on a regional level its understanding of unified monitoring and reporting methods. In doing so, the recommendation endorses the recognition of "one unified method of sampling and reporting of marine litter found on beach" and to "call upon different marine litter survey initiatives to use it in order to achieve comparable results."[760] In an attempt to harmonise and therefore increase the comparability of data, HELCOM has taken the beach litter monitoring approach as developed by OSPAR´s survey protocol.[761] A comparison between the two approaches supports the assumption that increased harmonisation between the monitoring methods in the different sea regions is sought after, which is also emphasised by recitals to HELCOM Recommendation 29/2 that provides for a regular review of marine litter and to "ensure harmonised approach on a global scale."[762]

---

757 *Ehlers,* Marine Environment Protection - The Baltic Sea Example, in *Ehlers/ Wolfrum/Borgese,* Marine issues (2002) 92–104, 102; *Ehlers,* The International Journal of Marine and Coastal Law 8 (1993) 191, 209.

758 HELCOM Recommendation 29/2 on marine litter within the Baltic Sea Region. No further definition of the term "marine litter" is provided in the recommendation.

759 Preamble, para.10 HELCOM Recommendation 29/2 (emphasis added).

760 Preamble, para.12 HELCOM Recommendation 29/2.

761 *HELCOM,* HELCOM 29th Meeting (29/2008), Agenda Item 3 Matters arising from the subsidiary bodies, Document Code 3/11, 2.

762 Preamble, paras.11 and 12 HELCOM Recommendation 29/2.

Also, the HELCOM Ministerial Declaration on the implementation of the HELCOM Baltic Sea Action Plan of 20 May 2010, the ministers of the environment of the Contracting Parties and the High Level EU representative agreed:

> to take further steps to be able to carry out national and coordinated monitoring of marine litter and identify sources of litter" and "to further investigate the potential harmful impacts to wildlife from microscopic plastic particles, an ingestion of which could lead to the transfer of toxic chemicals to the food chain.[763]

III. Preliminary Conclusion

The issue of marine litter in the Baltic Sea appears to have been of minor concern in the field of the pollution prevention regime. Notwithstanding this, one aspect has been covered under the primary law in that "synthetic and floating materials" are classified as a priority substance. It appears though that no further measures have been taken in that regard. Nevertheless, this classification could serve as an additional trigger point to take actions. Marine litter issues have been integrated in two ways: first, by adopting HELCOM Recommendation 29/2 and second, the amendment of HELCOM Recommendation 28E/10. However, recent changes have been made that serve as indicators that marine litter has been gaining increasing attention in this forum. In December 2012, the idea was proposed to establish a Task Group on "a project level to provide regional Baltic input to global and European work on Marine Litter."[764] This is now being implemented by establishing a new Working Group on Reduction of Pressures from the Baltic Sea Catchment Area (WG PRESSURE).[765] The Working

---

763 HELCOM Ministerial Declaration on the implementation of the HELCOM Baltic Sea Action Plan, 20.05.2010 (Moscow, Russia) (HELCOM Moscow Ministerial Declaration), 15.

764 *HELCOM*, HELCOM HOD 39th Meeting (39/2012), Agenda Item 3: Marine Litter in the Baltic Sea- Overview of present status and potential for further HELCOM actions, Document Code 3/19, 10.

765 The establishment of the Working Group PRESSURE is effected in the context of the rearrangement of HELCOM's structure as decided in September 2014: *HELCOM*, HELCOM HOD 46th Meeting, (46/2014), Agenda Item 3: Streamlining of HELCOM, 3.6, 3. The government of Germany has indicated a study reservation regarding the name until 24th September 2014.

Group addresses the input of different nutrients and hazardous substances and is also charged with coordinating the implementation on the Regional Action Plan on Marine Litter.[766] Additionally, the HELCOM Moscow Ministerial Declaration on the implementation of the HELCOM Baltic Sea Action Plan and the HELCOM Copenhagen Ministerial Declaration have stated that increased attention should be paid to marine litter considerations in the Baltic Sea.[767] This relates primarily to the Regional Action Plan on marine litter.[768] After a series of workshops to prepare this Action Plan, the Regional Action Plan on Marine Litter was adopted by HELCOM Recommendation 36/1 on a Regional Action Plan on Marine Litter (RAP ML) (hereinafter referred to as HELCOM RAP ML) in March 2015.[769] The HELCOM RAP ML integrates not only existing measures and approaches, but also moves beyond existing measures. It will be further analysed in a comparative manner to other Regional Action Plans in section F of this chapter.

With a view to specific instruments pertinent to marine litter it can be stated that the preventative pollution prohibition and the associated measures generally integrate several important sources of marine litter. The Helsinki Convention regime seems to contribute to the effective implementation of the global regime as it substantiates and fleshes out the rather vague provisions arising out of the global framework. In doing so, a very unique standard setting approach has been developed that is most strikingly discernible regarding the mandatory discharge prohibition and the no-special-fee-system.

Despite, or even because of, their non-binding character, the recommendations integrate progressive standards that have increasingly been adopted in other fora. The harmonisation of marine litter monitoring provisions indicates an increased coherence between the different regional agreements. In the following, the approach regarding marine litter as taken

766 *HELCOM,* HELCOM HOD 46th Meeting (46/2014), Annex 3: Terms of References for HELCOM Working Group on Reduction of Pressures from the Baltic Sea Catchment Area (WG PRESSURE).

767 See for a discussion section F. of this chapter.

768 See for a further analysis, section F. of this chapter.

769 . *HELCOM,* HELCOM Recommendation 36/1 on Recommendation 36/1 on a Regional Action Plan on Marine Litter (RAP ML), 04.03.2015. See for a detailed overview on the elemements of the HELCOM RAP ML, section F of this chapter.

in the North-East Atlantic will be analysed and contrasted, amongst others, with the regulatory regime of the Baltic Sea.

C. Marine litter regulations in the North-East Atlantic

The North-East Atlantic is a vast geographic area of 13,5 million km^2 which is home to a wide variety of different ecosystems. The regional ecology within the area varies immensely and is also, depending on the area, highly pressurised by human activities. Due to the presence of ports of global importance such as Rotterdam, Antwerp and Hamburg that serve as the logistical nexuses to continental Europe, shipping is intense in the area.[770] Due to the vast area and the multiplicity of activities that could potentially cause marine litter, "there are still gaps in the data characterising the status of marine litter in the region."[771] With this background in mind, particularly the issues of monitoring of marine litter will be studied, since it is notably in this regard that pertinent marine litter measures have been taken. After analysing relevant substantive provisions of the OSPAR Convention relating to marine litter, an attempt is made to put these obligations into the context of the strategic objectives on marine litter as adopted by the OSPAR Contracting Parties.

I. The regulatory framework of the North-East Atlantic

The OSPAR Convention is the Regional Sea Convention applicable to marine environmental protection of the North-East Atlantic.[772] The OSPAR Convention in its current form is a consolidated version of the Convention for the prevention of marine pollution by dumping from ships and aircraft

---

770 *Galgani/Fleet/van Franeker et al.,* Marine Strategy Framework Directive, Task Group 10 Report Marine Litter, 2010, 9; *Interviewes/Görlitz/Stöfen et al.,* Issue Paper to the "International Conference on Prevention and Management of Marine Litter in European Seas", 16.05.2013, 13.; *OSPAR Commission*, The OSPAR System of Ecological Quality Objectives for the North Sea (update 2010), Quality Status Report 2010, 2010, 11.

771 *UNEP*, Marine Litter: A Global Challenge, 2009, 107.

772 Its Contracting Parties are Belgium, Denmark, Finland, France, Germany, Iceland, Ireland, Luxemburg, the Netherlands, Norway, Portugal, Spain, Sweden, Switzerland, the United Kingdom and the European Union.

(Oslo Convention) from 1972[773] and the Convention for the prevention of marine pollution from land-based sources (Paris Convention) from 1974.[774] Even though the OSPAR Convention applies to the same geographic area, it moved the sectoral scope of its predecessors towards an integrated pollution approach that encompasses "all sources of pollution of the marine environment and the adverse effects of human activities upon it."[775] The OSPAR Convention is, similar to the Helsinki Convention, a framework convention in which some of the provisions of the treaty are substantiated by Annexes. By having a closer look at these Annexes, it becomes obvious that the OSPAR Convention exceeds that of a mere pollution prevention Convention.[776] The understanding of the inherent value of the marine environment of the North-East Atlantic as well as the importance of preserving an ecological equilibrium opens the regulatory scope beyond anthropogenic uses of the marine environment and provides a comprehensive protection instrument for this marine region.[777]

773 Convention for the Prevention of Marine Pollution by Dumping from Ships and Aircraft (Oslo) of 15 February 1972, in force 07 April 1974; 11 ILM 262 (1972). As amended by the Protocols of 2 March 1983 and 5 December 1989. The Oslo Convention on dumping also contained a reference to persistent plastic in Annex I (6) *Timagenis,* International control of marine pollution, op.1980, 205.

774 Convention for the Prevention of Marine Pollution from Land-Based Sources (Paris) of 04 June 1974, in force 06 May1978; 13 ILM 352 (1974). As amended by the Protocol of 26 March 1986. The OSPAR Convention from 1992 replaced these two conventions by virtue of Art. 31 OSPAR Convention. See for a discussion *Wettestad*, Marine Policy 18 (1994) 219.

775 Preamble, para.13 OSPAR Convention.

776 Annexes I, II and III OSPAR Convention deal with pollution from land-based sources, dumping and incineration and offshore pollution sources. Annex IV OSPAR Convention addresses the assessment of the quality of the marine environment. The wide material scope that goes beyond the pollution approach is also substantiated by its character as a framework convention that provides a mechanism to add further Annexes (Art. 15 in conjunction with Art. 16 OSPAR), see *De La Fayette,* The International Journal of Marine and Coastal Law 14 (1999) 247, 251. During the first ministerial meeting in Sintra, Portugal in 1998, Annex V and Appendix 3 on Criteria for Identifying Human Activities for the Purpose of Annex V were adopted. They substantiate the obligation contained in Art. 2 (1) (a) OSPAR Convention, see *Proelß,* Meeresschutz im Völker - und Europarecht, 2004, 229.

777 *Hilf,* Zeitschrift für ausländisches öffentliches Recht und Völkerrecht 55 (1995) 580, 582. Preamble, paras.2 and 4 OSPAR Convention.

The vast geographic area that is covered under the geographic scope extends to the Atlantic and Arctic Ocean and its dependent seas.[778] The regulatory technique of the OSPAR Convention is influenced by the geographic dimension of its subject of protection. The different sub-regions within the geographic scope differ in their degree of enclosure by land. Whereas some regions are to a certain extent enclosed by riparian States, such as the North Sea, other marine regions are "open" as "physical boundaries [...] in the open oceans are difficult, if not impossible, to define."[779] The different degrees of "openness" is, in regard to the discourse on marine litter, an important consideration as the differing ecological and oceanographic characteristics of each region require different priorities. In order to account for the factual context, the OSPAR Convention envisages a certain degree of regionalisation within its scope of application.[780] This regionalisation serves the purpose of integrating different ecological needs and economic conditions that may be addressed by proposing differing time frames in the implementation of the obligations arising out of the Convention.[781] For this purpose, five regions are determined that include: Arctic Waters, the Greater North Sea, the Celtic Sea, the Bay of Biscay and the Iberian Coast and the Wider Atlantic.[782] Particularly regarding marine litter, this distinction allows for a certain degree of flexibility in selecting adequate measures and for adjusting monitoring strategies and techniques to the specific prevailing geomorphic and hydrographic considerations.

This regionalisation is not limited but rather reinforced by the approach to cover the "maritime areas" as a whole that is defined as "the internal

778 Art. 1 (a) OSPAR Convention. These areas are delimited by the dependent seas that lie north of 36° north latitude and between 42° west longitude and 51° east longitude excluding the Baltic Sea and the Mediterranean Sea and are delimited by the Baltic and Mediterranean Sea and that part of the Atlantic Ocean north of 59° north latitude and between 44° west longitude and 42° west longitude.

779 See *Alexander,* The American Journal of International Law 71 (1977) 84, 86 (emphasis added) in: *Proelß,* Meeresschutz im Völker - und Europarecht, 2004, 39.

780 Art. 24 OSPAR Convention. *Hilf,* Zeitschrift für ausländisches öffentliches Recht und Völkerrecht 55 (1995) 580, 582.

781 Art. 24 OSPAR Convention; *De La Fayette,* The International Journal of Marine and Coastal Law 14 (1999) 247, 261.

782 In order to systematically order these sub-regions, a number has been provided for each part of the North-East Atlantic. Consequently, the Arctic is Region I, the Greater North Sea is Region II, the Celtic Seas is Region III, the Bay of Biscay and the Iberian Coast is region IV and the Wider Atlantic is Region V.

waters and the territorial seas of the Contracting parties, the sea beyond and adjacent to the territorial sea under the jurisdiction of the coastal state to the extent recognised by international law, and the high seas, including the bed of all those waters and its sub-soil."[783]

The OSPAR Convention establishes a fundamental prohibition to pollute in which the Contracting Parties are to "take all possible steps to prevent and eliminate pollution."[784] Irrespective of the pollution prevention aspect, the OSPAR Convention provides, furthermore, the ambitious goal of "where practicable, restore marine areas which have been adversely affected" from human activities.[785] The body of the OSPAR Convention contains the precautionary principle, a reference to Environmental Impact Assessment as well as monitoring and reporting obligations.[786] In the following, the approach to regulate ship-based pollution as a potential source of marine litter is studied.

II. Ship-based pollution prevention in the framework of the OSPAR Convention

In contrast to the source categories as envisaged by UNCLOS, the pollution sources addressed in the OSPAR Convention include land-based pollution, pollution by dumping and incineration and pollution from offshore sources. The substantive regulatory content and objectives thus differ somewhat from the Helsinki Convention's approach. This is most striking regarding the regulation of operational vessel-based pollution. Admittedly, pollution by dumping or incineration and offshore sources could include vessel-based pollution, but a reference to their definition clarifies this as being outside of the scope of the pertinent norm.[787] Dumping is defined as

> any deliberate disposal in the maritime area of wastes or other matter (1) from vessels or aircraft; (2) from offshore installations; (ii) any deliberate disposal in the maritime area of (1) vessels or aircraft; (2) offshore installations and

783 Art. 1 (a) OSPAR Convention.

784 Art. 2 (1) (a) OSPAR Convention.

785 *Ibid.*

786 See for an extensive discussion on these obligations: *Proelß,* Meeresschutz im Völker - und Europarecht, 2004 and section C.III of this chapter.

787 See also for a discussion on this aspect: *Heintschel von Heinegg,* The development of environmental standards for the north-east Atlantic including the North Ssea, in *Ehlers/Wolfrum/Borgese,* Marine issues (2002) 135–153, 137.

> offshore pipelines." In order to avoid conflicting norms, dumping does not include "the disposal in accordance with the International Convention for the Prevention of Pollution from Ships, 1973, as modified by the Protocol of 1978 relating thereto [...].[788]

The aim of the provision is however not to exclude any dumping, but only that type of disposal that is in conformity with the discharge standards of MARPOL.

Additionally, offshore sources are defined as "offshore installations and offshore pipelines from which substances or energy reach the maritime area."[789] Since vessel-based pollution, i.e. the disposal foreseen under MARPOL, does not fall under the scope of the regulated pollution, it is to be considered as "pollution from other sources" as provided for in Art. 7 OSPAR Convention.[790] The regulation of these types of pollution might be subject to action of the Contracting Parties. This right of initiative is limited to the extent that "the pollution is not already the subject of effective measures agreed by other international organisations or prescribed by other international conventions."[791]

Where actions regarding vessel-based pollution in the North-East Atlantic seem to be necessary, the OSPAR Commission may submit a request to IMO. The OSPAR Commission already made use of this rule regarding marine litter and has, for example, requested IMO to act on an amendment of MARPOL Annex V as early as 1998.[792] This provision

---

788 Art. 1 (f and g) OSPAR Convention.

789 Art. 1 (k) OSPAR Convention.

790 Art. 7 OSPAR Convention states that: "The Contracting Parties shall cooperate with a view to adopting Annexes, in addition to the Annexes mentioned in Articles 3-6 above, prescribing measures, procedures and standards to protect the maritime area against pollution from other sources, to the extent that such pollution is not already the subject of effective measures agreed by other international organisations or prescribed by other international conventions.".

791 Art. 7 OSPAR Convention.

792 OSPARCOM urged in the 42 MEPC meeting to "take appropriate action to strengthen the international co-operation within the maritime sector with the purpose of further reducing and controlling litter in the marine environment.", *IMO*, MEPC 42/22, Report of the Marine Environment Protection Committee on its Forty-Second Session, 16.11.1998, 48. In 2005, the proposition was made to expand the special area status of the North Sea under MARPOL Annex V to the same area as the Western European Waters PSSA: *OSPAR,* BCD 05/13/1-E, Summary Record of the Biodiversity Committee Meeting, Meeting of the Biodiversity Committee, Agenda Item 13, 25.02.2005, 24.

does not entirely exclude ship-based pollution from the scope of the OSPAR Convention. However, the OSPAR Commission´s role in this regard is that of a body charged with implementing global rules, rather than prescribing further substantiated or refined provisions. This could have several implications that also touch upon the question of marine litter.

III. Monitoring obligations under the OSPAR Convention

A very unique and highly pertinent obligation regarding marine litter consideration is stipulated in Art. 6 OSPAR Convention, in conjunction with Annex IV OSPAR Convention, on the assessment of the quality of the marine environment. The significance of this provision can be attributed to the fact that the norm is not only stipulated in the primary treaty body itself but also in an Annex which assigns concrete and detailed obligations. Art. 6 OSPAR Convention obliges the Contracting Parties to "undertake and publish at regular intervals joint assessments of the quality status of the marine environment and of its development, for the maritime area or for regions or sub-regions thereof" and to "include in such assessments both an evaluation of the effectiveness of the measures taken and planned for the protection of the marine environment and the identification of priorities for action."[793] This obligation reflects the understanding that an accurate assessment of the impacts of anthropogenic activities and good science must underpin policy.[794] The requirement to conduct monitoring activities is further substantiated by identifying its purpose and intention, therefore placing it within the overall OSPAR Convention system. The fundamental role in this context is the assessment of the quality of status of the marine environment that is then used as the basis for an assessment of the effectiveness of the measures taken. These two fundamental approaches also influence the work on marine litter. The need to acquire more insight knowledge on marine litter was introduced by Sweden in

793 Art. 6 (a and b) OSPAR Convention.

794 The idea to integrate science into policy and to therefore improve the establishment of adequate measures has been a focus in the (predecessor of the) OSPAR Convention since the late 1980s:*Ducrotoy/Elliott,* Marine Pollution Bulletin 34 (1997) 686, 687.

1996.[795] Following this impetus, a pilot project on monitoring was established in 1999 with the mandate to develop a methodology to monitor litter washed ashore (so-called beach litter) and to produce a first assessment on the trends of marine litter in the marine environment.[796]

Of particular relevance with regard to the OSPAR beach monitor pilot project is the approach adopted to distinguish between indicator items from five different sectors of activities that can be associated with specific sources. Consequently, the different types of marine litter are categorised, where possible, according to their potential origin: fishing, shipping, galley waste from ships, sanitary waste and tourism/recreation.[797] Following the pilot project, voluntary marine beach litter programmes were established that were based on the Guideline for monitoring marine litter on the beaches in the OSPAR Maritime Area.[798] Despite this very laudable approach, the marine litter monitoring regime is substantially weakened as the monitoring of litter is not mandatory and thus lacks financial support in some States.[799] To remedy this situation marine litter monitoring could be made mandatory as is the case of chemical or heavy metal monitoring activities, so that adequate funding would be permanently secured.[800]

795 *OSPAR Commission*, Work Programme for the Working Group on Impacts on the Marine Environment, 1996/1997, Annex 22, Ref.§ 10.27, 08.03.1996, 1.

796 *OSPAR Commission*, OSPAR Pilot Project on Monitoring Marine Beach Litter, Monitoring of marine litter in the OSPAR region, Steering Group, Biodiversity Series, 2007, 15. The time frame of the pilot project was from 2000-2006 It was however subdivided into two phases: 2000-2003 and 2004-2006: *ibid.*, 16.

797 *Ibid.*, 25.

798 *OSPAR Commission*, Guideline for monitoring marine litter on the beaches in the OSPAR Maritime Area, Agreement number 2010-02, 2010. The Agreements to conduct the Voluntary Beach Monitoring Programmes were adopted in 2007 and 2010: *OSPAR*, BDC 07/12/1-E, Draft Agreement for the Marine Beach Litter Monitoring Programme, Meeting of the Biodiversity Committee, Annex 10, Ref.§ 5.15, 26-30-03.2007; *OSPAR Commission*, Agreement on a Voluntary Marine Beach Litter Monitoring Programme, OSPAR Agreement: 2011-1, 2011, 1.

799 *UNEP*, Marine Litter: A Global Challenge, 119.

800 *Ibid.*

IV. The use of ecosystem quality criteria to assess the impact and presence of marine litter

The monitoring obligation under Annex IV OSPAR forms the legal basis for the Quality Status Report (QSR).[801] Because it combines scientific endeavour with political measures, *Ehlers* rightly calls it an "interface between science (assessment) and politics (measures)."[802] The particular significance of the QSR can also be explained by its evaluation of the condition of a vast marine region such as the North-East Atlantic in the context of the interactions and impacts of anthropogenic activities.[803] The specific role of the QSR is to make available adequate information on the status of the environment and to formulate results so as to be able to use these as a basis for taking measures.

A particular role in furthering this issue, also regarding marine litter, has been provided by the so-called North Sea Conferences which assembles North Sea riparian States to address problems facing "their" sea.[804] The North Sea Conferences have provided specific and valuable input since its participants; the governments of Belgium, Denmark, France, Germany, the Netherlands, Norway, Sweden, Switzerland and the UK first met in 1984.[805] The role of this sub-regional structure within the OSPAR Convention is, in principle, limited to propose specific measures for the North Sea, but it has at times impacted on the work of the OSPAR Convention overall.[806]

---

801 *Salchow,* The Quality Status Report (QSR 2000) for the North East Atlantic, in *Ehlers/Wolfrum/Borgese,* Marine issues (2002) 118–134, 120.

802 *Ehlers* in: *Salchow,* The Quality Status Report (QSR 2000) for the North East Atlantic, in *Ehlers/Wolfrum/Borgese,* Marine issues (2002) 118–134, 119.

803 *Ibid.*

804 See for an analysis between the North Sea Conferences and the OSPAR Convention *De La Fayette,* The International Journal of Marine and Coastal Law 14 (1999) 247, 259 *et seq.*

805 *Hilf,* Zeitschrift für ausländisches öffentliches Recht und Völkerrecht 55 (1995) 580, 581 *et seq.*

806 The North Sea Conferences, http://www.ospar.org/content/content.asp?menu=00590624000000_000000_000000, last accessed 27.08.2015. See only its role in introducing the precautionary principle to international policy: *Hilf,* Zeitschrift für ausländisches öffentliches Recht und Völkerrecht 55 (1995) 580, 585. The North Sea Conference recognised the problem of marine litter as early as 1987 in its London Declaration, in which shipping was identified as a potential source of marine litter. It was then concluded that in this regard action was need-

Among the recommendations originating from this intergovernmental forum is the development of a particular operational tool that implements the ecosystem approach contained in the OSPAR Convention.[807] The so-called Ecological Quality Objective (EcoQO) concept can be understood to stipulate concrete and measurable objectives for assessing the state of the ecosystem. Currently, the EcoQO is limited regarding its geographic scope to the North Sea and focuses on several key topics.[808] However, their outstanding value is that they establish, depending on the objective, limit values and indicators that provide either for a threshold when to act or as a yardstick for the effectiveness of already implemented measures. The concept underlying ecosystem quality criteria is the understanding that the marine environment has, to a certain degree, assimilative capacity towards anthropogenic impacts, i.e., it is able to compensate the impact and presence of certain substances. A particular challenge results from the interpretation of the scientific knowledge to a numerical quality standard that establishes a damage threshold.[809] The basis for a clearly defined standard requires that a fundamental understanding of the environmental system and also on the impacts and interactions of substances is available.[810]

One of the topical objectives of EcoQO is dedicated to the problem of marine litter. Nevertheless, the approach followed in this respect is limi-

---

ed to promote public awareness: Ministerial Declaration of the Second International Conference on the Protection of the North Sea, 25 November 1987 (London), 11. The 4th North Sea Conference in 1995 provided for concrete recommendations that envisaged measures to reduce vessel-based pollution. Among the proposed measures were for example "to develop regulations making it mandatory for ships to deliver all garbage to a port reception facility before leaving port": Ministerial Declaration of the Fourth Conference on the Protection of the North Sea, 9 June 1995 (Esbjerg), 39.

807 *Van Franeker/Heubecker/Fairchlough et al.,* 'Save the North Sea' Fulmar Study 2002-2004, 2005, 7.

808 These topical focuses of the EcoQOs are fish stocks, seals, harbour porpoises, guillemots and oil, impact of TBT, mercury in seabird eggs, organchlorines, restore large fish, eutrophication and litter. Additionally, the inclusion of other topics into the EcoQO and the geographic extension to other North-East Atlantic regions is currently under development. See for a further overview on each EcoQO and on the ongoing work, http://www.ospar.org/content/content.asp?menu=00690302200000_000000_000000, last accessed 27.08.2015.

809 *Elliott,* Marine Pollution Bulletin 32 (1996) 762, 762.

810 *Ibid.*

ted, as the litter EcoQO focuses exclusively on ingestible plastics for seabirds. The most striking contribution of the litter EcoQO is that it provides a limit value on the basis of a specific formula in that "there should be less than 10% of northern fulmars (*fulmarus glacialis*) having more than 0.1 g plastic particles in the stomach in samples of 50 to 100 beach-washed fulmars found from each of 4 to 5 areas of the North Sea over a period of at least five years."[811] At first sight, it seems surprising that no objective regarding the pilot study on beached litter has been chosen as an EcoQO. However, preference was given to an indicator species due to their ecological relevance given that fulmars are abundant in most of the North-East Atlantic. Tubenosed seabirds occur worldwide, allowing for comparisons to be made between trends of marine litter.[812] The numerical value of plastic in the stomach content is derived from the estimation that such a bird has more than 10 pieces of plastic in its stomach and that a mass indication rather than a quantity indication would be easier to follow up.[813] Consequently, the litter EcoQO makes use of a species monitoring approach in which a particular marine organism is used to monitor the presence of substances. Fulmars are believed to be suitable species because they are known to exclusively feed offshore. Unlike other species, fulmars do not regurgitate their food and retain slowly digesting substances.[814] Since fulmars′ foraging space covers a wide area, their stomach content has an informative value on the overall presence of (floating) plastics. Fulmars are surface feeders that cannot differentiate between their food and floating plastic particles when diving for prey.

Preliminary results from the pilot project reporting period of 2001-2006 demonstrate that between 40 and 60% of fulmars had more than 0.1g plastics in their stomach.[815] Whereas 45% of fulmars found in the Faroe Is-

---

811 *OSPAR Commission*, The OSPAR System of Ecological Quality Objectives for the North Sea, Quality Status Report 2010, 2010, 14.

812 Other tubenosed seabirds are for example albatrosses and petrels. Northern fulmars are also used as biological monitors of trends of plastic pollution in the eastern North Pacific *Avery-Gomm/O'Hara/Kleine et al.,* Marine Pollution Bulletin 64 (2012) 1776.

813 V*an Franeker/Heubecker/Fairchlough et al.,* 'Save the North Sea' Fulmar Study 2002-2004, 2005, 57.

814 *Ibid.*, 17.

815 *OSPAR Commission*, The OSPAR System of Ecological Quality Objectives for the North Sea, Quality Status Report 2010, 2010, 14. The stomach contents that contained more than 0.1g plastic varied depending on the identified sub-region.

lands regions had more than 0.1g plastic in their stomachs, the highest percentage of the study was found in the Channel area. This means that the current ecological status does not fulfil the threshold set by the litter EcoQO. One reason for this could be that the percentage of 10% or the 0.1g target was too ambitious with a view to the factual situation and that the problem is actually more acute than previously expected.

The key significance is, however, the agreement to put down numerical values that serve as a yardstick for legislative or prescriptive measures. While the selected values were initially too ambitious for a variety of reasons, it can be seen as a progressive and practical approach in addressing adverse consequences. The context of the EcoQO objectives as reflected in the diverse impacts and interactions of substances within the ecosystem make it a particularly important tool, in assessing the impact of marine litter. In order to be able to continuously measure the EcoQO on litter, the Biological Diversity Committee of OSPAR recommended to Contracting Parties to "meet their existing commitments on monitoring and assessment in relation to EcoQOs [...]."[816] The EcoQO establishes an indication of the quantities of floating litter in the marine environment and could be used as an indicator within the ambit of the Marine Strategy Framework Directive.[817]

V. Marine litter in the framework of OSPARCOM

In order to supervise the implementation of the Convention and to establish programmes and measures for the prevention and elimination of pol-

---

The remaining results were that besides the Faroe Islands and Channel area, the Scottish Islands (45%), East England (58%), Southern North Sea (56%) and the Skagerrak area (48%).

816 *OSPAR*, BDC 08/12/1-E, Summary record of the meeting of the Biodiversity Committee, Meeting of the Biodiversity Committee, Agenda Item 12, 25-29.02.2008, 8.

817 *OSPAR Commission*, Evaluation of the OSPAR System of Ecological Quality Objectives for the North Sea (update 2010), 2009, 13. See also, Directive 2008/56/EC of the European Parliament and of the Council of 17 June 2008 establishing a frame-work for community action in the field of marine environmental policy (Marine Strategy Framework Directive) (OJ 2008 L 164) (Marine Strategy Framework Directive), see further section B.VII.2. of chapter 4.

lution, the OSPAR Commission (OSPARCOM) was established.[818] Unlike HELCOM, it has the mandate to adopt legally binding decisions.[819] OSPARCOM is made up of representatives from the Contracting Parties that should meet at "regular intervals", at least once a year.[820] Additionally, a permanent secretariat is set up that is led by an Executive Secretary.[821] The working structure of the OSPARCOM differentiates between strategic and political work and the more technical aspects. Consequently, the OSPARCOM and the ministerial meetings determine the strategic orientation of the OSPAR Convention and its programmes and measures, whereas the Strategy Committees and their subordinated working groups implement these strategic orientations.[822]

The issue of marine litter was introduced to the work of OSPARCOM in the early 1990s by Sweden when it expressed concerns about solid waste in the environment.[823] Whereas marine litter was initially dealt with in the framework of a pilot project steering group on monitoring beach litter,[824] the issue was further institutionalised and refined by establishing an Intersessional Correspondence Group on Marine Litter (ICGML) in 2008.[825] The choice to further formalise the work on marine litter and to ensure regular meetings was made because the issue was seen as requiring more substantive work. The ICGML´s primary focus is on developing

---

818 Art. 10 (1 and 2) OSPAR Convention.

819 Art. 13 OSPAR Convention. Accordingly, "Decisions and recommendations shall be adopted by unanimous vote of the Contracting Parties. Should unanimity not be attainable, and unless otherwise provided in the Convention, the Commission may nonetheless adopt decisions or recommendations by a three-quarters majority vote of the Contracting Parties" (Art. 13 (1) OSPAR Convention). The decision is binding for every Contracting Party that has voted for it and that have not notified the Executive Secretary in writing that they are unable to accept the decision.

820 *Proelß,* Meeresschutz im Völker - und Europarecht, 2004, 199.

821 Art. 12 OSPAR Convention.

822 *Salchow,* The Quality Status Report (QSR 2000) for the North East Atlantic, in *Ehlers/Wolfrum/Borgese,* Marine issues (2002) 118–134, 120.

823 *OSPAR Commission*, OSPAR Pilot Project on Monitoring Marine Beach Litter, Monitoring of marine litter in the OSPAR region, Steering Group, Biodiversity Series, 2007, 11.

824 *OSPAR*, BCD 05/13/1-E, Summary Record of the Biodiversity Committee Meeting, Meeting of the Biodiversity Committee, Agenda Item 13, 25.02.2005, 24.

825 *OSPAR*, BDC 08/12/1-E, Summary record of the meeting of the Biodiversity Committee, Meeting of the Biodiversity Committee, Agenda Item 12, 25-29.02.2008, 34.

monitoring and evaluation practices regarding marine litter.[826] However, the ICGML´s position within the structure is weakened, as not every Contracting Party sends representatives to its meetings.[827]

Whereas initially the topic of marine litter was based on scientific research and more technical aspects, it has gained a more prominent role within the OSPAR system. The overall thematic directions of OSPAR-COM are established through non-binding strategies and working programs that establish general targets and implementation mechanisms. Irrespective of the non-binding, soft-law value of these strategies, such an assessment is valuable in order to understand what is seen as practicable regarding marine litter. The third Ministerial Meeting of the Contracting Parties in Bergen in 2010 adopted the Bergen Statement that clearly provided for a mandate to address the problem of litter.[828] It sets out to address the "unacceptable quantities" of marine litter in the region by providing, among other things, for an increased co-operation with IMO and to support the amendment of MARPOL Annex V.[829]

Moreover, the "Strategy of the OSPAR Commission for the Protection of the Marine Environment of North-East Atlantic 2010-2020" (NEAS) was adopted during the Ministerial Meeting, outlining thematic targets to be achieved by 2020.[830] Marine litter is identified as one of its objectives. Consequently the aim is to "substantially reduce marine litter in the OSPAR maritime area to levels where properties and quantities of marine

826 *OSPAR*, ICGML (4) –E, Fourth Meeting of OSPAR Inter-Sessional Correspondence Group on Marine Litter (ICGML), 11.05.2009, 4.

827 *OSPAR Commission*, Marine litter in the Northeast Atlantic Region, Assessment and priorities for response, London, 2009, 119.

828 *OSPAR Commission*, Ministerial Meeting Bergen 2010, Annex 49, Ref. M 6.2, 24.09.2010, 4. The Ministerial Meetings are not held on a regular basis. The first meeting was held in 1998 in Sintra, Portugal, the second meeting was held jointly with the Helsinki Commission in 2003 in Bremen, Germany. See for an account of the achievements of the Ministerial meeting in Sintra: *Heintschel von Heinegg,* The development of environmental standards for the north-east Atlantic including the North Sea, in *Ehlers/Wolfrum/Borgese,* Marine issues (2002) 135–153, 141; *De La Fayette,* The International Journal of Marine and Coastal Law 14 (1999) 247, 283.

829 OS*PAR Commission*, Ministerial Meeting Bergen 2010, Annex 49, Ref. M 6.2, 24.09.2010, 4.

830 *Ibid.*, 1; OSPAR Commission, the North-East Atlantic Environment Strategy (NEAS), Strategy of the OSPAR Commission for the Protection of the Marine Environment of the North-East Atlantic 2010–2020, OSPAR Agreement 2010-3.

litter do not cause harm to the coastal and marine environment".[831] Irrespective of the rather vague provision on the target levels, the NEAS has to be evaluated as an important document since it specifies measures to achieve this goal. Again, the progressive and forward-thinking approach taken within the OSPAR Convention can also be exemplified by the reference to the issue of microplastics as needing further attention.[832]

In the implementation process of the NEAS, two milestones are provided. First, by 2012 "regionally coordinated targets for marine litter" should be established that are based on available data on trends of marine litter. Second, based on these preliminary targets, a coordinated monitoring programme for marine litter is to be created.[833] These milestones are not chosen out of context, but are adapted to the time frame established by the Marine Strategy Framework Directive.[834] This assumption is also underlined that in following these strategic directions "facilitate the fulfilments of requirements under the EU Marine Strategy Framework Directive."[835] Additionally, a Regional Action Plan on marine litter has been prepared.[836]

VI. Preliminary Conclusion

The general legal framework provided by the OSPAR Convention establishes a comprehensive regulatory regime in which the sources of marine litter are also addressed. The OSPAR Convention does not, unlike the Helsinki Convention, regulate vessel-based pollution directly. In case it is seen as necessary, the OSPAR Commission has the mandate to make references regarding this type of pollution directly to IMO. A significant and

831 NEAS, 7. Marine litter is associated with the biodiversity and hazardous substances thematic strategy. The choice of addressing the issue of marine litter in these strategies demonstrates the integrated approach that is taken by OSPAR. The approach reflects on the diffuse and indirect interactions among substances but also between substances and the marine environment.

832 *OSPAR Commission*, Marine litter in the Northeast Atlantic Region, Assessment and priorities for response, London, 2009, 78; *UNEP*, Marine Litter: A Global Challenge, 2009, 118.

833 NEAS, 10.

834 See section B.VII.2.b.dd. of chapter 4 for further information.

835 NEAS, 11.

836 See section F. of this chapter.

unique provision under the OSPAR Convention refers to the assessment norm, allowing for a concerted and focused monitoring scheme. Even though the Helsinki Convention contains a similar approach, the OSPAR Convention further substantiates concrete obligations in a dedicated Annex that are also relevant to the issue of marine litter.

Marine litter has in the North-East Atlantic region been addressed since the 1990s. The establishment of the ICGML that particularly deals with marine litter can be seen as an institutional consolidation of the issue that guarantees a certain degree of consistency. The initiatives regarding marine litter were, however, primarily limited to the North Sea regions and mainly focused on monitoring and assessment aspects. The framework for these monitoring activities is established by the QSR and EcoQO respectively. The unique approaches that serve as an interface between science and policy have a role model function in that their key asset, the establishment of a concrete and measurable yardstick, has been implemented in the work of other fora. Nevertheless, the progressive scheme is weakened in that monitoring for marine litter is not mandatory and therefore lacks funding. Since monitoring effectively contributes to increased knowledge on the distribution and impacts of marine litter, a mandatory litter monitoring scheme could be a remedy to this situation.

In order to avoid a fragmented approach, the issue of marine litter was chosen to be one of the central objectives of the NEAS. The inclusion in this, admittedly, non-binding strategic document ensures that the issue is guaranteed to be on the agenda for the outlined time frame of ten years. Even though the knowledge of marine litter is an important source of information, particular in a vast geographic region as the North-East Atlantic, specific measures relating to preventing marine litter are currently missing. It is argued that presently this situation is changing due to the preparation and implementation of the Regional Action Plan on marine litter in the North-East Atlantic.

D. The regulation of marine litter in the Black Sea Region

The Black Sea is, similar to the Baltic Sea, a semi-enclosed sea that is linked to the aquatic system of the Mediterranean through the 35 km long and shallow Straits of Bosporus, and that is also connected to the Azov Sea through the Kerch Straits. The Black Sea covers 423 km^2 and drains a 1.9 million km^2 basin which extends to approximately one third of continental Europe. The rivers wash up to 350 km³ freshwater into the sea.[837] As the Black Sea is to 90% anoxic and the narrow straits only allow for a limited exchange of saltwater, the Black Sea marine environment is very susceptible to the impacts of pollutants.[838] The specific geomorphological structure also forms a unique ecological balance. The Black Sea is up to 2,212 m deep, and its water column is divided into two layers of different hydrochemical conditions. Whereas the oxygen rich upper layer of approximately 150m provides the basis for the Black Sea ecosystem, the underlying water layer is anoxic and saturated by hydrogen sulphide.[839]

Of particular importance, also regarding the legal regime, are the anthropogenic impacts on this very fragile environment of the 20 to 30 million people that live on the coast around the Black Sea. In the following, the applicable regulatory framework regarding marine litter will be assessed. Land-based pollution is afforded particular consideration as the Black Sea is a drainage for major tributaries. The role of the input of solid substances by way of international rivers is a key aspect for marine litter generally, but is particularly important in the Black Sea Region.[840] Furthermore, the issue of dumping is raised as it also represents an important source of marine litter.

I. The legal framework of the Black Sea Region

The vulnerable marine environment was recognised as early as 1973 by the IMO, when the Black Sea received the status of a Special Area for oil (MARPOL Annex I) and garbage (MARPOL Annex V).[841] The elabora-

---

837 *Alexandrov/Nicolaev/Mateescu et al.*, Integrated approaches to risk mitigation targeting conservation and sustainable development along the Romanian Black Sea coast, in *Czybulka,* Marine nature conservation and management at the borders of the European Union (2012) 103–119, 102. Amongst others the Rioni (Georgia), the Sakarya (Turkey), the Mzimta (Russian Federation), the Dniepro (Ukraine) and the Kamchia (Bulgaria) serve the Black Sea. The Don enters the Black Sea through the Sea of Azov: *Black Sea Commission*, Black Sea transboundary diagnostic analysis, 2007, 91.

838 *Kramm,* Introduction to the Black Sea region, in *Czybulka,* Marine nature conservation and management at the borders of the European Union (2012) 73–76, 74.

839 *Black Sea Commission*, Black Sea transboundary diagnostic analysis, 2007, 18.

840 *UNEP*, Marine Litter: A Global Challenge, 2009, 41.

841 MARPOL Annex V Special Area on garbage is not in force.

tion of a regional marine protection agreement of the Black Sea is disassociated from these early actions and is closely linked to the geopolitical changes following the collapse of the Soviet Union. The impetus of a new political landscape with now six riparian States, Romania, Bulgaria, Turkey, Georgia, Ukraine and the Russian Federation, led to the adoption of the Convention on the Protection of the Black Sea Against Pollution (Bucharest Convention or BlSC) in 1992.[842]

The Bucharest Convention came in force on 15 January 1994, after the Contracting Parties had declared in 1993 to "take action to ensure prompt ratification of the Convention on the Protection of the Black Sea against Pollution and its Protocols by all Black Sea coastal states."[843] The Bucharest Convention is a framework convention that consists of the primary convention text and four Protocols that substantiate some of the material provisions.[844] The Commission on the Protection of the Black Sea Against Pollution (Black Sea Commission) is established according to Art.XVII BlSC in order to "achieve the purpose of the Convention." The delegates to the Black Sea Commission of each Contracting Party meet at least once a year.[845]

The Black Sea Commission is assisted by a permanent Secretariat that is based in Istanbul, Turkey. The task of the Black Sea Commission is to

842 Convention on the Protection of the Black Sea against pollution (Bucharest) of 21 April 1992, in force 15 January 1994; ILM 110 (1992); 1764 UNTS 3. *Dupont/Kramm,* The legal framework for the protection of the marine environment of the Black Sea region and its implementation, in *Czybulka,* Marine nature conservation and management at the borders of the European Union (2012) 77–90, 78.

843 Odessa Declaration, Ministerial Declaration on the Protection of the Black Sea, 07.04.1993 (Odessa, Ukraine), para.18.

844 Besides the Protocols, the Commission can also produce so-called "Legally binding documents" which have been drafted since the early 1990s. This relates to the Draft Legally Binding Document (LBD) for Fisheries and Conservation of the Living Resources of the Black Sea, see further in section D.I.1 of this chapter. However, the legal status of such a LBD is controversially discussed and relates to "the lack of agreement as to the legal status of such a "document", whether as a protocol to the Bucharest Convention or as a distinct agreement/convention": *Dupont/Kramm,* The legal framework for the protection of the marine environment of the Black Sea region and its implementation, in *Czybulka,* Marine nature conservation and management at the borders of the European Union (2012) 77–90, 83.

845 The Black Sea Commission is chaired on a rotating annual basis by a Chairman (Art.XVII (3) BlSC).

provide recommendations on pollution prevention, reduction and control measures.[846] This forms the legal basis for the establishment of Strategic Action Plans for the Environmental Protection and Rehabilitation of the Black Sea (BlS SAP) that were issued in 1996, amended in 2002 and revised in 2009 respectively.[847] Even though the Bucharest Convention provides the competence to adopt recommendations, decisions and to adopt or amend Annexes to the Convention, it does not refer in this context to the BlS SAP. Even though Paragraph 1 BlS SAP refers to the document as an "agreement [...] to act in concert to assist in the continued recovery of the Black Sea", the BlS SAP is not a legally binding agreement. The overall wording and structure of the document implies that it is not the intention of the Black Sea States to adopt a legally binding document, but rather a document that sketches out the broad lines of co-operation. This is evident when examining Part 4 on the "Legal and Institutional Framework of SAP implementation."[848] The BlS SAP stipulates that "a legal framework shall enable the effective fulfilment of SAP *recommendations* [...] and the functions thereby delegated to the Black Sea Commission,"[849] but since recommendations are not legally binding, the BlS SAP simply establishes overall strategic orientation. Despite the legally non-binding value of these political strategy instruments, they "describe the policy actions required to meet the major environmental challenges now facing the Sea" and also include a "series of management targets."[850]

---

846 Art.XVIII (4) BlSC.

847 In the framework of the Bucharest Convention, the acronym "SAP" is used to refer to the Strategic Action Plans in the Black Sea. However, in the following the acronym BlS SAP is chosen so as to avoid any misunderstanding when comparing other similar strategies. See for a comprehensive overview on the development and role of the Strategic Actions Plans in the Black Sea Region: *Kramm,* Marine nature conservation and management at the borders of the European Union, in *Czybulka,* Marine nature conservation and management at the borders of the European Union (2012) 91–101.

848 Black Sea Commission, Strategic Action Plan for the Environmental Protection and Rehabilitation of the Black Sea, BlS SAP, 2nd ed., 17.04.2009 (Sofia, Bulgaria), 14.

849 *Ibid.* (emphasis added).

850 *Ibid.*, 2. Similar: *Tiroch* states that "the general politics in order to protect the Black Sea's marine environment are laid down in the Strategic Action Plan for the Rehabilitation and Protection of the Black Sea": *Tiroch,* Black Sea, in Max Planck Encyclopedia of Public International Law (MPEPIL), E.14. It reflects the overall understanding of the Contracting Parties towards necessary and accept-

The broad material scope of the Bucharest Convention is reflected, *prima facie*, in the pollution based approach that relates to pollution by hazardous substances or matter, land-based pollution, ship-based pollution, dumping, pollution by activities on the continental shelf, atmospheric pollution and pollution from transboundary movements or illegal trafficking of waste as well as biodiversity protection. Even though the Bucharest Convention was adopted simultaneously to the Helsinki Convention and the OSPAR Convention, its provisions do not reflect the prevailing *Zeitgeist* of that time. Consequently, there is no inclusion of the precautionary principle and the polluter-pays-principle, nor does it contain a reference to the principle of sustainable development.[851]

On the grounds of the limited (progressive) material provisions, the Bucharest Convention resembles those Regional Seas Conventions that were adopted in the 1970s and can therefore be categorised as a "first-generation" Regional Seas treaty as opposed to the more progressive revised "second-generation" 1992 Helsinki Convention for example.[852] Nevertheless, the necessity to reform the material obligations of the Bucharest Convention has been reflected in the ratification and drafting of progressive

---

able measures for preserving and restoring the Black Sea marine environment, see *Kramm,* The new strategic action plan for the environmental protection and rehabilitation of the Black Sea, in *Czybulka,* Marine nature conservation and management at the borders of the European Union (2012) 91–101, 93.

851 The drafting States of the Bucharest Convention took notice of the development following the Rio Declaration in the non-binding Odessa Declaration. They confirmed accordingly "their commitment to integrated management and sustainable development of coastal areas and the marine environment under their national jurisdiction and will base their policies on the following:
- precautionary approach
- The use of low and non-waste technologies
- Integration of marine environmental protection considerations into other policy areas
- Market mechanisms, including the development of economic incentives for using low and non-waste technologies, user fees, and the polluter pays principle
- Application of natural resource and environmental accounting and environmental impact assessment procedures to all sectors, including tourism" (Odessa Declaration, para. 9).

852 *Dupont/Kramm,* The legal framework for the protection of the marine environment of the Black Sea region and its implementation, in *Czybulka,* Marine nature conservation and management at the borders of the European Union (2012) 77–90, 84.

Protocols that could potentially change the scope of the Convention without necessarily amending its main text.

The geographical scope of the Bucharest Convention is not regulated uniformly and depends on the subject matter. The Bucharest Convention "applies to the Black Sea proper" and is delimited by the line that joins the Capes Kelagra and Dalyan.[853] The reference to the Black Sea environment includes usually the Exclusive Economic Zone and the territorial sea of each Contracting Party, "however, any Protocol to this Convention may provide otherwise for the purposes of that Protocol."[854] This means in practice that the adjacent Sea of Azov is not automatically covered by the geographical scope of the primary Bucharest Convention obligations. Whereas the Bucharest Convention does not include the Sea of Azov, it is included in the Protocol on the Black Sea Biodiversity and Landscape Protocol.[855] The variable geographical scope ultimately results in fostering legal uncertainty regarding the application of the Bucharest Convention´s provisions and, eventually, may lead to an increasing fragmentation of the respective regime.

Whereas the purpose and scope of the Bucharest Convention is, as already stipulated in the title, focused on pollution of the marine environment, certain measures are also aimed at ensuring the economic development of the area. It is apparent that such competing ambitions are, by their underlying nature, hardly compatible. The significance of the Black Sea coast as "a major international resort area where Black Sea Countries have made large investments in public health and tourism"[856] underlines this.[857] The primary Bucharest Convention obligations are substantiated by the

853 Art.I (1) BlSC.

854 Art.I (2) BlSC.

855 Black Sea Commission, The Black Sea Biodiversity and Landscape Conservation Protocol to the Convention on the Protection of the Black Sea Against Pollution, signed in Sofia 2002 (BlS Biodiversity Protocol). It has entered in force on 20 June 2011.

856 Preamble, para.9 BlSC.

857 The opposing interests between environmental protection and economic development have also been recognised by the Black Sea Commission: "the challenge which the region now faces is to secure a healthy Black Sea environment at a time when economic recovery and further development are also being pursued": *Black Sea Commission*, Implementation of the Strategic Action Plan for the Rehabilitation and Protection of the Black Sea, 2002-2007, 2009, chapter 2.6.

Land-Based Pollution Protocol(s)[858], the Protocol on Cooperation in Combating Pollution of the Black Sea Marine Environment by Oil and Other Harmful Substances in Emergency Situations, the Protocol on the Protection of the Black Sea Marine Environment Against Pollution by Dumping and the BlS Biodiversity Protocol.[859] Whereas the primary focus of the following sections is on land-based pollution and dumping, a critical analysis of pertinent obligations and on-going activities must be pursued in order to ensure a complete understanding of the regulatory regime of marine litter. Regarding pollution by vessels, Art.VIII BlSC stipulates that the Parties "shall take individually or, when necessary, jointly, all appropriate measures to prevent, reduce and control pollution of the marine environment of the Black Sea from vessels in accordance with generally accepted international rules and standards." This is clearly a reference to the competences of the IMO, as provided for by Art. 211 UNCLOS and MARPOL respectively. However, the increased protection standard of MARPOL Annex V Special Areas has not entered in force due to a lack of

858 The Land-Based Pollution Protocol is currently amended by a new Land-Based Pollution Protocol that was adopted in 2009 but has not yet entered in force.

859 In contrast to the BlS Biodiversity Protocol, the former three already formed an integral part of the Bucharest Convention and have binding legal effect since 1994: *Black Sea Commission*, Table of Main Legal Documents, http://www.blacksea-commission.org/_table-legal-docs.asp, last accessed 27.08.2015. The BlS Biodiversity Protocol stipulates an indirect protection approach as it aims to serve "as a legal instrument for developing, harmonizing and enforcing necessary environmental policies, strategies and measures in persevering, protecting and sustainably managing nature, historical, cultural and aesthetic resources and heritage of the Black Sea states for present and future generations." (Art. 1 (2) BlS Biodiversity Protocol). Even though pollution control is seen as a necessary measure to conserve and maintain biodiversity (Preamble, para.4 BlS Biodiversity Protocol), it is only addressed in a clause concerning the compensation of damage caused by pollution (Art. 11 (4) BlS Biodiversity Protocol). Regarding the issue of ghost fisheries, the current draft version of a "legally binding document (LBD)" on fisheries refers in Art. 10 (3) to the obligation to "agree on safe methods and gears in order to avoid use of and take measures for prohibition of the use for fishing or harvesting methods and gears of high risk of by-catch of non-target species or high adverse effect on the Black Sea ecosystem including but limited to explosive, poisonous and electric methods." The list of gears that are agreed upon should be included in Annex II to the LBD. However, currently those standards have not been established. Particularly from the wording that seems to omit some central words, it is clear that the document is still at a very early stage: *Black Sea Commission*, Draft Legally Binding Document (LBD) for Fisheries and Conservation of Living Resources of the Black Sea, undated.

adequate port reception facilities.[860] Despite the reference to the competence to the global regime, the Black Sea Commission envisages facilitating the establishment of port reception facilities so as to further the higher protection standards in the Black Sea. To achieve this, a MoU was signed between the IMO and the Black Sea Commission in 2009.[861] Both Parties agreed to provide assistance in matters that are of interest to both and to consult with the aim of harmonising their efforts "as far as possible."[862]

1. Measures to address riverine inputs and other land-based pollution

Given the specific hydrographic circumstances of the Black Sea, pollution by land-based sources is a key topic. Consequently, Art. VII BlSC provides

> the Contracting Parties shall prevent, reduce and control pollution of the marine environment of the Black Sea from land-based sources, in accordance with the Protocol on the protection of the Black Sea Marine Environment Against Pollution from Land-based Sources which shall form an integral part of the Convention.[863]

It is also in this context that the only (direct and indirect) reference to the problem of marine litter is made in the Bucharest Convention framework. The BlS LBP applies a classification approach in which substances are either to be "prevented or eliminated (Annex I substances: hazardous substances and matter)"[864] or "reduced (Annex II substances: noxious substances)."[865] The distinction between hazardous and noxious matters is made according to the toxicity, persistence and bioaccumulation characteristics of substances.[866] Even though marine litter is not explicitly mentioned, its characteristics are taken into consideration and "persistent synthetic materials which may float, sink or remain in suspension" are categorised as Annex I substances. Its status as an Annex I substance implies that it is categorised as a hazardous matter which involves a higher protec-

---

860 See section D.I.1.e. of chapter 2.

861 *Black Sea Commission*, Agreement of Cooperation between the International Maritime Organization (IMO) and the Commission on the Protection of the Black Sea Against Pollution (BSC), December 2009.

862 *Ibid.*, 1.

863 Art. VII BlSC is substantiated by the Protocol on Land-based Pollution.

864 Art. 4 (1) BlS LBP.

865 Art. 4 (2) BlS LBP.

866 Annex I BlS LBP.

tion standard than noxious substances. Notwithstanding the question whether the classification correctly represents the risk potential of each substance falling within the category of marine litter, the distinction between different substances according to their characteristics already represents an expression of a certain spirit of precaution or prevention. Since this is made in the context of polluting substances, this differentiated approach compensates, admittedly in a limited manner, for the lack of fundamental principles in the Bucharest Convention.

Irrespective of the material scope of the BlS LBP, the legal effect of Art. 4 (1) BlS LBP remains unclear. The vague, non-obligatory wording outlining that "the Contracting Parties *undertake* to prevent and eliminate pollution"[867] cannot be interpreted as an absolute obligation to act. The obligation to undertake measures, though, is strengthened by Art. 6 BlS LBP that stipulates the requirements to establish common emission standards and timelines which shall be prepared by the Contracting Parties. Accordingly, the emission standards should focus on four topical priorities that are seen as essential in combating land-based pollution. In this regard, two measures, namely the reduction of inputs from municipal sewage systems and industrial wastes are of importance for the issue of marine litter.[868]

The obligation to create emission standards is not absolute and it is indeed limited by the addendum that Annex I "does not apply to discharges which contain substances and matter listed below that are below the concentration limits defined jointly by the Contracting Parties."[869] This provision potentially provides a loophole for emitting certain concentrations of substances, however, to date no concrete limits have been established in the framework of the BlS LBP.[870] Contrary to the requirements on land-

867 Art. 4 sent.1 BlS LBP (emphasis added).

868 Art. 6 BlS LBP. The other two focal areas relate to cooling water from nuclear power plants and pollution from agricultural and forest areas that affect the water quality.

869 Annex I, para.2 BlS LBP.

870 *Churchill/Lowe,* The law of the sea, 2006, 386; *Vinogradov,* The International Journal of Marine and Coastal Law 22 (2007) 585, 601. The need to establish emission standards was also recognised in the 1993 Odessa Declaration, in which the Contracting Parties pledged to: "to develop, by 1996, [...] where possible, emission standards for inputs of substances listed in Annexes I and II to the 1992 BlS-LBS Protocol and to take the necessary measures to reduce inputs of these substances to the agreed levels" (harmful substances, § 1).

based pollution in the OSPAR and Helsinki Convention, the BlS LBP does not contain any reference to BAT or BEP that could potentially guide the implementation of the measures. The BlS LBP approach has nevertheless been reinforced by a MoU with the Convention on Cooperation for the Protection and Sustainable use of the Danube River (Danube River Protection Convention).[871] The Danube River Protection Convention enumerates as one of its objectives the reduction of "the pollution loads of the Black Sea from sources in the catchment area."[872] Thus, the Danube River Protection Convention not only integrates freshwater aspects but also establishes causation between inland pollution and the receiving sea.

The MoU between the Danube Commission and the Black Sea Commission adopted in 2001 with the common goal to "provide a legal basis and framework for future co-operation between the two international regimes and their respective institutional mechanisms" also reinforces the coordination of both regimes.[873]

871 Danube River Protection Convention (Sofia) of 29 June 1994, in force 22 October 1998; EMuT 994;411-41,583. The Contracting Parties are: Austria, Bosnia and Herzegovina, Bulgaria, Croatia, Czech Republic, Germany, Hungary, Republic of Moldova, Montenegro, Romania, Republic of Serbia, Slovakia, Slovenia, Ukraine and the European Union. See for a comprehensive overview on the Convention: *Beyerlin/Marauhn,* International environmental law, 2011, 107 *et seq.*; *Louka,* Water law & policy, 2008, 263. The Danube River Protection Convention is the legal basis for the International Commission for the Protection of the Danube River (ICPDR). See also the International Commission for the Protection of the Danube River (ICPDR) website on http://www.icpdr.org/main/, last accessed 27.08.2015.

872 Art. 2 (1) Danube River Protection Convention.

873 *Vinogradov,* The International Journal of Marine and Coastal Law 22 (2007) 585, 613.The MoU indicates that the Danube Convention and the Bucharest Convention are complementary to each other as the Bucharest Convention is a "shoreline Convention, *i.e.* itself holds no power over the inland activities of the States of the hydrographic drainage area discharging to the overall Black Sea" (Black Sea proper, Sea of Azov)" whereas the Danube Convention is "hydrographic basin convention", Black Sea Commission, Memorandum of Understanding between the International Commission for the Protection of the Black Sea (ICPBS) and the International Commission for the Protection of the Danube River (ICPDR) on common strategic goals, signed in Brussels on 26 November 2001, 1.

Revision of the Black Sea Land-Based Pollution Protocol in 2009

In 2002, the then forthcoming accession of Romania and Bulgaria to the EU provided an impetus to revise the BlS LBP.[874] The negotiations on the revised Protocol were dominated by the determination of the geographic scope, which could potentially allow for co-operation with third States that lie in the drainage basin of the tributaries.[875] During the Ministerial Meeting of the Black Sea States in April 2009, the revised BlS LBP was adopted and according to Art.XX (5) Bucharest Convention comes in force after the acceptance of the amendment by all Contracting Parties.[876]

The 2009 BlS LBP signifies in its legal approach a change in the regulatory regime as it stipulates not only the application of the precautionary principle and the polluter-pays-principle[877] but also contains detailed procedural requirements for the necessity to conduct Environmental Impact Assessment[878] and reporting activities. The material scope of the revised Protocol significantly exceeds its precursor and provides for measures related to addressing pollution from point and diffuse sources.[879] Consequently, the Contracting Parties are obliged to "take all appropriate measures [...] to prevent, control and to the maximum extent possible eliminate pollution of and other adverse effects on the marine environment or coastal areas of the Black Sea from land-based sources and activities."[880]

The implementation of the 2009 BlS LBP is significantly facilitated by the definitions on, *inter alia*, "harmful activities" or "diffuse and point sources" that substantiate its provisions. The detail and scope of the defi-

---

874 Ministerial Declaration of the Ministers of Environment of the Contracting Parties to the Convention on the Protection of the Black Sea Against Pollution, 14.07.2002 (Sofia) (Sofia Declaration), paras.8,11 and 32. *Vinogradov,* The International Journal of Marine and Coastal Law 22 (2007) 585, 603.

875 See for a discussion on the development of the revised 2009 BlS *ibid.*, 605–608.

876 Art. 24 (1) 2009 BlS LBP. Whereas all Contracting Parties have signed the 2009 BlS LBP, so far only Georgia has ratified it in 2009.

877 Art. 4 (2) (a and b) 2009 BlS LBP.

878 Art. 12 2009 BlS BP.

879 Art. 7 and 8 2009 BlS LBP. Additionally five Annexes further substantiate the provisions. They relate to activities and substances of concern (Annex I), diffuse sources of pollution from agriculture and forestry (Annex II), pollution transported through the atmosphere (Annex III), authorisation and regulation of emissions (Annex IV) and BAT and BEP (Annex V).

880 Art. 4 (1) 2009 BlS LBP.

nitions is unprecedented[881] and indeed addresses terms that were previously subject to controversial discussions during the negotiations. The significance of the 2009 BlS LBP, also with regard to marine litter, can be understood when examining the definitions of point and diffuse sources. Point sources are consequently defined as:

> sources of pollution where emissions and releases are introduced into the environment from any discernable, confined and discrete conveyance, including but not limited to pipes, outfalls, channels, ditches, tunnels, conduits or wells from which pollutants are or may be discharged.[882]

Diffuse sources are on the other hand defined as

> sources of pollution, other than point sources, from which substances enter the environment as a result of land run-off, precipitation, atmospheric deposition, drainage, seepage or by hydrologic modification or destruction of habitats.[883]

The 2009 BlS LBP thus applies to "emissions from polluting substances originating from land-based point and diffuse sources that may have a measurable adverse effect on the marine environment or coastal areas of the Black Sea."[884] Even though the material scope is limited to substances having a "measurable adverse effect", this restriction is compensated by the clause that the 2009 BlS LBP is also relevant for any activity that either directly or indirectly affects the marine environment.[885] With a view to the diverse sources and activities that cause marine litter, the scope and definitions contained in the Protocol provide concrete legal obligations which establish a robust regulatory framework.

Whereas the 1992 BlS LBP addresses marine litter in the form of "synthetic material", the 2009 BlS LBP explicitly mentions "marine litter" in Annex I B to the Protocol as a "substance of concern." It is defined in this context based on UNEP´s definition as "any persistent manufactured or processed solid material which is discarded, disposed of, or abandoned in the marine environment and coastal areas."[886] Consequently, once the 2009 BlS LBP comes in force, it will be the first legally binding instrument in the Black Sea Region that contains a definition of marine litter.

---

881 See only Art. 1 OSPAR Convention or Art. 2 HC.
882 Art. 2, para.14 2009 BlS LBP.
883 Art. 2, para.15 2009 BlS LBP.
884 Art. 3 (c) (i) 2009 BlS LBP.
885 Art. 3 (c) (iii) 2009 BlS LBP.
886 Annex I (B) (15) 2009 BlS LBP.

Similar to the regulatory technique of the 1992 BlS LBP, Annex I 2009 BlS LBP contains substances that need to be particularly considered when establishing measures to implement the Protocol. The 2009 BlS LBP, however, contains detailed specifications on measures of implementation, relating to the development and implementation of regional or national programmes that establish emission limit values and a timeframe in which these limits are to be achieved.[887] This approach deviates from the 1992 BlS LBP in which the attempt was made to jointly decide on specific concentration limits.[888]

Furthermore, each Contracting Party is obliged to assign an authority that coordinates the implementation process of the 2009 BlS LBP. The potential consequence arising from the fact that each State provides different emission limits values and timeframes is addressed in that the Black Sea Commission "periodically" reviews the measures.[889] While the Bucharest Convention does not assign substantive reporting obligations, the revised Protocol stipulates reporting obligations as outlined in Art. 16 2009 BlS LBP that include the provision of information on legal and regulatory measures, data on the discharge quantities of substances of concern and information on activities altering the coastline and habitats and related watersheds. These remarks demonstrate that the 2009 BlS LBP integrates different aspects that were identified as missing in the primary Bucharest Convention.

The entry into force would mean the introduction of the precautionary principle to the Bucharest Convention as well as a host of independent procedural obligations such as reporting or the obligation to conduct an EIA. Admittedly, this would only apply to the sectoral aspect of land-based pollution. The revised Protocol is a "substitute amendment" in the understanding that an overall revision of the Bucharest Convention is currently not feasible. Despite the sectoral and therefore limited protection approach to land-based pollution, the revision should in the context of the

887 Art. 5 (1) (a) 2009 BlS LBP. In establishing national or regional plans, marine litter could play a particular role as the action plans should be guided on certain hazardous characteristics of the substances concerned. Consequently, if the substances are amongst others persistent, likely to bioaccumulate or have a transboundary significance they need to be particularly taken into consideration (Annex I (C) (1, 3 and 8) 2009 BlS LBP).

888 Annex I, para.2 BlS LBP.

889 Art. 6 (2) (b) 2009 BlS LBP. However, no further substantiating provisions are stipulated.

overall regulatory technique be positively evaluated. Since land-based pollution poses factually the biggest threat to the Black Sea marine environment, the amendment of the Protocol can be seen as a first incremental step to improve the regulatory regime of the Bucharest Convention overall.

2. Critical analysis of the dumping regime as established by the Bucharest Convention

The Protocol on the Protection of the Black Sea Marine Environment Against Pollution by Dumping (Bucharest Dumping Protocol), that forms an integral part of the Bucharest Convention, is the legal instrument addressing the introduction of marine litter by dumping. It substantiates Art.X BlSC that provides for the obligation "to take all appropriate measures and co-operate in preventing, reducing and controlling pollution by dumping." A clause that prohibits dumping activities for third parties in the Black Sea region indicates that no absolute dumping prohibition exists.[890] Indeed the Protocol applies a listing approach in which substances listed in Annex I ('blacklist') to the Bucharest Dumping Protocol may not be dumped.[891] This provision is weakened further as these substances may be introduced in the case that only "trace contaminants of Annex I substances" are contained in dredged material.[892]

This is in particular relevant as "persistent synthetic materials which may float, sink or remain in suspension" are listed as Annex I substances

890 Art.X (2) BlSC: "The Contracting Parties shall not permit, within areas under their respective jurisdiction, dumping by natural or juridical persons of non-Black Sea States." The Protocol does not provide a definition of dumping.

891 Similar to a 'greylist'-approach Annex II substances and any other non -Annex I and II substances may be dumped after a specific permit has been issued by a competent national authority. According to Art. 6 Bucharest Dumping Protocol, Annex I substances may furthermore be dumped "when the safety of human life or vessel or aircraft at sea is threatened by complete destruction or total loss or in any other case when there is a danger to human life and when dumping appears to be the only way of averting such danger, and if there is every probability that the damage resulting from such dumping will be less than would otherwise occur (Art. 6 Bucharest Dumping Protocol) " In case dumping is pursued under the circumstances of Art. 6 Bucharest Dumping Protocol, the Black Sea Commission must be informed.

892 Art. 2, para.2 Bucharest Dumping Protocol.

and could consequently be included during dredging.[893] Furthermore, organohalogen compounds such as DDT or PCB are classified under Annex I (1) to the Bucharest Dumping Protocol. This regulatory approach is also of particular concern with a view to the causal relationship between those substances, since, to this date, no concentration limit has been defined.[894] The Bucharest Dumping Protocol thus resembles in its fundamental logic rather the regulatory approach of the London Convention than the London Protocol.

Consequently, three different dumping standards prevail around the Black Sea, a fact which is explained by different State practice regarding the accession to global agreements. Two States (Georgia and Bulgaria) have acceded to the LP, whereas Russia and Ukraine have merely ratified the older LC.[895] Romania and Turkey have neither signed or ratified either of those instruments and are merely obliged to implement the Bucharest Dumping Protocol. Since, for example, the Bucharest Dumping Protocol and the LP follow wholly contradictory protection regimes, a discrepancy regarding the regulatory approach and obligations exists among the Contracting Parties.

This naturally also has an impact on the prevention of the introduction of marine litter. The need to improve the Bucharest Dumping Protocol has already been called for in the first BlS SAP of 1996, only two years after the entry into force of the treaty itself.[896] Currently, the debate is still ongoing, and possible options include either amending the Bucharest Dumping Protocol or to collectively ratify the LP.[897] Having in mind the background of this study, the adoption of the LP by every Black Sea State appears to be a consequent step in establishing a general dumping prohibition while also ensuring a harmonised protection standard,[898] and the cur-

893 Annex I (5) Bucharest Dumping Protocol.

894 *Black Sea Commission/IMO*, Regional Workshop on Implementation of International Dumping Agreements in the Black Sea Region, Istanbul, February 2011, 14.

895 *IMO*, Status of Conventions, http://www.imo.org/About/Conventions/StatusOfConventions/Documents/Status%20-%202012.pdf, last accessed 27.08.2015.

896 Art. 45 1996 BlS SAP.

897 *Black Sea Commission/IMO*, Regional Workshop on Implementation of International Dumping Agreements in the Black Sea Region, Istanbul, February 2011, 145.

898 The Draft Strategic Action Plan for the Management and Abatement of Marine Litter in the Black Sea Region proposes a less ambitious step. It "promotes the

rent diversity in applicable legal regimes can only be described as utterly untenable if it is deemed necessary to avoid a "multi-speed" regulation of this issue in the area.

II. Marine litter in the overall regulatory framework of the Black Sea Commission

The preliminary remarks on the primary Convention law as established by the Bucharest Convention and its Protocols serve as a basis to understand the regulatory context of marine litter in the Black Sea region. Besides the reference to aspects of marine litter in both BlS LBPs, the issue has gained momentum through the Marine Litter MoUs between the Regional Seas Coordinating Office and the Black Sea Commission in 2005 and 2007 respectively.[899] Following the Marine Litter MoU´s approach, the activities in the Black Sea Region are primarily focused on collating a thorough database on the identification of sources and potential gaps in the regulatory framework both on a regional as well as national level.[900] The primary gaps identified were in this regard the inadequate waste management policies and "the imperfection and lack of balance of legal and administrative instruments developed for solid waste and marine litter management."[901] It was also noticed that

> no legal instrument dedicated specifically to the management of the marine litter problem in the Black Sea marine and coastal environment is established. Neither the concept of marine litter as a serious problem or indeed as a law term are formally accepted or even well-known in the Black Sea community.[902]

In order to remedy the situation, the development of a "Strategic Action Plan for the Management and Abatement of Marine Litter in the Black Sea

---

implementation by all Black Sea states of the principles of the London Convention" *Black Sea Commission*, Marine Litter in The Black Sea Region, 2009, 12.

899 *Ibid.*, 1.

900 *Ibid.* In this context, the review document "Marine litter in the Black Sea Region: A Review of the Problem" was completed in 2007 and adopted during the 15th Meeting of the Advisory Group on Pollution Monitoring and Assessment in October 2006 and the Meeting of the Black Sea Commission in November 2006.

901 *Black Sea Commission*, Marine Litter in The Black Sea Region, 2009, 10.

902 *Black Sea Commission*, Marine Litter in the Black Sea Region, 2007, Conclusion, para. 4.

region (BlS ML SAP)" was envisaged during the Advisory Group meeting in October 2006.[903] The BlS ML SAP as a substance-specific measure thus represents a "tailor-made" approach in which the specific regulatory and scientific issues are addressed. The aim of BlS ML SAP is to "consolidate, harmonise and implement necessary environmental policies, strategies and measures destined to develop sustainable integrated management of marine litter issues in the Black Sea region."[904]

The BS ML SAP approach is focused on the following key aspects: the consolidation of environmental policy, legislation and administrative instruments; organisational and institutional arrangements; research, monitoring and assessment; best available technologies to prevent and reduce marine litter pollution and public awareness, education and information exchange. With a view to efficiency, it is laudable that the action plan has identified key issues which primarily address the regulatory framework and research and monitoring questions. In this regard, it aims to provide adequate waste management policies and to enforce and "harmonise existing legal and administrative instruments relevant to the implementation of waste management policies in order to ensure their efficacy under the application with respect to marine litter issues."[905]

Consequently, the Action Plan follows a problem-oriented approach in which the primary problem of land-based pollution is principally addressed. The five key objectives are further substantiated by 41 "actions" to improve the situation of marine litter in the region. Even though the actions represent a summary of conceivable measures, the sheer amount of actions most likely prevents a complete and effective implementation and would appear to be counterproductive. For the purpose of increasing its efficiency and practicability, it would have been advisable to agree on a few

903 Draft Version of the Strategic Action Plan for the Management and Abatement of Marine litter in the Black Sea Region: *Black Sea Commission*, Marine Litter in The Black Sea Region, Overview and Draft Strategic Action Plan for the Management and Abatement of Marine Litter in the Black Sea Region, in: *UNEP*, Marine Litter: A Global Challenge, 2009, 39–52, 49 *et seq.*

904 *Ibid.*, 49.

905 *Ibid.* It is however questionable what this harmonization will exactly entail, since the implementation of waste management policies are only marginally and not necessarily legally binding regulated under the material scope of the Bucharest Convention, see for example Annex IV 2009 BlS LBP in which it is stated that the Contracting Parties "[…] shall evaluate and consider, as the case may be, the following factors […].".

key provisions. The BlS ML SAP is placed in the context of international and European legislation and thus calls for coordination with legal instruments "including management of wastes, water pollution, nature conservation, and relevant European criteria and standards."[906]

In this way, the BlS Ml SAP exceeds in its material scope the nature of a technical document as it addresses controversially discussed issues relating to amendments of primary Bucharest Convention obligations such as the revision of the Bucharest Dumping Protocol. Nevertheless, it does not provide any timeframes within which the action should be achieved. With regard to contents, the approach chosen is generally very ambitious. Originally, it was planned that the document was to be adopted individually by the Contracting Parties, therefore giving it a prominent role in the elaboration of the regulatory approach.[907] The BlS ML SAP was intended to serve as the "marine litter pillar" in the framework of the revised BlS SAP[908] and therefore intended to significantly increase the strategic orientation of the document. However, to date, the BlS ML SAP has not been officially adopted by the Contracting Parties and only some few provisions have been implemented in the 2009 BlS SAP. The 2009 BlS SAP provides, following the OSPAR EcoQO approach, management targets that are prioritised according to short, medium or long-term measures. Particular challenges to establishing an adequate regulatory regime in the region are the legacy of polluting activities and poor management practices of waste disposal.[909] Consequently, the urgency with which the revised 2009 BlS LBP is to be implemented is also reflected in the 2009 BlS SAP, as the adoption of the Protocol and the implementation of its integrated river basin man-

---

906 *Ibid.*

907 Whereas any references to the procedural options regarding the BlS ML SAP are missing in the draft document, the wording suggests an individual adoption of the BlS ML SAP. Consequently, it is stated that "before BS ML SAP coming into force the corresponding activities shall be conducted in line with provisions of the Strategic Action Plan for Rehabilitation and Protection of the Black Sea 1996, amended 2002": *Black Sea Commission*, Marine Litter in The Black Sea Region, Overview and Draft Strategic Action Plan for the Management and Abatement of Marine Litter in the Black Sea Region, in: *UNEP*, Marine Litter: A Global Challenge, 2009, 52.

908 *Ibid.*

909 *Black Sea Commission*, Strategic Action Plan for the Environmental Protection and Rehabilitation of the Black Sea, BlS SAP, 2nd ed., 17.04.2009 (Sofia, Bulgaria), 6 *et seq*.

agement are considered as being of "high priority".[910] Moreover, the development of regional and marine littering monitoring schemes and assessment methods and the development to amend waste strategies and coastal zone management plans can only be seen as marginally implementing the ambitious BlS ML SAP.[911]

III. Preliminary Conclusion

Whereas the Bucharest Convention in its current form indeed provides for a pollution prevention approach that integrates diverse sources of pollution, it fails to integrate important principles such as the precautionary and polluter-pays-principle that ought to guide its implementation and application. In addition, some weaknesses prevail that also have an impact on the regulation of marine litter. This relates in particular to the Protocols that outline the primary obligations of the Convention. Among others, the primary Convention obligations are not adequately substantiated in that coherent definitions are lacking, leading to legal and conceptual uncertainty. The somewhat rigid and outdated Convention is currently in the process of being amended.

This approach is not pursued by revising the overall Convention, as has been the case for example in the Helsinki Convention, but instead it has been decided to revise some of the Protocols to the Convention. Whereas the progressive 2009 BlS LBP has not entered in force yet, the Biodiversity and Landscape Conservation Protocol from 2002 entered in force nine years after its adoption. This Protocol marks a renunciation of the source-specific approach of the Protocols and applies an integrated protection approach according to which biodiversity should be protected as a whole. The revision and respectively successful ratification and entry into force can be seen as a first sign of momentum to change the regulatory regime of the Black Sea Region.

---

910 *Ibid.*, 10.

911 Other pertinent options refer to: Provide adequate port reception facilities for ship-generated wastes according to MARPOL Annex I, IV, V and establish a harmonised fee/cost recovery system on ship-generated waste. Furthermore, a system should be developed to identify illegal pollution sources from vessels and off-shore installations.

In the Bucharest Convention, marine litter is merely considered in both BlS LBPs, with the 2009 BlS LBP also providing a definition of the term itself. Since "synthetic materials" were formerly also defined, the material scope of both BlS LBP was not majorly changed due to the newly introduced definition. However, the inclusion of a definition of marine litter based on UNEP´s provisions indicates a legal harmonisation of the term itself that leads to a coherent application of its concept. The impetus to act on the subject of marine litter in the Black Sea region is derived from the MoU with UNEP´s Regional Seas Programme and the Black Sea Commission. The ambitious goal to establish a marine litter pillar as a complementary strategy to the 2009 BlS SAP has been, nevertheless, only partially achieved. The role of secondary legislation that is, admittedly, "soft-law" and therefore non-binding should particularly not be underestimated in the context of the Black Sea protection regime. As a political measure, the 2009 BlS SAP establishes progressive ideas such as the incorporation of the precautionary principle and the exigency to follow a causal chain analysis for substances. In this respect, marine litter is not only confined to certain specific sectoral instruments or strategies, but also indirect sources are taken into consideration. The reference to an integrated approach can only be seen as positive regarding the regulation of marine litter.

E. The regulatory scope of the Mediterranean regarding marine litter

The Mediterranean Sea is a semi-enclosed sea that is connected to the Atlantic Ocean through the Strait of Gibraltar which is merely 14 km wide.[912] The Mediterranean has 22 riparian countries, many of which have vastly divergent socio-economic states and different legal affiliations. Eight riparian States are EU-Member States. 460 million people live in the Mediterranean basin, whereas it is estimated that two-thirds of these live in urban spaces. In this regard, smoking-related activities account for 40% of the total marine litter in the Mediterranean.[913] A particular prominent factual problem is that marine litter from shoreline activities are continuously increasing, making it the major source of marine litter pollution in

---

912 *UNEP MAP-Plan Bleu*, State of the development and the environment in the Mediterranean, Athens, 2009, 18.

913 *UNEP*, Marine Litter: A Global Challenge, 98.

the Mediterranean Sea.[914] Furthermore, the Mediterranean Sea is an international shipping nexus in which 30% of international maritime traffic takes place, putting significant pressure on the marine environment.[915]

The environmental protection regime of the Mediterranean Sea is administered directly under the auspices of UNEP.[916] Each UNEP administered Regional Seas Programme is established by an Action Plan. In the case of the Mediterranean Sea, the Mediterranean Action Plan (MAP) was established in 1975 by 16 riparian States and the European Community and was the first Regional Seas Programme commissioned by UNEP.

The MAP envisaged both programmatic issues related to, *inter alia*, a monitoring and assessment approach of the state of ocean pollution and to normative provisions regarding the establishment of a framework Convention and related Protocols for the protection of the Mediterranean environment.[917] The MAP is coordinated by the Athens-based Coordinating Unit for the Mediterranean Action Plan (MEDU) that follows up and implements the legal issues associated with the MAP.[918] Only shortly after the adoption of the MAP, the Contracting Parties implemented its institutional and legal provisions by adopting the Convention for the Protection of the

914 *Ibid.* Approximately 52% of marine litter stems from shoreline and recreational activities.

915 *UN*, UNEP(DEPI)/MED WG.357/Inf.4, Assessment of the status of marine litter in the Mediterranean, Meeting of the MED POL Focal Points, 12.04.2011, 1.

916 *Busuttil* argues that the administrative link with UNEP, the MAP is a hybrid creation since its Convention is assigned to UNEP, whereas the elaboration is subject to the decision of Contracting Parties: *Busuttil*, Ocean Yearbook 21 (2007) 13, 15.

917 *Zoller,* Völker - und europarechtliche Aspekte des Mittelmeerumweltschutzes, 1996, 83. The other two pillars of MAP are: resource management of the Mediterranean Sea and institutional and financial implications of the Action Plan Mediterranean Action Plan (MAP), http://www.unepmap.org/index.php?module=content2&catid=001001002, last accessed 27.08.2015.

918 The main bodies of the MAP are the Meeting of the States Parties that provides strategic guidelines and budget issues and 6 Regional Activities Centers (RCA) that ensure coordinating functions between national focal points and MEDU and are in charge for a specifically defined function. The RCAs work primarily on interdisciplinary issues such as the Regional Marine Pollution Emergency Response Centre for the Mediterranean Sea (REMPEC) in Malta. National focal points are the link between States and the RACS and implement the obligations arising out of MAP, see for further information: http://www.unepmap.org/index.php?module=content2&catid=00101700.

Mediterranean Sea Against Pollution (Barcelona Convention 1976) in 1976.[919]

The Barcelona Convention 1976 is an umbrella treaty in which different sources are specifically addressed in substantiating Protocols.[920] Following the impetus of the Rio Conference in 1992, the Barcelona Convention 1976 was amended by the Convention for the Protection of the Marine Environment and the Coastal Region of the Mediterranean (Barcelona Convention, BC) which was adopted in 1995.[921] The Barcelona Convention came in force on 9 July 2004 and retained the regulatory technique of its predecessor, but exceeded, as the title already indicates, the stipulated pollution prevention approach. Similar to its sister-agreements in the Baltic and North-East Atlantic, the Barcelona Convention obliges the Contracting Parties to apply the precautionary principle and to utilise BAT and BEP.[922] It also contains a clause on monitoring that demands the establishment of a bilateral or multilateral "pollution monitoring system" for the Mediterranean which should be the result of close co-operation with international bodies "which they consider competent."[923]

---

919 Barcelona Convention (Barcelona) of 16 February 1976, in force 12 February 1978; 1102 UNTS, 27, 15 ILM 290 (1976). See for a discussion on the material obligations of the 1976 Barcelona Convention: *Zoller,* Völker- und europarechtliche Aspekte des Mittelmeerumweltschutzes, 1996.

920 See for a discussion on the development of legal measures in the Mediterranean: *Civili,* The Mediterranean Marine Environment: Pressures, State of Pollution and Measures (The Barcelona Convention and the Mediterranean Action Plan), in *Ehlers/Wolfrum/Borgese,* Marine issues (2002) 165–176.

921 Barcelona Convention (Barcelona) of 19 June 1995, in force 09 July 2004; 2102 UNTS 201, 16. Currently, there are 20 Contracting Parties to the BC which are: Albania, Algeria, Croatia, Cyprus, the European Union, Egypt, France, Greece, Italy, Israel, Libya, Malta, Monaco, Montenegro, Morocco, Slovenia, Spain, Syria, Tunisia and Turkey. Lebanon and Bosnia-Herzegovina are Contracting Parties to the 1976 Barcelona Convention and have not yet ratified the amended Convention, Signatures and Ratifications of the Barcelona Convention for the Protection of the Marine Environment and the Coastal Region of the Mediterranean and its Protocols as at 14th October 2014, http://www.unepmap.org/index.php?module=content2&catid=001001004, last accessed 27.08.2015.

922 Other than the Helsinki Convention, it includes a reference to sustainable development *Treves,* Regional Approaches to the Protection of the Marine Environment, in *Nordquist/Moore/Mahmoudi,* The Stockholm declaration and law of the marine environment (2003) 137–154, 145.

923 In regard to marine litter, this relates, *inter alia*, to the Food and Agricultural Organization, the Intergovernmental Oceanographic Commission (IOC), see only:

The fact that this approach aims at establishing a "system" indicates that the underlying intention of this provision is a harmonised monitoring scheme that facilitates the comparability of data and the exchange of good practice of monitoring techniques. These are important aspects also with a view to the multiplicity of sources of marine litter. The primary articles are substantiated by Protocols.[924] These relate to (different versions of) Protocols on Dumping,[925] Land-based Pollution,[926] Prevention of Pollution from ships, and, in cases of emergency,[927] Specially Protected Areas and

---

UNEP MAP, UNEP(DEPI)/MED WG.357/Inf.4, Assessment of the status of marine litter in the Mediterranean, Meeting of the MED POL Focal Points, 12.04.2011, 4.

924 Art. 4 (2) BC. Art. 4 (3) (a) and (4) (b) BC. According to Art. 29 BC "no one may become a Contracting Party to this [the Barcelona Convention] unless it becomes at the same time a Contracting Party to at least one of the Protocols. No one becomes a Contracting Party to a Protocol unless it is, or becomes at the same time, a Contracting Party to this Convention." In case it is proposed to amend a Protocol, three-thirds of the Contracting Parties to the Protocol in question have to be present in order to be able to make a decision (Art. 22 (2) BC). A three-fourths majority of these Parties must accept the amended in order that the Protocol enters into force (Art. 22 (4) BC). All Protocols are available under http://www.unepmap.org/index.php?module=content2&catid=001001001.

925 The 1976 and the 1995 versions of the Protocols for the Prevention and Elimination of Pollution of the Mediterranean Sea by Dumping from Ships and Aircraft or Incineration at Sea (Dumping Protocol). Even though two Dumping Protocols were developed in the framework of the Mediterranean Sea, only the first Protocol has entered in force. The Protocol for the Prevention of Pollution in the Mediterranean Sea by Dumping from Ships and Aircraft (Barcelona, Spain) of 16 February 1976, in force 12 February 1978. The subsequent amended Protocol for the Prevention and Elimination of Pollution in the Mediterranean Sea by Dumping from Ships and Aircraft or Incineration at Sea (Barcelona) of 10 June 1995, has not entered in force yet. See for a discussion on the Dumping Protocol: *Frank,* The European Community and marine environmental protection in the international law of the sea, 2007, 305.

926 The 1980 and 1996 version of Land-Based Pollution Protocol. The so-called Athens Protocol on Land-Based Pollution Protocol (Athens) of 17 May 1980, in force 17 June 1983. The Athens Protocol was revised in the form of the 1996 Protocol for the Protection of the Mediterranean Sea against Pollution from Land-Based Sources and Activities (Syracuse) (1996 LBSP) of 7 March 1996, in force 11 May 2008. See for a further discussion: *Hassan,* Protecting the marine environment from land-based sources of pollution, 2006, 129 *et seq.*

927 The first Protocol relates to the Cooperation in Combating Pollution of the Mediterranean Sea by Oil and other Harmful Substances in Cases of Emergency (Barcelona) of 16 February 1976, in force 12 February 1978. The replacing in-

Biological Diversity,[928] Offshore Pollution,[929] Transboundary Movements of Hazardous Wastes and their Disposal,[930] and Integrated Coastal Zone Management in the Mediterranean.[931] The regulatory landscape of these Protocols is complex, since some of the Protocols were revised or replaced, but not necessarily ratified by every Contracting Party, consequently there are now 9 Protocols currently in force.

The land-based pollution clause of Art. 8 BC is a central clause when dealing with marine litter.[932] Accordingly, the Contracting Parties are under an obligation to establish plans "for the reduction and phasing out of substances that are toxic, persistent and liable to bioaccumulate arising from land-based pollution."[933] The broad understanding of substances is limited to those that enter the sea from outfalls into the sea or coastal disposal and indirectly through rivers, canals or other watercourses such as run-offs.[934] Nevertheless, the listing of these land-based sources is very

---

strument is the Protocol Concerning Cooperation in Preventing Pollution from Ships and, in Cases of Emergency, Combating Pollution of the Mediterranean Sea (Malta) of 25 January 2002, in force 17 March 2004.

928 The Protocol concerning Mediterranean Specially Protected Areas (Geneva) of 3 April 1982, in force 23 March 1986. This Protocol has been replaced by the Protocol concerning Mediterranean Specially Protected Areas (Barcelona) of 19 June 1995, in force 12 December 1999.

929 The Protocol for the Protection of the Mediterranean Sea against Pollution Resulting from Exploration and Exploitation of the Continental Shelf and the Seabed and its Subsoil (Madrid) of 14 October 1994, in force 24 March 2011.

930 The Protocol on the Prevention of Pollution of the Mediterranean Sea by Transboundary Movements of Hazardous Wastes and their Disposal (Izmir) of 1 October 1996, in force 19 January 2008.

931 The Integrated Coastal Zone Management Protocol (Madrid) of 21 January 2008, in force on 24 March 2011. The ICZMP was signed on 21 January 2008 and entered in force on 24 March 2011. Currently, 9 States and the EU have ratified the ICZMP, http://www.pap-thecoastcentre.org/about.php?blob_id=56&lang=en#ratification, last accessed 27.08.2015.

932 Additionally, the BC covers in Art. 6 BC pollution from ships, in Art. 7 BC pollution resulting from exploration and exploitation of the continental shelf and the seabed and its subsoils and contains and in Art. 11 BC pollution resulting from the transboundary movements of hazardous waste and their disposal. Furthermore, an obligation to co-operate when dealing with pollution emergencies is established by Art. 9 BC.

933 Art. 8 BC.

934 Art. 8 (a) BC. Additionally, the provision also includes pollution from land-based sources that are transported via the atmosphere.

pertinent, as these primarily account for the most common marine litter sources.[935]

Besides the legal framework, the programmatic element of the MAP on pollution monitoring and assessment is of key importance to marine litter, as it resulted in the Programme for the Assessment and Control of Marine Pollution in the Mediterranean (MED POL). Whereas initially MED POL was established as the scientific pillar of the MAP in which data on the impacts of different substances or substance group on the marine environment were collected, its scope increasingly widened so as to integrate pollution controls measures.[936] MED POL oversees, among other things, the implementation of the Land-Based Pollution Protocols and the Dumping Protocol and it has the competence to act on issues regarding marine litter.[937] The legal basis for MED POL is, *inter alia*, Art. 5 BC on pollution by dumping and Art. 8 BC on pollution from land-based sources as well as their substantiating Protocols.[938]

I. Marine litter in the context of the Barcelona Convention and UNEP/MAP

Although, the topical orientation of measures that explicitly deal with the issue of marine litter in the Mediterranean has so far been primarily concerned with awareness raising and educational aspects as well as the pre-

935 *UNEP*, Marine Litter: A Global Challenge, 96.

936 *UNEP MAP*, UNEP(DEC)/MED IG. 16/5/Annex III, the MED POL– Phase IV Programme (2006-2013), 14th Ordinary Meeting of the Contracting Parties to the Convention for the Protection of the Marine Environment and the Coastal Region of the Mediterranean and its Protocols, 24.11.2005, 1 *et seq.* The MED POL competences and working scope were to this date developed in four phases: MED POL I, 1975-1980; MED POL II, 1981-1995; MED POL III, 1996-2005 and MED POL IV 2006-2013.

937 *UNEP MAP*, Guidelines on management of coastal litter for the Mediterranean, Athens, MAP Technical Reports Series (No 148), Athens, 2004, 2; *UNEP MAP*, UNEP(DEPI)/MED WG.357/7, Strategic Action Programme for the Management of Marine Litter in the Mediterranean, Meeting of the MED POL Focal Points, 01.04.2011, 2.

938 *UNEP MAP*, UNEP(DEC)/MED IG. 16/5/Annex III, the MED POL– Phase IV Programme (2006-2013), 24.11.2005, 2.

vention of coastal litter, this has changed in recent years.[939] The introduction of specific marine litter measures has primarily evolved independently of UNEP´s Marine Litter Initiative.

One of the early "landmark" activities regarding marine litter in the Mediterranean is the reference and definition of marine litter as a toxic substance in the Athens Protocol.[940] Also, a "persistent synthetic materials pilot survey" was conducted in 1988 in a joint co-operation between UNEP/MAP, IOC and FAO.[941] The Eleventh Meeting of Contracting Parties to the Barcelona Convention in 1999 addressed marine and coastal waste as a major source of pollution from solid waste as was previously identified in the pilot survey.[942] The subsequent assessment of coastal wastes

939 This relates for example to the guidelines on "medium term public awareness and education on management of marine litter" adopted in 2007: *UNEP MAP*, UNEP(DEPI)/MED WG. 316/Inf. 7, Medium Term Public Awareness and Education Campaign on Management of marine litter in the Mediterranean (Prepared by MIO-ECSDE, HELMEPA, Clean-up Greece), Meeting of MED POL National Coordinators, 13.06.2007. *UNEP MAP*, UNEP(DEPI)/MED WG. 316/Inf. 3, Progress Report of the implementation of MED POL activities during 2006-2007, Meeting of MED POL National Coordinators, 13.06.2007, 7; *UNEP MAP*, UNEP(DEPI)/MED WG. 334/3, Proposed activities to be carried out during the 2010-2011 Biennium as part of MED POL UNEP, Meeting of MED POL Focal Points, 19.05.2009, 19; *UNEP MAP*, UNEP(DEPI)/MED WG.357/Inf.5, Strategic Action Programme for the Management of Marine Litter in the Mediterranean, Financial Aspects of its Implementation, Meeting of the MED POL Focal Points, 01.04.2011, 5; *UNEP MAP*, UNEP (DEPI)/ MED WG.334/Inf.5, Results of the assessment of the status of marine litter in the Mediterranean, Meeting of the MED POL Focal Points, 19.05.2009, 52.

940 Annex I of the Athens Protocol makes reference to "persistent synthetic material which may float, sink or remain in suspension and which may interfere with any legitimate use of the sea", para.7 Athens Protocol. In conjunction with Annex I, the Contracting Parties are according to Art. 5 (1) Athens Protocol obliged to "[…] undertake to eliminate pollution […]" from land-based sources. Measures adopted thereunder are, *inter alia*, regular surveys and monitoring programmes and encouraging the use of biodegradable synthetic materials: Interviewes/ Görlitz/Stöfen *et al.*, Issue Paper to the "International Conference on Prevention and Manage-ment of Marine Litter in European Seas", 16.05.2013, 46. Also the 1996 version of the Land-Based Pollution Protocol contains a definition of marine litter as "any persistent manufactured or processed solid material which is discarded, disposed, or abandoned in the marine and coastal environment."

941 *UNEP MAP*, UNEP(DEPI)/MED WG.357/7, Strategic Action Programme for the Management of Marine Litter in the Mediterranean, Meeting of the MED POL Focal Points, 01.04.2011, 3.

942 *Ibid.*

sources, led to a strategy to assist local governments to improve the management of solid wastes.[943]

These activities and the amended scope of the 1995 Barcelona Convention form the basis of the thematic focus on coastal litter, which has influenced practice to this date. In 2004, the "Guidelines on Management of marine coastal litter for the Mediterranean Region" (Coastal Litter Guidelines) were established in the context of the Strategic Action Programme on land-based pollution.[944] Notwithstanding their status as "soft-law", the Coastal Litter Guidelines put an emphasis on two elements: assessment and management of waste and monitoring of coastal litter. Even though they provide rather detailed guidance for certain subjects, they are merely intended "to create a common reference framework."[945] They apply to "solid marine waste" which is defined as "any persistent, manufactured or processed solid material, visible to the naked eye."[946]

Even though the title might suggest differently, coastal litter is in this context primarily seen as an integrated part of the solid waste management.[947] The integration in a broader scheme is laudable, since in that way an incremental approach is avoided. This can be exemplified in that

---

943 *Ibid.*, 4. The review was based on questionnaires that were sent out to the riparian States which had to answer questions on litter management in the coastal zones of the Mediterranean. The main results of the review were that the primary sources of coastal litter were river run-offs and urban centers. It was chosen to first develop a strategy for coastal litter in the form of a pilot project in the municipality of Tripoli, Lebanon, *UNEP MAP*, UNEP(DEPI)/MED WG. 316/Inf. 3, Progress Report of the implementation of MED POL activities during 2006-2007, Meeting of MED POL National Coordinators, 13.06.2007, 6.

944 *UNEP MAP*, Guidelines on management of coastal litter for the Mediterranean, 2004. The Strategic Action Programme aims to address pollution from land-based activities and has been established according to Art. 5 of the 1996 Land-Based Pollution Protocol: *UNEP MAP*, UNEP(DEC)/MED WG.183/Inf.4, Litter Management in Coastal Zones of the Mediterranean Basin - Analysis of the Questionnaire and Proposals for Guideline, Meeting of the MED POL National Coordinators, 07.05.2001.

945 *UNEP MAP*, Guidelines on management of coastal litter for the Mediterranean, 2004, 2.

946 *UNEP MAP*, Guidelines on management of coastal litter for the Mediterranean, 3. The threshold of "naked eye" does not seem to be adequate particularly with regard to microplastics or smaller fragments. The formulation potentially ignores the impacts that these smaller particles could have on marine organisms; see the aspect of microplastics of chapter 1.

947 *Ibid.*, 8.

coastal-based litter in the Coastal Litter Guidelines is not only confined to land-based sources such as ports and harbours but also integrates offshore sources such as platforms and vessels.[948] The Coastal Litter Guidelines systematically address aspects such as waste collection as well as transport and the handling of waste which suggest that they follow an integrated approach to reduce coastal litter.[949] Following the impetus of the UNEP's Marine Litter Initiative, a regional strategy to address marine litter was developed. Initially the approach was primarily oriented towards coastal litter and was seen as a "multilevel watch dog system of the state of management of coastal litter in the region."[950] Its strategic orientation was subsequently broadened so as to encompass a comprehensive set of measures.[951]

In April 2011, the "Strategic Action Programme for the Management of Marine Litter in the Mediterranean" was adopted.[952] Its aim "is to minimise and further eliminate, to the fullest possible extent, marine litter in the Mediterranean Region through regional and national activities."[953] It applies to all Contracting Parties to the Barcelona Convention and not only to Contracting Parties to certain Protocols.[954] Due to its significant role in the context of the Mediterranean regime, it will be analysed in greater detail. The five elements contained therein demonstrate the fundamental

---

948 *Ibid.*, 9.

949 The Guidelines sensitise to consider the main producers of solid waste for example: *ibid.*, 5. They propose very pertinent and concrete recommendations for potential solutions. Consequently, they stipulate that proper management of coastal waste needs to be based on strict, on-going controls, which will be preventive, depending on the individual situation. Such controls can only be operational and effective if they are implemented within the framework of clear, consistent rules and regulations, and an economic and financial strategy based on two principles: "the polluter pays", and "production recovery": *ibid.*, 7.

950 *UNEP MAP*, UNEP(DEPI)/MED WG. 316/Inf. 3, Progress Report of the implementation of MED POL activities during 2006-2007, Meeting of MED POL National Coordinators, 13.06.2007, 7.

951 *UNEP MAP*, UNEP(DEPI)/MED WG.357/7, Strategic Action Programme for the Management of Marine Litter in the Mediterranean, 01.04.2011, 4.

952 *Ibid.*

953 *Ibid.*, 4. As already seen in the context of the 2009 BlS-LBP in the Black Sea region, the Strategy also applies the definition of marine litter as proposed by UNEP, *ibid.*, 4.

954 *Ibid.*, preamble, para.2.

ideas and approaches to successfully reduce the introduction of marine litter in the Mediterranean Sea.

The first two objectives intend primarily to adequately implement already existing legal obligations addressing explicitly municipal and coastal solid waste.[955] Objective one thus relates to the mapping of solid waste infrastructures such as landfills and to support institutional capacity to administer large scale waste management projects along the coast. The first objective primarily focuses on providing legal and institutional frameworks for addressing land and coastal based litter. In contrast, objective two focuses on *in-situ* litter that refers to plastics and smoking related marine debris that emanates from activities along the beach.[956] Hence, objective one and two are complementary as a substance-based focus is associated with activities along the shoreline.[957] Since littering is related to behavioural and environmental awareness, objective three is primarily focused on facilitating programmes that address these issues.[958]

Objective four addresses the options to establish a monitoring programme in the region that is based on UNEP´s guidelines on monitoring marine litter in order to achieve a harmonised framework.[959] The fifth objective is dedicated to furthering the co-operation of MAP with other pertinent legal agreements or programmes. The envisaged co-operation involves on the one hand MARPOL, more precisely, the legal aspects arising out of the MARPOL Annex V Special Area status and aspects related to ghost fisheries that are addressed in collaboration with the FAO Code of Conduct for Responsible Fisheries.[960] The role of the Marine Strategy Framework Directive is prominent as MED POL is instructed to "work with the EU to develop legally binding targets for the reduction of marine litter and align targets to Marine Strategy Framework Directive."[961] Most

---

955 *UNEP MAP*, UNEP(DEPI)/MED WG.357/Inf.5, Strategic Action Programme for the Management of Marine Litter in the Mediterranean, Financial Aspects of its Implementation, Meeting of the MED POL Focal Points, 01.04.2011, 8.

956 *UNEP MAP*, UNEP(DEPI)/MED WG.357/7, Strategic Action Programme for the Management of Marine Litter in the Mediterranean, 01.04.2011, 5.

957 *Ibid.*, 10 *et seq.*

958 *Ibid.*, 13.

959 The reference to UNEP´s Guidelines is the only explicit referral to this document in any of the four Strategic Action Plans.

960 *UNEP MAP*, UNEP(DEPI)/MED WG.357/7, Strategic Action Programme for the Management of Marine Litter in the Mediterranean, 01.04.2011, 20.

961 *Ibid.*, 22.

recently a Regional Action Plan on marine litter has been adopted in the Mediterranean.[962] This objective is particularly important in regard to the diverse sources and activities that cause marine litter and adequately recognise the challenges to regulate the introduction of marine litter.

II. Integrated Coastal Zone Management as an instrument to regulate coastal sources of marine litter

Since the results of the assessment of the status of marine litter in the Mediterranean indicate that shoreline activities are the primary sources of litter,[963] the pertinent instrument of the Barcelona Convention must be addressed. The regulation of coastal-based pollution is aggravated by the complexity of activities that fall, depending on their nature, under the jurisdiction of different competent authorities. This situation is also problematic as usually these competencies are strictly distributed according to land and maritime activities. As every State has a different administration in respect of the coastal zone, the establishment of integrated coastal zone management techniques that adequately encompass the different activities and competences could be a key instrument to address litter stemming from coastal areas.

The fundamental focus on coastal litter and the specific factual relevance require that the Protocol to the Barcelona Convention on Integrated Coastal Zone Management in the Mediterranean (ICZMP) will be analysed with a view to its role in preventing costal-based marine litter. With the entry in force of the ICZMP as the only legally binding instrument that addresses Integrated Coastal Zone Management (ICZM),[964] it establishes

962 See section B.VII.2.3.bb. of chapter 4.

963 *UNEP MAP*, UNEP(DEPI)/MED WG.357/Inf.4, Assessment of the status of marine litter in the Mediterranean, 12.04.2011, 24.

964 ICZM has been a particular focal point in the Mediterranean since MAP Phase II. The efforts of establishing coastal zone management approaches have been coined by local initiatives around the Mediterranean: *UNEP MAP*, UNEP(DEPI)/MED IG.20/8, Decision IG 20/2, Adoption of the Action Plan for the implementation of the ICZM Protocol for the Mediterranean (2012-2019), Report of the 17th Ordinary Meeting of the Contracting Parties to the Convention for the Protection of the Marine Environment and the Coastal Region of the Mediterranean and its Protocols, Annex II, 14.02.2012, 11. In contrary, the Helsinki Commission has also acted on the issue of ICZM and has adopted on 25

"a framework for the integrated management of the coastal zone."[965] ICZM means in the context of the ICZMP

> a dynamic process for the sustainable management and use of coastal zones, taking into account at the same time the fragility of coastal ecosystems and landscapes, the diversity of activities and uses, their interactions, the maritime orientation of certain activities and uses and their impact on both the marine and land parts.[966]

Since the integration of diverse activities and their impacts is the primary goal of the ICZMP, it is also highly relevant for addressing the sources of marine litter. The understanding of what constitutes a coastal zone is defined as:

> the geomorphological area either side of the seashore in which the interaction between the marine and landscape parts occurs in the form of complex ecological and resource systems made up of biotic and abiotic components coexisting and interacting with human communities and relevant socio-economic activities.[967]

The interactions contained therein set the framework for an integrated approach which comprehensively addresses the pollution of the marine environment by marine litter. Since marine litter in the Mediterranean area primarily stems from coastal activities, the demarcation of the coastal zone itself is of central importance as its designation has an influence on the covered activities. The geographic scope of the ICZMP applies to: "[t]he seaward limit of the coastal zone, which shall be the external limit of the territorial sea of Parties and the landward limit of the coastal zone, which shall be the limit of the competent coastal units as defined by the Parties."[968]

The definition of the area to which the ICZMP applies is thus not absolute and leaves a certain degree of flexibility for the Contracting Parties. Following the framework nature of the Protocol, general principles of inte-

---

June 2003 the non-binding HELCOM Recommendation 24/10 on the Implementation of Integrated Marine and Coastal Management of Human Activities in the Baltic Sea Area, 25.06.2003.

965 Art. 1 sent. 1 ICZMP.

966 Art. 2(f) ICZMP.

967 Art. 2 (e) ICZMP. The ratification law of the ICZMP in Croatia contains simultaneously a declaration on the geographical scope of the ICZMP in Croatia, *UNEP MAP*, Croatia Passes Law to Ratify the ICZM Protocol.

968 Art. 3 (a and b) ICZMP.

grated coastal zone management precede the more specific instruments.[969] The principles refer among others to allocation of uses and risk assessment of human activities. It can be seen as a key weakness of the Protocol, however, that these principles do not coincide with, for example, the precautionary or preventive principles.[970] A particular asset of the chosen approach is indeed the emphasis on both institutional and topical coordination between the different competent local, national and regional authorities in order to ensure an integrated approach.[971] This integrative approach has the advantage of addressing diffuse sources of marine litter by encompassing various administrative levels and therefore facilitating the development of integrated regulatory techniques.

Having these preliminary principles in mind, the ICZMP establishes elements that are to be considered in establishing ICZM laws. The elements are quite comprehensive as they are also activity-oriented and provide for measures that relate to specific economic activities and uses of the coastal zone. It is as well in the context of economic activities in which the issue of marine litter is most suitably addressed. Art. 9 ICZMP addresses these economic activities by stipulating that the Contracting Parties should generally ensure sound waste management and pay close attention "to economic activities that require immediate proximity to the sea."[972] This is a clear reference to, for example, waste managements in ports. Furthermore, it should be ensured that "the coastal and maritime economy is adapted to the fragile nature of coastal zones and that resources of the sea are protected from pollution."[973] Despite the absence of any reference to the preventive or precautionary principle, this provision reflects a "preventive spirit." In this regard, it needs to be emphasised that the Protocol not only refers to standard situations, but also refers to "risk affecting the coastal zone" which could be associated to natural disasters and also with the consequences of climate change.[974] This approach coincides with the international coordination objective of the Mediterranean Strategic Action Pro-

969 Art. 6 ICZMP.

970 Aspects of the precautionary and the preventive principle may be found in Art. 6 (i and j) ICZMP. The Contracting Parties are however obliged to apply the precautionary principle as contained in Art. 4 (3) (a) BC.

971 Art. 7 ICZMP.

972 Art. 9 (1) (a) ICZMP.

973 Art. 9 (1) (d) ICZMP.

974 Part IV ICZMP.

gramme for the Management of Marine Litter according to which increased attention ought to be paid to strong floods and heavy precipitation so as to avoid flush outs of litter.[975]

In an attempt to provide concrete measures that relate to specific activities such as fishing or tourism, the ICZMP fails to specify detailed provisions and merely stipulates broad proposals that relate to certain activities.[976] As an example, the Contracting Parties should "encourage sustainable coastal tourism that preserves coastal ecosystems, natural resources, cultural heritage and landscape."[977] In its regulatory approach, the ICZMP differentiates between elements that should be particularly considered in any ICZM law and instruments. ICZM instruments should thus include monitoring and observation mechanisms, environmental assessment provisions as well as economic, financial and fiscal aspects. With a view to marine litter, the diversity of instruments is of note. In particular, the proposal to establish a common regional framework for ICZM could ensure that the issue of solid waste is coherently addressed in different riparian States.[978]

The framework characteristics paired with the flexibility that automatically ensues from such broad obligations, has the disadvantage of only creating parameters that build, at most, a basic common denominator. This flexibility is, however, needed in particular regarding the diverse administrative and organisational structures that are differently competent in each

---

975 *UNEP MAP*, UNEP(DEPI)/MED WG.357/Inf.4, Assessment of the status of marine litter in the Mediterranean, 12.04.2011, 20.

976 The activities are agriculture and industry; fishing; aquaculture; tourism, sporting and recreational activities and the utilization of specific natural resources. Since the ICZM applies in principle to the territorial sea of each Contracting Party, it is quite surprising that fishing is mentioned in this context. In a strict interpretation, fishing that is conducted outside of the defined limits is outside of the scope of the ICZMP. This aspect also relates to Art. 9 (2) (g) ICZMP on maritime activities in which in a former proposal the referral was made to shipping. This was however changed and refers to "maritime activities" instead. *UNEP MAP*, UNEP(DEPI)/MED WG 305/4, Report of Third Meeting of the Working Group of experts designated by the Contracting Parties on the Draft Protocol on Integrated Coastal Zone Management (ICZM) in the Mediterranean, Third Meeting of the Working Group of experts designated by the Contracting Parties on the Draft Protocol on Integrated Coastal Zone Management (ICZM) in the Mediterranean, 16.07.2007, 4.

977 Art. 9 (d) (i) ICZMP.

978 Art. 17 ICZMP. Similarly, the ICZMP addresses specific elements such as specific coastal ecosystems, islands and coastal landscapes and provides for tailored measures.

Contracting Party. Since the overall outlook of the ICZMP integrates relevant aspects and provides general guidance, it can be, in principle, seen as a useful instrument to address coastal litter.

III. Preliminary Conclusion

Marine litter in the Mediterranean has been in focus since the 1980s. The regulatory emphasis was, also with a view to the factual situation and the extended scope of the Barcelona Convention, primarily on the regulation of coastal litter. This heritage has provided the background for follow-up programmes and initiatives that were addressed to reduce coastal litter. The assessment has demonstrated that a development from ad-hoc measures relating to the assessment of coastal litter to comprehensive and legally binding instruments has taken place which shows a political will to adequately address marine litter in the region. The Mediterranean regulatory framework already contains pertinent measures addressing sectoral sources of marine litter. In particular the ICZMP stipulates a complementary instrument that gives guidance on waste management and coastal activities. With a view to the multiplicity of activities along the coast that could contribute to marine litter, it contains broad elements and principles. In an attempt to further substantiate the provisions, it identifies certain economic activities that are believed to be important sectors that contribute to the potential degradation of the coastal zone. In this regard, however, the ICZMP does not demonstrate the adequate preciseness that would be required in order for it to be truly effective and it merely provides broad and flexible specifications.

The Strategic Action Programme for the Management of Marine Litter in the Mediterranean has defined objectives that are realistically drafted. With regard to the feasibility, it is laudable that it focuses on five key topics that are drawn from previous experiences on the topic. A noteworthy aspect is that the Strategic Action Programme is not formulated to stand on its own; rather it is embedded in the context of pre-existing measures. The orientation towards the EU is remarkable which is manifested in the intention not "to duplicate efforts in the region to de-pollute the Mediterranean."[979] It remains unclear how the Strategic Action Plan relates to the Regional Action Plan on Marine Litter in the Mediterranean.[980]

Notwithstanding the foregoing the established material framework is limited by the inadequate compliance and implementation of the overall regime.[981] *Papanicolopulu* outlines that despite the establishment of a compliance committee, "it is rather a "State-friendly" regime, in which the protection of Parties' interests seems to be the main concern [...]."[982] It is somewhat lacking in its ability to meaningfully further marine environmental protection in respect of marine litter.

F. Regional Action Plans

The development of Action Plans on marine litter in the four Regional Seas can be broadly derived from the impetus of the Marine Strategy Framework Directive and UNEP's Marine Litter Initiative. In April 2013, the "International Conference on Prevention and Management of Marine Litter in European Seas" in Berlin served the purpose to elaborate on the establishment and further coherence of Regional Action Plans on marine litter for the Regional Seas.[983]

The Baltic Sea Regional Action Plan on Marine Litter

In the Baltic Sea, the HELCOM Copenhagen Declaration indicated the development of a Regional Action Plan on Marine Litter in the Baltic Sea. The environmental ministers of the Contracting Parties and the EU Environment Commissioner reached an accord to "develop a regional action plan by 2015 at the latest with the aim of achieving significant quantitative

979 *UNEP MAP*, UNEP(DEPI)/MED WG.357/7, Strategic Action Programme for the Management of Marine Litter in the Mediterranean, 01.04.2011, 6.

980 See section F. of this chapter.

981 *Frank,* The European Community and marine environmental protection in the international law of the sea, 2007, 39.

982 *Papanicolopulu,* Procedures and Mechanisms on Compliance under the 1976/1995 Barcelona Convention on the Protection of the Mediterranean Sea and its Protocols, in *Treves/Pineschi/Tanzi et al.,* Non-compliance procedures and mechanisms and the effectiveness of international environmental agreements (2009) 155–168, 168.

983 *Interviewes/Görlitz/Stöfen et al.*, Issue Paper to the "International Conference on Prevention and Management of Marine Litter in European Seas", 16.05.2013, 6.

reduction of marine litter by 2025, compared to 2015, and to prevent harm to the coastal and marine environment."[984] Furthermore, the Regional Action Plan on Marine Litter should "carry concrete measures for prevention and reduction of marine litter from its main sources with the aim of achieving significant quantitative reductions focusing, *inter alia,* on working with the industry to reduce or phase out microbeads in certain products in the market." Also, it should serve to "develop and test technology for removal of microplastics and nanoparticles in municipal waste water treatment plants by 2020 and *inter alia* work with the industry to ban the use of microplastics and on the assessment of the use of nanoparticles within the production process."[985] With a view to develop a Baltic Regional Action Plan on Marine Litter, two workshops were organized in 2014.[986] The Baltic Regional Action Plan (HELCOM RAP ML) was adopted by HELCOM Recommendation 36/1 on a Regional Action Plan on Marine Litter (RAP ML) in March 2015.[987]

During the 48th Meeting of Heads of Delegations, the meeting considered and endorsed the proposed Annex to Recommendation 36/1 with regional actions and voluntary national actions as part of HELCOM Recommendation 36/1.[988] Both the regional actions as well as the voluntary na-

---

984 HELCOM Copenhagen Ministerial Declaration, 4 (emphasis added). Specific steps and possible targets in implementing the regional action plans in the four seas are outlined in the Issue paper to the International Conference on Prevention and Management of Marine Litter in European Seas": *Interviewes/Görlitz/Stöfen et al.*, Issue Paper to the "International Conference on Prevention and Management of Marine Litter in European Seas", 16.05.2013.

985 HELCOM Copenhagen Ministerial Declaration, 11. Other aspects include the identification of socio-economic and biological impacts of marine litter and the development of indicators and targets. The effectiveness of the regional action plan on marine litter is to be reviewed by 2020.

986 HELCOM LAND, 2nd Workshop on Regional Action Plan for Marine Litter (MARINE LITTER 2-2014), held in Stralsund, Germany from 22.10 to 23.10.2014.

987 *HELCOM,* HELCOM Recommendation 36/1 on Recommendation 36/1 on a Regional Action Plan on Marine Litter (RAP ML), 04.03.2015. See for a more general overview of primary and secondary Helsinki Convention provisions regarding marine litter in section B of this chapter.

988 HELCOM HOD 48th Meeting, (48/2015), Outcome of HOD 48-2015, Agenda Item 3: Matters arising from the HELCOM Groups 3.1. to 3.8, Document 3-1, 3 as well as HELCOM HOD 48th Meeting, (48/2015), Outcome of HOD 48-2015, Annex 2: Actions to reduce the input and presence of marine litter in the Baltic Sea as part of the HELCOM Regional Action Plan on Marine Litter, 16.

tional actions are clustered around three approaches: (1) actions addressing land-based sources, (2) actions on sea-based sources as well as (3) actions addressing education and awareness. The Annex outlines regional actions which require a joint approach by Contracting Parties and are of a large-scale, widespread and transboundary character.[989] The joint approach to address these actions are not only limited to actors within the Baltic Sea region, but also address other organisations such as the European Union or IMO. The collective actions addressing land-based sources of marine litter include measures on general improved waste prevention and management, measures to tackle "top items" such as microplastics and plastic bags, measures to seek coordination with third parties such as River Basin Commissions as well as remediation and removal actions. Some of the measures are based on existing guidance or recommendations that are adopted within HELCOM, which are to be developed within a specific time frame.[990] A second set of collective measures addresses actions regarding sea-based sources of marine litter, including actions on shipping related waste such as waste delivery in ports and actions on waste stemming from fisheries and aquaculture. Thirdly, the regional measures regarding education and awareness envisage, amongst others, a communication strategy on the HELCOM RAP ML.

The voluntary national actions are actions that can be selected by the Contracting Parties for voluntary implementation.[991] Proposed measures are to promote extended producer responsibility by requiring producers and manufacturers to take responsibility for the entire life cycle of a product or to promote the enforcement of MARPOL Annex V or certain EU Regulations on gear marking.

The diverse range of actions and specifications exemplifies the ambitious scope of HELCOM RAP ML. The implementation framework of the Action Plan is also strengthened by a reporting format on implemented actions[992], a reporting format on the effectiveness of the implemented ac-

---

989 *Ibid.*

990 *Ibid.* This relates amongst others to produce by 2020 a regional-wide map on landfills and dumpsites including historic ones which may eventually pose a risk to the marine environment. Other measures include to coordinate and share information among HELCOM Contracting Parties on the consumption of plastic bags on an annual basis by 2018 as well as to establish by 2019 a reduction target of plastic bags, taking into account the measures which are implemented nationally.

991 *Ibid.*, 21.

992 Ibid., Appendix I, 24.

tions[993] as well as a list of definitions of terms for the purpose of the Recommendation.[994]

The OSPAR Regional Action Plan on Marine Litter

In the context of the OSPAR Convention, the EIHA has adopted terms of references for a Workshop on the development of an OSPAR Regional Action Plan on Marine Litter that took place in November 2013 in Hamburg, Germany.[995] Altogether, three workshops were convened in the development and implementation of an OSPAR Regional Action Plan on Marine Litter (OSPAR RAP ML) so far.[996]

The OSPAR RAP ML was adopted as an Agreement during OSPAR 2014 in Cascais, Portugal.[997] An Agreement is a legally non-binding instrument under the OSPAR Convention. The OSPAR RAP ML is designed as a flexible tool providing a set of actions to address marine litter. The OSPAR RAP ML and its Implementation Plan aim to deliver, amongst others, measures on specific sources of marine litter that are of particular concern in different OSPAR regions or the entire OSPAR maritime region.[998] It is also closely linked to regionally coordinated reduction or operational targets which also take into consideration the MSFD targets that were submitted by EU Member States Contracting Parties to the European Union. The OSPAR RAP ML has four sections that comprehensively address the issue of marine litter. Section I addresses the objectives, scope and principles of the Action Plan. One of the main objectives is to prevent and reduce marine litter pollution in the North-East Atlantic and its im-

993 Ibid., Appendix II, 25.

994 Ibid, Appendix III, 26.

995 *OSPAR*, EIHA 13/10/1-E, Workshop on the development of an OSPAR Regional Action Plan on Marine Litter, Meeting of the Environmental Impact of Human Activities Committee, Annex 9, (Ref. § 4.17a), 15-19.04.2013.

996 *OSPAR WKRAP-ML*, Workshop on the development of an OSPAR Regional Action Plan on Marine Litter from 5 to 6 November 2013 in Hamburg Germany; *OSPAR WKRAP ML (2),* Second workshop on the development of an OSPAR Regional Action Plan on Marine Litter from 12 to 13 February 2014 in The Hague, the Netherlands and *OSPAR WKRAP ML*, Workshop on the Implementation of the OSPAR Regional Action Plan on Marine Litter from 9 to 10 October 2014 in The Hague, the Netherlands.

997 OSPAR, OSPAR Regional Action Plan on Marine Litter (OSPAR Agreement 2014-1) adopted in Cascais.

998 OSPAR RAP ML, 3.

pacts on marine organisms, habitats, public health and safety. The OSPAR RAP ML is guided by the precautionary and polluter-pays-principle as well as the ecosystem approach and highlights the importance of cross-sectoral cooperation.[999] Section II addresses the action items of the OSPAR RAP ML. The OSPAR RAP ML follows three different approaches: first, actions that require collective activities, second, national actions and third, actions that involve issues falling under the competence of other international organisations and competent authorities.[1000] In these, four themes are identified: (A) actions that combat sea-based and (B) land-based sources of marine litter, (C) actions for marine litter removal as well as (D) actions for education and outreach on the topic.[1001] The diversity of the actionable items demonstrate the ambitious and comprehensive scope of the OSPAR RAP ML. By way of exemplifying the scope, the collective actions regarding sea-based sources of marine litter addressing port reception facilities are ambitious given the on-going discussion within the European Union.[1002] The OSPAR RAP ML stipulates to ensure regional coordination on the implementation of EU Directive 2000/59/EC on port reception facilities for ship-generated waste in relation to MARPOL Annex V. According to OSPAR RAP ML, such coordination could deliver a cost recovery system which ensures that a maximum amount of onboard generated waste of MARPOL Annex V is delivered to port reception facilities. It could also facilitate the analysis of the implementation of the compulsory discharge of waste in each port for all ships leaving the OSPAR maritime area for non-EU ports, in line with EU Directive 2000/59/EC on port reception facilities for ship-generated waste.[1003]

Section III addresses monitoring and assessment in which reference is made to the comprehensive marine litter monitoring scheme that is established under the OSPAR Convention.[1004] This section also outlines how marine litter will be integrated in OSPAR's major assessment mechanisms, such as the QSR.[1005] Section IV stipulates the implementation and reporting mechanisms of the OSPAR RAP ML. It is to be noted that the imple-

999 OSPAR RAP ML, 4 and 5.
1000 OSPAR RAP ML, 3.
1001 OSPAR RAP ML, 5 and 6.
1002 See only section B.V.6. of chapter 4 of this study for further information.
1003 OSPAR RAP ML, 6 and 7.
1004 See only section C.III. of this chapter.
1005 OSPAR RAP ML, 12. See further on QSR, section C.IV of this chapter.

mentation period of the Action Plan is from 2014 to 2021, after which it shall be reviewed and updated. The time frame is coordinated with the new OSPAR Strategy as well as the assessments under the MSFD.[1006] The Implementation Plan of OSPAR RAP ML is outlined in Annex I and Contracting Parties will use the implementation reporting process to update OSPAR on their national implementation progress.[1007] Annex I on the OSPAR RAP ML Implementation Plan outlines a differentiated table in which the actions listed in the OSPAR RAP ML are outlined and the specific type of OSPAR measures are or will be described. In this regard, the implementation and substantiation of the action items could lead to legally binding measures in form of decisions. For each measure, it is envisage to determine a lead party or parties and to agree on a target year for developing the measure or implementing the actions.

The Regional Action Plan on Marine Litter Management in the Mediterranean

In the Mediterranean, the Contracting Parties committed themselves to make efforts to reach the target to intensify "efforts to curb pollution from land-based sources, such as marine litter, through the adoption and implementation of legally-binding measures, and pollution from offshore activities and sea based activities, through regional action plans"[1008] in 2012. This commitment was immediately implemented with the adoption of decision IG. 20/10 on "the adoption of the Strategic Framework for Marine Litter."[1009] In December 2013, the Contracting Parties adopted the Re-

1006 See section B.VI.2. of chapter 4 of this study.

1007 OSPAR RAP ML, 12.

1008 *UNEP MAP*, UNEP(DEPI)/MED IG.20/CRP.XX, Annex I, Paris Declaration, 17th Ordinary Meeting of the Contracting Parties to the Convention for the Protection of the Marine Environment and the Coastal Region of the Mediterranean and its Protocols, 10.02.2012, 3. 3. UNEP MAP, 3.

1009 *UNEP MAP*, UNEP(DEPI)/MED IG.20/8, Report of the 17th Ordinary Meeting of the Contracting Parties to the Convention for the Protection of the Marine Environment and the Coastal Region of the Mediterranean and its Protocols, 14.02.2012, 13. The different draft versions of the decisions are contained in: *UNEP MAP*, UNEP(DEPI)/MED IG.20/5, Draft decisions for the 17th Meeting of the Contracting Parties, 17th Ordinary Meeting of the Contracting Parties to the Convention for the Protection of the Marine Environment and the Coastal Region of the Mediterranean and its Protocols, 125, 12.01.2012, 125 and *UNEP MAP*, UNPE(DEPI)/MED, WG.387/11, "Draft Decision on the Regional Plan

gional Action Plan on Marine Litter Management in the Mediterranean (RAP ML Med) during their COP in Istanbul, Turkey.[1010] The RAP ML Med is based on Art. 5 and Art. 15 1996 LBSP. This implies that the measures and timetables of the RAP ML Med are made legally binding.[1011] Consequently, it is the first legally binding document that specifically focuses on marine litter. However, since the RAP ML Med is based on the 1996 LBSP, those Contracting Parties that have not accepted the amended 1996 LBSP are not legally bound by this.[1012]

The RAP ML Med has 22 Articles and is divided into five parts as well as Annexes on the work plan and timetables, potential research topics and elements for national reports. Its first part contains general provisions including the area and scope of application, definitions, objectives and principles. The second part addresses measures and operational targets that include the integration of litter measures into national action plans on land-based pollution, legal and institutional matters and prevention measures on marine litter as well as the removal of marine litter. A third part relates to

---

on Marine Litter Management" as discussed in the plenary as UNEP (DEPI)/MED WG.387/CRP.7; endorsed and agreed to be forwarded to COP 18, 18.07.2013.

1010 *UNEP MAP*, UNEP(DEPI)/MED IG.21/9, Decision IG.21/9 on a Regional Plan on Marine Litter Management in the Mediterranean in the Framework of Article 15 of the Land Based Sources Protocol. See for an overview on the institutional development toward the adoption, *UNEP MAP*, UNEP(DEPI)/MED WG. 379/ Inf.3, Draft Report of the Meeting to Review the Regional Action Plan on Marine Litter, MED POL Focal Points Meeting, 18.06.2013.

1011 Art. 5 (2) 1996 LBSP stipulates the elaboration and implementation of regional action plans. The procedures for adoption of this regional action plan are outlined in Art. 15 1996 LBSP. Consequently, the meeting of the parties has to adopt the regional action plans by a two-third majority (Art. 15 (1) 1996 LBSP). Accordingly, "[r]egional action plans and programmes […] shall be formulated by the Organization and considered and approved by the relevant technical body of the Contracting Parties […]. Such regional action plans and programmes shall be put on the agenda for the subsequent meeting of the Parties for adoption." (Art. 15 (2) Land-Based Pollution Protocol). Most importantly, Art. 15 (3) 1996 LBSP stipulates that "[s]uch measures and timetables become *binding* on the one hundred and eightieth day following the day of notification for the Parties which have not notified the Secretariat of an objection within one hundred and seventy-nine days from the date of notification" (emphasis added).

1012 These are Algeria, Bosnia and Herzegovina, Egypt, Lebanon and Libya as at 14. 10.2014. None of these have accepted the 1996 LBSP, http://www.unepmap.org/index.php?module=content2&catid=001001001, last accessed 27.08.2015.

the assessment of marine litter in the Mediterranean and a marine litter programme. Part four stipulates support for implementation that includes technical assistance, public awareness and education, stakeholder participation and reporting. Lastly, part V relates to implementation timetables, entry in force and enforcement of measures.

With a view to the requirements for an effective protection regime of marine litter, the RAP ML Med appears to be a highly suitable instrument. First, it is clearly drafted and outlines definitions including that of marine litter as consisting of "regardless of the size, means any persistent, manufactured or processed solid material discarded, disposed of or abandoned in the marine and coastal environment."[1013] The inclusion of objectives and principles such as the precautionary principle, preventive principle and the ecosystem-based approach guide the implementation of the subsequent measures.[1014] The RAP ML Med outlines the prevention of marine litter from land-based pollution and refers to urban waste solid waste management and prevention measures such as deposit and return systems.[1015] Also, the prevention of sea-based sources is outlined since the scope of RAP ML Med also extends to operational discharge from platforms.[1016] In this regard, among the proposed measures is the establishment of port reception facilities that can be used to a "reasonable" cost or the introduction of the no-special-fee-system are proposed measures.[1017] The RAP Ml Med aims to ensure an integrated approach that is characterised by institutional coordination between and among national and local authorities and regional organisations.[1018] The wording of the RAP ML Med remains, nonetheless, in some provisions vague and obliges Contracting Parries "to the extent possible" to take certain measures.[1019]

The Regional Action Plans on marine litter are important mechanisms to streamline marine litter measures and to ensure coherence. It remains to be seen what provisions will be selected by the Contracting Parties from

1013 Art. 3 RAP ML Med.

1014 Art. 4 RAP ML Med.

1015 Art. 9 (1-4) RAP ML Med. In this context, different timetables are outlined. Amongst others by the year 2020, Contracting Parties are to take measures on adequate waste water treatment plants to prevent run-off and riverine inputs of marine litter.

1016 Art. 2 RAP ML Med in conjunction with Art. 4 1996 LBSP.

1017 Art. 9 (5) RAP ML Med. However this is to be done "to the extent possible."

1018 Art. 8 RAP ML Med.

1019 See only Art. 9 (5-7) RAP ML Med.

the catalogue of available measures and actions. The adoption of a legally binding Regional Action Plan in the Mediterranean Sea indicates a paradigm change in that the document is legally binding and addressed marine litter in an integrated manner. This as well as the RAP MLs within HELCOM as well as OSPAR indicates that the issue is placed high on the agenda. It is in particular laudable, that an implementation and follow-up scheme is stipulated, which will hopefully encourage a constant follow-up and update of pertinent measures.

G. Conclusion on the scope and regulatory techniques for preventing marine litter contained in the four European Regional Seas Conventions

Even though UNEP's Global Initiative on Marine Litter provided for four fundamental elements that can be seen as systematically setting the framework and therefore stipulating the same elements, it is evident that these fundamental elements were differently interpreted and implemented in the different regions. The following table outlines a schematic overview on the material provisions and focal area taken in regard to marine litter in the four Regional Seas Conventions. Despite the risk of being too superficial, the table gives a first indication on whether a legally binding definition of marine litter exists in the Convention, whether a Regional Action Plan on marine litter has been adopted and whether land-based, coastal and ocean-based pollution provision are in place that address the sources of marine litter.

	Legally binding definition of marine litter	*ML RAP*	*Specific marine litter measures*	*Land-based pollution*	*Ocean-based pollution*
HC	**X**	√ HELCOM RAP ML	√ Monitoring, marine litter caught in fishing nets integrated in no-special-fee-system	√ Primary law, Recommendations (handling of waste/landfilling, municipal waste water treatment)	√ Port-reception facilities (no-special-fee-system), inclusion of marine litter caught in fisher nets
OSPAR Convention	**X**	√ OSPAR RAP ML	√ NEAS; Monitoring (QSR, EcoQO); ICGML	√ Primary law, Annex I	√ Annex II and III, Dumping, reference to IMO
Barcelona Convention	√	√ RAP ML Med	√ Coastal Litter Guidelines, Strategic Action Programme for the Management of Marine Litter in the Mediterranean	√ Primary law, Land-Based Pollution Protocols, ICZMP	√ Protocols on offshore-pollution, dumping and transboundary movement of hazardous waste

	Legally binding definition of marine litter	*ML RAP*	*Specific marine litter measures*	*Land-based pollution*	*Ocean-based pollution*
Bucharest Convention	(√) 2009 BlS LBP (not yet in force)	√	√ BlS ML SAP	√ Pertinent amendments in 2009 BlS LBP (not yet in force); MoU Danube Convention	√ Dumping: different standards

Table 1: Schematic overview on focal areas in the Regional Seas Conventions studied. Whereas "√" confirms the presence of measures or definition, "(√)" indicates that such measures are intended but not yet finalised in the context of institutional matters. "X" indicates that such a measure has (yet) not been taken.

Whereas in the Baltic Sea the issue of marine litter has until very recently not been considered as a major problem for the marine region, the situation was quite different in the North-East Atlantic, the Mediterranean and the Black Sea.

In the Baltic Sea, there does not exist a legally binding definition of marine litter. Specific actions on marine litter include the adoption of a legally non-binding recommendation on the monitoring of marine litter in which a monitoring scheme is proposed. Besides the monitoring approach, no further elements of the MoU have been applied. However, the regulatory approach of the Helsinki Convention is able to comprehensively address and integrate different sources of marine litter. The legally binding application of the precautionary principle and the polluter-pays-principle help to further guide and implement its provisions. A particular aspect regarding vessel-based pollution is the no-special-fee-system. The underlying approach of the no-special-fee-system is that no additional costs are imposed on the discharge of onboard generated garbage. In this way, the usual disposal expenses are indirectly covered through general harbour fees. Consequently, this is a key mechanism that serves the mitigation of vessel-based marine litter. Also, the no-special-fee-system has been extended by way of a legally non-binding recommendation to include marine litter caught in fisher nets. The adoption of Recommendation 36/1 on a Regional Action Plan on Marine Litter as well as the endorsement of its Annex including over thirty regional actions constitutes a paradigm shift within the region. With HELCOM RAP ML, an umbrella framework has been created under which the diverse regional and voluntary national measures and actions are integrated.

The comprehensive pollution approach taken within the OSPAR Convention allows for the integration of the sources of marine litter. Among one of the central provisions of the OSPAR Convention is the obligation to assess the quality of the marine environment. Its implementation entails a monitoring scheme in which also the impacts of consequences of polluting substances are assessed. Whereas the initial approaches were primarily focused on beach littering programmes, a more sophisticated assessment approach has been developed in the context of the North Sea region. The EcoQO approach provides for an interface between science and policy and entails the creation of certain objectives and limit values that can serve as a threshold of harm. Marine litter has been addressed as one parameter in this assessment. Even though the initial threshold of harm has initially not been met due to considerable levels of pollution, its integration in this context demonstrates the significance of establishing limit values. Notwithstanding their significant role, the ECQO are not legally binding and are geographically confined to the North Sea. Furthermore, the instalment of a standing working group with the mandate to address marine litter issues as seen in the framework of the OSPAR Convention is an important instrument to ensure a coherent regulatory approach. This institutionalization of the issue of marine litter ensures, on the one hand, a streamlined and continuous effort to address that issue, and creates a coordination unit for all measures and initiatives on the other. This is also strenghthened by the adoption of OSPAR RAP ML.

The regulation of marine litter in the Black Sea differs significantly from the approach taken in the other three agreements. This can be primarily explained by the weak and ambiguous provisions of the Bucharest Convention itself and its substantiating Protocols. The Bucharest Convention does not entail any implementation of the precautionary principle that could serve the Contracting Parties in engaging adequate marine pollution measures. The Bucharest Dumping Protocol, for example, applies a standard setting approach that resembles, in its nature that of the London Convention. Consequently, in order to adequately and comprehensively improve the environmental standard, the adoption of the London Protocol by all riparian States is seen as indispensable in mitigating dumping as a source of marine litter in this region. The only reference to marine litter in the Bucharest Convention is made in the context of the BlS LBPs. However, the approach of the BlS LBP entails provisions that do not adequately encompass the diverse requirements that are seen as necessary in addressing this source of pollution. The need to reform was acknowledged in 2009 and a more progressive Protocol was drafted. Even though the amended Protocol has not yet entered in force, it is to be considered a potentially key instrument in adequately addressing the issue of marine litter. The entailed precautionary principle and procedural obligations such as conducting an EIA would imply that these principles would for the first time be introduced into the legal framework of the Bucharest Convention, albeit only in the setting of land-based pollution.

Specific marine litter considerations are made in the framework of the BlS ML SAP. The non-binding BlS ML SAP is substantially weakened by the sheer amount of actions that are proposed to address the issue of marine litter in the region. In order to effectively increase its impact, it would have been advisable to reduce the strategic directions so as to focus on a few feasible priority issues. Effectiveness could still be maintained if States were to agree to concentrate on some of the goals at a time and address these systematically.

The marine environmental protection approach in the Mediterranean Sea is, once again, quite different from the three agreements mentioned above, given that it is directly administered under the auspices of UNEP. The primary obligations arising out of the Barcelona Convention and its substantiating Protocols provide a comprehensive framework that addresses several sources of marine litter. Marine litter has historically been thematically focused on the inputs of solid waste from coastal areas. In this regard, the assessment demonstrated that the regulation of this aspect has evolved from an ad-hoc assessment project to legally binding instruments. The ICZMP establishes a common regulatory framework for coastal based pollution throughout the entire region. This very pertinent approach is weakened by the absence of an application of the precautionary principle and the rather broad provisions that establish only a very flexible regulatory framework.

Even though UNEP´s Marine Litter MoU has no legally binding effect, it has had a measurable effect on the work of the different Regional Seas Conventions. In some contexts, it has introduced the issue of marine litter in the working programme of the Regional Seas Convention, or has, in other instances, enlarged the scope of pertinent activities so as to integrate a broader range of measures. The success of the programme is not only due to the thematic approach but also to its systematic strategy that draws both on scientific and regulatory expertise.

The Regional Seas agreements are, due to their specific regulatory approach, very suitable means to address the issue of marine litter. Their material scope always includes land-based as well as ocean-based pollution. In this way, it is possible to establish measures that integrate both primary sources of marine litter. Especially with a view to the diffuse nature of marine litter, the integration of horizontal issues such as solid waste management and coastal zone management, but also vertical integration between different regulatory levels such as public international, regional and European law, is indispensable.

In particular Regional Action Plans on marine litter hold a great potential in ensuring further integration between different sets of measures (technical, production, legislative and awareness) and sources of marine litter that can only be effective when approached in a coordinated manner. The development and preparation of (legally binding) Regional Action Plans constitutes a paradigm change. The Regional Action Plans serve as "thematic bridges" by ensuring that marine litter is addressed in an integrated manner, covering several sources and by convening international, regional and national actors. They therefore constitute, depending on the specific elaboration, a move away from a sectoral approach to the issue.

It is imperative that effective enforcement and application of the provisions and obligations that aim to reduce the introduction of marine litter is ensured. Regional Seas agreements are lacking or are at least limited in terms of the available enforcement and sanctioning mechanisms that could guarantee an increased compliance with primary and legislative obligations. Ultimately, the will to adequately and successfully address marine litter not only depends on the quality of the material scope and measures taken in each agreement, but most importantly on the implementation and application of pertinent provisions on a national, regional or local level.

Chapter 4: Marine litter in the regulatory context of European Union law

EU environmental law is distinguished, *inter alia*, by an increasing degree of integration of environmental matters in EU primary law.[1020] It is therefore to be differentiated from public international law and constitutes a legal order *sui generis*.[1021] The distinguishable element is based on the supranational character of this peculiar legal order that culminates in the well-known doctrine of direct effect.[1022]

1020 The development of EU environmental law covers six phases (the following overview is borrowed from: *Jans/Vedder,* European environmental law, 2012, 3 *et seq*). The first phase commenced with the entry in force of the European Economic Community Treaty (EEC Treaty) on 1 January 1958 and ended in 1972. It was coined by the predominant absence of environmental considerations, since the establishment of the common European market was the primary goal. In the second phase from 1972 to 1987, environmental considerations were initiated by the Declaration of the European Council in which it stressed the importance of European environmental policy. This marked also the start of the Environment Action Programme (EAPs) (see for a further analysis of these in section B.I of this chapter). Despite the absence of a legal base in the EEC Treaty, a further legislative development of environmental issues in the form of adopting pertinent Directives was pursued. The third phase of EU environmental law was marked by the entry in force of the Single European Act on 1 July 1987 and ended when the Treaty on the European Union (TEU) was made legally binding in 1993. In this phase, the environmental protection objective was introduced into EU primary law. Furthermore, the precautionary principle was included in EU primary law. The fourth phase was simultaneously influenced by the significant institutional change that was introduced by the "pillar-structure" of the European Union: *Craig/de Búrca,* EU law, 2008, 14. Additionally, the status of the EAPs changed as they were now subject to the co-decision procedure that involved also the participation of the European Parliament. In the fifth phase (1997-2007), the co-decision procedure (under the TFEU the ordinary legislative procedure) became the standard decision-making procedures for environmental protection instruments. The current sixth phase of EU Environmental Law has been introduced by the adoption of the Treaty on the Functioning of the European Union.

1021 C-6/64 *Flaminio Costa v. E.N.E.L.* [1964] ENEL I-585.

1022 C-26/62 *Van Gend en Loos v. Nederlands Belastingsadministratie* [1963] ECR I-1.

The following section examines legal approaches to marine litter in the European Union. Such an analysis is not a straight forward undertaking due to two factors. The legal assessment of EU law with regard to marine litter has always to be examined in the context of pre-existing international obligations. Additionally, EU law has developed a complex regulatory body which is increasingly substantiated by diverse implementing legislative acts. These two factors necessitate a twofold method to understand the potential of EU law in a marine litter regulatory framework. In a first step, the primary EU law is analysed. This relates to the Treaty on the Functioning of the European Union (TFEU),[1023] one of the key legal sources of EU law. This instrument sets out the competences of the EU institutions and the EU Member States to act on and address the issue of marine litter. In a second step, the substantive body of applicable EU secondary law is examined with a view to marine litter considerations. Here a selection and categorisation of possible measures is necessary in order to structure the discussion.

A. The distribution of competences of the EU institutions

The EU does not enjoy complete legal discretion when taking action in the field of environmental protection. The institutions of the EU, namely the European Parliament, the European Commission and the Council can only act within the framework of their competences. This understanding is based on Art. 13 (2) TEU which provides that "each institution shall act within the limits of the powers conferred on it in the Treaties and in conformity with the procedures, conditions and objectives set out in them." Depending on the specific policy in question, the EU is entrusted with shared or exclusive competences to act, which are enshrined in primary law. The delimitation of such horizontal questions is of relevance in the

1023 According to Art. 1 (2) TFEU, the TEU and the TFEU establish the European Union and are simultaneously applicable. See for an overview on the EU environmental policy provisions subsequently the entry into force of the TFEU: *Vedder,* Journal of Environmental Law 22 (2010) 285, 285. On 01.12.2009, the TFEU entered into force. In this context, Community law became European Union law. Therefore, any provisions in secondary law or Court of Justice of the European Union (CJEU) cases that refer to 'Community law' can be understood to also relate to EU law as it stands today.

context of decision-making and the competence to act on certain matters including environmental protection.[1024]

Marine litter poses, *prima facie,* a particular case in this respect. Its multifaceted origins constitute an intersecting topic in which several sectoral activities and policies are integrated. The legal basis in primary law for the fields of environment and transport (shipping) are a matter of shared competence between the European Union and its Member States.[1025] This situation is further complicated by considerations relating to the internal market as the legal basis to act which is also subject to shared competence.[1026] Given the roots of the EU as an economic union (European Economic Community and later European Communities), consideration of the internal market frequently play a role in regard to the legislative legal basis of a secondary act. The economic importance of plastics and plastic products is not to be underestimated, and this adds a further layer to an already complicated strata. In this context, a subsequent exclusivity is established in that Member States may only exercise their competences "to the extent that that the Union has not exercised its competence."[1027]

Among the different sectoral policies, the delimitation between fisheries and environmental protection in this internal horizontal legislative context seems to also present challenges. This relates to the case of ghost fisheries, discarded or lost fisher nets.[1028] In regard to the management and conservation of the living resources under the common fisheries policy, the EU has an exclusive competence, which is based on Art. 3 (1) (d) TFEU. In contrast, Art. 4 (2) (d) TFEU stipulates that, *inter alia*, fisheries, excluding the conservation of marine biological resources fall under the shared competence of the EU. Consequently, it is necessary to understand the scope and intention of the "conservation of marine biological resources" in regard to discarded and lost fishing gear. The European Commission has made it clear that even in instances where an environmental

---

1024 See for the role of the legal base in determining more stringent environmental protection measures: *Scott,* Flexibility in the Implementation of EC Environmental Law, in *Somsen,* Yearbook of European environmental law (2000) 37–60, 38 *et seq.*

1025 Art. 4 (2) (e and g) TFEU.

1026 Art. 4 (2) (a) TFEU.

1027 Art. 2 (2) TFEU.

1028 See chapter 2 on this aspect.

protection measure merely implies a reference to fisheries activities, the legal base should always be the provisions of the fisheries policy.[1029]

Consequently, a regulation that addresses the problem of ghost fisheries is to be based on Art. 3 (1) (d) TFEU and Art. 43 (2) TFEU respectively. Notwithstanding this, the integration principle of Art. 11 TFEU ("*Querschnittsklausel*") stipulates that "[e]nvironmental protection requirements must be integrated into the definition and implementation of the Union's policies and activities, in particular with a view to promoting sustainable development."[1030] This implies that even though a policy might not necessarily relate to environmental protection *per se*, environmental protection aspects must be nevertheless integrated. This principle stands as an important guideline in any other activities and issues that *prima facie* are not classified under the environmental policy. Particularly with a view to marine litter considerations, the integration principle is highly pertinent.

I. EU environmental objectives from a marine litter perspective

The regulatory structure of EU environmental law differentiates between the objectives and the legal base of environmental protection. With regard to the environmental protection measures as outlined in Art. 4 TFEU, this objective is substantiated by Title XX TFEU. The general objectives of the EU environmental policy are

> the preservation, protection and improvement of the quality of the environment, the protection of human health, the prudent and rational utilisation of natural resources and the promotion of measures at international level to deal with regional or worldwide environmental problems [...].[1031]

1029 *European Commission*, COM(2001) 143 final, Communication from the Commission to the Council and the European Parliament. Elements of a Strategy for the Integration of Environmental Protection Requirements into the Common Fisheries Policy, 16.03.2001, 7.

1030 See for a reference to this principle in the context of the Common Fisheries Policy: *ibid.*, 3; *Proelß,* Meeresschutz im Völker - und Europarecht, 2004, 384. See for further information on the principle: *Krämer,* The Genesis of EC Environmental Principles, in *Macrory/Havercroft/Purdy,* Principles of european environmental law (2004) 31–48, 33 *et seq.*; *Krämer*, EC environmental law, 2007, 21.

1031 Art. 191 (1) TFEU.

In a marine litter context, the reference to the quality of the environment, human health, rational use of natural resources and the mention of worldwide or regional environmental problems are of relevance. Since these objectives are broad and leave room for certain ambiguities regarding their exact scope and interpretation,[1032] a short analysis regarding their exact content is necessary. The general terms of Art. 191 (1) TFEU provides for a great deal of flexibility on what constitutes possible measures to achieve this objective.[1033] However, the CJEU has, in numerous cases, shaped the contours of this article.[1034] This relates, for example, not only to actions that results "directly in the improvement of the environment",[1035] but also those that indirectly contribute to environmental protection and preservation.[1036] Furthermore, the use of natural resources in the context of Art. 191 (1) TFEU is not quite clear.[1037] With a view to the absence of a further definition, a list of possible actions and sectors under this provision already provides a clarification. This objective can be found in legislations on industrial emissions, waste disposal, coastal areas and water policy.[1038]

Art. 191 indent 4 TFEU plays a particular interesting role with a view to the co-operation between international and regional actors such as UNEP or the Regional Seas Conventions. This provision underlines the understanding that environmental problems emanating from third countries could also impact on the environmental quality of the EU and that environmental problems occurring within the EU could potentially be of transboundary nature. Even though it is assumed that this provision merely reflects existing practice, a clarification of what constitutes "regional or worldwide" and "environmental problems" is missing, therefore creating a

1032 *Jans/Vedder,* European environmental law, 2012, 32.

1033 *Krämer,* EC environmental law, 2007, 2.

1034 This relates for example to the understanding and scope of the protection of human health: C-278/89 *Frans-Nederlandse Maatschappij voor Biologische Producten* [1981] ECR 3277; C-189/96 *United Kingdom vs. Commission* [1998] ECR I-2265 (BSE) and C-473/98 *Chemical Inspections v. Toolex* [2000] ECR 3. Also, C-284/95 *Safety Hi-Tech* [1998] ECR I-4301, para.8; C-302/86 *Commission v. Denmark* [1988] ECR 4607 (Danish Bottle); C-2/90 *Commission v. Belgium* [1992] ECR I-4431 (Walloon Waste); C-293/93 *Standley* [1999] ECR I-2603 and C-67/97 *Ditlev Bluhme* [2001] ECR I-8033.

1035 *Jans/Vedder,* European environmental law, 2012, 33.

1036 *Ibid.*

1037 *Jans/Vedder,* European environmental law, 2012, 37.

1038 *Ibid.*, 37; *Krämer,* EC environmental law, 2007, 14.

legal uncertainty.[1039] From a marine litter point of view, one can differentiate in this context between the geographical approach, *i.e.* the area in which the problem occurs, and the procedural aspect of the "problems." However, a clear demarcation between regional and global problems is in any case difficult to make with regard to the extremely transboundary dimension of the problem of marine litter.[1040] Notwithstanding these thoughts, the co-operation objective as laid out in Art. 191 indent 4 TFEU clearly extends to the issue of marine litter.

The EU´s environmental protection objectives are quite broad and potentially include a vast choice of actions. Notwithstanding any interpretational ambiguities regarding their exact material and conceptual content, it can be concluded that it is possible in a broad range of instances to address marine litter as an environmental problem. A further analysis of the subsequent actions taken will shed additionally light on possible questions relating to implementation.

II. The principles of EU environmental policy

The measures contained in part XX TFEU, are guided by the principles of EU environmental law as set out in Art. 191 (2) TFEU which stipulates that:

> Union policy on the environment shall aim at a high level of protection taking into account the diversity of situations in the various regions of the Union. It shall be based on the precautionary principle and on the principles that preventive action should be taken, that environmental damage should as a priority be rectified at source and that the polluter should pay.

Even though the definition of what constitutes a high level of protection leaves room for interpretation, it is established case law that this level of protection "does not necessarily have to be the highest that is technically feasible."[1041] In the development of EU environmental policy, the different environmental regional particularities occurring within the EU and the

---

1039 *Jans/Vedder,* European environmental law, 2012, 39.

1040 See chapter 1 on the distribution of marine litter worldwide.

1041 C-284/95 *Safety Hi-Tech*, para.49. This also provides in conjunction with Art. 193 TFEU, the possibility for the Member States to adopt an increased protection standard *Käller,* Artikel 191, in *Schwarze/Becker/Bär-Bouyssière,* EU-Kommentar (2012) 1834, 1840.

economic and social development of the EU has to be considered. However it remains unclear whether an assessment should include environmental standards or also covers economic, social and cultural aspects.[1042] Any subsequently adopted EU legislation has to be assessed whether it attempted to

> achieve a degree of balance between, on the one hand, the protection of health, environmental protection and consumer protection and, on the other hand, the economic interests of traders, while pursuing the objective assigned to it by the Treaty to ensure a high level of protection of health and environmental protection.[1043]

Therefore, the CJEU outlined that the EU institutions must exercise their discretion when adopting regulatory measures. This entails that every relevant aspect of the situation or aspect that is regulated must be considered.[1044]

The subsequent principles play a particular role in applying and implementing EU law. *Winter* argues that the EU environmental principles serve, *inter alia,* to support the exercise of Union competences, triggering actions by EU institutions and directing Member States.[1045] These principles are understood as *Leitmotivs* and a breach or non-application could, only in exceptional cases, lead to an infringement of EU primary law.[1046]

In the following the environmental principles contained in Art. 191 (2) TFEU will be individually considered not only with regard to their func-

---

1042 *Ibid.,* 1842. However, a first indication can be derived from Art. 11 TFEU that outlines that environmental protection requirements must be integrated "in particular with a view to promoting sustainable development." Even though the concept is too broad to create specific legal obligations for the institutions or the Member States, *Epiney* proposes that it could mean that "natural resources have to be protected and maintained in a long term perspective, and that economic development in particular has to respect this long-term perspective by avoiding the destruction of natural resources, with the effect that future generations can no longer benefit from these resources" *Epiney,* Environmental Principles, in *Macrory,* Reflections on 30 years of EU environmental law (2006) 17–40, 26.

1043 C-343/09 *Afton Chemical* [2010] ECR I-7027 (Afton Chemical), para.56.

1044 *Ibid.*, para.28.

1045 *Winter,* The Legal Nature of Environmental Principles in International, EC and German Law, in *Macrory/Havercroft/Purdy,* Principles of european environmental law (2004) 11–27, 22 *et seq*.

1046 Krämer, Droit de l'environnement de l'Union européenne, 2011, 55; *Krämer,* EC environmental law, 2007, 16.

tions but also with a particular focus on their relevance in a marine litter regulatory context.[1047]

1. The polluter-pays-principle

The polluter-pays-principle was introduced in the realm of the European Community in the 1970s when the European Commission declared that polluters should cover the costs of remedial actions.[1048] The TFEU does not contain a definition of the polluter-pays-principle and "the principle's outlines remain singularly difficult to trace at the legal level, despite the simplicity of its message."[1049] Its specific elaboration and elements in an EU context are substantiated by EU secondary legislation. With regard to liability, the polluter-pays-principle therefore requires the compensation of damages. The application of the principle is also limited by the difficulty to determine the polluter and the extent of (environmental) damage. Despite these intricacies, the importance of this principle with regard to marine litter can only be adequately acknowledged when looking at its specific implementation in EU secondary law. This is most dominantly visible in the context of waste legislation.[1050] Consequently, the Waste Framework Directive contains in recital 1, "in accordance with the polluter-pays principle, a requirement that the costs of disposing of waste must be borne by the holder of waste, by previous holders or by the producers of the product from which the waste came." Without wanting to enter into specific technical and legal intricacies of this requirement at this point,[1051] this exigency, from a marine litter point of view, relates to a straight for-

1047 See for a comprehensive historical overview on the development of the different principles in EU law: *Krämer,* The Genesis of EC Environmental Principles, in *Macrory/Havercroft/Purdy,* Principles of european environmental law (2004) 31–48.

1048 See further on the development of this principle in the context of the EU: *Krämer,* The Genesis of EC Environmental Principles, in *Macrory/Havercroft/Purdy,* Principles of european environmental law (2004) 31–48, 43.

1049 D*e Sadeleer,* The Polluter-pays Principle in EU Law – Bold Case Law and Poor Harmonisation, in *Bugge,* Teischrift (2012) 405–419, 418.

1050 *Ibid., 407.*

1051 This relates amongst others to the definition of holder: *De Sadeleer*, The Polluter-pays Principle in EU Law – Bold Case Law and Poor Harmonisation, in *Bugge*, Teischrift (2012) 405–419, 414.

ward obligation. Admittedly, the principle as such cannot be used as the basis for legal argument obliging holders to finance or conduct marine litter clean-ups at beaches that cannot be directly attributed to them.

In the European Union legal framework, there is one instrument that explicitly deviates from the application of the polluter-pays-principle. The Port Reception Facility Directive[1052] outlines that ships calling at a port of an EU Member State are obliged to contribute to the costs of port reception facilities and also the treatment and disposal of wastes notwithstanding their actual usage of these facilities.[1053] Admittedly, in this context it seems paradoxical that the Directive is explicitly based on the polluter-pays-principle.[1054] Vessels that do not deliver waste in harbours have nonetheless to cover these costs. This passage demonstrates the economic dimension of the principle, since it "answers to an economic logic,"[1055] thereby serving the function of correcting market failure and guiding remediation activities.[1056] The underlying logic behind the obligation is that therefore an incentive is created to deliver waste in every harbour without incurring additional cost. The preventative function[1057] of this application is compatible also with the aim of achieving a high level of environmental protection in the European Union.[1058]

1052 Directive 2000/59/EC of the European Parliament and of the Council of 27 November 2000 on port reception facilities for ship-generated waste and cargo residues (OJ 2000 L 332) (PRF Directive).

1053 Art. 8 (2) (a) PRF Directive. *Krämer,* The Genesis of EC Environmental Principles, in *Macrory/Havercroft/Purdy,* Principles of european environmental law (2004) 31–48, 46.

1054 Recital 1 PRF Directive. See also the discussion of this principle in section B.II. 2.bb of chapter 3.

1055 *De Sadeleer,* The Polluter-pays Principle in EU Law – Bold Case Law and Poor Harmonisation, *in Bugge, Teischrift (2012) 405–419, 418.*

1056 *Ibid.*, 408.

1057 *De Sadeleer*, The Polluter-pays Principle in EU Law – Bold Case Law and Poor Harmonisation, in Bugge, Teis-chrift (2012) 405–419, 406; *Kahl,* Umweltprinzip und Gemeinschaftsrecht, 1993, 24 *et seq.*

1058 Recital 1 PRF Directive.

2. The source-principle

The source-principle was introduced into primary law in 1985.[1059] In its core understanding, the principle indicates that the prevention of environmental damage shall be addressed temporally, locally und materially, in close proximity to the source.[1060] The principle therefore implies that environmental damage has already occurred or that it is known to be occurring.[1061] This distinguishes it from the precautionary principle.[1062] This approach is therefore applicable in regard to any legal measures that aim at specific and known sources of pollution.[1063] Moreover, as Art. 191 (2) TFEU states that measures should be preferably taken at the source, it indicates that measures to address consequences might also be permissible.[1064] In marine litter regulation, an application of the source principle necessitates the prevention at already identified sources of pollution and favours measures regulating emissions.[1065]

The source principle has several implications that are highly relevant for the marine litter discourse. Whereas it has been specifically addressed in the context of waste issues,[1066] it also targets producer responsibilities

1059 *Krämer*, The Genesis of EC Environmental Principles, in *Macrory/Havercroft/Purdy*, Principles of european environmental law (2004) 31–48, 41. See here also the role of the EAPs in paving the way to introduce this principle in EU law.

1060 *Käller, Art. 191*, in *Schwarze/Becker/Bär-Bouyssière,* EU-Kommentar (2012) 1834, 1843; *Epiney,* Environmental Principles, in *Macrory,* Reflections on 30 years of EU environmental law (2006) 17–40, 31. Critically of the objective of the principle: *Krämer,* EC environmental law, 2007, 26.

1061 *Käller*, Artikel 191, in *Schwarze/Becker/Bär-Bouyssière*, EU-Kommentar (2012) 1834, 1843; *Burgi,* Natur und Recht (1995) 11, 12 *et seq.*

1062 *Krämer,* The Genesis of EC Environmental Principles, in *Macrory/Havercroft/Purdy,* Principles of european environmental law (2004) 31–48, 39.

1063 *Käller*, Artikel 191, in *Schwarze/Becker/Bär-Bouyssière*, EU-Kommentar (2012) 1834, 1943.

1064 *Meßerschmidt,* Europäisches Umweltrecht, 2011, 305.

1065 *Ibid.*, 306. However, from this cannot be concluded that a general favorisation regarding emission standards versus quality standards or other measures exists *Käller,* Art. 191, in *Schwarze/Becker/Bär-Bouyssière,* EU-Kommentar (2012) 1834, 1844.

1066 *Lee*, EU environmental law, 2005, 227. See also. The CJEU states in C-221/06 *Stadtgemeinde Frohnleiten* [2007] ECR I-2613, para.61 that "pursuant to the principle of that environmental damage should as a matter of priority be remedied at source, which is consistent with the principle of proximity and self-suffi-

for their products.[1067] This relates thus on the one hand to analysing the entire life-cycle of a product, including its disposal,[1068] but also to aspects of product design.[1069] The application serves therefore as a legal argument to favour cleaner production over end-of-pipe-technology.[1070] With a view to the definition of end-of-pipe-technology as "[a]n approach to pollution control which concentrates upon effluent treatment or filtration prior to discharge into the environment, as opposed to making changes in the process giving rise to the wastes,"[1071] this elaboration of the source principle is highly significant regarding land-based marine litter sources. It implies that waste reducing measures must be taken preferably early in the production chain of a product in order to reduce the environmental impact of a product through, *inter alia,* decreased waste levels in an initial phase. The figurative language of this expression is taken from the exercise to install pipes that discharge effluents directly into the riverine or marine environment.[1072] That the elimination of such a practice is a worthy goal is clearly undisputed, particular with regard to marine litter considerations.

---

ciency." In 1992, the CJEU referred to the relevance of this principle in the context of a decree in which the Belgian province of Wallonia prohibited the transboundary shipment and storage, tipping or dumping of waste originating from other EU Member States or the two other Belgian regions, Brussels and Flanders. The CJEU found that the source principle "entails that it is for each region, municipality or other local authority to take appropriate steps to ensure that its own waste is collected, treated and disposed of; it must accordingly be disposed of as close as possible to the place where it is produced, in order to limit as far as possible the transport of waste: C-2/90 *Commission v. Belgium* [1992] ECR I-4431, para.34 (Walloon Waste).

1067 *Meßerschmidt,* Europäisches Umweltrecht, 2011, 307.

1068 The so-called cradle to grave analysis: *EEA*, Multilingual Environmental Glossary, cradle to grave analysis, http://glossary.eea.europa.eu/terminology/concept_html?term=cradle to grave, last accessed 27.08.2015.

1069 *Meßerschmidt,* Europäisches Umweltrecht, 2011, 307.

1070 *Ibid.*

1071 *EEA*, Eionet GEMET Thesaurus, End-of-pipe technology, last update 20.07.2012, last accessed 27.08.2015.

1072 *Meßerschmidt,* Europäisches Umweltrecht, 2011, 307.

3. The precautionary principle

The precautionary principle as embedded in the TFEU has a particular role with regard to marine litter considerations. The central focus point is the potentially associated risks of marine litter and microplastics and the corresponding uncertainties in this regard. The precautionary principle was only incorporated into EU law in the Treaty on European Union signed in Maastricht in 1992.[1073] The precautionary principle is not defined in the TFEU; therefore a further understanding on how this principle is applied and substantiated is necessary through case law. Whereas this section will outline the framework and central themes of the significance of the application of the precautionary principle in EU law, its specific relevance in the context of secondary instruments will be outlined further below.

With a view to the lack of a definition of the precautionary principle in EU primary law, the European Commission published a communication in 2000 to substantiate the understanding of its role and application in EU law. The European Commission identifies two major aspects that justify the application of the precautionary principle: (1) "the identification of potentially negative effects resulting from a phenomenon, product or process" and (2) "a scientific evaluation of the risk which because of the insufficiency of the data, their inconclusive or imprecise nature, makes it impossible to determine with sufficient certainty the risk in question."[1074]

The marine litter problem is a particular case, since it is a "death by a thousand cuts' phenomenon."[1075] Whereas marine litter is usually the sum of individual activities, it is *prima facie* not directly possible to single out a specific project that would have a significant individual effect on the marine litter problem. Notwithstanding this, precisely the many unidentified sources and consequences trigger recourse to the precautionary princi-

1073 Treaty on the European Union (Maastricht) (OJ C 325, 24.12.2002.).

1074 *European Commission*, COM(2000) 1 final, Communication from the Commission on the precautionary principle, 02.02.2000, 15.

1075 *Advocate General Sharpston* made reference to this expression raised by the European Commission as "cumulative habitat loss as a result of multiple, or at least a number of, lower level projects being allowed to proceed on the same site", CJEU, Opinion of the Advocate General Sharpston delivered on 22 November 2012 with regard to C-258/1 *Peter Sweetman*, para.67. Notwithstanding the different context of this metaphor, it also adequately reflects the inherent risks associated with marine litter.

ple.[1076] As will be demonstrated in the context of pertinent secondary legislation, the precautionary principle is also applied to determine threshold values and to assess the ecological and environmental status of the aquatic environment. Fundamentally, however the specific roles of the precautionary principle with regard to marine litter are, *inter alia*, aspects of causation and setting thresholds of risk. This not only relates to diffuse sources, but also to the potential toxicity of plastic, as the predominant material. The potential bioaccumulation and adverse consequences of the substances contained therein provide the major leverage point.[1077]

Despite the not entirely proven causation between the presence of marine litter and potential marine organisms and human health impacts, the approach to risk perception of plastic and its potential toxic characteristics are to be addressed in the scope and context of this principle. Thus a first consideration of the application is whether and how risks are perceived and are acceptable in EU law. Risk in this regard relates to the potential effects and impacts of the bioavailability of plastic to marine organisms and the potential transfer of chemicals to higher trophic levels, including humans, amongst others.

The Court of First Instance found in the *Pfizer case* that

> [i]t is never possible to prove conclusively that a chemical or pharmaceutical compound or anything created by modern technology represents a zero risk to public health now or that it will do so in the future. To apply such a test would quickly lead to the paralysis of technological development and innovation.[1078]

However, the Court went on to hold that

> [i]t follows, first, that as a result of the precautionary principle, as enshrined in Article 130r(2) of the Treaty, the Community institutions were entitled to take a preventive measure regarding the use of virginiamycin as an additive in feedingstuffs, even though, owing to existing scientific uncertainty, the reality and the seriousness of the risks to human health associated with that use were not yet fully apparent.[1079]

1076 *European Commission*, COM(2000) 1 final, Communication from the Commission on the precautionary principle, 15.

1077 See chapter 2.

1078 T-13/99 *Pfizer Animal Health SA v Council of the European Union* [2002] ECR II-3305, para.130.

1079 *Ibid.*, para.140.

In the *Afton Chemical* case, the CJEU outlined that

> [a] correct application of the precautionary principle presupposes, first, identification of the potentially negative consequences for health of the proposed use of MMT, and, secondly, a comprehensive assessment of the risk to health based on the most reliable scientific data available and the most recent results of international research.[1080]

Even though the CJEU had to judge in the Pfizer case on a more direct causal link of potential risks, namely that of the use of certain antibiotics as additives and increased resistance to those antibiotics in humans, the Pfizer and Afton Chemical cases clearly indicate the essence of the precautionary principle in EU law. What is different to the issue of marine litter in this case, is that the link of causation is more direct. The challenge to determine the risks associated with marine litter is that it is subject to several interlinked circumstances that may or may not likely occur. As a first step, the (micro) plastic in question needs to be discarded, (accidentally) lost or abandoned in the marine environment. As a second step, the type of marine litter must be bioavailable and subsequently ingested by marine organisms. The third step in this process relates to the potential toxic effects, bioaccumulation along the trophic chain and also possibly to humans that have ingested those affected organisms. Risks associated with marine litter are therefore not acute and locally confined, rather they are shaped by long-term and sub-threshold levels.

The precautionary principle in EU law plays an important role in determining (un)acceptable levels of risks and has been implemented in several secondary legislations that are also relevant for marine litter considerations.

B. Marine litter considerations in secondary EU law

In the following, substantive European Union secondary law addressing marine litter will be presented and analysed. A preliminary analysis of the overall strategic framework of EU environmental policy with regard to

---

1080 C-343/09 *Afton Chemical*, para.60. In the preliminary ruling, the CJEU had to decide on the validity of Article 1(8) of Directive 2009/30/EC of the European Parliament and of the Council of 23 April 2009 amending Directive 98/70/EC as regards the specification of petrol, diesel and gas-oil and introducing a mechanism to monitor and reduce greenhouse gas emissions.

marine litter considerations will be followed by an in-depth discussion of pertinent secondary instruments. With regard to the material issues of marine litter, it needs to be assessed whether EU secondary law also extends to the marine environment. The geographical application of EU law on the maritime zones has been subject to academic debate and certain CJEU rulings.[1081] According to Art. 52 TEU in conjunction with Art. 355 TFEU, the geographical scope of EU primary law extends to the territories of the EU Member States.[1082] In this regard, the distribution of competences to the EU is a key aspect. In cases where the Member States have given the EU a competence to act as enshrined in EU primary law, then the EU primary law is also applicable to the marine environment of the EU Member States. This also relates to EU secondary law.[1083] This is however to be assessed under the premise that the Member States have jurisdiction to act on the matter in the different jurisdictional zones as established under UNCLOS. The rights and obligations set out in UNCLOS create the regulatory framework in which the different activities are to take place.[1084]

I. Setting the background: marine litter in the overall strategic work

Before elaborating on the specific secondary legal framework in the EU regarding marine litter, it is necessary to put it into context so as to enable better relative understanding. Even though the environmental dimension of the problem is the central point of contact, other relevant issues relating to maritime or trade policy, for instance, also play a role.

The so-called Environment Actions Programs (EAP) have provided strategic direction to EU environmental policies since the 1970s.[1085] Since

---

1081 See for an overview on the development *Proelß,* Meeresschutz im Völker - und Europarecht, 2004, 276 *et seq.*

1082 Art. 52 TEU in conjunction with Art. 355 TFEU.

1083 *Proelß,* Meeresschutz im Völker - und Europarecht, 2004, 279. It is however possible to limit the spatial scope of secondary law.

1084 See chapter 2 section C.III-VI.

1085 *European Commission*, COM(2012) 710 final, Proposal for a Decision of the European Parliament and of the Council on a General Union Environment Action Programme to 2020 "Living well, within the limits of our planet", 29.11.2012, 2. First Environmental Action Programme 1973-1976 (OJ C 112, 20.12.73); Second Environmental Action Programme1977-1981 (OJ C 139, 13.6.77); Third Environmental Action Programme 1982-1986 (OJ C 46,

1993[1086] their development is obligatory under primary law with the participation of the European Parliament and the Council and after consultation with the Economic and Social Committee and the Committee of the Regions.[1087] The overall aim of the EAPs is to outline the over-arching strategic direction of EU environmental policy. It does so by making rather general and abstract statements.[1088] These guidelines are to be substantiated by Green and White papers[1089] or legislative measures. Even though the EU institutions are obliged to implement the strategies of the

---

17.2.83); Fourth Environmental Action Programme 1987-1992 (OJ C 328, 7.12.87); Fifth Environmental Action Programme 1993-2000 (OJ C 138, 17.5.93); Sixth Environmental Action Programme 2002-2012 (OJ L 242, 10.9.2002). See for a summary of the specific priorities and objectives: *Proelß,* Meeresschutz im Völker - und Europarecht, 2004, 341.

1086 *Krämer,* Thirty Years of Environmental Governance in the European Union, in *Macrory,* Reflections on 30 years of EU environmental law (2006) 553–576, 560. The legal basis for these programs was Art. 175 (3) Treaty establishing European Community (EC).

1087 Art. 192 (3) TFEU.

1088 *Kahl,* Art. 191- 193 AEUV, in *Streinz*, EUV/AEUV- Vertrag über die Europäische Union und Vertrag über die Arbeitsweise der Europäischen Union (2012) 1821, 1864.

1089 "Green Papers are documents published by the European Commission to stimulate discussion on given topics at European level. They invite the relevant parties (bodies or individuals) to participate in a consultation process and debate on the basis of the proposals they put forward. Green Papers may give rise to legislative developments that are then outlined in White Papers", *European Commission*, Glossary, Green paper, http://ec.europa.eu/green-papers/index_en.htm, last accessed 27.08.2015.
"Commission White Papers are documents containing proposals for Community action in a specific area. In some cases they follow a Green Paper published to launch a consultation process at European level. When a White Paper is favourably received by the Council, it can lead to an action programme for the Union in the area concerned", *European Commission*, Glossary, White paper, http://ec.europa.eu/white-papers/index_en.htm, last accessed 27.08.2015. Even though in 2006, the Commission published a Green Paper on a European vision for the oceans and seas, no explicit mention of the issue of marine litter was made in this regard. However, the paper raised several indirectly relevant questions such as Integrated Coastal Zone Management and the implementation of international conventions, *European Commission*, COM(2006) 275 final Volume II – ANNEX, Green Paper- Towards a future Maritime Policy for the Union: A European vision for the oceans and seas, 07.06.2006.

EAP, they have a certain degree of discretion in doing so.[1090] This has evoked criticism regarding the effectiveness and implementation of the EAPs.[1091]

With regards to its contents, the EAP requires the existence of a consensus among the EU institutions regarding the most pressing issues. As the EAPs cover approximately a time frame of four to ten years,[1092] one is able to gain an understanding of the priority setting in EU environmental policy that helps to estimate the direction of mid-term developments in EU environmental law.[1093] The adoption of a new EAP is preceded by negotiations with EU institutions, but also consultations of non-governmental organisations, national authorities, industry and individuals.[1094]

The issue of marine litter has only been introduced in the 7th and most recent EAP.[1095] Even though former EAPs addressed indirectly relevant issues such as waste management and pollution prevention, they did not explicitly identify marine litter as a strategic and pressing issue. The 7th EAP covers the timeframe until 2020 and is placed under the motto "living well, within the limits of our planet." It is dedicated to three thematic priority objectives that relate to natural capital, resource efficiency and health

---

1090 *Kahl*, Art. 191- 193 AEUV, in *Streinz*, EUV/AEUV - Vertrag über die Europäische Union und Vertrag über die Arbeitsweise der Europäischen Union (2012) 1821, 1864,.

1091 *Krämer,* Thirty Years of Environmental Governance in the European Union, in *Macrory,* Reflections on 30 years of EU environmental law (2006) 553–576, 568. *Krämer* argues in this context that the institutions were not effectively monitoring the implementation of the EAP and that targets and objectives were mostly ignored by the Member States.

1092 See the reasoning of the Commission for deciding on the length of the 7th EAP: *European Commission,* MEMO/12/908, New Environment Action Programme to 2020– questions and answers, 29.11.2012.

1093 With regard to the precision of the content of the EAP, an underlying conflict between the European Parliament, preferring concrete and detailed provisions, and the Council and the Commission, both usually opting for general formulations, exists: *Krämer,* Droit de l'environnement de l'Union européenne, 2011, 33.

1094 See for the development of the 7th EAP: *European Commission*, COM(2012) 710 final, Proposal for a Decision of the European Parliament and of the Council on a General Union Environment Action Programme to 2020 "Living well, within the limits of our planet", 29.11.2012.

1095 Decision No 1386/2013/EU of the European Parliament and of the Council of 20 November 2013 on a General Union Environment Action Programme to 2020 'Living well, within the limits of our planet' (OJ L 354/171, 28.12.2013) (7th EAP).

and well-being.[1096] Marine litter considerations are classified under priority objective 1 that that aims to protect and conserve the EU´s natural capital. Despite the somewhat brief reference to marine litter in the 7th EAP its specific mention and elaboration is worthy of note. The 7th EAP calls consequently for a "Union-wide quantitative reduction headline target for marine litter."[1097] Given the challenges experienced in the OSPAR-Convention,[1098] an EU-wide quantitative reduction target is a very ambitious goal. The inclusion and specific mention of marine litter in the context of the 7th EAP have two implications for the overall discussion of marine litter in the EU. First, it signifies that it is perceived as an environmental threat requiring actions by the EU institutions and the EU Member States. Second, the ambitious aim of achieving a quantitative reduction target could potentially have a trigger effect in the following years.[1099]

II. Secondary EU law–legislative procedure

The choice of the legal basis for an environmental protection measure has a decisive influence on the decision-making procedure and the subsequent possible legal actions of the EU Member States. With regard to environmental protection measures, Art. 192 (1) TFEU constitutes the explicit legal base. Consequently,

> [t]he European Parliament and the Council, acting in accordance with the ordinary legislative procedure and after consulting the Economic and Social Committee and the Committee of the Regions, shall decide what action is to be taken by the Union in order to achieve the objectives referred to in Article 191.

Thus, any legislative act that is adopted on the basis of Art. 192 TFEU is to be pursued in accordance with the ordinary legislative procedure.[1100]

1096 It also includes an "enabling framework" relating to aspects such as implementation, knowledge and investment and also a spatial dimension.

1097 7th EAP, Priority objective 1, para.28 (iii).

1098 See section C.IV. of chapter 3.

1099 See for an extensive discussion and the challenges to achieve this objective, section C.IV. of chapter 3.

1100 In the context of the common fisheries policy, the ordinary legislative procedure is also applied, see Art. 43 (2) TFEU. Other decision-making procedures relate to the special legislative procedure (Art. 289 (2) TFEU, formerly assent procedure) that gives the European Parliament a veto right without amending the act

The specific procedural steps of the ordinary legislative procedure are outlined in Art. 294 TFEU.[1101] In this context, the European Commission initiates proposals and has to submit these to the Parliament and Council.

Art. 288 TFEU outlines five legal acts: Regulations, Directives, Decisions, Recommendations and Opinions.[1102] Whereas the former three are legally binding, the latter two acts are not legally binding. A distinction must be made with respect to the material legal effect of the Regulations and Directives. Depending on the legal act, a difference degree of consolidation and harmonisation is achieved. Whereas the Regulations are entirely binding and applicable to all Member States from the date on which they enter in force, the Directive is binding regarding its aim; it leaves a margin of discretion to implementing Member States on the choice of form and methods.[1103]

In 2003, the European Commission estimated that of the 200 legal acts concerning environmental issues, 140 of these were Directives.[1104] Even though one can swiftly assume that today, the overall number of environmental protection legislation has increased since that date, the use of Directives in this field is dominant,[1105] the reason for this being, *inter alia*, the desire to provide Member States with a certain amount of discretion in selecting suitable implementation measures.[1106] This allows for tailor-made implementation taking into consideration the specific characteristics of the biogeographic regions and administrative systems within individual

in question). This is applicable in regard to Art. 192 (2) TFEU and relates to a member State's choice of energy sources and energy supply structure *Vedder,* Journal of Environmental Law 22 (2010) 285, 294.

1101 Art. 289 (1) TFEU.

1102 Art. 288 TFEU. This list is non-exhaustive, as further acts such as communication and memoranda which potentially could have a legally binding character if this is intended by the institutions: C-22/70 *Commission v. Council* [1971] ECR I-263 (ERTA), paras.38 and 42; *Schroeder*, Art. 288 AEUV, in *Streinz*, EUV/AEUV Vertrag über die Europäische Union und Vertrag über die Arbeitsweise der Europäischen Union (2012) 2413, 2442; V*on Bogandy/Bast/Arndt,* Zeitschrift für ausländisches öffentliches Recht und Völkerrecht 62 (2002) 77, 91.

1103 Art. 288 TFEU.

1104 *European Commission*, COM(2003) 745 final, Communication from the Commission to the Council and the European Parliament, 2003 Environment Policy Review - Consolidating the environmental pillar of sustainable development, 03.12.2003, 25.

1105 *Meßerschmidt,* Europäisches Umweltrecht, 2011, 189.

1106 *Krämer,* EC environmental law, 2007, 58.

States. The EU has, based on its conferred competences, enacted a broad range of legislative instruments that also address aspects of marine litter. Consequently, the following assessment is an attempt to synthesise and classify the enormous and condensed body of secondary legislation that is available in the EU regarding marine litter.

III. Categorisation of relevant secondary legal instruments touching on the question of marine litter

A vast body of secondary EU law is potentially applicable for the prevention and regulation of marine litter. Two elements will stand central in the analysis and discussion. This refers on the one hand to the prevention of marine litter at the source. This implies that a 'source-related' category of instruments has been chosen which serves as a mechanism to address the introduction of marine litter at the origin.[1107] A preliminary classification belonging to the source-category is made according to the following sectors: waste management, shipping, chemical regulation, transboundary movement of waste, industry, natural disasters and fisheries. It has to be noted in this context that in the EU, no legislative instruments exist that regulate the dumping of waste at sea and the pollution from exploitation of the seabed as foreseen in UNCLOS.[1108]

As a second category, the legal acts are divided into an 'impact-or quality related' legislation category.[1109] This refers to legislation that integrates scientific knowledge or quality standards as their underlying logic to prevent environmental degradation. The impact-or quality related legislation is affected by an integrated assessment approach in which the complex interactions of the environment are considered. This category is divided into legislation dealing with the marine environment, freshwater and biodiversity protection.

1107 *European Commission*, Commission Staff Working Document SWD(2012) 365 final, Overview of EU policies, legislation and initiatives related to marine litter, 31.10.2012.

1108 *Churchill,* The European Union and the Challenges of Marine Governance: From Sectoral Response to Integrated Policy?, in *Vidas/Schei,* The world ocean in globalisation (2011) 395–471, 410.

1109 *European Commission*, Commission Staff Working Document SWD(2012) 365 final, Overview of EU policies, legislation and initiatives related to marine litter, 31.10.2012.

Category of legislation	Sector	Secondary legislative instruments
Source-related legislation	Waste management	– Waste Framework Directive (2008/98/EC)[a] – Packaging and Packaging Waste Directive (94/62/EC), subsequently amended[b] – Directive on reducing the consumption of lightweight plastic carrier bags (2015/72)[c] – Landfill Directive (1999/31/EC)[d] – Urban Wastewater Treatment Directive (91/271/EEC), subsequently amended[e] – Batteries Directive (2006/66/EC)[f] – End-of-Life Vehicles Directive (2000/53/EC)[g] – Waste Electrical and Electronic Equipment (WEEE) Directive (2012/19/EU)[h]
	Ship-pollution	– Port Reception Facility Directive (2000/59/EC) – Community Vessel Monitoring Directive (2002/59/EC)[i]
	Chemicals	– REACH Regulation (1907/20067/EC)[j] – Directive establishing a framework for Community action on the sustainable use of pesticides (2009/128/EC)[k]
	Transboundary movement of waste	– Regulation on shipments of waste (1013/2006/EC)[l]
	Industry	– Industrial Emissions Directive (2010/75/EU)[m] – Directive on the management of waste from extractive industries (2006/21/EC)[n] – EU Ecolabel Regulation (66/2010/EC)[o]
	Natural disasters	– Flood Risk Directive (2007/60/EC)[p]
	Fisheries	– Common Fisheries Policy Regulation (2371/2002/EC)[q] – European Maritime and Fisheries Fund[r]

Category of legislation	Sector	Secondary legislative instruments
Impact-related legislation	Marine Environment	– Marine Strategy Framework Directive (2008/56/EC)[s] – Bathing Water Directive (2006/7/EC)[t]
	Freshwater	– Water Framework Directive (2000/60/EC)[u]
	Biodiversity protection	– Habitat Directive[v]
	Environmental Impact Assessment	– Environmental Impact Assessment Directive (2001/42/EC)[w]
Other proposals and initiatives		– Proposal calling for an EU wide ban on smoking in public places (COM (2009)328) – Recommendation providing for minimum criteria for environmental inspections in Member States (2001/331/EEC)[x]

Table 2: Overview on pertinent secondary legislation and proposals regarding marine litter considerations classified according to "source-related" and "impact-related" legislation.

Index:

a Directive 2008/98/EC of the European Parliament and of the Council of 19 November 2008 on waste and repealing certain Directives (OJ 2008 L 312/3).

b European Parliament and Council Directive 94/62/EC of 20 December 1994 on packaging and packaging waste (OJ 1994 L 365), subsequently amended.

c Directive (EU) 2015/720 of the European Parliament and of the Council of April 29 2015 amending Directive 94/62/EC as regards reducing the consumption of lightweight plastic carrier bags (OJ 2015, L 115).

d Council Directive 1999/31/EC on the landfill of waste of 26 April 1999.

e Council Directive 91/271/EEC of 21 May 1991 concerning urban waste water treatment, as amended by Commission Directive 98/15/EC of 27 February 1998 (OJ 1999 L 139).

f Directive 2006/66/EC of the European Parliament and of the Council of 6 September 2006 on batteries and accumulators and waste batteries and accumulators and repealing Directive 91/157/EEC (OJ 2006, L 266/1).

g Directive 200/53/EC of the European Parliament and of the Council of 18 September 2000 on end-of life vehicles (OJ 2000 L 269/34).

h Directive 2012/19/EU of the European Parliament and of the Council of 4 July 2012 on waste elec-trical and electronic equipment (WEEE) (OJ 2012 L 197).

i Directive 2002/59/EC of the European Parliament and of the Council of 27 June 2002 establishing a Community vessel traffic monitoring and information system and repealing Council Directive 93/75/EEC (OJ 2002 L 208/10).

j Regulation (EC) No 1907/2006 of the European Parliament and of the Council of 18 December 2006 concerning the Registration, Evaluation, Authorisation and Restriction of Chemicals (REACH), establishing a European Chemicals Agency, amending Directive 1999/45/EC and repealing Council Regulation (EEC) No 793/93 and Commission Regulation (EC) No 1488/94 as well as Council Directive 76/769/EEC and Commission Directives 91/155/EEC, 93/67/EEC, 93/105/EC and 2000/21/EC (OJ 2006 L 396/1).

k Directive (2009/128/EC) of the European Parliament and of the Council of 21 October 2009 estab-lishing a framework for Community action to achieve the sustainable use of pesticides (OJ 2009 L 309/71).

l Regulation (EC) No 1013/2006 of the European Parliament and of the Council of 14 June 2006 on shipments of waste (OJ 2006 L 190/1).

m Directive 2010/75/EU of the European Parliament and of the Council of 24 November 2010 on industrial emissions (OJ 2010 L 334/17).

n Directive 2006/21/EC of the European Parliament and of the Council of 15 March 2006 on the management of waste from extractive industries (OJ 2006 L 102/15).

o Regulation (EC) No 66/2010 of the European Parliament and of the Council of 25 November 2009 on the EU Ecolabel (OJ 2010 L 27).

p Directive 2007/60/EC of the European Parliament and of the Council of 23 October 2007 on the assessment and management of flood risks (OJ 2007 L 288).

q Council Regulation (EC) No 2371/2002 of 20 December 2002 on the conservation and sustainable exploitation of fisheries resources under the Common Fisheries Policy (OJ 2002 L 358/59).

r Regulation (EU) No 387/2012 of the European Parliament and of the Council of 19 April 2012 amending Council Regulation (EC) No 1198/2006 on the European Fisheries Fund, as regards certain provisions relating to financial management for certain Member States experiencing or threatened with serious difficulties with respect to their financial stability (OJ 2012 L129).

s Directive 2008/56/EC of the European Parliament and of the Council of 17 June 2008 establishing a framework for community action in the field of marine environmental policy (Marine Strategy Frame-work Directive) (OJ 2008 L 164).

t Directive 2006/7/EC of the European Parliament and of the Council of 15 February 2006 concern-ing the management of bathing water quality and repealing Directive 76/160/EEC (OJ 2006 L 64).

u Directive 2000/60/EC of the European Parliament and of the Council of 23 October 2000 estab-lishing a framework for Community action in the field of water policy (OJ 2000 L 327/1).

v Council Directive 92/43/EEC of 21 May 1992 on the conservation of natural habitats and of wild fauna and flora (OJ1992 L 206).

w Directive 2011/92/EU of the European Parliament and of the Council of 13 December 2011 on the assessment of the effects of certain public and private projects on the environment Directive (OJ 2012 L 26/1).

x Recommendation 2001/331/EEC of the European Parliament and of the Council of 4 April 2001 providing for minimum criteria for environmental inspections in Member States (OJ 2001 L 118/41).

The classification of these instruments, in this way, potentially runs the risk of ignoring inter-sectoral implications that exist between different instruments. It is hence admitted that potential interactions between waste management and marine environmental protection instruments are not taken into consideration in this classification. However, such a categorisation is a first and necessary step to provide a structured and focused approach. The subsequent analysis and discussion will also carve out existing, or as the case may be, necessary synergies between different legislative instruments stemming from both categories.

IV. Selection of most pertinent issues and instruments

Due to the vast amount of possibly applicable secondary instruments, a selection of the most pertinent instruments is necessary so as to avoid a trivial and superficial discussion. By way of introducing secondary EU law, it has to be remarked that the chosen legislation might not be specifically addressed to marine litter or waste considerations. Any interpretation of the following instruments therefore potentially leads to the conclusion that only a few instruments directly serve the purpose of reducing marine litter. This is explained by the comprehensive objectives and scope of the EU environmental policy that encompasses many issues and problems.

Thus the method of selection is also guided by a problem-oriented approach, in which the overall aim of the secondary instrument in question is considered from a marine litter perspective. It is intended to provide a better understanding of the specific scope and role that the different legislation can play in preventing and regulating marine litter. The legislation is looked at with regard to its regulatory approach and obligations for the issue of marine litter. In a second step, the analysis addresses possible loopholes and potential contradictions that have been identified during the initial assessment.

In the context of the source-related category, the system established by the Waste Framework Directive and subordinated instruments is analysed. It is argued that in particular the waste management system in the EU plays an important role in steering different land-based sources of marine litter pollution. Here, the Landfill Directive and Urban Waste Water Treatment Directive will be specifically analysed following this structure. Further, the PRF Directive will be analysed in relation to shipping as a potential source of pollution. Also, the ban of the use of non-biodegradable plastic bags that has been introduced in Italy is classified in the context of EU primary and secondary law.

With regard to the impact-related legislation, the Water Framework Directive and the Marine Strategy Framework Directive will be analysed with a view to assessing and monitoring marine litter aspects in their material scope.

V. Source-related legislation

Proceeding under the assumption that land-based pollution is the primary source of marine litter, waste management options play a central role in addressing this issue. Whereas illegal dumping or littering from recreational activities also play an important role, the systematic management of waste from municipalities and industrial activities is of key importance. Post-consumer plastic waste amounted to 24.9 Mt in the European Union, Norway and Switzerland.[1110] Considering these figures, it is not surprising that the body of waste related legislation in the EU is quite substantial. A particular aspect of this issue is that it is closely intertwined with economic interests, since the waste management sector has an important share in the EU economy.[1111]

1110 *BIOIS*, Plastic Waste in the Environment, 2011, 13.

1111 This relates for example to the landfilling industry and also incineration with energy recovery that are important economy sectors: *European Commission*, COM (2013) 123 final, Green Paper on a European Strategy on Plastic Waste in the Environment, 07.03.2013, 4.

1. The waste management system established by EU law

The fundamental pillar of the EU waste management system is the Waste Framework Directive,[1112] an umbrella framework that establishes the essential requirements and principles of EU waste management.[1113]

a) The regulatory system established by the Waste Framework Directive

The Waste Framework Directive has the aim of protecting the environment and also human health from adverse impacts following the generation and management of waste. This clearly provides a gateway for marine litter considerations.[1114] This 'spirit' is also reflected in recital 30 Waste Framework Directive in which the implementation of the precautionary principle in waste management states the aim of wanting to oblige the European Union and its Member States "to establish a framework to prevent, reduce and, in so far as is possible, eliminate from the outset the sources of pollution or nuisance by adopting measures whereby recognised risks are eliminated." The risk-based approach of these preliminary considerations is made legally binding in that the Member States are obliged to take "necessary measures to ensure that waste management is carried out without endangering human health, without harming the environment and […] without risk to water, soil, plants and animals."[1115] Even though this obligation is somewhat weakened through the restriction of "necessary," Member States are to apply the principle of precaution when developing waste legislation.[1116] Through this reference, the scope of potential measures is also extended to cases of scientific uncertainty or un-

---

1112 See for a general account of the development of the European Union waste management policy: *Williams,* Waste treatment and disposal, 2005, 7 *et seq*. The Waste Framework Directive repealed Directive 2006/12 (OJ 2006 L 114/9) that repealed Council Directive 75/442/EEC of 15 July 1975 on waste as amended by Directive 91/156 (OJ 1991 L 78/32).

1113 Recitals 1 Waste Framework Directive. See for the development of national municipal waste streams in a tabular overview: *Hafkamp,* Comparison of National Solid Waste Regimes in Trajectories of Change, in *Buclet,* Municipal waste management in Europe (2002) 7–26, 24.

1114 Art. 1 Waste Framework Directive.

1115 Art. 13 (a) Waste Framework Directive.

1116 Art. 4 (2) Waste Framework Directive.

predictable risk. Admittedly, the extent and potential of the concrete application of these obligations remains to be seen in the subordinated secondary legislation.

A waste hierarchy is established by the Waste Framework Directive with an order of preference for prevention, preparing for re-use, recycling, energy recovery and finally disposal.[1117] Prevention relates to any measure that is taken prior to a product becoming waste and that reduces the quantity of waste by the re-use of the product,[1118] or the extension of its life span, the reduction of adverse consequences of the generated waste on the environment and also to limit the content of harmful substances in materials and products.[1119]

When applying the waste hierarchy, measures to ensure the best environmental outcome should be preferred, even if this implies a deviation from the order of the waste hierarchy.[1120] The decisive criterion on whether a deviation is permissible is established by the life-cycle thinking that could serve as a justification.[1121] This demands that a product should not only be designed for the time of usages, but also for its post-consumer stage, therefore its disposal.[1122] Such thinking can also be found in the so-

---

1117 Art. 4 (1) (a-e) Waste Framework Directive. *Petersen* speaks in this context of a programmatic character of the hierarchy: *Petersen,* Zeitschrift für das Recht der Abfallwirtschaft 12 (2013) 2, 4. An argument for the flexible application of the waste hierarchy contained in the Waste Framework Directive is also that the Member States may depart from it when implementing life-cycle thinking (Art. 4 (2) Waste Framework Directive). See also for further guidance on the definition and scope of the elements of the waste hierarchy, the non-binding document issued by the European Commission: *European Commission*, Guidance on the interpretation of key provisions of Directive 2008/98/EC on waste, June 2012, 28-34. For an overview on the origins of the waste hierarchy: *Williams,* Waste treatment and disposal, 2005, 9.

1118 Re-use means: "any operation by which products or components that are not waste are used again for the same purpose for which they were conceived" (Art. 3 (13) Waste Framework Directive).

1119 Art. 3 (12 (a-c)) Waste Framework Directive.

1120 Art. 4 (2) Waste Framework Directive.

1121 Art. 4 (2) Waste Framework Directive.

1122 Life-cycling thinking is a constituent part of the "prevention element" of the waste hierarchy. See only Art. 3 (12) (a) and Annex IV, para.4 Waste Framework Directive, see for example Directive 2009/125/EC of the European Parliament and of the Council of 21 October 2009 establishing a framework for the setting of ecodesign requirements for energy-related products (OJ L 285, 31.10.2009) (Ecodesign Directive). Ecodesign means "the integration of envi-

called extended producer responsibility of Art. 8 Waste Framework Directive. Even though this concept is in legal terms not clearly outlined,[1123] the concept entails, *inter alia*, the responsibility for product designers and producers to create products that create less waste.[1124] Even though no absolute obligation is established to apply this in national law, the Directive indicates that measures implementing this principle could include "an acceptance of returned products and of waste that remains after those products have been used."[1125]

In order to be able to effectively use the recovery and recycling objectives as outlined in Art. 10 and 11 Waste Framework Directive, the Waste Framework Directive establishes a recycling target according to which by 2020 the re-use and recycling rate of waste materials including, *inter alia,* metal, plastic and glass should be at least 50% of overall weight.[1126] This recycling target is an important regulatory tool for the overall waste management approach in the EU. Depending on the envisaged recycling tar-

---

ronmental aspects into product design with the aim of improving the environmental performance of the product throughout its whole life cycle" (Art. 2 (23) Ecodesign Directive). The Ecolabel Regulation "links the life-cycle approach to a scheme whereby the reduced environmental impact is visualised through a sign (the flower logo)" *Jans/Vedder,* European environmental law, 2012, 378. Admittedly, both instruments are not directly integrated in the context of the Waste Framework Directive; however they reflect the implementation of the life-cycle assessment in EU law. See for further information on this issue: *Jans/ Vedder,* European environmental law, 2012, 378 *et seq.*

1123 *Onida,* Challenges and Opportunities in EC Waste Management, in *Somsen,* Yearbook of European environmental law (2000) 253–289, 282. Therefore, its implementation and meaning in the waste context can assume many different forms and fields of application.

1124 See in this regard recital 27 Waste Framework Directive.

1125 Art. 8 (1) Waste Framework Directive. The Member States "may take legislative and non-legislative measures that any natural or legal person has [...] extended producer responsibility" (Art. 8 (1) Waste Framework Directive. However, according to Art. 8 (4) Waste Framework Directive, the extended producer responsibility shall be applied without prejudice to the responsibility for waste management as outlined in Art. 15 (1) Waste Framework Directive and specific waste stream and product legislation.

1126 Art. 11 (2) (a) Waste Framework Directive. The second target aims to achieve "by 2020, the preparing for re-use, recycling and other material recovery, including backfilling operations using waste to substitute other materials, of non-hazardous construction and demolition waste excluding naturally occurring material defined in category 17 05 04 in the list of waste shall be increased to a minimum of 70% by weight" (Art. 11 (2) (a) Waste Framework Directive).

get, the subordinated instruments of EU waste management are to be adjusted. From a marine litter perspective, ambitious legally binding recycling targets are control items that increase the economic value of waste, therefore potentially reducing its (illegal) discharge. Despite the umbrella framework of the Directive, its general requirements and principles indicate that all subordinated legislation must be measured against an ambitious and comprehensive set of standards. [1127]

b) Marine litter in the context of the definition of waste under the Waste Framework Directive

The Waste Framework Directive defines key concepts and notions of EU waste legislation that have been subject to intensive legal dispute.[1128] Particularly the concept of waste itself stands central in this regard.[1129] Generally, a harmonised terminology and understanding of waste ensures a "level playing field" for industry and Member States in the implementation and application of the Directive and its subordinated instruments.[1130] Waste in the Waste Framework Directive is defined as "any substance or object which the holder discards or intends or is required to discard."[1131]

The wording therefore indicates that the intention of the holder is the central starting point, thus potentially excluding those substances that were unintentionally lost, from definition of Art. 3 (1) Waste Framework Directive. Since Art. 2 (2) (a) Waste Framework Directive excludes waste

---

1127 See only C-252/05 *Thames Water Utilities* [2007] ECR I-3883.

1128 *Jans/Vedder*, European environmental law, 2012, 473 *et seq*. The challenges to adopt an EU-wide definition of waste were related to the many different definitions and concepts of the term in the Member States. *Williams,* Waste treatment and disposal, 2005, 8. See for an account of the challenges to implement the definition of waste as was established by EU waste legislation into UK law: *Pocklington,* The law of waste management, 1997, 16.

1129 The challenges to adopt an EU-wide definition of waste were related to the many different definitions and concepts of the term in the Member States: *Williams,* Waste treatment and disposal, 2005, 8. See for an account of the challenges to implement the definition of waste as was established by EU waste legislation into UK law: *Pocklington,* The law of waste management, 1997, 16.

1130 *Pocklington,* The law of waste management, 1997, 15.

1131 Art. 3 (1) Waste Framework Directive. The CJEU has in the past played a significant role in shaping and substantiating the definition of norms: *Jans/Vedder,* European environmental law, 2012, 474.

water from the scope of the Directive to the extent that it is covered by other Union legislation, the relevance of waste water from sewage systems as a potential source of microplastics would be excluded from the definition. In the T*hames Water Utilities Case*, the CJEU had to decide whether sewage escaping from a sewage collecting system is to be considered as waste. The CJEU ruled that even though waste water is spilled accidentally, it still constitutes waste under the Waste Framework Directive.[1132] This is of relevance in the marine litter discourse, in that the understanding of waste is therefore quite broad and extends to intentional and unintentional discharge.

The broad understanding of the definition of waste under the Waste Framework Directive ensures the maintenance of a high protection level. The broad and comprehensive definition also implies that aspects of marine litter considerations, such as microplastics escaping from sewage systems are to be considered as waste. Whereas the geographical scope of the Waste Framework Directive does not explicitly apply to the marine environment, its protection standard as established in Art. 13 Waste Framework Directive indirectly extends also to the marine environment.[1133] Even though the Directive excludes gaseous effluents, radioactive waste, decommissioned explosives and faecal matter from its scope,[1134] most of the substances associated with marine litter clearly are subject to the application of the Waste Framework Directive.

1132 *Ibid.,* para.28.

1133 C-188/07 *Commune de Mesquer [2008] ECR I-04501*; C-387/97 *Commission v. Hellenic Republic* [2000] ECR I-05047, para.94. Also, the reference of Art. 13 (a) Waste Framework Directive to the "risk of water" indicates such an inclusion. Limiting this only to freshwater would undermine the EU´s environmental objective that also relates to the marine environment.

1134 Art. 2 (1) (a, d-f) Waste Framework Directive. It is admitted that in some studies, faecal matter or decommissioned explosive are considered as marine litter (see chapter 2). Notwithstanding this, these substances only marginally contribute to the overall abundance of marine litter. Furthermore, the Waste Framework Directive excludes certain issues from its scope to the extent that these are covered by other Union legislation: waste waters, animal by-products, carcasses of animals and waste resulting from prospecting, extraction, treatment and storage of mineral resources (Art. 2 (2) (a-d) Waste Framework Directive).

c) The relevance of the Waste Framework Directive in the marine litter context

The issue of marine litter can only be indirectly categorised under the provisions of the Waste Framework Directive.[1135] However, it is uncontested that the spirit and scope of this legislation clearly integrate the problem of marine litter. Despite its implicit mention in the Waste Framework Directive, several aspects and provision of this legislation are highly relevant for the marine litter context. The Directive establishes a high protection standard which aims to prevent adverse impacts of waste management such as risk to water without affecting the countryside and places of special interests.[1136] The CJEU stated in its judgement *Commission v. Greece* from 2000, that

> the obligation to dispose of waste without endangering human health and without harming the environment forms part of the very objectives of Community environmental policy as set out in Article 130r of the EC Treaty. The failure to comply with the obligation resulting from Article 4 of Directive 75/442 could, by the very nature of that obligation, endanger human health directly and harm the environment and must, in the light of the other obligations, be regarded as particularly serious.[1137]

Even though Art. 13 Waste Framework Directive does not specifically prescribe the measures that are to be taken in order to fulfil the environmental protection and human health obligations, certain circumstances have been held to constitute an infringement of its provisions. The CJEU has established, that despite the inherent discretion of Member States to achieve the objectives of the Waste Framework Directive,

> it is established that if that situation persists and leads in particular to a significant deterioration in the environment over a protracted period without any action being taken by the competent authorities, it may be an indication that

1135 Recital 30 Waste Framework Directive and Art. 13 Waste Framework Directive.

1136 Art. 13 (b and c) Waste Framework Directive.

1137 C-387/97 *Commission v. Hellenic Republic*, para.94. Art. 13 Waste Framework Directive is the corresponding obligation to Art. 4 of Council Directive 75/442/EEC of 15 July 1975 on waste. In the Judgement, Greece was taken to the CJEU since it had not fulfilled the obligations placed on it from an earlier judgement relating to a rubbish tip containing waste and toxic waste.

> the Member States have exceeded the discretion conferred on them by that provision.[1138]

In conjunction with Art. 36 Waste Framework Directive requiring Member States to prohibit the abandonment, dumping and uncontrolled management of waste, Art. 13 Waste Framework serves as the legal obligation for the Member States to control and prohibit illegal tipping and landfills.[1139] The framework that is established by the Waste Framework Directive can be seen as a fundamental stepping stone to regulating marine litter at the source. This relates on the one hand to the waste hierarchy and its associated obligations and also to the waste prevention programmes of Art. 29 Waste Framework Directive.

2. Addressing identified point sources of marine litter: the role of the Landfill Directive

Landfilling is a particularly prominent type of waste disposal with regard to marine litter. In EU waste management legislation, landfills are classified as a waste disposal operation.[1140] The Landfill Directive was adopted in 1999 and aims to establish operational and technical requirements for landfill operation so as to prevent or reduce any adverse consequences on the environment such as pollution and risk to human health.[1141]

1138 C-135/05 *Commission v. Italy* [2007] ECR I-03475, para.37; C-365/97 *Commission v. Italy* [1999] ECR I-7773, para.67 (San Rocco). The *San Rocco Case* addressed fly-tipping and illegal waste disposal in the Italian San Rocco valley.

1139 See only, *ibid.*

1140 D.1 and D 5 Annex I Waste Framework Directive.

1141 Art. 1 (1) Landfill Directive. See for a legislative overview on the development of the Landfill Directive: *Williams,* Waste treatment and disposal, 2005, 27; *Fischer/Petschow/Buclet,* The consequences of implementing directives in the national context: the correct answer to the friction between national regimes?, in *Buclet,* Municipal waste management in Europe (2002) 81–110, 96 *et seq*. The main controversies in the development of the instrument related to the proposed exemptions for rural areas and small islands, that according to the European Parliament covered 50% of the territory at that time: *ibid.*, 96. Potentially first order effects of landfills are: increase in ambient concentrations, chemical concentrations in receiving waters, noise emissions, visual impacts and vermins. Secondary effects are: nuisance, explosion risks, health effects and effects on vegetation: *Williams,* Waste treatment and disposal, 2005, 27.

The finality of the waste disposal is also reflected in the definition of landfill (Art. 2 (g) Landfill Directive):

> Landfill means a waste disposal site for the deposit of the waste onto or into land (i.e. underground), including
> - internal waste disposal sites (i.e. landfill where a producer of waste is carrying out its own waste disposal at the place of production), and
> - a permanent site (i.e. more than one year) which is used for temporary storage of waste.

The permanency criteria of Art. 2 (g) Landfill Directive implies that interim storage facilities fall under the scope of the Directive.[1142] The Directive prescribes a classification approach of landfills in which a differentiation[1143] is made between landfills for hazardous,[1144] non-hazardous and inert waste.[1145] This is necessary to limit the risks of potential chemical interactions between different types of waste.[1146]

a) Plastic in the context of the definition of non-hazardous waste under the Landfill Directive

With regard to the classification of the usual types of waste that could constitute marine litter, the Landfill Directive displays a certain inconsistency.

1142 The following facilities are excluded from the scope: "-facilities where waste is unloaded in order to permit its preparation for further transport for recovery, treatment of disposal elsewhere, and
-storage of waste prior to recovery or treatment for a period less than three years as a general rule, or
-storage of waste prior to disposal for a period less than one year" (Art. 2 (g) Landfill Directive).

1143 Art. 4 Landfill Directive.

1144 Hazardous waste is defined in Art. 2 (c) Landfill Directive and "means waste which is covered by Article 1 (4) of Council Directive 91/689/EEC of 12 December on hazardous waste" (OJ L 3377, 31.12.1999).

1145 See for example the definition of inert waste: "waste that does not undergo any significant physical, chemical or biological transformations. Inert waste will not dissolve, burn or adversely affect other matter with which it comes into contact in a way likely to give rise to environmental pollution or harm human health. The total leachability and pollutant content of the waste and the ecotoxicity of the leachate must be insignificant and in particular not endanger the quality of surface water and/or groundwater" (Art. 2 (e) Landfill Directive).

1146 *Meßerschmidt,* Europäisches Umweltrecht, 2011, 888.

According to the classification scheme of the Landfill Directive, municipal waste may be disposed in landfills holding non-hazardous waste.[1147] The provision implies that waste from households is, by its nature, categorised as non-hazardous.[1148] This classification appears *prima facie* to be somewhat over-simplified, since plastic has a significant share in household waste. Particularly with a view to potential effects of plastic such as leachate, it should be considered whether a somewhat differentiated approach to the classification of municipal waste is in order. From a normative point of view, Art. 2 (c) Landfill Directive defines hazardous under Art. 1 (4) of Council Directive 91/689/EEC of 12 December 1991 on hazardous waste (now Art. 3 (2) Waste Framework Directive).[1149] In this regard, hazardous waste is "waste which displays one or more of the hazardous properties listed in Annex III." Among the different criteria, H 14 Annex III Waste Framework relating to ecotoxicological properties appears particularly relevant. Ecotoxic is defined as: "waste which presents or may present immediate or delayed risks for one or more sectors of the environment."[1150] Whereas the objective of the Landfill Directive is to dispose of waste permanently, the definition of ecotoxic as presenting delayed risks could potentially be applicable in situations in which waste from landfills results in adverse consequences years after the date of initial disposal in the landfill.

The requirement that only one of the listed properties suffices for the classification not only demonstrates the high protection standard established by the Waste Framework Directive. It also indicates a differentiated definition and scope with regard to the classification of municipal waste as non-hazardous under the Landfill Directive. The consequence of a differentiated definition and classification of waste in the context of the Directive includes divergent environmental protection standards relating to landfills containing non-hazardous and hazardous waste.[1151]

1147 Art. 6 (c) (i) Landfill Directive.

1148 See definition of municipal waste in Art. 2 (b) Landfill Directive: "'Municipal Waste' means waste from households, as well as other waste which, because of its nature or composition, is similar to waste from households." Admittedly, the definition of municipal waste is in itself is ambiguous and potentially provide a significant degree of discretion when put to the test.

1149 This Directive has been repealed by the Waste Framework Directive.

1150 See only the results of chapter 2.

1151 See only the exceptions of Art. 3 (4) (a and b) Landfill Directive that relate to non-hazardous and inter waste stored disposed in landfills. In this regard Mem-

b) Evaluation of the regulatory approach of the Landfill Directive with a view to marine litter considerations

The long-term scale that is inherent in the Landfill Directive is taken into consideration through a permit approach.[1152] This implies that an operator has to apply for a permit to operate a landfill.[1153] Consequently, every landfill not operating with a valid permit is to be considered an illegal landfill.[1154] That these landfills pose a challenge particular with regard to the marine litter problem is obvious. Illegal landfills tend not to be properly managed and are therefore likely to constitute a significant threat to the environment.[1155]

The elements of the permit application cover issues relating to the planning, operation and post-closure phase of a landfill.[1156] Only after the permit granting authority is satisfied that the planned landfill is in compliance with every provision of the Landfill Directive and that the management of

---

ber States may exempt landfills in isolated settlements and landfills on islands with a capacity of 15 000 tonnes from certain obligations under the Directive. A particular weakness of these exemption clauses are the missing definition of what constitutes an isolated settlement. This potentially runs the risk to be misused in the context of the Directive.

1152 Art. 7 Landfill Directive.

1153 The Landfill Directive provides details on the content and condition of the permit (Art. 7 and 8 Landfill Directive).

1154 *European Commission*, Follow-up study on the implementation of Directive 1999/31/EC on the landfill of waste in the EU, 2007, 15. Litter abuse or random fly tipping has been formerly considered as illegal landfilling by some EU Member States, however it does not constitute illegal landfilling: *ibid.*, 15. Such a threshold applies when determining whether and when a dump site can be considered a landfill. Small and local activities of fly-tipping or dumping sites can potentially quickly become of larger scale, since they "invite" people to discharge their waste. Also, smaller dump sites might have a cumulative effect. Admittedly, the inclusion additionally puts constraints on the administrative system when monitoring these sites.

1155 That this aspect of the Landfill Directive is of a particular concern relates also to the available information about these landfills that are aggravated by the different statistics and definitions among the EU Member States: *European Commission,* Follow-up study on the implementation of Directive 1999/31/EC on the landfill of waste in the EU, 2007, 15. Some Member States only mention illegal landfills in their statistics but did not further indicate precise numbers, see only: *ibid.*, 27. This has of course repercussions on national measures to eliminate these illegal landfills.

1156 Art. 7 Landfill Directive.

the landfill is by competent and trained operators, may it grant the permit.[1157] It is submitted that the general requirements of the Directive contain highly pertinent provisions for marine litter considerations. The requirements established in Annex I require, *inter alia,* that when considering the location of the planned landfill, the existence of coastal water or nature protection zones in the area, the risk of flooding and also the distance from the boundary of the site to waterways or waterbodies are to be considered.[1158] These location requirements clearly establish the legal basis for preventive planning so as to ensure that the chosen site is not prone to lead to marine pollution. This is also reinforced by the obligation to minimise nuisance from wind-blown materials and birds.[1159] Birds can potentially destroy the cover material and lead in that way to unwanted leakages from the landfill that might be dispersed by wind. With a view to the absence of specific mention of marine pollution in the Directive itself, these provisions are important in a marine litter context. They form fundamental criteria that serve as basic rules to prevent the emission of waste from the landfill into the (marine) environment. Overall, the Landfill Directive clearly provides a framework which, in case properly implemented and managed, should not lead to emitted landfilled waste.

Furthermore, a particular aspect of the Landfill Directive is its strict and comprehensive control and monitoring procedures.[1160] The precise parameters that are to be adhered to are further substantiated in Annex III Landfill Directive, where, fundamental requirements for the control and monitoring obligations in the operational phase on, *inter alia,* emissions data of water, leachate and gas are listed.[1161] The operator is under an obligation to notify the competent authority in case "significant adverse environmental effects" are revealed during these monitoring and control exercises.[1162] These obligations not only relate to the operational phase but also to the

1157 Art. 8 Landfill Directive. Furthermore, the operator has to provide a financial security to be able to cover any obligations arising under the Directive.

1158 Section 1.1 (a, b and d) Annex I Landfill Directive.

1159 Section 5 Annex I Landfill Directive.

1160 Art. 12 Landfill Directive.

1161 Section 3 Annex III Landfill Directive. Accordingly, the volume and composition of the surface water has to monitored every three months during the operational phase and every six-months during the after-care phase. Furthermore, the requirements extend to meteorological data (Section 2), protection of groundwater (Section 4) and the topography of the landfill body (Section 5).

1162 Art. 12 (b) Landfill Directive.

post-closure, or after-care phase of the landfill. The responsibility of the operator to maintain, monitor and control extends also to closed landfills, notwithstanding if this situation arises if the permit conditions are met or on the request of the operator or the competent authority.

In order to prevent harm to the environment, the Landfill Directive stipulates uniform waste acceptance procedures for waste acceptable in landfills.[1163] As a fundamental rule, only waste that has been treated may be accepted into landfills. The treatment requirement of the Landfill Directive aims to reduce the potential negative impacts, the volume of waste generated and should also lead to enhanced recovery.[1164] Treatment includes thus "physical, thermal, chemical or biological processes, including sorting, that change the characteristics [...]."[1165] Despite this control mechanism, the Landfill Directive fails to provide precise obligations regarding the waste acceptance procedure. Annex II Landfill Directive merely outlines "principles and general procedures" of waste acceptance that only establish a vague legal framework for guiding Member States. Instead of providing concrete elements that are used in the waste acceptance procedure, Annex II merely outlines a non-exhaustive list of criteria that could be considered. Overall, the permit approach and reporting and monitoring obligations contained in the Landfill Directive serve in principle as central tools to ensure a reduction of pollution from landfills. However, the lack of precise obligations on waste acceptance do serve to weaken the practical effectiveness of this instrument.

Nonetheless, a central caveat in this regard relates to the ambition and scope of the Directive in general. The objective is to provide for measures that reduce "*as far as possible* negative effects on the environment, in particular the pollution of surface water, groundwater [...] and on the global environment, as well as any resulting risks to human health [...]."[1166] Even though it is admitted that the technical requirements of the Directive are highly pertinent regarding the issue of marine litter, the fundamental reasoning and spirit of the Directive soften the overall scope and application of these provisions. The wording implies that Member States enjoy discretion with regard to the development of measures which do not nec-

1163 Recital 20 Landfill Directive. See Art. 6 in conjunction with Annex II Landfill Directive.

1164 Art. 2 (h) Landfill Directive.

1165 Art. 2 (h) Landfill Directive.

1166 Art. 1 (1) Landfill Directive (emphasis added).

essarily have to ensure the highest possible protection standard. Admittedly, the Landfill Directive is subordinated under the system created by the Waste Framework Directive,[1167] therefore its high protection standards serves as a threshold. Notwithstanding this, an explicit and clear commitment to avoid any adverse consequences from landfilling could strengthen the implementation of this legislation.

c) Issues of implementation: the Zakynthos-case

The Landfill Directive has in the past been at the heart of several infringements procedures initiated by the Commission relating to shortcomings by certain Member States in terms of the Directive´s application and implementation. These implementation gaps become apparent when considering that in 2011 six Member States landfilled less than 3% of their municipal waste, 18 Member States landfilled 50% of their waste and some exceeding 90% of landfilling.[1168] Also, inadequately managed or illegal landfills falling under the scope of the Landfill Directive are a major factor in contributing to the marine litter problem in some regions.[1169]

In a recently referred case relating to the Landfill Directive, the CJEU was asked to decide on an infringement procedure about the implementation of the Directive in a marine protected area. Greece has established a landfill on the Zakynthos Island which is located in a marine park that was established with the aim of protecting the loggerhead turtle, *caretta caretta,* a species also protected under the Habitat Directive. It is estimated that 80% of the protected loggerhead turtles population in the Mediterranean nests on the six beaches around Zakynthos.[1170]

1167 See only: C-135/05 *Commission v. Italy*, para.37.

1168 *European Commission*, COM(2014) 397 final, Proposal for a Directive of the European Parliament and of the Council amending Directives 2008/98/EC on waste, 94/62/EC on packaging and packaging waste, 1999/31/EC on the landfill of waste, 2000/53/EC on end-of-life vehicles, 2006/66/EC on batteries and accumulators and waste batteries and accumulators, and 2012/19/EU on waste electrical and electronic equipment, 02.07.2014, 0.

1169 See chapter 1.

1170 *European Commission*, Commission takes Greece to Court over waste landfill and endangered turtles, Press Release, Brussels, 27.09.2012, IP/12/1023.

Inspections by Greek authorities have shown that leakages from the landfill have caused the release of plastic bags.[1171] Notwithstanding the consequences of litter such as entanglement and ingestion for adults of this species,[1172] their offspring is, in addition, particularly vulnerable to seagulls that are attracted by this waste.[1173] Consequently, the leakage of this landfill constitutes an identified point source that has a direct causal link to the marine litter issue in the Mediterranean Sea. The Greek authorities acknowledged this issue and commenced with constructing of a replacement facility.[1174] However, due to significant delay, the replacement landfill will not be operational until some time in 2014 and an interim solution, in which the waste would be stored in mobile units, was dismissed.[1175] Consequently, the European Commission has sent a reasoned opinion in January 2012 in which it indicated its concern regarding the continuous breach of the applicable law and the slow pace with which a remedy to the solution was being found and invited Greece to submit a statement.[1176] According to Art. 258 (sent.2) TFEU, the European Commission may bring the issue before the CJEU if the State in question does not comply with the opinion within the proposed time frame. By September 2012, no selection regarding the location of the replacement facility had been made. Consequently, the European Commission requested the CJEU to adjudicate on the matter.

This infringement procedure indicates the role of the CJEU in ensuring adequate implementation and application of substantive law. In 2014, 31%

1171 *European Commission*, Commission urges Cyprus and Greece to clean up waste landfills, Press Release, Brussels, IP/12/66, 26.01.2012.

1172 See chapter 1.

1173 *European Commission*, Commission urges Cyprus and Greece to clean up waste landfills, Press Release, Brussels, IP/12/66, 26.01.2012.

1174 *Ibid.* The first concerns regarding this landfill site emerged in 2009: *European Commission*, Commission takes Greece to Court over waste landfill and endangered turtles, Press Release, Brussels, 27.09.2012, IP/12/1023.

1175 *European Commission*, Commission urges Cyprus and Greece to clean up waste landfills, Press Release, Brussels, IP/12/66, 26.01.2012.

1176 Art. 258 (sent.1) TFEU. "If the Commission considers that a Member State has failed to fulfil an obligation under the Treaties, it shall deliver a reasoned opinion on the matter after giving the State concerned the opportunity to submit its observations." The reasoned opinion was not available for public and was not shared by the Commission on request. If the State concerned does not comply with the opinion within the period laid down by the Commission, the latter may bring the matter before the Court of Justice of the European Union.".

of all overall environmental infringement cases concerned waste legislation.[1177] The non-conformity and infringement in this particular sector has significant repercussions for the marine litter problem. Even though it is perhaps leaning a little too far out of the window to single out a specific activity given the manifold sources of marine litter, illegal landfilling is of particular concern. This relates on the one hand to the environmental impacts such as diffuse groundwater and surface water pollution, the instability of waste masses and potential human health concerns related to illegal landfills.[1178] On the other hand, delayed or incomplete implementation of EU standards also necessitates additional remedial costs and potentially causes a distortion of competition.[1179]

In 2013, the European Commission showed that 78 illegal landfills were still in operation and 318 currently rehabilitated landfills were not closed.[1180] This example demonstrates that there is a divergence between legislative requirements and effective implementation and enforcement of waste disposal by Member States.

1177 *European Commission*, Legal Enforcement, Statistics on infringements by environmental sector, available online at http://ec.europa.eu/environment/legal/law/statistics.htm, last updated 22.04.2015, last accessed 27.082.2015. Landfilling is a prominent issue in this regard, see only the first infringement procedures of 2013: *European Commission*, Environment: Commission takes Italy to Court over inadequate treatment of waste landfilled in Lazio, Press Release, Brussels, IP/13/250, 21.03.2013; *European Commission*, Environment: Commission takes Greece back to Court over illegal landfills and asks for fines, Press Release, Brussels, IP/13/143, 21.02.2013.

1178 *European Commission*, Follow-up study on the implementation of Directive 1999/31/EC on the landfill of waste in the EU, 2007, 81 *et seq.*

1179 *European Commission*, COM(2012) 95 final, Communication from the Commission to the European Parliament, the Council, the European Economic and Social Committee and the Committee of the Regions, Improving the delivery of benefits from EU environment measures: building confidence through better knowledge and responsiveness, 07.03.2012, 3.

1180 *European Commission*, Environment: Commission takes Greece back to Court over illegal landfills and asks for fines, Press Release, Brussels, IP/13/143, 21.02.2013.

d) The interlink between waste management law and biodiversity protection

The particular importance of the Zakynthos case with regard to marine litter, lies in the link between adequate waste management and its potential impacts on biological diversity. The connection between different environmental protection policies in the EU demonstrates the potential vigour of EU law. The primary (entanglement and ingestion) and secondary (danger to juveniles due to increase in seagulls) impacts of landfill leakages on the overall *caretta caretta* population are a suitable case study to understand the EU environmental protection legislation and the role of the CJEU in enforcing these. The *caretta caretta* population is listed under Annex IV Habitat Directive, establishing according to Art. 12 Habitat Directive, a system of strict protection in their natural range. The Member States are accordingly under the obligation to establish measures that prohibit, *inter alia*, the "deliberate disturbance of these species, particularly during the period of breeding, rearing, hibernation and migration"[1181] and the "deterioration or destruction of breeding sites or resting places."[1182]

The Zakynthos Island has in the past been subject to a ruling of the CJEU in which the Court had to decide whether Greece had implemented an effective system of strict protection for the local *caretta caretta* population. The CJEU held that the driving of mopeds on the breeding beaches and the presence of pedalos and small boats in the area constituted deliberate disturbances of the turtles and a deterioration or destruction of its breeding sites.[1183] The CJEU has therefore further defined the requirements for a strict protection system. In doing this, it has established a wide understanding of what kind of activities constitute a "deliberate disturbance" under Art. 12 Habitat Directive. Even though the case did not make reference to the disturbances of marine litter around Zakynthos, it demonstrates that the Habitat Directive adopts a high protection standard.[1184] Arguably, whereas the general causal link between the presence of marine litter and the coastal State is not necessarily established, the Zakynthos case that was opened in 2013, underlines that a significant point source, such as the Zakynthos landfill, potentially impacts the high protec-

1181 Art. 12 (1) (b) Habitat Directive.

1182 Art. 12 (1) (d) Habitat Directive.

1183 C-387/97 *Commission v. Hellenic Republic* (Zakynthos case), paras.36-39.

1184 *Jans/Vedder,* European environmental law, 2012, 413 *et seq.*

tion standard of the Habitat Directive. Under specific circumstances, it could also be argued by extension that an inadequately managed landfill that emits significant amount of plastics into the environment could potentially be considered as a disturbance under the Habitat Directive.

e) Role of reporting and information

The enforcement of existing standards and obligations will always depend on the amount and quality of information available. The information necessary to understand whether a breach of EU law has occurred cannot generally be directly inquired by the European Commission.[1185] The European Commission does not have inspection bodies or a specific structure and cannot systematically control the situation in each Member State.[1186] Information on the management and location of landfills is, however, a *conditio sine qua non* for an effective implementation of the Landfill Directive.[1187] Consequently, the Commission relies on external sources[1188] such as Member States[1189] and complainants.[1190] These form the knowledge basis of how and to what extent the specific legal act has been implemented.[1191]

1185 *Macrory,* Community Supervision in the Field of the Environment, in *Somsen,* Protecting the European environment (1996) 9–21, 18. *Macrory* comes to this conclusion while comparing the investigation powers of the European Commission in the field of competition law. See however the adoption of the Recommendation 2001/331/EEC of the European Parliament and of the Council of 4 April 2001 providing for minimum criteria for environmental inspections in Member States (OJ 2001 L 118/41).

1186 *Krämer,* EC environmental law, 2007, 427.

1187 This in particular refers to the issue of illegal or abandoned landfills that are not necessarily included in the national registers or are heterogeneously registered: *European Commission*, Follow-up study on the implementation of Directive 1999/31/EC on the landfill of waste in the EU, 2007, 3.

1188 *Macrory,* Community Supervision in the Field of the Environment, in *Somsen,* Protecting the European environment (1996) 9–21, 19.

1189 C-494/01 *Commission v. Ireland* [2005] ECR I-3382, para.43. The different legislative acts of the EU usually contain regular reporting obligations to the European Commission, see only Art. 15 Landfill Directive.

1190 This relates amongst others to citizen complaints, see further: *Krämer,* EC environmental law, 2007, 429.

1191 In 2012, the European Commission stressed the importance of inspection and surveilling in regard to EU legislation and proposed, *inter alia*, an assessment

With a view to illegal landfills in which different definitions and notions preexist, this information may vary and might therefore lead to differing legal conclusions with regard to non-compliance. The importance of complaints and questions of the European Parliament in this regard have become apparent in the case C-502/03 *Commission v. Greece* in which the European Commission has initiated a case on illegal landfills in Greece after receiving several objections.[1192] In *Commission v. Ireland,* the CJEU had to rule on the alleged systematic breach of the Waste Framework Directive by Ireland. Following twelve complaints of private parties about illegal waste handling activities effecting, *inter alia,* sensitive wetlands of particular ecological interest, the European Commission had initiated an infringement procedure. Ireland raised doubts as to the burden of proof in respect of the alleged breaches. It contented that the information contained in the complaints to which the European Commission referred, lead to the conclusion of drawing general assumption for alleged system failures.[1193]

In previous case law, the CJEU had already established that even though it is the European Commission's obligation to prove the non-compliance of a Member State, it may not rely on any particular presumption.[1194] However, Art. 4 (3) TEU stipulates an obligation on Member States to assist the Commission in ensuring the observance of the treaties.[1195] Thus, if the Commission has gathered sufficient evidence

for including specific provisions on inspection and surveillance for all new legislation and an EU level inspection and surveillance capacity: *European Commission*, COM(2012) 95 final, Communication from the Commission to the European Parliament, the Council, the European Economic and Social Committee and the Committee of the Regions, Improving the delivery of benefits from EU environment measures: building confidence through better knowledge and responsiveness, 07.03.2012, 6.

1192 C-502/03 *Commission v. Greece* [2005], not yet published (only available online), para.5.

1193 C-494/01 *Commission v. Ireland* [2005] ECR I-3382, para.40.

1194 C-96/81 *Commission v. the Netherlands* [1982] 1791, para.6. Rather, "[i]t is the Commission's responsibility to place before the Court the information needed to enable the Court to establish that the obligation has not been fulfilled, and in so doing the Commission may not rely on any presumption": C-408/97 *Commission v. the Netherlands* [2000] ECR I-6436, para.15.

1195 C-494/01 *Commission v. Ireland* [2005] ECR I-3382, para.42. *Hedemann-Robinson* outlines the role of the duty to co-operate in ensuring active as well as passive assistance from Member States in order to assist the European Commis-

> [i]n such circumstances, it is indeed primarily for the national authorities to conduct the necessary on-the-spot investigations, in a spirit of genuine cooperation and mindful of each Member State's duty [...] to facilitate the general task of the Commission.[1196]

It follows that the Member States are under an obligation to co-operate and indeed actively investigate the evidence used by the European Commission in order to comply with this obligation. This judgement consequently increases the burden on Member States to further investigate and indeed not to ignore complaints, providing that the European Commission has adduced sufficient evidence on the matter. It also reinforces the reporting obligation of the Landfill Directive that serves as a first indication of the correct implementation of the Directive. In broader terms, this and previous judgements on this matter indicate that Member States may not necessarily ignore systematic breaches of waste legislation that are illegal or inadequately managed landfills.

f) Excursus: Measures reducing the impacts of plastic from landfills

In 2008, 48.7% of generated plastic waste in the EU was landfilled.[1197] This implies that inadequately managed or illegal landfills could potentially be an important source of plastic waste. It is in this regard that the potential impact of landfilling for marine litter considerations could be addressed. In 2013, the European Commission published a Green Paper on a European Strategy on Plastic which served to initiate a broad consultation on issues relating to the problems associated with the impact of plastic in the environment.[1198] One of the issues raised in this context is whether the reduction or elimination of landfilling plastic waste would contribute to the re-use and recovery of plastic.[1199]

---

sion: *Hedemann-Robinson*, Enforcement of European Union environmental law, 2007, 58.

1196 C-365/97 *Commission v. Italy* [1999] ECR I-7773, para.85; C-494/01 *Commission v. Ireland* [2005] ECR I-3382, para.45.

1197 *European Commission*, COM (2013) 123 final, Green Paper on a European Strategy on Plastic Waste in the Environment, 07.03.2013, 4.

1198 See for an in-depth discussion, section B.VI.4. of this chapter.

1199 *European Commission*, COM (2013) 123 final, Green Paper on a European Strategy on Plastic Waste in the Environment, 07.03.2013, 11.

With this proposition in mind, it is submitted that generally such an approach must be addressed on the European Union level since uniform waste acceptance and classification procedures are one of the key aspects to ensure that minimum environmental protection standards are maintained in the different EU countries. Creating and maintaining such EU-wide common standards in respect of plastic waste specifically would represent a major step forward in harmonising protection standards across all Member States. Hence, notwithstanding the importance of the principle of subsidiarity in EU law, it is submitted that an EU-wide measure in the form of a (amended) Directive would represent the most efficient and most effective approach. This guarantees that waste is not transported to a different EU country in which its disposal is less costly due to lower protection standards. With regard to marine litter considerations, the classification of non-hazardous waste, as it currently stands, most likely represents the majority of source material of plastic. This refers amongst others to plastic bags and packaging.[1200] The logic of such an approach is that banning the landfilling of plastic potentially reduces the environmental impact of inadequately managed landfills. Generally, such an advance is in principle permissible under the regulatory scheme of the Landfill Directive. The option to do so relates to the ban or phasing-out of certain substances, possible under Art. 5 Landfill Directive. Given the current scope, the Member States are obliged to reduce the landfilling of biodegradable waste (phasing out)[1201] and to prohibit the landfilling of, *inter alia*, tyres or hospital or other clinical waste.[1202] Consequently, a similar step regarding plastic waste or certain type of plastic could in theory be possible; however such a step would require an amendment of the Directive. In concrete terms, this could be affected by adding a new category to Art. 5 Landfill Directive and to amend the waste acceptance criteria of Annex II Landfill Directive accordingly. However, the term "plastic" as used by the

1200 PVC waste is usually landfilled in the municipal solid waste stream: *European Commission*, The Behaviour of PVC in Landfill, Final report, 2000, 79.

1201 Art. 5 (2) Landfill Directive. The phasing-out is to be pursued in a three scale approach. The baseline of the phasing-out is the amount (weight) of produced biodegradable municipal waste in the year 1995. Thus the reduction target require that the biodegradable municipal waste going to landfills shall be reduced to 75% in 2006, 50% by 2009 and 35% by 2016 (Art. 5 (2) (a–c) Landfill Directive respectively.

1202 Art. 5 (3) Landfill Directive. Furthermore, also liquid waste, explosive, corrosive, oxidizing and highly flammable waste may not be landfilled.

European Commission appears to be generic and potentially includes several types of plastic. With a view to precise and concrete considerations, a specific option could be to ban all recyclable plastics. This proposition has however several economic, environmental and legal dimensions.

Such a ban or phasing out would also have a high impact on plastic waste management as a whole. Among the different options to dispose waste, landfilling is the cheapest form.[1203] This opens the question whether it would be proportionate to introduce such a ban that immediately requires alternatives such as a higher recovery or recycling rates of plastic waste. Arguably, with a view to the necessary structural and capacity changes of involved stakeholders such as the Member States, the landfill operators and the plastic industry, a phase-out would be more suitable to address the problem.

Notwithstanding the proportionality of the measure, a change in the material scope of the Landfill Directive to prohibit or phase-out recyclable plastic waste in landfills has to be accompanied by adequate waste management alternatives. If such an amendment were to be pursued in an isolated way, no incentives for alternative waste management options would accompany this development and the ban or phasing out would merely result in an increase of illegal landfills for plastic waste. A first consequent step would be to adapt the recycling targets of the Waste Framework Directive in order to compensate for different recycling needs and targets. With this in mind, the planned review of the Waste Framework Directive and also the Landfill Directive provides a highly suitable window of opportunity.[1204] Such a ban could, when integrated in the overall EU Waste Management Framework, serve as an incentive to reduce the impact of plastic through recycling.[1205] In its legislative proposal on amending certain waste streams that was issued as a result of the ongoing process of EU waste management revision, the European Commission proposes, among others, that by January 2025, Member States may not accept non-haz-

---

1203 *Fischer/Petschow/Buclet,* The consequences of implementing directives in the national context: the correct answer to the friction between national regimes?, in *Buclet,* Municipal waste management in Europe (2002) 81–110, 104.

1204 *European Commission*, COM (2013) 123 final, Green Paper on a European Strategy on Plastic Waste in the Environment, 07.03.2013, 7.

1205 *Forwarst*, Documentation of the contribution analysis and uncertainty assessment: Results interpretation identifying priority material flows and wastes for waste prevention, re-cycling and choice of waste treatment options, Sixth Framework Programme, 2010, 48.

ardous recyclable waste such as plastics, metals, paper and cardboard in landfills.[1206] Therefore the European Commission suggested a ban of landfilling plastics. It remains of course to be seen how this will be dealt with in the course of the decision-making procedure. The proposal stipulates an alteration of the material scope of the Landfill Directive, which, in line with the argumentation presented above, would increase the environmental protection standard when accompanied by appropriate measures. Concurrently, the proposal also outlines that by the first of January 2020, the recycling and preparing for re-use of municipal waste shall be at least 50% by weight, by first of January 2030, this should be increased by 75% respectively.[1207] However, the European Commission withdrew the proposal to review certain directives in March 2015 and announced to propose a new and ambitious new package to promote the circular economy at the end of 2015.[1208] It remains to be seen how this new proposal integrates this specific aspect.

g) Preliminary Conclusion

The regulation of landfills in the overall waste management scheme of the European Union is placed between the constraints of the need for disposal and environmental protection. Since it is seen as a last resort in the hierarchical order of preference as established in the waste hierarchy, it plays an important role in the marine litter discourse. The permit approach en-

---

1206 Proposal for a Directive of the European Parliament and of the Council amending Directives 2008/98/EC on waste, 94/62/EC on packaging and packaging waste, 1999/31/EC on the landfill of waste, 2000/53/EC on end-of-life vehicles, 2006/66/EC on batteries and accumulators and waste batteries and accumulators, and 2012/19/EU on waste electrical and electronic equipment, 25.

1207 Proposal for a Directive of the European Parliament and of the Council amending Directives 2008/98/EC on waste, 94/62/EC on packaging and packaging waste, 1999/31/EC on the landfill of waste, 2000/53/EC on end-of-life vehicles, 2006/66/EC on batteries and accumulators and waste batteries and accumulators, and 2012/19/EU on waste electrical and electronic equipment, 13.

1208 *European Commission*, COM(2014) 910 final, Annex to the Communication from the European Commission to the European Parliament, the Council, the European Economic and Social Committee and the Committee of the Regions on the Commission Work Programme 2015, 16.12.2014 and *European Commission*, Press Release, Commission confirms Withdrawal of 73 Pending Proposals Announced in 2015 Work Programme, IP/15/4567, 07.03.2015.

sures that specific requirements such as location, conditions and waste acceptance procedures are adhered to. In principle, the material obligations are a suitable framework to ensure safe storage without endangering the environment or human health. However, overall the Landfill Directive lacks an ambitious spirit that would increase its protection standard. Even though it is embedded in the framework and obligations of the Waste Framework Directive, the Landfill Directive allows for exemptions that reduce its purpose and objective.

Besides the material considerations, the implementation of the provisions of the Landfill Directive would increase the protection standard. However, the lack of compliance and inadequate implementation of the Landfill Directive pose a threat to the environmental protection overall and effectively prevent the achievement of its objectives. The exemplary case of the Zakynthos Island demonstrates that technical requirements arising out of the Landfill Directive have direct repercussions on the marine litter and marine biodiversity context. Even though judicial options are available in the EU, the sheer amount of systematic failures to implement and apply the Directive poses a challenge in addressing these. In particular the reporting obligations that are contained in the Landfill Directive theoretically play an important role in evoking infringement procedures. However, the limited capacity of the Commission to investigate possible infringements potentially limits an effective implementation of the Directive. Admittedly, the CJEU has shaped the obligation on the Member States to co-operate in this regard.

3. The adoption of more stringent national measures: the classification of a ban of plastic bags in EU law

In 2010, Europeans citizens used over 85, 3 billion plastics bags.[1209] Their economic lifetime of less than 30 minutes makes them a symbol of a modern throwaway society. As has been discussed in chapter 1, pollution of the marine environment by plastic bags is one of the major problems of marine litter. They are particular likely to be thrown away or to be lost due to their low economic value and the fact that they are easily blown away

1209 *European Commission*, Speech of Janez Potočnik (Commissioner for Environment): "Any Future for the Plastic Industry in Europe?", held in Wiesbaden, Germany, 21.9.2012, Press Release SPEECH/12/632 21/09/2012.

by wind. Among the different options on how to address this problem, the Italian ban on the sale of non-biodegradable plastic bags from 01 January 2011 is exemplary of the tensions involved in this challenging problem. Whereas a ban on the sale of non-biodegradable plastic bags has been primarily, but not exclusively, introduced at local or municipal levels,[1210] Italy´s step to introduce a nationwide ban of non-biodegradable plastic bags raises several questions on the legality of such national rules in the context of EU law. Italy has adopted in its Laws of 27 December 2006 No 296, Article 1, paras.1129, 1130 and 1131 a gradual ban on putting non-biodegradable carrier bags on the market that applies to all product sectors and all types of non-biodegradable carrier bags.[1211] The reasons for doing so are reducing CO_2 emissions, improving environmental protection and supporting the agri-industry on biomaterials.[1212] Even though the other reasons for this ban could also be subject to scrutiny under EU law, the following assessment exemplarily relates to the grounds of protecting the environment, notably its relation and impact with the issue of marine litter.

The core of the question is whether Member States are entitled to take more stringent national environmental measures. Such measures are permitted according to Art. 194 TFEU. The CJEU has, in its jurisprudence, held that if a Directive has provided for exhaustive harmonisation of national legislation, Member States cannot take recourse to provisions of the free movement of goods in the EU internal market.[1213] A starting point in this discussion is to understand whether the issue has been subject to regulation by the EU. In a second step, it has to be evaluated whether this regulation is exhaustive and whether and to what extent the pertinent EU regu-

---

1210 See only the ban for retailers to provide single-use plastic bags in San Francisco that has been in force already in 2007: *Romer,* Golden Gate University Environmental Law Journal 1 (2010) 439, 439. More recently, Seattle, United States of America and Toronto, Canada introduced ban on plastics bags in July 2012 and January 2013 respectively. In the case of Toronto, the decision to introduce the ban on plastic bags was made only 6 month after a five-cent levy on plastic bags has been introduced.

1211 *BIO Intelligence Service,* Assessment of impacts of options to reduce the use of single-use plastic carrier bags, 2011, Annex B to the study, case study of Italy.

1212 *Ibid.*

1213 C-169/89 *Gourmetterie v.d.Burg* [1990] ECR I-2143 (Red Grouse), para.8. *Temmink,* From Danish Bottles to Danish Bees: The Dynamics of Free Movement of Goods and Environmental Protection- a Case Law Analysis, in *Somsen,* Yearbook of European environmental law (2000) 61–102, 67; *Jans/Vedder,* European environmental law, 2012, 98.

lation harmonises national law.[1214] Here, the role and scope of the legal basis of the specific instrument determines whether and to what degree more stringent national measures may be pursued.

a) The applicability of the Packaging and Waste Packaging Directive

A first starting point whether the ban on plastic bags is subject to regulation by the EU is to assess if a legal instruments exists that covers this question, *i.e.* whether the Packaging and Waste Packaging Directive (Waste Packaging Directive)[1215] is applicable in this regard. The Waste Packaging Directive has a "dual"[1216] objective that intends to harmonise national rules with regard to different aims. These refer to preventing and reducing "the impact of packaging waste on the environment so as to provide a high level of environmental protection"[1217] and also to ensuring "the proper functioning of the internal market and avoiding obstacles to trade and distortion and restriction of competition within the Community."[1218]

Despite this twofold objective, the legal base of the Directive is exclusively Art. 114 TFEU[1219] stipulating the harmonisation of national

1214 *Holwerda,* Climate Law 2 (2011) 37, 44; *Temmink,* From Danish Bottles to Danish Bees: The Dynamics of Free Movement of Goods and Environmental Protection- a Case Law Analysis, in *Somsen,* Yearbook of European environmental law (2000) 61–102, 66.

1215 See for an overview on the challenges and intricacies in regulating the waste stream of packaging *Fischer/Petschow/Buclet,* The consequences of implementing directives in the national context: the correct answer to the friction between national regimes?, in *Buclet,* Municipal waste management in Europe (2002) 81–110, 83 *et seq.*

1216 *Jans/Vedder,* European environmental law, 2012, 485; C-463/01 *Commission v. Germany* [2004] ECR I-11705, para.37.

1217 C-444/00 *Mayer Perry Recycling Ltd.* [2003] ECR I-6163, para.71.

1218 C-463/01 *Commission v. Germany* [2004] ECR I-11705, para.37. See also Art. 1 (1) Waste Packaging Directive.

1219 Formerly, Art. 100a Treaty establishing the European Community and Art. 95 TEU. Accordingly, "the European Parliament and the Council shall, acting in accordance with the ordinary legislative procedure and after consulting the Economic and Social Committee, adopt the measures for the approximation of the provisions laid down by law, regulation or administrative action in Member States which have as their object the establishment and functioning of the internal market" (Art. 114 TFEU).

rules.[1220] It serves as a legal basis to ensure "the unity and cohesion of European" [1221] Union law. Art. 192 TFEU on environmental protection standards was not chosen as a legal base for this Directive.[1222] With a view to previous CJEU judgements, it appears peculiar why it was not decided to use both provisions as joint legal bases.[1223] The CJEU has outlined in previous judgments that where the legislative instruments in question "pursues a number of objectives or has several components that are indissociably linked, without one being secondary and indirect in relation to each other, such an act will have to be founded on the various corresponding legal bases."[1224] The elements that are regulated in this instrument and that are directly linked with each other are the harmonisation of national measures regarding packaging, the functioning of the internal market and environmental protection.

Art. 114 TFEU as the legal basis has thus consequences on the range of options of the EU Member States to introduce specific environmental protection standards.[1225] The primary goal of the Waste Packaging Directive is the prevention of the production of packaging waste which is supported by the concepts of reuse of packaging, recycling and therefore reducing

---

1220 See for a discussion on the development and role of this treaty provision *St Clair Bradley,* Powers and Procedures in the EU Constitution: Legal Base and the Court, in *Craig/de Búrca,* The Evolution of EU Law (2011) 85–110, 94 *et seq*.

1221 *Sevenster,* The Environmental Guarantee After Amsterdam, in *Somsen,* Yearbook of European environmental law (2000) 291–310, 293.

1222 In C-300/89 *Commission v. Council* [1991] I-2967 (Titanium Dioxide), the Court had to decide whether the regulation of titanium dioxide was to regulated on the basis of Art. 100a EEC or the environmental protection provision respectively. The CJEU stated that: "provisions which are made necessary by considerations relating to the environment and health may be a burden upon the undertakings to which they apply and, if there is no harmonization of national provisions on the matter, competition may be appreciably distorted. It follows that action intended to approximate national rules concerning production conditions in a given industrial sector with the aim of eliminating distortions of competition in that sector is conducive to the attainment of the internal market and thus falls within the scope of Article 100a, a provision which is particularly appropriate to the attainment of the internal market" (para.23).

1223 C-178/03 *Commission v. European Parliament and Council* [2006] ECR I-107, para.59 as well as C-300/89 *Commission v. Council* (Titanium Dioxide), see also *Jans/Vedder,* European environmental law, 2012, 485.

1224 C-178/03 *Commission v. European Parliament and Council*, para.43.

1225 See only: *Holwerda,* Climate Law 2 (2011) 37, 47 *et seq.*

the final disposal of this type of waste.[1226] The material scope of the Directive in terms of waste is comprehensive and includes "all packaging placed on the market in the Community and all packaging waste, whether it is used or released at industrial, commercial, office, shop, service, household or any other level, regardless of the material used."[1227] Here the Directive differentiates between differing purposes of the packaging, in which the so-called "transport packaging or tertiary packaging" as outlined in Art. 3 (1) (c) Waste Packaging Directive addresses the function of plastic bags. Packaging waste falling in this category is defined as "packaging conceived so as to facilitate handling and transport of a number of sales units or grouped packagings in order to prevent physical handling and transport damage [...]."

A direct reference to plastic carrier bags is made in the context of a further refinement of what constitutes packaging in which Art. 3 (1) (ii) Waste Packaging Directive refers to "items designed and intended to be filled at the point of sale and `disposable` items sold, filled or designed and intended to be filled at the point of sale shall be considered to be packaging provided they fulfil a packaging function." In order to fill out this rather laborious description, Annex I to the Waste Packaging Directive outlines "illustrative examples" of how this could be interpreted. Here, plastic carrier bags are listed as examples that could be subsumed under Art. 3 (1) (ii) Waste Packaging Directive. Consequently, the placement of plastic bags on the market is regulated in EU legislation.

b) Essential requirements under the Waste Packaging Directive

Since the placement of plastic bags is regulated, a further assessment is necessary whether this is done in an exhaustive manner because of shared competence. A central provision is that according to Art. 9 Waste Packaging Directive, packaging may only be placed on the market if it complies

1226 Art. 1 (2) Waste Packaging Directive. *Jans/Vedder,* European environmental law, 2012, 485.

1227 Art. 2 (2) Waste Packaging Directive. "Packaging" means "all products made of any materials of any nature to be used for the containment, protection, handling, delivery and presentation of goods, from raw materials to processed goods, from the producer to the user or the consumer. `Non-returnable' items used for the same purpose shall also be considered to constitute packaging.".

with all essential requirements that are defined by the Directive or Annex II Waste Packaging Directive. Among others, the essential requirements for packaging relate to the obligation to limit the weight and volume of packaging to a minimum in order to meet the required level of safety, hygiene and acceptability for consumers. Second, the packaging must be designed so as to allow its reuse, recovery or recycling. Third, the packaging shall be designed in such a way that the content of hazardous and noxious substances is minimised with regard to its emissions or leachates during incineration or landfilling.[1228] The essential requirements are only broadly formulated and therefore leave a broad margin of their interpretation. However, Art. 18 Waste Packaging Directive stipulates that "Member States shall not impede the placing on the market of their territory of packaging which satisfies the provisions of this Directive."

From this it can be concluded that Member States may not put in place a ban of a packaging product under the scope of the Directive, if the product is in line with the essential requirements of the Waste Packaging Directive. With regard to the aim of the Directive to ensure the functioning of the internal market, to avoid obstacles to trade and restriction of competition, it can be established that the placement of packaging also relating to a ban is exhaustively regulated.[1229]

1228 Paragraph 1, Annex II Waste Packaging Directive.

1229 See only the argumentation of the CJEU in C-428/08 *Monsanto Technology LLC v. Cefetra BV and Others* [2010] ECR I-6765, paras.58-60. The case relates to a preliminary ruling concerning the interpretation of Article 9 of Directive 98/44/EC of the European Parliament and of the Council of 6 July 1998 on the legal protection of biotechnological inventions (OJ 1998 L 213). One of the referred questions of the national court related to whether Art. 9 of the Directive 98/44/EC effects exhaustive harmonization (para.51). The CJEU held that "[…] as regards, in particular, Article 9 of the Directive […] reflects its intention to ensure the same protection for patents in all Member States. Uniform protection appears to be the means to eliminate or prevent differences between the Member States […] whereas, conversely, a minimalist harmonisation approach which would favour patent holders would, on the one hand, compromise the balance sought between the interests at stake and, on the other hand, only entrench or give rise to differences between the Member States, thereby fostering barriers to trade. It follows that the harmonisation effected by Article 9 of the Directive must be regarded as exhaustive.".

As a third step in the assessment, the degree of harmonisation envisaged by the Directive must be examined.[1230] In EU law, different methods of harmonisation have been developed, that differ in their harmonization impact and scope of discretion for Member States to adopt national laws. Generally, two types prevail: a total and a minimum harmonisation.[1231] A minimum harmonisation implies that the secondary instrument only stipulates minimum standards. States can therefore introduce more stringent environmental protection standards.[1232] A total harmonisation envisages that the environmental protection standard adopted in an EU instrument is binding and national implementing legislation must not deviate from these rules.[1233]

Since the inherent nature of Directive is that the aim is provided, yet it leaves discretion to Member States on the form and method of implementation, the question which form of harmonisation is stipulated in the Waste Packaging Directive can only be answered by taking recourse to CJEU jurisprudence. Accordingly, the degree of harmonisation has to be assessed according to wording, purpose and structure of the Directive.[1234] In *Aher-Waggon*, the CJEU found that "that the directive merely lays down minimum requirements, as is shown by the words 'in accordance with requirements which are at least equal to the applicable standards' […]. The directive thus allows the Member State to impose stricter noise limits."[1235]

In *Deutscher Apothekenverband*, the CJEU has found that in the absence of express reference to the possibility of laying down more restrictive or simply different rules, the provisions are subject to an exhaustive rule.[1236] Consequently since the Waste Packaging Directive does not in-

---

1230 *Temmink*, From Danish Bottles to Danish Bees: The Dynamics of Free Movement of Goods and Environmental Protection - a Case Law Analysis, in *Somsen*, Yearbook of European environmental law (2000) 61–102, 68.

1231 *Jans/Vedder,* European environmental law, 2012, 104 *et seq.*

1232 *Jans/Vedder,* European environmental law, 2012, 108.

1233 *Ibid.*, 104.

1234 C-52/00 *Commission v. France* [2001] ECR I-3827, para.16; C-154/00 *Commission v. Greece* [2002] ECR I-3887, para.12.

1235 C-389/96 *Aher-Waggon GmbH* [1998] ECR I-4473, para.15. The case dealt with a refusal of Germany to grant registration for a propeller-driven aircraft previously registered in Denmark on the ground that it exceeded the noise limit permitted in Germany.

1236 C-322/01 *Deutscher Apothekerverb*and [2003] ECR I-14951, para.144; C-374/05 *Gintec International Import-Export GmbH* [2007] ECR I-9541, para. 26.

clude a reference to the possibility to introduce more restrictive rules, it is argued that the Directive envisages a total harmonization in regard to the placement of products on the market. Also, the "market access clause"[1237] of Art. 18 Waste Packaging Directive usually indicates the intention of total harmonisation.[1238]

Taking the foregoing into account, it would be fair to conclude that the Italian plastic bag ban is not compatible with EU law. This is due to the fact that the essential requirement of the Waste Packaging Directive can be seen as a provision indicating total harmonisation. However, before a final assessment can be made, the derogation clause of Art. 114 (5) TFEU has to be analysed. Such an assessment is necessary since Art. 114 TFEU is the legal basis for the Waste Packaging Directive.

c) The derogation clause under Art. 114 TFEU

The legal basis of the Waste Packaging Directive is Art. 114 TFEU. In paragraph 5, the option to introduce national standards that derogate from the harmonisation measure as envisaged by Art. 114 TFEU is foreseen. Consequently, the introduction of a ban on using non-biodegradable plastic bags has to be mirrored with these provisions.

Accordingly, the derogation clause of Art. 114 (5) TFEU states that:

> [m]oreover, without prejudice to paragraph 4, if, after the adoption of a harmonisation measure by the European Parliament and the Council, by the Council or by the Commission, a Member State deems it necessary to introduce national provisions based on new scientific evidence relating to the protection of the environment or the working environment on grounds of a problem specific to that Member State arising after the adoption of the harmonisation measure, it shall notify the Commission of the envisaged provisions as well as the grounds for introducing them.[1239]

According to paragraph 5, harmonisation measures may be taken after the fulfilment of certain criteria. These include the necessity to base the rules

---

1237 *Jans/Vedder,* European environmental law, 2012, 112.

1238 *Ibid.*, 105.

1239 Whereas Art. 114 (4) TFEU refers to "maintain" national rules, paragraph is pertinent in the discussed case, since it is applicable in case new rules are introduced that deviate from "harmonisation measures taken in the framework of the internal market" *Jans/Vedder,* European environmental law, 2012, 123. See also: C-41/93 *France v. Commission* [1994] ECR I-1829.

on "new" and "scientific evidence" relating to the protection of the environment or on grounds of a "specific problem" to a Member State. Additionally, a Member State relying on this derogation standard has to notify the Commission and is under the obligation to produce reasons for adopting stricter environmental protection standards.

The derogation criteria of Art. 114 TFEU are cumulative which implies that "they must all be satisfied if the national derogating provisions are not to be rejected by the Commission."[1240] Generally, the cumulative nature of Art. 114 (5) TFEU poses certain limits for the Italian plastic bag ban. This stems in particular from the fact that the causality between the use of non-biodegradable plastic bags and their impact is not entirely proven. Depending on the interpretation of "new scientific evidence" the argument whether this requirement is fulfilled varies. From a strict interpretation of Art. 114 (5), one could conclude that only evidence that has been found after the adoption of the measure is to be taken into consideration.[1241] Taking into account that the awareness of a scientific problem is constantly evolving,[1242] the precautionary principle should be taken as the basis for any subsequent decision.[1243] These considerations speak in favour of confirming that the increasing body of knowledge on the risk of plastic bags theoretically speaks in favour of confirming the relevance of this requirement.

Even though it is established that plastic bags indeed have a significant share in marine litter, the alternative, biodegradable bags,[1244] potentially also pose several challenges in this context. Despite their role as an alter-

---

1240 C-512/99 *Germany v. Commission* [2003] ECR I-00845, para.81.

1241 *Sevenster,* The Environmental Guarantee After Amsterdam, in *Somsen,* Yearbook of European environmental law (2000) 291–310, 304.

1242 *Ibid.*

1243 C-405/07 P *Netherlands v. Commission* [2008] ECR I-8301, para.61. Accordingly, "[u]nder the first indent of Article 174(3) EC, the Commission is, as a rule, obliged to take account, in its decisions in the field of the environment, of all available new scientific and technical data. That obligation applies, particularly, to the procedure under Article 95(5) and (6) EC, for which taking account of new data forms the very foundation.".

1244 In this regard, one has to distinguish between biodegradable and bio-based plastic bags. Bio-based plastic bags are made of bio-based materials such as natural polymers from renewable sources such as starch and polymers synthesised from renewable sources such as polyactic acid (PPLA). A third source material can be polymers produced by micro-organism such as polyhydroxyalkanoates (PHAs): *BIO Intelligence Service*, Assessment of impacts of options to reduce

native to non-biodegradable plastic bags, most of the marketed biodegradable plastic bags do not degrade rapidly in the environment.[1245] Biodegradable plastic bags are usually designed to be composted under certain conditions such as micro-organisms and specific temperature that are not comparable to marine environmental conditions.[1246] Therefore, it is argued that a ban of non-biodegradable plastic bags has not necessarily a positive link to the issue of marine litter.[1247]

The CJEU has held that Art. 114 TFEU does not necessitate that the problem of concern has to be exclusively occurring in that Member State.[1248] However such an exclusive occurrence could be "highly relevant in guiding the Commission as to whether to approve or reject the notified national provisions."[1249] A strict application of the precondition that the problem is specific to a Member State would potentially impact the objective of achieving a high environmental protection standard.[1250] With regard to marine litter, it is undisputed that the problem is not confined from an environmental or economic point of view to the territory of Italy.

According to Art. 114 (6) TFEU, the Commission has 6 months to approve or object to the national measure from the date the notification is received.[1251] It examines whether the national measure constitutes an arbitrary discrimination, a disguised restriction on trade between Member State or a limitation of the effective functioning of the EU internal market.

---

the use of single-use plastic carrier bags, 2011, 26. Not every bio-based plastic carrier is also biodegradable.

1245 *Ibid., 32.*

1246 *BIO Intelligence Service*, Assessment of impacts of options to reduce the use of single-use plastic carrier bags, 2011, 32.26.

1247 It is admitted that the other reasons such as the agri-industry could benefit from the increased demand of renewable source such as starch that results from such a ban.

1248 C-3/00 *Denmark v. Commission* [2003] ECR I-2643, para.59. See also: *Sevenster,* The Environmental Guarantee After Amsterdam, in *Somsen,* Yearbook of European environmental law (2000) 291–310, 302.

1249 C-3/00 *Denmark v. Commission*, para.60.

1250 *Sevenster,* The Environmental Guarantee After Amsterdam, in Somsen, Yearbook of European environmental law (2000) 291–310, 302.

1251 The European Commission can, should this be justified by the complex circumstances, extend this time frame by six months (Art. 114 (6) para.3 TFEU. In the absence of a reaction by the European Commission within the provided timeline, the national measure is deemed to have been approved (Art. 114 (6) para.2 TFEU).

If the Commission authorises the introduction of national measures that derogate from a harmonization measure, it is also under the obligation to examine whether a proposal for amendment is in order.[1252] The notification obligation of Art. 114 (5) TFEU is therefore also applicable in the context of the Italian plastic bag ban. The Italian government adopted the law establishing the ban without notifying the European Commission.[1253] The European Commission was only informed of this national measure in April 2011.[1254]

d) Preliminary conclusion

The material and procedural obligations arising from EU primary and secondary law in this case render the result that the Italian plastic bag ban is incompatible with EU law. Admittedly, a change of certain parameters such as the type of plastic that is subject to the ban might change such an evaluation. It could be argued in this context that recourse to the polluter-pays-principle could lead to a contrary evaluation. Since it is known that plastic bags are a cause of marine litter, the corresponding obligations under this principle speak for a direct regulation of this source of marine litter. A possible (legal) option in this regard would be to amend the Waste Packaging Directive or to introduce an overall ban of plastic bags EU wide.

In 2013, the European Commission published a Proposal for a Directive of the European Parliament and of the Council amending Directive 94/62/EC on packaging and packaging waste to reduce the consumption of lightweight plastic carrier bags.[1255] The objective of the proposal was to limit the consumption of plastic carrier bags with a thickness below 50 mi-

---

1252 Art. 114 (7) TFEU.

1253 *BIO Intelligence Service*, Assessment of impacts of options to reduce the use of single-use plastic carrier bags, 2011, Annex B to the study, reference to Italy´s policy.

1254 *Ibid.*

1255 *European Commission*, COM(2013) 761 final, Proposal for a Directive of the European Parliament and of the Council amending Directive 94/62/EC on packaging and packaging waste to reduce the consumption of lightweight plastic carrier bags, 04.11.2013. See also the European Parliament resolution of 14 January 2014 on a European strategy on plastic waste in the environment (2013/2113(INI)).

crons (0.05mm) in the EU.[1256] It had not been chosen to adopt an EU-wide reduction target, rather the choice was made to opt for national implementation measures.[1257] The proposed amendments to the Waste Packaging Directive relate to the "measures that may include the use of national reduction targets, economic instruments as well as marketing restrictions in derogation from Article 18 of this Directive."[1258] Notwithstanding this, even though the amended version relates to "marketing restrictions", it also emphasises alternative options. In its first reading, the European Parliament adopted a resolution in which it favoured the reduction of consumption of lightweight carrier bags.[1259] Whereas the Commission proposal outlined national measures, the European Parliament argued for an EU wide-reduction target and contain specific provisions on biodegradable plastics.[1260]

This is laudable, since a plastic bag ban is a two-sided coin. From an environmental point of view, a ban on non-biodegradable plastic bags has the most effective environmental impact with regard to its prevention of marine litter.[1261] From a legal point of view, the ban appears to be too rigid. The CJEU held in case C-320/03 that before introducing a total ban, a Member State has the duty to carefully assess other possibilities that re-

---

1256 *European Commission*, COM(2013) 761 final, Proposal for a Directive of the European Parliament and of the Council amending Directive 94/62/EC on packaging and packaging waste to reduce the consumption of lightweight plastic carrier bags, 2.

1257 *Ibid.*, 3. An EU-wide target has been critically debated; see for a related proposal: *European Commission*, Commission seeks views on reducing plastic bag use, Press Release, Brussels, 18.05.2011, IP/11/580.

1258 *European Commission*, COM(2013) 761 final, Proposal for a Directive of the European Parliament and of the Council amending Directive 94/62/EC on packaging and packaging waste to reduce the consumption of lightweight plastic carrier bags, 7.

1259 *European Parliament*, European Parliament legislative resolution of 16 April 2014 on the proposal for a directive of the European Parliament and of the Council amending Directive 94/62/EC on packaging and packaging waste to reduce the consumption of lightweight plastic carrier bags (COM(2013)0761 – C7-0392/2013 –2013/0371(COD)) (Ordinary legislative procedure: first reading), 16.04.2014.

1260 *Ibid.*

1261 *BIO Intelligence Service,* Assessment of impacts of options to reduce the use of single-use plastic carrier bags, 2011, 95.

strict to a lesser degree the freedom of movement.[1262] It is argued that more proportional means of protecting the marine environment from discarded or lost plastic bags are already applied in other EU Member States. In the case of Ireland, a levy on the purchase of plastic carrier bags was introduced in 2002.[1263] Its revenues are paid into an environmental fund.[1264] The aim of the introduction of the levy, namely reducing the share of plastic bags in litter pollution, has been achieved with considerable success given that the share of plastic bags in litter pollution has dropped from 5% in 2001 to 0.25% in 2010.[1265]

As a result of the revision process, the Directive (EU) 2015/720 on reducing the consumption of lightweight plastic carrier bags[1266] has been adopted in April 2015. Directive 2015/720 stipulates binding national reduction targets for the consumption of lightweight carrier bags. Accordingly, Member States are obliged to take either or both of the following measures:

(a) the adoption of measures ensuring that the annual consumption level does not exceed 90 lightweight plastic carrier bags per person by 31 December 2019 and 40 lightweight plastic carrier bags per person by 31 December 2025, or equivalent targets set in weight. Very lightweight plastic carrier bags may be excluded from national consumption objectives or

---

1262 C-320/03 *Commission v. Austria* [2005] ECR I-9871, para.87. This infringement procedure dealt with the legality of a ban of lorries over 7.5 tonnes carrying certain goods from using certain main roads on the ground of ensuring the quality of ambient air in the area. Accordingly, "[...] before adopting a measure so radical as a total traffic ban on a section of motorway constituting a vital route of communication between certain Member States, the Austrian authorities were under a duty to examine carefully the possibility of using measures less restrictive of freedom of movement, and discount them only if their inadequacy, in relation to the objective pursued, was clearly established.".

1263 Other options include voluntary commitments of the retail sector not to provide single-use plastic bags or setting an EU–wide prevention target: *BIO Intelligence Service,* Assessment of impacts of options to reduce the use of single-use plastic carrier bags, 2011, 99 *et seq.*

1264 *Ibid.,* Appendix B to the study, see case study of Ireland.

1265 *BIO Intelligence Service,* Assessment of impacts of options to reduce the use of single-use plastic carrier bags, 2011, Appendix B to the study, case study of Ireland.

1266 Directive (EU) 2015/720 of the European Parliament and of the Council of April 29 2015 amending Directive 94/62/EC as regards reducing the consumption of lightweight plastic carrier bags (OJ 2015, L 115).

(b) the adoption of instruments ensuring that, by 31 December 2018, lightweight plastic carrier bags are not provided free of charge at the point of sale of goods or products, unless equally effective instruments are implemented. Very lightweight plastic carrier bags may be excluded from those measures.[1267]

Furthermore, the European Commission is required to assess the impact on the environment of oxo-degradable plastic materials, which fragment into small particles, and propose suitable measures. Also, by 2017, the European Commission will have to propose labelling and marking measures for an EU-wide recognition of biodegradable and compostable plastic bags.[1268]

4. The Green Paper on a European Strategy on Plastic Waste in the Environment and the proposal for amending waste legislation

The instruments analysed above have demonstrated that the European Union´s waste management and policy is from a material point of view, quite complex and relates to potentially many sources of marine litter. It is also in this context, that the European Commission has initiated one of the most explicit developments regarding marine litter. In March 2013 it published a Green Paper on a European Strategy on Plastic Waste in the Environment.[1269] It launched a public consultation phase to initiate a consultation on the issue of plastic in the environment with the ultimately aim to contribute to the review of EU waste legislation that was scheduled in 2014.[1270] During the period from 7th March 2013 to 7th June 2013 stakeholders were invited to express their views on challenges posed by plastic that are not specifically addressed in EU waste legislation.

Since the Green Paper was intended to stimulate discussion and collect feedback of several actors, it outlined and identified loopholes of the waste management policy. With regard to the study at hand, it is remarkable that the European Commission has focused the outline of the Green Paper almost exclusively on the issue of marine litter. Even though the

---

1267 Para. 1a Directive 2015/720.

1268 *Ibid.*

1269 *European Commission*, COM (2013) 123 final, Green Paper on a European Strategy on Plastic Waste in the Environment, 07.03.2013.

1270 *Ibid.*, 3.

scope of the paper was dominantly limited to source-related legislation, it addressed a broad range of issues falling within this scope. To steer the consultation phase, 26 questions were raised that relate, *inter alia*, to the application of the waster hierarchy, packing and design of plastics and also include the use of biodegradable plastics. Furthermore, the international dimension of the problem was assessed, highlighting the potential role of the Regional Seas Conventions, as well as the new EU´s Neighbourhood Policy.[1271]

The particular value of the Green Paper is that it also took account of issues that are currently not regulated under EU law, but that could potentially include a possible (partial) solution to the problem. This relates, for example, to a ban on plastics in landfills. Given its consultative status, the Green Paper also touched upon issues that are politically ambitious and controversially discussed, such as an EU wide quantitative reduction targets.[1272]

As a follow-up, the results of the consultation and academic and scientific reviews of different waste streams directives were published in April 2014.[1273] Whereas this study also addressed the identification of certain loopholes and overlap between certain legislative instruments, it partially also outlined certain marine litter aspects that were raised in the consultation phase. As an example, it addressed the role of the Packaging Waste Directive in creating marine litter.[1274] However, whereas the Green Paper clearly focused on environmental aspects of waste management, the study addressed besides these concerns, broader aspects such as smarter regulation in the EU.[1275] In July 2014, the European Commission adopted a proposal for amending, amongst others, the Waste Packaging Directive and the Landfill Directive.[1276] In the recitals to the proposal, the environ-

---

1271 *European Commission*, COM (2013) 123 final, Green Paper on a European Strategy on Plastic Waste in the Environment, 07.03.2013. 19 *et seq*.

1272 See also section B.VI.2.dd.of this chapter.

1273 *European Commission*, Ex-post evaluation of certain waste stream Directives Final report, 18.04.2014.

1274 *Ibid.*, 103.

1275 *European Commission*, Ex-post evaluation of certain waste stream Directives Final report, 18.04.2014, 7.

1276 *European Commission*, COM(2014) 397 final, Proposal for a Directive of the European Parliament and of the Council amending Directives 2008/98/EC on waste, 94/62/EC on packaging and packaging waste, 1999/31/EC on the landfill of waste, 2000/53/EC on end-of-life vehicles, 2006/66/EC on batteries and ac-

mental and economic impacts of littering, in particular plastics, is emphasised. It is suggested that specific measures such as waste management plans and obligatory measures to implement extended producer responsibility as well as proper enforcement could eradicate the problem.[1277]

As has been mentioned above, the proposal suggests among others that by January 2025, Member States may not accept non-hazardous recyclable waste such as plastics, metals, paper and cardboard into landfills.[1278] Also, it outlines that by the first of January 2020, the recycling and preparing for re-use of municipal waste shall be at least 50% by weight, by first of January 2030, this should be increased to 70%.[1279] Especially the ban of landfilling of non-hazardous and recyclable plastics is an ambitious and laudable proposal and it remains to be seen how it will be dealt with during the inter-instutional decision-making.

However, the European Commission withdrew the proposal for a Directive of the European Parliament and of the Council amending Directives 2008/98/EC on waste, 94/62/EC on packaging and packaging waste, 1999/31/EC on the landfill of waste, 2000/53/EC on end-of-life vehicles, 2006/66/EC on batteries and accumulators and waste batteries and accumulators, and 2012/19/EU on waste electrical and electronic equipment 28/10/2014 in March 2015.[1280] The reason for withdrawal being that the

---

cumulators and waste batteries and accumulators, and 2012/19/EU on waste electrical and electronic equipment, 02.07.2014. See also, *European Commission*, Commission Staff Working Document SWD/2014/0209 final, Ex-post evaluation of Five Waste Stream Directives, Accompanying the document Proposal for a Directive of the European Parliament and of the Council reviewing the targets in Directives 2008/98/EC on waste, 94/62/EC on packaging and packaging waste, and 1999/31/EC on the landfill of waste, amending Directives 2000/53/EC on end-of-life vehicles, 2006/66/EC on batteries and accumulators and waste batteries and accumulators, and 2012/19/EC on waste electrical and electronic equipment, 02.07.2014.

1277 *European Commission*, Proposal for a Directive of the European Parliament and of the Council amending Directives 2008/98/EC on waste, 94/62/EC on packaging and packaging waste, 1999/31/EC on the landfill of waste, 2000/53/EC on end-of-life vehicles, 2006/66/EC on batteries and accumulators and waste batteries and accumulators, and 2012/19/EU on waste electrical and electronic equipment, Recital 26.

1278 *Ibid.*, 25. See chapter 4 B.V.2.f.

1279 *Ibid.*, 13.

1280 *European Commission,* Press Release, Commission confirms Withdrawal of 73 Pending Proposals Announced in 2015 Work Programme, IP/15/4567, 07.03.2015.

circular economy package will be replaced by a new and more ambitious proposal by the end of 2015 to promote circular economy.[1281] It remains to be seen how the elements of a new proposal feed into the overall marine litter discourse in the EU and follow-up from the Green Paper.

5. Preliminary Conclusion

Waste management in the EU is at the same time boon and bane of the marine litter problem. Whereas it is potentially a major source of marine litter, its relevance to provide solutions in legal terms is undisputed. The Waste Framework Directive plays a particular important role in the overall structure of waste management. Its high environmental protection standard and principles serve as a threshold for marine litter considerations. In particular, the waste hierarchy and its associated obligations and options theoretically pave the way for effective waste prevention measures. However, the discussion has demonstrated that the logic and understanding of these elements are not coherently implemented in subsequent secondary law.

The analysis of the Landfill Directive addressing a point source of marine litter has revealed a central impediment to the effectiveness of this instrument. The infringement procedures of the CJEU, are symbolic for the divergence between legislative requirements and effective implementation and enforcement of waste management by Member States. The Zakynthos case has a prominent place in the marine litter context. It addresses the link between inadequately managed landfills and their potential impacts on marine biodiversity. This case symbolises the causal relationship between waste management and the marine litter problem. However, it also demonstrates that despite the specific role of the CJEU, judicial remedies to a known point source can be a lengthy procedure. Particularly with a view to the diverse and complex nature of such an inadequately managed landfill, taking immediate action is the only fundamental prerequisite to eliminate this source of marine litter.

1281 *European Commission*, COM(2014) 910 final, Annex to the Communication from the European Commission to the European Parliament, the Council, the European Economic and Social Committee and the Committee of the Regions on the Commission Work Programme 2015, 8, 16.12.2014.

6. Port Reception Facilities Directive–a mechanism to address operational vessel-based pollution

The European Union has developed a comprehensive set of secondary instruments that address maritime safety and marine environmental protection measures. Herewith, a new regulatory layer has been established that is positioned "between the national level of Member States′ legislation and the international (global) level composed of rules and standards adopted, mostly, by the International Maritime Organization […]."[1282] This implies certain challenges that relate to the relationship of the EU to regulatory systems of the Member States and to international conventions relating to the law of the sea.[1283] The EU legislation is "treated in much the same way as any national legislation by a single State in this field. Yet the EU is not a State […]."[1284] In the following, the Port Reception Facility Directive (PRF Directive) will be analysed, in which the EU has laid down requirements for all vessels entering EU ports.[1285] The PRF Directive is one of the primary instruments of EU law that explicitly addresses the issue of marine litter. Since it explicitly targets the illegal discharge of on-board generated waste into the marine environment, it is, amongst others, a key tool to address the source of operational vessel-based pollution. With a view to the overall scope and purpose of this study, the following analysis aims to understand how and to what degree this instrument serves the purpose of reducing the input of marine litter from vessels.

a) General framework

Notwithstanding its environmental protection approach, the classification of this Directive in the overall secondary legislation has to be differentiated from the instruments that have been discussed so far. This stems from the fact that the legal basis of the Directive is to be found in Art. 100 TFEU, a provision relating to transport. The PRF Directive, has at the in-

---

1282 *Ringbom,* The EU maritime safety policy and international law, 2008, 2.

1283 *Ibid.*, 3.

1284 *Ringbom,* The EU maritime safety policy and international law, 2008, 3.

1285 *Ibid.,* 258. *Long* states that "[t]he EU has used the Convention [UNCLOS] as a regulatory plinth to strengthen its position as a global leader in oceanic affairs" *Long,* The International Journal of Marine and Coastal Law 27 (2012) 711, 720.

tersection of maritime transport and environmental protection, a specific regulatory role that is ultimately linked to port State provisions. The PRF Directive is embedded in the international and regional public law context. This is on the one hand provided by the obligations of UNCLOS,[1286] MARPOL (Annex V) and the Regional Seas Conventions.[1287] Indeed the 'spirit' of the Directive is explicitly focused towards and adapted to integrate and modify the obligations arising out of those other instruments where necessary.[1288]

The purpose of the PRF Directive is the reduction of (illegal) discharges of ship-generated waste and cargo residues into the sea from vessels bound to EU ports.[1289] In doing so, the PRF Directive does not specify its geographic scope but imposes, in principle, an obligation on all ships headed into EU ports to deliver waste generated onboard in the ports of call, thereby avoiding potential jurisdictional issues relating to the geographical scope of the discharge prohibition thereby imposed.[1290] The material scope of the PRF Directive is, in essence, quite wide and includes all ships, but also fishing and recreational crafts regardless of the flag they are flying and also all ports of Member States that are normally visited by those vessels.[1291] Warships, naval auxiliary or other vessels that are owned or operated by a State for non-commercial service are excluded from this Directive.[1292]

The core instrument of the PRF Directive, as the name suggests is the port reception facilities (PRF) that are defined as "any facility, which is fixed, floating or mobile and capable of receiving generated waste or cargo residues."[1293] Bearing in mind the definition of ship-generated waste as

---

1286 Recital 2 PRF Directive.

1287 Recital 3 and 8 PRF Directive.

1288 Art. 4 (3) and Art. 15 PRF Directive.

1289 Art. 1 PRF Directive. In the following onboard generated waste is taken as a collective term when referring to both substances.

1290 *Ringbom,* The EU maritime safety policy and international law, 2008, 330.

1291 Art. 3 (a and b) PRF Directive.

1292 Art. 3 (a) PRF Directive. Notwithstanding this, Member States are obliged to ensure "as far as is reasonable and practicable" that the vessels in question deliver their onboard generated waste and cargo residues in accordance with the Directive (Art. 3 subsection 1 PRF Directive).

1293 Art. 2 (e) PRF Directive. Due to the scope of the study, the particular problems of reception facilities for cargo residues defined as "the remnants of any cargo material on board in cargo holds or tanks which remain after unloading procedures and cleaning operations are completed and shall include loading/unload-

"all waste, including sewage, and residues other than cargo residues, which are generated during the service of a ship and fall under the scope of Annexes I, IV and V to MARPOL and cargo-associated waste as defined in the Guidelines for the implementation of Annex V to MARPOL,"[1294] it is clear that the PRF Directive applies to marine litter considerations. With a view to the amendment and coming into effect of MARPOL Annex V in 2013, it has to be assessed how the newly adopted definition of garbage therein is to be integrated in the scope of the PRF Directive. The Directive stipulates that

> [t]he Annexes to this Directive, the definition in Article 2(b) and references to Community and IMO instruments may be amended in accordance with the procedure laid down in Article 14 (2) in order to bring them into line with Community or IMO measures which have entered in force, in so far as such amendments do not broaden the scope of this Directive.[1295]

Consequently, the provision is a dynamic reference to IMO and more specifically to MARPOL provisions. The procedure laid down in Article 14 (2) PRF Directive refers to Council Decision laying down the procedures for the exercise of implementing powers conferred on the Commission.[1296]

The wording of Art. 15 PRF Directive indicates that such an evolutive interpretation is admissible. However certain limitations are imposed. In particular the addendum that the amendments may not broaden the scope of the Directive could potentially pose a problem. This relates to the fact that the definition of MARPOL Annex V could change the scope of the PRF Directive. This is relevant, *inter alia,* to the determination of the adequacy of the port reception facilities regarding the delivered waste. However, due to the fact that the definition of onboard generated garbage is itself broadly defined in Art. 2 (c) PRF Directive, the newly amended definition of MARPOL Annex V is unlikely to have an impact on the scope of the Directive itself. Additionally, the Member States have ratified MAR-

---

ing excesses and spillage" (Art. 2 (d) PRF Directive) will not be considered in the following section.

1294 Art. 2 (c) PRF Directive.

1295 Art. 15 PRF Directive.

1296 In this regard Art. 5 and 7 of Council Decision of 28 June 1999 laying down the procedures for the exercise of implementing powers conferred on the Commission (1999/468/EC) (OJ 1999 L 184/23) shall apply while also regarding Art. 8 of the same instrument.

POL Annex V, whereas the EU is Contracting Party that makes reference to IMO, and more specifically, MARPOL instruments. This also implies that they are under the obligation to interpret provisions according to the newly amended MARPOL Annex V. Such an approach also assures harmonisation of standards on the international field as well as EU law, a much needed unity in an already fragmented regime.

The Member States have to ensure that their PRFs are adequately suited to meet the needs of those ships that normally use the port without causing "undue delay." From this wording, one can perceive that certain elements of the adequacy test are not entirely clear or remain vague. This refers, for example, to the requirement of "normally using" and also what constitutes "undue delay." However, the PRF Directive provides further elements that can be used when assessing the adequacy of PRF, such as the capacity of the port to receive the types and quantities of ship-generated waste while taking into account the operational needs of the users of the port, its size and geographical location.[1297]

b) Critical evaluation of the elements of the PRF Directive

In order to achieve the aim of reducing discharges of waste generated onboard, the PRF Directive supplements not only existing elements from MARPOL Annex V, but introduced new substantive elements.[1298] It is necessary to further scrutinise the notification requirements, the fee and cost recovery system, the inspections requirements and the importance of the waste handling plan with a view to their role in reducing marine litter.

aa) Notification

The primary obligation on vessels in the PRF Directive are the delivery of onboard generated waste into ports[1299] and the obligation to notify the next port of call within the EU of the intended amount and type of delivered waste (Art. 6 PRF Directive). The prior-notification duty of the PRF Directive has two 'dimensions.' The first dimension relates to the time

1297 Art. 4 (2) PRF Directive.
1298 *Ringbom,* The EU maritime safety policy and international law, 2008, 258.
1299 Art. 7 PRF Directive.

frame within which the vessels are to inform the authorities. Here, a notification of 24 hours prior of arrival serves as the fundamental rule so as to be able to adapt the organisational procedure in the port of call to accommodate the delivery of waste.[1300] This standard must only be adhered to when the next port of call is known. In case the voyage is shorter than 24 hours or the next port of call is known less than 24 hours prior to arrival, the notification may either be done immediately after the departure of the previous port or as soon as the port of call is known.[1301]

The procedural dimension of the notification obligation refers to the content of the notification. Annex II to the PRF Directive contains the fundamental information that is to be transmitted by the vessel in the form of a draft pro forma document.[1302] In this regard, the last and next ports of call are to be indicated, as well as the last port and date when ship-generated waste was delivered. Furthermore, the type and amount of delivered or, as the case may be, remaining waste on board is to be specified.[1303] The obligation to deliver ship-generated waste in a port is, in essence, mandatory. However, this provision is substantially weakened in that an exemption to this is established by Art. 7 (2) PRF Directive. Accordingly, if there is sufficient storage capacity for the onboard generated waste until the next port of delivery, the vessel may not be obliged to discharge its waste.[1304] Notwithstanding this, Member States are obliged to take "all necessary measures" "if there are good reasons to believe that adequate facilities are not available at the intended port of delivery, or if this port is unknown."[1305] Consequently, the Member States are not only obliged to administer the notification of incoming vessels and to receive and supervise the delivery of ship-generated waste, but they have to ensure the adequacy of PRF in the next port of call in the specific circumstance of Art. 7 (2) para.2 PRF Directive.

Although the determination of the adequacy of ports has principally a local scope, the prior notification obligation also has an impact on vessels

---

1300 Art. 6 (1) (a) PRF Directive.

1301 Art. 6 (1) (b and c) PRF Directive. See for a critical analysis Proelß, Meeresschutz im Völker - und Europarecht, 2004, 414.

1302 Art. 6 (1) PRF Directive.

1303 Annex II to the PRF Directive.

1304 The information whether sufficient dedicated storage capacity exists, is taken from the notification requirement as outlined in Art. 6 PRF Directive and also Annex II to the Directive (Art. 7 (2) PRF Directive).

1305 Art. 7 (2) second paragraph PRF Directive.

flying the flag of third States visiting the ports.[1306] In case these vessels are outside of the EEZ of the EU Member States at time of the notification obligation, the scope of the Directive is not applicable to them. However, upon entering the EEZ of any EU Member States, vessels flying the flag of third States are under the obligation to give prior notification.[1307] The notification system of the PRF Directive guarantees a stringent surveillance of the waste streams from ships throughout their journey in the European Union. With a functioning and harmonised notification scheme, it would be possible to monitor the levels of delivered waste and therefore ensure that no onboard generated waste is illegally discharged during the journey.[1308] To this end, a further substantiation of exemptions with precise obligations would, from an environmental protection point of view, increase the protection standard overall.

bb) The fee and cost-recovery system of the PRF Directive

The PRF Directive outlines requirements for fees and cost recovery systems for ship-generated waste. As has been demonstrated in the discussion on the no-special-fee-system envisaged by HELCOM,[1309] the cost recovery system plays a pivotal role in achieving lower illegal discharges rates, as it does reflect the polluter-pays-principle that is one of the guiding principles of the Directive.[1310] The Directive obliges Member States to "ensure that the costs of port reception facilities for ship-generated waste, in-

---

1306 *Ringbom,* The EU maritime safety policy and international law, 2008, 259 *et seq.*

1307 Critical: *Proelß,* Meeresschutz im Völker - und Europarecht, 2004, 414. A somewhat different interpretation applies in case the notification obligation extends to the operator, agent or master of the vessel. A detailed analysis of this difficult legal question relating to the hierarchy of international and surpranational norms would far exceed the scope of this study. For further discussion, see *ibid.* and *Ringbom*, The EU maritime safety policy and international law, 2008, chapter 5.

1308 Similar regarding the difficulties to monitoring the progress towards the objectives of the Directive, *European Commission*, Ex-post evaluation of Directive 2000/59/EC on port reception facilities for ship-generated waste and cargo residues, http://ec.europa.eu/transport/modes/maritime/studies/doc/2015-ex-post-evaluation-of-dir-2000-59-ec.pdf, 121 (last accessed 27.08.2015).

1309 See section B.II.2.a. of chapter 3.

1310 Recital 14 PRF Directive.

cluding the treatment and disposal of the waste, shall be covered through the collection of a fee from ships."[1311] All ships calling at a port of a Member States "shall contribute significantly to the costs […], irrespective of the actual use of the facilities."[1312] From this, the PRF Directive exempts fishing vessels and recreational crafts that do not carry more than 12 passengers.[1313]

The PRF Directive does not stipulate specific fee systems or principles that govern the cost recovery system. Rather, the cost recovery system adopts an inverse approach when it states that the system shall not provide incentives to vessels to discharge their waste into the sea.[1314] Also, recital 14 PRF Directive indicates that "in the interest of protecting the environment," the applied fee system should encourage the delivery of ship-generated waste. However, the PRF Directive remains vague and non-distinct with regard to how this is to be achieved. To this end, it proposes non-exhaustive options such as separate standards or differentiated waste fees relating to the category or size of ship.[1315] The fraction of the costs incurred that are not covered by the fee shall "be covered on the basis of the types and quantities of ship-generated waste actually delivered by the ship."[1316] This addendum serves to significantly minimise the underlying logic of reduced port reception fees so as to reduce potential illegal discharge. Due to economic considerations, ships may opt to deliver a small amount of waste so as to minimise the disposal fees.

A positive aspect of the cost recovery system is the possibility to reduce the fee for those vessels where the master can demonstrate that the vessel ´s environmental management, equipment, design and operation leads to reduced quantities of onboard generated waste.[1317] However, the wording

---

1311 Art. 8 (1) PRF Directive.

1312 Art. 8 (2) (a) PRF Directive.

1313 Art. 8 (2) PRF Directive.

1314 Art. 8 (2) PRF Directive.

1315 Art. 8 (2) (a) PRF Directive. The non-exhaustiveness is indicated by the wording "may be differentiated with respect to, *inter alia*, […]."

1316 Art. 8 (2) (b) PRF Directive.

1317 "[F]ees may be reduced […]," Art. 8 (2) (c) PRF Directive. In the EU, there are some initiatives that deal with the so-called green ships. The Rotterdam Green Award Bureau certifies vessels that have an environmental-friendly waste management system onboard, http://www.greenaward.org/346-requirements.html, last accessed 27.08.2015. To this end, it was recommedend to further refine this aspect during a possible revision of the Directive by defining minimal criteria

of this provision leaves a substantial amount of discretion for the Member States and ports, therefore creating a wide potential of heterogeneous implementation.[1318]

Even though the cost recovery system of the PRF Directive is in essence aimed at reducing incentives to discharge illegally, its substantiation lacks ambitions. This relates to the aspect of the applied fee system and the vague and non-committal exceptions for green vessels. With a view to the overall objective of achieving incentives to reduce illegal discharges, a harmonised cost recovery system on an EU scale would be preferable. Such a development could be effected in the context of a revised PRF Directive.[1319]

In this regard the principle of subsidiarity could be of possible application since "[i]n areas which do not fall within the Union's exclusive competence, the principle of subsidiarity, laid down in the Treaty on European Union, defines the circumstances in which it is preferable for action to be taken by the Union, rather than the Member States."[1320] According to

---

for a more uniform application of a discount on waste fees charged by port reception facilities, in collaboration with IMO, *European Commission*, Ex-post evaluation of Directive 2000/59/EC on port reception facilities for ship-generated waste and cargo residues, http://ec.europa.eu/transport/modes/maritime/studies/doc/2015-ex-post-evaluation-of-dir-2000-59-ec.pdf, 121, last accessed 27.08.2015.

1318 *Carl Bro a/s*, A Study on the Availability and Use of Port Reception Facilities for Ship-Generated Waste De-cember 2005, 11; *Ramboll*, EMSA Study on the Delivery of Ship-Generated Waste and Cargo residues to Port Reception Facilities in EU Ports, 2012, 52. This finding is also confirmed by the ex-post evaluation of the PRF Directive, *European Commission*, Ex-post evaluation of Directive 2000/59/EC on port reception facilities for ship-generated waste and cargo residues, http://ec.europa.eu/transport/modes/maritime/studies/doc/2015-ex-post-evaluation-of-dir-2000-59-ec.pdf, 115, last accessed 27.08.2015, which concluded that ports developed a large numer of different variations to the principle of cost recovery systems that ensure that all ships contribute to the costs of port reception facilities and that limits the transparency of the waste fees charged to port users.

1319 *European Commission*, Public consultation on an impact assessment for a possible revision of Directive 2000/59/EC of the European Parliament and of the Council of 27 November 2000 on port reception facilities for ship-generated waste and cargo residues, consultation period 14.07.-16.09.2011, http://ec.europa.eu/transport/modes/maritime/consultations/2011_09_16_prf_en.htm, last accessed 27.08.2015.

1320 The legal basis is Art. 5 (3) TEU and Protocol No.2 TFEU on the application of the principles of subsidiarity and proportionality. See for an overview on the ori-

Art. 5 (3) TEU, two (cumulative) preconditions exist that initiate the EU's competence to act: first, "the objective of the proposed action cannot be sufficiently achieved by the Member States, either at central level or at regional and local level, [second] but can rather, by reason of the scale or effects of the proposed action, be better achieved at Union level."[1321] Also, it has the function of serving as a justification by the various EU institutions when taking measures.[1322]

On its face harmonisation of cost recovery systems can be better implemented at EU level. The legal basis of the PRF Directive is subject to shared competence between the Member States and the EU. Determining a harmonised cost recovery system cannot be sufficiently achieved only by Member States, due to reasons of scale (competition and environmental protection) that necessitate EU-wide action.[1323] Protocol 30 on Subsidiarity and Proportionality annexed to the EC treaty,[1324] gives a preliminary hint. It provides guidelines that outline whether and when Union action can be justified. Accordingly if the issue has "[…] transnational aspects which cannot be satisfactorily regulated by action by Member States"[1325] and "actions by Member States alone or lack of Community action would conflict with the requirements of the Treaty (such as the need to correct distortion of competition) […] or would otherwise significantly damage Member States' interests […]"[1326] it should be dealt with by the Union.[1327] Depending on the specific elaboration of the cost-recovery system, an EU-

gin and role of this principle in the EU: *Chalmers/Hadjiemmanuel/Monti et al.,* European Union law, 2006, 219 *et seq.*

1321 EUV, AEUV, 2010, Art. 5 TEU.

1322 *Chalmers/Hadjiemmanuel/Monti et al.,* European Union law, 2006, 223.

1323 Admittedly, the precise context and requirements of these elements are vague and have been subject to academic debate and judicial review: *Chalmers/Hadjiemmanuel/Monti et al.,* European Union law, 2006, 219 *et seq.*

1324 Treaty establishing the European Community–D. Protocols annexed to the Treaty establishing the European Community-Protocol (30) on the application of the principles of subsidiarity and proportionality (OJ 2006, 321E, 29.12.2006). The EC treaty is not in force anymore.

1325 Para.5 first indent Protocol 30 on the principles of subsidiarity and proportionality.

1326 Para.5 second indent Protocol 30 on the principles of subsidiarity and proportionality.

1327 The wording in the text refers to the Community.

wide measure is preferable due to the "forum-shopping" of vessels among different ports that could potentially cause a distortion of competition.[1328]

cc) Inspections

The Member States are obliged to ensure that ship-waste is delivered and that a sufficient number of inspections are carried out.[1329] The PRF Directive establishes pre-departure port State enforcement.[1330] To this end, the PRF Directive outlines selection criteria for ships that are made subject to inspection. This refers thus on the one hand to vessels that have not complied with their notification obligation[1331] and also for those ships, where, after the study of the notification information, there are "other grounds to believe that the ship does not comply with this Directive."[1332] If in the view of the responsible authority, the inspections have rendered unsatisfactory results, the authority is obliged to ensure that the ship delivers its waste before it may leave the port.[1333]

If a vessel has already left the port and "clear evidence" indicates that it has not complied with its discharge requirements, the next port authority must be informed which may not permit the vessel to continue its journey until a further assessment of the alleged breach has been made.[1334]

1328 The recent ex-post evaluation of the PRF Directive recommended in this context that during a possible revision of the Directive, further additional guidance to Member States on key elements such as the cost recovery systems is recommended to encourage that the various approaches in the different sea basins around Europe are brought closer together, while respecting subsidiarity, *European Commission*, Ex-post evaluation of Directive 2000/59/EC on port reception facilities for ship-generated waste and cargo residues, http://ec.europa.eu/transport/modes/maritime/studies/doc/2015-ex-post-evaluation-of-dir-2000-59-ec.pdf (last accessed 27.08.2015), 123.

1329 Art. 11 PRF Directive.

1330 *Ringbom,* The EU maritime safety policy and international law, 2008, 327.

1331 Art. 11 (2) (a) first indent PRF Directive.

1332 Art. 11 (2) (a) second indent PRF Directive.

1333 Art. 11 (2) (c) PRF Directive.

1334 Art. 11 (2) (d) PRF Directive.

dd) Waste Handling Plans

Finally, the Member States are, according to Art. 5 (1) PRF Directive, obliged to develop "appropriate waste reception and handling plans." The importance of the waste reception and handling plans are their systematic place in ensuring the general framework relating to information on the competent authority for notification, the delivery of waste, the fee system for delivered waste[1335] and waste treatment.[1336] Furthermore, owing to the importance of the waste reception and handling plans, Annex I to the PRF Directive outlines requirements that must be covered in these plans. This refers, *inter alia*, to information on the capacity of the port reception facilities, the cost recovery system used in the port, procedures for consultation with port stakeholders such as waste contractors or terminal operators and description of the waste management and treatment of vessel-generated waste in the ports.[1337]

c) Proposal for a Port Reception Facility Directive

The analysis above has demonstrated that some aspects of the PRF Directive do not effectively serve to increase the delivery of waste generated onboard and therefore it fails to significantly reduce the purpose to prevent illegal discharges. In order to revise the PRF Directive and to collect feedback from several actors, the Commission initiated a formal review of the Directive in 2011 and launched a public consultation on an impact assessment in 2011.[1338] The completion of the impact assessment was expected

---

1335 This relates for example to the obligation to calculate the fees for waste delivery in a transparent and non-discriminatory manner (Art. 8 (3) PRF Directive).

1336 Art. 5 (1) PRF Directive.

1337 Annex I PRF Directive.

1338 *European Commission*, Public consultation on an impact assessment for a possible revision of Directive 2000/59/EC of the European Parliament and of the Council of 27 November 2000 on port reception facilities for ship-generated waste and cargo residues, consultation period. In an answer to a question of a Member of the European Parliament (Vladko Todorov Panayotov) in September 2010, the European Commissioner (Mr.Kallas) answered that such an impact assessment was expected towards the end of 2010: *European Parliament*, Parliamentary question, Answer given by Mr.Kallas on behalf of the Commission, P-6795/2010, 10.09.2010.

towards the end of 2011.[1339] In 2015, an ex-post evaluation of Directive 2000/59/EC on port reception facilities for ship-generated waste and cargo residues was published.[1340] The study concluded that the principle of mandatory delivery of ship-generated waste is relevant to reducing discharges at sea and improving the protection of the marine environment.[1341] It was also found that many ports do not collect the data on actual deliveries of ship-generated waste and cargo residues in a systematic and comparable way and that the increased volumes of garbage deliveries to port reception facilities indicates that the PRF Directive has been effective in increasing the delivery of garbage to port reception facilities.[1342] Moreover, Member States have interpreted various elements in the PRF Directive in different ways.[1343]

Based on the findings above, the recommendations of the study include that a possible revision of the PRF Directive should encourage the development of measures aimed at reducing the amount of on-board generated waste. In this context, it is suggested to improve the provisions on green shipping in collaboration with IMO by defining minimal criteria for a more uniform application of a discount on waste fees charged by port reception facilities.[1344] Furthermore, a revision of the PRF Directive should consider reporting on delivery statistics in EU ports as well as the systematic consultation of stakeholders in the development and updating of Waste Handling Plans.[1345] Other recommendations include to provide additional guidance to Member State on key elements of the Directive, such as mandatory delivery or relevant requirements on cost recovery systems.[1346]

1339 *Ibid.*

1340 European Commission, Ex-post evaluation of Directive 2000/59/EC on port reception facilities for ship-generated waste and cargo residues, http://ec.europa.eu/transport/modes/maritime/studies/doc/2015-ex-post-evaluation-of-dir-2000-59-ec.pdf (last accessed 27.08.2015).

1341 *Ibid.*, 113.

1342 *Ibid.*, 114.

1343 *Ibid.*, 118.

1344 *Ibid.*, 121.

1345 *Ibid.*

1346 *Ibid.*, 123.

d) Preliminary Conclusion

The PRF Directive is one of the few instruments in EU secondary law that specifically addresses a specific source of marine litter. It is embedded in the context of international and regional obligations. Therefore, it can be understood as a complementary instrument to MARPOL Annex V that aims to substantiate it while at the same time introducing new elements.[1347] This relates to the prior-notification obligation and the cost recovery and fee system. Despite the substantiation, the analysis has demonstrated that the PRF Directive entails certain weaknesses regarding its aim to protect the marine environment from (illegal) discharges of on board-generated waste and cargo residues. Even though the general obligation to discharge is laudable, the elements of the fee and cost recovery system appear to be too vaguely formulated. The exemptions covered therein potentially undermine the overall objective of the Directive.

7. Preliminary Conclusion

The source-related secondary legislation in the European Union covers a broad range of potential sources. The key regulatory system for the issue of marine litter overall is established by the EU waste management system, the reason being, the normative and material scope of the Waste Framework Directive that provides a context for all other subordinated secondary instruments. In this regard the waste hierarchy and its associated obligations are important principles that play a considerable role in waste prevention. Additionally, the environmental protection standards and objective of the Waste Framework Directive serves as a threshold and yardstick for any subsequent measures. The targets established in the Waste Framework Directive for specific waste streams, such as plastic waste, are important regulatory tools to increase the value of plastic as a commodity even after its initial use and to thereby reduce the likelihood of it ending up as marine litter.

In contrast to the high environmental protection standard established by the Waste Framework Directive, the Landfill Directive, addressing a point source of marine litter, is weakened by its somewhat lesser ambitious

---

1347 *Ringbom,* The EU maritime safety policy and international law, 2008, 258.

scope. The Directive does aim to establish technical requirements and is ultimately measured against the overall objective of the Waste Framework Directive. However, certain incongruities such as the undifferentiated categorisation of all municipal waste into landfills storing non-hazardous waste and differentiated protection standards demonstrate a lower environmental protection standard overall.

It is submitted that full compliance with waste legislation as it stands today clearly provides a key to addressing a large share of marine litter sources. However, infringement procedures in the context of waste management legislation account for one of the major shares in environmental law cases overall. Particularly the inadequately implemented and enforced provisions of the Landfill Directive clearly contribute to the issue of marine litter in this context. It is also in the context of waste management, that explicit marine litter related developments are initiated. Whereas the different legislative instruments only indirectly address the issue of marine litter, it has recently received increased attention within the EU institutions, most notably in the form of the Green Paper on a European Strategy on Plastic Waste in the Environment. Its specific aim to launch a consultation on potential solutions to the issue of plastic in the environment serves the purpose of putting the problem of the agenda of the EU institutions and other stakeholders. Since the result of the consultation will feed into the review process of the waste legislation, the value of the Green Paper cannot be underestimated. It opens up a window of opportunity to include explicit mention of the issue of marine litter into legislation.

VI. Impact related legislation

Whereas the source-related legislation discussed above for the most part directly targets potential marine litter sources, the impact-related legislation addresses the impact of human activities in the "receiving" environment. Two "sister" Directives must be analysed in this respect, the Water Framework Directive and the Marine Strategy Framework Directive. Even though the Habitat Directive is categorised under impact-related legislation, it will not be further analysed in this section, the reason being the difficulty as of yet of establishing to a sufficient degree the causation between the impact on biodiversity and the presence of marine litter.[1348]

1. The Water Framework Directive

The protection of the European Union's freshwater is, *inter alia,* regulated by the Water Framework Directive. The purpose and objective of the WFD is particularly ambitious and aims to establish a framework for the protection of surface,[1349] transitional waters,[1350] coastal[1351] and ground waters.[1352] Furthermore, an additional category of water is proposed, namely water bodies that are created by human activities may be labelled as artificial and heavily modified bodies of water.[1353]

The WFD aims to preventing further deterioration and to protect the aquatic ecosystems by way of targeted measures of the progressive reduction of discharges, emissions and losses of priority and hazardous sub-

---

1348 However, it is admitted that marine litter has potentially a negative effect on biodiversity, this is also subject to further scientific knowledge. See also in this regard section B.VII.2.cc. of this chapter.

1349 Surface waters "means inland waters, except groundwater; transitional waters and coastal waters, except in respect of chemical status for which it shall also include territorial waters" (Art. 2 (1) WFD).

1350 Transitional waters "are bodies of surface water in the vicinity of river mouths which are partly saline in character as a result of their proximity to coastal waters but which are substantially influenced by freshwater flows" (Art. 1 (6) WFD).

1351 Coastal water "means surface water on the landward side of a line, every point of which is at a distance of one nautical mile on the seaward side from the nearest point of the baseline from which the breadth of territorial waters is measured, extending where appropriate up to the outer limit of transitional waters" (Art. 2 (7) WFD).

1352 Art. 1 WFD. Groundwater "means all water which is below the surface of the ground in the saturation zone and in direct contact with the ground or subsoil" (Art. 2 (2) WFD).

1353 Art. 2 (8) WFD. A Member State may designate a body of surface water in this category in case "the changes to the hydromorphological characteristics of that body which would be necessary for achieving good ecological status would have significant adverse effects" on, *inter alia,* the wider environment (Art. 4 (3) (a) (i) WFD). See for an overview on the implications of this type of waters *Louka,* Water law & policy, 2008, 58 *et seq.*

stances.[1354] Marine litter considerations relate to "achieving concentrations in the marine environment near background values for naturally occurring substances and close to zero for man-made synthetic substances."[1355] Since litter is most likely to occur in surface waters, their specific environmental objectives as outlined in Art. 4 (1) (a) WFD will be specifically presented.[1356]

The boundary between the freshwater and marine environment is not only addressed from a material point of view under the objectives, but also extends to the geographical scope of the WFD. Consequently, transitional and coastal waters are included in the scope of the Directive and also play a role in determining the objectives of the Directive.[1357]

a) The management units of the WFD– the river basin districts

Before a material assessment of the WFD with regard to marine litter considerations is pursued, a preliminary discussion of the administrative units of the WFD is in order. The WFD follows a river basin approach defined as "the area of land from which all surface run-off flows through a sequence of streams, rivers and, possibly, lakes into the sea at a single river mouth, estuary or delta."[1358] Accordingly, Member States must identify the individual river basins that are then assigned to river basin districts (RBD).[1359] The definition of RBD under the WFD already demonstrate

---

1354 Art. 1 (c) WFD. See for an overview of the WFD *Blöch,* Journal for European Environmental & Planning Law 1 (2004) 170.

1355 Art. 1 (e) WFD. See only: *Lechner/Keckeis/Lumesberger et al.*, Environemntal Pollution 188 (2014) 177.

1356 Analogue provisions of environmental objectives for ground water and protected areas are Art. 4 (1) (b) and 4 (c) WFD respectively. It is important to note in this context that groundwaters contribute water to, or receive water from, surface waters. Therefore groundwater systems that are connected to surface waters theoretically could contain microplastics. However, no studies are currently available on this aspect.

1357 Art. 4 (1) (a) in conjunction with Art. 2 (1) and (18) WFD.

1358 Art. 2 (13) WFD.

1359 Art. 3 (1) WFD. During the drafting of the WFD, certain Member States were reluctant to create one or further competent authorities as the administrative units of the RBD. Concerns related to the costs of creating new units or coordination problems with existing authorities: *Louka,* Water law & policy, 2008, 52. See for an overview on the identified RBD and competent authorities under the

the importance of this management unit: "the area of land and sea, made up of one or more neighbouring river basins together with their associated groundwaters and coastal waters which is identified under Article 3(1) as the main unit for management of river basins." These are points of reference for procedural and material obligations of the WFD. The Member States are under the obligation to establish for each RBD within their territory a programme of measures.

The specific requirements for these are outlined in Art. 11 WFD and include a comprehensive set of elements such as measures for diffuse sources liable to cause pollution.[1360] Also, for each RBD the Member States are to establish river basin management plans in which, *inter alia,* a general description of the characteristics of the RBD is made, significant pressures outlined and details of measures to avoid the pollution of the marine waters are provided.[1361] The WFD follows a cyclical process since the river management plans are revised every six years.[1362] Additionally, the Member States are obliged to ensure that in case a river basin covers the territory of more than one Member State, the specific basin is assigned to an international river basin district (IRBD).[1363] Coastal waters are to be identified and assigned to the nearest or most appropriate RBD.[1364] This administrative approach is not only highly suitable for marine litter con-

---

WFD: *European Commission,* SEC(2007) 362, Commission Staff Working Document, Accompanying document to the Communication from the Commission to the European Parliament and the Council 'Towards Sustainable Water Management in the European Union', First stage in the implementation of the Water Framework Directive 2000/60/EC, 22.03.2007, Annex 3 and Annex 4.

1360 Art. 11 (3) (h) WFD. Pollution "means the direct or indirect introduction, as a result of human activity, of substances or heat into the air, water or land which may be harmful to human health or the quality of aquatic ecosystems or terrestrial ecosystems directly depending on aquatic ecosystems, which result in damage to material property, or which impair or interfere with amenities and other legitimate uses of the environment" (Art. 2 (33) WFD).

1361 Art. 13 WFD in conjunction with Annex VII WFD.

1362 *European Commission,* COM(2012) 670 final, Report from the Commission to the European Parliament and the Council on the Implementation of the Water Framework Directive (2000/60/EC) River Basin Management Plans, 14.11.2012. The Member States were to develop their first river basin management plans and programme of measures by 2009 and update these regularly.

1363 See for a further discussion on these administrative units, section B.VII.1.f. of this chapter. See for a legal discussion on the programme of measures *Baaner,* Journal for European Environmental & Planning Law 8 (2011) 82.

1364 Art. 3 (1) WFD.

siderations. In this way, transboundary effects are integrated into administrative structures that go beyond national jurisdictions.

b) The regulatory approach to protect surface waters under the WFD

The Member States are under the obligation to protect, enhance and restore all bodies of surface water with the aim of achieving good surface status by 2015.[1365] "[G]ood surface water status" is determined as the "status achieved by a surface water body when both its ecological status and its chemical status are at least 'good'."[1366] Consequently good status of the waters covered under the WFD can only be achieved upon the fulfilment of two cumulative criteria: Good Ecological Status (GEcS) and good chemical status.[1367] The Member States are obliged to monitor the water status with a particular focus on these criteria.[1368]

1365 Art. 4 (1) (a) (i) WFD. Body of surface water "means a discrete and significant element of surface water such as a lake, a reservoir, a stream, river or canal, part of a stream, river or canal, a transitional water or a stretch of coastal water" (Art. 2 (10) WFD). The artificial and heavily modified bodies of water are also to achieve by 2015 a good ecological potential and good surface water chemical status (Art. 4 (1) (a) (ii) WFD). Good ecological potential "is the status of a heavily modified or an artificial body of water, so classified in accordance with the relevant provisions of Annex V" (Art. 2 (23) WFD). The aim of achieving a good ecological potential already indicates that these categories are subject to a less stringent requirement profile in comparison to other surface bodies (1.2.5. Annex V WFD). *Reichert* criticises that good ecological potential represents a less ambitious and demanding objective compared to GEcS: *Reichert,* Der nachhaltige Schutz grenzübergreifender Gewässer in Europa, 298. *Jans* and *Vedde*r argue that the considerable leeway in this regard has important consequences on the applicable environmental objectives *Jans/Vedder,* European environmental law, 2012, 394.

1366 Art. 2 (18) WFD. See for a detailed analysis on the approach in this regard *Borja/Elliott/Carstensen et al.,* Marine Pollution Bulletin 60 (2010) 2175.

1367 Regarding the chemical status, surface water also includes territorial waters (Art. 2(1) WFD). *Reinhardt* argues that whereas the GEcS is an aim that is distinguished by its political clarity, its abstractness is not compatible with the requirement of certainty of law in the EU: *Reinhardt,* Natur und Recht 35 (2013) 765, 767.

1368 Art. 8 WFD.

aa) Determining GEcS

The WFD stipulates a definition of ecological status classification of surface waters. [1369] In this context, five categories of reference statuses are listed: high, good, moderate, poor or bad.[1370] Waters having generally 'high' or 'good' ecological status are considered as fulfilling the criteria of GEcS under the WFD.[1371] The WFD is relatively prescriptive since for each of the surface water types (rivers, lakes, transitional waters and coastal waters)[1372] reference conditions for a high, good and moderate status are given.[1373] *Reinhardt* identifies a weakness in the assessment criteria that are based, *inter alia*, on the "normal status" of a water body (see definition of high status), whose determination poses a challenge.[1374]

The GEcS of surface waters is defined by ecological quality elements as outlined in Annex V WFD.[1375] Here, different compartments and aspects of the surface water types are taken as elements in the assessment. These generally relate to biological elements, hydromorphological quality elements and physico-chemical quality (general elements such as transparency coastal or transitional waters such as transparency or specific pollutants).[1376] With regard to marine litter considerations, a preliminary assessment of the different reference conditions leads to the conclusion that no specific reference to litter or plastic is made.

1369 "Ecological status is an expression of the quality of the structure and functioning of aquatic ecosystems associated with surface waters, classified in accordance with Annex V" (Art. 2 (21) WFD).

1370 See only 1.2. Annex V WFD.

1371 For example, the general criteria for a high status are: "[t]here are no, or only very minor, anthropogenic alterations to the values of the physico-chemical and hydromorphological quality elements for the surface water body type from those *normally* associated with that type under undisturbed conditions. The values of the biological quality elements for the surface water body reflect those normally associated with that type under undisturbed conditions, and show no, or only very minor, evidence of distortion" (emphasis added) (Table 1.2. Annex V WFD).

1372 Annex II WFD.

1373 1.2.1-1.2.4. Annex V WFD. Additionally, short descriptions regarding the poor and bad statuses are outlined.

1374 *Reinhardt,* Natur und Recht 35 (2013) 765, 768. The determination of the "normality status" depends on normative substantiation that could be based on the status from twenty, fifty or hundred years ago.

1375 Art. 2 (22) WFD.

1376 See overview Annex V WFD.

bb) Good chemical status

Good chemical status for surface waters is defined as

> the chemical status achieved by a body of surface water in which concentrations of pollutants do not exceed the environmental quality standards established in Annex IX and under Article 16(7), and under other relevant Community legislation setting environmental quality standards at Community level.[1377]

In this context, the WFD refers to emission limit values and environmental quality elements only in regard to certain chemical contaminations instruments.[1378] An environmental quality standard is thus "the concentration of a particular pollutant or group of pollutants in water, sediment or biota which should not be exceeded in order to protect human health and the environment."[1379]

This source control as provided by the WFD is, in particular, valuable for those contaminants where there is confirmed scientific knowledge about the transport in the environment and dose-response relationship of a specific substance. However, criticism has been voiced in this regard since only certain parameters are taken into account in the assessment of a good chemical status. Even though the selected substances represent a broad range of important substances, they do not necessarily depict the diversity of potential substances and the factual status of surface waters.[1380] *Kotulla* argues that therefore a paradoxical situation is created in which waters have *prima facie* a good chemical status despite a significant exposure by pollutants that are not listed under the quality elements.[1381]

A preliminary assessment leads to the conclusion that no specifically relevant aspects for marine litter considerations are included in the WFD. Admittedly, the WFD constitutes an umbrella instrument that cannot explicitly target any substance or environmental issues. Its function is to

---

1377 Art. 2 (24) WFD. According to Art. 16 (6) WFD, the European Commission shall make proposals for the reduction of discharges and emissions and particularly a cessation or phasing-out of these substances, see also *Jekel/Munk,* Zeitschrift für Umweltrecht 10 (2013) 403.

1378 Annex IX WFD, see further section B.VII.1.b.bb. of this chapter.

1379 Art. 2 (35) WFD.

1380 *Kotulla,* Die Bewirtschaftungsziele der §§ 25a-25d, 32c, 33a WHG*, in: Hendler,* Jahrbuch des Umwelt- und Technikrechts (2005) 185–220, 202.

1381 *Ibid.*

"provide common principles and the overall framework for action."[1382] The question remains to be answered whether the issue of marine litter can be subsumed under the provisions of the WFD. A particular aspect will be whether the lack of a reference to solid waste or plastics constitutes a lacuna in the EU freshwater regulation approach.

c) Marine litter considerations despite a clear reference in the WFD?

The lack of explicit mention or reference of marine litter in the WFD could potentially lead to a situation in which the core instrument of the European Union to address freshwater pollution does not integrate marine litter considerations. This could further result in Member States being under no obligation to develop measures and to take actions to eliminate or reduce this substance under the WFD. However, even though the WFD does not explicitly address marine litter, several factors would seem to suggest the contrary.

aa) The use of quality elements for GEcS for the classification of marine litter

The prescriptive indications of quality elements for the different water surface types are the central starting point for the integration of marine litter into the WFD. It is argued that marine litter is relevant in the context of some of the quality elements and therefore its presence could have an impact on the status of the water. Since the WFD applies a differentiated regime regarding the surface water body, a selection of pertinent dedicated quality elements for rivers, lakes, transitional and coastal waters is made.

A first factor of relevance for marine litter considerations can be found in criteria for morphological conditions in which the structure and substrate of the river, lake or coastal bed respectively, the lake shore or the

1382 Recital 18 WFD. *Louka* describes it as a planning and process instrument in which the "focus of the directive is not so much on the accomplishment of specific, quantitative goals but on the establishment of an institutional structure and process that facilitates integrated water management": *Louka,* Water law & policy, 2008, 54.

river riparian zone are to be considered.[1383] In this regard, the presence of litter either on the river, lake or coastal bed can have an impact on its reference status. The 'high status' reference condition for lakes is: "[l]ake depth variation, quantity and structure of the substrate, and both the structure and condition of the lake shore correspond totally or nearly totally to undisturbed conditions." [1384] Additionally, the 'transparency' quality element as stipulated as under the physico-chemical quality element in lakes, transitional and coastal water is relevant in this context.[1385] The 'good' reference status for transitional water outlines that "[...] transparency [does] not reach levels outside the ranges established so as to ensure the functioning of the ecosystem and the achievement of the values specified above for the biological quality elements."[1386] The relevance of this element can be explained in that the presence of marine litter could reduce the transparency of these waters. However, this argument is simultaneously limited by the highly dynamic spatial distribution that is characteristic for litter. Litter can be rapidly dispersed through quickly moving streams and rivers after heavy rainfalls or snow melts, therefore being highly variable in its spatial distribution.

bb) Marine litter in the context of chemical pollution of surface waters

The strategy against pollution of water as stipulated in Art. 16 WFD indicates that "[t]he European Parliament and the Council shall adopt specific measures against pollution of water by individual pollutants or groups of pollutants presenting a significant risk to or via the aquatic environment [...]."[1387] In this regard, the European Commission is obliged to submit a proposal on priority substances that are selected among those contaminants mentioned in Art. 16 (1) WFD. According to Art. 16 (11) WFD this list was incorporated into the Directive in Annex X WFD. Currently, the

1383 1.1.1. and 1.1.2. Annex V WFD.

1384 1.2.1. Annex V WFD. Similar for coastal waters: "[t]he depth variation, structure and substrate of the coastal bed, and both the structure and condition of the inter-tidal zones correspond totally or nearly to the undisturbed conditions" 1.2.4. Annex V WFD.

1385 Presentation given by Leo *De Vrees,* The EU and its role on reducing marine litter, Conference: Marine Litter at the European level, Brussels, 13.03.2013.

1386 1.2.3. Annex V WFD.

1387 Art. 16 (1) WFD.

environmental quality standards are outlined in Annex I of the Directive 2008/105/EC on environmental quality standards in the field of water policy in 2008 (EQSD).[1388] The EQSD prescribes environmental quality standards for priority substances in surface waters and authorises the list of priority and priority hazardous substances.[1389] According to Art. 1 EQSD, good chemical status is reached for a water body when it complies with the environmental quality status for all the priority substances and other pollutants listed in Annex I EQSD.

Annex II WFD confirms the list of priority substances and lists certain priority substances that are also associated with plastics.[1390] In this context the plasticisers *di-2-ethylhexylphthalat (DEHP)*[1391] and also *nonylphenol*[1392] are listed as priority substances.[1393] The possibility of leaching of these two substances from the plastic into the environment[1394] is thus theoretically an option in constructing the argument that chemical aspects of marine litter are covered under the WFD. A possible causation between these two substances and the presence of plastic in the water body could serve as an indicator for the presence of marine litter under the WFD.[1395]

However, such a hypothesis based on a possible causation between the presence of certain plasticisers and plastics has significant limits. Even though the presence of additive-derived chemicals in the context of marine

---

1388 Directive 2008/105/EC of the European Parliament and of the Council of 16 December 2008 on environmental quality standards in the field of water policy, amending and subsequently repealing Council Directives 82/176/EEC, 83/513/EEC, 84/156/EEC, 84/491/EEC, 86/280/EEC and amending Directive 2000/60/EC of the European Parliament and of the Council (OJ 2008 L 348/84).

1389 See only Annex I in conjunction with Art. 3 EQSD.

1390 Presentation given by *Leo De Vrees,* The EU and its role on reducing marine litter, Conference: Marine litter at the European level, Brussels, 13.03.2013.

1391 *Ibid.*; *Sasakawa/Mitomi,* Vox Sanguinis 34 (1978) 81.

1392 *Loyo-Rosales/Rosales-Rivera/Lynch et al.,* J. Agric. Food Chem 52 (2004) 2016, 2016.

1393 Number 12 and 24 respectively Annex II EQSD.

1394 Presentation given by *Leo De Vrees,* The EU and its role on reducing marine litter, Conference: Marine litter at the European level, Brussels, 13.03.2013.

1395 A different aspect could also be polyaromatic hydrocarbons (PAH) that are also listed as priority substance and priority hazardous substance (number 28) under Annex II EQSD. Furthermore, PCB and also Bisphenol A are listed as those substances under Annex III EQSD that are subject to review as being identified as either priority or priority hazardous substances. See for a discussion on their role with regard to the ecotoxicty of marine litter, chapter 1.

litter has been confirmed,[1396] the reservations can be explained. First, *nonylphenol* does not necessarily have to be contained in every type of plastic. The use and application of *nonylphenol* is not only limited to plastics, since *nonylphenol*, for example, also originates from the degradation of *nonylphenol ethoxylates* that are used as industrial surfacants.[1397] In this context, no direct correlation between additives and plastic exists. Moreover, the marketing and use of *nonylphenol* and *nonylphenol ethoxylate,* for example, is restricted in the European Union.[1398]

The WFD follows a comprehensive monitoring scheme in which the Member States are, *inter alia,* required to establish monitoring programmes for water status in their different river basin district, including for surface waters as well as monitoring for ecological and chemical status and ecological potential.[1399] An intercalibration exercise stipulated in the WFD ensures that the reference statuses are consistent among Member States.[1400] Taken from the preliminary assessment above, this monitoring does not necessarily include litter or plastics. However, some of the possibly pertinent quality elements are covered under the monitoring programmes. In this context, the monitoring frequency stipulated in Annex V WFD can also be regarded as an aspect that is relevant in the context of the marine litter discourse.[1401] Here, the quality elements of the WFD are coupled with specific time frames in which exemplarily the morphology of rivers, lakes, transitional and coastal waters are to be monitored every 6 years.[1402] The limits of this frequency are that the problem of marine litter can build up much quicker than the proposed 6 years.

In summary, even though the WFD does not explicitly address aspects of litter pollution in freshwaters covered under its scope, certain aspects can be subsumed under its provisions. This relates to certain quality ele-

---

1396 *Teuten/Saquing/Knappe et al.,* Philosophical Transactions of the Royal Society B: Biological Sciences 364 (2009) 2027, 2037.

1397 *Soares/Guieysse/Jefferson et al.,* Environment International 34 (2008) 1033, 1033.

1398 Directive 2003/53/EC of the European Parliament and of the Council of 18 June 2003 amending for the 26th time Council Directive 76/769/EEC relating to restrictions on the marketing and use of certain dangerous substances and preparations (nonylphenol, nonylphenol ethoxylate and cement) (OJ 2003, L 178/43).

1399 Art. 8 (1) (ii) WFD.

1400 1.4.1. Annex V WFD.

1401 1.3.4. Annex V WFD.

1402 1.3.4. Annex V WFD.

ments and also some aspects with regard to chemical pollution. Admittedly, the construction of the relevance of litter aspects is somewhat cumbersome and does not entirely render a completely convincing result. Nonetheless, certain aspects of the WFD indirectly relate to important aspects of litter pollution in freshwater. This relates on the one hand to the combined approach to control point, general monitoring obligations for diffuse sources and the no deterioration principle.

The precise application, content and binding effect of the no deterioration principle as contained in the WFD has been subject to dispute.[1403] This is explained, *inter alia*, by the vague definition of the principle of no deterioration in the WFD that leaves leeway for interpretation.[1404] Also, the precise point at which deterioration occurs is disputed. According to the status-quo-theory, every adverse consequence on the water implies deterioration, even though it has not resulted in a categorisation in a lower reference status overall. [1405] On the other hand, the step-theory implies that deterioration occurs in case a change from a higher reference condition into a lower reference condition as outlined by the WFD ensues.[1406] In order to clarify this, the European Commission has issued a "Guidance Document on Exemptions to the Environmental Objectives" in 2009.[1407] It states that the deterioration is "expressed in terms of classes,"[1408] consequently favouring the step-theory.[1409] With a view to the need to further

---

1403 See only: *Faßbender/Kurt,* EurUP (2/2013) 70, 74 *et seq*. Also among EU Member States, the application of the no deterioration principle is differently understood.

1404 See Art. 1 (a) WFD "prevents further deterioration […]" and Art. 4 (1) (a) (i) and (b) (i) WFD. However, despite the comprehensive catalogue of definitions in Art. 2 WFD, the concept of deterioration has not been defined *Wabnitz,* Das Verschlechterungsverbot für Oberflächengewässer und Grundwasser, 2010, 252.

1405 See for a comprehensive and detail review of the different aspects of the interpretation of the non-deterioration principle in the WFD *Wabnitz,* Das Verschlechterungsverbot für Oberflächengewässer und Grundwasser, 2010; *Faßbender/Kurt,* EurUP (2/2013) 70.

1406 *Faßbender/Kurt,* EurUP (2/2013) 70, 74.

1407 *European Commission/DG ENV*, Guidance Document on Exemptions to the Environmental Objectives, Guidance Document No.20, Common Implementation Strategy for the Water Framework Directive (2000/60/EC), 2009. The Guidance Document is not legally binding.

1408 European Commission, Guidance Document No.20 on Exemptions to the Environmental Objectives, 27.

1409 *Faßbender/Kurt,* EurUP (2/2013) 70, 79.

clarify the extent and content of the deterioration principle of the WFD in general,[1410] its relevance to (micro) plastics is currently only limited.

d) The combined approach to control point and diffuse sources–addressing microplastics

The WFD explicitly stipulates a combined approach to point and diffuse sources. It targets water pollution directly at the source. The source-based approach is developed in Art. 10 WFD and obliges Member States to "ensure that all discharges referred to in paragraph 2 into surface waters are controlled according to the combined approach […]."[1411] The obligations regarding point sources are to be addressed by establishing or implementing emission controls that are based on best available techniques and emission limit values.[1412] The approach of the WFD regarding diffuse sources is a significant aspect as it relates to quality criteria in the receiving environment, "therefore putting an end to the old dispute between these two antagonist approaches."[1413]

The integration provision of Art. 10 (c) WFD establishes that the control of these sources are to follow "as appropriate" best environmental practice as established in certain EU instruments. Among the listed instruments, the Urban Waste Water Directive (UWWTD) is particularly relevant with a view to household waste as a potential source of marine litter.[1414] This Directive targets the effluents of waste water plants into the environment. The UWWTD addresses the collection, treatment and discharge of certain industrial sectors and urban waste waters.[1415] Its objective is to protect the environment from the adverse effects of these waste

1410 *Faßbender* suggests a preliminary reference to the CJEU on this matter: *Faßbender/Kurt,* EurUP (2/2013) 70, 84.

1411 Art. 10 (1) WFD.

1412 Art. 10 (2) (a and b) WFD.

1413 *Olazábal,* Europe and the environment, in *Onida,* Europe and the environment (2004) 157–172, 167.

1414 Amongst others the WFD also lists Council Directive 91/676/EEC of 12 December 1991 concerning the protection of waters against pollution caused by nitrates from agricultural sources (OJ 1991 L 375) and also the Directives listed in Annex IX WFD and Art. 16 WFD (Art. 10 (2) (c) WFD).

1415 Art. 1 UWWTD.

waters.[1416] All agglomerations are accordingly to provide a collecting system for waste water.[1417] With a view to the aspect of microplastics from personal care products or clothing,[1418] the definition of urban waste water is highly indicative for these kind of sources. Urban waste water itself refers to "domestic waste water or the mixture of domestic waste water with industrial waste water and/or run-off rain water."[1419] In consequence, the definition of domestic waste water as "waste water from residential settlements and services which originates predominantly [...] from household activities"[1420] clearly outlines the relevance of this Directive for marine litter considerations.

The Directive goes onto outline that urban waste water collecting systems of agglomerations of more than 2000 inhabitants must ensure that these waters have been subject to secondary treatment or equivalent before their discharge into freshwaters and estuaries.[1421] Waste water that has been discharged under these circumstances, has thus been subject to primary treatment in which suspended and floating solids are removed from the sewage and also secondary treatment. Here, the sewage is usually exposed to aerobic biological processes in which dissolved organic matters are removed by microorganisms. Despite these standards, it is believed that primary microplastics in particular are released through the effluents of waste water treatment plants.[1422]

As a preliminary hint, it is submitted that even though larger pieces of plastic are removed from sewage during primary treatment, the filters of

1416 Art. 1 UWWTD.

1417 Art. 3 UWWTD.

1418 See on these aspects chapter 1.

1419 Art. 2 (1) UWWTD.

1420 Art. 2 (2) UWWTD.

1421 Art. 4 (1) UWWTD. The UWWTD establishes a system of different obligations regarding different waste water treatment systems. This relates, *inter alia,* to differentiated obligations regarding waste water effluents in so-called sensitive areas (Art. 5 in conjunction with Annex II UWWTD) and less sensitive areas (Art. 6 in conjunction with Annex II UWWTD). Here the time frames when different collecting systems are to be implemented are associated to population equivalents, see only Art. 4 (1) UWWTD). See for an overview on the UWWTD: *Jans/Vedder,* European environmental law, 2012, 413 *et seq.*

1422 *Browne/Galloway/Thompson,* Integrated Environmental Assessment and Management 3 (2007) 559, 561; *Browne/Crump/Niven et al.,* Environmental Science & Technology 45 (2011) 9175.

treatment plans are not specially designed to collect microplastics.[1423] Usually, solid material in waste water treatment plants is removed through screens which differ in their sizes, depending on the target material. Coarse or so-called bar screens with more than 6mm openings are the main part of the first unit treatment process and remove solid waste that could potentially interfere with the downstream operators of the treatment plant such as pumps and valves.[1424] Fine screens have an opening between 1, 5-6 mm. Only under circumstances where the standard of secondary effluents is intended to increase to tertiary standards are microscreens of openings between 1 μ and 0,3 mm used.[1425]

For agglomerations of less than 2000 inhabitants situated close to estuaries or freshwater or agglomerations of less than 10000 inhabitants that discharge directly into coastal waters, the waste water treatment has to receive "appropriate" treatment.[1426] Appropriate treatment is defined as "treatment of urban waste water by any process and/or disposal system which after discharge allows the receiving waters to meet the relevant quality objectives and the relevant provisions of this and other Community Directives."[1427] Even though the direct reference to the WFD is laudable, the absence of pertinent litter elements in the WFD limits the purpose of the reference norm, therefore also weakening the scope and purpose of the UWWTD with regard to marine litter considerations.

Additionally, the sludge of waste water treatment plants that accumulates, *inter alia*, during the biological treatment processes of waste water could be a source of microplastics. Since it has been confirmed that terrestrial soils having received sewage, for example as organic fertilisers, con-

---

1423 *Ibid.*, 9176. Note that the discussion regarding the pathways of primary microplastics is still subject to uncertainties and knowledge gaps, see chapter 1 for further information.

1424 *Vesilind/Rooke*, Wastewater treatment plant design, 2003, chapter 4, 2; *Walker*, Principles of ecotoxicology, 2006, 24.

1425 *Vesilind/Rooke*, Wastewater treatment plant design, 2003, chapter 4, 2.

1426 Art. 7 UWWTD.

1427 Art. 2 (9) UWWTD. The UWWTD also relates to transboundary effects in which Member States are under an obligation to notify and consult with each other (Art. 9 UWWTD). Furthermore, the UWWTD also the competent authorities in the Member States are not only obliged to monitor discharges of waste water (Art. 15 UWWTD) but also to publish reports on urban waste water effluents and the disposal of sludge (Art. 16 UWWTD).

tain microfibers,[1428] their run-offs could also be a source of marine litter. The legislative answer to the risk associated with sewage sludge is that the UWWTD requires that "disposal routes shall minimise the adverse effects on the environment."[1429] The former commonly used practice of dumping sewage sludge into surface waters by vessel or pipeline[1430] has been prohibited by virtue of Art. 14 (3) UWWTD since 31st December 1998. The combined-source approach of the WFD is a highly relevant regulatory technique for marine litter considerations. The explicit mention of the UWWTD in the context of the WFD strengthens the indispensable link between source-related and impact-related legislations.

e) Preliminary remarks

The interpretation of the WFD with regard to marine litter considerations has shown that this aspect is not explicitly mentioned in the instrument. The 'construction' of possible relevant issues is cumbersome and necessitates a wide understanding of several elements. In this respect, the quality elements for ecological status such as "transparency" only partially result in a successful integration of litter aspects into the WFD. The attempt to construct the relevance of chemical pollution monitoring in the context of the presence of chemicals associated with plastics, is significantly aggravated by the difficult causation chain between their presence in the environment and the occurrence of plastics. Thus, the potential applicable scope of the WFD with regard to this aspect is highly dependent on coincidences such as the presence of litter during routine monitoring. The somewhat intricate construction, in which the presence of litter in the surface water bodies of the WFD is only covered under certain circumstances, runs the risk of ignoring the fact that land-based sources account for up to 80% of marine litter. In this context, however, the combined source approach of the WFD strengthens the indispensable link between source-related and impact-related legislations. This is in particular relevant with a view to the UWWTD.

1428 *Zubris/Richards,* Environmental Pollution 138 (2005) 201, 211.

1429 Art. 14 (1) UWWTD.

1430 *Browne/Crump/Niven et al.,* Environmental Science & Technology 45 (2011) 9175, 9176.

f) The transboundary co-operation obligations of the WFD in light of marine litter considerations

The different material obligations contained in the WFD such as the coordination to achieve the environmental objectives of Art. 4 WFD or the programme of measures are aligned in the context of RBD.[1431] The implementation of the WFD is based on an institutionalised co-operation for the whole of the RBD.[1432] For IRBD, the necessary coordination may be pursued through the "use [of] existing structures stemming from international agreements."[1433] The obligation to co-ordinate also relates to RBD that extends beyond EU territory and in this context the concerned Member State or Member States "shall endeavour to establish appropriate coordination with the relevant non-EU Member States, with the aim of achieving the objectives of this Directive throughout the river basin district."[1434] In so doing, the concerned Member States shall for IRBD "together ensure this coordination and may, for this purpose, use existing structures stemming from international agreements."[1435] The competent authorities required under Art. 3 (2) WFD can, according to Art. 3 (6) WFD, refer to an "existing national or international body." The references relate to conventions and also subsequently created commissions that deal with different aspects of freshwater protection such as the allocation of water resources or pollution control in Europe.[1436]

As a result, an instrument of international law is used to implement EU law. With a view to the transboundary issue of marine litter, an analysis is necessary whether the procedural obligations under the WFD to coordinate in the framework of IRBD have an impact on marine litter regulation in a freshwater context. The reasoning being that, similar to the Regional Seas Conventions, the work on marine litter in these fora potentially has also a programmatic impact on marine litter regulation from land-based

---

1431 Art. 3 (4) WFD.

1432 *Bruha/Maaß Christian A.,* Integrierte Gewässerpolitik in Europa, in *Bruha/ Koch,* Integrierte Gewässerpolitik in Europa (2001) 69–118, 104.

1433 Art. 3 (4) in conjunction with Art. 3 (6) WFD. Also, the Member States are also obliged to attribute a competent authority to each river basin district lying within their territory (Art. 3 (2) WFD).

1434 Art. 3 (5) WFD. *Louka,* Water law & policy, 2008, 54.

1435 Art. 3 (4) WFD.

1436 See for an overview on freshwater resources legislation and case law: *Beyerlin/ Marauhn,* International environmental law, 2011, chapter 11.

pollution. Hence an additional regulatory layer would reinforce and strengthen the freshwater protection regime relating to marine litter. In order to understand the possible role of these conventions, a short introduction on a few conventions sketches out the scope and major leverage for marine litter in their established system. Subsequently, it will be analysed whether and to what degree marine litter is considered and how a potential absence affects the regulatory regime.

Pertinent international agreements cover, depending on the case, either entire river-basins or sub-basins.[1437] In this case study three rivers will be analysed since they are major tributaries in Europe: the Danube, Elbe and Rhine. In the following the coordination platforms for these rivers under the WFD will be analysed with a view to their potential role in addressing marine litter.[1438] The international river convention addressing the protection of the Danube is the Danube River Protection Convention.[1439] Amongst one of the goals of the Danube River Protection Convention is the reduction of pollution loads of the Black Sea from sources in the catchment area.[1440] The Convention on the International Commission for the Protection of the Elbe is the legal basis for the establishment of the In-

1437 *Epiney/Felder,* Überprüfung internationaler wasserwirtschaftlicher Übereinkommen im Hinblick auf die Implementierung der Wasserrahmenrichtlinie, 2002, 150. This relates for example to the Mosel River that is a tributary to the Rhine but that also has a specific regulatory protection regime, see for further information the homepage of the International Commission for the protection of the Mosel and Saar, http://www.iksms-cipms.org/servlet/is/391/, last accessed 27.08.2015.

1438 The protection regime of Europe´s freshwaters also relate to issues of navigation and specific sectoral agreements: see only for an overview on the protection system of the Rhine: *Kiss/Shelton,* International environmental law, op. 2004, 408 *et seq*.

1439 See section D.I. of chapter 3. See for an account of the plastic pollution in the Danube river: *Lechner/Keckeis/Lumesberger et al.*, Environemntal Pollution 188 (2014) 177.

1440 Art. 2 (1) Danube River Protection Convention. The catchment area of the Danube River is defined as "the hydrological river basin as far as it is shared by the Contracting Parties" (Art. 1 (b) Danube River Protection Convention). See on a comprehensive overview on the development of the Danube river protection regime and the interaction between a "shoreline instrument" and a "watercourse specific regime" in the context of the Danube and the Black Sea: *Vinogradov,* The International Journal of Marine and Coastal Law 22 (2007) 585.

ternational Commission for the Protection of the Elbe River (ICPER).[1441] One of the central tasks of the ICPER is to reduce substantially the pollution of the North Sea from the Elbe area.[1442] The pertinent protection agreement for the River Rhine is the Convention on the Protection of the Rhine of 1990.[1443] It establishes the International Commission for the Protection of the Rhine (ICPR).[1444] This agreement is also dedicated to reduce the inputs of pollutants into the North Sea.[1445] Even though the different agreements differ somewhat with regard to their specific mandate and approach, the three international river conventions studied for the Elbe, Danube and Rhine share, *inter alia,* one common denominator: their aim to reduce the pollution loads of the rivers into the respective receiving marine environment.

In this regard, marine litter considerations could, in principle, be included in the work of these commissions, therefore potentially influencing or complementing the implementation and coordination requirements under the WFD. In particular with a view to land-locked States, the coordination requirements under the WFD in the context of these freshwater protection commissions could contribute to address this issue far inland and also beyond national and, as the case may be, EU borders.[1446] Admittedly, identi-

---

1441 (OJ 1991 L 321 23.11.1991). The ICPER is established following the Protocol to the Convention of 8 October 1990 between the Governments of the Federal Republic of Germany and the Czech and Slovak Federal Republic and the European Economic Community on the International Commission for the Protection of the Elbe (OJ 1993 L 045, 23.02.1993). Please note however that even though major tributaries of the river Elbe also stem from the territories of Poland and Austria, they are only observers to the ICPER. See for further information the ICPER´s homepage, http://www.ikse-mkol.org/index.php?id=1&L=2, last accessed 27.08.2015.

1442 Art. 1 (2) (c) Convention on the International Commission for the Protection of the Elbe.

1443 Convention on the Protection of the Rhine (Bern) of 12 April 1999, in force 01 January 2003; EMuT 999:28; (OJ 2000 L 289, 16.11.2000). The Contracting Parties are: Germany, European Union, France, Luxemburg, the Netherlands, Switzerland. See for a preliminary overview on this Convention *Beyerlin/ Marauhn,* International environmental law, 2011, 109.

1444 See for further information the ICPR´s homepage http://www.iksr.org/index.php?id=58, last accessed 27.08.2015.

1445 Art. 3 Convention on the Protection of the Rhine.

1446 See only the institutional adjustments to adapt to procedural requirements under the WFD in the context of the ICPER: Workgroup on the Implementation of the EU Water Framework Directive in the Elbe River basin (WFD), http://

fying relevant marine litter aspects in the overall context of the work of these commissions is, in principle, too simplistic, given their complex and historically developed mandates.[1447] A preliminary analysis, however, indicates that pertinent provisions such as the obligation to provide general rules to establish emission limits of waste water discharges[1448] or point and diffuse sources[1449] are envisaged.

An understanding of whether aspects of the marine litter issue can be found either in the material law of these conventions or in their organisational structure or work is necessary in order to understand the synergies and differences between EU freshwater law and international law. This approach is, nevertheless, limited by two conditions. First, this relates on the one hand to the fact that these commissions can only in a functionally limited way serve as coordination mechanisms for the WFD since their material and geographical scope and competences do not cover all aspects of the WFD.[1450] The nexus between public international and European Union law potentially poses certain limitation with regard to the role and scope of each agreement with regard to the instrument of EU law. Therefore only certain aspects of the WFD are implemented in the framework of IRBD.[1451] As *Epiney* and *Felder* point out, the commissions are, *inter alia,* able to carry out the obligations to monitor and analyse as is required under Art. 6 - 8 WFD.[1452] This would thus be marginally relevant for ma-

www.ikse-mkol.org/index.php?id=76&L=2, last accessed 27.08.2015. See also *Louka,* Water law & policy, 2008, 345.The ICPDR has been nominated as the implementation platform for the adoption of river management plans for the Danube under the WFD: *Louka,* Water law & policy, 2008, 276.

1447 See for an overview on the regime pertinent to transboundary water pollution as existent in 1993: *Nollkaemper,* The legal regime for transboundary water pollution, 1993, 9. See the historical development of the freshwater protection regime of the River Rhine: *Nollkaemper,* International watercourses law for the 21st century, in *Subedi,* International watercourses law for the 21st century (2005) 151–166.

1448 Art. 5 (4) (a) Convention on the Protection of the Rhine, Art. 7 (1) Danube River Protection Convention.

1449 Art. 2 (1) (f) ICPER.

1450 *Epiney/Felder*, Überprüfung internationaler wasserwirtschaftlicher Übereinkommen im Hinblick auf die Implementierung der Wasserrahmenrichtlinie, 2002, 151 *et seq.*

1451 *Reichert,* Der nachhaltige Schutz grenzübergreifender Gewässer in Europa, 340 *et seq*.

1452 *Epiney/Felder*, Überprüfung internationaler wasserwirtschaftlicher Übereinkommen im Hinblick auf die Implementierung der Wasserrahmen-

rine litter considerations.[1453] Second, the institutionalised co-operation between different countries in the context of these commissions addresses the transboundary nature of the problem of water pollution in a coordinated manner. This is also reinforced by the co-operation between certain freshwater protection commissions and marine protection conventions. Such a co-operation, acknowledging the interdependence of the water system, can be seen in the observer status of the ICPR to the OSPAR Commission.[1454]

Marine litter located at the intersection of these regulatory nexuses is a "suitable" polluting substance that can be the subject of attention for both fora. However, with regard to the significance of land-based pollution in marine litter pollution, it is interesting to note that the ICPR, ICPDR and ICPER have not dedicated any further attention to this issue at international level, at this stage.[1455] Therefore, a further reinforcement or mutual influence and contribution of considerations relating to marine litter through these international river commissions is not discernible at this stage. Even though they would serve as highly suitable coordination platforms, these conventions and co-operation structures currently do not serve as addi-

---

richtlinie, 2002, 152. They also refer to the establishment of management plans and the related reporting duties (Art. 13 and 15 WFD), public participation obligation (Art. 14 WFD) and coordination duties (Art. 3 (4) and (5) WFD).

1453 See only the limited relevance of marine litter related aspects of monitoring, B.VII.1.b. of this chapter.

1454 OSPAR Commission Observers, http://www.ospar.org/content/content.asp?menu=00120000000028_000000_000000, last updated 27.08.2015, last accessed 27.08.2015. As an example, the regional measures of the HELCOM RAP ML to strengthen collaboration with River Basin Management is also a mechanism to strengthen collaboration between Regional Seas Organisations as well as River Basin Commission, see for further information Chapter 3.F of this document.

1455 This information has been gathered by means of written correspondence with members of staff of the ICPR (date of answer to the inquiry: 03 May 2013), ICPDR (date of answer to the inquiry: 07 May 2013) and ICPER (date of answer to the inquiry: 13 May 2013). The electronic correspondence is present with the author. The ICPDR administers an inventory of accident risk spots in which *inter alia* contaminated sites also including landfills and dumps in areas liable to flooding are registered, http://www.icpdr.org/main/issues/accidental-pollution, last accessed 27.08.2015. In the setting of the Green Danube Partnership, the ICPDR was involved in a bottle collection and recycling project in the river Tisza.

tional regulatory layers to address the sources and pathways of land-based marine litter.

g) Preliminary Conclusion

The WFD intends to contribute, *inter alia,* to protect surface waters and applies in this context a drainage basin approach. The aim of the WFD is to achieve GEcS and good chemical status of all surface waters. It does so by using a "deconstructing, structural approach" in that it differentiates between the different constituent parts of the ecosystem.[1456] The assessment of these elements is then used to define the status of the surface body water. Even though the WFD applies a comprehensive regulatory scope with regard to several ecosystem elements, it does not cover explicitly marine litter under its scope. In the assumption that land-based pollution accounts for 80% of the sources of marine litter, the importance of the WFD, with regard to its management, cannot be underestimated. However, the synopsis of categorising marine litter into the scope of the WFD by applying and interpreting its material law, does not render entirely satisfactory results.

The no deterioration principle could serve as an indicator that cumulative and low-threshold damages such as those caused by (micro) plastics are also to be considered under the WFD. The debate on its content and application however poses significant limits on the evaluation of its relevance for litter considerations in surface waters. A particularly laudable aspect of the WFD is the combined approach for point and diffuse sources in which existing source-related legislation is included in the regulatory method. In this way, the potential impacts from these sources are to be addressed in the context of the WFD. The Member States only enjoy a limited degree of discretion in that the specific instruments are explicitly mentioned in the WFD. However, with a view to the factual situation and also the combined approach to control point and diffuse sources, the explicit inclusion of marine litter aspects would increase the legal certainty of this

1456 *Borja/Elliott/Carstensen et al.,* Marine Pollution Bulletin 60 (2010) 2175, 2176. A deconstructing approach "can be summed up as taking the ecosystem, separating it (deconstructing it) into its constituent parts, or at least those parts considered important, the so-called BQE, then assessing the individual quality of each BQE, then using a combining rule to put these back together and then assume that the outcome summarises and protects the whole ecosystem […]."

instrument regarding the issue of marine litter. This relates not only to its integration in the ecological quality elements that would then extend to the monitoring of plastics, for example. Without claiming that the explicit inclusion of plastics in the WFD would solve the issue of marine litter in the European seas, it could however contribute to increase knowledge regarding its sources and impacts in fresh waters.

With regard to the overall structure of the WFD, it is submitted that given its nature and *raison d'être* as an instrument aiming at facilitating such an ambitious and complex undertaking as to protect and preserve the body of surface water and groundwater in the European Union, marine litter or plastics respectively cannot be a central consideration. Certainly, an argument can be made that in the end, marine litter occurs in and impacts on the marine environment and marine organisms respectively. This lays the ground for the argumentation that the Marine Strategy Framework Directive is the applicable instrument for marine litter. Such an understanding could result in a potential transfer of the core of the problem from the context of freshwater legislation (source) to the receiving environment, the oceans (impacts). A specific and explicit integration of aspects of marine litter or plastics in the WFD would also be in line with the precautionary principle and the source principle that are not only embodied in EU primary law but also explicitly mentioned in recital 11 WFD.

2. The Marine Strategy Framework Directive in the context of the marine litter discourse

The Marine Strategy Framework Directive (MSFD) does not set out to address a specific sectoral source of pollution or activity, but rather establishes a regulatory framework for the marine environment in general.[1457] It is also in this context, that the issue of marine litter is directly considered and mentioned in EU secondary legislation. The following assessment aims to understand and apply the relevance of its geographical and material scope to marine litter considerations.

1457 "This Directive establishes a framework […]" Art. 1 (1) MSFD. See generally, *Juda,* Ocean Development & International Law 38 (2007) 259; *Barreira,* Environmental Law Network International (2012) 46.

a) The geographical scope of the MSFD

The geographical scope of the MSFD extends to marine waters that are defined according to Art. 3 (1) (a) MSFD as

> waters, the seabed and subsoil on the seaward side of the baseline from which the extent of territorial waters is measured extending to the outmost reach of the area where a Member State has and/or exercises jurisdictional rights, in accordance with the Unclos, with the exception of waters adjacent to the countries and territories mentioned in Annex II to the Treaty and the French Overseas Departments and Collectivities […].

Consequently, the WFD and the MSFD somewhat overlap in their geographical scope in that both instruments apply to coastal waters, as defined in Art. 3 (1) (b) MSFD.[1458] However, the fundamental approach of the MSFD does not necessarily correspond to the zonation system as envisaged by UNCLOS, but is organised according to "large marine ecosystems."[1459] These refer to the "marine regions or sub-regions" as outlined in Art. 4 MSFD. The MSFD covers those marine waters in the Baltic Sea, the Black Sea, the North–East Atlantic and the Mediterranean Sea that are under the jurisdiction of the EU Member States. Depending on the sea in question, the marine regions, as delineated by Art. 4 (1) MSFD, cover a vast space and could therefore face differing issues and problems. To this end, the MSFD opens the possibilities to integrate the specificities of subdivisions in the marine regions by developing measures in predefined areas. In this context, the MSFD does not leave the determination of these sub-regions on a Member State level, but proposes four sub-regions in the North-East Atlantic and the Mediterranean.[1460]

1458 Coastal waters are defined as: "coastal waters as defined by Directive 2000/60/EC, their seabed and their subsoil, in so far as particular aspects of the environmental status of the marine environment are not already addressed through that Directive or other Community legislation." Also, the WFD applies in its chemical status also to the territorial sea, see section B.VII.1. of this chapter.

1459 *Barnes/Metcalfe*, Current Legal Developments: The European Union, The International Journal of Marine and Coastal Law 25 (2010) 81, 82.

1460 The MSFD remains silent on possible sub-regions in the Baltic or Black Sea, Art. 4 (2) (a and b) MSFD. Accordingly, the sub-regions in the North East Atlantic are: the Greater North Sea, including the Kattegat and the English Channel; the Celtic Sea; the Bay of Biscay and the Iberian Cost and in the Atlantic Ocean, the Macaronesian biogeographic region, being the waters surrounding the Azores, Madeira and the Canary islands. These coincide largely with those

b) The aim to achieve a Good Environmental Status by 2020 and the context of "polluting effects"

The MSFD aims to establish a framework in which Member States are obliged to take measures so as to achieve or maintain a good environmental status (GES) in the marine environment by 2020.[1461] The GES is analogously developed to the GEcS of the WFD.[1462] However, the concrete application differs. In abstract terms the GES is defined as:

> the environmental status of marine waters where these provide ecologically diverse and dynamic oceans and seas which are clean, healthy and productive within their intrinsic conditions, and the use of the marine environment is at a level that is sustainable, thus safeguarding the potential for uses and activities by current and future generations.[1463]

These broad and unspecified conditions are further sketched out in the following paragraphs which, due to their significance, are worthy of reproduction in full:

> (a) the structure, functions and processes of the constituent marine ecosystems, together with the associated physiographic, geographic, geological and climatic factors, allow those ecosystems to function fully and to maintain their resilience to human-induced environmental change. Marine species and habitats are protected, human-induced decline of biodiversity is prevented and diverse biological components function in balance;
> (b) hydro-morphological, physical and chemical properties of the ecosystems, including those properties which result from human activities in the area concerned, support the ecosystems as described above. Anthropogenic inputs of

---

regions used in the framework of the OSPAR Convention, see section C.I. of chapter 4. In the Mediterranean the proposed sub-regions are the Western Mediterranean Sea; the Adriatic Sea; the Ionian Sea and the Central Mediterranean Sea and the Aegean-Levantine Sea. From a preliminary analysis, none of the subregions have been specifically targeted for marine litter measures. Rather the options so far relate to taking measures on a regional scale, such as the development of Regional Action Plans for marine litter. See also *Juda,* Ocean Development & International Law 41 (2010) 34, 41.

1461 Art. 1 (1) MSFD.

1462 *Juda,* Ocean Development & International Law 41 (2010) 34, 37. See for a comparative analysis regarding the challenges relating to the development and implementation of the GEcS of the WFD and the GES (MSFD) *Borja/Elliott/Carstensen et al.,* Marine Pollution Bulletin 60 (2010) 2175.

1463 Art. 3 (5) MSFD.

> substances and energy, including noise, into the marine environment do not cause pollution effects[1464]

Even though these provisions remain very broad and include a wide range of indistinct possible variables that can be subsumed under the GES, the last sentence of Art. 3 (5) (b) MSFD requires specific attention. It refers, *inter alia,* to the input of substances which should not cause pollutive effects. Clearly, this sentence has implications for marine litter. The objective to avoid a "pollutive effect" is related to the determination of thresholds. When assessing the definition of pollution under the MSFD, it becomes quickly visible that the aim to avoid any pollutive effect is extremely ambitious. Pollution thus means:

> direct or indirect introduction into the marine environment, as a result of human activity, of substances or energy, including human-induced marine underwater noise, which results or is likely to result in deleterious effects such as harm to living resources and marine ecosystems, including loss of biodiversity, hazards to human health, the hindering of marine activities, including fishing, tourism and recreation and other legitimate uses of the sea, impairment of the quality for use of sea water and reduction of amenities or, in general, impairment of the sustainable use of marine goods and services.[1465]

Reading Art. 3 (5) (b) MSFD in conjunction with the definition of pollution, reaching the threshold that is thus created by the avoidance of a polluting effect is an enormous undertaking. The objectives, as outlined in the definition of pollution, touch upon highly relevant aspects, also with regard to marine litter. This relates to aspects of hazards to human health, harm to living health, tourism and recreation and the impairment of the quality for the use of sea water. Particularly with regard to the consideration that the deleterious effects of a substance could "likely" occur, therefore incorporating the precautionary principle, these provisions indicate the ambitious scope of the Directive.

c) Cyclical assessment of the marine environment

The central instruments of the MSFD are the so-called marine strategies that are to be developed and implemented in the framework of each of the

---

1464 Art. 3 (5) (a and b) MSFD.
1465 Art. 3 (8) MSFD.

marine regions or subregions.[1466] The Member States are not to develop marine strategies exclusively for waters under their jurisdiction, rather they are obliged to co-operate with all other Member States sharing a marine region or sub-region.[1467] The MSFD establishes the parameters for a common approach that aims to ensure that a coordinated and comparable plan of action is developed specific to the different regions.[1468] The elements of this "plan of action" are defined in the framework of the Directive and refer, first, to a preparation phase of the marine strategies[1469] and, second, to the establishment of programme of measures.[1470] In doing this, it follows a dynamic approach in which the "protection and management of the marine environment be flexible and adaptive and take account of scientific and technological developments."[1471]

The MSFD includes a complex set of tasks and obligations that are combined with a stringent and very ambitious time frame. The fundamental elements of the first phase are (1) the preliminary assessment of the marine waters,[1472] (2) the determination of the GES,[1473] (3) the establishment of environmental targets,[1474] all of which were supposed to be developed and implemented by 15 July 2012.[1475] Also, in the first phase a monitoring programme is to be established and implemented by 15 July 2014.[1476] The second phase refers to the development of programme of measures by 2015 which are then applied and made operational by 2016.[1477] In the following these regulatory elements will be analysed with a view to addressing marine litter in the MSFD.

1466 Art. 3 (3) and Art. 5 MSFD:.

1467 Art. 5 (2) MSFD. See for a critical evaluation of the proposal for the MSFSD in which *Salomon* criticises that only the EU Member States are responsible for developing environmental objectives *Salomon,* Marine Pollution Bulletin 52 (2006) 1328.

1468 Art. 5 (2) MSFD.

1469 Art. 5 (2) (a) in conjunction with chapter II MSFD.

1470 Art. 5 (2) (b) in conjunction with chapter III MSFD.

1471 Recital 34 MSFD. See also *Juda,* Ocean Development & International Law 41 (2010) 34, 39.

1472 Art. 5 (2) (a) (i) MSFD in conjunction with Art. 8 MSFD.

1473 Art. 5 (2) (a) (ii) MSFD in conjunction with Art. 9 (1) MSFD.

1474 Art. 5 (2) (a) (iii) MSFD in conjunction with Art. 10 (1) MSFD.

1475 Art. 5 (2) (a) (i-iii) MSFD.

1476 Art. 5 (2) (a) (iv) MSFD in conjunction with Art. 11 (1) MSFD.

1477 Art. 5 (2) (b) (i and ii) MSFD in conjunction with Art. 13 MSFD.

aa) Assessment of marine waters

The assessment of marine waters as embodied in the MSFD represents the understanding that a complete and comprehensive knowledge of the impacts of human activities on marine environment is a prerequisite for any subsequent measure. In the initial assessment stage the assessment is not confined to activities that are particularly prone to cause polluting effects or are hazardous, but also includes aspects where there is no significant risk to the marine environment.[1478] This assessment is understood as a fundamental baseline study that is taken as the point of reference for any subsequent steps.[1479] The MSFD proposes a three stage assessment procedure.[1480] This relates, first, to an analysis of features and characteristics and the *status quo* of the environmental status of the marine waters.[1481] In order to guide the Member States the assessment is to be based on the non-exhaustive lists of elements enumerated in table 1 of Annex III MSFD that include, *inter alia,* biological and physical and chemical features.[1482] In a second step, predominant pressures and impacts from human activities are analysed.[1483] Elements in this assessment relate to cumulative and synergetic effects and also assessment that have been effected in existing EU legislation.[1484] Additionally, the indicative table 2 of Annex III MSFD enumerates pressures that might be included in the assessment.[1485] The in-

1478 Art. 14 (4) MSFD: "Member States shall develop and implement all the elements of marine strategies referred to in Article 5(2), but shall not be required, except in respect of the initial assessment described in Article 8, to take specific steps where there is no significant risk to the marine environment, or where the costs would be disproportionate taking account of the risks to the marine environment, and provided that there is no further deterioration."

1479 See only Art. 10 (1) MSFD on the establishment of environmental targets that must be based on the initial assessment made according to Art. 8 (1) MSFD.

1480 Art. 8 (1) MSFD. *Barnes/Metccalfe*, Current Legal Developments: The European Union, The International Journal of Marine and Coastal Law 25 (2010) 81, 82.

1481 Art. 8 (1) (a) MSFD.

1482 Art. 8 (1) (a) MSFD in conjunction with table 1 Annex III MSFD.

1483 Art. 8 (1) (b) MSFD.

1484 Art. 8 (1) (b) (ii and iii) MSFD.

1485 Elements of table 2 Annex III MSFD relate *inter alia* to physical loss, contamination by hazardous substances, biological disturbances and systematic and/or intentional release of substances.

tegration of marine litter is made through an explicit reference[1486] and can also be included under the element of systematic and/or intentional release of substances.[1487] Thirdly, the MSFD requires an economic and social analysis of the use of those waters and of the cost of degradation of the marine environment.[1488]

Since the lists of characteristics (table 1 Annex III MSFD) and pressures (table 2 Annex III MSFD) are indicative, the Member States may also choose to include additional aspects in their assessment that go beyond the predefined elements, *i.e.* the MSFD enumerates a set of minimum standards. Consequently giving them a certain degree of flexibility to develop specifically suitable assessment for the marine region or subregion in question.[1489] However, Art. 8 (3) (a) MSFD stipulates that the assessment methodologies are to be "consistent across the marine or sub-region," thus limiting the leeway in decision-making of the individual Member State in this exercise.[1490]

With regard to marine litter considerations, these multi-layered assessment requirements pose a challenge regarding the spatial and temporal scales of marine litter. Agreeing on consistent methodologies for this assessment requires agreement on the appropriate variables and parameters, a task that is very challenging given the diverse occurrences and impacts of marine litter. A certain structure and framework in the selection of methodologies is provided in this context in Art. 8 (2) MSFD, which requires Member States to

> [...] take into account elements regarding coastal, transitional and territorial waters covered by relevant provisions of existing Community legislation, in particular Directive 2000/60/EC. They shall also take into account, or use as their basis, other relevant assessments such as those carried out jointly in the context of Regional Sea Conventions, so as to produce a comprehensive assessment of the status of the marine environment.

1486 Marine litter as an element of pressure or impact is enumerated under "other physical disturbances" (table 2 Annex III MSFD).

1487 Table 2 Annex III MSFD.

1488 Art. 8 (1) (c) MSFD.

1489 *Barnes/Metcalfe*, Current Legal Developments: The European Union, The International Journal of Marine and Coastal Law 25 (2010) 81, 83.

1490 *Ibid.*

bb) The challenge to determine the GES for marine litter

The assessment of Art. 8 MSFD forms the baseline for any further measures. It also serves the aim of achieving a GES of marine waters. As this concept is *prima facie* fairly broad and vague, Member States should use the findings of the assessment in determining a set of characteristics to describe the GES for each marine region or sub-region.[1491] In order to streamline this exercise, the MSFD outlines elements that serve as variables in the assessment.[1492] Member States are obliged to draw on the compulsory qualitative descriptors in determining good environmental status as outlined in Annex I MSFD.

Annex I MSFD lists eleven descriptors that are to be applied. These relate to biological diversity (descriptor 1), non-indigenous species (descriptor 2), commercially exploited fish and shellfish (descriptor 3), marine food web (descriptor 4), eutrophication (descriptor 5), sea-floor integrity (descriptor 6), permanent alteration of hydrographical conditions (descriptor 7), concentration of contaminants (descriptor 8), contaminants in fish and other seafood for human consumption (descriptor 9), *marine litter (descriptor 10)* and introduction of energy including noise pollution (descriptor 11).[1493] Should a Member State choose not to apply one descriptor, it must notify this to the European Commission.[1494] Since descriptor 10 ad-

---

1491 Upon the finalization of the assessment made pursuant to Art. 8 (1) and the determination of the set of characteristics for good environmental status, the Member States are to notify the European Commission on these developments not later than three months after their completion (Art. 9 (2) in conjunction with Art. 12 MSFD).

1492 See also Art. 24 (2) (a) MSFD.

1493 In particular descriptor 3 on commercially exploited fish and shellfish has been subject to academic debate, due to its relevance to the nexus between marine conservation and the Common Fisheries Policy of the EU, see *Salomon/Dross,* Marine Policy 42 (2013) 142, 145; *Markus/Schlacke/Maier,* The International Journal of Marine and Coastal Law 26 (2011) 59, 77 *et seq.*

1494 Annex I MSFD in conjunction with Art. 9 (2) MSFD. This provision also stipulates that a Member State must notify the European Commission after it has completed the assessment according to Art. 8 (1) MSFD and determined the GES as envisaged by Art. 9 MSFD three months after the completion of the latter. *Juda* outlines that the "Directive mandates a series of actions at the level of member states, it clearly provides an oversight and coordinating role at the Community level through the European Commission" *Juda,* Ocean Development & International Law 41 (2010) 34, 42.

dresses marine litter, it is, in the context of this study, the key variable in determining a GES for the marine environment. However, the diverse nature of marine litter also necessitates a reference to other pertinent descriptors such as on biological diversity (descriptor 1), non-indigenous species (descriptor 2), sea floor integrity (descriptor 6), contaminants in fish and other sea food for human consumption (descriptor 9). The thematic relevance of all these descriptors should be used to overcome the sectoral approach towards addressing one descriptor but to also see the specific issue in its context.

cc) Descriptor 10 on marine litter: legal challenges

Descriptor 10 is dedicated exclusively to the purpose of marine litter. The target state for a GES for marine litter is achieved when: *"[p]roperties and quantities of marine litter do not cause harm to the coastal and marine environment* (emphasis added)." Its content appears to be vague and somewhat difficult to grasp at first sight.[1495] Moreover, the concept of "“‘goodness” is not a property that is intrinsic to nature but an extension of our human value system."[1496] On the contrary, for some species, marine litter is beneficial. It provides "mobile homes" for barnacles and polychaete worms.[1497] Additionally, the aim to create a GES generally is also associated with the knowledge about the 'as-is state' of the marine environment as a starting point. Particularly in regard to marine litter, the current state of the environmental status, the actual amount of marine litter in the marine environment can only be broadly estimated at best.[1498]

1495 See for a similar critical remark regarding the "somewhat unclear descriptors": *Markus/Schlacke/Maier,* The International Journal of Marine and Coastal Law 26 (2011) 59, 76.

1496 *Mee/Jefferson/Laffoley et al.,* Marine Pollution Bulletin 56 (2008) 187, 190.

1497 *Barnes,* Nature 416 (2002) 808, 808. Admittedly, the negative impacts and consequences significantly prevail over these "positive" aspects. The examples is made on the basis of the example of *Mee et al.*who argue that "[a] naturally eutrophic lagoon is "good" for jellyfish or small pelagic fish, for example" *Mee/Jefferson/Laffoley et al.,* Marine Pollution Bulletin 56 (2008) 187, 190.

1498 See chapter 1.

The challenge in the current form is to understand the legal meaning of the concepts of "properties", "quantities", "marine litter" [1499] and "coastal and marine environment"[1500] and most importantly their concrete influence on the notion of "harm." Depending on its interpretation and understanding, the notion of harm can potentially have many meanings and different consequences. In the end, a GES for marine litter is achieved only when, among many other aspects, marine litter does not cause harm to the coastal and marine environment.

(1) Interpretation of the wording of the provision

The interpretation of the wording of the provision is based on an analysis of the words and structure of the sentence.[1501] The words coastal and marine environment indicate that any human health considerations are not included in the assessment of whether harm occurs or not. Additionally, the parameters properties and quantities potentially leave a wide margin of discretion to determine what kind of elements are integrated in the assessment. The scientific knowledge of the impacts and consequences of marine litter is continuously increasing. Nevertheless substantial knowledge gaps still prevail that need also to be considered.

1499 No legally binding definition of marine litter can be found in the primary or secondary law today. A definition of what constitutes marine litter is given in the Task Group report on descriptor 10 from 2010: *Galgani/Fleet/van Franeker et al.*, Marine Strategy Framework Directive, Task Group 10 Report Marine Litter, 2010, 4. However, this definition is in itself not legally binding.
The definition is based on the definition provided by UNEP: "Marine litter is any persistent, manufactured or processed solid material discarded, disposed of or abandoned in the marine and coastal environment.
Marine litter consists of items that have been made or used by people and deliberately discarded or unintentionally lost into the sea or coastline including such materials transported into the marine environment from land by rivers, drainage or sewage systems or wind. For example marine litter consists of plastics, wood, metals, glass, rubber, clothing, paper etc. This definition does not include semi-solid remains of for example mineral and vegetable oils, paraffin and chemicals that sometime litter sea and shores.".

1500 Even though the MSFD defines marine and coastal waters (Art. 3 (1) MSFD), it is argued that the marine and coastal environments are different from these definitions.

1501 *Seyr,* Der effet utile in der Rechtsprechung des EuGH, 2008, 32.

The descriptor prescribes an extremely ambitious goal in that its target is to achieve "no harm" by marine litter. Consequently one could conclude that zero harm is the aim of this provision. "Harm"[1502] also indicates that a concrete occurrence of damage must be discernible in order to be classified as such. When looking at the provision in other languages, a similar conclusion is supported. Thus, in the German version it is stated "Die Eigenschaften und Mengen der Abfälle im Meer haben *keine schädlichen Auswirkungen* auf die Küsten- und Meeresumwelt" and in the French version it says "Les propriétés et les quantités de déchets marins *ne provoquent pas de dommages* au milieu côtier et marin."[1503] Consequently, among the three versions, the French version is clearly relating to damages, which aggravates the determination regarding the "objective" (economic damage, human health, environmental damage). Looking exclusively at the wording of descriptor 10 MSFD provides a somewhat limited picture that cannot be entirely taken as a final interpretation. It could be argued that the legislators deliberately left the concepts and notions as vague as possible in order to leave a margin of discretion for its implementation. This is however limited by the different nouns that are taken in the various linguistic versions.

(2) Legislative historical interpretation

The content and elements of descriptor 10 have been the subject of considerable and often protracted negotiations. The CJEU has several times used the recitals as a means to interpret a provision.[1504] Considering recital 34 MSFD, it becomes visible that the status of GES is, in essence, also subject to developing scientific knowledge that potentially influences the understanding of harm. It reads as follows:

> [i]n view of the dynamic nature of marine ecosystems and their natural variability, and given that the pressures and impacts on them may vary with the evolvement of different patterns of human activity and the impact of climate change, it is essential to recognise that the determination of good environmental status may have to be adapted over time. Accordingly, it is appropriate that

1502 See for an overview on the types and levels of environmental harm: *Trouwborst,* Precautionary Rights and Duties of States, 2006, 39 *et seq*.

1503 Emphasis added.

1504 *Seyr,* Der effet utile in der Rechtsprechung des EuGH, 2008, 78.

> programmes of measures for the protection and management of the marine environment be flexible and adaptive and take account of scientific and technological developments […].

The approach taken in the recital indicates that the notion of harm should be understood as a concept that is open for development, depending on the scientific and technological *status quo*.

Additionally, in the course of the negotiation phase of the MSFD, the aim and content of descriptor 10 was amended. It was formerly defined as the situation where "the quantity of litter in marine and coastal environments has been reduced to a level which ensures that it does not pose a threat to marine species and habitats, human health and the safety and economy of coastal communities." [1505] Even though the definition itself retains somewhat ambiguous concepts such as levels that do not pose a threat to the safety and economy, it does contain more tangible elements that potentially increase a legal certainty in the application of the provision. In particular, the reference to threat indicates the relevance of the precautionary principle.[1506] However, the Council aimed to reduce the detailedness of the descriptors of Annex I "bearing in mind that the proposal is for a framework Directive that should not burden implementation with too much technical detail."[1507] Nevertheless, this provision is in essence preferable to the content of the descriptor as it stands now, since it made reference to certain variables that would have acted as more concrete thresholds or parameters to evaluate the impact of marine litter. A mere interpretation of the wording of descriptor 10 does not render entirely satis-

---

1505 *European Parliament*, A6-0373/2006, Report on the proposal for a directive of the European Parliament and of the Council establishing a Framework for Community Action in the field of Marine Environmental Policy (Marine Strategy Directive), Committee on the Environment, Public Health and Food Safety, 24.10.2006, 43.

1506 See only the elaboration of the precautionary principle in the Rio Declaration: "In order to protect the environment, the *precautionary principle* shall be widely applied by States according to their capabilities. Where there are *threats o*f serious or irreversible damage, lack of full scientific certainty shall not be used as a reason for postponing cost effective measures to prevent environmental degradation" (emphasis added), see section B of chapter 2.

1507 *Council*, 9388/07 ADD1, Draft Statement of the Council´s Reasons, Common position adopted by the Council with a view to the adoption of a Directive of the European Parliament and of the Council establishing a Framework for Community Action in the field of Marine Environmental Policy (Marine Strategy Directive), 12.07.2007, 3.

factory results. The CJEU has additionally stipulated that "[i]n order to interpret that provision, therefore, it is necessary to consider its context and the objective of the rules in question."[1508]

(3) The effet utile interpretation of descriptor 10 MSFD

EU law recognises, the *effet utile* as an additional means of interpretation.[1509] The CJEU does not define its understanding of the *effet util,*[1510] however, it implies that the interpretation of a provision leads to a "full effect of Community law."[1511] *Ormand* outlines three different functions of the effet utile: it serves as a mechanism to avoid that the interpretation leads to an inadequate result, second it guarantees that a provision achieves a minimum of effectiveness and it allows a provision to ensure a maximum of effectiveness.[1512]

The function of descriptor 10 is to provide on the one hand a tangible target that serves as a variable in the assessment of a GES in the MSFD. The MSFD foresees accordingly the application of

> an ecosystem-based approach to the management of human activities, ensuring that the collective pressures of such activities is kept within levels compatible with the achievement of good environmental status and that the capacity of marine ecosystems to respond to human-induced changes is not compromised, while enabling the sustainable use of marine goods and services by present and future generations.[1513]

1508 C-11/76 *Netherlands v. Commission* [1979] ECR 00245. The CJEU had to decide in this case on the content and meaning of a provision in the light of ambiguities and differences in wording in different linguistic versions of a provision.

1509 See for an overview on the development of the *effet utile* from its roman origins to its application in international public law and European Union law: *Seyr,* Der effet utile in der Rechtsprechung des EuGH, 2008, 94 *et seq.*

1510 *Seyr,* Der effet utile in der Rechtsprechung des EuGH, 2008, 273. The *effet utile* method of interpretation has been subject to extensive academic debate. In the context of this study it cannot be analysed whether the effet utile is congruent with the teleological interpretation.

1511 C-441/93 *Panagis Pafitis v. Trapeza Kentrikis Ellados A.E. and others* [1996] ECR I-1347, para.70.

1512 *Ormand,* La notion de "l'effet-utile" des traités communautaires dans la jurisprudence de la Cour de justice des Communautés européennes, 1975, 44 *et seq. Ormand* speaks of "*résultat impropre ou absurd*", "*efficacité minimale*" and "*maximum d'efficacité*" respectively.

1513 Art. 1 (3) MSFD.

In reading the ecosystem-based approach of the MSFD, the understanding of the concept coastal and marine environment cannot be seen as strictly relating only to the environmental aspects. With regard of the aim of the EU to also protect and improve the quality of the environment and the protection of human health,[1514] the concept of "coastal and marine environment" should therefore be seen as encompassing a broader perspective.[1515] This can also be confirmed when reading descriptor 10 in context with some of the other descriptors that form a "framework" for the assessment of GES.[1516] Consequently, the other descriptors also integrate human health considerations. Therefore, the scope of the understanding of 'harm' in the context of descriptor 10 MSFD not only covers environmental considerations but also extends to potential human health impacts and socio-economic impacts.[1517]

1514 Art. 191 (1) TFEU.

1515 Admittedly, such a conclusion can also be made after studying the legislative history of the MSFD. In EU law, no general definition of coastal and marine environment exists. What is more, it appears to be a collective term that is relevant depending on the specific instrument in question. Thus, it covers aspects such as 'coastal and marine waters' (Water Framework Directive or MSFD), the 'coastal zone' as contained in Art. 3 (1) of: *European Commission*, COM (2013) 133 final, Proposal for a Directive of the European Parliament and the Council establishing a framework for maritime spatial planning and integrated coastal zone man-agement, 12.03.2013, or 'international coastal waters' as is envisaged by Art. 1 (b) of the Directive 76/464/EEC on water pollution by discharges of certain dangerous substances that has been integrated into the WFD.

1516 See section B.VII.2c.aa. of this chapter.

1517 *Galgani* identifies three general categories for the concept of harm in the MSFD exist: "(i) social harm, *i.e.* loss in aesthetic value and public health; (ii) economic harm, such as the cost to tourism, damage to vessels (net and ropes in propellers) and fishing gear and facilities and cleaning costs; and (iii) ecological harm e.g. mortality of, or sublethal effects on, animals through entanglement by e.g. ghost nets, derelict traps, pots or other fishing gear, or harm resulting from ingestion of litter, including the uptake of microparticles (mainly microplastics)": *Galgani/Hanke/Werner et al.,* ICES Journal of Marine Science 70 (2013) 1055, 1060.

(4) The challenge to determine "harm" in the context of descriptor 10 MSFD

The ambitious aim to prevent harm is not only quite difficult to grasp, but it also poses a challenge in legal term. Whereas the "no harm" doctrine is an important concept in particular relating to transboundary damage in international environmental law,[1518] the concept of harm in the MSFD entails a somewhat different understanding. Harm is a normative concept that indicates that a certain threshold of harm or damage exists.[1519] However, the wording as it is formulated in descriptor 10 leads to the conclusion that a zero tolerance or zero harm approach has been chosen in this regard. Consequently, the acceptance of harm of marine litter is very low if not indeed utterly non-existent or even prohibited. With regard to the persistency of marine litter and the many primary and secondary harmful impacts, the concept of harm appears to be ambiguous and attackable. *Trouwborst* argues that

> the taking of human risks by human society can never be banned completely given that, by definition, all human behaviour has some impact on the environment. As long as people walk the face of the earth, it will not be possible to prevent all levels of anthropogenic environmental damage, which makes it imperative to draw a line somewhere.[1520]

Nevertheless, the established threshold of the adverse consequences of marine litter is quite high and establishes an extremely high, perhaps even unattainable, environmental protection standard. Even though an increasingly large body of scientific knowledge is available and a basic understanding of causation and potential cumulative harm exists, many lacunae such as the fate and impact of microplastics prevail. The determination of what constitutes harm is thus also always a choice on the values.[1521] In this regard, the deterministic approach to define harm could be based on the intrinsic value of the marine and coastal environment or it could refer to the "harm with respect to human interests."[1522] This necessitates a decision on the reference state or baseline that is considered as being accept-

1518 See only A.II. of chapter 2.

1519 *Trouwborst,* Precautionary Rights and Duties of States, 2006, 43.

1520 *Ibid.,* 45.

1521 *Lin,* Wisconsin Law Review (2006) 898, 900; *Mee/Jefferson/Laffoley et al.,* Marine Pollution Bulletin 56 (2008) 187, 189.

1522 *Lin,* Wisconsin Law Review (2006) 898, 979.

able in terms of environmental quality or impacts respectively.[1523] Understanding the "dimensions" of this provision, also relates to the boundaries of what constitutes harm. What kind of levels does it include? Harm to a single marine organism, harm to a population level, harm for human beings or should it also relate to long-term (as of today not perceivable) consequences.

With regard to establishing the boundaries of harm, *Galgani/Hanke/Werner et al.* pointed out that "[i]t is not generally feasible for assessments to provide information on the extent of harm at the population, community or ecosystem level and it is actually unlikely that we can develop an assessment procedure that can show effects at a population or ecosystem level."[1524] Even though it is fundamentally known that marine litter causes harm, the MSFD thus requires translating this scientific knowledge into a legislative context. The MSFD proposes a scientists–orientated approach in which the scientists have to assume the role of advising on the environmental status of the marine environment that must then be measured against societal expectations.[1525] Even though such a knowledge-based approach is highly suitable to the requirements of an effective marine litter regulatory framework, it has certain limitations, primarily the lack of knowledge on the complex interactions and ecosystem structures of the marine environment, particularly with regard to marine litter.

A further decisive point is whether a reactionary or a precautionary approach to the definition of harm should be taken. A reactionary approach would be to first determine the damage of marine litter or microplastics before adequate measures are taken. A precautionary approach would widely integrate potential damages that can, with current knowledge, only be vaguely assumed. The MSFD implements in certain aspects a reactionary approach that is certainly needed to be able to fully address the scope of the problem. This is visible in the approach to first pursue an assessment of the status of the marine environment before a programme of measures is devised. However, dealing with marine litter issues also clearly calls for a precautionary approach. Even though this principle is not

---

1523 *Mee/Jefferson/Laffoley et al.,* Marine Pollution Bulletin 56 (2008) 187, 192.

1524 *Galgani/Hanke/Werner et al.,* ICES Journal of Marine Science 70 (2013) 1055, 1061.

1525 *Mee/Jefferson/Laffoley et al.,* Marine Pollution Bulletin 56 (2008) 187, 190; somewhat different (on the draft MSFD): *Fletcher,* Marine Pollution Bulletin 54 (2007) 1881.

contained in the legally binding body of the MSFD, it is mentioned in the recital of the MSFD, therefore undoubtedly paving the way for its consideration in this regard.

(5) Establishing criteria and indicators for descriptor 10: the Commission Decision on criteria for good environmental status of marine waters

The MSFD introduces a provision requiring the Commission to propose further criteria and standards and on the basis of Art. 9 (3) MSFD, the Commission adopted in 2010 the Commission Decision on criteria for good environmental status of marine waters.[1526] This Decision on GES makes technical suggestions on the concrete implementation and application of the standards of the MSFD, while referring primarily to Annex I and Annex III MSFD.[1527] The Decision on GES is structured in a general Part A and a Part B that lays out specifications of the descriptors as listed in Annex I MSFD. The descriptors give an interpretation of what constitutes GES in more concrete terms. These criteria for achieving GES are considered as a starting point that merely form an initial basis for further knowledge and developments.[1528] This understanding that these descriptors are open for further development reflects the challenges that arise with regulating complex marine environmental issues. The Decision on GES aims to further interpret and animate the broad specifications of descriptor 10 as contained in Annex I MSFD. Consequently, the Decision on GES outlines that "[t]he temporal and spatial scale of impacts varies considerably depending on the type and the sensitivity of the ecosystem com-

1526 Commission Decision (2010/477/EU) of 1 September 2010 on criteria and methodological standards on good environmental status of marine waters (OJ 2010 L 232/14, 02.09.2010) (Decision on GES). In the follow-up of the adoption of the Decision on GES, a technical subgroup under the Working Group on GES was established. The subsequently established Technical Subgroup on Marine Litter (TSG ML) is chaired by IFREMER (French Research Institute for the Exploration of the Sea, France), the Umweltbundesamt (Germany) and the Joint Research Center: *Galgani/Hanke/Werner et al.,* ICES Journal of Marine Science 70 (2013) 1055, 1056.

1527 Recital 1 Decision on GES. 29 criteria and 56 methodological standards for the 11 descriptors are established *Salomon/Dross,* Marine Policy 42 (2013) 142, 145.

1528 Recital 1 Decision on GES.

ponents affected."[1529] Therefore it has further defined criteria that are then substantiated by indicators. Given the crucial role of these indicators in interpreting and fleshing out the MSFD, it is worth reproducing it in full.

> The distribution of litter is highly variable, which needs to be taken into consideration for monitoring programmes. It is necessary to identify the activity to which it is linked including, where possible, its origin. There is still a need for further development of several indicators, notably those relating to biological impacts and to micro-particles, as well as for the enhanced assessment of their potential toxicity.
> 10.1. Characteristics of litter in the marine and coastal environment
> – Trends in the amount of litter washed ashore and/or deposited on coastlines, including analysis of its composition, spatial distribution and, where possible, source (10.1.1)
> – Trends in the amount of litter in the water column (including floating at the surface) and deposited on the sea-floor, including analysis of its composition, spatial distribution and, where possible, source (10.1.2)
> – Trends in the amount, distribution and, where possible, composition of micro-particles (in particular micro-plastic) (10.1.3)
> 10.2. Impacts of litter on marine life
> – Trends in the amount and composition of litter ingested by marine animals (e.g.stomach analysis) (10.2.1)
> This indicator needs to be developed further, based on the experience in some sub-regions (e.g. North Sea), to be adapted in other regions.

The descriptor thus broadly differentiates between spatial distribution and the impacts of marine litter. Whereas other descriptors provide for specific aims,[1530] descriptor 10 remains non-specific and broad.[1531] The explanation for this dearth of specificity is contained in the introductory section of descriptor 10, outlining that the "distribution of litter is highly variable."

1529 Para.5, Part A Decision on GES.

1530 This is for example visible in the context of descriptor 11 that addresses the introduction of energy and underwater noise. With regard to impulsive sounds, indicator 11.1.1 takes into consideration the "[p]roportion of days and their distribution within a calendar year over areas of a determined surface, as well as their spatial distribution, in which anthropogenic sound sources exceed levels that are likely to entail significant impact on marine animals measured as *Sound Exposure Level (in dB re 1μPa 2.s) or as peak sound pressure level (in dB re 1μPa peak) at one metre, measured over the frequency band 10 Hz to 10* kHz" (emphasis added).

1531 See also: *Markus/Schlacke/Maier,* The International Journal of Marine and Coastal Law 26 (2011) 59, 78 *et seq.* Even though the authors mistakenly label the descriptor 11 on the introduction of energy and sound as descriptor 2, they correctly conclude that also that descriptor remains unclear.

Defining and agreeing on common variables is, with a view to the manifold sources and impacts indeed quite a challenge.

Among the descriptors listed in Part B, descriptor 10 therefore seems to be one of the least developed. In the preparation phase in the lead up to the Decision on GES, reports corresponding to the descriptors referred to in Annex I MSFD were prepared. Also, a Task Group for each qualitative descriptor was established. The Task Group on Marine Litter published its report in April 2010 in which it outlined the scope and elements of descriptor 10.[1532] Among others, the Task Group on Marine Litter addressed the overall aim of the descriptor and proposed that "[a]n overriding objective will be a measurable and significant decrease (e.g. 10%/year for litter on coastlines) in the total amount of litter in the environment by 2020."[1533] However, apparently this consideration did not find its way into the indicator of this descriptor.

The reference towards the further development in the regions and subregions indicates that a clear mandate is given to goals being pursued in the Regional Seas Conventions. Due to its incomplete nature, one can conclude that the vague content of this descriptor makes it difficult to determine concrete legal standards. Notwithstanding this, an obligation exists to implement the monitoring and scientific research programmes as outlined by the different indicators so as to be able to fulfil the obligations both provided for in the preparatory stages as outlined in Art. 5 (2) (a) MSFD and the programme of measures as stipulated in Art. 5 (2) (b) MSFD. Additionally, the target setting exercise in this regard could potentially compensate for any vague notions and concepts of harm.

dd) Determination of targets for marine litter

According to Art. 10 MSFD, the Member States are under the obligation to "[…] establish a comprehensive set of environmental targets and asso-

---

1532 Galgani/Fleet/van Franeker *et al.*, Marine Strategy Framework Directive, Task Group 10 Report Marine Litter, 2010.

1533 *Galgani/Fleet/van Franeker et al.*, Marine Strategy Framework Directive, Task Group 10 Report Marine Litter, 2010, 1; *European Commission/Joint Research Center*, MSFD GES Technical Subgroup on Marine Litter, Marine litter technical recommendations for the implementation of MSFD requirements, JRC Scientific and Technical Reports, 14.12.2011, 77.

ciated indicators for their marine waters so as to guide progress towards achieving good environmental status [...]."[1534] An environmental target is defined as "a qualitative or quantitative statement on the desired condition of the different components of, and pressures and impacts on, marine waters in respect of each marine region or subregion [...]."[1535] The exercise of target setting serves several functions with regard to marine litter. It can be used to create awareness and serves as a point of reference in a political and legal debate.[1536] Foremostly however, it establishes a link to the GES and therefore forms a measurable threshold for its achievement. However, exactly on this account, the determination of concrete and measurable requirements poses a challenge in legal terms. Even though the determination of environmental targets of Art. 10 MSFD should take into account Table 2 of Annex III and Annex IV MSFD,[1537] the Member States enjoy a wide margin of discretion to determine their targets.

The MSFD stipulates the establishment of targets by 15 July 2012.[1538] In this regard, additional sub-targets are provided that are distinguishable by their nature and scope. The environmental targets of Art. 10 MSFD relate to (1) targets establishing desired conditions based on the GES; (2) measurable targets and associated indicators that allow for monitoring and (3) operational targets that refer to concrete implementation measures.[1539] In the development of these targets, the Member States are to consider the "application of relevant existing environmental targets laid down at national, Community or international level in respect of the same waters, ensuring that these targets are mutually compatible [...]."[1540] In concrete terms, these relate for example to the commitments made during the Rio +20 conference and those made for example under the OSPAR Conven-

1534 Art. 10 (1) MSFD. The European Commission needs to be notified about the environmental targets within three months of their establishment (Art. 10 (2) in conjunction with Art. 12 MSFD).

1535 Art. 3 (7) MSFD.

1536 Presentation given by *Leo de Vrees*, Marine litter targets for European seas, International Conference on Prevention and Management of Marine Litter in European Seas, 10.04.2013, http://www.marine-litter-conference-berlin.info/downloads.php, last accessed 27.08.2015.

1537 Art. 10 (1) MSFD.

1538 Art. 5 (2) (a) (iii) MSFD.

1539 Para.2 (a-c) Annex IV MSFD.

1540 Art. 10 (1) MSFD.

tion.[1541] Also for the Contracting Parties to the Barcelona Convention that are bound by the RAP ML Med, the therein stipulated targets are certainly pertinent in this regard.[1542] This also relates to the HELCOM RAP ML and the OSPAR RAP ML.

Additionally, the MSFD also requires the integration of targets from other relevant legislation and instruments.[1543] In this connection, the recycling targets of the Waste Framework Directive are thus relevant targets that could potentially have an influence on the issue of marine litter. Target setting under the MSFD is the link between source-related and impact-related legislation. Bridging those two categories of legislation is a key element to ensure that measures are adequate and indeed target the source of the problem. A particular caveat in the context of target setting in the MSFD is the discretion of the Member States to determine their targets. Depending on Member State, these can be chosen to be ambitious or lesser ambitious, therefore leading to differentiated protection standards and weakening the overall purpose of the Directive.

In April 2013, the European Commission presented the targets as referred to in Art. 10 MSFD that were reported by the EU Member States to that date. Consequently, 14 out of 22 Member States reported qualitative reduction targets for marine litter.[1544] Three Member States set quantified reduction targets on the plastic content in fulmar stomachs that refer to the OSPAR EcoQO.[1545] Four Member States established targets for land-based pollution such as improved waste collection in coastal municipali-

1541 Presentation given by *Leo de Vrees*, Marine litter targets for European seas, International Conference on Prevention and Management of Marine Litter in European Seas, 10.04.2013. See chapter 2 and chapter 4 respectively.

1542 Art. 8 RAP ML Med.

1543 Art. 10 (1) MSFD.

1544 *Interviewes/Görlitz/Stöfen et al.*, Issue Paper to the "International Conference on Prevention and Management of Marine Litter in European Seas", 16.05.2013, 30; Presentation given by Leo de Vrees, Marine litter targets for European seas, International Conference on Prevention and Management of Marine Litter in European Seas, 10.04.2013.

1545 Interviewes/Görlitz/Stöfen *et al.*, Issue Paper to the "International Conference on Prevention and Manage-ment of Marine Litter in European Seas", 16.05.2013, 30. Other indicator species that are used are turtles, lobster and cetaceans (dolphins and porpoises).

ties and reduced input of litter from rivers and sewers.[1546] One Member State has targeted a change in social behaviour as well as the performance of waste management.[1547] Another target relates to floating litter that has been fished.[1548] Several Member States also outlined targets addressing the knowledge gap regarding seabed monitoring, the impact on species and habitats and the microplastics in the water column.[1549]

The European Commission has stipulated in this regard an ambitious proposal in the 7th EAP. It calls for an Union-wide quantitative reduction headline target for marine litter."[1550] Even though such a call appears *prima facie* to be a fairly simple and straight forward suggestion, the manifold aspects and the complexity of the issue pose certain difficulties. An EU-wide target on marine litter thus implies that all Member States agree on one single identifiable target that is applicable to all European Seas. This would in principle be somewhat inconsistent with the regional approach of the MSFD. Notwithstanding this, an EU-wide target would not only reflect the transboundary impact of marine litter, but it is also indicative of a genuine desire to make tangible progress in respect of this issue.[1551] Consequently, an EU-wide target would have to be applicable to all EU Member States. Nevertheless, the differences of sources and activities leading to marine litter among the four European Seas necessitate a twofold approach to the target setting in the MSFD. First, an EU-wide target needs to be complemented with regional and specific operational targets and indicators that address the particular challenges in the marine region in question.[1552] In September 2014, the European Commission proposed in its Communication on a circular economy a headline reduction

---

1546 *Ibid.* Also a target was established that related to the no-special-fee-system. Additionally, several Member States addressed the prevailing knowledge gaps regarding marine litter.

1547 *Interviewes/Görlitz/Stöfen et al.*, Issue Paper to the "International Conference on Prevention and Manage-ment of Marine Litter in European Seas", 16.05.2013, 30.

1548 *Ibid.*

1549 *Interviewes/Görlitz/Stöfen et al.*, Issue Paper to the "International Conference on Prevention and Manage-ment of Marine Litter in European Seas", 16.05.2013, 30 *et seq.*

1550 7th EAP, Priority objective 1, para.28 (iii).

1551 Similar to the OSPAR Convention´s reduction target on nutrients: *Interviewes/Görlitz/Stöfen et al.*, Issue Paper to the "International Conference on Prevention and Management of Marine Litter in European Seas", 16.05.2013, 31.

1552 *Ibid.*, 33.

target on marine litter which states: "reducing marine litter by 30% by 2020 for the ten most common types of litter found on beaches, as well as for fishing gear found at sea, with the list adapted to each of the four marine regions in the EU."[1553] The proposed headline target is made in the context of the so-called circular economy package that is envisaged within the framework of the review of EU waste management and recycling targets.[1554] This further strengthens the role of the MSFD as a vehicle to "frame" and impact other related policies. However, the European Commission withdrew the proposal to review certain directives in March 2015 and announced to propose a new and amibitious new package to promote circular economy at the end of 2015. It remains to be seen how this new proposal integrates these objectives.[1555]

The legal assessment regarding questions relating to whether Member States are in non-compliance in case they do not reach their targets is particularly challenging. This relates to the fact that the current targets are also always embedded in a greater political, legal or scientific context, such as those relating to waste management or knowledge gaps. However, the Member States are certainly under an obligation to establish targets.

ee) Monitoring programmes

The fourth step of the preparation phase, relates to the development of monitoring programmes that are based on the knowledge gained during

1553 *European Commssion*, COM (2014) 398 final, Communication from the Commission to the European Parliament, the Council, the European Economic and Social Committee and the Committee of the Regions, Towards a circular economy: A zero waste programme for Europe, 02.07.2014, 12. With regard to the quantitative reduction target of marine litter, a public consultation was held: *European Commission*, Consultation on the establishment of a quantitative reduction headline target for marine litter, consultation period 25.09.2013 to 18.12.2013.

1554 See in particular section B.V.4. of this chapter for further information on the planned review of different waste stream directives. :

1555 *European Commission*, (COM(2014) 910 final, Annex to the Communication from the European Commission to the European Parliament, the Council, the European Economic and Social Committee and the Committee of the Regions on the Commission Work Programme 2015, 16.12.2014 and *European Commission*, Press Release, Commission confirms Withdrawal of 73 Pending Proposals Announced in 2015 Work Programme, IP/15/4567, 07.03.2015.

the initial assessment of Art. 8 MSFD. In this context, Member States sharing one marine region or subregion are obliged to

> draw up monitoring programmes [...] and shall, in the interest of coherence and coordination, endeavour to ensure that
> (a) monitoring methods are consistent across marine region or subregion so as to facilitate comparability of monitoring results;
> (b) relevant transboundary impacts and transboundary features are taken into account.[1556]

The establishment and implementation of the monitoring programmes is to be achieved by 15 July 2014. The list of the roles and functions of monitoring in Annex V MSFD demonstrates the ambitious scope of this element. The manifold requirements and needs that have to be met by the monitoring scheme demonstrate the complexity and challenges of its role, but also its function as a principal tool in the overall system of the MSFD. Its significance can not only be derived from the requirements to provide information for the assessment of the environmental status, but also as a tool to generate knowledge that is used for developing indicators for environmental targets and to allow the assessment of the impacts of measures.[1557]

With a view to the harmonisation and coherence of monitoring approaches, the MSFD additionally stipulates that the monitoring programmes for marine regions shall build on and be compatible with assessment and monitoring provisions that are established by Union legislation and/or international agreements.[1558] This avoids duplication of efforts and fosters comparability.[1559] While this provision is relevant for other descriptors, marine litter constitutes a particular case. Besides the criteria and indicators of the Decision on GES that serve as monitoring elements, no other explicit monitoring or assessment provisions for marine litter can be found in Union legislation. However, some relevant requirements can

---

1556 Art. 11 (2) (a and b) MSFD. The Member States must notify the European Commission within three months of the establishment of the monitoring programmes (Art. 11 (3) MSFD in conjunction with Art. 12 MSFD).

1557 Paras.1, 11 and 12 Annex V MSFD.

1558 Art. 11 (1) second paragraph MSFD.

1559 See only paras. 9 and 10 Annex V MSFD. See also *Juda,* Ocean Development & International Law 41 (2010) 34, 42 who stresses the importance of the consistency.

be found in the Regional Seas Conventions.[1560] This is of itself not unproblematic, since the different monitoring obligations in the Regional Seas Conventions differ immensely with regard to their scope, objects to be studied and legal nature.[1561] However, the harmonisation of monitoring methodologies is not only necessary within the Regional Seas Conventions but also across the European Union and potentially beyond. Here, a particular challenge arises, for example, when looking at biota monitoring. The considered species might not necessarily be present in all European Seas, therefore creating potential inconsistencies between data.[1562]

The TSG ML has the mandate to describe data needs and methods for marine litter assessment and to make recommendations on monitoring protocols for beach litter, floating macro litter, seafloor litter, litter in biota and microplastics.[1563] The evidence gained from these comprehensive monitoring exercises also play an important role to address the lack of knowledge and therefore further assist in defining harm and to understand the risks and uncertainties in the marine litter setting.

d) Marine Strategies: Programme of measures

The second phase of the MSFD will be introduced by the programmes of measures that are to be developed by 2015 at the latest.[1564] One year later, these programmes are to enter into operation.[1565] The programmes of measures entail those measures that have been identified to achieve or maintain GES.[1566] According to the overall structure of the MSFD, they are to be based on the initial assessment of Art. 8 MSFD and must indicate how they contribute to achieving the environmental targets as outlined in Art. 10 (1) MSFD. When devising those measures, the Member States

---

1560 *Zampoukas/Piha/Bigagli et al.*, Monitoring for the Marine Strategy Framework Directive: Requirements and Option, 2012, 17.

1561 See chapter 3 .

1562 See for example section C.IV and V. of chapter 3 on the target species used in the framework of the OSPAR Convention. Therefore, pertinent indicators and monitoring approaches need to be developed: *Galgani/Hanke/Werner et al.,* ICES Journal of Marine Science 70 (2013) 1055, 1062.

1563 *Ibid.,* 1059.

1564 Art. 5 (2) (b) (i) MSFD.

1565 Art. 5 (2) (b) (ii) MSFD.

1566 Art. 13 (1) MSFD.

must take into account relevant Union legislation.[1567] In this context, the MSFD refers particularly to the UWWTD and the Bathing Water Directive, even though the explicit mention of these two instruments appears to be somewhat arbitrary.[1568] Moreover, the measures must take into consideration "forthcoming legislation on environmental quality standards in the field of water policy, or international agreements."[1569] With a view to the transboundary nature of the marine environment, the Member States must consider the impacts of their programme of measures beyond their marine waters.[1570]

Also, the Member States are to give due consideration to sustainable development and the social and economic impacts of the planned measures.[1571] These aspects are particularly relevant for marine litter considerations. They indeed create a regulatory dimension in which the measures are not necessarily confined to specific environmental instruments, but that allow for certain flexibility in the selection of suitable provisions.[1572] The broad flexibility of choices for measures potentially undermines the effectiveness, since Member States may opt to choose the least ambitious options to address the objectives of the MSFD.

The MSFD delimits to some degree the choice of options. First, the Member States must notify their programme of measures to the European Commission,[1573] which assesses whether they constitute an appropriate framework and correspond to the objectives and targets of the Directive. In this context, the European Commission must inform all Member States,

1567 Art. 13 (2) MSFD.

1568 The enumeration is non-exhaustive therefore leaving a wide discretion for Member States.

1569 Art. 13 (2) MSFD.

1570 Art. 13 (8) MSFD.

1571 Art. 13 (3) MSFD.

1572 This flexibility is however to some extent limited by Art. 13 (4) and (5) MSFD in which it is outlined that the programmes of measures are to include spatial protection measures that contribute to a coherent and representative networks of marine protected areas (Art. 13 (4) MSFD). Also, where a human activity is likely to have a significant impact on the marine environment, the Member States are under the obligation to, either individually or jointly, address the competent authority or international organization to ensure the achievement of the aims of the Directive.

1573 Art. 13 (9) MSFD. The notification has to be submitted at the latest three months after their development. The notification obligation also extends to other EU Member States.

after receiving all notifications, whether the programme of measures is compatible with the MSFD. The Commission can also provide guidance and suggestions on modification.[1574]

Furthermore, the content of the programmes of measures are also framed by the reference to Annex VI MSFD.[1575] In this regard, eight possible measures are listed that are highly relevant for the marine litter framework. Among others, possible measures could relate to output controls, management coordination measures, economic incentives and communication and raising public awareness. With regard to the transboundary nature of the marine litter problem and its intersection with several Community policies, Art. 15 MSFD provides a gateway to use the MSFD as a vehicle to amend and review Community legislation.

The provision states that:

> [w]here a Member State identifies an issue which has an impact on the environmental status of its marine waters and which cannot be tackled by measures adopted at national level, or which is linked to another Community policy or international agreement, it shall inform the Commission accordingly and provide a justification to substantiate its view.[1576]

Furthermore, "[w]here action by Community institutions is needed, Member States shall make appropriate recommendations to the Commission and the Council for measures regarding the issues referred to in paragraph 1."[1577] "As appropriate," the Commission can "reflect the recommendations when presenting related proposals to the European Parliament and to the Council."[1578] Even though the European Commission is not legally bound to further act on or transfer these recommendations, the provision could be used to reinforce considerations for amending or developing pertinent legislation. It can be certainly used as an argument to influence the planned review of the waste legislation.[1579]

In this regard, the MSFD also outlines exceptions which lead to a situation in which a Member State cannot achieve the environmental targets or GES. One particular aspect is highly relevant in a marine litter context.

1574 Art. 16 MSFD.

1575 Art. 13 (1) MSFD.

1576 Art. 15 (1) MSFD. The European Commission is under the obligation to respond to the information within six months.

1577 Art. 15 (2) MSFD.

1578 Art. 15 (2) MSFD.

1579 See for more information on this in section B.VI.4. of this chapter.

This relates to Art. 14 (1) (e) MSFD regarding to "natural conditions which do not allow timely improvement in the status of the marine waters concerned."[1580] In order to prevent the abuse of these exception clauses, the Member States must identify these circumstances in their programme of measures and must substantiate their reasons for doing so to the European Commission.[1581]

e) The reference to a public international law instrument by EU law

As has been numerously mentioned in the cyclical approach, the MSFD does not primarily focus on the application and implementation of the obligations by individual Member States but rather follows a regional or transboundary approach.[1582] This approach clearly reflects the importance to consider the interconnectedness of marine ecoystems. In this regard, a preliminary assessment of the EU as an actor in public international law is necessary in order to understand the basic rules governing this issue. In a second step, the legal intricacies and potential benefits of the approach taken by the MSFD will be highlighted with a view to the specific requirements for addressing marine litter.

1580 Other instances are according to Art. 14 (1) MSFD: (a) action or inaction for which the Member State concerned is not responsible, (b) natural causes, (c) force majeure, (d) modifications or alterations to the physical characteristics of marine waters brought about by actions taken for reasons of overriding public interest which outweigh the negative impact on the environment, including any transboundary impact. See further on this aspect: *Markus/Schlacke/Maier,* The International Journal of Marine and Coastal Law 26 (2011) 59, 81 *et seq.*

1581 Art. 14 (1) second paragraph MSFD.

1582 The development of the MSFD was coined by discussions on placing the EU's marine environmental protection measures in their international context: *Salomon,* Marine Pollution Bulletin 52 (2006) 1328.

aa) EU as an actor in international public law

The EU is a Contracting Party to the Helsinki Convention,[1583] the OSPAR Convention and the Barcelona Convention. The competence to conclude international agreements derives from the legal personality of the EU.[1584]. The external competence and internal competences are inextricably linked. This legitimates the EU to conclude international agreements lying within their scope of its competences. In this regard, two legal competences can be distinguished: First, when an express power to conclude international agreements is conferred by virtue of an express provision of primary legislation, generally the TFEU. Second, the CJEU has developed the theory of external implied powers according to which the EU can conclude international agreements not only when a legal basis is provided in primary law, but also in the case of the exercise of such primary competences through the adoption of binding internal acts.[1585] Whereas previously, a referral to this doctrine was necessary, the TFEU introduced a new article so as to clarify this situation. Thus, Art. 216 TFEU relates to the "implied power doctrine" which signifies that "internal competences can also be used in respect of external policy."[1586] To this end,

> [the] Union may conclude an agreement [...] where the conclusion of an agreement is necessary in order to achieve, within the framework of the Union´s policies, one of the objectives referred to in the Treaties, or is provid-

1583 Due to political distrust in respect of its membership ambitions and the consequences thereof the EC (and its predecessor, the EEC) was merely an observer to the 1974 Helsinki Convention. Yet the EU acceded as a Contracting Party to the Helsinki Convention after lengthy discussion. The legal base conferring on it the capability to be a party is provided by Art. 35 HC, an accession clause according to which a regional economic integration organization (REIO) interested in fulfilling the objectives and purpose of the convention can accede under the condition of the invitation of all Contracting Parties. A participation clause aimed at addressing unclear distribution of competences between the EU Member States which are Contracting Parties and the EU sets out the conditions of participation.

1584 *Cremona,* External relations and external competence of the European Union, in *Craig/de Búrca,* The evolution of EU law (2011) 217–268, 260.

1585 C-22/70 C-22/70 *Commission v. Council* (ERTA).

1586 *UNEP*, Marine litter, an analytical overview 2005, 59.

ed for in a legally binding Union act or is likely to affect common rules or alter their scope.[1587]

With this in mind, the obligations arising from these conventions play an important role in EU law since "[c]ommunity legislation must, so far as possible, be interpreted in a manner that is consistent with international law, in particular where its provisions are intended specifically to give effect to an international agreement concluded by the Community."[1588] Thus, the European Commission participates in three Regional Seas Conventions both in its capacity as a Contracting Party as well as in its functions of Guardian of the treaties.

bb) Regional Seas Conventions as an instrument to implement the MSFD

The underlying aim of the MSFD to establish marine strategies is to be pursued by Member States sharing a marine region.[1589] They "shall cooperate to ensure that, within each marine region or subregion, the measures required to achieve the objectives of this Directive […] are coherent and coordinated across the marine region or subregion concerned […]."[1590]

This explicit obligation to co-operate is also strengthened by a specifically dedicated provision in which the fundamental structures of regional co-operation are laid down. Art. 6 (1) MSFD thus establishes that in the envisaged co-operation the "[…] Member States shall, where practical and appropriate, use existing regional institutional cooperation structures, including those under Regional Sea Conventions, covering that marine region or subregion." Despite the 'softer' formulated obligation to make use of existing structures, this reference provides for a clear mandate not to use possible European Union co-operation platforms, but to direct the level of co-operation to regional public international law. In this way, the Regional Seas Conventions can serve as "administrators" of EU considera-

1587 Art. 216 TFEU. In this context, the so-called necessity-text, developed by the CJEU was integrated into primary law. Accordingly, the necessity-test confers the competence to conclude international agreements in the absence of internal legislation, in the event that "the action seems to be *necessary* for the obtainment of one of the Community´s objective" (Joined Cases 3,4 and 6/76 *Kramer* [1976] ECR 1279, para.36 (emphasis added)).

1588 C-284/95 *Safety Hi-Tech,* para.22.

1589 Art. 5 (2) MSFD.

1590 Art. 5 (2) MSFD.

tions in these Regional Seas.[1591] This obligation is even made more explicit with regard to third countries sharing the same marine region:

> [f]or the purpose of establishing and implementing marine strategies, Member States shall, within each marine region or subregion, make every effort, using relevant international forums, including mechanisms and structures of Regional Sea Conventions, to coordinate their actions with third countries having sovereignty or jurisdiction over waters in the same marine region or subregion.[1592]

This approach can be considered as sustainable, as it follows an understanding in which attempts are made to streamline and harmonise approaches to marine environmental protection at the regional level, therefore ignoring artificial borders established by international conventions. The integration of complex environmental interactions is also reflected in the provision to extend the required co-operation, where appropriate, to land-locked EU Member States that lie in the catchment basin of a marine region.[1593]

The institutionalised co-operation through public international public law contributes the reduction of the potential for fragmentation of international environmental law in that the standards and methodological approaches are aligned. However, the Contracting Parties to the Regional Sea Conventions that are not concurrently EU Member States are not under the legal obligations to co-operate in the framework of the MSFD. This could thus lead to a situation in which the EU Member States co-operate according to the MSFD in setting particular standards such as targets or programmes of measures in order to fulfill their obligations under the Directive. The third States are simultaneously not bound by EU law and do not necessarily have to agree on specific targets and measures.

A lack of consensus between all Contracting Parties to the Regional Seas Conventions on certain measures could lead to the consequence of either inactiveness of the fora on the matter or the creation of specific subregional measures particular to the EU Member States. Both consequences have, from an environmental protection view, a negative impact and could

---

1591 They do so albeit in a functionally limited manner, namely that of implementing the specific provisions of the MSFD.

1592 Art. 6 (2) MSFD.

1593 Art. 6 (2) third paragraph MSFD. See also section B.VII.1.f. of this chapter on a similar obligation in the WFD.

lead to a divergence of standards.[1594] Even though the EU Member States cannot legally bind their non-EU counterparts, they can exert political and financial pressure to follow the action plans as provided by the MSFD. The necessary co-operation of third States in this regard is also acknowledged in the recitals of the MFSD which states that these should be "invited to participate" so as to facilitate the attainment of the GES.[1595]

The EU Member States are thus obliged "as far as possible" to "build upon existing programmes and activities developed in the framework of structures stemming from international agreements such as Regional Sea Conventions."[1596] Existing programmes and activities in this sense could thus include recommendations, monitoring schemes or action plans.[1597]

cc) Aspects of institutionalised co-operation by means of the integration of marine litter related MSFD issues in the work and programs of the Regional Seas Conventions

The Member States were required not only to designate by 15 July 2010 a competent authority for the implementation of the Directive in their marine waters, but also to inform the Commission on the competent international bodies in which they participate and that are relevant for the implementation of the Directive.[1598] In the framework of the Helsinki Convention, the commitment to serve as the coordination body was made well before the required deadline.[1599]

1594 *Stöfen,* The role of the Marine Strategy Framework Directive in the protection of the marine environment at the EU´s borders (and beyond), in Czybulka, Marine nature conservation and management at the borders of the European Union (2012) 151–158, 155.

1595 Recitals 20 MSFD.

1596 Art. 6 (2) second paragraph MSFD.

1597 See only the pertinent measures in the Regional Seas Conventions regarding marine litter.

1598 Art. 7 (1) third paragraph MSFD.

1599 *HELCOM*, HELCOM HOD 27th Meeting (27/2008), Agenda Item 2: Use of HELCOM´s work in implementing other international legislative frameworks, Document Code 2/4/Rev. 1, 4. During the Ministerial Meeting 2010, the Contracting Parties officially established "for those HELCOM Contracting States being also EU-Member States, the role of HELCOM as the coordinating platform for the regional implementation of the EU Marine Strategy Framework Directive (EU MSFD) in the Baltic Sea including striving for harmonised national

Marine litter is a fairly recent issue in the regulatory realm of the Regional Seas Conventions and therefore the exercise of standard setting is currently in the process. The RAP ML Med is "committed to increased efforts to tackle the regional challenges for the management of marine litter in an efficient and effective way to achieve good environmental status in synergy with EU Marine Strategy Framework Directive [...]."[1600] Also, the Contracting Parties "shall make best effort" to implement the measures and operational targets of the RAP ML Med "in a coherent manner to achieve good environmental status and relevant targets on marine litter."[1601] Similar references can be found both in the OSPAR RAP ML as well as the HELCOM RAP ML.[1602] The OSPAR RAP ML has as one of the main objectives to "support Contracting Parties in the development, implementation and coordination of their programmes for litter reduction, including those for the implementation of the Marine Strategy Framework Directive."[1603]

As has been demonstrated in chapter 4, the MSFD has had a significant impact in steering the agenda of the Regional Seas Conventions with regard to marine litter. Even though certain projects and approaches have been initiated before the adoption of the MSFD, the repercussions are not to be dismissed. The influence of the MSFD is not only visible with regard to material law but also institutional developments.[1604]

---

marine strategies for achieving good environmental status according to the HELCOM Baltic Sea Action Plan and the EU MSFD": HELCOM Ministerial Declaration on the implementation of the HELCOM Baltic Sea Action Plan 20 May 2010, 5. See also for an early account of the endorsement of both the OSPAR Commission and HELCOM with regard to a European Marine Strategy: *OSPAR Commission/ HELCOM*, First Joint Ministerial Meeting of the Helsinki and OSPAR Commissions, Statement on the European Marine Strategy, What HELCOM and OSPAR can bring to the development of the European Marine Strategy, 25-26.06.2003 (Bremen, Germany).

1600 Preamble, indent 13 RAP ML Med.

1601 Art. 6 RAP ML Med.

1602 HELCOM RAP ML, 3. See for a further analysis of these Regional Action Plans section F of chapter 3.

1603 OSPAR RAP ML, 4.

1604 See only the establishment of the Correspondence Group on Good Environmental Status (GES) and targets- Pollution and Litter Cluster in the context of UNEP/MAP: *UNEP MAP*, UNEP(DEPI)/MED WG.372/4, Report of the Meeting of the Correspondence Group on Good Environmental Status (GES) and targets-Pollution and Litter Cluster from 12.11.2012 as discussed in the UNEP(DEPI)/MED WG.379/Inf.4, Meeting of the Correspondence Group on

f) Marine litter in the context of the GES by 2020

When considering the overall aim of the MSFD to establish a GES by 2020, it is unlikely that, in regard to marine litter, this will be achieved, on time. Reasons for this delay include the legacy of polluting activities, the persistency of plastic and continuous influx of waste. Marine litter is thus a show case to understand how incomplete knowledge and scientific uncertainty is integrated in a legislative setting. It is submitted that the failure to achieve GES for marine litter by 2020, is mainly due to the adopted time frame. Admittedly, agreeing on an ambitious time frame is to be welcomed within the MSFD. Yet, the exercise to agree on a time frame has possible impacts on subsequent legislative and policy developments in the European Union[1605] and a long-term target is much more realistic in achieving a significant reduction of marine litter. In the OSPAR Convention, a long-term target for the continuous reduction of the emission, losses and discharges of hazardous substances was adopted in 1995.[1606] Analogous to this, a generational target covering approximately 25 years for synthetic material seems to be a realistic time frame to entirely address marine litter. Notwithstanding this, the cyclical steps of the MSFD with its continuous adaptation of targets, measures and monitoring serves as a very suitable tool to reach this aim. A successful integration is always highly dependent on the political will of Member States to comprehensively address the issue. An approach in which the Member States can define their own standards throughout the course of the implementation of the Directive poses thus the risk that the requirements are only partially implemented and applied. The Member States have in this regard a wide competence to act and to establish material standards and thresholds.

The probable failure of the MSFD to achieve GES with regard to marine litter has also been admitted in the 7th EAP. Consequently, the GES is "coming under severe pressure, due to […] pollution (including underwa-

---

Good Environmental Status (GES) and targets-Pollution and Litter Cluster, MED POL Focal Point Meting, 31.05.2013.

1605 *European Commission*, COM (2013) 123 final, Green Paper on a European Strategy on Plastic Waste in the Environment, 07.03.2013, 19.

1606 *The North Sea Secretariat*, The North Sea – An Integrated, Ecosystem Approach for Sustainable Development, April 1999,10.

ter noise and marine litter […]."[1607] Given the fact that this statement is made approximately 7 years before the 2020 deadline, it can be interpreted as being self-reflected and demonstrating an unusual level of direct self-criticism. On the other hand it could also be interpreted as an advance excuse for failure to effectively implement and enforce arising standards. Whether this assumption has to be affirmed, will have to be determined in the coming years.

g) Preliminary conclusion

The MSFD is an important tool in the European Union´s regulatory framework for addressing marine litter. This is not only due to the explicit inclusion of it in the context of descriptor 10, but also due to the overall approach of the MSFD. The cyclical approach of the MSFD and its ambitious aim address a comprehensive set of factors that also (indirectly) relate to the marine litter problem. The elements of the cyclical approach (assessment, determination of GES, monitoring programmes, establishment of targets and the programme of measures) can be seen as important elements in a marine litter setting. Also, the socio-economic and public consultation and information elements that are to be taken into consideration are important variables in the MSFD. The Commission as a "supervisory" agent that collects and evaluates different elements serves to ensure a certain degree of coherence in this highly complex instrument.

The GES regarding marine litter will, however, not be achieved by 2020. This is for the largest part due to the present of marine litter in the marine environment. The definition, and therefore the target, of descriptor 10 relating to marine litter is an important aspect. Without wanting to ignore the importance of target setting on a broader scale, the specific elaboration of the descriptor 10 has to be critically evaluated. The analysis has demonstrated that understanding descriptor 10 is somewhat limited by its ambiguous elements. This relates most importantly to the understanding of

1607 7th EAP, Priority objective 1, para.19. In the draft of the 7th EAP a somewhat "stronger" formulation was chosen that lists fishing and marine litter as the two major factors. Accordingly, "[…] there is also a risk that the Marine Strategy Framework Directive target to achieve 'good environmental status' by 2020 may be missed, inter alia due to continued overfishing and the presence of marine litter in Europe's seas."

harm and also to the concept of coastal and marine environment. A discussion on the interpretation of the constituent elements of descriptor 10 has demonstrated that the approach to achieve "no harm" poses several legal challenges. The GES on marine litter taken from a verbatim interpretation gives the impression that "no-harm" for the coastal and marine environment should be achieved, potentially excluding the human health dimension. The legislative history has demonstrated that in the course of the negotiations leading to the adoption of MSFD, a proposal for a GES on marine litter was made that would, in principle, be preferable to the form as it stands today. In particular, the application of the precautionary principle in this regard serves as a threshold to determine the level of accepted risk.

In the current form the objective to achieve "no harm" is significantly hampered by the factual situation of a legacy of polluting activities and the persistency of marine litter. Therefore, it is proposed the provision should be understood with the aim to ensure full effectiveness of EU law. With a view to the scope of the MSFD, the coastal and marine environment approach not only relates *sensu stricto* to biological or ecosystem considerations but also to human health issues.

The emphasis of the MSFD to refer to a coordinated regulatory approach on a regional level has several implications for the marine litter discourse. The use of the Regional Seas Conventions as coordination platforms in the four European Seas serves on the one hand to develop adequate protection standards and monitoring methods that correspond to the ecosystem needs and specific marine litter sources of the region. On the other hand, pertinent measures and provisions that already prevailed in the Regional Sea can be used to further implement the MSFD. Therefore, a consistency can be ensured that also strengthens the protection approach of the Regional Seas Conventions. Depending on the Regional Sea in question, the MSFD has had as an impetus on the further development of specific marine litter considerations. The influence of the MSFD in regard to the Regional Seas Conventions can be, *inter alia*, seen in the institutionalization of working groups addressing the implementation of MSFD provision's and the specific references newly developed instruments.

Generally, the process-oriented approach of the MSFD ensures that continuously new scientific knowledge and developments are included in its scope. The MSFD is however a complex instrument for a complex task. *Juda* is correct in saying that "[...] the MSFD must be seen for what it is: not the end, but rather another step, in an ongoing process of policy evolution and in the development of an important part of an integrated, ecosystem-based framework for a management regime for the marine areas of Europe."[1608]

C. Conclusion concerning EU law

European Union law has a particular role in addressing the prevention of marine litter in the four European seas which surround it. It is apparent that the material EU law as its stands today is, in principle, already in itself a key to successfully combat major sources of marine litter due to the wealth of material law, but also through the means of compliance control in the form of infringement procedures.

With regard to the instruments that are to be considered when analysing the issue of marine litter in EU secondary law, a certain categorisation assists in classifying the different possible regulatory responses that are available in the EU. Broadly speaking, these refer to source-related instruments and impact-related instruments. The former category addresses marine litter sources. The latter category addresses the assessment and monitoring of the environment and potential impacts of pollution on the ecosystem and serves in theory as a baseline to further understand and identify the sources and impacts of marine litter.

A key conclusion of this chapter is the relevance of the so-called combined sources approach. This approach links source-related legislation with impact-related instruments. In that way, the effectiveness of source-related measures is, in principle, linked to their factual impact, an approach that is highly important in a marine litter context, due to the prevailing knowledge gaps. In this regard, monitoring of the impacts and consequences of legislative measures is an essential step to develop adequate regulatory responses.

The discussion on source-related instruments and aspects has demonstrated that several sources of marine litter are covered by Union legislation. In particular, the EU waste management system established by the Waste Framework Directive plays a pivotal role. The Waste Framework Directive establishes high environmental protection standards and pertinent principles that serve as a threshold in the overall system it establishes. However, depending on the time of drafting, the subordinated legislation

---

1608 *Juda,* Ocean Development & International Law 41 (2010) 34, 45.

more or less integrates aspects of marine litter. This is visible in regard to the Landfill-Directive which provides an adequate framework to be able to address point sources of marine litter. The discussion has identified the challenges posed by non-compliance by EU Member States hindering the effective management of this source. Even though the legally binding effect of CJEU jurisprudence for the parties is a key factor of success to enable enforcement of environmental protection standards, the Zakynthos case has demonstrated that a legal remedy may span several years and therefore a solution is often delayed. A possible remedy in this regard is to either phase out or ban landfilling overall or a specific waste stream such as plastic, an endeavour that would require systematic revision of the overall EU waste management regime.

The revision of the EU waste management system is currently in preparation, therefore presenting a highly suitable window of opportunity to adjust it so as to integrate focused measures directed also on marine litter considerations. In this regard, the Green Paper on Waste in the Environment published by the Commission contains several highly applicable and constructive approaches to this issue. It remains to be seen how the therein proposed suggestions will be integrated into existing legislation or lead to new legislative proposals.

This is also the more relevant, as the European Commission withdrew the proposal for a Directive of the European Parliament and of the Council amending Directives 2008/98/EC on waste, 94/62/EC on packaging and packaging waste, 1999/31/EC on the landfill of waste, 2000/53/EC on end-of-life vehicles, 2006/66/EC on batteries and accumulators and waste batteries and accumulators, and 2012/19/EU on waste electrical and electronic equipment 28/10/2014 in March 2015.[1609] The reason for withdrawal being that it the circular economy package will be replaced by a new and more ambitious proposal by the end of 2015 to promote circular economy.[1610] It remains to be seen how the elements of a new proposal feed into the overall marine litter discourse in the EU.

1609 *European Commission,* Press Release, Commission confirms Withdrawal of 73 Pending Proposals Announced in 2015 Work Programme, IP/15/4567, 07.03.2015.

1610 *European Commission*, COM(2014) 910 final, Annex to the Communication from the European Commission to the European Parliament, the Council, the European Economic and Social Committee and the Committee of the Regions on the Commission Work Programme 2015, 8, 16.12.2014.

Other aspects of waste management relate to the regulation of urban waste water which is suggested as a potential source of microplastics contained in personal care products. The established standards of the UWWTD have been identified as failing to address the aspect of this source of pollution in its regulatory scope. Taking a step back, the waste management sector of the EU is currently under review. Admittedly, targeting only certain sectoral instruments such as the UWWTD would be an end-of-pipe-solution that only in a limited manner, systematically and long-term, reduces the input of marine litter through inadequate waste management approaches. It is argued that structural changes in the waste management system overall such as changing recycling targets would be important to that end.

With regard to the impact-related instruments, two instruments have been specifically assessed: the WFD addressing, *inter alia*, the EU´s surface waters and the MSFD, applicable to the marine environment. Even though both instruments are understood as sister-instruments and, in principle, follow the same aim of assessing and monitoring their respective ecosystems, their approaches vary with a view to the marine litter issue. The WFD aims to achieve GEcS and good chemical status and measures this according to ecological quality elements. The prescriptive obligations of the WFD indicate certain parameters and substances according to which the monitoring has to be carried out. An analysis of these parameters has resulted in the conclusion that aspects of marine litter are not directly mentioned in the material scope of the WFD.

In a second step, an attempt to subsume or identify possible elements of marine litter in this context proved to be rather complicated. Aspects of this relate, *inter alia*, to the transparency of the surface waters or chemical associated with plastics. It is argued that the missing explicit mention or reference of plastic and possibly microplastics does not reflect the factual relevance of land-based pollution as a major source of marine litter. Arguably, the no deterioration principle of the WFD also relates to impacts and negative adverse consequences caused by the presence of litter in surface waters. However, the application of the no deterioration principle is limited for litter issues, due to its unclear content and application.

The objective of the WFD to create consistent and coordinated management plans and associated obligations such as monitoring and reporting throughout the designated river basin districts is relevant in the context of rivers located in more than one country. Since the WFD opens the possibility of coordinating measures for these rivers in the framework of international river commissions, it was analysed whether potential synergies with regard to marine litter are to be expected. Since these commissions are mandated and have the aim of reducing the pollution load from their catchment area into the receiving sea, an involvement of their role regarding pertinent marine litter aspects was assumed. However, a further study of their programs and direct communication with their staff has shown that these commissions have not yet explicitly addressed the issue of land-based litter in the context of their work, as of yet.

The MSFD is the fundamental driver in addressing marine litter. Its significance stems not only from the fact that it is one of the first explicit references to marine litter aspects in EU legislation, but also from its impact-related approach. Among the elements defining GES by 2020, marine litter is one of the eleven variables. This gives the issue a prominent place in the comprehensive cyclical assessment and monitoring system of the MSFD. The MSFD has a very low acceptance for harm of marine litter. Even though defining the content and boundary of harm is difficult, the established protection standard is high.

The inherent assessment and monitoring approach of the MSFD allows prevailing uncertainties and knowledge gaps to be addressed. Even though it is suitable to address marine litter in this connection, the MSFD remains broad and gives the Member States a high degree of discretion in selecting suitable monitoring methodologies, admittedly this to be expected in a Framework Directive. In order to address the potential for fragmentation and an unfocused monitoring approach, the MSFD stipulates that the monitoring programmes for the marine regions shall build on and be compatible with assessment and monitoring provisions that are established by Union legislation and/or international agreements. With a view to the prevailing knowledge gap, focused scientific data collection is an important prerequisite for any subsequent actions. The cyclical assessment serves as a mechanism to apply up-to-date scientific knowledge and methodologies that potentially ensure the integration of best available knowledge. Particularly in regard to marine litter aspects, this aspect is a central provision.

The obligation to establish targets linked to the outcome of the assessment and monitoring obligations serves as the key factor of success of this instrument. This serves as a bridging element to integrate source-related legislation in its scope. In the end, it is not measures under the MSFD that effectively reduce the input of marine litter, but other source-related legislation. In this regard, the adoption of ambitious and quantifiable targets is indispensable in effectively using this opportunity in legislation. Since the exercise of target setting is made at the level of Member States, a complementary EU-wide target would frame the different national targets. Even though it is important to establish tailor-made national targets addressing the specific sources and impacts in the environment, such an EU-wide target would serve the purpose of depicting a broad objective that can be integrated into the review of the waste management system for example. With a view to the urgency of the issue and the non-achievement of the GES for marine litter by 2020, a quantified reduction target would be highly suitable. However, in the overall context, the legal value of such a target cannot be entirely estimated. Such an EU-wide target probably serves as a political statement and overall point of reference without necessarily having legal consequences after non-compliance. Notwithstanding this, it could be a yardstick for any other subsequent legislation addressed to reduce or eliminate the introduction of marine litter in the European Union.

Conclusion and Summary

Marine litter is not merely a marine issue. It is a transfer problem where the causal relation between its introduction and its adverse consequences are often far apart from one another. With regard to a regulatory response to marine litter, it is fairly safe to make this assertion. From this assumption, one is already able to draw several conclusions when seeking regulatory responses. Consequently, regulating marine litter, poses certain challenges as the control of the effectiveness of (legal) measures is aggravated due to the dynamic nature of the problem. The role of a legal framework can be to create a level playing field in highly competitive economic activities (such as port reception facilities), coordination of legal measures and responses, to steer and frame economic activities, to ensure legal certainty for stakeholders, express acceptable level or risks and uncertainties and to foster research and technology on the issue with a view to optimising policy and legal instruments.

There are three central conclusions of this study. First, the many consequences and sources of marine litter pose a particular challenge to regulating marine litter. Fundamentally, having a basic knowledge on the sources of marine litter is a prerequisite to establishing effective regulative answers. Even though research and monitoring activities have only been in place for a few short years, the collection of data and knowledge has found its way into several regulatory instruments. Most notably, the MSFD is the first instrument in which a harmonised and structured monitoring scheme is in place. Other monitoring and data collection measures were also developed in the OSPAR region, however, these remain mostly geographically limited. Nevertheless, their design and approach have had an influence on the development of corresponding obligations in other fora. Even though marine litter emanates for the most part from land-based sources, the current regulatory regimes addressing freshwater bodies do not integrate monitoring provisions for litter. The many risks and uncertainties surrounding the consequences of marine litter trigger the application of the precautionary principle that can also be used to determine threshold of acceptable harm.

Second, boon and bane of the marine litter problem is waste management. Whereas it is potentially a major source of marine litter, its relevance to provide solutions in legal terms is undisputed. While the issue of waste management is only marginally addressed in public international law, some Regional Seas Conventions establish requirements regarding waste management both on land as well as in ports. Even though these obligations stem mostly from soft law instruments, they provide a guideline and approach on how to improve waste management in the respective fields. In the EU, waste management law is substantiated by the Waste Framework Directive and several daughter directives that together comprise a comprehensive body of regulation. Even though the substantive standard established by these instruments is very high in itself, the incomplete implementation substantially reduces the effective protection standard. Consequently, having in place adequate substantive law is not the only effective means to reduce the input of marine litter, the established standards have to be implemented and enforced. The CJEU has handed down several judgments that have had an influence on reinforcing environmental standards through addressing specific point sources but also to underline the Member States′ duty to co-operate and actively investigate infringements of EU law. It is to be expected and indeed welcomed from an environmental protection perspective if the European Commission should continue its prior proactive approach to taking infringement proceedings in this area with a view to improving compliance in the mid-term.

Third, due to the manifold direct and indirect sources of marine litter, a regulatory regime relying entirely on sectoral approaches does not effectively address the complexity of the issue. Therefore, a suitable regime must rely on integrated provisions and instruments that are based on the coordination of measures and cooperation among actors. In that way, the sectoral approach to regulate sources of marine litter is overcome, facilitating the development of suitable measures that are adapted to reduce the input of marine litter from every source. An early approach of coordination with regard to marine litter consideration is the Partnership Agreement between the London Convention and London Protocol and the UNEP Global Plan of Action for the Protection of the Marine Environment from Land-based Activities as well as UNEP′s Marine Litter Initiative and the Regional Seas Conventions. In particular UNEP′s Marine Litter Initiative has triggered actions on a regional level. Notwithstanding this, the central and most noteworthy instruments in this regard are the Regional Action Plans on Marine Litter that are (intended) to be adopted under the Regional Seas Conventions. They constitute a paradigm shift away from the ad-hoc and sectoral approach to marine litter and establish long-term and strategic objectives for the sea region in question. The Regional Action Plans not only stipulate substantive requirements for specific regional sources and activities leading to marine litter, they also provide for monitoring and awareness raising aspects. Their role is also reinforced by the cooperation requirements of the MSFD.

Scientific Uncertainties

Marine litter is a complex issue that is framed by a high degree of uncertainty and considerable knowledge gaps. The environmental impacts of marine litter are diverse and can range from entanglements in ghost nets to ingestion of marine litter and litter as a vector for alien species. The dynamic nature and many levels of potential harm create a challenge to define the boundaries of the problem. In particular, the continuous fragmentation of litter and the introduction of primary microplastics constitute important considerations with regard to the assessment of harm and consequences. Microplastics stemming both from primary or secondary plastics sources pose a particular risk due to their size that facilitates their further bioavailability. The particle toxicity of these microparticles can be explained by the adsorbed POPs or additives contained therein. The bioavailability of these contaminants is suspected to be influenced by factors such as the accumulation and translocation of microplastics in the marine organism. The monitoring of the effectiveness of (legal) measures is hindered one the one hand by the dynamic nature of the pollutant in the marine environment and on the other hand by the legacy of polluting activities and the persistency of the material. Additionally, uncertainties still prevail regarding engineered plastic nanoparticles that could be ingested by filter feeders.[1611] The relevance of scientific knowledge is also linked to the role it can play in translating potential risks into a legal sphere. The regulatory context then serves as a vehicle to define environmental, human or economic risks that are acceptable or unacceptable.

Marine litter in public international law

Before an analysis of specific agreements applicable to marine litter, three applicable principles of public international law were assessed with a view

---

1611 *Andrady,* Marine Pollution Bulletin 62 (2011) 1596.

to their role on in guiding decisions and regulatory options in a marine litter context as well as means of interpretation: the polluter-pays-principle, the preventive principle and the precautionary principle. The polluter-pays-principle has a preventive function since its application dissuades potential polluters from polluting in order to reduce the financial consequences of their actions. With regard to marine litter considerations, the polluter-pays-principle faces limitations as diffuse sources with no clearly distinguishable polluter poses a challenge to impose potential sanctions. Also, the application of the principle is limited to determine the extent of damage that was caused by singular sub-threshold activities for example. The polluter-pays-principle can be found in provisions on port reception facilities for example.

The preventive principle applies to those circumstances in which the sources of marine litter are known. The exact content and application of the principle is disputed, however the preventive principle has been substantiated by the Pulp Mills Case in which the ICJ further refined its elements. The ICJ related to the duty of due diligence as an obligation to adopt not only adequate regulations but also to enforce these. The implementation in different agreements has demonstrated that the application of the principle integrates the use of best available techniques, best environmental practice and also clean technology.

The precautionary principle plays a particular important role in a marine litter regulatory context since it is impossible to speak about a quantified or even quantifiable risk. The application and elements of the principle are disputed and differently applied in treaties; however the essence of the precautionary principle is to take anticipatory decisions in order to avoid uncertain future risks. The principle applies in particular to the issue of microplastics, with their diverse risks and uncertainties and can be used when establishing thresholds of harm. When assessing risks or uncertainties regarding such a polluting substance, an important parameter is the boundary of the risk. The boundary of risks thus relates, *inter alia*, to threshold values that seem to suggest that there exists an acceptable amount of pollution and an inacceptable amount. An implementation of the precautionary principle is for example the differentiation between hazardous or non-hazardous substances or zero discharge provisions.

A chronological overview on the development of regulatory responses to marine litter has demonstrated that it was only until recently almost always subsumed under the broader marine pollution framework. Within public international law, a largely sectoral and fragmented approach of the different legal conventions and approaches relating to marine litter is pursued. The differentiation between ocean-based regulations and land-based regulatory approaches can be seen as an expression of the territorial sovereignty of States. Different degrees of regulations are therefore discernible in the regulatory context of public international law regulating marine litter. The adoption of the London Convention constitutes one of the early events addressing a sectoral aspect of marine litter from dumping activities. The London Convention established, in principle, a prohibition of dumping synthetic materials in the marine environment. Plastic has been listed as one of the substances placed on the 'black list' that must not be dumped. However, the London Convention allows for exceptions that potentially undermine the prohibition of the London Convention.

The 'reverse listing' approach of the London Protocol, as well as its corresponding obligation to integrate a precautionary approach, establishes, a much more suitable approach to eliminate dumping as a source of marine litter. The prohibition of dumping of all other wastes except that of Annex 1 LP, implies that a broad range of types of marine litter are covered. However, the vague definitions of the substances of Annex 1 LP potentially provide loopholes for marine litter considerations. Also, the dumping of sewage from municipal treatment plants potentially allow for the introduction of microplastics or microfibers from these sources into the environment.

The MARPOL Convention establishes with Annex V on vessel-based garbage the global regulatory framework for vessel-based pollution. Whereas MARPOL was adopted in the 1970s, the effectiveness of its regulatory standards has been very limited. The recent amendment of MARPOL Annex V has significantly increased legal certainty due to the introduction of further definitions and increased discharge standards resulting in an approximation between areas outside and areas inside Special Areas. Three European seas are subject to an increased protection standard that is established by the adoption of Special Areas under MARPOL Annex V.

On a public international law level, no pertinent legally binding instrument regarding land-based pollution exists. However, the Global Action Programme of Land-based Pollution is, despite its non-binding status, an important programme for marine litter. Marine litter is one of the priority substances under the GPA that puts it in a prominent position. The importance of the GPA regarding marine litter can be summarised as attempting to overcome the fragmentation of its regulation (co-operation between the

London Convention and London Protocol on dumping and the GPA) and the advisory role on (waste) management of marine litter from land-based pollution.

Marine litter in the European Regional Seas Conventions

The four instruments of regional international law relating to marine environmental protection play a particular role in addressing marine litter in the European Seas. Their specific geographical role addressing a confined regional ecosystem allows for tailor-made solutions to be developed so as to target the specific sources and activities leading to pollution by marine litter in the region. Also, their scope usually follows an integrated approach in that ocean-based and land-based pollution are, to a certain degree, commonly regulated. Almost all of them contain monitoring and assessment clause that are highly pertinent regarding the knowledge gap. Each of the different agreements has pursued somewhat different approaches to the issue of marine litter. Since marine litter is a "newly emerging" regulatory aspect, it serves as a case study on how marine litter considerations are integrated into existing agreements.

In the Baltic Sea, the issue of marine litter was for some time perceived as a problem of lower importance. However, the general structure established by the Helsinki Convention contains highly suitable regulations addressing both offshore and land-based sources of marine litter. Synthetic and floating materials are considered as a priority substance under the Helsinki Convention. Additionally, marine litter monitoring has been the subject of a recommendation. The no-special-fee-system assumes the most prominent role in a marine litter context as it serves as an incentive to reduce illegal discharge of vessel-based garbage. With the adoption of HELCOM RAP ML, both the collective regional measures as well as the voluntary national measures form a comprehensive "implementation umbrella" that addresses land-based as well as sea-based sources of marine litter and also highlights the importance of awareness and education actions.

The OSPAR Convention has specific monitoring and assessment provisions that have had repercussions on the approach towards marine litter. Accordingly, monitoring projects on marine litter were initiated and established that serve as role models in other regulatory frameworks such as the EU. Amongst others, the EcoQO on litter found in the stomachs of fulmars is an important biomonitoring approach that will be implemented in other regions. Furthermore, the establishment of a working group focusing on marine litter can be seen as an institutional consolidation of the issue that guarantees a certain degree of consistency.

The Bucharest Convention relating to the protection of the Black Sea has addressed the issue in a sectoral manner. Whereas the BlS ML SAP potentially serves as an indication that the issue has previously received attention, its vague and broadly formulated provisions significantly reduce its effectiveness. Merely the newly adopted and not yet in force 2009 BlS LBP contains the only definition of marine litter in the Black Sea regime.

The Barcelona Convention addressing the protection of the Mediterranean Sea has been dealing with the issue of (coastal) marine litter since the 1980s. The Athens Protocol from 1980 already contains a provision on synthetic and floating material. An analysis of the ICZMP has demonstrated that whereas it contains highly pertinent aspects regarding land-based marine litter sources, its provisions remain fairly vague and broad. The adoption of the RAP ML Med is an important milestone in marine litter regulation in the European Union. It is the first legally binding document specifically addressing in an integrated manner the issue of marine litter in the European Union. Even though it is not legally binding for every Contracting Party to the Barcelona Convention, its drafting and spirit demonstrate a comprehensive approach. Among other things, it includes a definition of marine litter, the inclusion of the precautionary principle, specific targets for offshore and land-based pollution and provisions on awareness raising.

The singular most important feature in the context of the Regional Seas Conventions is the Regional Action Plans on marine litter. Most notably, the RAP ML in the Mediterranean is of particular importance since it is made legally binding. It is interesting to note that the HELCOM RAP ML, for example, focuses on already existing measures that are taken within the framework of HELCOM and also moves beyond measures discussed within the existing governance structure. Its implementation is strengthened through reporting formats on implementation of actions as well as on their effectiveness. It remains to be seen how the Regional Action Plans on marine litter are integrated in the overall structure of the agreements. The elaboration of these Action Plans is also an important show case to understand the prioritisation of marine litter in the conventions. They potentially serve as a "bridge" between the different requirements that were outlined above and therefore can be seen as important developments that will change the context of marine litter regulations in Europe.

European Union framework

The European Union legal framework is a key regulatory instance to eliminate or reduce the introduction of marine litter in the four European Seas. Its complex structure of obligations stemming from primary and secondary EU law integrate (indirectly or directly) a diverse range of marine litter problems. Also, the possibility of judicial review in the form of infringement procedures ensures the coherent and uniform implementation of EU law.

The comprehensive body of secondary EU law necessitates a categorisation of two central types of instruments: source-based instruments and impact-related instruments. It is submitted that not one category on its own can effectively address marine litter, but an interplay between both categories is a fundamental prerequisite to address the problem. This can be explained by the fact that the impact-related instruments need to serve as the basis for knowledge upon which effective and source-oriented legislative answers can be developed. It also serves the purpose of controlling and monitoring whether the chosen mitigation or prevention measures were successful and indeed serve their purpose.

The diversity of pertinent measures to eliminate or reduce the introduction of marine litter makes it a complex problem. In order to illustrate the diversity of the problem, the following table schematically outlines possible responses, structural problems and potential regulatory gaps in the current marine litter regulatory *status quo* in the four European Seas.

Schematic overview on regulatory measures

Regulatory level	Types of regulatory measures
Global	– Dumping: Prohibition of dumping of synthetic materials through London Protocol (and London Convention) – Shipping: MARPOL Annex V on vessel-based pollution: increased discharge standards through Special Areas and revision of Annex V, Port State Control – Land-based pollution: no legally binding measures – Co-operation initiated by UNEP GPA (however limited effect) **Regulatory gaps**: Compliance, microplastics, fragmentation according to sources of marine litter, land-based solutions are not regulated, no specific marine litter monitoring aspects
Regional	– Integrated approach towards different sources of marine litter – Environmental targets (EcoQO) – Regional Action Plans on Marine Litter as important vehicles to ensure an integrated approach – ICZM – Divergence of effectiveness and legal nature of the documents in the different Regional Seas Conventions – Awareness raising **Regulatory gaps:** Compliance, microplastics (partially)
EU law	– Waste management (structural solutions) on land – Infringement procedures (CJEU) – Vessel-based pollution: Port Reception Facilities Directive – Biodiversity protection (link with waste management) – Technical solutions: UWWTD – Impact assessment: MSFD – Market-mechanisms (PRF Directive, Waste Framework Directive) – Public Participation (MSFD and WFD) **Regulatory gaps**: few explicit mention of marine litter aspects, microplastics

Table 3: Schematic overview on regulatory measures in public international and regional law and EU law

The schematic overview indicates that the density of pertinent regulatory measures is increasing from global to the EU level. One central conclusion is however, that with regard to land-based pollution, international law has no legally binding instrument to address this important source of pollution. A major source of pollution is therefore not covered. Despite the different levels and specificities of measures, it is clear that not one single jurisdictional level can adequately address the issue. What is more, an effective regime has to be determined by broad and long-term policy or coordination goals and also by measures of a technical nature. In the end, a robust regulatory framework that integrates different intersections and approaches and effectively addresses loopholes is an essential prerequisite for effective marine litter management.

Compliance

The environmental protection standards of agreements regulating marine litter aspects are characterised by the frequent problems posed by non-compliance with their standards. Even though to date no accepted definition of compliance control exists, compliance can be defined as "the fulfilment by the contracting parties of their obligations under a multilateral environmental agreement and any amendments to the multilateral environmental agreement."[1612] In a marine litter context, compliance with internationally binding norms relates for example to the discharge prohibition of vessel-based pollution under MARPOL Annex V or dumping of materials other than the grey list under the London Protocol. It is argued that, in principle, these standards are clear obligations whose compliance would significantly increase the protection standard regarding the prevention of marine litter. Notwithstanding this, the issue of non-compliance remains one of the central themes in international law of the sea and will most likely increase due to the continuous regulation of the high seas.

Marine litter–institutional aspects

The issue of marine litter has, because of its diverse sources, the potential to be ineffectively regulated due to the inherently fragmented nature of international law. The expansion and continuous growth of the body of international environmental law, however, has the benefit to allow for a differentiated regulation of the issue of marine litter. In the regulatory framework it has not been dealt with as a subject-matter on its own, but as a rather sectoral or fragmented (sub-) aspect. In the role of limiting or avoid-

1612 This definition is taken from the 2002 UNEP Guidelines on Compliance with and Enforcement of Multilateral Environmental Agreements, part 1, http://www.unep.org/delc/Portals/119/UNEP.Guidelines.on.Compliance.MEA.pdf, last accessed 27.08.2015.

ing the introduction of marine litter, a broad range of actors can be determined. The manifold sources of marine litter and potential regulatory solutions seemingly lead to measures that are not connected and harmonised.

However, particularly with a view to diffuse sources, harmonisation is necessary in the context of integrated approaches. Therefore, the increased strive for harmonisation in the different regulatory levels is highly laudable. In this regard, three central actors play an important role. On a global level, this relates to the role of the GPA and UNEP that have had a significant impact on coordinating and initiating of programs and processes. Even though their mandates are in the context of marine litter limited to non-binding measures, the analysis has demonstrated that soft–law measures potentially have a regulatory influence. This is clearly visible in the regard to UNEP`s Marine Litter Initiative.

The second regulatory level consists of the Regional Seas Conventions that face a particular challenge to integrate Contracting Parties with diverse stages of economic development, different societal problems and environmental protection standards. Because of these circumstances, they play an important role in the marine litter regulatory structure. The RAP ML Med, for example constitutes, a paradigm shift since, for the first time, a legally binding document has been adopted that addressed exclusively several aspects of marine litter. The subsequent Regional Action Plans on marine litter in the Baltic Sea and North East Atlantic are important measurable results of co-operation and coordination efforts with a view to reduce or eliminate the introduction of marine litter.

On a third level, the regulatory framework of the European Union plays an important role in initiating and streamlining pertinent measures. In this regard, the MSFD as a driver for monitoring activities and target setting is an important element. Its coordination potential is on the one hand derived from the jurisdictional integration of the Regional Seas Conventions as a platform of coordination. On the other hand, an important leverage point is the integration of source-based solutions as targets and measures. It remains to be seen whether the EU Member States integrate this important opportunity.

These actors demonstrate that an institutionalised and streamlined approach to address the issue of marine litter is the fundamental element of any marine litter regulatory framework, not only accounting for the transboundary impact of marine litter but also contributing to create synergies in research and development of measures. Even though it is undisputed that all actors are indispensable, the role of the Regional Seas Conventions is particularly highlighted. Even though their work is on occasion coined by incomplete implementation, financial constraints and limited mandates to act, they have the competence to address all (contracting) States around a specific marine region.

Marine litter as a societal question

Even though an effective regulatory framework regarding the introduction of marine litter is indispensable, an approach only limited to judicial questions would quasi deny the complex societal questions that are associated with it. The problem of marine litter is highly dynamic and not linear in nature. Marine litter is a societal problem that necessitates that a broad range of measures are taken in order to be able to effectively reduce or eliminate its introduction into the aquatic environment.

Resource efficiency

Marine litter demonstrates how society deals with waste that can be seen as a resource. Admittedly, the concept of resource efficiency has been used as a catch-phrase in the political context; its underlying understanding and potential implementation are still relevant. The European Commission has presented its understanding of the notion among others in the Communication "Roadmap to a Resource Efficient Europe" from 2011[1613] in which the different steps towards achieving this aim are highlighted. Whereas centrally it implies the use of resources in a sustainable way, it represents one of the key strategies to reduce marine litter from a waste management perspective. The underlying idea is to restore the value of a used product, therefore reducing its overall impact on the environment. The concept of the cradle to cradle approach, also known as open loop production that was elaborated by *Wiliam McDonough* and *Michael Braungart* is an important issue in this respect.[1614] The field of operation of the cradle to cradle approach is a circular economy in which the product is produced, used and then recycled instead of disposed. Through recycling of already used raw materials the overall demand for new material is reduced. Applying this understanding of a circular economy would there-

---

1613 *European Commission*, COM (2011) 571 final, Communication from the Commission to the Council and the European Parliament, Roadmap to a Resource Efficient Europe, 20.09.2011.

1614 *McDonough/Braungart,* Cradle to cradle: remaking the way we think, 2002.

fore be a necessary paradigm change that could target the issue of marine litter at its source. Therefore, the circular economy package as proposed by the European Commission is a promising step towards achieving the reduction of waste which in turn potentially reduces the emission of it into the (marine environment).[1615] However, after the withdrawal of a proposal on amending certain directives as part of the circular economy package,[1616] it remains to be seen what can be understood by the promise to replace the package by a new and more ambitious proposal.[1617]

Education and awareness

Another aspect that is also very relevant is whether a threshold in regard to a sociably accepted pollution exists. Similar to other environmental catastrophes, any heavy pollution incidents are mostly acknowledged after they have resulted in disastrous effects (such as Exxon Valdez or Deep Water Horizon) or affect the individual in their daily life or holidays. This basic premise also plays an important role in the regulation of marine litter. A study that addresses the regulatory framework to prevent marine litter, can only address individual behaviour marginally. In this aspect, environmental awareness and education are key approaches that help to clarify the negative consequences that these actions could have on the environment and also human health itself. The role of public perception of the issue of marine litter or microplastics is an important guidance in steering the (un)acceptability of plastic pollution. In this regard, public participation is an important vehicle in creating awareness. As has been outlined, several instruments such as the Regional Action Plans on marine litter have dedicated specific provisions on this aspect. Amongst others clean-up activities are suitable measures to increase awareness.[1618]

1615 See for further information on this topic, chapter 4 B.V.4.

1616 See also section C of chapter 4. *European Commission,* Press Release, Commission confirms Withdrawal of 73 Pending Proposals Announced in 2015 Work Programme, IP/15/4567, 07.03.2015.

1617 *European Commission*, COM(2014) 910 final, Annex to the Communication from the European Commission to the European Parliament, the Council, the European Economic and Social Committee and the Committee of the Regions on the Commission Work Programme 2015, 8, 16.12.2014.

1618 *Martin,* Marine Pollution Bulletin 74 (2013) 165, 168.

Outlook

Marine litter regulation is constantly shifting. Whereas it has been formerly concluded under sectoral pollution control, it has increasingly gained momentum and has been identified as a singular important pollutant. Even though microplastics are labelled as "emerging pollutants", their first reference as being in the marine environment can be dated to the 1990s. Nevertheless, approximately 20 years later, the issue of microplastics and also marine litter have gained increasing attention.

During the recent G7 Summit which was hosted by Germany in June 2015, the leaders of the G7 group acknowledged in their Summit Declaration that "[…] marine litter, in particular plastic litter, poses a global challenge, directly affecting marine and coastal life and ecosystems and potentially also human health. Accordingly, increased effectiveness and intensity of work is required to combat marine litter striving to initiate a global movement." Further, the G7 Summit "commits to priority actions and solutions to combat marine litter as set out in the annex, stressing the need to address land- and sea-based sources, removal actions, as well as education, research and outreach."[1619]

In the Annex to the G7 Summit Declaration, the G7 Action Plan to Combat Marine Litter is presented.[1620] Overarching principles are defined as an umbrella structure that include, amongst others, a reference to support regional or national action plans to prevent marine litter as well as removal efforts. Furthermore, and very importantly, the principles also include to opt for a broad range of policy toolkits and instruments including economic incentives and market based instruments to support effective marine litter prevention measures. The Action Plan evolves around four action pillars. The first action pillar addresses priority for land-based sources.[1621] The Action Plan identifies the improvement of countries' waste management and the encouragement of reusing and recycling as key working areas. Furthermore, the Action Plan encourages industry to develop sustainable packaging and remove ingredients from products to gain environmental benefits, such as by a voluntary phase-out of microbeads. With regard to the second action pillar on sea-based sources of marine lit-

1619 G7, Leader's Declaration G7 Summit: Think Ahead. Act Together - An morgen denken. Gemeinsam handeln, G7 Germany, Schloss Elmau, 7-8 June 2015.

1620 G7, Annex to the Leader's Declaration, G7 Summit Germany, Schloss Elmau, 7-8 June 2015, 9.

1621 *Ibid.*, 10.

ter, the Action Plan outlines, amongst others, to work towards maximizing the amount of waste delivered to port reception facilities and disposed of properly in accordance with Annex V of the International Convention for the Prevention of Pollution from Ships (MARPOL).[1622] The third action pillar addresses priority removal actions, which envisage to "support the removal of litter where it poses a threat to sensitive marine ecosystems, in an environmentally sound way, taking into account the socioeconomic aspects including cost effectiveness, thereby using best available techniques (BAT) and best Environmental practice (BEP) and engaging partners where possible."[1623] Lastly, the fourth action pillar addresses priority actions on education, research and outreach.[1624] The actions referred to include promoting outreach and education activities that might lead to individual behaviour change with the aim to reduce the amount of litter entering the seas. Furthermore, it is aimed to support the initiation of a harmonized global marine litter monitoring effort as well as supporting the efforts of UNEP to understand the sources, pathways and impacts of marine litter.

In the following years and decade, several targets and associated time lines are set. The consequence thereof will be increased scientific research and development regarding the issue that will ultimately lead to a larger body of acquired knowledge that contributes to reduce the uncertainties surrounding the issue. The multitude of targets however runs the risk of remaining only political goals that are merely lip service.

Some of the different targets and time lines are delimited underneath:

Year	Instrument/document
2015	GEcS WFD
2015	HELCOM RAP ML
2020	GES MSFD
2025	Rio+20: "States take action by …[…]"
2025	HELCOM: Aim is to achieve by then a significant quantitative reduction of marine litter by 2025
2025	GPA: Aim is to achieve adequate waste services for all urban populations

Table 4: Outlook on the relevant marine litter targets in different instruments.

1622 *Ibid.*, 11.
1623 *Ibid.*, 10.
1624 *Ibid.*, 11.

Despite the importance to determine goals and objective to focus regulatory measures, the risk potentially prevails that States rely on the legacy of polluting activities and the persistency of the material as a potential excuse not to take adequate actions. That this risk possibly prevails is also visible from the outcome document of the UN Conference on Sustainable Development "Rio +20." In this context, States "commit to take action to, by 2025, based on collected scientific data, achieve significant reductions in marine debris to prevent harm to the coastal and marine environment."[1625] Even though the document clearly aims towards a harmonised data collection effort, the weak commitment to take actions could be understood to effect a postponement of measures until after the outcome of scientific undertakings. Notwithstanding the importance of verified evidence as a precondition for effective measures, a postponement to take action or enforce material law in the EU would clearly counteract the aim of reducing marine litter by 2020. Additionally, such an approach would be incompatible with the precautionary principle as enshrined in EU primary law.

1625 *UNGA*, A/RES/66/288, United Nations General Assembly, Resolution 66/288 on "the Future we want", Annex, Conference Report Rio+20 United Nations Conference on Sustainable Development, 11.09.2012, para.163.

Bibliography

I. International instruments and cases

1. International Conventions

1945 Statute of the International Court of Justice (San Francisco) of 26 June 1945, in force 24 October 1945; 1946 UKTS 67

1948 Convention on the International Maritime Consultative Organization (Geneva) of 06 March 1948, in force 17 March 1958; 289 UNTS 175

1969 Convention on the Law of Treaties (Vienna) of 25 May 1969, in force 27 January 1980; 1980 UKTS 58

1969 Agreement for Co-operation in Dealing with Pollution of the North Sea by Oil (Bonn) of 09 June 1969, in force 09 August 1969; 704 UNTS as revised in 1983, in force 01 September 1989

1972 Convention for the Prevention of Marine Pollution by Dumping from Ships and Aircraft (Oslo) of 15 February 1972, in force 07 April 1974; 11 ILM 262 (1972)

1972 Convention on the Prevention of Marine Pollution by Dumping of Wastes and Other Matter (London Convention) (London, Mexico-City, Moscow, Washington) of 29 December 1972, in force 30 August 1975; 11 ILM 1294 (1972)

1973 International Convention for the Prevention of Pollution from Ships (MARPOL) (London) of 2 November 1973, in force 2 October 1983 as amended by the 1978 Protocol (London), of 01 June 1978; 1340 UNTS 61

1974 Convention on the Protection of the Marine Environment of the Baltic Sea Area (1974 Helsinki Convention) (Helsinki) of 22 March 1974, in force 03 May 1980; 13 ILM 546 (1974)

1974 Convention for the Prevention of Marine Pollution from Land-Based Sources (Paris) of 04 June 1974, in force 06 May1978; 13 ILM 352 (1974)

1976 Convention for the Protection of the Mediterranean Sea against Pollution (Barcelona) of 16 February 1976, in force 12 February 1978; 1102 UNTS, 27, 15 ILM 290 (1976), as amended by the Convention for the Protection of the Marine Environment and the Coastal Region of the Mediterranean of 19 June 1995, in force 09 July 2004; 2102 UNTS 201, 16

1976 Protocol to the Convention for the Protection of the Mediterranean Sea Against Pollution (Barcelona Convention) on the Prevention and Elimination of Pollution of the Mediterranean Sea by Dumping from Ships and Aircraft (Barcelona) of 6 February 1976, in force 12 February 1978

1982 United Nations Convention on the Law of the Sea (UNCLOS) (Montego Bay) of 10 December 1982, in force 14 November 1994; 1833 UNTS 3

1982 Memorandum of Understanding on Port State Control (Paris MoU) (Paris) of 26 January 1982, in effect 01 July 1982

1990 Convention of the International Commission for the Protection of the Elbe (Magdeburg) of 08 October 1990 (OJ L 321, 23.11.1991)

1991 Protocol to the Convention of 8 October 1990 between the Governments of the Federal Republic of Germany and the Czech and Slovak Federal Republic and the European Economic Community on the International Commission for the Protection of the Elbe (OJ 1993 L 045, 23.02.1993), in force 13 August 1993

1992 Convention on the Protection of the Marine Environment of the Baltic Sea Area (Helsinki Convention) (Helsinki) of 09 April 1992, in force 17 January 2000; 33 ILM 1540 (1992)

1992 Convention on the Protection of the Black Sea against pollution (Bucharest) of 21 April 1992, in force 15 January 1994; ILM 110 (1992) ; 1 1764 UNTS 3

1992 Convention for the Protection of the Marine Environment of the North-East Atlantic (OSPAR Convention) (Paris) of 22 September 1992, in force 25 March 1998; 2354 UNTS 67; 32 ILM 1069 (1993)

1994 Convention on Co-operation for the Protection and Sustainable Use of the River Danube (Sofia) of 29 June 1994, in force 22 October 1998; EMuT 994:49

1994 Protocol to the Convention for the Protection of the Marine Environment and the Coastal Region of the Mediterranean on the Protection of the Mediterranean Sea against Pollution Resulting from Exploration and Exploitation of the Continental Shelf and the Seabed and its Subsoil (Madrid) of 14 October 1994, in force on 24 March 2011

1995 Protocol to the Convention for the Protection of the Marine Environment and the Coastal Region of the Mediterranean concerning Mediterranean Specially Protected Areas (Barcelona) of 19 June 1995, in force 12 December 1999

1996 Protocol to the Convention for the Protection of the Marine Environment and the Coastal Region of the Mediterranean on the Prevention of Pollution of the Mediterranean Sea by Transboundary Movements of Hazardous Wastes and their Disposal (Izmir) of 1 October 1996, in force 19 January 2008

1996 Protocol to the 1972 Convention on the Prevention of Marine Pollution by Dumping of Wastes and Other Matter (London Protocol) (London) of 07 November 1996, in force 24 March 2006; 36 ILM 1 (1997)

1999 Convention on the Protection of the Rhine (Bern) of 12 April 1999, in force 01 January 2003; EMuT 999:28

2001 Convention on Persistent Organic Pollutants (Stockholm Convention) (Stockholm) of 22 May 2001, in force 17 May 2004; 40 ILM 532 (2001)

2008 Protocol to the Convention for the Protection of the Marine Environment and the Coastal Region of the Mediterranean. on Integrated Coastal Zone Management in the Mediterranean (Madrid) of 21 January 2008, in force 24 March 2011

2. Permanent Court of International Justice

1927 The Lotus case (France v. Turkey), Judgement of 07 September 1927, PCIJ, Ser.A, No 10

3. International Tribunal for the Law of the Sea (ITLOS)

1999 The Southern Bluefin Tuna Cases (Australia v. Japan; New Zealand v. Japan), Request for Provisional Measures, Order of 27 August 1999, ITLOS Reports 1999, 280

2001 The Mox Plant Case (Ireland v. United Kingdom) Request for Provisional Measures and Statement of Cases in Ireland of 9 November 2001, ITLOS Reports 5 (2001), 95

2011 Responsibilities and Obligations of States Sponsoring Persons and Entities with Respect to Activities in the Area, Advisory Opinion, Seabed Dispute Chamber of 01 February 2011 (No 17), ILM 50 (2011), 455

4. International Court of Justice

1949 Corfu Channel Case (United Kingdom of Great Britain and Northern Ireland v. Albania), Merits, Judgement of 9 April 1949, ICJ Rep.1949, 4 (Corfu Channel)

2010 Pulp Mills on the River Uruguay (Argentina v. Uruguay), Judgement of 20 April 2010, ICJ Rep.2010, 14 (Pulp Mills)

5. Arbitrations

1905 Trail Smelter (United States of America v. Canada), RIAA III, 1905, 1938

6. United Nations

U.N. Doc. A/Conf.48/14/Rev. 1(1973), Declaration of the United Nations Conference on the Human Environment of 16 June 1972 (Stockholm Declaration); 11 ILM 1416 (1972)

UNCLOS Third Committee, 5th Meeting July 15-16 1974, UNCLOS III 312-13, Delegate of Sweden: Mr. Delin

World Commission on Environment Development, Our Common Future 1987, transmitted to the General Assembly as an Annex to document A/42/427 - Development and International Co-operation.

Rio Declaration on Environment and Development of 13 June 1992, 31 ILM 876 (1992)

A/CONF.151/26, Agenda 21: Programme of Action and Sustainable Development, 13.06.1992

A/RES/51/189, United Nations General Assembly Resolution on Institutional arrangements for the implementation of the Global Programme of Action for the Protection of the Marine Environment from Land-based Activities, 21.02.1997

UN/ECLAC, LC/CAR/L.24, Major issues in the management of enclosed or semi-enclosed seas, with a particular reference to the Caribbean Sea, 18.11.2004

A/RES/60/30, United Nations General Assembly, Resolution 60/30 on Oceans and the law of the sea, 08.03.2006

A/RES/65/37, United Nations General Assembly, Resolution 65/37 on Oceans and the law of the sea, 17.03.2011

United Nations Conference on Sustainable Development, Rio Ocean Declaration, Calling for strong and immediate action to meet the sustainable development goals for oceans, coasts, and small island developing States (SIDS) at Rio+20 and beyond, Co-Chairs' Statement of The Oceans Day at Rio+20 (Rio de Janeiro, Brazil), 16.06.2012

A/RES/66/288, United Nations General Assembly, Resolution 66/288 on "the Future we want", Annex, Conference Report Rio+20 United Nations Conference on Sustainable Development, 11.09.2012

United Nations Development Programme- Lebanon, The Rehabilitation of Saida Dumpsite, Project document, available online at http://www.lb.undp.org/content/dam/lebanon/docs/Energy%20and%20Environment/Projects/3244.pdf, updated 10.05.2013, last accessed 27.08.2015

UNEP/EA.1/10, United Nations Environment Assembly of the United Nations Environment Programme, Resolution 1/6. Marine plastic debris and microplastics, 02.09.2014

7. UNCTAD

UNCTAD/RMT/2011, Review of Maritime Transport 2011

8. UNEP (UNEP and GPA)

UNEP, Protection of the Marine Environment Against Pollution from land-Based Sources" (Montreal Guidelines), Environmental Policy and Law, Vol.14, 1985, 77

UNEP/IOC/FAO, Assessment of the State of Pollution of the Mediterranean Sea by persistent synthetic materials which may float, sink or remain in suspension, Athens, MAP Technical Reports Series, 56, 1991

UNEP(OCA)/LBA/IG.2/7, Global Programme of Action for the Protection of the Marine Environment from land-based Activities (GPA), Intergovernmental Conference to adopt a Global Programme of Action for the Protection of the Marine Environment from Land-Based Activities, 05.12.1995

UNEP/EAS/GPA/HS. 1/4. UNEP East Asian Seas Regional Co-ordinated Unit, Report on the Regional Workshop on Identification of Pollution Hot Spots in the East Asian Seas Region, 2002

UNEP, Marine litter, an analytical overview, Nairobi: UNEP, 2005

UNEP, Marine Litter: A Global Challenge, Nairobi: UNEP, 2009

TBD IGR-3 25-27, UNEP/ Division of Environmental Policy Implementation, Global Partnership on Waste Management, Marine Litter (ML) Work Plan for 2012-2016, November 2011

UNEP/GPA/IGR.3/3, Policy guidance for implementing the Global Programme of Action for the Protection of the Marine Environment from Land-based Activities over the period 2012–2016, Intergovernmental Review Meeting on the Implementation of the Global Programme of Action for the Protection of the Marine Environment from Land-based Activities, Third session, 01.11.2011

UNEP/GPA/IGR.3/INF/3/Rev. 1, Progress in implementing the Global Programme of Action for the Protection of the Marine Environment from Land-based Activities at the National Level, Intergovernmental Review Meeting on the Implementation of the Global Programme of Action for the Protection of the Marine Environment from Land-based Activities Third session Manila, 04.01.2012

UNEP/GPA/IGR.3/INF/9, Honolulu Strategy– a global framework for prevention and management of marine debris, Intergovernmental Review Meeting on the implementation of the Global Programme of Action for the Protection of the Marine Environment from Land-based Activities Third session, Manila, 12.01.2012

UNEP/GPA/IGR.3/INF/6, Progress in the implementation of UNEP's marine litter activities 2007-2011 and the way forward from 2012 to 2016, Intergovernmental Review Meeting on the implementation of the Global Programme of Action for the Protection of the Marine Environment from Land-based Activities, Third session, Manila, 12.01.2012

UNEP/GPA/IGR.3/CRP.1/Rev. 1., Manila Declaration on Furthering the Implementation of the Global Programme of Action for the Protection of the Marine Environment from Land-based Activities, Intergovernmental Review Meeting on the Implementation of the Global Programme of Action for the Protection of the Marine Environment from Land-based Activities Third session, Manila, 26.01.2012

UNEP/CBD, Report of the Expert Workshop Report of the Expert Workshop to Prepare Practical Guidance on Preventing and Mitigating the Significant Adverse Impacts of Marine Debris on Marine and Coastal Biodiversity and Habitats (UNEP/CBD/MCB/EM/2014/3/2), 2-4.12.2014, Annex IV, https://www.cbd.int/doc/?meeting=MCBEM-2014-03, last accessed 27.08.2015.

9. International Conferences on the Protection of the North Sea

1984 Ministerial Declaration of the First International Conference on the Protection of the North Sea, 1 November 1984 (Bremen)

1987 Ministerial Declaration of the Second International Conference on the Protection of the North Sea, 25 November 1987 (London)

1990 Ministerial Declaration of the Third International Conference on the Protection of the North Sea, 8 March 1990 (The Hague)

1995 Ministerial Declaration of the Fourth Conference on the Protection of the North Sea, 9 June 1995 (Esbjerg)

10. IMO[1626]

Assembly resolution A.466 (XII) on Procedures for the Control of Ships, 1981

Assembly resolution A.787 (19) on Procedures for Port State Control, 23.11.1995

LC 19/10, Report of the Nineteenths Consultative Meeting of Contracting Parties to the Convention on the Prevention of Marine Pollution by Dumping of Wastes and Other Matter, 14.11.1997

MEPC 42/22, Report of the Marine Environment Protection Committee on its Forty-Second Session, 16.11.1998

Assembly resolution A.882 (219) on Amendments to the Procedures for Port State Control, 25.11.1999

IMO, Comprehensive manual on port reception facilities, 1999, 2nd ed., London

IMO, Guidelines for ensuring the adequacy of port waste reception facilities, 2000, London

Resolution MEPC.83(44), Guidelines for ensuring the adequacy of port waste reception facilities, 13.04.2000 as contained in Annex 2 of the Report of the Marine Environment Protection Committee on its Forty-Fourth Session, MEPC 44/20, 12.04.2000

LC/SG 24/2/Add.4, Waste Assessment Guidance: Completion of the Reformatting of the Waste-Specific Guidelines adopted in 2000, Twenty-Fourth Meeting of the London Convention and London Protocol Scientific Group, 23.02.2001

LC/SG 21/11, Report of the Twenty-Fourth Meeting of the of the London Convention and London Protocol Scientific Group, Twenty-Fourth Meeting of the Scientific Group, 24.07.2001

Assembly resolution Res.A.882(21), Procedures for Port State Control, amending Resolution A.787(19), 2001, London

LC 26/WP.4/Add.1, Draft Report of the Twenty-sixth Consultative Meeting (continued), Twenty-Sixth Consultative Meeting of Contracting Parties to the Convention on the Prevention of Marine Pollution by Dumping of Wastes and Other Matter 1972, 04.11.2004

LC 27/16, Report of the 27th Consultative Meeting of Contracting Parties to the Convention on the Prevention of Marine Pollution by Dumping of Wastes and Other Matter 1972, 06.12.2006

1626 The IMO documents are available at: http://www.imo.org/about/pages/default.aspx. The differing names and title names and dates are due to the inconsistent labelling of some IMO documents.

IMO, Guidelines for the implementation of Annex V of MARPOL, 2006, 2nd ed., London

Assembly resolution A 24/Res.982, Assembly Resolution on Revised Guidelines for the Identification and Designation of Particularly Sensitive Sea Areas, adopted on 01. December 2005, 06.02.2006

MEPC 54/21, Report of the Marine Environment Protection Committee on its Fifty-Fourth Session, 27.02.2006

LC/SG 29/8, Status Report of the Joint London Convention/MEPC Correspondence Group, Coastal Management issues associated with activities to prevent marine pollution: Collaboration with MEPC to clarify boundary issues between the London Convention/Protocol and MARPOL 73/78, 09.06.2006

LC 28/15, Report of the Twenty-Eight Consultative Meeting of Contracting Parties to the Convention on the Prevention of Marine Pollution by Dumping of Wastes and Other Matter 1972 and First Meeting of Contracting Parties to the 1996 Protocol to the Convention on the Prevention of Marine Pollution by Dumping of Wastes and Other Matter 1972, 06.12.2006

LC 29/17, Report of the Twenty-Ninth Consultative Meeting and the Second Meeting of Contracting Parties, 14.12.2007

MEPC.1/Circ.469/Rev. 1, Revised Consolidated Format For Reporting alleged Inadequacies of Port Reception Facilities, 13.07.2007

MEPC 58/6/5, Interpretations of and amendments of MARPOL and related instruments, status Report on the Review of MARPOL Annex V, 01.08.2008

MEPC 59/6/3, Interpretations of and amendments to MARPOL and related Instruments, Report of the Correspondence Group for the Review of MARPOL Annex V, 02.04.2009

LC/SG 32/8, Coastal Management issues associated with activities- Initial proposals for co-operation between the London Convention and Protocol and the UNEP Global Programme of Action for Protection of the Marine Environment from Land-based Activities (GPA) discussed during the Thirty-Second Meeting of the Scientific Group of the London Convention and the Third Meeting of the Scientific Group of the London Protocol Scientific Group, 24.04.2009

MEPC 59/6/14, Interpretations of, and Amendments to, MARPOL and related Instruments, comments on the Report of the Correspondence Group for the Review of MARPOL Annex V, 22.05.2009

LC/SG 32/15, Report of the Thirty-Second Meeting of the Scientific Group of the London Convention and the Third Meeting of the Scientific Group of the London Protocol, 29.06.2009

MEPC.1/Circ.67. MEPC, Guide to Good Practice for Port Reception Facility Providers and Users, 20.07.2009

LC 31/15, Report of the Thirty-First Consultative Meeting and the Fourth Meeting of Contracting Parties, 30.11.2009

MEPC 60/6/8, Solving the problem of marine litter by making MARPOL Annex V SMART, submitted by Friends of the Earth International (FOEI), 15.01.2010

MEPC 61/7/2, Interpretations of, and amendments to, MARPOL and other related instruments, Report of the Correspondence Group for the Review of MARPOL Annex V, submitted by New Zealand, 28.06.2010

MEPC 62/6/2, Issues arising from the Committee's work on the revision of MARPOL Annex V, sub-mitted by the Clean Shipping Coalition (CSC), 23.05.2011

LC/SG 34/15, Report of the Thirty-Fourth Meeting of the Scientific Group of the London Convention and the Fifth Meeting of the Scientific Group of the London Protocol, 24.05.2011

LC 33/15, Report of the Thirty-Third Consultative Meeting and the Sixth Meeting of the Contracting Parties, 08.11.2011

Resolution MEPC.201(62), Amendments to the Annex of the Protocol of 1978 relating to the International Convention for the Prevention of Pollution from ships, 1973, Revised MARPOL Annex V, 15.07.2011

LP-CG 4/1/1, Fourth Meeting of the Compliance Group under the London Protocol, 21.08.2011

MEPC 63/7, Report of the Intersessional Correspondence Group on Reviewing the Guidelines for the Implementation of MARPOL Annex V and the Guidelines for the Development of Garbage Management Plans, 25.11.2011

MEPC 63/9, Identification and Protection of Special Areas and Particularly Sensitive Sea Areas, Consequential amendments to the Guidelines for the Designation of Special Areas under MARPOL, 25.11.2011

Assembly resolution A.1052(27), Procedures for Port State Control, 2011, 20.12.2011

LEG/MISC.7, Implications of the United Nations Convention on the Law of the Sea for the International Maritime Organization, Study by the Secretariat of the International Maritime, 19.01.2012

Resolution MEPC .219(63), 2012 Guidelines for the Implementation of MARPOL Annex V, 02.03.2012

Resolution MEPC .220(63), 2012 Guidelines for the development of Garbage Management Plans, 02.03.2012

MEPC 64/INF.29, Outcomes of the joint session of the Scientific Groups under the London Convention and Protocol in relation to the management of spoilt cargoes, Note by the Secretariat, 27.07.2012

MEPC 65/7, Interpretations of, and Amendments to MARPOL and related instruments, Draft revised guidance to manage spoilt cargoes, 03.01.2013

LC-LP.1/Circ.58, Revised Guidance on the Management of spoilt cargos, 03.07.2013

LC 35/15, Report of the Thirty-Fifth Consultative Meeting and the Eight Meeting of Contracting Parties, Annex 9 Information flyer on spoilt cargos–managing spoilt cargo, 21.10.2013

11. HELCOM[1627]

HELCOM Recommendation 21/2 on Amendments to Annex IV "Prevention of Pollution from Ships" of the Helsinki Convention, 20.03.2000

HELCOM Recommendation 22/3 on Unified interpretations to ensure a harmonised and effective implementation of the strategy for port reception facilities for ship-generated wastes and associated issues, 21.03.2001

HELCOM Recommendation 24/10 on the Implementation of Integrated Marine and Coastal Management of Human Activities in the Baltic Sea Area, 25.06.2003

HELCOM Recommendation 23/1 on Notification on ship´s waste, 06.03.2002

HELCOM Recommendation 28E/10 on the Application of the no-special-fee system to ship-generated wastes and marine litter caught in fishing nets in the Baltic Sea Area, 15.11.2007

HELCOM News, 1/2008 Newsletter, Marine litter a concern, but not a major problem

HELCOM 29th Meeting (29/2008), Agenda Item 3 Matters arising from the subsidiary bodies, Document Code 3/11

HELCOM Recommendation 29/2 on marine litter within the Baltic Sea Region, 05.03.2008

HELCOM HOD 27th Meeting (27/2008), Agenda Item 2: Use of HELCOM´s work in implementing other international legislative frameworks, Document Code 2/4/ Rev. 1

HELCOM, Ecosystem Health of the Baltic Sea 2003–2007: HELCOM Initial Holistic Assessment, Baltic Sea Environmental Proceedings (No 122), 2010

HELCOM Ministerial Declaration on the implementation of the HELCOM Baltic Sea Action Plan, 20.05.2010 (Moscow, Russia) (HELCOM Moscow Ministerial Declaration)

HELCOM Recommendation 31E/4 on Proper handling of wastes/landfilling, 20.05.2010

HELCOM HOD 35th Meeting (35/2011), Agenda Item 3: Matters arising from the HELCOM Groups -Draft Criteria for Green Baltic Spots, Document Code 3/12

HELCOM Land 17th Meeting (17/2012), Agenda Item 6: Joint Comprehensive Environmental Action Programme - Request for additional information for the decision to delete hot spots No.54 in Lithuania, Document code 6/16

HELCOM HOD 39th Meeting (39/2012), Agenda Item 3: Marine Litter in the Baltic Sea - Overview of present status and potential for further HELCOM actions, Document Code 3/19

1627 All documents available at: http://www.helcom.fi/helcom-at-work/meetings/. The date of the documents are not necessarily congruent with the dates of the meetings

HELCOM Copenhagen Ministerial Declaration "Taking Further Action to Implement the Baltic Sea Action Plan - Reaching Good Environmental Status for a healthy Baltic", 03.10.2013 (Copenhagen, Denmark) (HELCOM Copenhagen Ministerial Declaration)

HELCOM HOD 46th Meeting, (46/2014), Outcome of HOD 46-2014, Agenda Item 3:Streamlining of HELCOM, Document Code 3.6, 3

HELCOM HOD 46th Meeting (46/2014), Outcome of HOD 46-2014, Annex 3: Terms of References for HELCOM Working Group on Reduction of Pressures from the Baltic Sea Catchment Area (WG Pressure), 19

HELCOM LAND, 2nd Workshop on Regional Action Plan for Marine Litter (MARINE LITTER 2-2014), held in Stralsund, Germany from 22.10 to 23.10.2014

HELCOM Recommendation 36/1 on a Regional Action Plan on Marine Litter (RAP ML), 04.03.2015

HELCOM HOD 48th Meeting, (48/2015), Outcome of HOD 48-2015, Agenda Item 3: Matters arising from the HELCOM Groups 3.1. to 3.8, Documents 3-1, 3

HELCOM HOD 48th Meeting, (48/2015), Outcome of HOD 48-2015, Annex 2: Actions to reduce the input and presence of marine litter in the Baltic Sea as part of the HELCOM Regional Action Plan on Marine Litter, 16.

12. Black Sea

Ministerial Declaration on the Protection of the Black Sea, 07.04.1993 (Odessa) (Odessa Declaration)

Black Sea Commission, Memorandum of Understanding between the International Commission for the Protection of the Black Sea (ICPBS) and the International Commission for the Protection of the Danube River (ICPDR) on common strategic goals, signed in Brussels on 26 November 2001

The Black Sea Biodiversity and Landscape Conservation Protocol to the Convention on the Protection of the Black Sea Against Pollution (Sofia) of 14 June 2002, in force 20 June 2011

Ministerial Declaration of the Ministers of Environment of the Contracting Parties to the Convention on the Protection of the Black Sea Against Pollution, 14.07.2002 (Sofia) (Sofia Declaration)

Black Sea Commission, Black Sea transboundary diagnostic analysis, 2007

Black Sea Commission, Marine Litter in the Black Sea Region, 2007

Black Sea Commission, Agreement of Cooperation between the International Maritime Organization (IMO) and the Commission on the Protection of the Black Sea Against Pollution (BSC), December 2009

Black Sea Commission, Implementation of the Strategic Action Plan for the Rehabilitation and Protection of the Black Sea, 2002-2007, Publication of the Commission on the Protection of the Black Sea Against Pollution, 2009

Black Sea Commission, Marine Litter in The Black Sea Region, Overview and Draft Strategic Action Plan for the Management and Abatement of Marine Litter in the Black Sea Region, in: UNEP (ed.): Marine Litter: A Global Challenge, Nairobi, Kenya: Regional Seas, United Nations Environment Programme, 2009, 39–52

Black Sea Commission, Strategic Action Plan for the Environmental Protection and Rehabilitation of the Black Sea, BlS SAP, 2nd ed., 17.04.2009 (Sofia, Bulgaria)

Black Sea Commission/IMO, IMO/MoEF/BSC Regional Workshop on Implementation of International Dumping Agreements in the Black Sea Region, Istanbul, 23-25 February 2011, available online at http://81.8.63.74/Downloads/RegionalDumping WorkshopReportFeb2011Istanbul.pdf

Black Sea Commission, Draft Legally Binding Document (LBD) for Fisheries and Conservation of Living Resources of the Black Sea

13. UNEP/MAP[1628]

UNEP MAP MED POL, Strategic action programme to address pollution from land-based activities, MAP Technical Reports Series (No 119), Athens, 1999

UNEP(DEC)/MED WG.183/Inf.4, Litter Management in Coastal Zones of the Mediterranean Basin - Analysis of the Questionnaire and Proposals for Guideline, Meeting of the MED POL National Coordinators, 07.05.2001

UNEP MAP, Guidelines on management of coastal litter for the Mediterranean, Athens, MAP Technical Reports Series (No 148), Athens, 2004

UNEP(DEC)/MED IG. 16/5/Annex III, the MED POL– Phase IV Programme (2006-2013), 14th Ordinary Meeting of the Contracting Parties to the Convention for the Protection of the Marine Environment and the Coastal Region of the Mediterranean and its Protocols, 24.11.2005

UNEP(DEPI)/MED WG. 316/Inf.8, Elaboration of a Regional Action Plan for the Management of Macro-Waste in the Coastal Area of the Mediterranean Basin, Meeting of the MED POL National Coordinators, 13.06.2007

UNEP(DEPI)/MED WG. 316/Inf. 7, Medium Term Public Awareness and Education Campaign on Management of marine litter in the Mediterranean (Prepared by MIO-ECSDE, HELMEPA, Clean-up Greece), Meeting of MED POL National Coordinators, 13.06.2007

UNEP(DEPI)/MED WG. 316/Inf. 3, Progress Report of the implementation of MED POL activities during 2006-2007, Meeting of MED POL National Coordinators, 13.06.2007

1628 The information are available at http://www.unepmap.org/index.php?module=content2&catid=001001004 (Protocols) and http://www.unepmap.org/index.php?module=content2&catid=001003001 (meeting documents). The date of the documents are not necessarily congruent with the dates of the meetings.

UNEP(DEPI)/MED WG 305/4, Report of Third Meeting of the Working Group of experts designated by the Contracting Parties on the Draft Protocol on Integrated Coastal Zone Management (ICZM) in the Mediterranean, Third Meeting of the Working Group of experts designated by the Contracting Parties on the Draft Protocol on Integrated Coastal Zone Management (ICZM) in the Mediterranean, 16.07.2007

UNEP(DEPI)/MED WG. 334/3, Proposed activities to be carried out during the 2010-2011 Biennium as part of MED POL UNEP, Meeting of MED POL Focal Points, 19.05.2009

UNEP (DEPI)/ MED WG.334/Inf.5, Results of the assessment of the status of marine litter in the Mediterranean, Meeting of the MED POL Focal Points, 19.05.2009

UNEP MAP-Plan Bleu, State of the development and the environment in the Mediterranean, Athens, 2009

UNEP(DEPI)/MED WG.357/7, Strategic Action Programme for the Management of Marine Litter in the Mediterranean, Meeting of the MED POL Focal Points, 01.04.2011

UNEP(DEPI)/MED WG.357/Inf.5, Strategic Action Programme for the Management of Marine Litter in the Mediterranean, Financial Aspects of its Implementation, Meeting of the MED POL Focal Points, 01.04.2011

UNEP(DEPI)/MED WG.357/Inf.4, Assessment of the status of marine litter in the Mediterranean, Meeting of the MED POL Focal Points, 12.04.2011

UNEP/MAP, Signatures and Ratifications of the Barcelona Convention for the Protection of the Marine Environment and the Coastal Region of the Mediterranean and its Protocols as at 31 December 2011, 2011

UNEP(DEPI)/MED IG.20/5, Draft decisions for the 17th Meeting of the Contracting Parties, 17th Ordinary Meeting of the Contracting Parties to the Convention for the Protection of the Marine Environment and the Coastal Region of the Mediterranean and its Protocols, 125, 12.01.2012

UNEP MAP, Croatia Passes Law to Ratify the ICZM Protocol, 2012

UNEP(DEPI)/MED IG.20/CRP.XX, Annex I, Paris Declaration, 17th Ordinary Meeting of the Contracting Parties to the Convention for the Protection of the Marine Environment and the Coastal Region of the Mediterranean and its Protocols, 10.02.2012

UNEP MAP, UNEP(DEPI)/MED IG.20/8, Report of the 17th Ordinary Meeting of the Contracting Parties to the Convention for the Protection of the Marine Environment and the Coastal Region of the Mediterranean and its Protocols, 14.02.2012, 3.

UNEP(DEPI)/MED IG.20/8, Decision IG 20/2, Adoption of the Action Plan for the implementation of the ICZM Protocol for the Mediterranean (2012-2019), Report of the 17th Ordinary Meeting of the Contracting Parties to the Convention for the Protection of the Marine Environment and the Coastal Region of the Mediterranean and its Protocols, Annex II, 14.02.2012

UNEP(DEPI)/MED WG.372/4, Report of the Meeting of the Correspondence Group on Good Environmental Status (GES) and targets-Pollution and Litter Cluster from 12.11.2012 as discussed in the UNEP(DEPI)/MED WG.379/Inf.4, Meeting of the Correspondence Group on Good Environmental Status (GES) and targets-Pollution and Litter Cluster, MED POL Focal Point Meting, 31.05.2013

UNEP(DEPI)/MED WG. 379/Inf.3, Draft Report of the Meeting to Review the Regional Action Plan on Marine Litter, MED POL Focal Points Meeting, 18.06.2013

UNPE(DEPI)/MED, WG.387/11, "Draft Decision on the Regional Plan on Marine Litter Management" as discussed in the plenary as UNEP (DEPI)/MED WG.387/CRP. 7; endorsed and agreed to be forwarded to COP 18, 18.07.2013

UNEP MAP, UNEP(DEPI)/MED IG.21/9, Decision IG.21/9 on a Regional Plan on Marine Litter Management in the Mediterranean in the Framework of Article 15 of the Land Based Sources Protocol

14. OSPAR[1629]

OSPAR Commission, Work Programme for the Working Group on Impacts on the Marine Environment, 1996/1997, Annex 22, Ref.§ 10.27, 08.03.1996

OSPAR Recommendation 2000/1 on Best Environmental Practice (BEP) for the Reduction of Inputs of Agricultural Pesticides to the Environment through the Use of Integrated Crop Management Techniques, Annex 8, Ref. § 5.25a adopted in Copenhagen, 2000

OSPAR Commission/ HELCOM, First Joint Ministerial Meeting of the Helsinki and OSPAR Commissions, Statement on the European Marine Strategy, What HELCOM and OSPAR can bring to the development of the European Marine Strategy, 25-26.06.2003 (Bremen, Germany)

BDC 04/14/1-E, Summary Record of the Biodiversity Committee, Meeting of the Biodiversity Committee, Agenda Item 14, 20.02.2004

BCD 05/13/1-E, Summary Record of the Biodiversity Committee Meeting, Meeting of the Biodiversity Committee, Agenda Item 13, 25.02.2005

BDC 06/10/1-E, Summary Record of the Biodiversity Committee, Meeting of the Biodiversity Committee, Agenda Item 10, 17.03.2006

OSPAR Commission, OSPAR Pilot Project on Monitoring Marine Beach litter, Monitoring of marine litter in the OSPAR region, OSPAR Pilot Project on Monitoring Marine Beach Litter, Steering Group, Biodiversity Series, 2007

BDC 07/12/1-E, Summary Record of the Biodiversity Committee, Meeting of the Biodiversity Committee, Agenda Item 12, 26-30.03.2007

BDC 07/12/1-E, Draft Agreement for the Marine Beach Litter Monitoring Programme, Meeting of the Biodiversity Committee, Annex 10, Ref.§ 5.15, 26-30-03.2007

1629 The documents are available at: http://www.ospar.org/. The dates of the documents are usually not congruent with the dates of the meetings.

BDC 08/12/1-E, Summary record of the meeting of the Biodiversity Committee, Meeting of the Biodiversity Committee, Agenda Item 12, 25-29.02.2008

OSPAR Commission, Evaluation of the OSPAR System of Ecological Quality Objectives for the North Sea (update 2010), Biodiversity Series, 2009

OSPAR Commission, Marine litter in the Northeast Atlantic Region, Assessment and priorities for response, London, 2009

ICGML (4) –E, Fourth Meeting of OSPAR Inter-Sessional Correspondence Group on Marine Litter (ICGML), 11.05.2009

OSPAR Commission, the North-East Atlantic Environment Strategy (NEAS), Strategy of the OSPAR Commission for the Protection of the Marine Environment of the North-East Atlantic 2010–2020, OSPAR Agreement 2010-3

OSPAR Commission, Guideline for monitoring marine litter on the beaches in the OSPAR Maritime Area, Agreement number 2010-02, 2010

OSPAR Commission, The OSPAR System of Ecological Quality Objectives for the North Sea (update 2010), Quality Status Report 2010, 2010

OSPAR Commission, Ministerial Meeting Bergen 2010, Annex 49, Ref. M 6.2, 24.09.2010

OSPAR Commission, Agreement on a Voluntary Marine Beach Litter Monitoring Programme, OSPAR Agreement: 2011-1, 2011

OSPAR EIHA 11/10/1-E, Terms of Reference for ICG Marine Litter (ICG-ML), Meeting of the Environmental Impact of Human Activities Committee, Annex 8, Ref. § 4 6, 31.01.-04.02.2011

OSPAR Recommendation 2012/5 for a risk-based approach to the Management of Produced Water Discharges from Offshore Installations (OSPAR 12/22/1, Annex 18), adopted in Bonn, 2012

EIHA 13/10/1-E, Workshop on the development of an OSPAR Regional Action Plan on Marine Litter, Meeting of the Environmental Impact of Human Activities Committee, Annex 9, Ref. § 4.17a, 15-19.04.2013

OSPAR Commission, OSPAR Marine Litter Regional Action Plan, OSPAR 14/3/2-E, 27.06.2014

OSPAR, Regional Action Plan for the Prevention and Management of Marine Litter in the North-East Atlantic, OSPAR Agreement 2014-1.

II. European Union

1. EC/EURATOM/EU/TFEU Treaties

1957 Treaty establishing the European Economic Community (Rome) of 25 March 1957, in force 01 January 1958

Treaty establishing the European Atomic Energy Community (Rome) of 25 March 1957, in force 01 January 1958

1987	Single European Act (Luxembourg) of 17 February 1986, in force 01 July 1987 (OJ L 169, 26.09.1987)
1992	Treaty establishing the European Community (Maastricht) (OJ C 325, 24.12.2002)
	Treaty on the European Union (Maastricht) (OJ C 325, 24.12.2002)
1997	Protocol 30 on the Application of the Principles of Subsidiarity and Proportionality annexed to the Treaty of Amsterdam (OJ C 340/105)
2007	Treaty on the Functioning of the European Union (TFEU) consolidated version 2012 (OJ C 326, 26.10.2012)

2. European Court of Justice Cases[1630]

C-26/62 *Van Gend en Loos v. Nederlands Belastingsadministratie* [1963] ECR I-1 (Van Gend en Loos)

C-6/64 *Flaminio Costa v. E.N.E.L.* [1964] ENEL I-585 (Costa Enel)

C-22/70 *Commission v. Council* [1971] ECR I-263 (ERTA)

Joined Cases 3,4 and 6/76 *Kramer* [1976] ECR 1279

C-11/76 *Netherlands v. Commission* [1979] ECR 00245

C-61/79 *Amministrazione delle finanze dello Stato v. Denkavit italiana* [1980] ECR 01205

C-96/81 *Commission v. the Netherlands* [1982] ECR I-1791

C-302/86 *Commission v. Denmark* [1988] ECR 4607 (Danish Bottle)

C-169/89 *Gourmetterie v.d.Burg* [1990] ECR I-2143 (Red Grouse)

C-278/89 *Frans-Nederlandse Maatschappij voor Biologische Producten* [1981] ECR 3277

C-300/89 *Commission v. Council* [1991] I-2967 (Titanium Dioxide)

C-2/90 *Commission v. Belgium* [1992] ECR I-4431 (Walloon Waste)

C-41/93 *France v. Commission* [1994] ECR I-1829

C-293/93 *Standley* [1999] ECR I-2603.

C-441/93 *Panagis Pafitis and others v. Trapeza Kentrikis Ellados A.E. and others* [1996] ECR I-1347

C-284/95 *Safety Hi-Tech* [1998] ECR I-4301

C-189/96 *United Kingdom vs. Commission* [1998] ECR I-2265

C-203/96 *Dusseldorp* [1998] ECR I-4075

C-389/96 *Aher-Waggon GmbH* [1998] ECR I-4473

C-67/97 *Ditlev Bluhme* [2001] ECR I-8033

C-365/97 *Commission v. Italy* [1999] ECR I-7773 (San Rocco)

C-387/97 Commission v. Hellenic Republic [2000] ECR I-05047

C-408/97 *Commission v. the Netherlands* [2000] ECR I-6436

1630 All cases are available at: http://curia.europa.eu/jcms/jcms/j_6/.

C-473/98 *Chemical Inspections v. Toolex* [2000] ECR 38

C-512/99 *Germany v. Commission* [2003] ECR I- I-00845

C-154/00 *Commission v. Greece* [2002] ECR I-3887

C-3/00 *Denmark v. Commission* [2003] ECR I-2643

C-52/00 *Commission v. France* [2001] ECR I-3827

C-103/00 *Commission v. Greece* [2003] ECR I-1147

C-444/00 *Mayer Perry Recycling Ltd.* [2003] ECR I-6163

C-322/01 *Deutscher Apothekerverband* [2003] ECR I-14951

C-463/01 *Commission v. Germany* [2004] ECR I-11705

C-494/01 *Commission v. Ireland* [2005] ECR I-3382

C-320/03 *Commission v. Austria* [2005] ECR I-9871

C-178/03 *Commission v. European Parliament and Council* [2006] ECR I-107

C-502/03 Commission v. Greece [2005], not yet published

C-252/05 *Thames Water Utilities* [2007] ECR I-3883

C-374/05 *Gintec International Import-Export GmbH* [2007] ECR I-9541

C-221/06 *Stadtgemeinde Frohnleiten* [2007] ECR I-2613

C-308/06 *Intertanko and others* [2007] ECR I-4057

C-405/07 P *Netherlands v. Commission* [2008] ECR I-8301

C-188/07 *Commune de Mesquer* [2008] ECR I-04501

C-428/08 *Monsanto Technology LLC v. Cefetra BV and Others* [2010] ECR I-6765 (Monsanto)

C-343/09 *Afton Chemical* [2010] ECR I-7027 (Afton Chemical)

3. Court of First Instance

T-70/99 *Alpharma Inc. v Council* [2002] ECR II-3506

T-13/99 *Pfizer Animal Health SA v Council of the European Union* [2002] ECR II-3305

4. European Union/Community Environmental Action Programmes

1973 First Environmental Action Programme, (OJ C 112, 20.12.1973)

1977 Second Environnemental Action Programme, (OJ C 139, 13.06.1977)

1983 Third Environmental Action Programme, (OJ C 46/1, 17.02.1983)

1987 Fourth Environmental Action Programme (OJ C 328, 07.12.87)

1992 Fifth Environmental Action Programme "Toward Sustainability" (OJ C 138, 17.05.1993)

2001 Sixth Environmental Action Programme "Environment 2010: Our Future, Our Choice" (OJ L 242, 10.09.2002)

2013 General Union Environment Action Programme to 2020 "Living Well, within the Limits of our Planet" (Seventh Environmental Action Programme) (OJ L 354/171, 28.12.2013)

5. European Union secondary instruments

Council Directive 91/271/EEC of 21 May 1991 concerning urban waste water treatment, as amended by Commission Directive 98/15/EC of 27 February 1998 (OJ 1999 L 139)

Council Directive 92/43/EEC of 21 May 1992 on the conservation of natural habitats and of wild fauna and flora (OJ 1992 L 206)

European Parliament and Council Directive 94/62/EC of 20 December 1994 on packaging and packaging waste (OJ 1994 L 365), subsequently amended

Directive 2000/53/EC of the European Parliament and of the Council of 18 September 2000 on end-of life vehicles (OJ 2000 L 269/34)

Directive 2000/59/EC of the European Parliament and of the Council of 27 November 2000 on port reception facilities for ship-generated waste and cargo residues (OJ 2000 L 332)

Directive 2000/60/EC of the European Parliament and of the Council of 23 October 2000 establishing a framework for Community action in the field of water policy (OJ 2000 L 327/1)

Recommendation 2001/331/EEC of the European Parliament and of the Council of 4 April 2001 providing for minimum criteria for environmental inspections in Member States (OJ 2001 L 118/41)

Decision 2455/2001/EC of the European Parliament and of the Council of 20 November 2001 establishing the list of priority substances in the field of water policy and amending Directive 2000/60/EC (OJ 2001 L 331/1)

Directive 2002/59/EC of the European Parliament and of the Council of 27 June 2002 establishing a Community vessel traffic monitoring and information system and repealing Council Directive 93/75/EEC (OJ 2002 L 208/10)

Regulation (EC) No 2371/2002 of 20 December 2002 on the conservation and sustainable exploitation of fisheries resources under the Common Fisheries Policy (OJ 2002 L 358/59)

Directive 2003/53/EC of the European Parliament and of the Council of 18 June 2003 amending for the 26th time Council Directive 76/769/EEC relating to restrictions on the marketing and use of certain dangerous substances and preparations (nonylphenol, nonylphenol ethoxylate and cement) (OJ 2003 L 178/43)

Directive 2006/7/EC of the European Parliament and of the Council of 15 February 2006 concerning the management of bathing water quality and repealing Directive 76/160/EEC (OJ 2006 L 64)

Directive 2006/21/EC of the European Parliament and of the Council of 15 March 2006 on the management of waste from extractive industries (OJ 2006 L 102/15)

Regulation (EC) No 1013/2006 of the European Parliament and of the Council of 14 June 2006 on shipments of waste (OJ 2006 L 190/1)

Directive 2006/66/EC of the European Parliament and of the Council of 6 September 2006 on batteries and accumulators and waste batteries and accumulators and repealing Directive 91/157/EEC (OJ 2006 L 266/1)

Regulation (EC) No 1907/2006 of the European Parliament and of the Council of 18 December 2006 concerning the Registration, Evaluation, Authorisation and Restriction of Chemicals (REACH), establishing a European Chemicals Agency, amending Directive 1999/45/EC and repealing Council Regulation (EEC) No 793/93 and Commission Regulation (EC) No 1488/94 as well as Council Directive 76/769/EEC and Commission Directives 91/155/EEC, 93/67/EEC, 93/105/EC and 2000/21/EC (OJ 2006 L 396/1)

Protocols annexed to the Treaty establishing the European Community-Protocol (30) on the application of the principles of subsidiarity and proportionality (OJ 2006, 321E, 29.12.2006)

Directive 2007/60/EC of the European Parliament and of the Council of 23 October 2007 on the assessment and management of flood risks (OJ 2007 L 288)

Directive 2008/56/EC of the European Parliament and of the Council of 17 June 2008 establishing a framework for community action in the field of marine environmental policy (Marine Strategy Framework Directive) (OJ 2008 L 164, 25.06.2008)

Directive 2008/98/EC of the European Parliament and of the Council of 19 November 2008 on waste and repealing certain Directives (OJ 2008 L 312/3)

Directive 2008/105/EC of the European Parliament and of the Council of 16 December 2008 on environmental quality standards in the field of water policy, amending and subsequently repealing Council Directives 82/176/EEC, 83/513/EEC, 84/156/EEC, 84/491/EEC, 86/280/EEC and amending Directive 2000/60/EC of the European Parliament and of the Council (OJ 2008 L 348/84)

Directive (2009/128/EC) of the European Parliament and of the Council of 21 October 2009 establishing a framework for Community action to achieve the sustainable use of pesticides (OJ 2009 L 309/71)

Regulation (EC) No 66/2010 of the European Parliament and of the Council of 25 November 2009 on the EU Ecolabel (OJ 2010 L 27)

Commission Decision (2010/477/EU) of 1 September 2010 on criteria and methodological standards on good environmental status of marine waters (OJ 2010 L 232/14, 02.09.2010)

Directive 2010/75/EU of the European Parliament and of the Council of 24 November 2010 on industrial emissions (OJ 2010 L 334/17)

Directive 2011/92/EU of the European Parliament and of the Council of 13 December 2011 on the assessment of the effects of certain public and private projects on the environment Directive (OJ 2012 L 26/1)

Directive 2012/19/EU of the European Parliament and of the Council of 4 July 2012 on waste electrical and electronic equipment (WEEE) (OJ 2012 L 197)

Directive (EU) 2015/720 of the European Parliament and of the Council of April 29 2015 amending Directive 94/62/EC as regards reducing the consumption of lightweight plastic carrier bags (OJ 2015, L 115)

6. European institutions and agencies

COM(2000) 1 final, Communication from the Commission on the precautionary principle, 02.02.2000

European Commission DGXI.E.3, The Behaviour of PVC in Landfill, Final report, 07.04.2000

COM(2001) 143 final, Communication from the Commission to the Council and the European Parliament. Elements of a Strategy for the Integration of Environmental Protection Requirements into the Common Fisheries Policy, 16.03.2001

COM(2003) 745 final, Communication from the Commission to the Council and the European Parliament, 2003 Environment Policy Review- Consolidating the environmental pillar of sustainable development, 03.12.2003

COM(2006) 275 final Volume II – ANNEX, Green Paper- Towards a future Maritime Policy for the Union: A European vision for the oceans and seas, 07.06.2006

European Parliament A6-0373/2006, Report on the proposal for a directive of the European Parliament and of the Council establishing a Framework for Community Action in the field of Marine Environmental Policy (Marine Strategy Directive), Committee on the Environment, Public Health and Food Safety, 24.10.2006

European Commission, SEC(2007) 362, Commission Staff Working Document, Accompanying document to the Communication from the Commission to the European Parliament and the Council 'Towards Sustainable Water Management in the European Union', First stage in the implementation of the Water Framework Directive 2000/60/EC, 22.03.2007

Council, 9388/07 ADD1, Draft Statement of the Council´s Reasons, Common position adopted by the Council with a view to the adoption of a Directive of the European Parliament and of the Council establishing a Framework for Community Action in the field of Marine Environmental Policy (Marine Strategy Directive), 12.07.2007

European Commission, Follow-up study on the implementation of Directive 1999/31/EC on the landfill of waste in EU- 25, Final Report- Findings of the Study, 30.07.2007

COM(2008) 773 final, Communication from the Commission to the European Parliament, the Council, the European Economic and Social Committee and the Committee of the Regions on implementing European Community Environmental Law, 18.11.2008

European Commission/DG ENV, Guidance Document on Exemptions to the Environmental Objectives, Guidance Document No.20, Common Implementation Strategy for the Water Framework Directive (2000/60/EC), 2009

European Parliament, Parliamentary question, Answer given by Mr.Kallas on behalf of the Commission, P-6795/2010, 10.09.2010

European Commission/DG ENV, Plastic Waste in the Environment, April 2011

European Commission, Commission seeks views on reducing plastic bag use, Press Release, Brussels, 18.05.2011, IP/11/580

European Commission, Public consultation on an impact assessment for a possible revision of Directive 2000/59/EC of the European Parliament and of the Council of 27 November 2000 on port reception facilities for ship-generated waste and cargo residues, consultation period from 14.07.2011 to 16.09.2011

COM (2011) 571 final, Communication from the Commission to the Council and the European Parliament, Roadmap to a Resource Efficient Europe, 20.09.2011

European Commission, Impact assessment for a possible revision of Directive 2000/59/EC of the European Parliament and of the Council of 27 November 2000 on port reception facilities for ship-generated waste and cargo residues, consultation period 14.07.-16.09.2011, http://ec.europa.eu/transport/modes/maritime/consultations/2011_09_16_prf_en.htm, last accessed 27.08.2015.

European Commission, SEC(2011) 1255 final, Commission Staff Working Paper, Relationship between the initial assessment of marine waters and the criteria for good environmental status, 14.10.2011

COM(2011) 804 final, Proposal for a Regulation of the European Parliament and of the Council on the European Maritime and Fisheries Fund [repealing Council Regulation (EC) No 1198/2006 and Council Regulation (EC) No 861/2006 and Council Regulation No XXX/2011 on integrated maritime policy, 02.12.2011

European Commission/Joint Research Center, MSFD GES Technical Subgroup on Marine Litter, Marine litter technical recommendations for the implementation of MSFD requirements, JRC Scientific and Technical Reports, 14.12.2011

European Commission, Commission urges Cyprus and Greece to clean up waste landfills, Press Release, Brussels, IP/12/66, 26.01.2012

COM(2012) 95 final, Communication from the Commission to the European Parliament, the Council, the European Economic and Social Committee and the Committee of the Regions, Improving the delivery of benefits from EU environment measures: building confidence through better knowledge and responsiveness, 07.03.2012

European Commission, Environment: Commission takes Greece to Court over waste landfill and endangered turtles, Press Release, Brussels, 27.09.2012, IP/12/1023

COM(2012) 629 final (Vol.1/2), Communication from the Commission to the European Parliament, the Council, the European Economic and Social Committee and the Committee of the Regions, Commission Work Programme 2013, 23.10.2012

European Commission, Commission Staff Working Document SWD(2012) 365 final, Overview of EU policies, legislation and initiatives related to marine litter, 31.10.2012

COM(2012) 670 final, Report from the Commission to the European Parliament and the Council on the Implementation of the Water Framework Directive (2000/60/EC) River Basin Management Plans, 14.11.2012

COM(2012) 662 final, Report from the Commission to the Council and the European Parliament, Contribution of the Marine Strategy Framework Directive (2008/56/EC) to the implementation of existing obligations, commitments and initiatives of the Member States or the EU at EU or international level in the sphere of environmental protection in marine waters, 16.11.2012

European Commission, Proposal for a new EU Environment Action Programme to 2020, Public Consultation on the EU environment policy priorities for 2020: Towards a 7th EU Environment Action Programme, available online at http://ec.europa.eu/environment/newprg/results.htm, last updated 28.11.2012

European Commission, Legal Enforcement, Statistics on environmental infringements, available online at http://ec.europa.eu/environment/legal/law/statistics.htm, last updated 12.04.2013

European Commission/DG ENV, Guidance on the interpretation of key provisions of Directive 2008/98/EC on waste, June 2012

European Commission, Speech of Janez Potočnik (Commissioner for Environment): "Any Future for the Plastic Industry in Europe?" held in Wiesbaden, Germany, 21.9.2012, Press Release SPEECH/12/632 21/09/2012.

European Commission-MEMO/12/908, New Environment Action Programme to 2020– questions and answers, 29.11.2012

COM(2012) 710 final, Proposal for a Decision of the European Parliament and of the Council on a General Union Environment Action Programme to 2020 "Living well, within the limits of our planet", 29.11.2012

European Environment Agency, Late lessons from early warnings: science, precaution, innovation, EEA Report 01/2013, 23.01.2013

European Commission, Environment: Commission takes Greece back to Court over illegal landfills and asks for fines, Press Release, Brussels, IP/13/143, 21.02.2013

COM (2013) 123 final, Green Paper on a European Strategy on Plastic Waste in the Environment, 07.03.2013

COM (2013) 133 final, Proposal for a Directive of the European Parliament and the Council establishing a framework for maritime spatial planning and integrated coastal zone management, 12.03.2013

European Commission, Environment: Commission takes Italy to Court over inadequate treatment of waste landfilled in Lazio, Press Release, Brussels, IP/13/250, 21.03.2013

European Commission, Consultation on the establishment of a quantitative reduction headline target for marine litter, consultation period 25.09.2013 to 18.12.2013

COM(2013) 761 final, Proposal for a Directive of the European Parliament and of the Council amending Directive 94/62/EC on packaging and packaging waste to reduce the consumption of lightweight plastic carrier bags, 04.11.2013

European Parliament resolution of 14 January 2014 on a European strategy on plastic waste in the environment (2013/2113(INI))

European Parliament legislative resolution of 16 April 2014 on the proposal for a directive of the European Parliament and of the Council amending Directive 94/62/EC on packaging and packaging waste to reduce the consumption of lightweight plastic carrier bags (COM(2013)0761 – C7-0392/2013 – 2013/0371(COD)) (Ordinary legislative procedure: first reading), 16.04.2014

European Commission, Ex-post evaluation of certain waste stream Directives Final report, 18.04.2014

COM(2014) 397 final, Proposal for a Directive of the European Parliament and of the Council amending Directives 2008/98/EC on waste, 94/62/EC on packaging and packaging waste, 1999/31/EC on the landfill of waste, 2000/53/EC on end-of-life vehicles, 2006/66/EC on batteries and accumulators and waste batteries and accumulators, and 2012/19/EU on waste electrical and electronic equipment, 02.07.2014

European Commission, Commission Staff Working Document SWD/2014/0209 final, Ex-post evaluation of Five Waste Stream Directives, Accompanying the document Proposal for a Directive of the European Parliament and of the Council reviewing the targets in Directives 2008/98/EC on waste, 94/62/EC on packaging and packaging waste, and 1999/31/EC on the landfill of waste, amending Directives 2000/53/EC on end-of-life vehicles, 2006/66/EC on batteries and accumulators and waste batteries and accumulators, and 2012/19/EC on waste electrical and electronic equipment, 02.07.2014

COM (2014) 398 final, Communication from the Commission to the European Parliament, the Council, the European Economic and Social Committee and the Committee of the Regions, Towards a circular economy: A zero waste programme for Europe, 02.07.2014

(COM(2014) 910 final, Annex to the Communication from the European Commission to the European Parliament, the Council, the European Economic and Social Committee and the Committee of the Regions on the Commission Work Programme 2015, 16.12.2014

European Commission, Press Release, Commission confirms Withdrawal of 73 Pending Proposals Announced in 2015 Work Programme, IP/15/4567, 07.03.2015

European Commission, Ex-post evaluation of Directive 2000/59/EC on port reception facilities for ship-generated waste and cargo residues, http://ec.europa.eu/transport/modes/maritime/studies/doc/2015-ex-post-evaluation-of-dir-2000-59-ec.pdf (last accessed 27.08.2015)

III. The Group of 7 (G7)

G7, Leader's Declaration G7 Summit: Think Ahead. Act Together, An morgen denken. Gemeinsam handeln, G7 Germany, Schloss Elmau, 7-8 June 2015, https://www.g7germany.de/Content/EN/_Anlagen/G7/2015-06-08-g7-abschluss-eng_en.pdf?__blob=publicationFile&v=3, last accessed 27.08.2015.

G7, Annex to the Leader's Declaration, G7 Germany, Schloss Elmau, 7-8 June 2015, https://www.g7germany.de/Content/EN/_Anlagen/G7/2015-06-08-g7-abschluss-annex-eng_en.pdf?__blob=publicationFile&v=2, last accessed 27.08.2015.

IV. Literature

Acha, Eduardo M./Mianzan, Hermes W./Iribarne, Oscar, et al., The role of the Rio de la Plata bottom salinity front in accumulating debris, Marine Pollution Bulletin 46 (2003) 197–202.

Agardy, Tundi/Alder, Jacqueline, Coastal Systems, in: *Hassan, Rashid M./Scholes, Robert/Ash, Neville* (eds.), Ecosystems and human well-being, Washington (DC), Covelo (Calif.), London (2005) 513–548.

Alexander, Lewis M., Regionalism and the law of the sea: The case of semi-enclosed seas, Ocean Development & International Law 2 (1974) 151–186.

Alexander, Lewis M., Regional Arrangements in the Oceans, The American Journal of International Law 71 (1977) 84–109.

Alexandrov, Laura/Nicolaev, Simion/Mateescu, Alexandru et al., Integrated approaches to risk mitigation targeting conservation and sustainable development along the Romanian Black Sea coast, in: *Czybulka, Detlef* (ed.), Marine nature conservation and management at the borders of the European Union, 1.ed., Baden-Baden (2012) 103–119.

Alexy, Robert, Theorie der Grundrechte, Frankfurt am Main 1986.

Aliani, Stefano/Molcard, Anne, Hitch-hiking on floating marine debris: macrobenthic species in the Western Mediterranean Sea, Hydriobiologia 503 (2003) 59–67.

Allan, Sarah E./Smith, Brian W./Anderson, Kim A., Impact of the Deepwater Horizon Oil Spill on Bioavailable Polycyclic Aromatic Hydrocarbons in Gulf of Mexico Coastal Waters, Environmental Science & Technology 46 (2012) 2033–2039.

Anderson, David, Port States and Environmental Protection, in: *Boyle, Alan E./Freestone, David* (eds.), International law and sustainable development, Past achievements and future challenges, Oxford, New York (1999) 325–344.

Andrady, Anthony. L. (eds.), Plastics and the environment, Hoboken, N.J 2003.

Andrady, Anthony L., Common Plastics Materials, in: *Andrady, A. L.* (eds.), Plastics and the environment, Hoboken, N.J 2003.

Andrady, Anthony L., Microplastics in the marine environment, Marine Pollution Bulletin 62 (2011) 1596–1605.

Applegate, John S. (ed.), Environmental risk, Aldershot, Hants, England, Burlington, VT 2004.

Arthur, Cortney/Baker, Joel/Bamford, Holly(eds.), Proceedings of the International Research Workshop on the occurrence, effects, and fate of microplastic marine debris, September 2008, NOAA Technical Memorandum NOS-OR&R-30.

Ashton, Karen/Holmes, Luke/Turner, Andrew, Association of metals with plastic production pellets in the marine environment, Marine Pollution Bulletin 60 (2010) 2050–2055.

Avery-Gomm, Stephanie/O'Hara, Patrick D./Kleine, Lydia et al., Northern fulmars as biological monitors of trends of plastic pollution in the eastern North Pacific, Marine Pollution Bulletin 64 (2012) 1776–1781.

Baaner, Lasse, The Programme of Measures of the Water Framework Directive – More than just a Formal Compliance Tool, Journal for European Environmental & Planning Law 8 (2011) 82–100.

Baird, Robin W./Hooker, Sascha K., Ingestion of Plastic and Unusual Prey by a Juvenile Harbour Porpoise, Marine Pollution Bulletin 40 (2000) 719–720.

Ballance, A. Ryan Peter Turpie J.K, How much is a clean beach worth? The impact of litter on beach users in the Cape Peninsula, South Africa, South African Journal of Science 96 (2000) 210–213.

Bang, Ho-Sam, Is Port State Control an Effective Means to Combat Vessel-Source Pollution? An Empirical Study of the Practical Exercise by Port States of Their Powers of Control, The International Journal of Marine and Coastal Law 23 (2008) 715–759.

Bang, Ho-Sam, Port State Jurisdiction and Article 218 of the UN Convention on the Law of Sea, Journal of Maritime Law & Commerce 40 (2009) 291-307.

Bang, Ho-Sam/Jang, Duck-Jong, Recent Developments in Regional Memorandums of Understanding on Port State Control, Ocean Development & International Law 43 (2012) 170–187.

Barco, Susan G./D'Eri, Linda R./Woodward, Becky L. et al., Spectra® fishing twine entanglement of a bottlenose dolphin: A case study and experimental modeling, Marine Pollution Bulletin 60 (2010) 1477–1481.

Barnes, David K. A., Invasions by marine life on plastic debris, Nature 416 (2002) 808–809.

Barnes, David K. A./Galgani, Francois/Thompson, Richard C. et al., Accumulation and fragmentation of plastic debris in global environments, Philosophical Transactions of the Royal Society B: Biological Sciences 364 (2009) 1985–1998.

Barnes, Richard/Metcalfe, Daniel, Current Legal Developments: The European Union, The International Journal of Marine and Coastal Law 25 (2010) 81–91.

Barnet, F.G (Jerry), Shipping and Marine Debris in the Wide Caribbean: Answering a Difficult Challenge, in: *Coe, James M./Rogers, Donald B.* (eds.), Marine debris, Sources, impacts, and solutions, New York (1997) 219–228.

Barral, Virginie, Sustainable Development in International Law: Nature and Operation of an Evolutive Legal Norm, European Journal of International Law 23 (2012) 377–400.

Barreira, Ana, The legal protection of the marine environment: The Marine Strategy Framework Directive and its implementation in Spain, Environmental Law Network International (2012) 46–53.

Baur, Donald/Iudicello, Suzanne, Stemming the Tide of Marine Debris Pollution: Putting Domestic and International Control Authorities to Work, Ecology Law Quarterly 17 (1990) 71–95.

Bean, Michael J., Legal strategies for reducing persistent plastics in the marine environment, Marine Pollution Bulletin 18 (1987) 357–360.

Bergmann, Melanie/Klages, Michael, Increase of litter at the Arctic deep-sea observatory HAUSGARTEN, Marine Pollution Bulletin 64 (2012) 2734–2741.

Beyerlin, Ulrich/Marauhn, Thilo, International environmental law, Oxford, Portland, 2011.

BIO Intelligence Service, Assessment of impacts of options to reduce the use of single-use plastic carrier bags, Final report prepared for the European Commission - DG ENV , 2011.

Birnie, Patricia, Impact on the Development of international law on Cooperation, in: *Nordquist, Myron H./Moore, John Norton/Mahmoudi, Said* (eds.), The Stockholm declaration and law of the marine environment, The Hague, New York (2003) 85–100.

Birnie, Patricia W./Boyle, Alan E./Redgwell, Catherine, International law and the environment, 3. ed., Oxford, New York 2009.

Blanco-Bazán, Augustín, The Environmental UNCLOS and the Work of IMO in the Field of Prevention of Pollution from Vessels, in: *Kirchner, Andree* (ed.), International marine environmental law, Institutions, implementation and innovations, The Hague, New York, Frederick, MD (2003) 31–47.

Blöch, Helmut, European Water Policy and the Water Framework Directive: an Overview, Journal for European Environmental & Planning Law 1 (2004) 170–178.

BMT Group, Study on the Economic, Legal, Environmental and Practical Implications of a European Union System to Reduce Ship Emissions of SO2 and NOx, Appendix 4 (Legal Analysis: Prescription, Enforcement and Observance), Report No. 3623 2000, http://ec.europa.eu/environment/enveco/air/index.htm#_Toc240787022, last accessed 27.08.2015.

Board, P.A, The fate of rubbish in the Thames Estuary, Marine Pollution Bulletin 4 (1973) 165–166.

Bodansky, Daniel, The art and craft of international environmental law, 1.ed., Cambridge 2011.

Bodansky, Daniel/Brunnée, Jutta/Hey, Ellen (eds.), The Oxford handbook of international environmental law, Oxford, New York 2007.

Boerger, Christiana M./Lattin, Gwendolyn L./Moore, Shelly L. et al., Plastic ingestion by planktivorous fishes in the North Pacific Central Gyre, Marine Pollution Bulletin 60 (2010) 2275–2278.

Borja, Ángel/Elliott, Mike/Carstensen, Jacob et al., Marine management – Towards an integrated implementation of the European Marine Strategy Framework and the Water Framework Directives, Marine Pollution Bulletin 60 (2010) 2175–2186.

Bothe, Michael/Dolzer, Rudolf/Kau, Marcel et al. (eds.), Völkerrecht, 6. ed., Berlin, Boston, Mass 2013.

Boyle, Allan, Polluter Pays, in: Max Planck Encyclopedia of Public International Law (MPEPIL), http://opil.ouplaw.com/view/10.1093/law:epil/9780199231690/law-978 0199231690-e1602?rskey=xQGtuB&result=4&prd=EPIL, last updated March 2009, last accessed 27.08.2015.

Boyle, Alan E./Freestone, David (eds.), International law and sustainable development, Past achievements and future challenges, Oxford, New York 1999.

Boyle, A., Land-based sources of marine pollution Current legal regime, Marine Policy 16 (1992) 20–35.

-Marine Pollution under the Law of the Sea Convention, The American Journal of International Law 79 (1985) 347–372.

Brown Weiss, Edith, Environmental Equity: The Imperative for the Twenty-First Century, in: *Lang, Winfried* (ed.), Sustainable development and international law, London, Boston (1995) 17–33.

Brown, Chester, International Tribunal for the Law of the Sea, The International Journal of Marine and Coastal Law 17 (2002) 267–288.

Brown, James/Macfayden, Graeme, Ghost fishing in European waters: Impacts and management responses, Marine Policy 31 (2007) 488–504.

Browne, Mark A./Dissanayake, Awantha/Galloway, Tamara S, et al., Ingested Microscopic Plastic Translocates to the Circulatory System of the Mussel, Mytilus edulis (L.), Environmental Science & Technology 42 (2008) 5026–5031.

Browne, Mark A./Galloway, Tamara S./Thompson, Richard C., Spatial Patterns of Plastic Debris along Estuarine Shorelines, Environmental Science & Technology 44 (2010) 3404–3409.

Browne, Mark Anthony/Crump, Phillip/Niven, Stewart J. et al., Accumulation of Microplastic on Shorelines Worldwide: Sources and Sinks, Environmental Science & Technology 45 (2011) 9175–9179.

Browne, Mark Anthony/Galloway, Tamara/Thompson, Richard, Microplastic—An Emerging Contaminant of Potential Concern?, Integrated Environmental Assessment and Management 3 (2007) 559–566.

Busuttil, Regional Governance in the Mediterranean: An almost Metaphysical Note, Ocean Yearbook *21 (2007) 13-21.*

Butler, J.R.A./Gunn, R./Berry H.L. et al., A Value Chain Analysis of ghost nets in the Arafura Sea: Identifying trans-boundary stakeholders, intervention points and livelihood trade-offs, Journal of Environmental Management *123 (2013) 14-25.*

Brubaker, Douglas, Marine pollution and international law, Principles and practice, London, Boca Raton, 1993.

Bruha, Thomas/Koch, Hans-Joachim (eds), Integrierte Gewässerpolitik in Europa, Gewässerschutz, Wassernutzung, Lebensraumschutz, 1. ed., Baden-Baden 2001.

Bruha, Thomas/Maaß Christian A., Schutz der Süßwasserressourcen im Völkerrecht-Prinzipen, Instrumente, neue Entwicklungen, in: *Bruha, Thomas/Koch, Hans-Joachim* (eds.), Integrierte Gewässerpolitik in Europa, Gewässerschutz, Wassernutzung, Lebensraumschutz, 1. ed., Baden-Baden (2001) 69–118.

Brusendorff, Anne Christine/Ehlers, Peter, The HELCOM Copenhagen Declaration: A Regional Environmental Approach for Safer Shipping, The International Journal of Marine and Coastal Law 17 (2002) 351–395.

Buclet, Nicolas (eds.), Municipal waste management in Europe, European policy between harmonisation and subsidiarity, Dordrecht, Boston 2002.

Burgi, Martin, Das Schutz-und Ursprungsprinzip im europäischen Umweltrecht, Natur und Recht (1995) 11–15.

Campani, Tommaso/Baini, Matteo/Giannetti, Matteo et al., Presence of plastic debris in loggerhead turtle stranded along the Tuscany coasts of the Pelagos Sanctuary for Mediterranean Marine Mammals (Italy), Marine Pollution Bulletin 74 (2013) 225–230.

Carlo Bro a/s, A Study on the Availability and Use of Port Reception Facilities for Ship-Generated Waste December 2005.

Carpenter, Angela/Macgill, Sally, Charging for Port Reception Facilities in North Sea Ports: Putting Theory into Practice, Marine Pollution Bulletin 42 (2001) 257–266.

Carpenter, E. J./Anderson, S. J./Harvey, G. R. et al., Polystyrene Spherules in Coastal Waters, Science 178 (1972) 749–750.

Chalmers, Damian/Hadjiemmanuel, Christos/Monti, Giorgio et al., European Union law, Text and materials, Cambridge 2006

Chesire, Anthony/Adler, Ellik/Barbière, Julian et al., UNEP/IOC Guidelines on Survey and Monitoring of Marine Litter, UNEP Regional Seas Reports and Studies No.186, 2009.

Chua, Evan/Shimeta, Jeff/Nugegoda, Dayanthi et al., Assimilation of Polybrominated Diphenyl Ethers from Microplastics by the Marine Amphipod, Environmental Science & Technology (2014), just accepted script 02.06.2014.

Churchill, Robin, The European Union and the Challenges of Marine Governance: From Sectoral Response to Integrated Policy?, in: *Vidas, Davor/Schei, Peter Johan* (eds.), The world ocean in globalisation, Climate change, sustainable fisheries, biodiversity, shipping, regional issues, Leiden, Boston (2011) 395–471.

Churchill, Robin Rolf/Lowe, Alan Vaughan, The law of the sea, 3. ed., Yonkers, NY 2006.

Civili, Francesco Saverio, The Mediterranean Marine Environment: Pressures, State of Pollution and Measures (The Barcelona Convention and the Mediterranean Action Plan), in: *Ehlers, Peter/Wolfrum, Rüdiger/Borgese, Elisabeth Mann* (eds.), Marine issues, From a scientific, political and legal perspective, The Hague, London (2002) 165–176.

Clark, R. B., Marine pollution, 5.ed., Oxford 2007.

Coe, James M./Rogers, Donald B. (eds.), Marine debris, Sources, impacts, and solutions, New York 1997.

Colabuono, Fernanda Imperatrice/Taniguchi, Satie/Montone, Rosalinda Carmela, Polychlorinated biphenyls and organochlorine pesticides in plastics ingested by seabirds, Marine Pollution Bulletin 60 (2010) 630–634.

Cooper, David A./Corcoran, Patricia L., Effects of mechanical and chemical processes on the degradation of plastic beach debris on the island of Kauai, Hawaii, Marine Pollution Bulletin 60 (2010) 650–654.

Costanza, Robert/Bartmann, Herrmann, Einführung in die ökologische Ökonomik, Stuttgart 2001.

Craig, P. P./Búrca, Grainne de, EU law (eds.), Text, cases, and materials, 4. ed., Oxford, New York 2008.

Craig, Paul/Búrca, Grainne de (eds.), The Evolution of EU Law, 2. revised ed., Oxford 2011.

Cremona, Marise, External relations and external competence of the European Union, in: *Craig, Paul/Búrca, Gráinne de* (eds.), The evolution of EU law, 2. revised ed., Oxford (2011) 217–268.

Czybulka, Detlef (ed.), Marine nature conservation and management at the borders of the European Union, 1. ed., Baden-Baden 2012.

Davidson, Timothy M., Boring crustaceans damage polystyrene floats under docks polluting marine waters with microplastic, Marine Pollution Bulletin 64 (2012) 1821–1828.

Davies, Gareth, Deep-sea sludge dumping—an opportunity for business and research, Marine Pollution Bulletin 19 (1988) 2.

Davis, W.Jackson, Global aspects of marine pollution policy, Marine Policy 14 (1990) 191–197.

Debenest, T./Gagné, F./Petit, A.-N. et al., Ecotoxicity of a brominated flame retardant (tetrabromobisphenol A) and its derivatives to aquatic organisms, Comparative Biochemistry and Physiology Part C: Toxicology & Pharmacology 151 (2010) 407-412.

Denuncio, Pablo/Bastida, Ricardo/Dassis, Mariela et al., Plastic ingestion in Franciscana dolphins, Pontoporia blainvillei (Gervais and d'Orbigny, 1844), from Argentina, Marine Pollution Bulletin 62 (2011) 1836–1841.

Derraik, José G.B, The pollution of the marine environment by plastic debris: a review, Marine Pollution Bulletin 44 (2002) 842–852.

De Sadeleer, Nico, The Polluter-pays Principle in EU Law – Bold Case Law and Poor Harmonisation, in: *Bugge, Hans Christian* (ed.), Teischrift, Oslo (2012) 405–419.

- The effect of uncertainty on the thresholds levels to which the precautionary principle appears to be subject (1), in: *Applegate, John S.* (ed.), Environmental risk, Aldershot, Hants, England, Burlington (2004) 454–479.

- Environmental Principles, From political slogans to legal rules, Oxford, New York 2002.

Di Schiano Pepe, Lorenzo, Port Sate Control as an Instrument to Ensure Compliance with International Marine Environmental Obligations, in: *Kirchner, Andree* (ed.), International marine environmental law, Institutions, implementation and innovations, The Hague, New York, Frederick, MD (2003) 137–156.

Dotinga, Harm G./Oude Elferink, Alex G., Acoustic Pollution in the Oceans: The Search for Legal Standards, Ocean Development & International Law 31 (2000) 151–182.

Ducrotoy, Jean-Paul/Elliott, Michael, Interrelations between science and policy-making: the North Sea example, Marine Pollution Bulletin 34 (1997) 686–701.

Dupont, Claire/Kramm, Lars, The legal framework for the protection of the marine environment of the Black Sea region and its implementation, in: *Czybulka, Detlef* (ed.), Marine nature conservation and management at the borders of the European Union, 1. ed., Baden-Baden (2012) 77–90.

Dworkin, Ronald, Taking rights seriously, Cambridge 1977

Dzidzornu, David M., Marine Environment Protection under Regional Conventions: Limits to the Contribution of Procedural Norms, Ocean Development & International Law 33 (2002) 263–316.

Ebbesson, A Critical Assessment of the 1992 Baltic Sea Convention*, German Yearbook of International law 43(2000) 38.*

Ebbesson, Jonas, Protection of the Marine Environment of the Baltic Sea Area-The impact of the Stockholm Declaration, in: *Nordquist, Myron H./Moore, John Norton/ Mahmoudi, Said* (ed.), The Stockholm declaration and law of the marine environment, The Hague, New York (2003) 155–164.

Editor of Marine Pollution Bulletin, American News, Medical wastes on New York beaches, Marine Pollution Bulletin 19 (1988) 554.

Ehlers, Peter, The Helsinki Convention, 1992 Improving the Baltic Sea Environment, The International Journal of Marine and Coastal Law 8 (1993) 191–243.

- Marine Environment Protection- The Baltic Sea Example, in: *Ehlers, Peter/Wolfrum, Rüdiger/Borgese, Elisabeth Mann* (eds.), Marine issues, From a scientific, political and legal perspective, The Hague, London (2002) 92–104.

Ehlers, Peter/Lagoni, Rainer (eds.), International maritime organisations and their contribution towards a sustainable marine development, Hamburg 2006.

Ehlers, Peter/Wolfrum, Rüdiger/Borgese, Elisabeth Mann (eds.), Marine issues, From a scientific, political and legal perspective, The Hague, London 2002.

Elliott, M., The derivation and value of ecological quality standards and objectives, Marine Pollution Bulletin 32 (1996) 762–763.

Emanuelli, Claude, La pollution maritime et la notion de passage inoffensif, The Canadian yearbook of international (1973) 13–37.

Epiney, Astrid, Environmental Principles, in: *Macrory, Richard* (ed.), Reflections on 30 years of EU environmental law, A high level of protection?, Groningen (2006) 17–40.

Epiney, A./Felder, A.,(ed.), Überprüfung internationaler wasserwirtschaftlicher Übereinkommen im Hinblick auf die Implementierung der Wasserrahmenrichtlinie, Umweltbundesamt Texte 17/02, Forschungsbericht 20121 213, 2002.

Epiney, Astrid/Scheyli, Martin, Strukturprinzipien des Umweltvölkerrechts, Vol. 29, 1. ed., Baden-Baden 1998.

Eriksen, Marcus/Lebreton, Laurent/Carson, Henry et al., Plastic Pollution in the World's Oceans: More than 5 Trillion Plastic Pieces Weighing over 250,000 Tons Afloat at SeaPlos One (2014), 10 December 2014.

Eriksen, Marcus/Maximenko, Nikolai/Thiel, Martin et al., Plastic pollution in the South Pacific subtropical gyre, Marine Pollution Bulletin 68 (2013) 71–76.

Eriksson, Cecilia/Burton, Harry, Origins and Biological Accumulation of Small Plastic Particles in Fur Seals from Macquarie Island, AMBIO: A Journal of the Human Environment 32 (2003) 380–384.

Farrell, Paul/Nelson, Kathryn, Trophic level transfer of microplastic: Mytilus edulis (L.) to Carcinus maenas (L.), Environmental Pollution 177 (2013) 1–3.

Faßbender/Kurt, Zur aktuellen Diskussion um das Verschlechterungsverbot der Wasserrahmenichtlinie, EurUP (2/2013) 70–84.

Fendall, Lisa S./Sewell, Mary A., Contributing to marine pollution by washing your face: Microplastics in facial cleansers, Marine Pollution Bulletin 58 (2009) 1225–1228.

Fenichell, Stephen, Plastic: The making of a synthetic century, New York 1996.

Fischer, Lilo/Petschow, Urlich/Buclet, Nicolas, The consequences of implementing directives in the national context: the correct answer to the friction between national regimes?, in: *Buclet, Nicolas* (ed.), Municipal waste management in Europe, European policy between harmonisation and subsidiarity, Dordrecht, Boston (2002) 81–110.

Fitzmaurice, Malgorzata, OSPAR Tribunal: Dispute Concerning Access to Information Under Article 9 of the OSPAR Convention (Ireland v United Kingdom and Northern Ireland), The International Journal of Marine and Coastal Law 18 (2003) 541–558.

- The 1974 Convention on the Protection of the Marine Environment of the Baltic Sea Area, in: *Platzöder, Renate/Verlaan, Philomène* (eds.), The Baltic Sea, New developments in national policies and international cooperation, The Hague 1996.

- International legal problems of the environmental protection of the Baltic Sea, Dordrecht, Boston, Norwell, MA, USA 1992.

Fletcher, Stephen, Converting science to policy through stakeholder involvement: An analysis of the European Marine Strategy Directive, Marine Pollution Bulletin 54 (2007) 1881–1886.

Forwarst, Documentation of the contribution analysis and uncertainty assessment: Results interpretation identifying priority material flows and wastes for waste prevention, recycling and choice of waste treatment options, Sixth Framework Programme, 2010, http://forwast.brgm.fr/Documents/Deliverables/Forwast_D63.pdf, last accessed 27.08.2015.

Fossi, Maria Cristina/Panti, Cristina/Guerranti, Cristiana et al., Are baleen whales exposed to the threat of microplastics? A case study of the Mediterranean fin whale (Balaenoptera physalus), Marine Pollution Bulletin 64 (2012) 2374-2379.

Franckx, Erik, Regional Marine Environment Protection Regimes in the Context of UNCLOS, The International Journal of Marine and Coastal Law 13 (1998) 307–324.

Frank, Veronica, The European Community and marine environmental protection in the international law of the sea, Leiden, Boston 2007.

Freestone, David/Rayfuse, Rosemary, Ocean iron fertilization and international law, Marine Ecology Progress Series 364 (2008) 227–233.

Freestone, David/Barnes, Richard/Ong, David M. (eds.), The law of the sea, Progress and prospects, Oxford, New York 2006.

Frias, J.P.G.L/Sobral, P./Ferreira, A.M, Organic pollutants in microplastics from two beaches of the Portuguese coast, Marine Pollution Bulletin 60 (2010) 1988–1992.

Fritz, Simone, Integrierter Umweltschutz im Völkerrecht, Berlin 2009.

Fry, D. Michael/Fefer, Stewart I./Sileo, Louis, Ingestion of plastic debris by Laysan Albatrosses and Wedge-tailed Shearwaters in the Hawaiian Islands, Marine Pollution Bulletin 18 (1987) 339–343.

Galgani, F./Fleet, David/van Franeker, J., et al., Marine Strategy Framework Directive, Task Group 10 Report Marine Litter, ICES/JRC/IFREMER Joint Report No 31210 – 2009/2010), Luxembourg 2010.

Galgani, F./Hanke, G./Werner, S. et al., Marine litter within the European Marine Strategy Framework Directive, ICES Journal of Marine Science 70 (2013) 1055–1064.

Galgani, F./Leaute, J.P/Moguedet, P, et al., Litter on the Sea Floor Along European Coasts, Marine Pollution Bulletin 40 (2000) 516–527.

Gavouneli, Maria, Functional jurisdiction in the law of the sea, Publication on ocean development Vol.62, Leiden, the Netherlands, Boston 2007.

Geiger, Rudolf/Khan, Daniel-Erasmus/Kotzur, Markus (eds.), EUV, AEUV, Vertrag über die Europäische Union. Vertrag über die Arbeitsweise der Europäischen Gemeinschaft, 5. ed., München 2010.

GESAMP, Joint Group of Experts on the Scientific Aspects of Marine Environmental Protection, Bowmer, T. and Kershaw, P.J.(eds.), Proceedings of the GESAMP International Workshop on plastic particles as a vector in transporting persistent, bio-accumulating and toxic substances in the oceans, GESAMP Report No. 82, 2010.

GESAMP, *Joint Group of Experts on the Scientific Aspects of Marine Environmental Protection, Kershaw, P.J.* (ed.), Sources, fate and effects of microplastics in the marine environment: A global assessment, GESAMP Report No.90, 2015.

Gold, Edgar, Gard Handbook on Protection of the Marine Environment, 3. ed., Arendal, Norway 2006.

Good, Thomas P./June, Jeffrey A./Etnier, Michael A. et al., Derelict fishing nets in Puget Sound and the Northwest Straits: Patterns and threats to marine fauna, Marine Pollution Bulletin 60 (2010) 39–50.

Graf Vitzthum, Wolfgang, Begriff, Geschichte und Rechtsquellen des Seerechts, *in*: Graf *Vitzthum, Wolfgang* (ed.), Handbuch des Seerechts, München (2006) 1–134.

- Raum und Umwelt im Völkerrecht, in: *Graf Vitzthum, Wolfgang* (ed.), Völkerrecht. 4. ed., Berlin (2007) 387–490.

Graf Vitzthum, Wolfgang (ed.), Völkerrecht. 4. ed., Berlin 2007.

Graf Vitzthum, Wolfgang (ed.), Handbuch des Seerechts, München 2006.

Grandjean, Philippe, Science for precautionary decision-making, in: *EEA*, Late lessons from early warnings: science, precaution, innovation, EEA Report 01/2013 (2013) 623–642.

Gray, Holly/Lattin, Gwendolyn L./Moore, Charles J., Incidence, mass and variety of plastics ingested by Laysan (Phoebastria immutabilis) and Black-footed Albatrosses (P. nigripes) recovered as by-catch in the North Pacific Ocean, Marine Pollution Bulletin 64 (2012) 2190-2192.

Gray, John S., Statistics and the precautionary principle, Marine Pollution Bulletin 21 (1990) 174–176.

Gregory, Murray. R., Environmental implications of plastic debris in marine settings--entanglement, ingestion, smothering, hangers-on, hitch-hiking and alien invasions, Philosophical Transactions of the Royal Society B: Biological Sciences 364 (2009) 2013–2025.

Gregory, Murray R., Plastic 'scrubbers' in hand cleansers: a further (and minor) source for marine pollution identified, Marine Pollution Bulletin 32 (1996) 867–871.

Gregory, Murray R./Andrady, Anthony L., Plastics in the Marine Environment, in: *Andrady, A. L.* (ed.), Plastics and the environment, Hoboken, N.J (2003) 379–403.

Güner-Özbek, Meltem Deniz, Paris Memorandum of Understanding- an Example of International Co-operation and its Perspectives, in: *Ehlers, Peter/Lagoni, Rainer* (eds.), International maritime organisations and their contribution towards a sustainable marine development, Hamburg (2006) 105–134.

Habib, Daniel/Locke, David C./Cannone, Leonard J., Synthetic fibers as indicators of municipal sewage sludge, sludge products, and sewage treatment plants effluents, Water, Air and Soil Pollution 103 (1998) 1–8.

Hafkamp, Wim, Comparison of National Solid Waste Regimes in Trajectories of Change, in: *Buclet, Nicolas* (ed.), Municipal waste management in Europe, European policy between harmonisation and subsidiarity, Dordrecht, Boston (2002) 7–26.

Hafner, Gerhard, Kapitel: Meeresumwelt, Meresforschung und Technologietransfer, in: *Vitzthum, Wolfgang* (ed.), Handbuch des Seerechts, München (2006) 347–460.

Hammer, Jort/Kraak, Michiel H. S./Parsons, John R., Plastics in the Marine Environment: The Dark Side of a Modern Gift, in: *Whitacre, David M.* (ed.), Reviews of Environmental Contamination and Toxicology, New York, NY (2012) 1–44.

Hardin, Garret, The Tragedy of the Commons, Science 162 (1968) 1243–1248.

Hartwig, Eike/Clemens, Thomas/Heckroth, Mathias, Plastic debris as nesting material in a Kittiwake-(Rissa tridactyla)-colony at the Jammerbugt, Northwest Denmark, Marine Pollution Bulletin 54 (2007) 595–597.

Hassan, Daud, Protecting the marine environment from land-based sources of pollution, Towards effective international cooperation, Aldershot, Hants, England, Burlington, VT 2006.

Hassan, Rashid M./Scholes, Robert/Ash, Neville (eds.), Ecosystems and human well-being, Washington, Covelo, London 2005.

Hedemann-Robinson, Martin, Enforcement of European Union environmental law: Legal issues and challenges, London, New York 2007.

Heintschel von Heinegg, Wolff, The development of environmental standards for the north-east atlantic including the north-sea, in: *Ehlers, Peter/Wolfrum, Rüdiger/ Borgese, Elisabeth Mann* (eds.), Marine issues, From a scientific, political and legal perspective, The Hague, London (2002) 135–153.

Henderson, John R., A Pre- and Post-MARPOL Annex V Summary of Hawaiian Monk Seal Entanglements and Marine Debris Accumulation in the Northwestern Hawaiian Islands, 1982–1998, Marine Pollution Bulletin 42 (2001) 584–589.

Hewison, Grant J., The Precautionary Approach to Fisheries Management: An Environmental Perspective, The International Journal of Marine and Coastal Law 11 (1996) 301–332.

Hidalgo-Ruz, Valeria/Thiel, Martin, Distribution and abundance of small plastic debris on beaches in the SE Pacific (Chile): A study supported by a citizen science project, Marine Environmental Research 87-88 (2013) 12–18.

Hilf, Juliane, The Convention for the Protection of the Marine Environment of the North-East Atlantic - New Approaches to an Old Problem?, Zeitschrift für ausländisches öffentliches Recht und Völkerrecht 55 (1995) 580–603.

Hjorth, Ronnie, Baltic environmental cooperation, A regime in transition, Linköping 1996.

Holmström, Arne, Plastic films on the bottom of the Skagerack, Nature 255 (1975) 622–623.

Holwerda, Marijn, Deploying carbon capture and storage "safely": The scope for Member States of the EU to adopt more stringent CO2 stream-purity criteria under EU law, Climate Law 2 (2011) 37–61.

Horsman, Paul V., The amount of garbage pollution from merchant ships, Marine Pollution Bulletin 13 (1982) 167–169.

Brown, James/ Magnus, Jessica, Policy framework for improving management of the deep-water net fishery of the West and North of Great Britain and Ireland, IEEP, 2006.

Institute for European Environmental Policy/Poseidon Aquatic Resource Management Ltd joint report, Ghost Fishing by Lost Fishing Gear, Final Report to DG Fisheries and Maritime Affairs of the European Commission, 2005, http://www.consult-poseidon.com/reports/Ghost%20fishing%20final%20report.pdf, last accessed 27.08.2015.

International Institute for Sustainable Development, Summary of the Third Intergovernmental Review (IGR-3) Meeting on the Implementation of the Global Programme of Action for the Protection of the Marine Environment from Land-based Activities (GPA) convened in Manila, the Philippines, from 25-26 January 2012, Earth Negotiations Bulletin 25 (2012).

Interviewes/Görlitz/Stöfen et al., Issue Paper to the "International Conference on Prevention and Management of Marine Litter in European Seas", 16.05.2013, http://www.marine-litter-conference-berlin.info/userfiles/file/Issue%20Paper_Final%20Version.pdf, last accessed 27.08.2015.

Ivar do Sul, Juliana A./Costa, Monica F., Marine debris review for Latin America and the Wider Caribbean Region: From the 1970s until now, and where do we go from here?, Marine Pollution Bulletin 54 (2007) 1087–1104.

Jans, J. H./Vedder, Hans, European environmental law, 4. ed., Groningen 2012.

Jeftic, Ljubomir/Matte-Baker, Andrea/Schomaker, Mirjam, The state of the marine environment, Trends and processes, Hague 2006.

Jekel, Heide/Munk, Hans-Hartmann, Phasing-out für prioritäre gefährliche Stoffe-Was regelt die EG-Wasserrahmenrichtlinie wirklich?, ZUR (2013) 403–407.

Jenisch, Uwe K., The Development of Environmental Standards in the Baltic Sea, in: *Ehlers, Peter/Wolfrum, Rüdiger/Borgese, Elisabeth Mann* (eds.), Marine issues, From a scientific, political and legal perspective, The Hague, London (2002) 63–72.

Jenisch, Uwe K., The Baltic Sea: The Legal Regime and Instruments for Co-operation, The International Journal of Marine and Coastal Law 11 (1996) 47–67.

Johnston, Douglas M./Chircop, Aldo E./McDorman, Ted L./Rolston, Susan (eds.), The future of ocean regime-building, Essays in tribute to Douglas M. Johnston, Leiden, Boston 2009.

Jonge, Victor N. de/Elliott, Finn M./Brauer, Verena S., Marine monitoring: Its shortcomings and mismatch with the EU Water Framework Directive's objectives, Marine Pollution Bulletin 53 (2006) 5–19.

Joyner, Christopher C./Frew, Scott, Plastic pollution in the marine environment, Ocean Development & International Law 22 (1991) 33–69.

Juda, Lawrence, The European Union and Ocean Use Management: The Marine Strategy and the Maritime Policy, Ocean Development & International Law 38 (2007) 259–282.

Juda, Lawrence, The European Union and the Marine Strategy Framework Directive: Continuing the Development of European Ocean Use Management, Ocean Development & International Law 41 (2010) 34–54.

Kachel, Markus J., Particularly sensitive sea areas, The IMO's role in protecting vulnerable marine areas, Berlin 2008.

Kahl, Wolfgang, Art. 191- 193 AEUV, in: *Streinz, Rudolf (ed.),* EUV/AEUV, München (2012) 1821–1889.

Kahl, Wolfgang, Umweltprinzip und Gemeinschaftsrecht, Eine Untersuchung zur Rechtsidee des bestmöglichen Umweltschutzes im EWG-Vertrag, Augsburger Rechtsstudien Vol. 17, Heidelberg 1993.

Käller, Anja, Artikel 191, in: *Schwarze, Jürgen/Becker, Ulrich/Bär-Bouyssière, Bertold* (eds.), EU-Kommentar, 3.ed., Baden-Baden, Wien, Basel (2012) 1834-1849.

Keselj, Tatjana, Port State Jurisdiction in Respect of Pollution from Ships: The 1982 United Nations Convention on the Law of the Sea and the Memoranda of Understanding, Ocean Development & International Law 30 (1999) 127–160.

Kirchner, Andree (ed.), International marine environmental law, Institutions, implementation and innovations, The Hague, New York, Frederick, MD 2003.

Kiss, Alexandre/Shelton, Dinah, International environmental law, 3. ed., Ardsley, NY 2004.

Koch, Hans-Joachim/Lagoni, Rainer (ed.), Meeresumweltschutz für Nord- und Ostsee, Zum Zusammenspiel von Völkerrecht und nationalem Umweltrecht, 1. ed., Baden-Baden 1996.

Koelmans, Albert A./Besseling, Ellen/Foekema, Edwin M., Leaching of plastic additives to marine organisms, Environmental Pollution 187 (2014) 49-54.

Koelmans, Albert/Gouin, Todd/Thompson, Richard et al., Plastics in the Marine Environment, Environmental Toxicology and Chemistry 33 (2014) 5-10.

Koelmans, Albert/Besseling, Ellen/Wegner, Anna et al., Plastic as a Carrier of POPs to Aquatic Organisms: A Model Analysis, Environmental Science & Technology 47 (2013) 7812-7820.

König, Doris, Marine Environment, International Protection, in: Max Planck Encyclopedia of Public International Law (MPEPIL), http://opil.ouplaw.com/view/10.1093/law:epil/9780199231690/law-9780199231690-e1594?rskey=Y3SHaP&result=3&prd=EPIL, last updated April 2011, last accessed 27.08.2015.

Koss, Lawrence J., Dealing with Ship-Generated Plastics Waste on U.S. Navy Surface Ships, in: *Coe, James M./Rogers, Donald B.* (eds.), Marine debris, Sources, impacts, and solutions, New York (1997) 263–270.

Kotulla, Michael, Die Bewirtschaftungsziele der §§ 25a-25d, 32c, 33a WHG, in: *Hendler* (ed.), Jahrbuch des Umwelt- und Technikrechts, Berlin (2005) 185–220.

Koutsodendris, Andreas/Papatheodorou, George/Kougiourouki, Ourania et al., Benthic marine litter in four Gulfs in Greece, Eastern Mediterranean; abundance, composition and source identification, Estuarine, Coastal and Shelf Science 77 (2008) 501–512.

Krämer, Ludwig, Droit de l'environnement de l'Union européenne, Bâle 2011.

EC environmental law, 6. ed., London 2007.

- Thirty Years of Environmental Governance in the European Union, in: *Macrory, Richard* (ed.), Reflections on 30 years of EU environmental law, A high level of protection?, Groningen (2006) 553–576.

- The Genesis of EC Environmental Principles, in: *Macrory, Richard/Havercroft, Ian/ Purdy, Ray* (eds.), Principles of european environmental law, Groningen (2004) 31–48.

Kramm, Lars, Introduction to the Black Sea region, in: *Czybulka, Detlef* (ed.), Marine nature conservation and management at the borders of the European Union, 1.ed., Baden-Baden (2012) 73–76.

-The new strategic action plan for the environmental protection and rehabilitation of the Black Sea, in: Czybulka, Detlef (ed.), Marine nature conservation and management at the borders of the European Union, 1.ed., Baden-Baden (2012) 91–101.

Kremser, Ulrich, The Baltic Sea Joint Comprehensive Environmental Action Programme, in: *Ehlers, Peter/Wolfrum, Rüdiger/Borgese, Elisabeth Mann* (eds.), Marine issues, From a scientific, political and legal perspective, The Hague, London (2002) 105–118.

Kühn, Susanne/van Franeker, Jan A., Plastic ingestion by the northern fulmar (Fulmarus glacialis) in Iceland, Marine Pollution Bulletin 64 (2012) 1252–1254.

Kujawinski, Elizabeth B./Kido Soule, Melissa C./Valentine, David L. et al., Fate of Dispersants Associated with the Deepwater Horizon Oil Spill, Environ. Sci. Technol 45 (2011) 1298–1306.

Kwiatkowska, Barbara, The Ireland v United Kingdom (Mox Plant) Case: Applying the Doctrine of Treaty Parallelism, The International Journal of Marine and Coastal Law 18 (2003) 1–58.

La Fayette, Louise de, The London Convention 1972: Preparing for the Future, The International Journal of Marine and Coastal Law 13 (1998) 515–536.

-The OSPAR Convention Comes into Force: Continuity and Progress, The International Journal of Marine and Coastal Law 14 (1999) 247–297.

- The Protection of the Marine Environment-1999, Environmental Policy and Law 30 (2000) 51–60.

- The Role of the United Nations in International Ocean Governance, in: *Freestone, David/Barnes, Richard/Ong, David M.* (eds.), The law of the sea, Progress and prospects, Oxford, New York (2006) 63–74.

Lagoni, Rainer, Das OSPAR-Übereinkommen von 1992 und der Schutz der Nordsee: Einwirkungen auf das deutsche Umweltrecht, in: *Koch, Hans-Joachim/Lagoni, Rainer* (eds.), Meeresumweltschutz für Nord- und Ostsee, Zum Zusammenspiel von Völkerrecht und nationalem Umweltrecht, 1.ed., Baden-Baden 1996.

Laist, David W., Impacts of Marine Debris: Entanglement of Marine Life in Marine Debris Inclduing a Comprehensive List of Species with Entanglement and Ingestion Records, in: *Coe, James M./Rogers, Donald B.* (eds.), Marine debris, Sources, impacts, and solutions, New York (1997) 99–140.

Lang, Winfried (ed.), Sustainable development and international law, London, Boston 1995.

Laughthon, Anthony S., Using the ocean wisely, The waste problem, Marine Policy 18 (1994) 453–456.

Lavranos, Nikolaos, Protecting Its Exclusive Jurisdiction: The Mox Plant-judgment of the ECJ, The Law & Practice of International Courts and Tribunals 5 (2006) 479–493.

-The MOX Plant and IJzeren Rijn Disputes: Which Court Is the Supreme Arbiter?, Leiden Journal of Inernational Law 19 (2006) 223-246.

Law, K. L./Moret-Ferguson, S./Maximenko, N. A. et al., Plastic Accumulation in the North Atlantic Subtropical Gyre, Science 329 (2010) 1185–1188.

Lazar, Bojan/Gračan, Romana, Ingestion of marine debris by loggerhead sea turtles, Caretta caretta, in the Adriatic Sea, Marine Pollution Bulletin 62 (2011) 43–47.

Lechner, A./Keckeis, H./Lumesberger, B.et al., The Danube so colourful : a potpourri of plastic litter outnumbers fish larvaes in Europe´s second largest river, Environmental Pollution 188 (2014) 177-81.

Lee, EU environmental law: challenges, change and decision-making, Oxford, Portland, 2005.

Lentz, Sally Ann, Plastics in the marine environment: Legal approaches for international action, Marine Pollution Bulletin 18 (1987) 361–365.

Liebermann, Susan/Yang, Joan, Rio+20 and the Oceans: Past, Present and Future, Ocean Yearbook 27 (2013) 67–87.

Liebezeit, Gerd/Dubaish, Fatehi, Microplastics in Beaches of the East Frisian Islands Spiekeroog and Kachelotplate, Bulletin of Environmental Contamination and Toxicology 89 (2012) 213–217.

Liebezeit, Gerd/Liebezeit, Elisabeth, Non-pollen particulates in honey and sugar, Food Additives & Contaminants: Part A (2013) 1–5.

Lin, Albert C., The Unifying Role of Harm in Environmental Law, Wisconsin Law Review (2006) 898–985.

Lobelle, Delphine/Cunliffe, Michael, Early microbial biofilm formation on marine plastic debris, Marine Pollution Bulletin 62 (2011) 197–200.

Long, Ronán, The European Union and Law of the Sea Convention at the Age of 30, The International Journal of Marine and Coastal Law 27 (2012) 711–721.

Louka, Elli, Water law & policy, Governance without frontiers, Oxford, New York 2008.

Loyo-Rosales, Jorge E./Rosales-Rivera, Georgina C./Lynch, Anika M. et al., Migration of Nonylphenol from Plastic Containers to Water and a Milk Surrogate, J. Agric. Food Chem 52 (2004) 2016–2020.

Jones, A. Ingolfsson E. Olafsson/Helgason, Gudmundur V./K. Gunnarsson &. J. Svavarsson (eds.), Migrations and dispersal of marine organisms, in: Proceedings of the 37th European Marine Biology Symposium held in Reykjavik, Iceland, 5-9 August 2002, Dordrecht, Boston 2003.

Macrory, Richard, Community Supervision in the Field of the Environment, in: *Somsen, Han* (ed.), Protecting the European environment, Enforcing EC environmental law, London (1996) 9–21.

*Macrory, Richard (*ed.), Reflections on 30 years of EU environmental law, A high level of protection?, Groningen 2006.

*Macrory, Richard /Havercroft, Ian/Purdy, Ray (*eds.), Principles of European environmental law, Groningen 2004.

Madzena, Azwifarwi/Lasiak, Theresa, Spatial and temporal variations in beach litter on the Transkei coast of South Africa, Marine Pollution Bulletin 34 (1997) 900–907.

Mansell, John N. K., Flag state responsibility, Historical development and contemporary issues, Berlin 2009.

Markus, Till/Schlacke, Sabine/Maier, Nina, Legal Implementation of Integrated Ocean Policies: The EU´s Marine Strategy Framework Directive, The International Journal of Marine and Coastal Law 26 (2011) 59–90.

Marr, Simon, The precautionary principle in the law of the sea, Modern decision making in international law, The Hague, New York 2003.

Martin, Jeannie Miller, Marine debris removal: One year of effort by the Georgia Sea Turtle-Center-Marine Debris Initiative, Marine Pollution Bulletin 74 (2013) 165–169.

Martinez, Elodie/Maamaatuaiahutapu, Keitapu/Taillandier, Vincent, Floating marine debris surface drift: Convergence and accumulation toward the South Pacific subtropical gyre, Marine Pollution Bulletin 58 (2009) 1347–1355.

Mato, Yukie/Isobe, Tomohik/Takada, Hideshige et al., Plastic Resin Pellets as a Transport Medium for Toxic Chemicals in the Marine Environment, Environmental Science & Technology 35 (2001) 318–324.

Maurmann, Dorothee, Rechtsgrundsätze im Völkerrecht am Beispiel des Vorsorgeprinzips, Studies on environmental law Vol.38, 1. ed., Baden-Baden 2008.

McCoy, Floyd W., Floating megalitter in the eastern Mediterranean, Marine Pollution Bulletin 19 (1988) 25–28.

McDonough, William/Braungart, Michael, Cradle to cradle, Remaking the way we make things, 1.ed., 2002.

McDorman, Ted L., Port State Enforcement: A Comment on Article 218 of the 1982 Law of the Sea, Journal of Maritime Law & Commerce 28 (1997) 305–322.

Meadows, Donella H./Randers, Jørgen/Meadows, Dennis L., Grenzen des Wachstums: das 30-Jahre-Update, Signal zum Kurswechsel, Stuttgart 2006.

Mee, Laurence D./Jefferson, Rebecca L./Laffoley, Dan d'A et al., How good is good? Human values and Europe's proposed Marine Strategy Directive, Marine Pollution Bulletin 56 (2008) 187–204.

Mensah, Thomas A., The International Legal Regime for the Protection and Preservation of the Marine Environment from Land-based Sources of Pollution, in: *Boyle, Alan E./Freestone, David* (ed.), International law and sustainable development, Past achievements and future challenges, Oxford, New York (1999) 298–324.

Meßerschmidt, Klaus, Europäisches Umweltrecht, München 2011.

Milan, Shapour S., The Legal Status of the Persian Gulf as a Semi-Enclosed Sea, Archiv des Völkerrechts 25 (1987) 92–105.

Molenaar, Erik Jaap, Port State Jurisdiction: Toward Comprehensive, Mandatory and Global Coverage, Ocean Development & International Law 38 (2007) 225–257.

- Port State Jurisdiction: Towards Mandatory and Comprehensive Use, in: *Freestone, David/Barnes, Richard/Ong, David M.* (eds.), The law of the sea, Progress and prospects, Oxford, New York (2006) 192–209.

- Coastal State Jurisdiction over Vessel-Source Pollution, The Hague, Boston 1998.

Moore, C.J/Moore, S.L/Leecaster, M.K, et al., A Comparison of Plastic and Plankton in the North Pacific Central Gyre, Marine Pollution Bulletin 42 (2001) 1297–1300.

Moos, Nadia von/Burkhardt-Holm, Patricia/Köhler, Angela, Uptake and Effects of Microplastics on Cells and Tissue of the Blue Mussel Mytilus edulis L. after an Experimental Exposure, Environmental Science and Technology 46 (2012) 11327–11335.

Morét-Ferguson, Skye/Law, Kara Lavender/Proskurowski, Giora, et al., The size, mass, and composition of plastic debris in the western North Atlantic Ocean, Marine Pollution Bulletin 60 (2010) 1873–1878.

Morritt, David/Stefanoudis, Paris V./Pearce, Dave, et al., Plastic in the Thames: A river runs through it, Marine Pollution Bulletin 78 (2014) 196-200.

Mulder, Jan de, Case Note, Review of European Community & International Environmental Law 19 (2010) 263–269.

Nakashima, Etsuko/Isobe, Atsuhiko/Magome, Shinya et al., Using aerial photography and in situ measurements to estimate the quantity of macro-litter on beaches, Marine Pollution Bulletin 62 (2011) 762–769.

Nelson, L. Dolliver M., Reflections on the 1982 Convention on the law of the Sea, in: *Freestone, David/Barnes, Richard/Ong, David M.* (eds.), The law of the sea, Progress and prospects, Oxford, New York (2006) 28-39.

Ninaber, Ellen, MARPOL Annex V, Commercial Ships, and Port Reception Facilities: Making it Work, in: *Coe, James M./Rogers, Donald B.* (eds.), Marine debris, Sources, impacts, and solutions, New York (1997) 239–251.

Nollkaemper, André, The legal regime for transboundary water pollution: between discretion and constraint, Dordrecht, Boston, Norwell, MA 1993.

- Legal Regulation of Upland Discharges of marine debris: From Local to Global Controls and Back, in: *Coe, James M./Rogers, Donald B.* (eds.), Marine debris, Sources, impacts, and solutions, New York (1997) 293–305.

- The Evolution of the Regime for the River Rhine, in: *Subedi, Surya P.* (eds.), International watercourses law for the 21st century, The case of the river Ganges basin, Aldershot (2005) 151–166.

Nordquist, Myron H./Moore, John Norton/Mahmoudi, Said (eds.), The Stockholm declaration and law of the marine environment, The Hague, New York 2003.

Öko-Institute.V., Study on the land-sourced litter (LSL) in the marine environment, 2012.

Olazábal, Claudia, Community Legislation on Water Protection, in: *Onida, Marco* (ed.), Europe and the environment, Legal essays in honour of Ludwig Krämer, Groningen (2004) 157–172.

Onida, Marco, Challenges and Opportunities in EC Waste Management, in: *Somsen, Han* (ed.), Yearbook of European environmental law, Oxford, New York, Athens <etc.> (2000) 253–289.

Onida, Marco (ed.), Europe and the environment, Legal essays in honour of Ludwig Krämer, Groningen 2004.

Ormand, Robert, La notion de "l'effet-utile" des traités communautaires dans la jurisprudence de la Cour de justice des Communautés européennes, Paris 1975.

Panko, Julie M./Chu, Jennifer/Kreider, Marisa L. et al., Measurement of airborne concentrations of tire and road wear particles in urban and rural areas of France, Japan, and the United States, Atmospheric Environment 72 (2013) 192–199.

Papanicolopulu, Irini, Procedures and Mechanisms on Compliance under the 1976/1995 Barcelona Convention on the Protection of the Mediterranean Sea and its Protocols, in: *Treves, Tullio/Pineschi, Laura/Tanzi, Attila et al.* (eds.), Non-compliance procedures and mechanisms and the effectiveness of international environmental agreements, The Hague, Netherlands, West Nyack, NY (2009) 155–168.

Parmentier, Rémi, Greenpeace and the Dumping of Waste at Sea: A Case of Non-State Actors' Intervention in International Affairs, International Negotiation 4 (1999) 435–457.

Petersen, Frank, Die fünfstufige Abfallhierarchie- Funktionen und Probleme, Zeitschrift für das Recht der Abfallwirtschaft (2013) 2–12.

Pham, C.K/Gomes-Pereira, J.N/Isidro, E.J et al., Abundance of litter on Condor seamount (Azores, Portugal, Northeast Atlantic), Deep Sea Research Part II: Topical Studies in Oceanography 98 Part A (2013) 204-208.

Plasman, Cathy, The State of the Marine Environment of the North Sea and of the Baltic Sea: A Comparison in Relation to Dangerous Substances, The International Journal of Marine and Coastal Law 13 (1998) 325–336.

Plasticeurope, Plastics the fact 2013, An analysis of European latest plastic production, demand and waste data 14.10.2013, http://www.plasticseurope.org/Document/plastics-the-facts-2013.aspx?FolID=2., last accessed 27.08.2015.

Platzöder, Renate/Verlaan, Philomène (eds.), The Baltic Sea, New developments in national policies and international cooperation, The Hague 1996.

Pocklington, David, The law of waste management, Crayford 1997.

Possatto, Fernanda E./Barletta, Mário/Costa, Monica F. et al., Plastic debris ingestion by marine catfish: An unexpected fisheries impact, Marine Pollution Bulletin 62 (2011) 1098–1102.

Posselt, Jens-Christian, Umweltschutz in umschlossenen und halbumschlossenen Meeren, Münster, Hamburg 1995.

Proelß, Alexander, Raum und Umwelt im Völkerrecht, in: *Bothe, Michael/Dolzer, Rudolf/Kau, Marcel et al.* (eds.), Völkerrecht. 6. ed., Berlin, Boston (2013) 352–438.

- Das Urteil des Internationalen Gerichtshofs im Pulp Mills-Fall und seine Bedeutung für die Entwicklung des Umweltvölkerrechts, in: *Ruffert, Matthias* (eds.), Dynamik und Nachhaltigkeit des Öffentlichen Rechts, Festschrift für Professor Dr. Meinhard Schröder zum 70. Geburtstag, Berlin (2012) 611–625.

- Meeresschutz im Völker - und Europarecht, Das Beispiel des Nordostatlantiks, Tübinger Schriften zum internationalen und europäischen Recht Vol. 71, Berlin, Tübingen 2004.

Proelss, Alexander, International Environmental Law and the Challenge of Climate Change, German Yearbook of International Law 53 (2010) 65–87.

Purdy, Ray/Havercroft, Ian, Carbon Capture and Storage: Developments under European Union and International Law, Journal for European Environmental & Planning Law 4 (2007) 353–366.

Ramboll, Final Report, EMSA Study on the Delivery of Ship-Generated Waste and Cargo residues to Port Reception Facilities in EU Ports, EMSA/OP/06/2011, August 2012.

Raum-Suryan, Kimberly L./Jemison, Lauri A./Pitcher, Kenneth W., Entanglement of Steller sea lions (Eumetopias jubatus) in marine debris: Identifying causes and finding solutions, Marine Pollution Bulletin 58 (2009) 1487–1495.

Rayfuse, Rosemary Gail, Non-flag state enforcement in high seas fisheries, Publications on ocean development Vol. 46, Leiden 2004.

Reichert, Götz, Der nachhaltige Schutz grenzübergreifender Gewässer in Europa, Tübinger Schriften zum internationalen und europäischen Recht Vol. 76, Berlin, Tübingen 2005.

Reinhardt, Michael, Inventur der Wasserrahmenrichtline, Die rechtliche Fortwentwicklung der europäischen Gewässerschutzpolitik im Streit um Fristen, Ziele und Deutungshoheiten, Natur und Recht 35 (2013) 765–773.

Ringbom, Henrik, The EU maritime safety policy and international law, Publications on ocean development Vol. 64, Leiden, Boston 2008.

Ringbom, Henrik (ed.), Competing norms in the law of marine environmental protection, Focus on ship safety and pollution prevention, London, Boston 1997.

Rochman, Chelsea M./Manzano, Carlos/Hentschel, Brian T. et al., Polystyrene Plastic: A Source and Sink for Polycyclic Aromatic Hydrocarbons in the Marine Environment, Environmental Science & Technology 47 (2013) 13976 - 13984.

Röckmann, Christine, International Co-operation for Sustainable Fisheries in the Baltic, in: *Ehlers, Peter/Lagoni, Rainer* (eds.), International maritime organisations and their contribution towards a sustainable marine development, Hamburg (2006) 239–258.

Romer, Jennie Reilly, The Evolution of San Francisco's Plastic-Bag Ban, Golden Gate University Environmental Law Journal 1 (2010) 439–465.

Rothwell, Donald/Stephens, Tim, The international law of the sea, Oxford, Portland, 2010.

Ryan, P.G/Connell, A.D/Gardner, B.D, Plastic ingestion and PCBs in seabirds: Is there a relationship?, Marine Pollution Bulletin 19 (1988) 174–176.

Ryan, Peter G./Moore, Charles J./van Franeker, Jan A., et al., Monitoring the abundance of plastic debris in the marine environment, Philosophical Transactions of the Royal Society B: Biological Sciences 364 (2009) 1999–2012.

Ryan, Peter.G/Jackson, Scott, The lifespan of ingested plastic particles in seabirds and their effect on digestive efficiency, Marine Pollution Bulletin 18 (1987) 217–219.

Saila, S.B, Container dumping in the North Sea, Marine Pollution Bulletin 2 (1971) 125–127.

Salchow, Roland, The Quality Status Report (QSR 2000) for the North East Atlantic, in: *Ehlers, Peter/Wolfrum, Rüdiger/Borgese, Elisabeth Mann* (eds.), Marine issues, From a scientific, political and legal perspective, The Hague, London (2002) 118–134.

Salomon, Markus/Dross, Miriam, Challenges in cross-sectoral marine protection in Europe, Marine Policy 42 (2013) 142–149.

Salomon, Markus, The European Commission proposal for a Marine Strategy: Lacking substance, Marine Pollution Bulletin 52 (2006) 1328–1329.

Sand, Peter H., The Evolution of International Environmental Law, in: *Bodansky, Daniel/Brunnée, Jutta/Hey, Ellen* (eds.), The Oxford handbook of international environmental law, Oxford ;, New York (2007) 31–43.

Sands, Philippe/Peel, Jacqueline, Principles of international environmental law, 3. ed., Cambridge, New York 2012.

Sasakawa, Shigeru/Mitomi, Yoshitada, Di-2-ethylhexylphthalate (DEHP) Content of Blood or Blood Components Stored in Plastic Bags, Vox Sanguinis 34 (1978) 81–86.

Schroeder, Werner, Art. 288 AEUV, in: *Streinz, Rudolf* (ed.), EUV/AEUV, Vertrag über die Europäische Union und Vertrag über die Arbeitsweise der Europäischen Union. 2. ed., München (2012) 2413–2456.

Schwarze, Jürgen/Becker, Ulrich/Bär-Bouyssière, Bertold (eds.), EU-Kommentar, 3.ed., Baden-Baden, Wien, Basel 2012.

Scott, Joanne, Flexibility in the Implementation of EC Environmental Law, in: *Somsen, Han* (ed.), Yearbook of European environmental law, Oxford, New York, Athens (2000) 37–60.

Selke, Susan E.M, Plastics in Packaging, in: *Andrady, A. L.* (ed.), Plastics and the environment, Hoboken, N.J (2003) 139–183.

Sevenster, Hannah, The Environmental Guarantee After Amsterdam, in: *Somsen, Han* (ed.), Yearbook of European environmental law, Oxford, New York, Athens (2000) 291–310.

Seyr, Sibylle, Der effet utile in der Rechtsprechung des EuGH, Schriften zum europäischen Recht Vol.135, Berlin 2008.

Shany Yuval, The First MOX Plant Award: The Need to Harmonize Competing Environmental Regimes and Dispute Settlement Procedures, Leiden Journal of International Law 17 (2004) 815–827.

Sheavly, S. B./Register, K. M., Marine Debris & Plastics: Environmental Concerns, Sources, Impacts and Solutions, J Polym Environ 15 (2007) 301–305.

Shelton, Dinah, Stockholm Declaration (1972) and Rio Declaration (1992), in: Max Planck Encyclopedia of Public International Law (MPEPIL), http://opil.ouplaw.com/view/10.1093/law:epil/9780199231690/law-9780199231690-e1608?rskey=9rJMrg&result=5&prd=EPIL, last updated July 2008, last accessed 27.08.2015.

Simmonds, Mark Peter, Cetaceans and Marine Debris: The Great Unknown, Journal of Marine Biology 2012 (2012) 1–8.

Soares, A./Guieysse, B./Jefferson, B. et al., Nonylphenol in the environment: A critical review on occurrence, fate, toxicity and treatment in wastewaters, Environment International 34 (2008) 1033–1049.

Sohn, Louis Bruno/Noyes, John E., Cases and materials on the law of the sea, Ardsley N.Y 2004.

Somsen, Han (ed.), Protecting the European environment, Enforcing EC environmental law, London 1996.

Somsen, Han (ed.), Yearbook of European environmental law, Oxford, New York, Athens 2000.

St Clair Bradley, Kieran, Powers and Procedures in the EU Constitution: Legal Base and the Court, in: *Craig, Paul/Búrca, Grainne de* (eds.), The Evolution of EU Law, 2. revised edition, Oxford (2011) 85–110.

Steinbeck, John/Ricketts, Edward F., The log from the Sea of Cortez, The narrative portion of the book, Sea of Cortez (1941) by John Steinbeck and E.F. Ricketts, London 1995.

Stephanis, Renaud de/Giménez, Joan/Carpinelli, Eva et al., As main meal for sperm whales: Plastics debris, Marine Pollution Bulletin 69 (2013) 206–214.

Stephens, Tim, International courts and environmental protection, Cambridge, UK, New York 2009.

Stöfen, Aleke, The role of the Marine Strategy Framework Directive in the protection of the marine environment at the EU´s borders (and beyond), in: *Czybulka, Detlef* (ed.), Marine nature conservation and management at the borders of the European Union, 1. ed., Baden-Baden (2012) 151–158.

Streinz, Rudolf (ed.), EUV/AEUV, Vertrag über die Europäische Union und Vertrag über die Arbeitsweise der Europäischen Union, 2. ed., München 2012

Suarez, Suzette V., Towards sustainable Ocean Development: The Participation and Contribution of Non-governmental Organisations to the Work of International Organizations in the Ocean Sector, in: *Ehlers, Peter/Lagoni, Rainer* (ed.), International maritime organisations and their contribution towards a sustainable marine development, Hamburg (2006) 53–75.

Subedi, Surya P. (ed.), International watercourses law for the 21st century, The case of the river Ganges basin, Aldershot 2005.

Talsness, Chris E./Andrade, Anderson J. M./Kuriyama, Sergio N. et al., Components of plastic: experimental studies in animals and relevance for human health, Philosophical Transactions of the Royal Society B: Biological Sciences 364 (2009) 2079–2096.

Tan, Alan Khee-Jin, Vessel-source marine pollution, The law and politics of international regulation, Cambridge, New York 2006.

Tanaka, Yoshifumi, Regulation of Land-based Marine Pollution in International Law, A Comparative Analysis Between Global and Regional Legal Frameworks, Zeitschrift für ausländisches öffentliches Recht und Völkerrecht 66 (2006) 533-574.

Täufer, Katrin, Introduction to the Baltic Sea, in: *Czybulka, Detlef* (ed.), Marine nature conservation and management at the borders of the European Union, 1. ed., Baden-Baden (2012) 25–28.

Temmink, Harrie, From Danish Bottles to Danish Bees: The Dynamics of Free Movement of Goods and Environmental Protection- a Case Law Analysis, in: *Somsen, Han* (ed.), Yearbook of European environmental law, Oxford, New York, Athens (2000) 61–102.

Teuten, Emma L./Rowland, Steven J./Galloway, Tamara S. et al., Potential for Plastics to Transport Hydrophobic Contaminants, Environ. Sci. Technol 41 (2007) 7759–7764.

Teuten, Emma L./Saquing, Jovita M./Knappe, Detlef R. U. et al., Transport and release of chemicals from plastics to the environment and to wildlife, Philosophical Transactions of the Royal Society B: Biological Sciences 364 (2009) 2027–2045.

Thompson, R. C., Lost at Sea: Where Is All the Plastic?, Science 304 (2004) 838.

Thompson, Richard C./Moore, Charles J./Vom Saal, Frederick S. et al., Plastics, the environment and human health: current consensus and future trends, Philosophical Transactions of the Royal Society B: Biological Sciences 364 (2009) 2153–2166.

Thompson, Richard C./Swan, Shanna H./Moore, Charles J. et al., Our plastic age, Philosophical Transactions of the Royal Society B: Biological Sciences 364 (2009) 1973–1976.

Timagenis, Gregorios J., International control of marine pollution, Dobbs Ferry, Alphen aan den Rijn 1980.

Tiroch, Katrin, Black Sea, in: Max Planck Encyclopedia of Public International Law (MPEPIL), http://opil.ouplaw.com/view/10.1093/law:epil/9780199231690/law-9780199231690-e1260?rskey=6PDTSX&result=1&prd=EPIL, last updated March 2011, last accessed 27.08.2015.

Toope, Stephen J., Formality and Informality, in: *Bodansky, Daniel/Brunnée, Jutta/Hey, Ellen* (eds.), The Oxford handbook of international environmental law, Oxford, New York (2007) 107–124.

Treves, Tullio, Regional Approaches to the Protection of the Marine Environment, in: *Nordquist, Myron H./Moore, John Norton/Mahmoudi, Said* (eds.), The Stockholm declaration and law of the marine environment, The Hague, New York (2003) 137–154.

-Law of the Sea, in: Max Planck Encyclopedia of Public International Law (MPEPIL), http://opil.ouplaw.com/view/10.1093/law:epil/9780199231690/law-9780199231690-e1186?rskey=6dmbBZ&result=3&prd=EPIL, last updated April 2011, last accessed 27.08.2015.

Treves, Tullio/Pineschi, Laura/Tanzi, Attila et al. (eds.), Non-compliance procedures and mechanisms and the effectiveness of international environmental agreements, The Hague, Netherlands, West Nyack, NY 2009.

Trouwborst, Arie, Managing Marine Litter: Exploring the Evolving Role of International and European Law in Confronting a Persistent Environmental Problem, Utrecht Journal of International and European Law 27 (2012) 4–18.

- Prevention, Precaution, Logic and Law, The Relationship between the Precautionary Principle and the Preventative Principle in International Law and Associated Questions, Erasmus Law Review 2 (2009) 106–127.

- Precautionary Rights and Duties of States, Leiden, Boston 2006.

Van Cauwenberghe, Lisbeth/Vanreusel, Ann/Mees, Jan et al., Microplastic pollution in deep-sea sediments, Environmental Pollution 182 (2013) 495–499.

Van Cauwenberghe, Lisbeth/Janssen, C.R., Microplastics in bivalves cultured for human consumption, Environmental Pollution 193 (2014) 65-70.

Vandenberg, L.N./Hauser, R./Marcus, M./ Olea, N. et al, Human exposure to Bisphenol A, Reproductive Toxicology 24 (2007) 139-177.

Van Franeker, Jan A./Blaize, Christine/Danielsen, Johannis et al., Monitoring plastic ingestion by the northern fulmar Fulmarus glacialis in the North Sea, Environmental Pollution 159 (2011) 2609–2615.

Van Franeker, Jan Andries/Heubecker, M./Fairchlough, M. et al., 'Save the North Sea' Fulmar Study 2002-2004, Wageningen 2005.

VanderZwaag, David L./Daniel, Anne, International Law and Ocean Dumping: Steering a Precautionary Course Aboard the 1996 London Protocol, but Still an Unfinished Voyage, in: *Johnston, Douglas M./Chircop, Aldo E./McDorman, Ted L. et al.* (eds.), The future of ocean regime-building, Essays in tribute to Douglas M. Johnston, Leiden, Boston (2009) 515–571.

Vauk, Gottfried J.M/Schrey, Eckart, Litter pollution from ships in the German Bight, Marine Pollution Bulletin 18 (1987) 316–319.

Vedder, H., The Treaty of Lisbon and European Environmental Law and Policy, Journal of Environmental Law 22 (2010) 285–299.

Vernet, Paula María, Pulp Mills on the River Uruguay (Argentina v Uruguay), in: Max Planck Encyclopedia of Public International Law (MPEPIL), http://opil.ouplaw.com/view/10.1093/law:epil/9780199231690/law-9780199231690-e1983?rskey=snPqoB&result=2&prd=EPIL, last updated July 2010, last accessed 27.08.2015.

Verschuuren, Jonathan, Principles of environmental law, The ideal of sustainable development and the role of principles of international, European, and national environmental law, Studies on environmental law Vol. 30, 1.ed., Baden-Baden 2003.

Vesilind, P. A./Rooke, R. L. (eds.), Wastewater treatment plant design, Alexandria, London 2003.

Vidas, Davor/Schei, Peter Johan (eds.), The world ocean in globalisation, Climate change, sustainable fisheries, biodiversity, shipping, regional issues, Leiden, Boston 2011.

Vinogradov, Sergei, Marine Pollution via Transboundary Watercourses — An Interface of the' Shoreline ' and ' River-Basin ' Regimes in the Wider Black Sea Region, The International Journal of Marine and Coastal Law 22 (2007) 585–620.

Von Bogandy, Armin/Bast, Jürgen/Arndt, Felix, Handlungsformen im Unionsrecht, Empirische Analysen und dogmatische Strukturen in einem vermeintlichen Dschungel, Zeitschrift für ausländisches öffentliches Recht und Völkerrecht 62 (2002) 77–162.

Votier, Stephen C./Archibald, Kirsten/Morgan, Greg et al., The use of plastic debris as nesting material by a colonial seabird and associated entanglement mortality, Marine Pollution Bulletin 62 (2011) 168–172.

Wabnitz, Sabine Erika, Das Verschlechterungsverbot für Oberflächengewässer und Grundwasser, Art. 4 WRRL und §§ 25a, 25b, 32c und 33a WHG, Schriftenreihe Umweltrecht in Forschung und Praxis Vol. 47, Hamburg 2010.

Wade, Barry A., The Challenges of Ship-Generated Garbage in the Caribbean, in: *Coe, James M./Rogers, Donald B.* (eds.), Marine debris, Sources, impacts, and solutions, New York (1997) 229–238.

Wagner, Martin/Oehlmann, Jörg, Endocrine disruptors in bottled mineral water: total estrogenic burden and migration from plastic bottles, Environmental Science and Pollution Research 16 (2009) 278–286.

Walker, C. H., Principles of ecotoxicology, 3. ed., Boca Raton 2006.

Walker, George K. (ed.), Definitions for the law of the sea, Terms not defined by the 1982 Convention, Leiden 2012.

Walker, T.R/Reid, K./Arnould, J.P.Y, et al., Marine debris surveys at Bird Island, South Georgia 1990–1995, Marine Pollution Bulletin 34 (1997) 61–65.

Wallace, Barbara, A Strategy to reduce, control and minimize Vessel-Source Marine Debris, in: *Coe, James M./Rogers, Donald B.* (eds.), Marine debris, Sources, impacts, and solutions, New York (1997) 277–288.

Watters, Diana L./Yoklavich, Mary M./Love, Milton S. et al., Assessing marine debris in deep seafloor habitats off California, Marine Pollution Bulletin 60 (2010) 131–138.

Weimann, Joachim, Umweltökonomik, Eine theorieorientierte Einführung, 2. ed., Berlin 1991.

Whitacre, David M. (ed.), Reviews of Environmental Contamination and Toxicology, New York, NY 2012.

Wick, Peter/Malek, Antoine/Manser, Pius et al., Barrier Capacity of Human Placenta for Nanosized Materials, Environ Health Perspect 118 (2009) 432–436.

Widmer, Walter Martin/Hennemann, Mariana Coutinho, Marine Debris in the Island of Santa Catarina, South Brazil: Spatial Patterns, Composition, and Biological Aspects, Journal of Coastal Research 26 (2010) 993–1000.

Wilcox, C./Hardesty, B.D/Sharples, R., et al., Ghostnet impacts on globally threatened turtles, a spatial risk analysis for northern Australia, Conservation Letters 6 (2013) 247–254.

Williams, A.T/Simmons, S.L/Fricker, A., Off-shore sinks of marine litter: A new problem, Marine Pollution Bulletin 26 (1993) 404–405.

Williams, Paul T., Waste treatment and disposal, 2. ed., Chichester, West Sussex, England, Hoboken, NJ, USA 2005.

Winter, Gerd, The Legal Nature of Environmental Principles in International, EC and German Law, in: *Macrory, Richard/Havercroft, Ian/Purdy, Ray* (eds.), Principles of european environmental law, Groningen (2004) 11–27.

Wither, Andrew/Bamber, Roger/Colclough, Steve et al., Setting new thermal standards for transitional and coastal (TraC) waters, Marine Pollution Bulletin 64 (2012) 1564–1579.

Woodall, Lucy./ Sanchez-Vidal, Anna./ Canals, Miquel., et al., The deep sea is a major sink for microplastic debris, Royal Society Open Science 1 (2014) 140317.

Wolfrum, Rüdiger, General International Law (Principles, Rules, and Standards), in: Max Planck Encyclopedia of Public International Law (MPEPIL), http://opil.ouplaw.com/view/10.1093/law:epil/9780199231690/law-9780199231690-e1408?rskey=n2rEIv&result=7&prd=EPIL, last updated December 2010, last accessed 27.08.2015

Wettestad, Science, politics and institutional design: The case of the North-East Atlantic land-based pollution regime, Marine Policy 18 (1994) 219-232.

Wright, Stephanie L./Thompson, Richard C./Galloway, Tamara S., The physical impacts of microplastics on marine organisms: A review, Environmental Pollution 178 (2013) 483-492.

Yamashita, Rei/Takada, Hideshige/Fukuwaka, Masaaki et al., Physical and chemical effects of ingested plastic debris on short-tailed shearwaters, Puffinus tenuirostris, in the North Pacific Ocean, Marine Pollution Bulletin 62 (2011) 2845–2849.

Yankov, Alexander, The Law of the Sea Convention and Agenda 21: Marine Environment Implications, in: *Boyle, Alan E./Freestone, David* (eds.), International law and sustainable development, Past achievements and future challenges, Oxford, New York (1999) 271–295.

Ye, Song/Andrady, Anthony L., Fouling of floating plastic debris under Biscayne Bay exposure conditions, Marine Pollution Bulletin 22 (1991) 608–613.

Yoon, Jong-Hwan/Kawano, Shiro/Igawa, Shuzo, Modeling of marine litter drift and beaching in the Japan Sea, Marine Pollution Bulletin 60 (2010) 448–463.

Zarfl, Christiane/Fleet, David/Fries, Elke et al., Microplastics in oceans, Marine Pollution Bulletin 62 (2011) 1589–1591.

Zarfl, Christiane/Matthies, Michael, Are marine plastic particles transport vectors for organic pollutants to the Arctic?, Marine Pollution Bulletin 60 (2010) 1810–1814.

Zoller, Alexandra, Völker- und europarechtliche Aspekte des Mittelmeerumweltschutzes, Baden-Baden 1996.

Zubris, Kimberly Ann V./Richards, Brian K., Synthetic fibers as an indicator of land application of sludge, Environmental Pollution 138 (2005) 201–211.

Zylstra, E.R, Accumulation of wind-dispersed trash in desert environments, Journal of Arid Environments 89 (2013) 13–15.

V. Internet sources

BBC News, Japan tsunami ´ghost ship' drifting to Canada, http://www.bbc.co.uk/news/world-us-canada-17500008, last accessed 27.08.2015.

CNN, Alessio Vinci, Why Naples is drowning in garbage, http://edition.cnn.com/2008/WORLD/europe/01/07/naples.rubbish.background/, last accessed 27.08.2015

NOAA, Japan Confirms Dock on Washington Coast Is Tsunami Marine Debris, 18.01.2013, http://usresponserestoration.wordpress.com/2013/01/18/japan-confirms-dock-on-washington-coast-is-tsunami-marine-debris/%C3%A4, last accessed 27.08.2015.

Zürich Museum, Birth of a new continent, http://www.domusweb.it/en/design/the-seventh-continent-musings-on-the-plastic-garbage-project/, last accessed 27.08.2015.

VI. Presentations

Leo De Vrees, The EU and its role on reducing marine litter, Conference: Marine Litter at the European level, Brussels, 13.03.2013.

Leo de Vrees, Marine litter targets for European seas, International Conference on Prevention and Management of Marine Litter in European Seas, 10.04.2013.